TWELVE YEARS IN HELL

THE LOCHLAINN SEABROOK COLLECTION

AMERICAN CIVIL WAR
Abraham Lincoln Was a Liberal, Jefferson Davis Was a Conservative: The Missing Key to Understanding the American Civil War
Confederacy 101: Amazing Facts You Never Knew About America's Oldest Political Tradition
Confederate Blood and Treasure: An Interview With Lochlainn Seabrook
Everything You Were Taught About African-Americans and the Civil War is Wrong, Ask a Southerner!
Everything You Were Taught About the Civil War is Wrong, Ask a Southerner!
Give This Book to a Yankee! A Southern Guide to the Civil War For Northerners
Heroes of the Southern Confederacy: The Illustrated Book of Confederate Officials, Soldiers, and Civilians
Lincoln's War: The Real Cause, the Real Winner, the Real Loser
The Great Yankee Coverup: What the North Doesn't Want You to Know About Lincoln's War!
The Ultimate Civil War Quiz Book: How Much Do You Really Know About America's Most Misunderstood Conflict?
Women in Gray: A Tribute to the Ladies Who Supported the Southern Confederacy

CONFEDERATE MONUMENTS
Confederate Monuments: Why Every American Should Honor Confederate Soldiers and Their Memorials

CONFEDERATE FLAG
Confederate Flag Facts: What Every American Should Know About Dixie's Southern Cross
What the Confederate Flag Means to Me: Americans Speak Out in Defense of Southern Honor, Heritage, and History

SECESSION
All We Ask Is To Be Let Alone: The Southern Secession Fact Book

RECONSTRUCTION
Twelve Years in Hell: Victorian Southerners Expose the Myth of Reconstruction, 1865-1877

SLAVERY
Everything You Were Taught About American Slavery is Wrong, Ask a Southerner!
Slavery 101: Amazing Facts You Never Knew About America's "Peculiar Institution"
The Bittersweet Bond: Race Relations in the Old South as Described by White and Black Southerners

NATHAN BEDFORD FORREST
A Rebel Born: A Defense of Nathan Bedford Forrest - Confederate General, American Legend (winner of the 2011 Jefferson Davis Historical Gold Medal)
A Rebel Born: The Screenplay (film about N. B. Forrest)
Forrest! 99 Reasons to Love Nathan Bedford Forrest
Give 'Em Hell Boys! The Complete Military Correspondence of Nathan Bedford Forrest
I Rode With Forrest! Confederate Soldiers Who Served With the World's Greatest Cavalry Leader
Nathan Bedford Forrest and African-Americans: Yankee Myth, Confederate Fact
Nathan Bedford Forrest and the Battle of Fort Pillow: Yankee Myth, Confederate Fact
Nathan Bedford Forrest and the Ku Klux Klan: Yankee Myth, Confederate Fact
Nathan Bedford Forrest: Southern Hero, American Patriot - Honoring a Confederate Icon and the Old South
Saddle, Sword, and Gun: A Biography of Nathan Bedford Forrest For Teens
The God of War: Nathan Bedford Forrest As He Was Seen By His Contemporaries
The Quotable Nathan Bedford Forrest: Selections From the Writings and Speeches of the Confederacy's Most Brilliant Cavalryman

QUOTABLE SERIES
The Alexander H. Stephens Reader: Excerpts From the Works of a Confederate Founding Father
The Quotable Alexander H. Stephens: Selections From the Writings and Speeches of the Confederacy's First Vice President
The Quotable Jefferson Davis: Selections From the Writings and Speeches of the Confederacy's First President
The Quotable Nathan Bedford Forrest: Selections From the Writings and Speeches of the Confederacy's Most Brilliant Cavalryman
The Quotable Robert E. Lee: Selections From the Writings and Speeches of the South's Most Beloved Civil War General
The Quotable Stonewall Jackson: Selections From the Writings and Speeches of the South's Most Famous General
The Unquotable Abraham Lincoln: The President's Quotes They Don't Want You To Know!

CIVIL WAR BATTLES
Encyclopedia of the Battle of Franklin - A Comprehensive Guide to the Conflict that Changed the Civil War
Nathan Bedford Forrest and the Battle of Fort Pillow: Yankee Myth, Confederate Fact
The Battle of Franklin: Recollections of Confederate and Union Soldiers
The Battle of Nashville: Recollections of Confederate and Union Soldiers
The Battle of Spring Hill: Recollections of Confederate and Union Soldiers

CONSTITUTIONAL HISTORY
America's Three Constitutions: Complete Texts of the Articles of Confederation, Constitution of the United States of America, and Constitution of the Confederate States of America
The Articles of Confederation Explained: A Clause-by-Clause Study of America's First Constitution
The Constitution of the Confederate States of America Explained: A Clause-by-Clause Study of the South's Magna Carta

CHILDREN
Honest Jeff and Dishonest Abe: A Southern Children's Guide to the Civil War
Saddle, Sword, and Gun: A Biography of Nathan Bedford Forrest For Teens

VICTORIAN CONFEDERATE LITERATURE
I, Confederate: Why Dixie Seceded and Fought in the Words of Southern Soldiers
Rise Up and Call Them Blessed: Victorian Tributes to the Confederate Soldier, 1861-1901
Support Your Local Confederate: Wit and Humor in the Southern Confederacy
The Bittersweet Bond: Race Relations in the Old South as Described by White and Black Southerners
The God of War: Nathan Bedford Forrest As He Was Seen By His Contemporaries
The Old Rebel: Robert E. Lee As He Was Seen By His Contemporaries
Victorian Confederate Poetry: The Southern Cause in Verse, 1861-1901

ABRAHAM LINCOLN
Abraham Lincoln: The Southern View - Demythologizing America's Sixteenth President
Lincolnology: The Real Abraham Lincoln Revealed in His Own Words - A Study of Lincoln's Suppressed, Misinterpreted, and Forgotten Writings and Speeches
Lincoln's War: The Real Cause, the Real Winner, the Real Loser
The Great Impersonator! 99 Reasons to Dislike Abraham Lincoln
The Unholy Crusade: Lincoln's Legacy of Destruction in the American South
The Unquotable Abraham Lincoln: The President's Quotes They Don't Want You To Know!

NATURAL HISTORY
North America's Amazing Mammals: An Encyclopedia for the Whole Family
The Concise Book of Owls: A Guide to Nature's Most Mysterious Birds
The Concise Book of Tigers: A Guide to Nature's Most Remarkable Cats

PARANORMAL
Carnton Plantation Ghost Stories: True Tales of the Unexplained from Tennessee's Most Haunted Civil War House!
UFOs and Aliens: The Complete Guidebook

FAMILY HISTORIES
The Blakeneys: An Etymological, Ethnological, and Genealogical Study - Uncovering the Mysterious Origins of the Blakeney Family and Name
The Caudills: An Etymological, Ethnological, and Genealogical Study - Exploring the Name and National Origins of a European-American Family
The McGavocks of Carnton Plantation: A Southern History - Celebrating One of Dixie's Most Noble Confederate Families and Their Tennessee Home

MIND, BODY, SPIRIT
Autobiography of a Non-Yogi: A Scientist's Journey From Hinduism to Christianity (Dr. Amitava Dasgupta, with Lochlainn Seabrook)
Britannia Rules: Goddess-Worship in Ancient Anglo-Celtic Society - An Academic Look at the United Kingdom's Matricentric Spiritual Past
Christ Is All and In All: Rediscovering Your Divine Nature and the Kingdom Within
Christmas Before Christianity: How the Birthday of the "Sun" Became the Birthday of the "Son"
Jesus and the Gospel of Q: Christ's Pre-Christian Teachings As Recorded in the New Testament
Jesus and the Law of Attraction: The Bible-Based Guide to Creating Perfect Health, Wealth, and Happiness Following Christ's Simple Formula
Seabrook's Bible Dictionary of Traditional and Mystical Christian Doctrines
Sea Raven Press Blank Page Journal: For Reflections, Notes, and Sketches
The Bible and the Law of Attraction: 99 Teachings of Jesus, the Apostles, and the Prophets
The Book of Kelle: An Introduction to Goddess-Worship and the Great Celtic Mother-Goddess Kelle, Original Blessed Lady of Ireland
The Goddess Dictionary of Words and Phrases: Introducing a New Core Vocabulary for the Women's Spirituality Movement
The Martian Anomalies: A Photographic Search for Intelligent Life on Mars
Victorian Hernia Cures: Nonsurgical Self-Treatment of Inguinal Hernia
Vintage Southern Cookbook: 2,000 Delicious Dishes From Dixie

WOMEN
Aphrodite's Trade: The Hidden History of Prostitution Unveiled
Princess Diana: Modern Day Moon-Goddess - A Psychoanalytical and Mythological Look at Diana Spencer's Life, Marriage, and Death (with Dr. Jane Goldberg)
Women in Gray: A Tribute to the Ladies Who Supported the Southern Confederacy

REPRINTS
A Short History of the Confederate States of America (author Jefferson Davis; editor Lochlainn Seabrook)
Prison Life of Jefferson Davis (author John J. Craven; editor Lochlainn Seabrook)
Life of Beethoven (author Ludwig Nohl; editor Lochlainn Seabrook)
The New Revelation (author Arthur Conan Doyle; editor Lochlainn Seabrook)
The Rise and Fall of the Confederate Government (author Jefferson Davis; editor Lochlainn Seabrook)

Lochlainn Seabrook does not author books for fame and glory, but for the love of writing and sharing his knowledge.

SeaRavenPress.com

TWELVE YEARS IN HELL

VICTORIAN SOUTHERNERS EXPOSE THE MYTH OF RECONSTRUCTION, 1865-1877

CONCEIVED, COLLECTED, EDITED, ARRANGED, & DESIGNED, WITH AN INTRODUCTION BY
"THE VOICE OF THE TRADITIONAL SOUTH," HISTORIAN COLONEL

LOCHLAINN SEABROOK

SCV MEMBER AND JEFFERSON DAVIS HISTORICAL GOLD MEDAL WINNER

Diligently Researched and Generously Illustrated
by the Author for the Elucidation of the Reader

2023

Sea Raven Press, Park County, Wyoming, USA

TWELVE YEARS IN HELL

Published by Sea Raven Press
Cassidy Ravensdale, President
Park County, Wyoming, USA
SeaRavenPress.com

Copyright © all text and illustrations Lochlainn Seabrook 2023
in accordance with U.S. and international copyright laws and regulations, as stated and protected under the Berne Union for the Protection of Literary and Artistic Property (Berne Convention), and the Universal Copyright Convention (the UCC). All rights reserved under the Pan-American and International Copyright Conventions.

PRINTING HISTORY
1st SRP paperback edition, 1st printing, July 2023 • ISBN: 978-1-955351-28-7
1st SRP hardcover edition, 1st printing, July 2023 • ISBN: 978-1-955351-29-4

ISBN: 978-1-955351-28-7 (paperback)
Library of Congress Control Number: 2023942478

This work is the copyrighted intellectual property of Lochlainn Seabrook and has been registered with the Copyright Office at the Library of Congress in Washington, D.C., USA. No part of this work (including text, covers, drawings, photos, illustrations, maps, images, diagrams, etc.), in whole or in part, may be used, reproduced, stored in a retrieval system, or transmitted, in any form or by any means now known or hereafter invented, without written permission from the publisher. The sale, duplication, hire, lending, copying, digitalization, or reproduction of this material, in any manner or form whatsoever, is also prohibited, and is a violation of federal, civil, and digital copyright law, which provides severe civil and criminal penalties for any violations.

Twelve Years in Hell: Victorian Southerners Expose the Myth of Reconstruction, 1865-1877, by Lochlainn Seabrook. Includes an introduction, illustrations, index, endnotes, appendix, and bibliography.

ARTWORK
Front and back cover design and art, book design, layout, font selection, and interior art by Lochlainn Seabrook
All images, image captions, graphic design, and graphic art copyright © 2023 Lochlainn Seabrook
All images selected, placed, manipulated, cleaned, colored, tinted, and/or created by Lochlainn Seabrook
Cover image: "The Desolate Home: A Picture of the Suffering in the South"; wood engraving of Reconstruction period in Dixie, from Frank Leslie's Illustrated Newspaper, published February 23, 1867, artist unknown

All persons who approve of the authority and principles of Colonel Lochlainn Seabrook's literary work, and realize its benefits as a means of reeducating the world about facts left out of mainstream books, are hereby requested to avidly recommend his titles to others and to vigorously cooperate in extending their reach, scope, and influence around the globe.

WRITTEN, DESIGNED, PUBLISHED, PRINTED, & MANUFACTURED IN THE UNITED STATES OF AMERICA

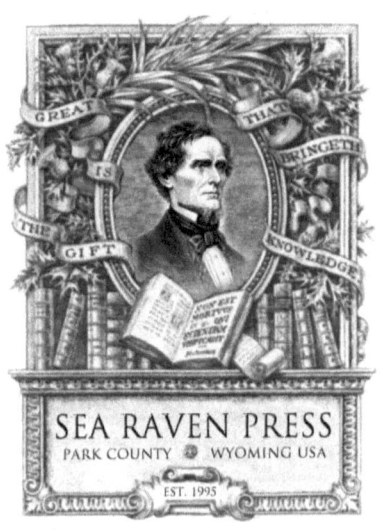

"Books invite all; they constrain none."
Hartley Burr Alexander (1873-1939)

Our President, Conservative Democrat Jefferson Davis, 1867.

Dedication

*To my Victorian Southern ancestors —
They fought in and survived two Wars:
The War for the Constitution
and the War of Reconstruction.*

The remnants of Richmond, Virginia, April 1865.

Epigraph

... The twelve tragic years that followed the death of Lincoln ... were years of revolutionary turmoil, with the elemental passions predominant, and with broken bones and bloody noses among the fighting factionalists. The prevailing note was one of tragedy.... Never have American public men in responsible positions, directing the destiny of the Nation, been so brutal, hypocritical, and corrupt. The Constitution was treated as a doormat on which politicians and army officers wiped their feet after wading in the muck. Never has the Supreme Court been treated with such ineffable contempt, and never has that tribunal so often cringed before the clamor of the mob.

... That the Southern people literally were put to the torture is vaguely understood, but even historians have shrunk from the unhappy task of showing us the torture chambers.

... The story of this Revolution is one of desperate enterprises, by daring and unscrupulous men, some of whom had genius of a high order. In these no Americans can take pride. The evil that they did lives after them. They changed the course of history, and whether for ultimate good or bad is still on the lap of the gods. The story carries lessons that are well worth pondering.

Claude G. Bowers, 1929

CONTENTS

Reconstruction: Pertinent Quotes ❧ 13
Notice: Terms Boycotted in Confederate Veteran ❧ 14
Notes to the Reader, by Lochlainn Seabrook ❧ 15
Reconstruction Time Line in Brief ❧ 24
Introduction, by Lochlainn Seabrook ❧ 25
Important Note From the Author-Editor ❧ 38

SECTION 1
RECONSTRUCTION: HISTORICAL ESSAYS

CHAP. 1: THE SOUTH SINCE THE WAR - STEPHEN DILL LEE ❧ 41
CHAP. 2: THE TRAGIC ERA - CLAUDE GERNADE BOWERS ❧ 119
CHAP. 3: THE RECONSTRUCTION ERA - SAMUEL GIBBS FRENCH ❧ 131
CHAP. 4: THE PRIVATION OF A CITIZEN - MARCUS B. TONEY ❧ 155
CHAP. 5: POSTWAR DIXIE - JOHN LESSLIE HALL ❧ 163
CHAP. 6: RECONSTRUCTION - LEON CUSHING PRINCE ❧ 191
CHAP. 7: PERSONAL REMINISCENCES - WILLIAM HENRY MORGAN ❧ 201
CHAP. 8: AFTER THE WAR - AUGUSTUS PITT ADAMSON ❧ 209
CHAP. 9: THE BLACK TERROR - CECIL EDWARD CHESTERTON ❧ 215
CHAP. 10: IN THE DAYS OF RECONSTRUCTION - JAMES H. MCNEILLY ❧ 237
CHAP. 11: DESTRUCTION & RECONSTRUCTION - RICHARD TAYLOR ❧ 249

SECTION 2
RECONSTRUCTION: PERSONAL VIEWS

CHAP. 12 ❧ 279
CHAP. 13 ❧ 295
CHAP. 14 ❧ 313
CHAP. 15 ❧ 331
CHAP. 16 ❧ 347
CHAP. 17 ❧ 363
CHAP. 18 ❧ 381
CHAP. 19 ❧ 397
CHAP. 20 ❧ 413
CHAP. 21 ❧ 429
CHAP. 22 ❧ 445

Appendix: Commies in the White House ❧ 457
Notes ❧ 459
Bibliography ❧ 469
Index ❧ 479
To Enemies of the Truth: ❧ 515
Meet the Author-Editor ❧ 517
Learn More ❧ 519

RECONSTRUCTION: PERTINENT QUOTES

Reconstruction Defined
"Radical misrule that cost the South more heartaches in 12 years than four years of war." — Verne Seth Pease, 1900

The Word Reconstruction
"The word 'reconstruction,' as the whole world now knows, is merely another term for murder, rapine, and robbery." — Confederate veteran A. F. Fry, 1919

Misrepresentation
"Probably no people, their character and institutions, were ever so thoroughly misunderstood and so malignantly misrepresented as were those of the Southern section of the United States by the leaders of so-called moral and religious sentiment in the Northern section. . . . Especially is this true as to the nature and results of the war of 1861-65." — Reverend James Hugh McNeilly, 1916

Reconstruction: The Untold Story
"Reconstruction: The history of that period, the reconstruction period of the South, has never been fully told. It is only beginning to be written." — Thomas Nelson Page, 1892

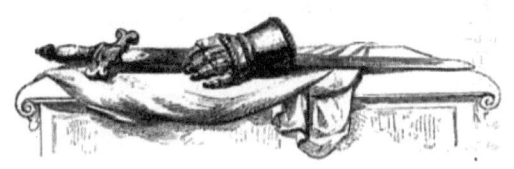

Notice

TERMS BOYCOTTED IN *CONFEDERATE VETERAN*

Will correspondents for the *Veteran* please take notice that the two detestable terms "new South" and "lost cause," will not be printed. Many a fairly good article is turned down by use of that last term. They both originated assuredly in the minds of prejudiced Northerners, and they both so reflect upon the Southern that the *Veteran* will not use articles where substitutes are not admissible.

A notice published in *Confederate Veteran* magazine, December 1902

NOTES TO THE READER

"NOTHING IN THE PAST IS DEAD TO THE MAN WHO WOULD
LEARN HOW THE PRESENT CAME TO BE WHAT IT IS."
WILLIAM STUBBS, VICTORIAN ENGLISH HISTORIAN

THE TWO MAIN POLITICAL PARTIES IN 1860

☛ In any study of America's antebellum, bellum, and postbellum periods, it is vitally important to understand that in 1860 the two major political parties—the Democrats and the newly formed Republicans—were the opposite of what they are today. In other words, the Democrats of the mid 19th Century (founded by what we now call "right-wingers" or "traditionalists")[1] were Conservatives, akin to the Republican Party of today, while the Republicans of the mid 19th Century (founded by what we now call "left-wingers" or "progressives")[2] were Liberals, akin to the Democratic Party of today.[3]

Thus the Confederacy's Democratic president, Jefferson Davis, was a Conservative (with libertarian leanings); the Union's Republican president, Abraham Lincoln, was a Liberal (with socialistic leanings).[4] This is why, in the mid 1800s, the conservative wing of the Democratic Party was known as "the States' Rights Party,"[5] as opposed to the Republican Party, which was widely known to have been created in 1854 by "progressive elements."[6]

Hence, the Democrats of the Civil War period referred to themselves as "conservatives," "confederates," "anti-centralists," or "constitutionalists" (the latter because they favored strict adherence to the original Constitution—which tacitly guaranteed states' rights—as created by the Founding Fathers). The Civil War Republicans, on the other hand, called themselves "liberals," "nationalists," "centralists," or "consolidationists" (the latter three because their goal was to nationalize the central government and consolidate political power in Washington, D.C.).[7]

The author's cousin, Confederate Vice President and Democrat Alexander H. Stephens: a Southern Conservative.

More evidence comes from a common phrase used at the time, "states' rights Democrats," a term that could have only applied to Conservatives, since then, as today, Liberals are squarely against states' rights (unless, in hypocritical fashion, they find that states' rights benefit their agenda in some way).[8]

In 1889 President Davis, who referred to the 1860 Democrats as "the conservative power of the country,"[9] himself explained the political situation at the time this way:

> . . . the names adopted by political parties in the United States have not always been strictly significant of their principles. In general terms it may be said that the old Federal party [Liberal] inclined to nationalism [then a term for big government], or consolidation [that is, consolidation of power in the Federal government], and that the Whig party [liberalistic], which succeeded it, although not identical with it, was favorable, in the main, to a strong Central Government [liberalism, socialism, communism]. On the other hand, its opponent, the Republican [Conservative], afterward known as the Democratic party, was dominated by the idea of the sovereignty of the States and the federal or confederate character of the Union [Americanism, traditionalism, conservatism]. Although other elements have entered into its organization at different periods, this has been its vital, cardinal, and abiding principle.[10]

We will note here that, while Davis would not live to witness the transition, a mere six years after he penned these words (during the 1896 U.S. presidential election), the two major parties would reverse positions, the Democratic Party adopting a Left-wing platform, the Republican Party adopting a Right-wing platform—the status they hold to this day.

Since this idea is new to most of my readers, let us further demystify it by viewing it from the perspective of the American Revolutionary War. If Davis and his Conservative Southern constituents (the Democrats of 1861) had been alive in 1775, they would have sided with George Washington and the American colonists, who sought to secede from the

The War for Southern Independence set Northern Liberals (then the Republican Party) against Southern Conservatives (then the Democratic Party).

tyrannical government of Great Britain; if Lincoln and his Liberal Northern constituents (the Republicans of 1861) had been alive at that time, they would have sided with King George III and the English monarchy, who sought to maintain the American colonies as possessions of the British Empire. It is due to this very comparison that we Southerners often refer to our secession from the U.S. as the Second Declaration of Independence, and the "Civil War" as the Second American Revolutionary War.

Without a basic understanding of these facts, the American "Civil War" will forever remain incomprehensible. For a full discussion of this all-important topic see my book, *Abraham Lincoln Was a Liberal, Jefferson Davis Was a Conservative: The Missing Key to Understanding the American Civil War.*

THE TERM "CIVIL WAR"
☛ As I heartily dislike the phrase "Civil War," its use throughout this book (as well as in my other works) is worthy of explanation.

Our entire modern literary system refers to the conflict of 1861 using the Northern term the "Civil War," whether we in the South like it or not. Of course, this is purposeful, for America's book industry, which determines everything from how books are categorized and designed to how they are marketed and sold, is almost solely controlled by Liberals, socialists, globalists, collectivists, and communists, individuals who will do anything to prevent the truth about Lincoln's War from coming out. An important aspect of this wholesale revisionism of American history is the use of the phrase "Civil War," which Yankee Liberals thrust into the public forum even as big government Left-winger Lincoln was diabolically tricking the Conservative South into firing the first shot at the Battle of Fort Sumter in April 1861.[11]

The American "Civil War" was not a true civil war as Webster defines it: "A conflict between opposing groups of citizens of the *same* country." It was a fight between two individual countries; or to be more specific, two separate and constitutionally formed confederacies: the C.S.A. and the U.S.A.

The progressives' blatant American "Civil War" coverup continues to this day, one of the more overt results which pertains to how books are coded, indexed, and identified.[12] Thus, as all book searches by readers, libraries, and retail outlets are now performed online, and as all bookstores categorize works from or about this period under the heading "Civil War," honest book publishers and authors who deal with this particular topic have little choice but to use this deceptive term. If I were to refuse to use it, as some of my Southern colleagues have suggested, few people would ever find or read my books.

Add to this the fact that scarcely any non-Southerners have ever heard of the names we in the South use for the conflict, such as "the War for Southern Independence," "the War Against Northern Aggression," "Lincoln's War," or my personal preference, because it is the most accurate: "the War for the Constitution." It only makes sense then to use the term "Civil War" in most commercial situations, historically inaccurate though it is.

We should also bear in mind that while today educated persons, particularly educated Southerners, all share an abhorrence for the phrase "Civil War," it was not always so. Confederates who lived through and even fought in the conflict regularly used the term throughout the 1860s, and even long after. Among them were Confederate generals such as Nathan Bedford Forrest, Richard Taylor, and Joseph E. Johnston, not to mention the Confederacy's vice president, Alexander H. Stephens.

Confederate General Nathan Bedford Forrest, just one of many Southern officials who referred to the conflict of 1861 as the "Civil War."

In 1895 Confederate General James Longstreet wrote about his military experiences in a work subtitled, *Memoirs of the Civil War in America*, while in 1903 Confederate General John Brown Gordon, the first commander-in-chief of the United Confederate Veterans, entitled his autobiography, *Reminiscences of the Civil War*. Even the Confederacy's highest leader, President Jefferson Davis, used the term "Civil War,"[13] and in one case at least, as late as 1881—the year he wrote his brilliant exposition, *The Rise and Fall of the Confederate Government* (see the Sea Raven Press reprint of this book, of which I am the editor, collector, technician, and designer).[14]

Authors writing for *Confederate Veteran* magazine sometimes used the phrase well into the early 1900s,[15] and in 1898, at the Eighth Annual Meeting and Reunion of the United Confederate

Veterans (the forerunner of today's Sons of Confederate Veterans), the following resolution was proposed: that from then on the Great War of 1861 was to be designated "the Civil War Between the States."[16]

A WORD ON EARLY AMERICAN MATERIAL

☛ In order to preserve the authentic historicity of the antebellum, bellum, and postbellum periods, I have retained the original spellings, formatting, and punctuation of the early Americans I quote. These include such items as British-English spellings, long-running paragraphs, obsolete words, and various literary devices peculiar to the time. However, I have corrected misspelled names to prevent confusion, and also *where possible*, inaccurate dates and locations (the inevitable result of aging faulty memories). Bracketed words are my additions and clarifications (added mainly for my new, foreign, and young readers), while italicized words are (where indicated) my emphasis.

Union General August von Willich: Typically labeled a "Radical" in mainstream history books, Willich was actually a card-carrying communist who led a revolutionary workers' party, studiously followed the teachings of Karl Marx, and participated in the failed European socialist revolution of 1848—all before joining Lincoln's army in 1861.

19TH-CENTURY CODE WORDS

☛ An early American *Southern* abolitionist was someone who simply desired the end of slavery. *Northern* abolitionists, however, were something quite different altogether: they identified themselves with socialism and communism. Also, as noted above, our modern political party names have different meanings than those of the mid 1800s. Hence, one must bear the following in mind when reading 19th-Century literature:

1. "Abolitionist" (Northern): A 19th-Century Left-wing euphemism for a socialist or communist.
2. "Radical" (Northern): Also a 19th-Century Left-wing euphemism for a socialist or communist.
3. "Republican": Between 1854 and 1896 the Republicans were the major Left-wing or Liberal party of that era. (See Appendix.)
4. "Democrat": Between 1828 and 1896, the Democrats were the major Right-wing or Conservative party of that era.

For more information on items 1 and 2 above, see my introduction in my book *The Bittersweet Bond: Race Relations in the Old South As Described by White and Black Southerners.*

For more information on items 3 and 4 above, see my books *Abraham Lincoln Was a Liberal, Jefferson Davis Was a Conservative: The Missing Key to Understanding the American Civil War*, and *Lincoln's War: The Real Cause, the Real Winner, the Real Loser.*

PRESENTISM

☛ As a historian I view *presentism* (judging the past according to present day mores and customs) as the enemy of authentic history. And this is precisely why the Left employs it in its ongoing war against traditional American, conservative, and Christian values. By looking at history through the lens of modern day beliefs—and, just as heinous, fabricating obviously fake history based on emotion, opinion, and political ideology—they are able to distort, revise, and reshape the past into a false narrative that fits their ideological agenda: the liberalization and Northernization of America, the enlargement and further centralization of the national government, and total control of American political, economic, educational, and social power, the same plan that Lincoln championed.[17]

Judging our ancestors by our own standards is dishonest, unfair, unjust, misleading, and unethical.

This book rejects presentism and replaces it with what I call *historicalism*: judging our ancestors based on the values of their own time.

To get the most from this work the reader is invited to reject presentism as well. In this way—along with casting aside preconceived notions and the fake history churned out by our Left-wing education system—the truth in this work will be most readily ascertained and absorbed; truth that has been rigorously researched and forensically uncovered by myself using the scientific method. In 1901 Confederate Colonel Bennett H. Young noted:

> History is valuable only as it is true. Opinions concerning acts are not history; acts themselves alone are historic.[18]

THE DIFFERENCE BETWEEN OPINIONS & FACTS
It must go without saying that I do not agree with every sentiment expressed in the following pages. I do not agree, for example, that one race is superior or inferior to another, that the U.S. is "a white man's country," that the "average black person" is lazy and immoral, that "all whites" are racists, or that Lincoln was a noble soul who, had he not been assassinated in April 1865, would have enacted a more "temperate and humane reconstruction policy" than his ruthless successors. Where such notions are expressed as *opinions* by the writers I cite, I have let them stand.

A peaceful antebellum river scene in Dixie.

However, I have edited out false views that are expressed as *factual history*, for, whenever I am aware of it, I will not promote fake history. For clarity, where necessary I have made note of my edits, either in the text or in the endnotes.

CONTINUE YOUR SOUTHERN HISTORY EDUCATION
☛ Lincoln's War on the Constitution and the American people can never be fully understood without a thorough knowledge of the South's perspective. As this book is only meant to be a brief introductory guide to these topics, one cannot hope to learn the complete story here. For those who are interested in additional material from Dixie's viewpoint, please see my comprehensive histories listed on pages 2 and 3.

There is not and can never be true neutrality on this subject, which is why there is no such thing as a purely "neutral" book on the War Between the States—despite the claims of many pro-North partisans. Thus in the year 1900, former Confederate General John Brown Gordon wrote:

> Neutrality has no place in masterful minds nor in heroic hearts. Neutrality has never yet developed a great character nor characterized a great people nor written one sparkling page in human history.[19]

FINAL THOUGHTS: HOW TO HONOR BOTH OUR SOUTHERN & OUR AMERICAN HERITAGE

☛ To all Americans: It is time to resurrect the South's true history. It is time to allow the authentic chronicle of past events to be told accurately and honestly. It is time to disseminate this knowledge far and wide, guilelessly and decisively. It is time to shine the Light of Truth into the dark corners of ignorance, malice, divisiveness, and deceit fomented by the gaslighting enemies of the South.[20]

Then and only then do we truly honor our gallant Confederate ancestors, do justice to their names, military service, and memories, and confer upon them the respect and reverence so they richly deserve as American patriots.

LOCHLAINN SEABROOK, 2023

"Steps must be taken to preserve from oblivion, or worse, from misrepresentation, a civilization which produced, as its natural fruit, Washington and Jefferson. Lee and Jackson. Their stories must be told and their deeds must be sung through the ages—not what its enemies thought it to be, but what in truth it was.

"We are not willing to be handed down to the coming generation as a race of slave-drivers and traitors. So let the North lay aside her prejudice and hatred, and seek the truth instead. She should reveal that the [Southern] Cavalier, as well as the [Northern] Puritan, was on the continent from the earliest days, and has been the most conspicuous element in its progress and its freedom. She should admit that the South has a heart of feeling and honor, and is worthy of justice."

Arthur Marshall, 1893

Keep Your Body, Mind, & Spirit Vibrating at Their Highest Level

YOU CAN DO SO BY READING THE BOOKS OF

SEA RAVEN PRESS

There is nothing that will so perfectly keep your body, mind, and spirit in a healthy condition as to think wisely and positively. Hence you should not only read this book, but also the other books that we offer. They will quicken your physical, mental, and spiritual vibrations, enabling you to maintain a position in society as a healthy erudite person.

KEEP YOURSELF WELL-INFORMED!

The well-informed person is always at the head of the procession, while the ignorant, the lazy, and the unthoughtful hang onto the rear. If you are a Spiritual man or woman, do yourself a great favor: read Sea Raven Press books and stay well posted on the Truth. It is almost criminal for one to remain in ignorance while the opportunity to gain knowledge is open to all at a nominal price.

We invite you to visit our Webstore for a wide selection of wholesome, family-friendly, well-researched, educational books for all ages. You will be glad you did!

Unique Books & Gifts for the Whole Family!

SeaRavenPress.com

LochlainnSeabrook.com
TheBestCivilWarBookEver.com
AmbianceGoneWild.com

WAR FOR THE CONSTITUTION & WAR OF RECONSTRUCTION

Time Line in Brief

- March 20, 1854: Socialist Horace Greeley selects the name "Republican," around which Socialist Alvan E. Bovay forms the Republican Party at Ripon, Wisconsin; Socialist Galusha A. Grow is named "the Father of the Republican Party";[21] in 1856 the party selects Socialist John C. Frémont as its first presidential candidate.[22]
- November 6, 1860: Big government Liberal Republican Abraham Lincoln elected, becoming America's 16th President.
- December 20, 1860: The first of the Southern states, South Carolina, secedes.
- April 12, 1861: Lincoln tricks the South into firing the first shot of the "Civil War" at Fort Sumter, South Carolina.
- November 8, 1864: Lincoln "elected" to a second term.
- April 9, 1865: Confederate General Robert E. Lee surrenders his troops at Appomattox, Virginia. The Confederate capitol at Richmond, Virginia, falls, inaugurating the official start of 12 years of Reconstruction.
- April 14, 1865: Lincoln is assassinated by Yankee John Wilkes Booth.
- April 15, 1865: Southern Conservative (then a Democrat) Andrew Johnson, Lincoln's vice president, becomes 17th U.S. president.
- December 24, 1865: Formation by Conservative Confederate veterans of the original Ku Klux Klan (no relation to the modern KKK), which became a pro-Constitution paramilitary organization and social welfare group whose purpose was to help Southerners of all races survive Reconstruction. Officially closed in 1869 when its goals had been attained.
- March 2, 1867: The Reconstruction Act of 1867 becomes law, dividing the former Confederate states (except Tennessee) into five military districts.
- March 4, 1869: Yankee Liberal (then a Republican) and former Union General Ulysses S. Grant elected America's 18th president. He serves two terms.
- March 4, 1877: Yankee Liberal (then a Republican) Rutherford B. Hayes is elected America's 19th president.
- April 24, 1877: President Hayes withdraws the last U.S. troops from the South, officially ending 12 years of Reconstruction.

John Charles "the Pathfinder" Frémont: Explorer, Union general (lost a battle with Stonewall Jackson), American socialist, and major supporter of the then Left-wing Republican Party—the first sectional party ever formed in the U.S. In 1856 Frémont was selected as the Republican Party's first presidential candidate, but lost the election to Conservative Democrat James Buchanan. To increase their chances of winning the 1860 election, the party chose a more moderate Left-winger, big government Liberal Abraham Lincoln, as its presidential nominee.

INTRODUCTION

by Lochlainn Seabrook

"My purpose is not to arouse any antagonisms nor to create bitterness. The cold, clear facts of history ought never to be distasteful to any people. Truth cannot hurt any cause or any man." — Confederate officer Bennett Henderson Young, 1916

ASK THE AVERAGE MAN OR woman on the street to describe so-called "Reconstruction" and you will most likely hear something similar to the following: "Reconstruction was the culmination of Abraham Lincoln's great plan to save the Union; a necessary step in chastising the traitorous South, bringing the wayward states back into the fold, ending the inhumanity of slavery, and humbling the arrogant Dixiecrat."

While this tidy mainstream summation reads well to the uneducated ear, it is wholly untrustworthy. More to the point, it is an outrageous fiction. This is because, like nearly *all* mainstream history, it was written and fabricated by the Left, making it a Victorian aspect of what I call "The Great Yankee Coverup."[23]

Battle at Thoroughfare Gap, Virginia.

In the 1860s, the Left—then operating under the name the Republican Party, but today known as the Democratic Party—is the same political group that President Donald J. Trump refers to as "the party of disinformation."[24] Why? Because gaslighting the public via books, articles, and news filled with purposefully manufactured, misleading information, is one of the specialities of Liberals, Socialists, and Communists. And these brazen Left-wing disinformationists, after all, made up the bulk of the Yankees who opposed the Conservative South during the 16 years between 1861 and 1877.

WHY THE SOUTH WAS PUNISHED
The truth is that Reconstruction was primarily and above all the Liberal North's effort to penalize, humiliate, disgrace, and injure the Conservative South economically, politically, and socially. As it was nothing but a thinly veiled Left-wing police state mercilessly imposed on the South at the tip of a bayonet to keep Liberals in power, Yankee Socialists and Communists openly—and for once honestly—labeled Reconstruction a "punishment, repentance, and regeneration" program,[25] revealing that Reconstruction was indeed not inspired by compassion, empathy, brotherly love, or even patriotism, as our mainstream history books teach, but by anger, hatred, jealousy vengeance, and retaliation.

But for what? What were Southerners being punished for?

For being independent-thinking, Constitution-loving, traditional, happy, successful, and Christian. In fact, the "Civil War," which Southern statesman Thomas Clendinen Catchings called "the most stupendous drama of all the ages,"[26] was the Victorian version of the same Liberal-versus-Conservative

C.S. ironclad *Chicora*, at Charleston, South Carolina.

battle that rages today, and that has been raging since the dawn of prehistoric humanity; the same Left-wing/Right-wing conflict recorded in ancient Greek myths and other early sacred writings, such as the Epic of Gilgamesh, the Bhagavad Gita, the Torah, and the New Testament; an archetypal, age-old battle that was best summarized by an ancient biblical poet, who wrote:

> "The heart of the wise inclines to the right, but the heart of a fool to the left."[27]

THE COMMUNIST REVOLT THAT WAS RECONSTRUCTION
The foolish Left's four-year campaign to overturn the Constitution and subdue the freedom-loving American people—a conflict described by a Conservative Southerner in 1921 as "the war that was to end in the complete overthrow of the government originated and founded by the fathers of the republic"[28]—was followed by over a decade of additional suffering, illegalities, outrages, and humiliation. Our history books deceitfully label this period "Reconstruction"; but *it was, as we shall see, actually a Left-wing, Yankee-inspired communist uprising*, one rightly known to Victorian Southerners as "the Bolshevik Period,"[29] or more precisely, "the red ordeal of Bolshevik Reconstruction."[30] Nothing like this—"the most horrible reconstruction period the world ever saw,"[31] "the darkest period of American history"[32]—had ever occurred on our continent

before. And we can only hope that nothing remotely like it will ever occur again.

THE WAR OF RECONSTRUCTION
I, like other traditional Southerners, use the phrase "so-called Reconstruction" intentionally, for it was anything but a sincere and conciliatory attempt to "help rebuild the South" after the War, as is so often claimed. In fact, the 12 horrific years following the War Between the States was actually a second conflict, one which we might most accurately refer to as "The War of Reconstruction."[33] This particular battle, as will become evident, pitted several million Union soldiers against the South's new postwar army: the Conservative, pro-Constitution, pro-law, Southern social welfare organization: the Ku Klux Klan, comprised of some 500,000 members.

The antebellum South.

WHAT NEED WAS THERE TO "REPAIR" THE SOUTH?
To begin with, "reconstruction," which means "the process of repairing something," was not needed in the Southern states before, during, or after the conflict. What was there to fix, improve, or restore? Dixie was not only thriving before the War, at the time she was superior to the North in almost every area, from economics to natural resources to education and religiosity. And as the American abolition movement had begun in the South (in Virginia in the 1600s), abolition was being widely discussed in 1860, with the entire institution on the verge of being demolished across the South.[34]

Dixie, the compassionate heart of Christian America, needed no assistance in that department. She was well on her way to determining how to end the practice—an institution which, we will note, had begun in the North (in Massachusetts in 1638), and which was later thrust upon the South by Yankee slave-owners, who came to decide that they did not like black people and preferred an all-white Northeast.[35]

So we must ask again: what need was there for a war on the soft-hearted, agrarian South, whose humble farmers and genteel landowners produced a vast proportion of America's wealth? And why did she need "mending" afterward? Why the need for what even one Yankee officer referred to as "the infamy, the degradation and the despoilation of the reconstruction period"?[36]

Such questions must be asked, especially considering that *both* the War and Reconstruction were not only immoral, unethical, and unjustified, they were unconstitutional—and therefore illegal.

THE ROOTS OF RECONSTRUCTION

The facts behind what Claude G. Bowers rightly called "the tragic era" are not difficult to uncover. Unless one is an alethophobe.

For one thing, the majority of Liberal Yankees (members of the then Left-wing Republican Party) absolutely detested not only the Southern people, but her beautiful lands as well. One of them, William Henry Seward, President Abraham Lincoln's secretary of state, spoke for many progressive Yankees when he haughtily informed the Pan-American Congress that "there was nothing worth visiting South of the Potomac River."[37]

Then there was the problem of Yankee jealousy, which stands out as yet another motivation behind the Yanks' communist revolution—deceptively labeled "Reconstruction" by the mainstream. In 1894 Confederate General Bradley Tyler Johnson wrote:

> "The habit of control and the practice of masterdom made the Southern man reliant, positive, and forceful. He controlled the formative period of the new [colonial American] society. He formed the Union under the Constitution, and he directed the policy of the Union for the first seventy years of its existence. His power was the logical result of the institution by which he was formed. His whole energy was directed to the art of governing. The assertion of intellectual predominance and the exhibition of material power in the South produced irritation, envy, and ill will [in Yankeedom]. [Thus, for] thirty years prior to 1860 the North had been gradually making up its mind for the overthrow of the predominance in the South. . . ."[38]

Yet such childish emotions could hardly be responsible for the whole of Reconstruction, a demonically controlled period in the South that I have termed "Twelve Years in Hell." Let us turn now to the more powerful and influential factors.

CONQUERING THE PROSTRATE SOUTH

Vituperative, South-hating, ethnomasochist (one who hates his own race) and Yankee Socialist Thaddeus Stevens saw Reconstruction as a necessary means to Northern ends, calling it the "Conquered Province" policy, one whose chief aim was to confiscate the entire South to pay for the costs of the War, then allow only those seceded Southern states to be readmitted to the Union that had been "redeemed;" that is, thoroughly cleansed of their "rebellious attitudes"—that is, their states' rights movements and independent way of thinking; in other words, their *Southernness*.[39]

Stevens, who once openly declared that his primary goal was to "put the white South under the heel of the black South,"[40] delivered the following words before the U.S. House of Representatives in 1865:

"*The whole fabric of southern society must be changed* [my emphasis, L.S.] and never can it be done if this opportunity is lost. . . . If the South is ever to be made a safe republic let her lands be cultivated by the toil of the owners or the free labor of intelligent citizens. This must be done even though it drive her nobility into exile. If they go, all the better."[41]

These were sentiments which all radical Left-wing Yankees like Stevens could agree with and support.

Earlier, in 1863, for example, another rabid Yankee South-hater, Christian clergyman Henry Ward Beecher, avowed that a Northern (that is, a Liberal) win over the Southern Confederacy would allow the North to spread "New England ideas" across miserable, backwards, inbred, uncultured Dixie. Such ideas included radically Left-wing notions such as Fourierism, free-loveism, "and the whole brood of Yankeeisms." According to Beecher, culturally Northernizing the South would assure a victory more thorough than the bloody path Lincoln had chosen.[42] This was vitally important to Liberal Yankees like Beecher, for, as the far Left historically inaccurate *Encyclopedia Britannica* then assured its readers, 19th-Century Southerners were "a semi-barbarous people who could only be saved by Northern civilization."[43]

San Antonio, Texas, in the 1800s.

RACIAL DIVISION, IMPOVERISHMENT, & SEIZURE OF PRIVATE PROPERTY

In turn, the South's "salvation" could be gained only by turning her upside down, putting, as the Victorian Left arrogantly phrased it, the "bottom rail on top." This meant, in essence, not *black equality*—as Left-wing history books claim—but *black supremacy*, revealing the insidious and entrenched institutional racism that was, and still is, part and parcel of the Left's plan take and maintain governmental control.

In initiating their program to install black supremacy, educated whites would be ousted from positions of power and replaced with uneducated blacks. The New York *Herald* wrote at the time (1868):

"Here we have the full focus of negro efforts of civilization. In drawing the picture of Haiti we are only photographing on the American mind in advance the picture [U.S.] Congress is trying to impress on the United States by false and barbaric legislation. Radical [socialist-communist] rule means, down with the white, up with the black. Down with civilization, up with barbarism."[44]

That same year the Ohio Democratic [then Conservative] platform noted that

> "the practical effect of the reconstruction acts is to deliver over the Southern states to the political and social control of negroes, to place the lives, liberties and fortunes of the whites in the hands of a barbarous people."[45]

In addition to promoting black supremacy, dividing the races, and stirring up racial discord, the Yankee Left intended to "impoverish" the South through, among other things, confiscation of property, which would then be freely redistributed to blacks. In plain English, white-owned, multi-million dollar mansions (along with their farmland and livestock) were to be given to uneducated former black servants ("slaves" to Yankees), most who not only could neither read or write, but did not have the slightest understanding of finances or the many responsibilities of home ownership. Radical Left-winger Thaddeus Stevens, who publicly referred to the seceded Southern states as "dead carcasses lying within the Union,"[46] voiced the vengeful, South-hating tone of the times in this excerpt from one of his many speeches:

The steamer *Great Republic*, a Mississippi river boat.

> "The laws of war authorize us to take their [the Southern peoples'] property by our sovereign power. You behold at your feet a conquered foe and an atrocious enemy. We have the right to impose confiscation of all their property, to impoverish them. This is strict law and good common sense. To this issue I devote the small remnant of my life."[47]

This is the same South-loathing Yankee socialist who, on January 3, 1867, made the following comments before the House of Representatives concerning passage of the first Reconstruction Bill. Stevens admits that his support for the bill was motivated in great part by, not concern for black civil rights, but both "party purpose" and revenge on the South:

> "Another good reason [for voting for this bill's passage] is that it would insure the ascendancy of the Union Party [a 19th Century nickname for the then Left-wing Republican Party]. . . . [Without passage of this bill, the rebels,] with their kindred Copperheads of the North, would always elect the President and control Congress. . . . For these, among other reasons, I am for negro suffrage in every rebel state. If it be just, it should not be denied; if it be necessary, it should be adopted; if it be a punishment for traitors, they deserve it."[48]

Here the Victorian Left exposes itself and its social engineering scheme in all its shameless glory, perfectly reinforcing the words of Lincoln's chief justice, Yankee Liberal Salmon P. Chase, who once asserted that he would rather never see another black person "set his foot upon Ohio soil." When asked why he felt that way, Chase responded:

> "Because their [that is, Africa-Americans] moral influence is degrading. . . . I do not wish the slave emancipated because I love him, but because I hate his [white Southern] master."[49]

CONFISCATION, KILLING, COLONIZING, & SETTLING

Socialists and Communists in Lincoln's administration, military, and party heartily concurred with the ideas voiced by men like Chase, Stevens, and Beecher, demanding that before there could be true reconciliation between the two sections, the "misguided" Southern states would first have to be "drastically remade."[50]

Remade into what?

A hint comes from the "revolutionary" Union General William Tecumseh Sherman (to this day still considered a war criminal in the South), who penned the following missive from Memphis, Tennessee, to his brother, fellow South-hating, Yankee Liberal Senator John Sherman,[51] on August 13, 1862:

Ohio Senator John Sherman, brother of Union General William T. Sherman, both identified with socialism. The Liberal Yankee Congressman (a member of the then Left-wing Republican Party) was instrumental in strengthening and enforcing brutal Reconstruction measures in the South.

> "My dear brother: I have not written to you for so long that I suppose you think I have dropped the correspondence. For six weeks I was marching along the road from Corinth to Memphis, mending roads, building bridges, and all sorts of work. At last I got here and found the city contributing gold, arms, powder, salt and everything the enemy wanted. It was a smart trick on their part thus to give up Memphis that the desire of gain to our Northern merchants should supply them with the things needed in war.
>
> "I stopped this at once and declared gold, silver, treasury notes and salt as much contraband of war, as powder. I have one man under sentence of death for smuggling arms across the lines, and hope Mr. Lincoln will approve it. But the mercenary spirit of our people is too much and my orders are reversed and I am ordered to encourage the trade in cotton, and all orders prohibiting gold, silver and notes to be paid for it are annulled by orders from Washington. [Union General Ulysses S.] Grant promptly ratified my order, and all military men here saw at once that gold spent for cotton went to the purchase of arms and munitions of war. But what are the lives of our soldiers to the profits of the merchants?
>
> ". . . Of course I approve the confiscation act, and *would be willing to*

revolutionize the government [my emphasis, L.S.] so as to amend that article of the Constitution which forbids the forfeiture of [Confederate] land to . . . [their Southern] heirs. My full belief is, we must colonize the country *de novo* ["again"], beginning with Kentucky and Tennessee, and should remove [that is, import and settle] 4,000,000 of our people [Liberal Yankees] at once south of the Ohio River, taking the farms and plantations of the Rebels. I deplore the war as much as ever, but if the thing has to be done, let the means be adequate.

". . . The weather is very hot and [Confederate General Braxton] Bragg can't move his forces very fast; but I fear he will give trouble. My own opinion is we ought not to venture too much into the interior until the river is safely in our possession, when we could land at any point and strike inland. To attempt to hold all the South would demand an army too large even to think of.

"We must colonize and settle as we go South, for in Missouri there is as much strife as ever.

"Enemies must he killed or transported to some other country. Your affectionate brother, W. T. Sherman."[52]

"Confiscate, kill, colonize, and settle." Here we begin to discover the true motivations behind the Liberal North's Reconstruction plan.

We get even closer to the truth in the following excerpt from an essay by Arthur Marshall, which appeared in an 1893 issue of *Confederate Veteran*:

". . . The war left the South exhausted to the last degree. The ragged, half-starved Confederate soldier, crushed with defeat, returned to his once happy and beautiful home to find his house in ruins, his farm devastated, his slaves free, his stock killed, his barns empty, his trade destroyed, and his money worthless.

"The North took advantage of this helpless condition, and under the euphemism of reconstruction made an attempt to destroy the South. She was dismembered, disfranchised, denationalized, and turned into military provinces. Besides the war having rendered to the torch and sword three billion dollars' worth of property, she has been robbed from her poverty of a billion dollars in twenty years to pension Northern soldiers. [Pro-South Virginian and President Woodrow Wilson's Ambassador to Italy] Thomas Nelson Page is reported to have made this strong statement: 'It was intended that the South should be no more.'"[53]

STAGE ONE & TWO OF THE NORTH'S NEFARIOUS PLAN
The conquest and obliteration of the Conservative Christian South could only come by way of total war, the first phase of Lincoln's plan to "save the Union." As the Yankee soldier's war cry was "beauty and booty!" apparently two of the Left's primary war goals were the molestation and rape of Southern females and the wholesale theft of Southern goods and property.[54]

The merciless violence, massive destruction, emotional shock, unspeakable horrors, widespread homelessness, and senseless deaths of hundreds of

The cotton plant.

thousands of men, women, and children (of all races) via four years of war, was intended to wear the Southern people down, preparing them for the second stage—the Left-wing Yankee's ultimate goal: the complete economic, political, social, educational, and military takeover of the South, including the seizing of her businesses, banks, schools, churches, farms, land, and natural resources by Union soldiers. *In essence, the brazen plan called for the total Northernization of the South under threat of further death and destruction.*

The result of Reconstruction would be, as authentic history shows, the near ruination of Dixie, with millions of Southerners turned into bankrupt, starving, homeless refugees. One of the better known victims of the Yankee Left's satanic campaign to destroy the righteous South was the much beloved Southern bard Henry Timrod, the well-known "poet of the Confederacy," who died of "insufficient nourishment" at Columbia, SC, October 7, 1867.[55] Timrod, a hapless casualty of the Left's savage communist reconstruction program, was only 38 years old.

And here we arrive at the final and most damning piece of evidence of all, revealing the Left's true motivation for inappropriately named "Reconstruction."

According to Interior Department official T. J. Barnett, very early on, in 1862, during the second year of the War, he had a private conversation with President Lincoln. It was during this startling discussion that the megalomaniacal chief executive told Barnett that not only was he going to alter the purpose of the war to one of "subjugation," but that "the South was to be destroyed and replaced with new propositions and ideas"—namely, Left-wing Yankee propositions and ideas.[56] In other words, as Lincoln's communist followers phrased it, the "misguided South would have to be drastically remade."[57]

Of course, this shocking admission by America's Liberal 16th chief executive never made into mainstream history books—and for obvious reasons.

First, as some of my 19th- and early 20th-Century writers assert in the following pages, Lincoln himself did not publicly announce or publish *all* of his statements and plans for fear that his cabinet and the public would not sanction them. Thus, he kept many to himself, only revealing them to those who "needed to know."[58]

Big government Liberal (then a Republican) President Abraham Lincoln, circa 1858, the original architect of Reconstruction.

Second, Lincoln's statement to Barnett goes against the bogus, hate-filled narrative that the Left has foisted upon the public for the past century and a half, right into the current day: "Conservatives, whites, Christians, and Southerners in particular, are terrible people who do not deserve to be a part of America's social, political, economic, or educational institutions." According to its own warped vision of America, only the Left was qualified.[59] Here was more motivation for launching Reconstruction in postwar America.

MILITARY DISTRICTS, MILITARY FASCISM, MILITARY STATE

The Left knew, however, that it could not *legally* and *peacefully* force white, Christian, Conservative Southerners out of power. And so it would have to do it *illegally* and *violently*. And this is precisely what it did, beginning with the establishment of martial law across the former Confederacy (unconstitutional since civil courts were still open in Dixie).[60]

After cruelly banning the wearing of Confederate uniforms and the display of Confederate flags across the South,[61] in early 1867 a new Reconstruction Act, known to be "the most brutal proposition ever introduced into the Congress of the United States by a responsible committee," divided the South's ten states (her eleventh, Tennessee, having been exempted from reconstruction several years earlier by Tennessean Andrew Johnson) were divided into five military districts, "conquered territories," each overseen by a Northern officer. The five districts and their commanding officers were:

View of the James River below Lynchburg, Virginia.

1) Virginia: U.S. General John M. Schofield.
2) North Carolina and South Carolina: U.S. General Daniel E. Sickles.
3) Alabama, Florida, and Georgia: U.S. General John Pope.
4) Arkansas and Mississippi: U.S. General Edward O. C. Ord.
5) Louisiana and Texas: U.S. General Philip H. Sheridan.

Each officer was in charge of "supervising elections," setting up new governments, and writing new state constitutions.[62]

In the typical style of the Northern oppressors, the five commanding officers were given unlimited powers with no time limit on military rule; nor did they need to answer to President Johnson; only to General Grant, a Left-wing slave owner. In other words, Generals Schofield, Sickles, Pope, Ord, and Sheridan were given complete free reign in Northernizing their districts, the worst course of action possible for the independent-minded, ruggedly individualistic South.⁶³

In each of the ten Southern states now under military rule, the constitutional right of secession was repealed and the emancipation of all slaves was recognized (even though slavery continued openly in some areas of the North). The ten Southern states were then further divided into subdistricts, each headed by Yankee "military commissioners" who were given police powers to "suppress disorder and violence"—basically, the Left-wing giving itself permission to censor and silence all those who disagreed with it. No public acts were allowed without their authorization. In support of the commissioners, provost marshals were stationed across each state whose job was to "regulate local affairs."⁶⁴

Command centers were set up across the five districts and the streets were patrolled by unruly, vengeful, often violent, armed U.S. troops, many of them made up of angry blacks inculcated (that is, communized) by Left-wing Yanks to hate their former owners. On every corner was posted an armed Yankee guard, and governmental buildings in principle Southern cities were "completely surrounded by a cordon of sentinels." As if this was not enough torment for the Southern people, the legislatures of the Southern states were either forcibly ejected or seized, then replaced by hand-picked Union men who were paid to implement the North's Radical Left-wing Reconstruction agenda.⁶⁵

SAVING THE PAST FOR THE FUTURE

Victorian Southerners were well aware of what lay behind the diabolical Northernization plans of their arrogant Left-wing cousins above the Mason-Dixon line. And, after the close of the "Conquered Province" program in 1877, they were eager to tell the world about them.

Confederate monument, Montgomery, Alabama.

Tragically, however, they were not the ones who wrote the mainstream history of either the War or Reconstruction—a horrendous 16 year communist insurrection whose evil consequences have endured into the 21ˢᵗ Century, and which have given rise to many of the societal ills we are experiencing today due to the Left-wing takeover of our political structures, media, schools, churches, and commercial industries.

Because mainstream book publishers had intentionally rejected their manuscripts, those Southerners who were determined to get the truth out to the public made a valiant attempt at self-publishing. But, as we shall see, these brave honest souls were quickly silenced by the dishonest fact-hating Left: Liberal reviewers panned their books, socialist-owned bookstores refused to carry them, and government-controlled libraries banned them.[66] Suppression, oppression, and censorship: long standard communist tools of the trade.

Thus, the truth about what Southerners called "the heart-rending conditions of Reconstruction" never found their way into the pages of American history.[67] Instead, the facts were supplanted by the Left's heavily rewritten, redacted, reworked version of the events, one carefully calculated to portray the *Conservative South* as a villainous traitor, one whose citizens were nothing more than cowardly deserters, violent rebels, and lynch-happy racists; the *Liberal North*, on the other hand, was depicted as being comprised of heroic patriots, intrepid loyalists, obedient citizens, and color-blind egalitarians—despite copious evidence to the contrary.

The Mississippi State Capitol at Jackson.

And where is this all-important evidence to be found?

Fortunately for us, much of it was recorded in non-mainstream chronicles, such as *Confederate Veteran* magazine, the massive 12-volume work *Confederate Military History*, and *The Journal of Southern History*. My book, *Twelve Years in Hell*, is a record of some of these recollections, described in detail by Victorian Southern men and women, nearly all of them eyewitnesses—and even a few sympathetic, understanding, educated Yanks and foreigners.

Thankfully, by 1877, Reconstruction ultimately failed, for the South was able to displace the radical socialist and communist influences (originating in the then Liberal Republican Party) and regain near total control of her land. Reviving herself, she rose Phoenix-like from the ashes of Left-wing intolerance, sadism, perversion, racism, and savagery.

However, the dangers posed by both the Victorian Left and the Victorian Liberal North have not fully passed.

Not only is Dixie still recovering from Reconstruction—a period that Major J. C. C. Black called "the darkest, blackest, most damning chapter in the history of any civilized nation"[68]—but today a second wave of "Yankeefication" is sweeping over the South, with ever increasing industrialization, liberalization, and Northernization taking root in every Southern state. In point of fact, Reconstruction of the South has never completely stopped.

I know because, as a Southerner who has lived and traveled extensively across my ancestral home region, I have seen and experienced it firsthand, and I continue to see and experience it firsthand. For example, just as the Victorian Left did to truth-telling Southern writers 150 years ago, the modern Left censors, spreads disinformation about, and tries to prevent the sales of my books. The volume you now hold in your hand will almost certainly be suppressed and banned by Leftists (and even some uneducated Conservatives) in an attempt to prevent the Truth about Reconstruction from coming out.

The timeworn battle between good and evil continues.

Lincoln's dream of turning slow-paced, religious, agricultural Dixie into a facsimile of the fast-paced, atheistic, manufacturing North is indeed never far away, and traditional and Conservative Southerners must be on constant guard to protect their homeland, their culture, their history, their traditions, their schools, their beliefs, their symbols—their very way of life.

It is hoped that the truths I have compiled in *Twelve Years in Hell* concerning America's disgraceful and reprehensible 12-year "carnival of crime"[69] will aid in this endeavor. I pray too that these fact-based reminiscences will touch the hearts and minds of this and future generations, and help restore and maintain the valor, memory, and reputation of America's Southern "Civil War" generation. Their sole goal—as they repeatedly stated themselves[70]—was the preservation of the Constitution as it was originally constructed by the Founding Fathers. Thus, as true patriots, they have earned no less and deserve much more.

LOCHLAINN SEABROOK (unreconstructed)
Park County, Wyoming, USA
July 2023
In Nobis Regnat Christus

Important Note From the Author-Editor

In reading the following pages, I ask my readers to refuse to succumb to presentism—a favored tactic of the Left, which, in its ongoing effort to dominate and control us, it uses to suppress facts, rewrite history, and weaken society by sowing division, enmity, and distrust amongst its members.

Instead, bear in mind the extraordinariness of the period, the atypical milieu in which the events recorded in my book take place: 1865 to 1877; a time when anti-white socialists and communists in the then Left-wing Republican Party were in control of the U.S., and were sadistically punishing the South for wanting to be free and for thinking independently—which Liberals still refer to as "rebellion." This 12-year span, intentionally and deceptively named "Reconstruction" by the North, was marked, not by "reconciliation," as mainstream history books disingenuously teach, but by corruption, robbery, racism, intolerance, rapine, sadism, violence, and general immorality. Not on the part of the Conservative South, as we have been taught, but, as my readers shall see, on the part of the Liberal North.

All of the North's brutal postwar policies had an adverse effect on the South and directly influenced her reactions to Reconstruction. But none so much as the Left's "bottom rail on top" policy, in which—using minorities as political pawns, as it always does—the Left indoctrinated African-Americans with hatred for white Southerners, then placed them in positions of sociopolitical domination and financial and legal power. Thus a great deal of my writers' words are devoted to what they called "the race problem." More to the point, much of the white supremacy sentiment expressed by some of my writers was nothing more than a reaction to the institutional black supremacy being forced upon the South by white-hating Yankee Liberals.

Lastly, keep in mind that the words recorded in the following pages were penned over a century ago, in some cases far earlier. The world at that time, including what was acceptable and what was unacceptable concerning social norms, values, mores, customs, ethics, conventions, morals, manners, standards, behavior, and racial views, were obviously very different than they are today—just as social norms will be very different a century from now.

Judge not lest ye be judged.

We are all products of the time and place we are born in and live in. Let us pray that our descendants are more tolerant and less judgmental toward us than we have been toward our ancestors.

Lochlainn Seabrook

SECTION 1

RECONSTRUCTION: HISTORICAL ESSAYS

CHAPTER 1
THE SOUTH SINCE THE WAR

An Essay Written 1897-1898 by Confederate General

Stephen Dill Lee

THE DAY THE WAR ENDED
☛ THE WAR BETWEEN THE STATES came suddenly and finally to an end in the spring of 1865. The effort which the seceded States made to maintain their independence brought under demand every resource of the people, and they utterly exhausted everything they had in order to make their cause a success.

Confederate General Stephen Dill Lee.

The army of Gen. Robert E. Lee, in Virginia, surrendered April 9th; that of Gen. Joseph E. Johnston, in North Carolina, April 26th; that of Gen. Richard Taylor, in Mississippi, May 4th, and that of Gen. E. Kirby Smith, west of the Mississippi river, May 26, 1865. All other organized bodies of Confederate troops, as well as individual soldiers, wherever they happened to be, reported to the nearest officer in command of Union troops, surrendered and received their paroles. The surrender of the Confederate armies and soldiers was universal and sincere, so much so that there was not a Confederate soldier under arms throughout the South from Maryland to Mexico, by June 9, 1865, or two months from the date of the surrender of General Lee's army in Virginia. There was no reservation in this surrender, no desire or effort to continue the struggle as guerrillas or otherwise.

There was complete submission to the authority of the United States government by all in official and private station. President Jefferson Davis, Vice-President A. H. Stephens, Governor [Joseph E.] Brown of Georgia, Governor [Charles] Clark of Mississippi, Gen. Howell Cobb, and Senator [Benjamin H.] Hill of Georgia, and other distinguished citizens of various parts of the South, were immediately arrested and imprisoned. The members of the Confederate cabinet were either prisoners, fugitives or exiles. The Confederate congress was disbanded, the judiciary inoperative, the treasury empty, and the finances, resources and civil power of the Confederate States of America perished in the death struggle.

The complete and sudden collapse of the Confederate government officially was typical of the complete exhaustion and prostration of the South in the almost superhuman effort she had made to sustain herself against the great odds in men and resources which the United States government had brought to bear against her. The seceded States had put in the field more than their white arms-bearing population; when we consider how soon the border States were overrun and occupied, and remember how soon large portions of the territory of these seceded States were also guarded by the Union armies as to prevent any effort to further recruit the Southern armies, this is the more apparent. The Confederacy had enlisted an army of a little over 700,000 men and had fought over 2,200 battles. The struggle was made over nearly every foot of her territory. She had lost the flower of her youth in the death of 325,000 men from the casualties of war (about one-half her enlisted strength), and many more were disabled and ruined in health. It is a moderate estimate to say that 20 per cent of the white bread-winners of the South were killed or disabled by the war. There was scarcely a home from which one or two had not been taken. The mortality of the Southern troops was enormously greater in proportion than was that of the Union troops, which was only 359,000 men in all, while that of the Southern troops was 325,000 men, the forces of the former outnumbering the latter by over 2,000,000. The contending armies had moved to and fro over the Confederate territory, leaving many cities in ashes and tracts of country in almost every State in waste. The desolation of war had reached nearly every locality and home. The people were utterly impoverished. Nearly all business was destroyed, and the farms gone to wreck. There was no money in circulation; the banks were generally broken; there was no credit system; most of the commercial agencies were inoperative or suspended. The work stock used in making crops had been mostly destroyed or carried away. Provisions were scarce, having been taken by the one or the other of the contending armies. The paroled soldiers returned to find their homes desolate, and they were disheartened and humiliated by failure. They had nothing at hand with which to begin life anew, except their land and the brave hearts which had carried them through four years of war, which ended in the defeat of a cause they deemed just and honorable.

They found at home 4,000,00 slaves suddenly emancipated as a result of the war. They realized that the greatest problem any people had ever had to solve on sudden notice faced them. The negroes, as was natural that it should be, were greatly demoralized, and had but a faint conception of the responsibility of the freedom that was theirs, and that they knew had been brought about by the defeat of the Southern armies. Large numbers of them thought that freedom meant a cessation of labor on their part, and that the great government which had freed them by force of arms would feed, clothe and provide for them [just as their white Southern owners had]. They generally left their work in the fields and went in crowds to the cities and towns, where they were fed and cared for at the expense of the United States government. All this added greatly to the chaos and confusion of the time.

Private debts that had been incurred in a period of great prosperity, prior to 1861, and were unpaid at the beginning of the war, were still unpaid, and the property, on which most of these debts were contracted, no longer existed. The railroads and other means of transportation were almost wrecked. All factories and other industries were generally destroyed. Agriculture, the main means of support in the South, was almost demoralized by the need of work animals and on account of the disorganized labor. To add to the general confusion, the country was flooded with adventurers from the North, camp followers of the Union armies, and others who rushed to the South as soon as they realized that the war was over. These men, imbued with the prejudices and passions which existed at the North during the war, at once began to inflame the negroes against their recent masters, and offered themselves as their friends and advisers in their new condition of freedom. In many portions of the South, the property of private individuals was seized and claimed as abandoned property (under the Freedmen's Bureau law), and taken possession of for the use of the United States, and this property assigned for use to negroes who had left their homes and work. The new advisers generally led [that is, gaslit] the negroes to believe that the Southern people were going to try to put them back into slavery, and that the United States government would give to each able-bodied negro man at least forty acres of land and a mule.

To add to the general gloom, great apprehension was felt regarding the future. The war had been waged cruelly toward the close, as was evidenced by the track of desolation and devastation (without a parallel in modern warfare for its pitiless barbarity), averaging 50 miles in breadth, from the Tennessee line through Georgia to Savannah, and through South Carolina by Columbia to North Carolina, by the Union army under Gen. W. T. Sherman; and the desolation in the valley of Virginia by General [Philip H.] Sheridan, surpassing if anything that caused by Sherman's march to the sea. Everything the South fought for was lost and surrendered. The general feeling which was mingled with apprehension and fear found expression (by [Mississippi Senator Lucius Q. C.] Lamar) as follows:

> "We have given up the right of a people to secede from the Union; we have given up the right of each State to judge for itself of the infraction of the Constitution and the mode of redress; we have given up the right to frame our own domestic institutions. We fought for all these and we lost in that controversy."

It is difficult to estimate the pecuniary loss of the South in the war, but it may be partially estimated by comparing her conditions in 1860 and 1870 according to the United States census. In 1860 the total assessed value of property in the United States was $12,000,000,000. The assessed value in the South was $5,200,000,000 (44 per cent), and at that time the South was increasing in wealth faster than any other portion of the United States. The census of 1870 showed the assessed valuation in the South to be $3,000,000,000 only, a decline of $2,200,000,000 since the census of 1860, and the property of the South decreasing in value instead of increasing. This, too, in face of the fact that the total assessed value in the whole country was $14,170,000,000, an increase of $4,370,000,000 in the North, showing that the North had gotten rich during the war while the South was impoverished.

Though the valuation of property by census is used to estimate the values officially, it is always considerably less than the real value. The loss of the South is only partially shown by the census. If we consider what was spent by the South to carry on the war, the destruction of property during the war, and the other losses incident to so great and complete a failure, it is estimated that the total loss of the South will not fall below $5,000,000,000. Alexander H. Stephens, in his history of the United States, says the war cost both sides $8,000,000,000, three-fourths of the assessed value of property in the whole United States at the beginning of the war. When we consider that the war debt incurred by the United States government alone was $3,000,000,000, the estimate given is less than a reasonable one, for the cost to the North in actual loss and expense in prosecuting the was far beyond the war debt—the cost being estimated by some writers at $8,000,000,000.

Such was the condition of the South at the time (1865) exhausted, prostrated, disarmed, and in the presence of the victorious North, which then had an army, perhaps the best the world ever saw, of over 1,000,000 soldiers under arms. "Thus ended the war between the States," says Mr. Stephens. "It was waged by the Federals with the sole object, as they declared, of 'maintaining the Union under the Constitution,' while by the South it was waged with the great object of maintaining the inestimable sovereign right of local self-government on the part of the Southern States." The war had lasted four years and the battles fought were among the greatest of modern times, great patriotism and generalship being displayed on both sides. The successes and defeats during most of the time were nearly equally divided, until finally the South fell from exhaustion before overwhelming numbers and resources. Over 2,000,000 soldiers had been brought against her, over and above her total force, with a navy numbering 700 vessels of war, manned by 105,000 sailors, not including chartered vessels numbering near 3,000. This great fleet was used in occupying and holding the numerous rivers in Confederate territory, in [illegally] blockading the coast from Maryland to the Rio Grande, and in transporting armies and supplies around territory which could not be crossed or occupied directly.[71]

POLITICAL CONDITIONS BEFORE THE WAR, & AT ITS CLOSE

☛ To understand thoroughly the events which followed the close of the war, it is necessary to allude briefly to the political conditions of the North and South previous to the war, and the theories which each side acknowledged and adhered to to its close. For the first time in its history the great [U.S.] republic, which in its progress had grown in power, prosperity, resources and wealth so as to astonish the world, met the shock of revolution. Intricate questions difficult to solve and existing from the very formation of the government itself, had grown in intricacy with increase in power, population and prosperity, until the great political parties had divided on sectional lines [the Democrats, in 1860, being

Conservative, the Republicans being Liberal], and the solution of the questions culminated in the war between the States, the greatest war of modern times. Slavery, State rights and acquisition of territory were the irritating causes. The two sections fought against each other, though neither of them departed, except as the exigencies of the war temporarily demanded, from the great American principle of government as they had construed it, namely, the sovereignty of the States composing the respective confederations. The Congress of the United States, in July, 1861, while controlled by the Republican [then Liberal] party (the great war party), solemnly declared that the war was waged "to defend the Constitution and all laws in pursuance thereof, and to preserve the Union with all the dignity, equality, and rights of the several States unimpaired; that as soon as these objects were accomplished the war ought to cease." This was the accepted theory to the close of the war.

The seceded States, in their sovereign capacity and through constitutional conventions (the accepted method), severed their connection with the United States, formed a confederated government for common defense and adopted a constitution virtually the same as that of the United States, from which they had separated. They maintained for four years a government which was recognized as belligerent and *de facto* by other powerful nations, and at the close of that period, in theory, these States were still in the Confederacy, although it was *de facto* dead. In the theory of the Confederate government, and also of the United States government, the States composing each had been regarded as free and sovereign. They were as capable of maintaining self-government as they had been from the earliest days of the United States government. They as States had seceded from the United States in their sovereign capacity, and were capable of legally reconsidering their former action and again uniting with the other States of the Union, The people in the seceded States, as they understood it, had fought to perpetuate the Constitution of their fathers. They believed in State sovereignty in its broadest sense. This question had been an unsettled one always. They believed in the reserved rights of the States. They believed in the decisions of the Supreme court as finally settling all constitutional questions. They had looked to the Constitution to protect their property in slaves. They did not know what to expect next when fourteen of the States of the Union practically nullified the acts of Congress and the decisions of the highest court of the land in the matter of the fugitive slave laws. They had fought to maintain the constitution of

1789 as framed by a common ancestry. They felt and believed that they were actuated by as pure and lofty a spirit of liberty as had ever actuated and governed any people, and their devotion and sacrifices in the war were the evidence of this belief. The North entertained different views as to these questions. They wanted their views to prevail in the construction of the Constitution, and they wanted the Union to remain as it was. They had a majority of votes. The war came and the two irritating causes of difference, slavery and secession, were finally and forever settled against the South. They were eliminated as causes of dissension and difference and that, too, by the highest appeal known to man—that of arms.

The South could do nothing but accept the result of the war. This they were anxious to do, and desirous to claim the protection of the Constitution of their fathers, framed by common ancestry, North and South. They were ready to accept the results with the same honesty and sincerity with which they had been ready to sacrifice their lives and their property, and with which they had endured privations, hardships, and other trials not surpassed by any people in history. But while this was the case, they felt that they had borne themselves honorably and as a brave people, believing that they were right in the great struggle through which they had passed. All that they had left after that struggle were their integrity, their honor, and their deep-seated love for the American form of government. They were incapable of doing anything which would throw dishonor on their record, or of taking any action by which they would stultify themselves as to that record. They were in the frame of mind to patiently await the action of the United States government in restoring them to the places they had formerly occupied among the States of the Union before the war. They hoped that they would be treated generously, and they determined to submit to any reasonable demand made on them by the victorious North. They knew that they would have to accept what was meted out to them, whether it was good or bad, whether it was generous or ungenerous, as they were utterly incapable of resorting to arms again.

The status of the seceded States immediately after the War, politically, was as follows: The States of Virginia, Georgia, North Carolina, South Carolina, Mississippi, Texas and Florida had governments organized under their respective constitutions which they had in 1861. Tennessee, Arkansas (spring, 1864), and Louisiana (spring, 1864) were under bogus governments, organized and sustained by the military forces of the United States, not by the free will of its citizens. The States of Maryland, Missouri and

Kentucky had never seceded regularly [that is, fully and constitutionally] from the Union, and their State governments were quickly subdued and controlled by troops of the United States, and, because a large portion of the citizens of those States sympathised with the South, were held under strict surveillance during the entire war. This surveillance was carried to the extent of arresting legislators in Maryland, suspending the writ of *habeas corpus* in counties and localities everywhere, and arresting and imprisoning thousands suspected of disloyalty to the United States government. Editors of [Northern] newspapers were arrested for criticising the [U.S.] government, and martial law existed generally in the border States—all being violations of the Constitution.[72]

PROPER LEGAL WAY OF RESTORING THE SECEDED STATES

☞ The proper legal course which should have been pursued by the United States, if the Union was "an indissoluble Union of indestructible States," as afterward stated by the Supreme court of the United States, and if the Constitution of the United States was to be the guide, was as follows:

> "With the cessation of hostilities against the power of the United States, nothing remained to be done but for the sovereigns, the people of each State, to assert their authority and restore order. If the principle of the sovereignty of the people, the corner-stone of our political institutions, had survived and was still in force was necessary only that the people of each State should reconsider and revoke their ordinances of secession and again recognize the Constitution of the United States as the supreme law of the land. This simple process would have placed the Union on its original basis, and would have restored what had ceased to exist—the Union.[73] Unfortunately such was not the intention of the conqueror. Henceforth there was to be established a union by force." [Confederate President Jefferson Davis]

These views were also entertained by [Confederate] Vice-President Alexander H. Stephens, and seemed to have been entertained by [Union] Generals Grant and Sherman in arranging with [Confederate] Generals Lee and [Joseph E.] Johnston for the surrender of the Southern armies. Certainly they were the true, legal, and non-political views, unless, now that the war was over the Constitution was to be further strained and violent coercive measures inaugurated after the South had laid down her arms. There can be little doubt now that most of the conservative Democrats at the North, and even conservative [leaning] Republicans [then the Liberal party], entertained these views, until the breach between the [U.S.] President and [the U.S.] Congress became so wide and bitter, and the President so violent in his denunciation of Congress.[74]

PROBLEMS TO BE SOLVED
☛ There were many complex problems to be solved as a result of the war. The responsibility of their solution necessarily rested in the greater degree upon the United States government. It had been completely victorious in the struggle. It had all the power in its hands, and it was evident, as every foot of the lately seceded States was occupied by its troops, that the South could only expect such treatment as it dictated. These problems may be stated generally as follows: To restore the seceded States to the Union; to establish tranquillity throughout the Union; to legally abolish slavery, and invest the negro with the civil rights necessary for his protection; to provide ways and means for liquidating the vast war debt incurred on both sides by both governments and by the individual States; to determine whether there was criminality in secession or in the conduct of the war by the Confederates; to preserve the essential radical principles of the Constitution and prevent change in the structure of the United States government; to reinstate fraternal feelings among the late antagonists.

The main question was not as to the freedom of the negroes, for their freedom was unquestionable—not doubted by any one—as a result of the war, the success of the Union armies, the proclamation of President Lincoln, and the establishment of the Freedmen's bureau by the Congress of the United States. Nor was the question whether secession should be made forever illegal by positive law. For no statesman would subject himself to ridicule by attempting to deny all right of future popular revolutions by the mere force of a statute, or by a clause in the Constitution. Nor was it whether treason be made odious by degrading great States and harassing a vast body of peaceful people; for jurists were saying that no treason had been committed, and that States cannot be tried by courts. Only some politicians, partisans and not patriots, were crying with reference to the Southern people, "Let them be made odious." Nor should it have been whether party supremacy must be maintained. That is, shall the party which caused the war, fought for the war, and pressed it to the success of the conquest—shall its supremacy and security be the main questions? Some partisans so desired, and acted on their wishes. But the conditions of the era should have raised all issues above the fetid atmosphere of politics. It was not the time to be either a Democrat [Conservative] or a

Republican [Liberal]—but a patriot.[75]

RECONSTRUCTION

☞ *What is known as the reconstruction of the seceded States is a very sad epoch to recall, and no American who loves his country likes to bring back its harsh memories* [my emphasis, L.S.]. Yet it is a matter of history and it needs be recorded in order that the part which the North and the South played during that period should be fully understood. It began under President Lincoln before the close of the war, and was carried on by President [Andrew] Johnson after the assassination of President Lincoln, during the years 1865 and 1866. *Afterward there was a second phase of reconstruction, or "destruction," known as the congressional plan, which undid all that had been done by Presidents Lincoln and Johnson. This latter period was the greatest trial that the South had to bear* [my emphasis, L.S.], not excepting the terrible ordeal of war. To understand properly the surroundings, it is necessary to enumerate briefly the events which occurred early in 1865, and the directions given by President Johnson to the military officers of the United States. First, I would mention the death of Mr. Lincoln himself, which was regarded as the greatest calamity that could have happened to the people of the South. The arrest and imprisonment of [Confederate] President Davis and many of the Confederate soldiers and statesmen have been already related. The treatment of Mr. Davis was very harsh indeed, complicity in the assassination of Mr. Lincoln being cruelly imputed to him, and a large reward offered for his capture. He was placed in prison and shackled with irons in the strongest fortress in the Union, and a military guard placed over him day and night.[76] Every town, village and district was occupied rapidly by the Union troops as the Confederate resistance melted away, and all civil government was ignored. The governors of most of the seceded States attempted to call their legislatures together to conform to the results of the war

U.S. President Andrew Johnson.

and take steps for their restoration to the Union. They did this, believing that the American principle of government—the sovereignty and indestructibility of the States—would be respected and that these prompt proceedings would be favored as the constitutional plan of restoration. They did this also believing it absolutely necessary to preserve civil government, and to show by legislative enactment complete submission to the results of the war in repealing their ordinances of secession and in accepting the freedom of the negro.

The order issued by General [James H.] Wilson, of the United States army in Georgia, when the legislature was called to meet, was to this effect:

> "Neither the legislature nor any other political body will be permitted to assemble under the call of the rebel State authorities."

The spirit of this order was carried out in all the seceded States. Existing civil government was ignored everywhere, and military rule inaugurated in municipal and local communities. The only government allowed was that of the local military officers, or under their supervision.

This harsh action of the United States authorities, civil and military, immediately following the collapse of the Confederate government, caused all prominent actors in the war to feel insecure. They did not know what to expect. It was not known how general the arrests and imprisonments would be, and many leading men, civil and military, escaped to foreign lands, and for the time expatriated themselves. Gen. Jubal Early, with others, escaped to Cuba. Generals [William W.] Loring, Graves, and a few other officers went to Egypt and took service under the khedive. Hons. Robert Toombs, J. C. Breckinridge and many others went to Europe. Gov. Isham G. Harris, Gens. J. Bankhead Magruder, [Thomas C.] Hindman and [Sterling] Price went to Mexico; in fact, prominent citizens and soldiers everywhere felt great apprehension as to the course of the [U.S.] government, even with their paroles. It was even contemplated by President Johnson and his advisers to arrest and imprison Gen. Robert E. Lee, who had surrendered his army to General Grant and had been paroled. General Grant, however, entered a vigorous protest against such action, and insisted that men who had surrendered with arms in their hands were entitled to the usual laws recognized by all civilized nations, and that their paroles should be respected. This action on his part, and the advice of Gen. Robert E. Lee and the leading statesmen, officers, and soldiers of all the lately seceded States, caused it to be thought best for all to remain in their respective States and share whatever fate was in store for the South. The feeling of expatriation was greatly allayed when such prominent men advised against it.[77]

PRESIDENTIAL RECONSTRUCTION

☛ President Lincoln began to reconstruct the seceded States when he issued his amnesty proclamation in December, 1863, which offered pardon to all who were in arms if they would lay them down and take an oath to support the government of the United States. He said he would recognize a State government as a loyal government, provided as many as one-tenth of the number who voted in 1860 would organize a State government and comply with certain conditions named in the proclamation. It was evident also, that he followed the spirit of the resolution passed by Congress in July, 1861, as to preservation of the Union, "with all the dignity, equality and rights of the several States unimpaired," although in the progress of the war, the Constitution was greatly strained, and had been, at times, ignored [by Lincoln] to secure success which he regarded as paramount to a restored Union. He tried personally to keep as near the principles of the Constitution as was possible in war. His object was to restore the Union. This was the one object near his heart. His theory was,

> "that the States were never out of the Union; that the people of these States, when they returned to their allegiance, had the power of reconstruction in their own hands."

His views as to the qualification of voters were given in his proclamation of 1863, referred to in his message of December 21, 1863, viz:

> "Being a qualified voter by the election laws of the State, existing immediately before the so-called act of secession and excluding all other, shall re-establish a State government."

He believed in the people; to the extent that the people in the seceded States, notwithstanding the war, should and must be trusted. There can be no doubt as to Mr. Lincoln's intention in reconstructing the Southern States, and time has demonstrated that his statesmanship was correct, and that his principles were based on the proper theory of the organization of the government. The decisions of the Supreme court since the war clearly sustain his general views.

When he visited Richmond early in April, 1865, after the city had been occupied by the Union troops, he conversed freely with leading citizens, and after leaving the place and arriving at City Point (near Richmond), on his way back to Washington, on April 6, 1865, he sent written authority to [Union] General [Godfrey] Weitzel, commanding the United States forces in Richmond, "to permit the assembling of the legislature of Virginia;" and a formal call was issued, signed by prominent citizens and approved by the general commanding. In his letter he directed the general to extend his "permission" and "protection" to the assembly until it should attempt any action hostile to the United States. He intended at that time to restore the States through their existing legislatures and executives, acknowledging the State as a political authority, and as represented by them through its constituted authority. If he had not so considered the matter before, he thought so now that he saw the war was virtually over. He was ready to restore the Union as far as he was able in accordance with the principles and resolutions promulgated over and over again in the halls of Congress during the war, and that, too, in the most expeditious way.

On his return to Washington from Richmond, he [Lincoln] changed his mind as to [correctly and legally] restoring Virginia to the Union through the executive and legislature as then existing under the constitution of that State, and he recalled the [original] order given [to Union] General [Godfrey] Weitzel [to allow Virginia to do so]. It is not known why he did so, but he evidently was informed that he would again have trouble with the extreme men of his party [that is, Republican—then the Left-wing party—socialists and communists] if he pursued this policy; and he deemed it best to revoke the order and await events then rapidly following the collapse of the Confederate government. A few days afterward he was assassinated (April 14th). This monstrous crime was a great calamity both to the North and to the South. Lincoln was a statesman and had a good heart. He had the prestige of success. His brain and heart were then grappling with the problems of restoring the seceded States to the Union. He had maturely digested the plan, had discussed it with his cabinet, and they had agreed with him. Restoration had in fact proceeded so far that the proclamation to restore civil government in North Carolina had been prepared. Mr. Lincoln had great tact in controlling men and bringing them to his views without irritating those who differed with him, as all conceded his patriotism, his love of the Union, and his sincerity.

The effect of [Lincoln's] death on the people of the North and the South was electrical. At the North it intensified hatred and revengeful feelings toward the crushed South, and gave excuse to extremists [socialists and communists] to push their views to the injury of the people of the seceded States in their extreme helplessness. At the South, the people were shocked at the tragedy and condemned it in their brave hearts. They felt that Lincoln was the most moderate and kind-hearted of the men in power at the North, and believed that he, if any one could, would hold in check all extreme measures and stand between them and all unnecessary severities.[78]

It is not certain, however, that Mr. Lincoln's policy would have been otherwise than the "reconstruction" policy of Congress. He intended to attempt to carry out his matured plan if possible [my emphasis, L.S.]. His pocket veto of the bill of Congress in 1864, relative to reconstructing the seceded States, and his giving no official explanation in his next message to Congress, showed that he was adhering his prerogative of restoring the States as he had determined. He knew that there was great opposition by extremists in his party [Republican socialists and communists] to his proposed plan of action, yet Congress had not renewed its claims to the extent of antagonizing him again before his death. Congress and a majority of the Northern people had confidence in his ability, and apparently were disposed to give him the right of way by adjourning, March, 1865.

Mr. Lincoln, however, was a party man; his fealty to his party dominated him. Before his death, many of the party leaders demanded a reconstruction that would enable them to control the South as well as the North. The [then Left-wing] Republican majority distrusted the Northern Democrats [that is, Yankee Conservatives], who were less disposed to violate the Constitution by going too far out of the beaten tracks of the past. Mr. [Edwin M.] Stanton, the great [U.S.] war secretary, said, "If he (Lincoln) had lived, he would have had a hard time with his party, as he would have been at odds with it on reconstruction." His speech made in answer to a serenade immediately preceding his death, showed that, although he had recalled permission for the Virginia legislature to meet at Richmond, he still adhered to a liberal view of reconstructing and restoring the Southern States.

He would certainly have met the opposition of many in his party, and whether or not his persuasive tact in dealing with such matters would have prevented the extremes to which his party carried legislation after his death, is a matter of speculation. It is believed that *the appointment of provisional governors was a concession to the extreme* [socialist/communist] *party in Congress even before his death* [my emphasis, L.S.]. He recognized that the States had control of suffrage, and that negroes had no legal right to vote except as that boon was given them by the State. It is generally agreed now, that the death of Mr. Lincoln was at least a great blow to early reconciliation, if it did not end the last hope entertained for a conservative and wise policy of reconstruction.[79]

RECONSTRUCTION BY ANDREW JOHNSON

☛ President Andrew Johnson was of a different temperament from his predecessor—most combative, aggressive, and abusive to those who differed with him, and not a safe man for such a great emergency. While he was a great Union man, his ideas were generally Democratic [then Conservative] rather than Republican [then Liberal], in that he was more conservative [that is, like a majority of Conservatives then as now, quite literal-minded] in his construction of the Constitution.

President Johnson was sworn into office April 14, 1865, immediately after the death of Mr. Lincoln. Congress had adjourned early in March, and the field was open to him to act independently and without congressional interference. His first act was to retain the entire cabinet of Mr. Lincoln, and he proceeded at once to adopt and follow out the plan which had been decided upon by his predecessor. The States of Arkansas, Louisiana and Tennessee had already had their new governments approved and accepted by Mr. Lincoln, and under the conditions of his proclamation of 1863. Virginia had been dismembered in 1862, and forty counties out of one hundred and forty in the State had been erected into a new State known as West Virginia [illegally pushed and allowed by Lincoln in an effort to provide additional electoral votes for himself in his 1864 bid for reelection].[80] Before this was done, these counties had a State government which had been recognized as the true loyal government of Virginia. When this government became the separate State of West Virginia, Francis H. Pierpont, who had been governor, had an election in a few counties so he could hold on as a governor. He was elected, and moved out of the west of the old State and set up as governor in the city of Alexandria, near Washington, where, at pleasure, he had a convention or legislature composed of not over sixteen members, and claimed to be the loyal governor of Virginia.

The proclamation for the restoration of civil government in North Carolina had already been matured by Mr. Lincoln and his cabinet. This paper was presented by Mr. Stanton in Mr. Johnson's cabinet meeting, was approved and accepted by him, and promulgated on May 29, 1865. In this instrument, he appointed W. H. Holden provisional governor, with authority to call a convention to frame a constitution for the State. The voters were designated as those who were entitled to vote under the constitution of the State at the time it seceded. Amnesty was offered to all who had taken part in the war with certain exceptions, viz., all [Confederate] military officers above the rank of colonel, naval officers above the rank of lieutenant, governors, judges of courts, West Point officers, all civil officers of the Confederate government, and all citizens worth over $20,000. A fair estimate is that this exclusion fell upon at least 120,000 men in the South. The excluded persons were required to make application for pardon. Each voter had to take an oath as follows:

> "I, _____, do solemnly swear or affirm in presence of Almighty God that I will hereafter faithfully support and defend the Constitution of the United States and the Union thereunder, and that I will in like manner abide by faithfully and support all laws and proclamations which have been made during the existing rebellion with reference to the emancipation of slaves. So help me God."

Similar proclamations were issued for the States of South Carolina, Georgia, Alabama, Mississippi, Florida and Texas. In all the proclamations, the feature mainly noted was that voters were qualified by the laws of the State in force at the time they seceded, and these voters were to restore the State to the Union. Without any reservation, every citizen and former soldier determined to make the reconstruction plan of President Johnson a success;[81] even those who were excluded from amnesty by proclamation, gave their moral support and advice for every one who could take part to do so, and as soon as possible, restore civil law and get from under military rule. Every one was anxious to see order come from the confusion then existing, so that a beginning could be made in restoring prosperity, building up waste places, and with brave hearts, removing the scars of war evident in every spot in the South. There was great unanimity in all the States in expediting the process. The provisional governors quickly issued their proclamations, generally restoring civil and local law as far as possible by continuing in office all persons who had been holding State and county offices, till others could be regularly appointed or elected. In the confusion and chaos of the times, there were local frictions occasionally. The military officers interfered frequently, but the governors considered this as incident to the surroundings and took no exceptions. The people showed great evenness of temper and displayed most remarkable forbearance. The [Republicans' socialist-communist run] Freedmen's bureau was in operation, and its [radical] administration tended to inflame both races and produce collisions.

During this trying period, the people of the South did as best they could amid the great trials and perplexities which surrounded them, and the civil and military pressure brought to bear on them. Provost guards [U.S.] were set up over municipal government. Military courts [U.S.] were established [across the South], and many of the best [Southern] citizens were arrested on frivolous complaints of irresponsible negro men and women, and under military guard, forced to appear at county seats before these [socialist-communist] courts and undergo trial. Bayonet rule [that is, a ruthless military state] was the order of the day; [Southern] civil officers were disregarded and humiliated.

Repudiation of State war debts was pressed as a necessity for success in restoring States. The pressure was brought to bear by the [U.S.] president [Johnson] and Secretary Seward. This repudiation was done under protest upon the behest of Federal power. The [tyrannical] reign of the provisional [U.S.] governors and [U.S.] military officers was very odious, and the humiliating conditions, not necessary to mention now, developed a spirit of forbearance, sacrifice, and discretion remarkable in a people high-strung and liberty-loving although crushed.

By the fall of 1865, the States were reorganized, and the program of the president carried out to the letter, so much so that when Congress met in December he was able to report in his message that civil government had been restored in the States of North Carolina, South Carolina, Georgia, Alabama, Mississippi, Louisiana and Tennessee. These States had adopted new constitutions, elected governors, senators and representatives in congress, and State and county officers. Great prudence and good taste were displayed in the elections. Generally those who had originally opposed secession and were considered as Union in sentiment were elected to the new offices. Those who had been in any way prominent in urging resistance took back seats and did not aspire to official positions. It is true, however, that nearly all who had originally opposed separate State action went with their States in the war and determined to share the common fate.

The people, however, did not stultify themselves by electing Republicans to office; in fact, there was none to be elected then. Welded together by common misfortunes, there was but one party in the South, the white man's party. While all were ready to accept the results in a dignified and manly way, they were not ready to humiliate themselves by any voluntary act reflecting on the motives which impelled them to go into the war. The States had repealed their ordinances of secession which had taken them out of the Union. Five of the States had ratified the Thirteenth amendment to the Constitution abolishing slavery, making in all eleven of the former slave-holding States and sixteen free States, and their votes were accepted and counted to make up the necessary two-thirds needed to ratify it and make it law. Civil law was in force. State and county officers were in the exercise of the functions of their offices. The president, by a proclamation issued April 2, 1866, finally announced the full restoration of every one of the seceded States, stating that "no organized armed resistance" existed anywhere; that the laws "can be sustained and enforced therein by proper civil authority, State and Federal; that the people of said States are well and loyally disposed, and have conformed or will conform in their legislation to the condition of affairs growing out of the amendment to the Constitution prohibiting slavery within the borders and jurisdictions of the United States." He named Georgia, South Carolina, North Carolina, Virginia, Tennessee, Alabama, Louisiana, Arkansas, Mississippi and Florida as included. He pronounced the insurrection "at an end and henceforth to be so regarded." This proclamation may be regarded as the end of the presidential [Reconstruction] plan.

The States, excepting Texas, had perfected what they had been required to do, and but for the friction caused by the armed forces of the Union everywhere, the tendency to race collisions in the [socialist-communist] administration of the [ethnomasochistic, white-people hating] Freedman's bureau, and grave apprehension as to the future action of Congress, matters were beginning to assume normal conditions in the re-establishment of civil government, which had been destroyed immediately after the close of armed resistance throughout the South.[82]

CONGRESSIONAL RECONSTRUCTION

☛ Congress had adjourned in March and left matters entirely in the hands of President Lincoln, so that when it met December 4, 1865, there had been a recess of over eight months, in which Presidents Lincoln and Johnson had had time to carry out their plans coincident with the rapid happening of events incident to the sudden collapse of the Confederate government. Upon the meeting of Congress a concurrent resolution was immediately passed by a party vote in both houses to appoint a committee of fifteen, nine representatives and six senators, with instructions to look into the condition of the seceded States, and to advise Congress as to whether or not they should be represented in Congress under the organization effected through the plan of President Johnson. The committee, as conceded by leading men of the time, was really to look after the interests of the Republican [that is, Liberal] party, and to devise some scheme to perpetuate its power. It was admirably organized for this purpose, and was composed of twelve Republicans [Liberals] and three Democrats [Conservatives]. Its duty was to visit the States lately at war with the United States and take testimony on which to formulate a report. In the meantime the senators and representatives elected to Congress under the president's plan were in Washington seeking to be admitted to their seats. Their names were not put on the rolls in organizing the two houses of Congress, and they were left in expectancy, awaiting the pleasure of Congress, until February 26, 1866, when another concurrent resolution was passed in both houses to the effect that neither house should admit any members from the late insurrectionary States until the committee of fifteen, known as the "reconstruction committee," made its report, and Congress had taken action on it. It was resolved also that the Union troops should be kept in the South [to continue to enforce the military state] till Congress recalled them.

As this illustration from the July 25, 1868, edition of Harper's Weekly clearly shows, the Freedmen's Bureau, a creation of South-loathing Left-wing Yankees, further divided and antagonized the races—its primary purpose to begin with.

On February 6, 1866, another [racist, anti-white] Freedmen's bureau bill, enlarging the powers of the bureau and with much severer conditions than the preceding one, was passed, but was [understandably] vetoed by the president [a Tennessee Democrat, that is, a Southern Conservative]. In March, a "civil rights" bill was passed, making all persons born in the United States and not subject to any foreign power "citizens of the United States," and affixing penalties to cover the execution of the law. Each measure bore severely on the white people of the South and enlarged the rights and political conditions of the negroes lately enfranchised, and both showed a determination to override the president and make Congress the sole authority in all matters relating to the reconstruction of the lately seceded States. In June, the Fourteenth amendment to the Constitution was proposed to the States for adoption. The object of this [second anti-South] amendment was to put into the fundamental law the provisions of the "civil rights" bill, which had been passed over the president's veto. Congress had now full power, since it had the majority necessary to pass its bills over the veto of the president. This fourteenth amendment meant negro citizenship and *white disfranchisement* [my emphasis, L.S.] and it reduced representation in Congress, taking the right to regulate suffrage from the States and putting it in the hands of Congress, thus conforming to the provision of the "civil rights" bill. It refused Federal [U.S.] offices to all prominent civil and military officers of the late Confederacy until pardoned by Congress; enforced the repudiation of all debts or obligations "incurred in the aid of insurrection or rebellion against the United States." The States had to accept this amendment or remain without the restoration of civil government.

In July, another [racist] Freedmen's bureau bill was passed over the president's veto, extending the provisions [and authority] of the [anti-white] bureau, enlarging the power of the commissioner and appointing [hostile South-hating] agents in almost every locality, and appropriating as much as $6,887,700 for its support. Military protection was given to the agents everywhere to enforce the provisions of the act. In fact, every agent was in himself a court with military power back of him. Every agent had to be able to take the ironclad oath which necessarily confined the appointments mainly to newcomers in the different States. *A more ingenious law to show distrust and alienate the negroes and whites of the South who had to live together, could not have been framed* [my emphasis, L.S.].

The State of Tennessee was admitted to congressional representation July 24, 1866, having ratified both the [anti-South] Thirteenth and Fourteenth amendments to the Constitution.

The committee of fifteen had rendered its report June 18th, and Congress adjourned the latter part of July, 1866. The action of Congress during this session, from December 4, 1865, to July 28, 1866, inaugurated by its legislation a fierce war against the executive branch of the government. There was a great gulf between them. The president [Andrew Johnson] considered the war as over, Congress said it was not over and that the lately seceded States had forfeited all claim to protection or appeal to the Constitution; that they were conquered provinces and not "indestructible States of an indissoluble union." This, too, was said in spite of the resolution passed in 1861, "that this war is not waged on our part in any spirit of oppression, nor for the purpose of conquest or subjugation, nor for the purpose of interfering with or overthrowing the rights of established institutions of the States."[83]

RETROSPECT

☞ At the close of this first session of the Thirty-ninth Congress, which showed the great divergence between the executive and legislative branches of the government, and which also *included the beginning of a darker and more revengeful period of reconstruction for the South* [my emphasis, L.S.], it is necessary to take a retrospective view of certain conditions not already considered. When Congress met in December, 1865, the president [Johnson] accompanied his message with a report of a tour which [Union] General Grant had made through the South during the latter part of November preceding the assembling of Congress. This report, coming from the highest possible authority, confirmed the president as to the correctness of his message in regard to the feeling of the people of the South. It was to this effect:

> "With the approval of the president and secretary of war, I left Washington on the 27th of last month for the purpose of making a tour of inspection in the Southern States. . . . I am satisfied that the mass of thinking men of the South accept the present situation of affairs in good faith. . . . There is universal acquiescence in the authority of the general government. . . . *My observations lead to the conclusion that they [the citizens of the Southern States] are anxious to return to self-government within the Union as soon as possible* [my emphasis, L.S.]; that they are in earnest in wishing to do what they think is required by the government, not humiliating to them as citizens, and if such a course was pointed out they would pursue it in good faith."

General Grant could not have given a more correct or accurate statement as to the animus of the people of the South in the winter of 1865. His testimony in reference to the Freedmen's bureau, obtained during that same trip, is of most valuable character, showing the estimate of its workings as noted by a man not a politician, but a great soldier, and one who was most instrumental in attaining success to the Union armies. From conscientious agents administering the workings of the bureau, he learned that the "belief widely spread among the freedmen [emancipated former black servants] of the Southern States that the lands of their former owners will at least in part be divided among them, came from agents of this bureau. This belief is seriously interfering with the willingness of the freedmen to make contracts for the coming year. ... Many, perhaps the majority of the agents of the bureau, advise the freedmen that by their own industry they must expect to live. ... In some instances, I am sorry to say, the freedman's mind does not seem to be disabused of the idea that he had a right to live without care or provision for the future [just as he formally had as a "slave"]. The effect of this belief in the division of lands is idleness and accumulation in camps, towns and cities." This is as General Grant saw it in the winter of 1865, and *under the act extending and enlarging the scope and powers of the bureau, it was ten times worse after war. He evidently then saw the drift of the work of the [anti-white] bureau and the aim and object of the [anti-South] agents. Nearly every agent became a politician in the near future and was a candidate for office. Under the congressional reconstruction they were elected to nearly all of the Federal, State and county offices by virtue of their influence over the ignorant [that is, uneducated] negroes, and in effecting the organization of [nefarious] "Union League" clubs* [my emphasis, L.S.].

It was to the interest of the agents to create distrust and suspicion on the part of the negroes toward all Southern whites, and to cause them to look only to themselves (the agents) for justice and their rights. So long as they could cause friction, encourage idleness by raising false hopes of support and obtaining lands from the government, and create the impression that their rights could only be obtained through them, it would prolong the necessity of their offices being continued. All this unsettling work was done through men nearly all whom were not born in the South and had never been citizens of the South, but who had all the prejudices and bad blood of the times toward the South [my emphasis, L.S.].[84]

OBJECTIONS URGED AGAINST PRESIDENTIAL RECONSTRUCTION

☛ There were some features in the new constitutions adopted and in the laws being passed by the legislature under these constitutions, which were to be seized upon by the Republican party [a Left-wing party at the time] as an excuse for a more severe reconstruction by Congress. I mention first that suffrage was confined to the whites alone; even the most conservative element [Democrats at the time], which had taken the lead in restoring the States, did not think their recent slaves fit subjects for the great boon of the ballot.[85] A good many of the Northern [that is, Liberal] States did not allow negroes to vote; in fact, several States even after the war defeated acts proposing to give them the ballot, when there were only a few negroes within their borders. This suffrage feature had much to do with the States not being admitted. Public opinion at the North, under the lead of [anti-South socialist] Mr. Thaddeus Stevens, of Pennsylvania, and other extreme [Left] partisans, was fast drifting in favor of universal suffrage and the adoption of a disciplinary and coercive legislation toward the South, forgetting that nearly all negroes lived at the South, with but few at the North to be affected by such legislation.[86] It was a great problem, yet hostility toward the South turned the scale to the enfranchisement of the negro and disfranchisement of enough whites to create negro domination in the South [part of the Left's plan to sew discord in order to weaken Dixie and take control].

[Union] General Grant, in his description of the Freedmen's bureau, stated enough to show that legislation was necessary to check the demoralization among the negroes, and to influence them to return to habits of industry and self-support. As he stated, *large numbers had quit work in the fields, and considered their newly-acquired freedom as relieving them from labor. Somehow they felt that the [U.S.] government would feed, clothe and care for them [a way of life they had become accustomed to as "slaves"]. This was being done by the bureau, and large numbers had assembled in cities and towns to be supported* (my emphasis, L.S.]

If the new State governments were to take charge, as State governments did in other States, and as was the case before secession, wisdom admonished the legislator to provide for this condition of things and correct it. *The Southern people had lived with the negroes; they understood them far better than did the Northern people and the politicians of the North* [my emphasis, L.S.]. Some legislatures, to meet this condition of affairs, passed certain laws known as vagrant laws, similar to many found on the statute books of the Northern States, possibly a little different because the surroundings were different. The North, however, in the desire to protect the negro from imposition, not fully understanding matters, took great offense at this, and felt that it was an effort to re-enslave the negro, and defeat the purpose of his freedom. A careful analysis of these vagrant laws, so called, and similar laws on the statute books of the North framed to meet conditions far less aggravated and void of the prejudices and bad blood of the time, will show there was no ground for this excuse seized upon to defeat presidential reconstruction. These laws were of little import anyway, for *the bureaus of refugees, freedmen and abandoned lands, backed by military force, were overriding everything in a supposed protection of the rights of the negroes, encouraging them in idleness and inculcating vicious ideas and hostility toward the Southern whites* [my emphasis, L.S.][87]

COMMITTEE OF FIFTEEN

☛ The committee of fifteen was carefully selected to carry out its purpose, viz.. to perpetuate the power and continued existence of the Republican party [then the major Liberal party]. It was the duty of this committee to visit the lately seceded States and take testimony for the guidance of Congress in coming to a correct conclusion. It was divided into sub-committees. There being but three Democrats [then Conservatives] on the committee, most of the sub-committees visiting more than one-half of the States had no Democrat on them to cross-question witnesses or call for witnesses to present the side of the people to be investigated. It may be stated generally here that the Democrats [Conservatives] in Congress and in the North were opposed to the extreme and radical [socialist-communist] measures of reconstruction, and joined with the president [Johnson] to hinder and alleviate all harsh legislation against the South. They [Yankee Conservatives] were the only ones in those days who said a kind word for the South, or tried to befriend her, although they had been good Union men and had done their full duty to the North in the war against the South.

The people to be investigated and inquired into were of the whole South. They had not a single representative in Congress to speak for them, and the Democrats [Conservatives] who did speak were classed as copperheads, sympathizing with the South in her war against the Union. *A more one-sided, partisan, unfair, ungenerous investigation was never set on foot against a helpless people* [my emphasis, L.S.]. A fair sample of the work of this committee is given when they investigated Alabama.

> "As to the condition of Alabama, only five persons who claimed to be citizens were examined. They were all Republican [Liberal] politicians. The testimony of each was bitterly partisan. Under the government of the State as it then existed, no one of these witnesses could hope for official preferment. In his testimony each was striving for the overthrow of his State government and the setting up of some such [Left-wing] institutions as followed under congressional reconstruction. When this reconstruction finally had taken place, the first of these five became governor of his State; the second became a senator, and the third secured a life position in one of the departments in Washington. The fourth became a judge of the supreme court of the District of Columbia, all as Republicans."

Of all the people of Alabama who had gone into the war (a

number over her arms-bearing population [white] by the census of 1860), the people who were to be investigated in that State, not a single witness was called. Every witness was a selfish, prejudiced one, anticipating a reward for the kind of testimony he had given, and which reward he duly received. This one-sided testimony is a sample of the testimony taken in all the States by this committee, having the lives and fortunes of a brave people in its power. The people on trial before this partisan court were allowed no witnesses, had no voice or testimony in the matter. The committees summoned only such witnesses as they desired, and who would be likely to give the testimony needed to carry out the [Left-wing] purposes for which they were selected. They were pitiless in their work, for they saw and knew how prostrated and helpless the South was. But, *seeing as they did, the poverty and destruction of the property of the South, it is strange that even a committee of politicians working for party supremacy could deliberately recommend so terrible an ordeal as was congressional reconstruction* [my emphasis, L.S.].[88]

The committee made its report June 18, 1866, near the close of the first session of Congress, a report

> "admirably adapted to serve as a manifesto and campaign document, for a new House of Representatives was to be elected before Congress should again convene. It declared that the governments of the States recently in secession were practically suspended by reason both of the irregular character of the governments which had been set up, and of the reluctant acquiescence of the Southern people in the results of the war; and that it was essential to the preservation of the Union that they should not be reinstated in their former privileges by Congress until they should have given substantial pledges of loyalty and submission." [Woodrow Wilson]

This is certainly a very different conclusion from that arrived at by General Grant.[89]

ANOTHER STEP IN RECONSTRUCTION
☛ The Republicans [Liberals], at the close of the first session of the Thirty-ninth Congress, with the report of the committee of fifteen as a campaign document, inaugurated a most bitter partisan campaign at the North in the election of the new House of Representatives in the fall of 1866. *Although the war had been over since April, 1865, the Southern people were represented as still in insurrection and not reconciled to the results of the war, notwithstanding the fact that they had reorganized their State governments, repealed their ordinances of secession, and ratified the Thirteenth amendment abolishing*

slavery. All the bitterness and hatred of the war were revived by the Republicans [Liberals] in this campaign, and every possible unfair accusation was launched against the sincerity and motives of the people of the lately seceded States. They affirmed that they still intended hostility toward the Union, and had a fixed purpose to defeat the legitimate results of the war. So wrought up were the people of the North that they returned the Republican party [Liberal] to power with an increased majority [my emphasis, L.S.].

The last session of the Thirty-ninth Congress met in December, 1865, feeling safe in pushing the bitter legislation against the South and in their ability to overrule any veto of President Johnson's. A caucus committee of the Republican party [then Liberal] was appointed to take special charge of this legislation and *push it forward with the radical* [socialist-communist] *rules* of a bitter caucus program. Hostile [that is, anti-South, anti-white] legislation was at once started in the shape of a tenure of office law to tie the hands of the President and prevent his removal of persons in office who were in sympathy with the [Left-wing] policy of Congress. *This and other legislation was intended to open the way for more radical [socialist-communist] legislation toward the South to follow in the near future* [my emphasis, L.S.]. It was also provided that the first session of the new Congress (Fortieth) should meet immediately upon the close of the Thirty-ninth Congress, on March 4th, instead of December, 1867. This was to give a continuous session of Congress till the [radical Left-wing] congressional reconstruction plan was fairly put in operation, and so that the President could not cause delay. General Grant's power as commander-in-chief of the army was increased, and he was made in a measure independent of the President.

On March 2nd, just before the close of the Thirty-ninth Congress, the "reconstruction" law was passed over the President's [Johnson] veto, to the effect that the reconstruction already completed by the President was null and void. And the work was to be done under the direction of Congress. *The ten States were divided into five [U.S.] military districts, under the absolute command and control of generals of the [U.S.] army, backed by a sufficient military force to carry out any program. They were to ignore State organizations and officers, to treat the State governments as illegal and not affording protection to life and property. These generals were to give this protection, and use their pleasure in trying offenders by military commissions, or by suspended local civil tribunals, if they so desired, but such cases were to be reviewed by them* [my emphasis, L.S.] The generals were to proceed to register as voters all male citizens, whites and blacks, over twenty-one years of age, of whatever race or previous condition, who had been in the State for one year, except such as were disfranchised under the proposed Fourteenth amendment for participation in the war. A convention was to be called under stringent regulations to form a constitution, which should provide that such persons as Congress had designated should have suffrage, and contain such other conditions as had also been named. The constitution passed by this convention was to be submitted to the same voters who called the convention, and, when adopted, to be passed on by Congress. The legislature called by the State constitution was to ratify the Fourteenth amendment. The States were to remain as provisional till this amendment was ratified and became a part of the Constitution of the United States. No disfranchised person was eligible to any office.

The Fourteenth amendment was to be ratified under compulsion. "The amendment reduced representation in Congress and based it upon voting population; provided that no person should hold office under United States authority, who, having taken an oath as a Federal [U.S.] or State officer to support the Constitution, had subsequently engaged in the war against the Union." *The insuperable objection to the [Left's wholly anti-South] Fourteenth amendment was to be found in the clause which required the Southern people to disfranchise their own leaders, to brand with dishonor those who had led them in peace and in war. The North [the Left] now intended to force this amendment under the terrible compulsion of the congressional reconstruction law* [my emphasis, L.S.] It is recalled here, too, that five of the restored States had already ratified the [equally anti-South] Thirteenth amendment and their votes had been accepted and counted as valid in the ratification promulgated by the secretary of state of the United States (Mr. Seward). Without these votes the amendment would have lacked the necessary three-fourths of the States needed. *The question arises, Was the ratification legal or illegal under the Constitution. This made little difference then with Congress* [my emphasis, L.S.].

A supplementary act was passed by the new Congress in March, specifying details for the government of the generals commanding the five military districts, carrying out the same bitter spirit in the enforcement of the law.

The Southern people regarded this new legislation as harsh in the extreme, and ungenerous to them in their prostrate and helpless condition. Just as they thought they were being restored to civil government and could begin to rebuild their homes and repair their losses caused by the war, they were again thrown into confusion worse than ever, and under military law in its most severe administration. *It was plain to them that the disfranchising scheme would eliminate all citizens who had had any experience in law making, and in sufficient numbers to turn the whites over bodily to the negroes led by Northern [Left-wing] men and the inexperienced and worse element of Southern whites [scalawags], those who had generally shirked in taking part with either government in the war. It amounted to placing the bayonet at the breast of every white citizen of the South and saying: You must keep your hands off and let this reconstruction plan go through, or we will take your life and property, or send you to prison* [my emphasis, L.S.].

It will be impossible in this short chapter to go into detail in each State, and only the salient features of *those terrible and dark days* [my emphasis, L.S.] will be given. Details must be found in the accounts given of each State by others. The people of the South could not willing stultify themselves by acceding to what they considered *the dishonorable conditions of the Fourteenth amendment* [my emphasis, L.S.], and the legislatures under presidential organization generally declined to ratify the amendment. It was deemed even better to endure patiently military government until "passions generated by the war subside and better counsels prevail at the Federal capital, maintaining meanwhile law and order and addressing ourselves to industrial pursuits." (Governor [Charles J.] Jenkins of Georgia.) Leading citizens protested against the harsh measures. Governor [William L.] Sharkey, of Mississippi, filed a bill in the supreme court to test its constitutionality. His bill was dismissed. Governor Jenkins, of Georgia, also filed a bill for the same purpose, and employed Jeremiah S. Black, Robert J. Brent, Edgar Cowan, and Charles O'Connor from the North as counsel. The bill was ably argued by Mr. O'Connor and Mr. Walker, of Mississippi, but it was dismissed by the court. The McCardle case from Mississippi was at last presented on its merits. "The argument was concluded on the 9th of March, 1868, and the court took the case under advisement. While it was being so held, to prevent a decision of the question, a bill

Judge Jeremiah Black.

was rushed through both houses and finally passed, March 27, 1868, over the president's [Johnson] veto depriving the court of jurisdiction over such appeals." This was the course in all similar cases involving a constitutional decision, which certainly was revolutionary [that is, communist-leaning], and showed a fear that the court would pronounce the law unconstitutional.

The Fourteenth amendment was now presented to the Southern people again. Its behests and the reconstruction acts were carried out in legislation by the bayonet. The States were negroized in succession. "Its practice operation was of course revolutionary in its effects upon the Southern State governments. The most influential [Conservative] white men were excluded from voting for the delegates who were to compose the constitutional conventions, while the [communized] negroes were all admitted to enrollment. Unscrupulous adventurers appeared to act as the leaders of the inexperienced blacks in taking possession first of conventions, and afterward of State governments; and in States where the negroes were most numerous or their [Left-wing] leaders most shrewd and unprincipled, an extraordinary carnival of public crime set in under the form of law. Negro majorities gained complete control of State governments, or rather [angry, freshly propagandized] negroes constituted the legislative majorities and submitted to the unrestrained authority of small but masterful groups of [far Left] white men, whom the instinct for plunder had drawn from the North [my emphasis, L.S.].

> "Taxes were multiplied, the proceeds mostly going into the pockets of the white [Yankee] rascals and their confederates [that is, associates] among the negroes. Immense debts piled up by processes both legal and fraudulent, and most of the money borrowed reached the same destination. In several of the States, it is true that after the conventions had acted, the white vote was strong enough to control when united, and in these, reconstruction, when completed, reinstated the whites in power almost at once, but it was in these States, in several cases, that the process of reconstruction was longest delayed, just because the [Conservative Southern] white voters could resist the more obnoxious measures of the [Left-wing controlled] conventions, and in the meantime, there was [U.S.] military rule. By the end of June, 1868, provision had been made for the readmission of Arkansas, the two Carolinas, Florida, Georgia, Alabama, and Louisiana to representation in Congress. Reconstruction was delayed in Virginia, Mississippi and Texas because of the impossibility of securing popular majorities for the constitution framed by the reconstruction conventions, and Georgia was again held off from representation because her laws had declared negroes ineligible to hold office [Note: This was because most were still uneducated at the time, not because they were black, L.S.]. It was not until January, 1871, therefore, that all of the States were once more represented in Congress." [Woodrow Wilson]

The above is the account given by a fair writer, but being represented then, was not the desired panacea which was to end the *hostile legislation* [my emphasis, L.S.] or woes of the helpless Southern people.[90]

FACTS, PHASES & COLORINGS OF RECONSTRUCTION

☛ Besides trying to bring the law before the supreme court, prominent citizens in every State protested against the infamy. Among them may be mentioned H. V. Johnson, B. H. Hill, and others. When Governor Jenkins of Georgia issued an address to the people of the State, advising against acceptance of the Sherman bill, [Union] General [John] Pope [still considered a war criminal in the South], the military commander of the district, issued an order forbidding officials to influence the people on reconstruction, and quickly and peremptorily notified him that State officers would not be permitted to denounce the act of Congress. The general soon after relieved Governor Jenkins, the State treasurer and comptroller-general, and appointed army officers to execute their functions. Governor [James W.] Throckmorton, of Texas, and the governor of Alabama [Wager Swayne] were also removed [my emphasis, L. S.].

The judiciaries were subjected to the rule of the sword. All judges held their places by sufferance. Even superior court judges were summarily ousted from the bench. The same was true of county officers, and mayors and aldermen of cities. Citizens were arrested, and the only authority given was that of the soldiers who made the arrests. Then citizens were confined at Fort Pulaski and other most convenient fortresses, generally under false and malicious charges urged by irresponsible parties. Two thousand Federal [U.S.] arrests were made in Louisiana, mostly during the Republican [Left-wing] rule of eight years. When the people of a State evinced a disposition not to comply with the severe conditions given, a new act of Congress was passed, as in the case of Georgia, December 22, 1869: "An act to promote the reconstruction of Georgia," *imposing still more stringent conditions* [my emphasis, L.S.].

The Alabama constitution was submitted according to the reconstruction law to the registered voters, which required a majority of registered votes should be cast. At the election it was defeated, because it lacked the support of this majority. The conservatives [then politically represented by the Democratic Party] registered, but did not vote and thus caused the defeat of the constitution. [Union] General [George G.] Meade, commanding the district, [disingenuously] reported. "The registered voters do not desire to be restored under the Constitution." He reported that the Constitution failed of ratification by 8,114 votes, yet Congress took the matter entirely in its control. It lumped Alabama and its odious constitution in the general bill admitting the other States, and thus made a constitution which the people had refused to ratify. The same thing was done in the case of Arkansas.

A correct idea may be had of the officeholders of Alabama from the State ticket put out by Republicans [Liberals] for election in February, 1868, including the following members of the [far Left] Freedmen's bureau: [Andrew J.] Applegate, of Ohio, for lieutenant-governor; Miller, of Maine, for secretary of state; Reynolds, of Maine, for auditor; Keifer, of Ohio, for commissioner of internal revenue. For legislators, from Montgomery county, Albert Warner of Ohio; Shoeback of Austria. For probate judge, Early of New York. The same rule was followed in the county and local offices in every State and municipality. *Illiterate negroes, also, were elected or appointed to highly responsible positions* [my emphasis, L.S.].

The State militia, as organized, was composed mainly of [communized] negroes to enforce the odious State laws enacted by a legislature even more radical [Left-wing] in legislation than the examples given by Congress. To illustrate: In the election in Alabama, in November, 1869, for governor and members of the legislature, the Republicans [Liberals] asked Governor [William H.] Smith to call out the negro militia to protect the courts. For political purposes, [fabricated] complaint was made, in 1870, that there were violent measures used by Democrats [Conservatives] in courts and at the polls. Governor Smith, the Republican [then Left-wing] governor, denounced Sibley and others as agitators

> "who would like to have a Ku Klux outrage every week to assist in keeping up strife between the whites and the blacks, that they might be more certain of the votes of the latter. He would like to have a few colored men killed every week, to furnish semblance of truth to Spencer's libels upon the people of the State generally."[91]

The legislature of Alabama, put in by Congress, contrary to law,

> "sat nearly the entire year. As soon as it got fairly down to business, it increased the former State aid to railroads by authorizing endorsements to the extent of $16,000 per mile. *Bribery and corruption became common* to pass these pernicious grants of the State's credit. Only one road was completed. Five were built a few miles and abandoned. *Fraudulent bonds were demanded and issued.* The bond brokers and railroad schemers conspired to *rob the State of many millions of dollars.* The legislature also authorized cities, towns, and counties to issue bonds to railroad builders, and *many were fleeced*, as these same

organizations were controlled by the same [radical Left-wing] element elected in the same way as was the legislature.

"*The North Carolina legislature authorized the governor to proclaim martial law in every county, to arrest and try all accused persons by court-martial . . . to raise two regiments to execute his will . . . one regiment of [communized] negroes and the other of renegades . . . and proceeded to arrest honorable citizens to be tried by court-martial in time of peace.* With rare patience, the people of North Carolina restrained their indignation and resolved to await the election of 1870. [my emphasis, L.S.]."

This procedure was general in all the States under the reconstruction law.

The Republican party [Liberal] accomplished its object, in preserving its power, but only for a time. In the Forty-first Congress, beginning March 5, 1871, the twelve Southern States were represented as follows: Twenty-two Republican [Liberal] senators, 2 Democratic [Conservative] senators, 48 Republican [Liberal] representatives, and 13 Democratic [Conservative] representatives. Most of the members of Congress were from the North. President Lincoln had made a supposed case of this kind in 1862, and thus criticised it:

"To send a parcel of Northern men here as representatives, elected as it would be understood and perhaps really so, at the point of the bayonet, would be disgraceful and outrageous."[92]

Under the iron hand of military government, both Federal and State, the [anti-South] Fourteenth and Fifteenth amendments were ratified and the credit of every State exhausted, but *at the sacrifice of every principle of local self-government* [my emphasis, L.S.].

South Carolina is a sample of the other States (in 1873).

"But the treasury of South Carolina has been so thoroughly gutted by the thieves who have hitherto had possession of the State government, there is nothing to steal. The note of any negro in the State is worth as much on the market as a South Carolina bond. It would puzzle even a Yankee carpet-bagger to make anything out of the office of State treasurer under the circumstances."

[South Carolina] Governor [Daniel H.] Chamberlain, a Republican [Liberal], said that when at the end of the [Franklin J.] Moses [Jr.] administration, he entered on his duties as governor, "two hundred trial justices were holding office by executive appointment, who could neither read nor write the English language."[93]

BORDER STATES

☛ If anything, the border States of Maryland, Kentucky, West Virginia and Missouri, while passing through the same ordeal of adjustment, between war and peace, *had a more revengeful and vindictive experience* than the States which were reconstructed by Congress. *The population of these States sympathized with the people of the South, but a minority, upheld by the army of the Union, were kept in power; and their legislation was bent to but one purpose, to retain themselves in power, which they did by disfranchising all who sympathized or were suspected of sympathizing with the South* [my emphasis. L.S.]. In West Virginia, test oaths were freely used, and the laws framed only by those who could take them. To illustrate:

> "*For five years after the war, in West Virginia, an ex-Confederate was not a citizen, could not hold office, could not practice law, could not sit as a juror, could not teach school, could not sue in the courts, could not make a defense for charges brought during his absence, could not be administrator or executor.* [my emphasis, L.S.]."

This policy was pursued with more or less severity in the other border States. In Missouri, the constitution framed was most proscriptive, and could not be excelled in this particular.[94]

UNION LEAGUES

☛ The [radical far-Left] Union League in the South was formed to establish the black man's party, and bind the negroes by secret organization to the [then Left-wing] Republican party, so they could be detached and taken entirely from under the control of the white people of the South. The

> "Union League is the right arm of the Union Republican [Liberal] party of the United States, and no man should be initiated into the league who does not heartily endorse the principles and policies of the [Left-wing] Union Republican party."

There were two divisions of the league, one for the whites and the other almost entirely for negroes, with a few whites to instruct and lead them. With few exceptions, *the whites of the South were excluded*. Even brigadier-generals, commanding States, entered the league for political purposes (Swayne.) The league was surrounded by mystery, had [secret hand] grips and mysterious signs, and the negroes were sworn "to vote only for and for none but those who advocate and support the great principles set forth by the league to fill any office of honor, profit, or trust in either State or general government." (By-Laws of the League.)

This [radical Left] league, in practice, taught that the white men of the South were enemies of the negroes, and it excited the latter to deeds of disorder and interference in every way with the whites. The poor negro could not withstand the strong will of the [Liberal] whites from the North, who were controlling him, against all advice and friendly appeal from the Southern whites. Friction, conflict, disorder between whites and blacks were incited to prolong the important and lucrative offices held by the carpet-baggers. It was the stock in trade of the Republicans [Liberals] in the South to keep up the vindictive and hostile legislation of Congress, and it is needless to say that members of the league had the ear of Congress [my emphasis, L.S.].

> "But there was a companion to this abominable dynasty in the dangerous order of the Ku Klux Klan. The one caused the other. The [original Victorian] Ku Klux Klan [not to be confused with the modern 20th Century KKK] was the perilous effect of which the odious [Left-wing Union] league was the unhealthy cause. The [original Victorian] Klan was a veritable [Southern, Christian, Conservative] body, founded in a holy object [constitutionalism], and often prostituted to violence [by imposters who infiltrated the Klan for nefarious purposes] under great provocation. The writer knows all about it, and shared in its legislative work. *It combined the best men of the State, old, virtuous, settled, cautious citizens [that is, Conservative Southerners]. Its object was the preservation of order and the protection of [Southern] society.* It used mystery as its weapon. It was intended to aid the law, and prevent crime. In the license of the era, it was a matter of self-defense against plunder, assassination, and rape.[95] Both the [Union] league and the Ku Klux Klan were excrescences of reconstruction, and the natural outcome of abnormal politics and abortive government."[96]

The writer of this chapter [that is, General Stephen Dill Lee] never knew personally of this Klan. He saw the effect of it in a negro county of Mississippi (Noxubee), where there were ten negroes to one white person. The lawlessness and tendency to riot and override the laws of social life, became so great that a crisis appeared to be near, as shown by abusive language, disorderly meetings, and incendiary proceedings [the very intention of Northern Left-wingers]. This existed for months. One night about two hundred white men clothed in white sheets, in single file on horseback, without uttering a word, rode through the thickly-settled negro portions of the county. They appeared without warning at dark. They disappeared just before dawn. The effect was electrical. The negroes gave little more trouble in that county, notwithstanding the [Union] league and their secret organization.⁹⁷

THE CARPET-BAGGER

☞ "His like the world has never seen from the days of Cain or of the forty thieves in the fabled time of Ali Baba. Like the wind, he blows and we hear the sound thereof, but no man knoweth whence it cometh or whither it goeth. National historians will be in doubt how to class him. Ornithologists will claim him, because in many respects he is a bird of prey. He lives only on corruption, and takes his flight as soon as the carcass is picked. He is no product of the war. He is a 'canker of a calm world' and of peace, which is despotism enforced by bayonets. His valor is discretion; his industry perpetual strife; and his eloquence 'the parcel of a reckoning' of chances as he smells out a path which may lead from the White House to a custom house, a postoffice, the internal revenue bureau, or perchance, to either wing of the Federal capitol. His shibboleth is 'The [Left-wing] Republican Party.' From that party he sprung as naturally as a maggot from putrefaction. Where two or three or four negroes are gathered together, he, a leprous spot, is seen, and his cry, like the daughter of the horse leech, is always, Give, give me office. Without office he is nothing; with office, he is a pest and public nuisance. Out of office he is a beggar; in office he grows rich till his eyes stick out with fatness. Out of office he is, hat in hand, the outside ornament of every negro's cabin, a plantation loafer and the nation's *lazzarone*; in office he is an adept in 'addition, division and silence.' Out of office he is the orphan ward of the administration and the general sign-post of penury; in office he is the complaining suppliant for social equality with Southern gentlemen."⁹⁸ [Thomas Norwood]

This is a splendid picture in general of the carpet-bagger during the days of reconstruction.

Alabama had become insolvent, and "Governor [David P.] Lewis, Republican [Liberal], said to the legislature that he could not sell for money any of the State bonds." The State debt had grown to the enormous sum of $25,500,000, besides county and city debts of vast sums.

> "Corruption marked the Republican management as its own. The scoundrel class was in office. Strife between whites and blacks still stirred up by Spencer and his henchmen. Immigration was prevented, emigration from the State by whites going steadily on. Capital shrank from the State into which it had corruptedly rushed a few years ago. For six years the State had been losing at all outlets."

Such was Alabama. It was even worse in South Carolina, Louisiana and other States.

In North Carolina, July 4, 1868,

> "this new State government was organized. Senate, 38 Republicans [Liberals], 12 Democrats [Conservatives], 12 carpet-baggers. Outside the legislature, in the lobby, a swarm of the same kind, . . . all of them disreputable. The treasury was robbed, the school fund stolen to pay per diems. The educational investments in securities were sold out at nearly one-third their par value to the Republican [Liberal] treasurer for himself and his associates. . . . In less than four months, this legislature authorized a State debt of over $25,000,000 in bonds, in addition to $16,000,000 for various minor schemes. The entire debt imposed by reconstruction on North Carolina exceeded $38,000,000, while the taxable wealth of the State at that time was returned at only $120,000,000. . . . Similar corruption in municipal bonds. Yet not a mile of railroad was built, although $14,000,000 in bonds were actually issued. Not a child, white or black, was educated for two years; not a public building erected, no State improvements anywhere."[99]

Alabama's debt, before Republican [Left-wing] rule, was $8,336,083; at the end, $25,503,593.

In North Carolina, the assessed property in 1860 was $292,000,000; taxes, $543,000. In 1870, assessed property, $130,000,000; taxes, $1,160,000, showing a difference between local government and enforced military government under carpet-baggers.

In South Carolina, in 1860, the taxable property was $490,000,000; taxes, $400,000. In 1870 (Republican [Left-wing] rule), assessed property, $184,000,000; taxes, $2,000,000 a year.

In Georgia, in 1860, the taxable property was $672,3 22,777; in 1870, $226,329,767. When Governor [Rufus B.] Bullock became governor, the State debt was $5,827,000; at the date of his flight, the debt was reported to be $12,500,000; bond endorsements amounted to $5,733,000, aggregate over $18,000,000.

In Florida, property decreased in value 45 per cent in eight years of Republican [Left-wing] rule, from 1867 to 1875. In Mississippi, 6,400,000 acres of land were forfeited to the State in payment of excessive taxation, and large amounts were collected as taxes and squandered.

In Louisiana, during Republican [Left-wing] rule, New Orleans city property decreased in value $58,104,864 in eight years. County property decreased more than one-half, or from $99,266,839 to $47,141,690. One hundred and forty millions of dollars were squandered with nothing to show for it; State debt increased more than $40,000,000; city property depreciated 40 per cent, county property 50 per cent.[100]

SUMMARY

☛ *The terrible ordeal of reconstruction may be said to have lasted from 1865 to 1876 [1877], twelve years, before the [Conservative Southern] whites got hold of the States again. No people had to undergo so dark a period with such complications, having 4,000,000 of slaves suddenly enfranchised, with no preliminary training to fit them for the great responsibility of the ballot [or freedom]* [my emphasis, L.S.].

> "Our ancestors placed suffrage upon the broad common-sense principle that it should be lodged in and exercised by those who could use it most wisely and most safely and most efficiently, to serve the ends for which government was instituted . . . not upon any abstract or transcendent notion of human rights, which ignored the existing facts of social life. . . . I shall not vote to degrade suffrage. I shall not vote to pollute and corrupt the foundation of political power in this country, either in my own State or in any other State." [Senator Charles R. Buckle of Pennsylvania]

It seems strange now that statesmen of the Republican [Liberal] party in control of the government, even after so terrible a war, and mad with absolute power, could have gone so far in error as to place those who had been slaves but a few years before, and were now led by corrupt and reckless adventurers, in charge of framing governments for the Anglo-Saxon race in the South. It seems now that they could have seen they were attempting an impossible problem; but they did not, even when warned by cool-headed statesmen who did see it. Passion [emotions] and prejudice [fueled by communist ideologies] reigned supreme. Those who were conservative [at the time, the Democrats] were misled by the colored representations of designing partisans. The negroes were as clay in the hands of the potter. *They had never before felt the strong hand of strong men, ruling them and using them in affairs, in which they had had no experience, for political ascendancy* [my emphasis, L.S.].[101] The negroes were never very much blamed by the Southern people, for the whites felt that the influences surrounding the negro, backed by military power and the moral support of the [U.S.] government of the great republic and of the State governments, were irresistible under the circumstances.

The conduct of the true citizens of the South during the days of reconstruction surpassed in wisdom, endurance, patience, and subordination

Primarily uneducated and illiterate, (making them gullible and manipulable) emancipated Southern black servants were easy targets for the then Left-wing Republican Party, which used them as unwitting pawns in their campaign to overturn the Constitution, subjugate the American people, and assume control of the U.S. government. Under their new name, the Democratic Party, today's Leftists continue to use the same strategies (e.g., race-baiting, race-swapping, race-hustling, race warfare), and for the same purposes: the exploitation of racial tensions for political advantage and party supremacy.

to law (military law), any traits they had displayed in the war. They never yielded moral support to the corrupt [Left-wing] legislation surrounding them, but patiently waited for the time when they could act together to restore local self-government [my emphasis, L.S.]. This time came when the corrupt influences of those in power had passed beyond endurance. The better element of the Republicans [Liberals] in the South, composed of Northern men, could not stand the stealing and general corruption which threw the spoils mainly into the hands of the few officeholders. They began to separate from the extremists as they "saw the handwriting on the wall," and to approach the true citizens of the State. All thinking men now saw that there was no doubt that white civilization itself, the very existence of society, was at stake. The white people arose as one man to correct the evil. They appealed to all to help (white and black), no matter what had occurred in the past. The moral pressure and presentation of the open frauds and crimes accomplished under form of law, were irresistible. It amounted almost to another revolution, and one after another, the States were recovered by the white people within their borders. Illegal and corrupt returning boards, under semblance of law, prevented the consummation for a time, as the Federal [U.S.] power was slow to relax its hold, but it was seen on every hand that the end was near, and that the corrupt governments, set up under the reconstruction law, remained only because [they were] held up on the points of the bayonets of the United States army.

The carpet-bag government in Louisiana fell in a day (September 14, 1874), and was powerless when the military

(United States troops) were not interfering. One company of United States troops, after a few days, reinstated the corrupt government for a time. This was an object-lesson that every citizen of the North could understand, and the conservative men [that is, Yankee Democrats] there began to change their views in regard to the South, and to understand that Congress had made a mistake in its zeal, as it supposed, to gather in the results of the war, and afford protection to the negro race in its freedom. It was shown, too, that no change could be made under Republican [Liberal] rule in the South, as was demonstrated by Governor Chamberlain's effort in South Carolina. Their regime was a stench in the nostrils of every respectable man, North or South. It could only be done under the Democratic party [then Conservative], and all good citizens flocked to its standard and worked under it, till what was desired was accomplished.

> "The conduct of the Republican party in the South was such as to repel patriotism and decency . . . and a monumental warning to those who seek party advantage through illegitimate legislative enactment."[102]

The cost to the South was great, but her citizens did not repine, but began to work with a will to revoke and improper and corrupt legislation, to restore economy in public expenditures, to reduce taxation, to do away with useless offices, to make the schools efficient, and to build up the waste places. The conservative element in Congress [then the Democrats] was strong enough to enforce "hands off." In fact, Congress, as early as May, 1872, had passed a general amnesty bill removing political disabilities from almost all citizens who had been disfranchised, still excepting those who had been officers in the judicial, military, or naval service of the Confederate States. The carpet-baggers had taken their "carpet-bags" and gone to a more congenial clime, where they lost their identity as a class, having the scorn and contempt of all respectable citizens.

The supreme court, too, had rendered several decisions tending to recall [the then Left-leaning U.S.] Congress from its proneness to legislate beyond the limits of the Constitution. The negroes, who could not resist being led to extremes in the hands of the "masterful" carpet-baggers, now easily and readily yielded to the will of the Southern whites, and began to return to more industrious habits and conditions, and were less disposed to spend their time as politicians and lawmakers. They began to realize that they were not competent to withstand the nerve and moral pressure of the white man, whether he was a carpet-bagger and using him for his own advantage, and for corrupt and vindictive purposes, or the Southern white man who intended to rule and preserve white civilization and society at all hazards. The normal condition of the Southern States, being again ruled by the whites, by the educated people and the property-holders, was accepted by the people of the North as the only true solution in the reconstruction of the States. The restoration of the governments of the States to their own people, left them heavily burdened with debts put upon them under the guise of law. They had to start with this great burden upon them in their work of restoration. Even after the States were restored, for many years there was a large element of the Republican [Liberal] party that still desired to interfere in the internal management of the States. Some force bills were passed by Congress to carry into effect the Fourteenth and Fifteenth amendments. This uncertainty, in again resorting to extreme legislation, kept capital away and made it timid. It had become thoroughly panic-stricken during the corrupt days of reconstruction, and had fled from the South and sought other channels, mainly in the development of the Northwest. It showed no disposition to return for many years, even after recuperation had begun in earnest with Southern hands and Southern capital.

The struggle of Southern men during reconstruction, in fact, of the whole Southern people, under adverse political, social and commercial circumstances, was the most remarkable feature in those dark days. They never lost confidence in themselves, patiently bided their time, and achieved a most remarkable victory over all malign influences [my emphasis, L.S.]. Although they had had such sad experience once with the carpet-baggers, they at once invited immigration to assist in building up the South, but they preferred bona fide citizens, not the class which had lived off of them so long, and which had fled when the purse and power had been stripped from them.

It cannot now be a question that the policy of the Northern statesmen [that is, Yankee Liberals] was a failure, and that the wisdom of Southern leaders was superior in their ideas of reconstruction. "Reconstruction accomplished not one useful result and left behind not one pleasant reflection." History will certainly condemn the legislation that entailed such misery, such corruption, such profligate expenditure of the money of an impoverished and crushed people, and in establishing negro governments at a time when the whites of the South had the best intentions of protecting the negroes in their new given freedom [my emphasis, L.S.].

"The experiment being tried, all interests, not least those of the blacks themselves, were found to require that the superior race should rule. It seems strange that even any were so dull as to expect success of the opposite policy."

Governor Chamberlain, of South Carolina (Republican) [Liberal], said:

> "The Republican party in power was not all nor nearly all Northern adventurers, Southern renegades, or depraved negroes. Among all the classes so described were worthy and able men, but the crude forces with which they dealt were temporarily too strong for their control or their resistance. Corruption ran riot; dishonesty flourished in shameless effrontery; incompetency was the rule in public offices."[103]

Louisiana, South Carolina and Florida were not entirely reclaimed till after [U.S.] President [Rutherford B.] Hayes was inaugurated in 1877. One of the first acts of the new president was to order the withdrawal of the United States troops from the South. As soon as this was done, the Republican [Left-wing] governments in the Southern States at once fell to pieces, and the Democratic [Conservative] State governments, which had been legally elected and had claimed to be the true governments, took their places. The rule of the white people was once more inaugurated in all the lately seceded States. They had governed these States from their earliest colonial or territorial days, until the reconstruction policy of the presidents (Lincoln and Johnson) was overturned by the armed forces of the [Left-wing U.S. Republican] government, as the Confederate government had been overturned by the same force in 1865, and the negro governments established in their places in 1867, under the reconstruction laws of Congress. As already explained, this reconstruction might be styled "destruction," for it took what little the Southern people had left after coming out of the war which had impoverished them, and left their country devastated and devoid of nearly all property.

The assessed property in 1876 was about one-third of what it was in 1860. Two-thirds of the wealth of the Southern people had been swept away, and the South was helpless and bankrupt. However, as soon as the white people realized that they again had control of their country, that the eleven years' trial of negro lawmaking and legislation was about ended, they at once went work with a will to correct the corrupt and vicious legislation of the experiment of negro suffrage, in administering the affairs of the great States, and with heart and soul to reassert their influence and rights in the union of their fathers.

In so far as their material resources were concerned, they were about in the same fix that they were in 1865, in fact, worse off than when they laid down their arms. At that date the total debts of the States were about $87,000,000. They had been compelled to repudiate all debts contracted for carrying on the war. In the ten years of negro legislation and government, conducted under carpet-baggers, the additional debt of $300,000,000 was added to the burdens of the people of the South.

> "The Republicans [Liberals] in Congress gave the ballot to the negroes as a weapon of defense of their freedom and to keep the [Left-wing] party in power. But the first result of negro suffrage was a saturnalia of ignorant and corrupt government such as the world has seldom seen. The debts of the Southern States were rolled up to enormous extent. At the close of the war the debts had aggregated $87,000,000. Reconstruction added $300,000,000, and a great part of this was squandered."[104]

Public and private debts remained as a legacy to remind the people of the war and its consequences. These debts were paid by many, compromised by many, and in many cases could not be paid at all. As yet, the [Southern] people were not sure that there were not to be further attempts at readjustment ["reconstruction"]. Capital had long since fled from the South, and was diverted in other directions. Money could only be had at enormous rates of interest (75 per cent to 80 per cent). The North and West were enjoying the greatest financial prosperity in their history. All capital was being used in booming and building up the Northwest into new States and increasing their material wealth. This was being done to its utmost limit, and there was no money to help the South. The great Western railroads were being built, backed by enormous grants of public lands by Congress, and these roads were planting immigrants (500,000 foreign) and citizens from other States in the West. Immigration had even gone westward from the people of the South who had despaired of better days. There was no immigration southward. The increase in population was only the natural one. There were but few banks, and Southern men had few friends among the great financiers anywhere. The South, in its looted and prostrated condition, offered no invitation to capital which promised even prospective returns. Northern capital strictly avoided the South in those gloomy days. To all appearances, the South was paralyzed. Her great wealth, as shown by the census of 1850 and 1860, which had been the accumulation from the earliest days, in slave property and material investments in all possible directions, had been swept away.

The social fabric of the people had been uprooted and turned upside down. The negroes had not only been freed as the result of the South's failure in the war, but they had been made lawmakers and put to governing States, whose people had been as progressive [that is, forward-looking] and aggressive as any element of the Anglo-Saxon race in any part of the world. The [Conservative] Southern people had before them the lamentable failure of their [Liberal] brothers at the North to restrain their bad blood and forego Anglo-Saxon determination, indifferently to friend or foe, to carry out their own [Left-wing] purposes by putting negro governments over men of their own race for whom they showed at that time no sympathy or generosity.

But the white people of the South began to realize again that their destinies had fallen into their own hands. They recalled the terrible ordeal through which they had passed, a fiery furnace, as it were, of devastating war and reconstruction and destruction of over fifteen years. Every true citizen realized the fearful conditions surrounding him to begin social, political and material life anew. A condition without a precedent in history confronted them. Their brothers of the North were still hostile, suspicious, distrustful, and watching them with vigilant eyes, possibly to try a new experiment in restoration.

Yet they were at least able to face the future and apply their wisdom and statesmanship to the upbuilding of a new civilization, having to accept the Thirteenth, Fourteenth and Fifteenth amendments to the Constitution irrevocably, although fastened on them by the bayonet and having negro suffrage as a fixed fact, and that, too, in face of the great burdens imposed on them in the ten years' experiment. It looked as if the effort they could not avoid in the solution of the intricate problem was made hopeless by the conditions they had to accept. Two races differing in almost every respect, one a governing race with a proud prestige of success, the other a docile, inexperienced, uneducated race without a record, had to live side by side with equal political power and rights.[105]

The new problem which Southern statesmen had to face and solve, was surrounded by every possible adverse condition. At the same time, the need most pressing above all others was to restore confidence and prosperity and provide employment to hands made idle by destruction of all manufacturing enterprises and all employments not strictly agricultural. Although the South was mainly agricultural, because her peculiar conditions made her so before the war, still she had been proportionally doing her share in all lines of development before the struggle. The almost total destruction of all these lines of industry, reduced her people in starting, to the one primitive pursuit of every people—agriculture, as an immediate way of making a living. The Southern people knew their great unequaled resources in climate, soil, rivers, seacoast, rainfall, iron, coal, timber, agriculture, and everything necessary to make a people rich and prosperous. They knew that they had every condition essential to success. They realized that the race question was settled possibly for a time, and with discretion on their part, passion and prejudice must necessarily die out. They knew that with patriotism, patience, and fidelity and good principles, success might be assured. They were conscious that in the ordeal through which they had passed, they had preserved their self-respect and honor, and there was nothing to be ashamed of in their conduct. And they now determined to enter with courage and skill the great future before them, relying on their strong arms and hearts and on their own meager resources, for it has been shown that there were no friends at hand to aid them materially. The only friends they had politically were the Democrats [then Conservatives] at the North, and these friends had never deserted them from the time the war closed.[106]

PLUCK, ENERGY & PUSH OF THE SOUTHERN PEOPLE

☞ Before showing what rapid strides the South made after the white people got control, in material development, in educational progress, social restoration, and in reinstating prosperity in every line of progress and industry, it is not inappropriate to show that the same pluck, energy and push which had always animated the people of the South still existed, and that those who now led in this restoration of prosperity were the same people who in ante-bellum days made the South the richest section of the great republic [the U.S.A.]. Her record before the war in all branches showed her sons abreast not only with the citizens of any other section, but with the citizens of any other country in the world in every respect, in energy, thrift, and progress. There are those who would have the world believe that her citizens were slothful, that they were incapable of using that energy and skill necessary to rebuild the waste places left by the war. Many writers in leading books of reference, showed a lack of knowledge and an untruthfulness as to facts that make it necessary to present proof. To show the falsity of their record, the last *Encyclopedia Britannica*, for instance, says:

"Since the revolutionary days, the few thinkers of America born south of Mason and Dixon's line are outnumbered by those belonging to the single State of Massachusetts; nor is it too much to say, that mainly by that mainly by their connection with the North, the Carolinas have been saved from sinking to the level of Mexico and the Antilles."

No country has been so persistently falsified in history as the South has been; hers has been to make history, unfortunately, not to write it [my emphasis, L.S.]. Dr. J. L. M. Curry says:

> "History, poetry, art, public opinion have been most unjust to the South. By perverse reiterations its annals, its acts, its inner feelings, its purposes have been grossly misrepresented. History, as written, if accepted, in future years will consign the South to infamy."

In connection with this section or article, other articles will show that the people of the South were abreast with the people of any other section of the republic in fighting its battles, in commanding its armies, in protecting the national honor, in adding to the territory of the Union, in leading in judicial, political, and social development, in fact in all branches calling for the exercise a progressive [that is, forward-looking] and aggressive citizenship, in aiding and taking part in the growth of our common country.

The manhood of the South has been equal to any emergency, political, judicial, material or social. I will treat only of the capacity for material and industrial growth by the Southern people, to show that there was no difference in these particulars in the decade from 1850 to 1860, preceding the war, from that developed in the decade 1880 to 1890 and afterward; that they were able to do even more in face of disaster and untoward conditions than when surrounded by wealth and increasing prosperity; that they could create conditions to build up prosperity. When all the capital of the country was being used in building up the West, it was caused to seek the South (after a time) in its own interest, by a prosperity brought about in spite of unfavorable surroundings, and by the Herculean effort of her own impoverished people.

It is now proposed to show briefly that the white people of the South have always been abreast with their brethren of the North and West, and displayed as much push and business capacity as men of any other section of the country. Different conditions faced them, but with these different conditions they created wealth equally with other sections. Let us draw the record of the census of 1850 and 1860 to examine the facts. In this decade, the South only had one-fourth of the white population of the whole country, and counting slaves, her population was one-third of the entire population. Yet the census shows that in railroading, which is a good index of a country's progress, the South built in the ten years 7,562 miles, an increase of 400 per cent, while New England and the Middle States built 4,712 miles, an increase of 100 per cent. In 1850, the two Northern sections exceeded the South in miles by 2,463; in 1860, the South had caught up and was 387 miles ahead, thus showing how she was gaining in wealth then. The South increased her mileage 319 per cent, while the whole country increased only 234 per cent during the ten years. She also had a mile of railroad to as many people as the North had proportionally. She expended in the ten years, $220,000,000 in building new railroads, mostly her own capital.

In diversified manufacturing enterprises, she was making rapid strides; for example, she made 24 per cent increase in manufacturing flour and meal. She made more than one-third increase in the amount of manufactured plain and sawed lumber. In the iron industry, her gain was greater than in the whole country. In steam engines and machinery, she made a gain of over 200 per cent. The rest of the country made a gain of only 40 per cent. In cotton manufacturing in 1860, she had gained $1,000,000 over 1850. She was just then realizing what a mine of wealth she had in her great product.

In banking capital, the South had 30 per cent of the total amount in the country. In 1860, of the total assessed property in the whole country, she had nearly one-half, or 44 per cent. In 1850 the South had 48 per cent of all the live stock (about one-half). She grew over one-half of all the corn raised, and, singular as it may seem now, she had over 56 per cent of all the hogs in the country, and 25 per cent of all the sheep.

In that decade the South raised more than one-half of all the agricultural products, besides producing all the cotton, sugar, rice and molasses. She also produced 44 per cent of all the corn raised, and nearly the entire crop of tobacco and sweet potatoes. She had 48 per cent of all the live stock of the country, one-half of the beeswax and honey. She slaughtered 33 per cent of all animals killed. In home manufacturing she made over 67 per cent of that of the whole country. She owned one-third of the total value of farms, and in the decade she increased their value $1,300,000 over what it was in 1850. She had over 38 per cent of the total investment agricultural implements in the whole country. The per capita valuation of property in the South, including slaves who owned no property,[107] was $568, while in New England and the Middle States (the richest) it was only $528.

In educational income of all institutions, the South had about one-third of the amount for the one-fourth of the white population, as no education was provided for tho negroes.[108] In religious matters she had about as many churches in proportion to population as had the North and West, although that section had claimed precedence in morals. Fortunately the census is better authority than prejudiced writers in treating of the South. Certainly no unprejudiced person could say from this record that the people of the South lacked energy or thrift before the war. With a white population of only one-fourth, and only one-third including negroes, they were ahead in products, and had begun to climb up in those manufacturing industries claimed as showing peculiar energies and enterprise in our Northern brethren.

The Arkansas State Capitol, Little Rock.

Before taking up the rapid recuperation of the South, in contrast with the progress made at the North and West from 1880 (for really no start had been made before then), let us glance again for a moment at her enormous loss in property. As before stated, she had lost valued property amounting to over $5,000,000,000.

> "This vast sum is eight times as great as the combined capital of all the national banks in the United States, and is nearly as great as the aggregate capital invested in manufactures in the whole country. Blot out of existence in one night every manufacturing enterprise in the whole country, with all the capital employed, and the loss would not equal that sustained by the South as the result of the war."[109]

In 1880, when the real start in recuperation was made, the real and personal property by the census was valued at $7,641,000,000; that of the entire country at $43,642,000,000. This shows that the South had about 17½ per cent of the total valuation of the entire country, against 44 per cent of that valuation twenty years previous, showing her greatly changed position as result of the war.[110]

MATERIAL & INDUSTRIAL DEVELOPMENT OF THE SOUTH

☞ Let us see what the South did in the decade 1880 to 1890, at first, almost alone. She increased the value of her property by $3,800,000,000, while New England and the Middle States increased the value of their property by $3,900,000,000. The South gained over 50 per cent while the latter two sections gained 22 per cent only. In 1880 the total farm assets were valued at $2,314,000,000. In 1890 the valuation was $3,182,000,000, a gain 37 per cent, while the increase in the rest of the country was 30 percent, and that, too, in face of the very large inflow of immigrants and capital from Europe. The value of farm products in the South in 1880 was $666,000,000, while in 1890 she produced $773,000,000, a gain of 16 per cent during the ten years. At the same time the rest of the country gained only 9 per cent. Referring to the value of farm assets in 1880, the South, with one-fourth of that value, produced in 1890, 43 per cent of all the products raised. The South made, in 1890, 24 per cent on her investments in farming, while the rest of the country made only 13 per cent.

> "The South, in 1896, made one-third of the corn crop of the whole country, and has sold more corn than it bought; makes more than one-half of the wheat used." [Tradesman]

The cotton crop in 1880 was 5,000,000 bales; in 1895, 9,750,000 bales. The South produced in 1894 nearly three-fourths of the entire of the crop.

In manufacturing, which has been the special industry of many sections of the North, the South has made her most rapid progress. In 1880 the South had $257,244,561 invested in manufactures. In 1890 it was $659,008,817, or a gain of 156 per cent. The gain in the entire country was 120¾ per cent. The value of manufactured products increased 100 per cent, while in the rest of the country it was only 69½ per cent. In 1890, in cotton manufacture, the South had $21,976,000 invested. By 1895 the capital invested was about $107,000,000. Twenty-five thousand miles of railroad have been built in the South in the last fifteen years, over $1,000,000,000 having been spent in new roads and in improving old ones since 1880.

In 1880 the South produced 397,301 tons of pig iron; in 1895, 1,900,000 tons. In 1880 the South produced 6,048,000 tons of coal; in 1895, 30,000,000 tons. In 1880 there were 40 cottonseed-oil mills, with a capital of $3,500,000; in 1896 there were 300 mills, with a capital of $30,000,000. This is almost entirely a new industry, cottonseed furnishing both oil and the cake used as fertilizer and cattle feed.

The facts given are sufficient to show that the South is forging ahead in all manufacturing industries. She is establishing woolen mills, manufacturing establishments of all kinds, to work her crude materials into finished articles of commerce, into furniture, tools, building material, etc. She is using marble, granite, copper, clay, terra cotta and other minerals, and diversifying her industries in every way, producing what she needs rather than importing it. Before the war her agricultural resources paid so well, in fact so much better than her other industries, that she mainly confined herself to them. Now she is diversifying her agriculture on still more varied and scientific principles, keeping up in her great local advantages in this industry, and at the same rapidly increasing her industries in every other line, providing employment for her people and all who cast their lot with her. In diversifying her agriculture, she has met with the success which always follows such a course. Her great cotton yield has been brought about by better selection of seed, in better handling of the staple, and in better fertilizing of the soil. While this is true, proportionally large crops of other kinds are planted and raised—sugar, corn, oats, wheat, tobacco, sorghum, rice and potatoes. She raises every crop raised at the North and West, and many others besides, which cannot be raised in those sections.

She is raising her own food and not buying nearly to the extent she did immediately following the war. Then she bought grain and meat almost exclusively, and confined her crops mainly to cotton, sugar and tobacco. Everything was needed in the way of furniture and family supplies, and had to be bought anew, and in those dark days, only cotton brought money at once on the market, so this crop only could be mortgaged to get these necessaries. Now this drain is all over, and the South is developing a great industry in early fruits and vegetables, amounting to $50,000,000 a year in her oranges, apples and vegetables now shipped North. The South is reversing matters, and beginning to send food products North, having a surplus over her needs. Her great cotton crop and other staple crops are now becoming surplus crops since she is feeding herself, and to-day the Southern planter and farmer is generally as comfortable as he was in the better days before disaster overtook him.

The growth of manufactures in the South is fully brought out by the statistics given in detail, and we may sum up the bearing of these industries by stating that in the ten years 1880 to 1890, the

South so firmly established herself as to more than compete with the Middle and New England States in the manufacture of iron and cotton goods. The conditions are so favorable in economic advantage, the iron, coal and limestone frequently being found in juxtaposition in the same mountain, as to enable the mills almost to do away with the cost of transportation of ore, coal and coke as compared with this item of expense which in the North involves an average distance of from 300 to 600 miles. As early as 1884 and 1885 the South began shipping pig iron to eastern markets. Southern iron was sold at a profit, after paying freight rates, of from $3 to $5 per ton, and at all periods when the business is not profitable at the North, and the mills and furnaces shut down or run on short time, the Southern furnaces and mills continue to work and make money and supply the deficit caused by the shutting down at the North. It is now an established fact that the South can more than compete with Northern furnaces, and it remains to be seen what the great iron manufacturing interests in Pennsylvania and the North generally will do to counteract the advantages in this industry in the South. It is not only in the manufacture of pig iron that the South has demonstrated her economic advantages, but she is now diversifying her work in iron in every possible way, by putting up other manufacturing establishments, such as rolling mills, pipe works, car and wheel works, foundries and machine shops, and turning out finished products, such as stoves, agricultural implements, car wheels, iron pipe, in fact every variety of articles and machines, even to the construction of locomotives and the smallest kinds of iron goods sold on the market. This new feature saves the cost of transportation on iron to the North, and also the freight on the finished product returned to the South, and affords employment to laborers and mechanics at the shops, giving employment and retaining money at Southern centers.

While this is going on, more and more iron is being shipped northward and sold at the doors of Northern furnaces. Shipments are even going beyond the borders of the United States, and it is conceded now that Southern manufacturers of iron will control the market in prices and facilities.

> "Those who have visited the districts were impressed with its remarkable advantages for the production of cheap iron. The ore, coke, coal and excellent limestone are in contiguity, and it is figured that the total cost of material at the furnace in the Birmingham [Alabama] district will average about $1.12½ per ton of iron produced, against $4 and $5 in the Lehigh and Schuylkill valleys [in Pennsylvania]." [R. W. Raymond, mining engineer]

"But dealing with the industry as it exists today, a candid survey of the situation will lead to the admission that if it should come to a struggle between furnaces in eastern Pennsylvania, New Jersey and New York, which produce chiefly foundry brands for open market, and the makers of the South, no inconsiderable number of the former would be unable to survive long." [*Iron Age*]

"It is idle for Pennsylvania and other great iron and coal-producing States to close their eyes to the fact that we have reached the beginning of a great revolution in those products. . . . The tread of the iron and coal diggers of Alabama threatens the majesty of the Northern iron and coal fields." [No source listed]

With scarcely less advantage in economic condition, are the immense iron and coal fields of West Virginia, southwest Virginia, western North Carolina, east Tennessee, Georgia and Kentucky, an inexhaustible field of ores 700 miles in length and 200 miles in breadth, as rich almost in timber as in coal and iron. In 1896 the production of pig iron was 8,623,181 tons in the United States, less by 823,181 than the amount produced in 1895. There were produced in the South 1,834,451 tons, an increase of 132,000 tons over 1895, a shortage for the North, and an increase for the South. The South to-day presents the most inviting field for investment of any section of the Union.

The coal fields in the South are as extensive as the iron fields, and as already stated, coal and iron are frequently mined out of the same mountain, and the supply is inexhaustible. Coal and iron together give to the South advantages, from an economic standpoint, to be found in no other section of the same area in the world.

The cotton crop of the South alone is a wonderful source of wealth and gives her advantages possessed by no other country of equal area. She produces about 70 per cent of the entire cotton crop of the world, and her climatic conditions will give her this advantage for all time. This crop alone from 1865 to 1890 was valued at $7,867,113,555, of which $5,161,000,000 was exported. This crop is every year becoming more and more a surplus crop, and will be a mine of wealth to the country, now that she has resumed her normal condition as a rich section well supplied with everything lost during the dark period of twenty years from 1861 to 1881. More and more of the money obtained for this crop will remain in the South, as she is now producing her own food crops and is self-sustaining. A great part of the money heretofore went North and West for manufactured products of iron, for coal and for provisions now produced at home. Statistics have already shown that the strides made in establishing mills for manufacturing in the South are very great.

It is fully understood now that the South has even greater advantages in cotton than in the iron industry for competing with the North. It is not whether she can do this, but whether the North can hold her own with the South. The coarser fabrics are now shipped to the East and sold at a profit at the doors of Northern mills, and the finer fabrics are being rapidly manufactured at cheaper rates. It is only a matter of time when the South, by multiplying her mills, will dictate prices to the world in cotton goods, coarse and fine. She has the advantage of from $4 to $6 start in having the mills in the cotton fields, as it takes that amount for freight, compressing, insurance, etc., necessary in transporting to the New England mills.

> "The mills of the Southern States possess a decided advantage over the mills of the North and Great Britain, in that they have the raw cotton at their doors, and that this alone represents a money value sufficient to give them control of the coarse goods has been fully demonstrated within the last ten years. This difference can be clearly shown by the following illustration: Let us assume a 40,000-spindle mill is located at any well-situated site in the cotton-growing section of the Southern States. This mill properly equipped with the latest and most approved style of machinery for the manufacture of standard 4-4 sheeting to Nos. 12 and 14 yarns, would cost complete $800,000, and would consume 20,000 bales of cotton per annum. It is variously estimated that the difference in cost of a bale of cotton, 490 lbs., between the mills in Augusta, Ga., and Fall River, Mass., is from $4 to $6 a bale. Assume the lowest estimate of $4 a bale, and you have 20,000 times 4, or $80,000, in favor of the Augusta mill, or a saving of 10 per cent on the complete cost of the mill in cotton alone." [C. R. Makepeace]

This is a mathematical demonstration in favor of the South, of a splendid profit before starting in manufacturing, provided skilled labor is obtained. The premises, too, are not well taken in the reason given to bolster up the Northern mills. The labor in the Southern mills is cheaper for the same grade of skill than that of the employees in Northern mills, and is becoming more and more skilled, and equal to the turning out of the finest products. The mills are now yearly increasing their output in this direction, and adding the necessary machinery for the finer products, and all new mills are equipped with the latest and best machinery. The climate, too, is demonstrating the economic values in its effect on material, and the less expense in heating buildings owing to the milder temperature.

In its other crops the South has made great strides. She has more than doubled her grain crops, as well as cotton, since 1870. The percentage of gain in corn has been greater than that of any other section of the whole country. In corn, cotton, wheat, oats, potatoes and other crops, the South in 1889 increased their value $25,000,000 over what it was in 1879. The agricultural products of the South amounted to about $850,000,000 in 1889. She increased the value of her live stock in the decade $177,747,296. Stock [livestock] is fed at the South at a profit in saving winter shelter and feed, covering at least from three to four months, owing to the climate and longer grazing.

In foreign commerce, the South got one-half of the increase of the whole country. In banking there was an increase of surplus of 146 per cent, while it was only 63½ per cent in the rest of the country. While in 1879 the South had only 220 banks, with a capital stock of $45,408,985, in 1889 she had 472 banks with a capital of $76,454,510. In 1889 she had increased her banks 113 per cent, while at the North the increase was only 13 per cent and in the West 80 per cent. In capital stock she increased the amount 70 per cent against the 4 per cent in the North and 95 per cent in the West. In 1897 the bank clearings in January, as compared with January, 1896, give a gain of 6 per cent; the Middle States a gain of 22 per cent, and a decrease of from 5 per cent to 11 per cent in the West and on the Pacific coast.

What the South may be said to have accomplished, may be summed up in the language of Mr. D. A. Tompkins, who said:

> "(1) It has shaken off the idea of dependence on the negro as a laborer, and the latter is falling into the relation of helper to the white laborer. (2) It has accumulated capital enough to undertake very extensive manufacturing without, in many cases, the need to borrow capital from the North. (3) It has demonstrated that the Southern man makes as successful a manufacturer and skilled mechanic as the Northern man or the Englishman, and that the climate is rather advantageous than otherwise to successful and profitable work. (4) In iron, cotton and lumber manufacturing, it is not a question whether the South can hold its own against other sections, but whether other sections can compete with the South."

Mr. Frederick Taylor, a banker of New York, said in 1889, after visiting the South:

> "The new South has been built up by the indomitable energy and by the hard work of the Southern people themselves."

Hon. H. B. Pierce, of Massachusetts, said:

> "I predict for the new South an era of prosperity which shall eclipse any which has ever been achieved in any other section of our great country, so remarkable for its success in that line."

There is no portion of the Union surpassing the South in its lumber resources. The annual lumber produced is valued at $400,000,000, almost equaling the value of the cotton crop.

In education, equally great progress has been made. As soon as the whites secured control, they proceeded to perfect the system of public school education established in the days of reconstruction, but which was only organized to raise money to be squandered in those corrupt and looting days. Before the war, only such white children as could not be educated by their parents were educated at the public expense. Education was mainly provided in private schools by those able to educate their children. In the twenty years from 1875 to 1895, the South increased in population 54 per cent, in school attendance 130 per cent, school property from $16,000,000 to $51,000,000—$2,000,000 a year. In 1896, Dr. A. D. Mayo, an educational expert, reports that education has cost the South since the war $250,000,000, of which amount $75,000,000 has been expended in the education of the negro in public schools, though he pays little tax toward their support. Dr. Mayo also says:

> "The sixteen Southern States are to-day paying as much for the public schools as the British parliament votes every year for the public school system of the British islands, between $20,000,000 and $30,000,000. Population of the British islands, 38,104,973."

In Georgia, "the whites pay taxes on $436,000,000, while the negroes pay on $15,000,000." Yet the negroes share the fund in common; no separation of the fund between the races, the separation is in the schools. The proportion of school population in 1893 between the races in Georgia was as 55 whites to 47 blacks. The tax in the other States to educate negroes, where they outnumber the whites, is still more burdensome on the white taxpayers. The tax paid by the South, when we consider the great difference in wealth and area between the two sections, approximates in amount to that paid by the wealthier section, and when we consider how little tax is paid by the negro (not exceeding 5 per cent), is unsurpassed in generosity by any people in the world toward a class doing so little for their own education, or for the accumulation of wealth and consequent benefit from taxation for education.

> "The six New England States, with 66,000 square miles area and a population of 5,000,000, had in 1890 a total assessed valuation of $3,500,000,000. The whole South, with twelve times the area and four times the population, had $3,750,000,000, practically the same amount of property from which to support schools for four times as many children, and those scattered over twelve times the area as New England. It is evident, then, that New England with the same levy can support her schools three times as long as the South, even when we omit from the estimate the facts that in the South the children are scattered over twelve times the area, and that a double set of schools must be maintained. These two factors greatly militate against effective concentration in organizing, administering and supporting a school system." [Supt. J. R. Preston, of Mississippi]

The attendance in the colleges and universities in fifteen years has increased from 10,000 to 25,000—150 per cent. So it is seen the South has shrunk from no expense or effort to keep up an efficient system of education. She is doing more in proportion to her means than any other section.

The cities of the South have increased rapidly in wealth and population. The old cities have grown steadily in every way. Knoxville, Tenn., had in 1880, 9,000 inhabitants; assessed value of property, $3,485,000. In 1890 she had 42,000 inhabitants, and property valued at $9,500,000. Louisville, Ky., increased from 123,000 population to 227,000; Nashville, from 46,000 to 110,000; and other cities in like proportion in population and wealth. New towns like Birmingham, Anniston, Roanoke, Dallas, have sprung up as if by magic.

The inauguration of President [Grover] Cleveland in 1885, when the South was making its great effort to restore its prosperity, gave good heart to the Southern people everywhere. His administration brought about the first genuine confidence between the people of the North and the South. He led the Southern people away from the traditions and many of the prejudices of the great war. He revived in them the spark of national patriotism, which needed some master spirit to ignite and cause it to glow with the spirit of their ancestors, who had defended the national honor when other sections were slow to do so. He called Southern men to offices of trust and honor. His was the happy privilege of doing more to bind up sectional wounds than any other president. He did it, too, without sacrifice of any vital principle established by the victory of the Union armies. The South owes Mr. Cleveland a debt of gratitude.

U.S. President Grover Cleveland.

It is proper to state that while the South did by far the most in the great industrial upheaval in the decade of 1880 to 1890, she did this with her own resources, capital and manhood; that when the great revolution was apparent in 1885, Northern men began to notice it, and to lend their helping hands and capital. But the capitalists of the North did not fully realize the situation till the latter part of the decade, and now Northern capital and energies are mingling with those of the South in the development of wealth in the South, which beyond doubt now presents the safest field for investment of capital in all the Union. She is but at the very threshold of her industrial development.

The whole Southern people in the decade of 1880 to 1890 exerted themselves in every way to develop their resources, by State agricultural and mechanical exhibitions, by interstate farmers' conventions, by public meetings in various cities. To foster commerce between the North and South, bankers' associations assembled in various places where Northern and Southern men met together to discuss finance. The great Southern exposition at New Orleans in 1884, and afterward in Atlanta (1895), did much to encourage the Southern people, and showed the people of the North our splendid natural resources, and displayed the push and earnestness of the Southern people.

Not long after the inauguration of President Cleveland (1885), [former Union] General [Ulysses S.] Grant, the great leader of the Union armies and twice president of the United States, died under peculiarly touching surroundings. A deadly disease seized him, and he passed slowly away before its steady progress. His heart seemed then to turn on the happy reunion of his country, and his utterances tended to bury sectional animosities. He said, "Let us have peace," and this terse epigram found lodgment in the hearts of his countrymen North and South. While the reconstruction policy was put in execution, during the time he was president, in all its rigor, still a retrospective view caused the Southern people to believe he had befriended them when he could judiciously do so. The temper of the victorious North was not such that any one man, however influential, no matter what his generous instincts were, could anticipate any change of policy prematurely. They felt that he had been generous to the soldiers of the South during the war whenever he had the power to be generous; also, that in executing the policy of Congress he was obeying orders in the spirit of his military training rather than in sympathy with that policy. He felt, too, as he stated, that if a law were wrong and impracticable, it would work out a good result by its strict enforcement, and this was really the effect in the consolidation and in the irresistible effort of the Southern people in wresting from the wreck the white civilization of the South, an effort almost equal to a revolution. They believed that his great common sense enabled him to understand the surroundings at the time better than any one else. At an opportune moment he did befriend the people of the South in procuring additional legislation expediting reconstruction, and he did this at as early a moment as would have been prudent. He also foreshadowed the removal of [U.S.] troops from the South. He became impatient at the frequent calls for troops to hold up the rotten [Left-wing] carpet-bag governments, and prepared public opinion at the North for the removal of troops from the South by his successor [former Union General Rutherford B. Hayes].

At his funeral, the president [Hayes] and his cabinet, composed in part of several eminent Southerners, many Southern statesmen and surviving Confederate soldiers, took part, and marched side by side with the mourning North in doing honor to the great dead. All over the South flags were lowered at halfmast in his honor, and legislatures passed suitable resolutions of respect.[111]

NATIONAL PATRIOTISM AT THE SOUTH

☛ These two circumstances first evoked a display of national patriotism by the South. The people were then intensely considering the happy restoration of local self-government in their respective States. The national government, by its severe and radical [Left] treatment, had partially destroyed local self-government everywhere. Under its policy enormous debts had been piled upon them while they were facing the bayonet in the hands of the military power. To them local self-government and a stoppage of corrupt government were the great present boon, and the growth of national feeling was slow but steady, as the two sections better understood each other. Their time was taken up in undoing the false legislation then in force, and when necessary, in constructing new constitutions, in steering between Scylla and Charybdis by keeping within the new amendments, and at the same time in holding the political power in the hands of the white people; also in preventing a return to power of the negro element [at that stage still largely uneducated and unskilled, and so not yet prepared for the enormous responsibilities of political life; in other words, in the parlance of the late 19th Century, he was not yet "fitted for citizenship"], which was in a majority in many sections of the South.

To accomplish this required the greatest skill, courage and patience. The means resorted to at times varied as the occasion demanded, not always approved by the best citizenship, but deemed necessary generally to effect the purpose. This period was a very trying one, and brought out prominently the leading characteristics of the Southern people in their resolve never again to submit to negroism and its baneful results. The Southern people knew that they alone could solve the great social problem of the races. They, white and black, lived together [in racial harmony]; they had seen that the effort made by [Left-wing] strangers from the North, who had attempted to administer their affairs when local self-government had been suppressed [during Reconstruction], had proved to be a woeful failure.

They felt that the people of the North would soon see that it was better to permit the people of the South to solve their own difficult problems themselves and without further interference. As the people felt more secure, a more liberal legislation and policy were adopted toward the negro race, and they themselves see how much better everything works since they ceased to give so much attention to politics and more to their material wants and education. This period from 1885 to 1895 was really a period of readjustment to normal conditions in the South, and the people were really too busy and too anxious in their hard work of restoration and in making permanent their new boon of self-government, to take any great interest in national affairs.

The year 1895 was really the year when the North and South were again permanently cemented together in good feeling and in a broad national spirit. It is true this feeling had grown steadily since the inauguration of President Cleveland, but it bore substantial fruit in 1895. Then were the three prominent events of the year to emphasize fraternal feeling, and to encourage and broaden the people of the South in their attachment to the government. They now fully recognize that theirs was the best government in the world; that the people had more freedom than under any other government; that all were getting back substantially to the government of their fathers; that the Constitution was once more erect in its majesty, true without the principles for which they had fought (states' rights), but with a restoration of prosperity and a full acceptance of results, a good and beneficent government to them.

The first notable event was the dedication of a monument at Chicago to the Confederate soldiers who died during the war in prison in that city. The money to build this monument was mainly raised by broad-minded citizens of Chicago [my emphasis, L.S.],[112] and showed that the bloody chasm was a myth, and that we were again in heart and spirit one people with the same national aspirations. At first great opposition was manifested, as the dedication occurred on Decoration day of the dead Federal soldiers under the auspices of the Grand Army of the Republic. The officials of that organization objected, but its members, many of them, still aided in their unofficial capacity. The surviving Confederate generals and soldiers who attended the ceremony were most hospitably received and entertained. They had to pass through several hundred thousand people in going to the cemetery, and there was not a word, motion or sign in that vast assemblage or during a stay of several days that did not betoken the best of feeling and a broad nationality. The fable of the bloody chasm, it was found, did not exist. The First regiment of the Illinois National Guard (under Colonel Turner), 800 strong, fired three volleys at the close of the ceremonies and many of the Grand Army men in uniform listened attentively to [Confederate] Gen. Wade Hampton, who delivered the address.

Another significant event was the dedication of the battlefield of Chickamauga, in Georgia, as a national military park by the law of Congress. *The liberal legislation in this work, in putting Federal and Confederate conditions on an equality, in erecting out of the public treasury monuments, similar in every respect, over spots where Union and Confederate generals lost their lives, and equally honoring the valor of both as American soldiers rather than as former foes, had a wonderful effect* [my emphasis, L.S.]. Then, too, cabinet officers, statesmen of all political parties, soldiers of the Union and of the Confederacy, assembled on the field and commingled in friendly intercourse, fighting the battle over again. Soldier organizations, North and South, held reunions and even reunions in common, attesting a new era of good feeling; indeed, all were now satisfied to be covered by the common flag of a common country. The addresses delivered were also of a marked character, breathing that free atmosphere of equality natural to American citizenship. No principle was sacrificed by either side in the maintenance that each side believed that it had been right in the advocacy of the principles for which men had fought on the great field.

The Atlanta exposition occurred also in 1895, and showed with what vigor the Southern people were progressing in their material development in every line. It gave the people who visited that great Southern city new life, new aspirations. They discovered in that great display that they were once more a rich people and had made great strides. All went to their homes feeling that they need not again have a return of despondency, but with renewed effort they could equal any section of the country in wealth and real prosperity.[113]

FUTURE OF THE SOUTH

☛The South is now really at the very beginning of her industrial development. Her great advantages in the extent of her resources, incident to her mild climate and wonderful natural proximity of ores, and demonstrated advantages in the manufacture of her cotton and wood products, where the crop and timber are most convenient, her facilities for the raising of stock of all kinds, in feeding for a less time by several months, owing to milder climate, and the growing of almost every grass suitable for hay and feed—all these advantages have been fully demonstrated since 1880. Capitalists in Europe and this country now have no doubt as to the favorable surroundings for investment, and the large development of her newly discovered fields of industry in every line will surpass the sanguine expectations of her most ardent enthusiasts. In the North, owing to an earlier development and diversified industries, her fields are more fully occupied and opportunities for capitalists are not so encouraging or inviting.

It is a fact, too, that nearly all new railroad enterprises are pointing southward. The shipment of grain eastward from Chicago and the West to Boston, New York, Philadelphia and Baltimore for water transportation to Europe and South American ports, is about being diverted to south Atlantic and Gulf ports, which will shorten the land transportation and substitute the cheaper water transportation from one-third to one-half the distance. The Illinois Central railroad has erected docks and elevators in New Orleans equaling, if not surpassing, facilities and conveniences in this line at eastern ports, and thousands of carloads of grain have traveled over this road to these elevators. Kansas City, backed by foreign capital, is building a railroad to a gulf port, lessening the rail transportation of grain eastward by 767 miles.

The Mobile & Ohio railroad is now building a line from Columbus, Miss., to Montgomery, Ala., connecting with the great Plant system, giving direct lines to Brunswick, Ga., Jacksonville, Pensacola, and Tampa, Fla. This road now has extensive wharves and elevators in Mobile, Ala. These new lines and connections now being perfected by other roads will be ready for not only transporting grain from the North and West, but the iron, cotton, and timber products (one-half of all the standing timber being in the South at the present time), to be manufactured into the various articles of commerce. The South is now making enough for home consumption, and is shipping largely besides, and will increase annually these shipments. These are no longer doubted facts, and there is now going on a movement toward the South of larger manufacturing interests, of capital, of railroad builders, of population. A most significant illustration of how immigration is increasing is the locating of a colony, composed of veterans of the Union army, in South Georgia, by ex-Governor [William J.] Northen of that State. Scarcely over two years ago there was established in the piney woods of that State a town of 6,000 inhabitants with constant accessions in population and capital. The settlement has sprung up almost like magic, and has attracted great attention. It is one of the many such colonies now being contemplated and being established throughout the South, and must necessarily continue, as nearly all of the available arable land fit for settlement is now in the South, while much of the land settled by agriculturists in the extreme Northwest has been found unsuitable as farming land, owing to uncertain seasons and little rainfall.

The class immigrating southward is a most desirable class, being mainly Americans, or foreigners who have become thoroughly Americanized, and who prefer the South on account of the very cold weather in the North. Nearly all new emigrants from Europe prefer the North at first. The cotton and iron manufacturing enterprises in the South did not experience the effects of the depression in money matters in the panics of 1892 and 1893 as did similar plants at the North. At Fall River, Mass., and other manufacturing centers, mills were run on half time; in fact, for many years the loss on this account in wages and income has been almost one-half, while similar plants in the South have run on full time steadily and have supplied the shortage caused by the closing of the manufactories at the North.[114]

THE NEGRO PROBLEM

☞ With the account of the great strides made by the South since 1880, one will ask, What became of the great negro problem, which for nearly three hundred years has been a running sore in this country? In nearly every stage of our history, this vexed problem has caused division, irritation, bitter political discussions, sectional animosities, and conflicting interests in material development. Even in the constitutional convention of 1789, our wisest statesmen knew and said that the States were divided between those having slaves and those not having them, or about getting rid of them. This division existed down to the war between the States; in fact, slavery was the irritating cause which divided the North and the South on sectional lines in the construction of the Constitution. *The negro since the war was still the irritating cause which kept the sections wide apart, and was responsible for the harsh reconstruction epoch. He owed his freedom to a war necessity.*[115] *He was the cause of the drastic political experiments inaugurated by [Left-wing] Northern statesmen* [my emphasis, L.S.]. From a slave he was made a full citizen, with full political rights.

These were thrust upon him suddenly, without any previous training or preparation. At the same time he was made to face the white man in the great problem of competition, while his aspirations and instincts were entirely different from the stronger ruling race; the one race thrifty, dominating, accumulative and full of enterprise and progress, the other not inclined to lay up wealth or better its condition. For awhile the negro was the ward of the nation, and money was lavishly spent to hold him in his new responsible position, but this had its end. Thinking men knew that while he was not expected, owing to his unfortunate past, to be able to fight the battles of life with the superior race, still it was disappointing, as shown by the statistics, that the masses [of negroes thus far] have been but little advanced in the acquisition of property and education. He is inclined to be wasteful and improvident; inclined to spend his money in baubles rather than in surrounding himself with comforts. It cannot be denied that he has improved in many ways, educationally, materially and morally, but as yet the signs are not of the most encouraging character that he will ever be successful in the great competition in life, which he will necessarily encounter side by side with the white man.

I hardly think it can be denied that prejudice exists against him as a race, both North and South. In his work he cannot compete with the white man in quality or amount. It is also evident that in all lines of employment except agriculture, he is steadily disappearing in numbers at the North, as compared with his hold in those employments years ago, when there was a sentiment in his favor. He is being more and more restricted in all the avenues of the various industries affording a living to workers. The places are being filled more and more by white employees. He is constantly failing in his ability to keep abreast of the white man in the struggle for employment. He is being pushed aside as the white man needs work and tries to get it, to such an extent that at the North he has but few lines of employment now left. Labor unions are discriminating against him in all mechanical trades, and in fact in all lines of work controlled by guilds, and this discrimination also exists where there are no labor unions. For a long time and until recently this feeling did not pervade the South, but it is growing, and where many negro mechanics got work for a long time, white mechanics are now strongly competing and demanding preference, and as they generally give better work, they are getting it more and more to the exclusion of the negro. The white immigrants, too, from the North to the South, have little use for the negro after a few years, and more and more the negro will have to fight and struggle for a living like every other race; and it remains to be seen how he can run side by side with his more progressive and assertive white neighbor, as the white race outnumbers him more and more, and becomes more aggressive.

Mr. Henry Garnett, in the summary of negro statistics in the Census Bureau for 1890, gives the following results:

> "The negroes, while increasing rapidly in this country, are diminishing in number relative to the whites. They are moving southward from the border States into those of the South Atlantic and the Gulf. They prefer rural life rather than urban life. The proportion of criminals among the negroes is much greater than among the whites, and that of the paupers is at least as great. In the matter of education, the number of negro attendants at school is far behind the number of whites, but is gaining rapidly on that race."

These statistics show that in one hundred years the whites have multiplied eighteen times and the negroes nearly ten times. In 1790, the whites were 80.73 per cent of the population, the negroes 19.27 per cent. In 1890 the negroes constituted only 12½ per cent of the population.

In the criminal statistics, the proportion of negroes in jails was nearly four times as great as that of native white extraction, and the commitment of negroes for petty offenses is in much greater proportion than among the white race. The negroes also marry earlier and their lives are shorter than in the white race. The Rev. L. W. W. Manaway, missionary of the African Methodist church in Mississippi, who has carefully collated statistics as to his race, says:

> "A great many of my race say that the white people send them to prison. I differ from them. . . . I found that out of 78 convictions of

colored people, the testimony on which the convictions were had in 77 cases was furnished by colored people, and that the man convicted by white testimony received a sentence of one year in the penitentiary, and the average sentence of those convicted on colored testimony was from two to five years. Last year there were twenty- two negroes killed over the crap table. . . . It is said abroad that the white people in the South are killing off the negroes. The statistics of crime which I have kept for years disprove the charge. It is true that pernicious crimes are committed which cause lynchings, but the same causes bring the same results in other States of the Union. I must not be understood as defending lynchings. Lynchings are wrong whenever or wherever engaged in. Every lyncher is a murderer. . . .The majority of crimes are not committed by the best colored citizens, but by shiftless people who float from one community to another with no visible means of support."[116]

From a statistical standpoint, the outlook for the negro is not encouraging. I do not believe that any one can forecast the future of the negro. One thing is certain, when left to himself without the strong will and example of the white man in the black belts, he tends to retrograde; when outnumbered by the whites in the white belts, he assimilates more to the habits of white men, becomes a better laborer and a better citizen. The negro is certainly improving as a laborer all over the South since the last three or four years, and farming is getting more and more in its normal condition. Experimenting is passing away and both white and black races understand each other better, and all work is more strictly on business principles. Labor has got over its disorganization, and is realizing that unless good service is rendered, it is difficult to get on good lands or with good employers. Both white and black have paid old debts and are more careful in incurring new ones. Many mortgages have been lifted in the last three or four years, and good crops have been produced. The white people are realizing fully now that the negro is a constant quantity at the South; that he has no idea of moving away and settling at the North and elsewhere; that he must be educated and fitted for citizenship as rapidly as possible; that it is better to help and encourage him than to repress him; and the whole drift now is to elevate him by education. *It is worthy of remark that although he was freed [by Lincoln] as a war measure, still the great [U.S.] government which freed him has done nothing to remove his illiteracy, poverty and ignorance; but the great burden has fallen on the impoverished white people of the South mainly, which was the most disorganized section of the Union as a result of the war, and they are taxing themselves with as liberal and unselfish a spirit as has been shown by any people under similar circumstances anywhere on the globe* [my emphasis,

L.S.]. It is not just to say either that the negro, who was and is the principal farm laborer, is not entitled to a large credit for the great and valuable crops raised in the South since 1880. It is true he was directed by the white people who owned the land, but the crops were made mostly through his labor. The white people went to work also on the farms and made a large part of the crops themselves. They worked harder and more industriously than ever, and in the white belts raised a large per cent of the crops. I believe that the next census will show a much better record for the colored race. I remark, then, that the great progress of the South is explained in the energy and push of the Southern whites, under the great necessity to retrieve and save their country and transmit its Anglo-Saxon civilization unimpaired, and as far as possible untarnished by negroism or its consequences; that the rapid accumulation of wealth was brought about in spite of the incubus of an inferior race, which was forcibly carried along and made to do its part. The negro has seen the great difference and feels it is best for both races. Repression of the negro vote will gradually pass away, and he will become as regular a voter as his white brother, when he loses his identity as a political factor separate and distinct from others [my emphasis, L.S.]. White immigrants will move so rapidly now that the negro will be overshadowed everywhere, as he is now in the localities where the whites outnumber him two or three to one; they will be assimilated to the whites in thrift and citizenship; never the equal but always the weaker vessel which must not be imposed upon but must be protected.[117]

After creating what was then called "negroism," Yankee Liberals pushed the responsibility for it onto the South, then used this fabrication as a weapon to subdue her people.

MORALITY OF SOUTHERN PEOPLE

☞ The morality of the Southern white people will compare favorably with any country or section in the world. Unsympathizing pens have not considered their untoward surroundings in having contact with "an unassimilated and inferior race," that the "submersion of brains, political experience, land ownership, and habits of domination by ignorant members could have but one issue," which was plainly brought out in the reconstruction days and for many years following. The white people have given evidence of their morality in the growth of the religious denominations, and more especially in the prevalence of prohibition in the liquor business by local option laws, especially in Mississippi and Arkansas. About 90 per cent of the counties of Mississippi have prohibition by virtue of local option. It is even better in Arkansas, but in all these elections, the negro votes almost solid for whisky.[118]

SOCIAL MATTERS
☛ It is a wise provision also that the races are kept separate in the schools, in churches and in railroad cars. Equal accommodations are granted under the laws. In some of the States no separation appears in railroad cars, and soon it will be the rule in all the States in this particular, but it will be a long time, if ever, before the children of the two races will attend schools in common, so long as the negro is numerous in particular localities. The race instinct is implanted by a stronger hand than that of man, and a different arrangement where the races are anyway equal or the blacks more numerous, would result in constant collision and disorder. The young generations of whites and blacks have far less disposition to adjustment in such matters than the older members of the respective races. The sensible negro never aspires to social equality; the broad men of the race distinctly state this; and any tendency in this direction is found only with the worse element and those disposed to create disorder and trouble. *At the North it is hypocrisy to pretend that the negro is admitted in social circles equally with the whites. He is held more at arm's length than even at the South* [my emphasis, L.S.], this, too, in face of the fact that the negro is the exception there and seldom met, as compared with the South, where in several States he outnumbers the whites, and in many localities, the same condition exists in almost every State.

Of late years one hears more of negroes not being admitted to hotels and restaurants and public resorts at the North than at the South [my emphasis, L.S.]. Social equality is not recognized North or South, and the sentiment is the same among the whites and blacks in both sections.[119]

LYNCHINGS
☛ Lynching to the extent it has existed in the South is indefensible. The crime [blacks raping white women] invoking it began and has

been continued solely by the irrepressible and worst element of the negro race, inaugurating a new crime, which was unknown and impossible in the days of slavery, and which, from that fact and the existence of slavery, invested it with peculiar horror and atrocity. That the race instinct is strongly implanted in human society is undeniable; and when this crime is committed under the peculiarly harrowing surroundings of isolation in sparsely-settled communities, upon helpless and unprotected white women, combined with the murder in many cases of the outraged female, it arouses a fierceness and revengeful spirit uncontrollable at times. It should be borne in mind, too, that a most abnormal state of society had preceded the advent of this crime of rape, for which the Southern people were not alone responsible and which they tried to prevent. What is now regarded as a great political mistake was committed in the sudden enfranchisement and investment of the negro race with all the privileges of citizenship, including suffrage, lawmaking, and governing at the point of the bayonet a superior race, who had always been aggressive in the assertion of every political right. *This race was under a ban as a punishment for so-called rebellion and insurrection. Their hands were tied when this great political and social reversion of the races was put in operation and upheld by the military government of the United States from 1867 to 1880 (almost). When the military power of the government in this period stood aside, apparently to see what the new State governments would do alone, those governments inaugurated a similar system only worse, in that negro militia, armed to the teeth, took the place of the white United States troops, and most offensively flaunted their newly-invested rights in the faces of the white people of the South, a proud, sensitive race. conventions and legislatures, called to inaugurate new State governments, were divested of every essence of the theory and tradition of local self-government, composed mainly of designing men called carpet-baggers, who could not succeed at their former homes, with not a particle of sympathy for the people who had always governed. They were their avowed enemies, using a large number of the most ignorant of the negro race to assist them* [my emphasis, L.S.]. To illustrate: In the convention in Alabama, out of ninety-seven members of the one hundred and thirty-one, thirty-one were from Vermont, Connecticut, Massachusetts, Pennsylvania, Maine, New Jersey, New York, Ohio, Canada, and Scotland; bearing in mind, too, that these were mainly white strangers to the people, and that they controlled the negro element. Some of the Southern whites, who could not get office from the people among whom they lived, except in such upheavals of society, united with them and were even more extreme than the white aliens; they, too, were striving for influence among the negroes to hold office by their votes, and had to keep abreast of or surpass their alien white colleagues to allay their suspicions of loyalty to the new order of things, in order to win the confidence of the negroes by posing as their foremost defenders in their newly given rights obtained by military power.

There were some good white men in these conventions and legislatures intent on trying to get the best possible government, but these were silenced. Instead of realizing the dangerous situation, the new lawmakers began discussing, with most inflammatory language and bearing, the matter of intermarriage of the races, the further disfranchisement of classes of whites who might throw obstacles to their proposed plans, and mixed schools in common for all children, white and black. When it is recalled now that in some of the States the negroes were largely in the majority, and in others nearly equally divided, this complete social upheaval was enough to turn the heads of the worst element of a more fortunate race than that of the negro. But even with these temptations the crime of rape was not committed then, for the shrewd carpet-bagger knew that this one offense would not be tolerated, and so long as they remained, it did not occur except in most isolated cases. *The older negroes, too, and pleasure is taken in stating it, under the influence of even the great temptations and their previous living among the white people as slaves, never dreamed of such a crime, and held their growing sons for a time under that control which they had had under the system of slavery. No other race, under similar temptations and surroundings, would have done better. They had no revenges of a personal character to inaugurate against their former masters. This new and hideous crime remained to be inaugurated by a [communized] younger generation of negroes, raised amidst the upheaval of those troublous times, while their fathers were mainly engaged in listening to inflammatory appeals, many of a social coloring, by designing and robbing [Left-wing] strangers who held political power* [my emphasis, L.S.], and while their fathers themselves had laid aside their industrious habits of life and were leading a careless, wandering existence in their new-born freedom, not one-third of their time being given to productive labor.

Amid such surroundings the new generation of negro boys and men was raised. *Parents, in a measure, gradually lost control of their boys in that loose period, and they grew up in idleness and with distorted and ugly ideas of their rights. They felt that they had to assert those rights personally by insolence and bravado toward the white males and females, among whom they had lived* [my emphasis, L.S.]. The young negroes remembered that their fathers were held in place by the white troops of the government which had given them freedom. They saw soldiers of their own race parading almost every plantation and town to keep down the whites and hold the negroes in power. Even an ignorant negro boy could see that the "black man's party" [that is, the then Left-wing Republican Party] was in power, and the "bottom rail on top."

Under these conditions, when the brains of the carpet-baggers were lost to the negroes by a change of government into the hands of the Southern property-holders and educated class, the young negroes could scarcely appreciate the import of the change, and they found that dreams of social equality had vanished forever. This dream had never taken strong hold on the older blacks, but it had seized the younger ones. They recalled all the discussions and talks of the dark days as to the intermarrying of the races, and the crime of raping a white woman came into existence as a sequence. It occurred generally under most revolting and harrowing circumstances. It was in sparsely-settled districts where the crime was committed, in secluded paths and roads, when young girls were going to or returning from school, when wives were alone in their homes with children, their husbands being at work in the fields or otherwise engaged in the great struggle of bread-winning, and in communities generally where the blacks predominated in numbers. The feeling of utter lack of protection existed in places, and those who lived under such terrible facts, felt that the sanctity of their homes could only be protected by taking the law into their own hands and meting out punishment to the brutes. They did it just as they would turn out to kill a mad dog in a small town, or crush a rattlesnake under their feet, when beloved ones were in such peril. Women were afraid to go about without a guard. Life became unbearable; for the peace and security of home are gone when rape is committed. They felt that if the brute was not lynched, the wretch might get loose and repeat the same crime.

These acts of lynching, of course, always shocked every law-abiding citizen. They struck terror to the negro. The law-abiding sentiment was weakened whenever a lynching occurred. The crime was indefensible; but those who condemn it must not forget the abnormal conditions. Those who engaged in lynching put themselves outside of the law, but at the same time those who committed rape put themselves also outside of the law. It would always be better to abide by the law, for human society and civilization are based on the principle that the individual gives up his right of protection of life and property to the State which must perform this duty. But in the isolated spots where the crime was generally committed, it was almost impossible in many cases to get this legal protection promptly, and when it was needed, the community was swayed by a terrible cyclone of excitement and horror.

The conditions evoked, too, are most peculiar. The whites felt themselves outraged, and by a state of tutelage of the negro for which they were not responsible. This is no excuse for the crime of lynching. It is only stated to bring out the unfortunate facts incident to a great political crime in thrusting responsibilities on a weak and unfortunate race by a too rapid hotbed process of development, a procrustean operation.

The negroes felt outraged, too, for it appeared to them that only their race was lynched for the crime. They did not remember that white men, however loose in morals, did not find it necessary, in gratifying their beastly impulses for the other race, to commit the crime. This is no excuse for the white man to indulge his lustful desires. It was the misfortune of the negro race that in its condition of slavery and in the little time for improvement since free, habits of purity and chastity among them were not of a high grade. It was not to be expected that it should be otherwise. This is as much regretted by the conservative element of the negroes themselves as by their best well-wishers. At any rate, the negro was, as was natural, shocked and sullen and felt aggrieved. The two races in similar frame of mind from the peculiar circumstances, did not view, and have not as quickly viewed, the crime as it should have been. The example of the whites has been a bad one for the negroes themselves, for they, too, follow in the tracks of their neighbors. Only two years ago a negro girl near Enterprise, Miss., had to go through a lonely swamp to her home from work. She got a negro man to go with her for protection. Her dead body was found and her would-be protector was a fugitive, while outraged negroes, to protect their race from the great crime even among themselves, scoured the swamps, woods and everywhere to catch the brute and lynch him. *It should not be forgotten, too, that lynchings occur sometimes at the North under similar atrocious surroundings. Outraged communities in all parts of the world take the law in their own hands and lynch those who endanger the sanctity of home and society* [my emphasis, L.S.].

The negro element is hardly perceptible at the North; it is not in sufficient numbers to cause much friction. Still it does do it. Even mixed schools, where a small percentage of the scholars are negroes, have stirred up many communities, and considerable friction has resulted from the inborn race feeling implanted in every bosom. This presentation of facts is not given to excuse the lynching of negroes and whites, but to exhibit afresh the surroundings in the South in that new formative period after the war with its consequent chaos in society and morals. It is possible that some few lynchings may have been meted out to innocent parties, but barely possible. The greatest harm done always is in familiarizing public sentiment in witnessing such violations of law, and breaking down reliance on the law to redress grievances. The remedy lies in both races trying to put a stop to the crime which produces the violation of law by lynching.

The statistics show that the number of lynchings in 1896 within the limits of the United States was 131; 107 occurred in the South, and 24 in other parts of the Union, in Colorado, Illinois, Indiana, Minnesota, New York, Indian Territory and Oklahoma Territory. *Of the negroes, 80 were lynched (40 for the crime of rape, 20 for murder and house burning). Fifty-one whites were lynched. So it appears that lynching is not meted out to negroes alone, but that nearly 40 per cent of those lynched were white men, and of the negroes 50 per cent of those lynched were killed for the crime of rape, and 18 per cent of the lynchings occurred out of the South.*[120]

The law-abiding citizens everywhere have always tried to prevent lynching. Leading citizens in every State have, from the inception of the crime, done all they could, by pen and speech, to hinder and check it. Every leading paper in the South, in fact I will say the press generally, has done its duty to stop it. Governors have exercised all their power, and have often prevented it. In South Carolina legislation disfranchises an officer who even appears to play into the hands of a mob, and debars him from office. It renders the county liable in damages to the amount of $2,000 to go to the family of the lynched person. It is more frequent now that culprits are lodged in jail to await the slow process of law. Officers are doing their duty in protecting criminals and getting them beyond the reach of lynchers. Public sentiment is growing stronger and stronger in condemnation of the act. Whites and blacks alike are now working more together to root out the crime of rape, and have offenders tried as other criminals. Bishop W. J. Gaines, a colored man of the Methodist African church, says:

> "I am as emphatic in my condemnation of the lawless and godless crime of lynching as Bishop Turner can be, but he is entirely too radical. The best element of the white people is opposed to lynching as much as are the negroes. The governors and peace officers of the Southern States are doing all they can to bring about a proper condition of affairs. The best remedy for our evils is education and Christianity. The crimes for which lynching is the punishment are

committed by the most ignorant of our race. It will take time to educate them."

This is what he says in reply to Bishop Turner of the same race, who would have the negroes arm themselves and virtually inaugurate neighborhood war, and which some vile negroes would construe as a protection for those who committed rape, and which would result in the greatest calamity to the blacks if started. It is fortunate that so good an adviser is to be found as Bishop Gaines, I remark that the people of the South are as moral and law-abiding as any people anywhere in the world. It would be well if those who judge them harshly would consider what they would have done themselves, surrounded by the most grave social problem the world has ever seen; viz., the race problem in its ugliest presentation in the South, and by the provocation of the mistake of [Left-wing] statesmen.[121]

SUPPLEMENTARY

☛ The preceding part of this article was completed in 1897. Since that time the great Republic, in the year 1898, has made wonderful strides in history making. It has engaged in a most successful war with Spain, to put an end to the bad government of Spanish rule in Cuba. The people of the United States, on the score of humanity, forced the legislative and executive departments to put an end to the apparently endless bad government and inhumanity, emphasizing the rule of Spain of her colonies in the Western continent. The destruction of the warship *Maine*, in the harbor of Havana by being blown up; the victory of Admiral [George] Dewey at Manila; the destruction of Admiral [Pasqual] Cervera's fleet by Commodores [William T.] Sampson and [Winfield S.] Schley off Santiago de Cuba, and the capture of Santiago de Cuba by the American army under General [William] Shafter, have been rapidly recurring events, which have thrilled the heart of every patriotic American with pride. These naval and military events, which may be classed almost alone for their brilliancy, when we consider the little loss of life incurred, and the results following in acquisition of territory to the United States, make an historical era hitherto unsurpassed in the history of our country.

One of the most remarkable results of this [Spanish-American] war has been the display of national patriotism and unity among the citizens of this great country—North, South, East and West. All sectional lines have apparently been blotted out forever; all bad blood, if any still lingered either North or South, as a result of the great civil strife from 1861 to 1865, has disappeared and no longer exists.[122] The President of the United States [William McKinley], upon the declaration of war by Congress, called for 200,000 volunteer troops to defend the honor of the flag, and to carry out the wishes of Congress in making war against Spain. These troops were apportioned among the several States in the Union in accordance with their population, and the call met with a prompt response from the citizenship of every State. *In no part of the republic was the response more patriotic, more earnest, or more enthusiastic than in the ex-Confederate States which had been engaged in the war against the Union. About one-third of the volunteers called for by the President were furnished by the Southern States. The officers and enlisted men of these volunteer organizations were composed of ex-Confederate soldiers, their sons and their grandsons. Their conduct in the service of the United States was equally as honorable, as patriotic, and as enthusiastic as that of the troops from any other section of the Union. In camp, and while being hardened to service, they endured hardships and sacrifices with a spirit that showed they were worthy descendants of the men who, from 1861 to 1865, gave such evidence of manhood and heroism, in combating against superior numbers and resources* [my emphasis, L.S.].

In the preceding pages of this article, it was stated, that at the close of the war in 1865, the people of the South yielded to the inevitable with honesty and integrity of purpose; that in June, 1865, a little over two months after the surrender of Gen. Robert E. Lee's army in Virginia, there was not an armed Confederate soldier to be found anywhere; that the people of the South were ready, and showed their willingness to accept any results which the Federal government deemed necessary to impose upon them; that they gave most hearty support to the policies of Presidents Lincoln and Johnson, in inaugurating and putting into effect what was termed the "presidential reconstruction;" that they endured with great patience and calm judgment, the dark days of congressional reconstruction, and while protesting against what seemed to them undue harshness in the legislation of Congress, they bode their time, till *the corrupt negro governments established during the reconstruction period, virtually fell of their own weight and impracticability* [my emphasis, L.S.]; that so soon as the white people of the South again came into possession of their State governments, their prosperity began to dawn; that they devoted their time and energies to the preservation of that local self-government, rescued from ignorance and corruption, but not considered finally established; that they began to repeal all bad laws, and to work for the restoration of their waste places resulting from four years of dreadful war and twelve years of bad negro government, and that during all this period the people of the South conscientiously tried to perform their full duty as citizens of the United States. Their delicate surroundings under the peculiar circumstances, did not admit of undue demonstration of national feeling, but whenever an opportunity was offered them, they gave unmistakable signs of that love of country and true patriotism which was their heritage from revolutionary forefathers.

President Cleveland was the first great official who trusted the people of the South frankly, and gave typical Southerners cabinet positions, appointing them also on the supreme bench and as ambassadors to foreign courts and to other federal appointments. His administration evoked intense satisfaction among the citizens of the South, as it enabled them to show the sincerity of their avowed good feeling toward the restored Union [my emphasis, L.S.]. The death of General Grant, in 1885, who had always been generous to the Confederates in war; the dedication of Chickamauga park, and of the Confederate monument in the city of Chicago to the Confederate dead, brought forth displays of patriotism toward the general government on the part of the people of the South. Her senators and representatives in Congress, during the great riot in Chicago, also brought to the surface their patriotic love of the Union.

U.S. President, slave owner, and former Union general, Ulysses S. Grant. A Southerner himself, Grant proved to be somewhat lenient with General Lee at the time of the great Confederate chieftain's surrender. However, during Reconstruction our 18th President succumbed to the influences of his party's radical element, allowing a myriad of outrages and illegalities to be committed against the Southern people.

But it remained for the year 1898 and the war between Spain and the United States to cause this national feeling, this love of country, to burst into a flame that left no doubt as to the national patriotism of the people of the ex-Confederate States.

The writer of this article [Gen. Stephen D. Lee]—an ex-Confederate soldier—although he was always loyal to the Stars and Stripes from the moment he laid down his arms as a soldier of the Confederacy and took the oath of allegiance to the restored Union; although he had conscientiously performed his duty as a citizen under that oath of allegiance, and although he was ready at any time to defend the Stars and Stripes had it become necessary, as a duty still, when he heard of the great victory of Admiral Dewey at Manila, his heart leaped with joy and pride because he was a citizen of the United States. There was no longer a doubt as to his possessing real and true love for his reunited country. While he would not positively say that this was the feeling of every ex-Confederate soldier, he believes that this patriotic emotion which found expression from his own heart, found also a response in the heart of almost every ex-Confederate.

The tour of the President of the United States, Mr. McKinley, through the South, and his speeches of patriotism and good-will everywhere, evoked unbounded enthusiasm and patriotism in every portion of the South. Although he is the representative of the great Republican party, the party toward which the people of the South felt unkindly, because of the ordeal of reconstruction, still, in their display of patriotism they have forgotten everything in the past that stood in the way of a complete obliteration of sectional lines and bad blood. [Note: Gen. Lee is confused here: The Republican Party became Conservative during the presidential election of 1896, while, during the same election, the Democratic Party became Liberal. Thus at the time of this writing (1898), McKinley was a Conservative, one possessing the same patriotic sentiments and pro-Constitution views that Lee and the rest of the Confederacy held before, during, and after the War. L.S.].[123]

It should be a source of intense satisfaction to the people of the South, and also of the North, that there can no longer be any doubt of the unity of the people of the United States. It is certainly a most remarkable event in history, that the people of this country should be so reunited after the terrible civil war through which this country passed thirty-five years ago, and that, too, while so many of the participants of that mighty and heroic struggle are still living. From this time henceforth, no unpleasant accusations should be made in references to that great struggle. When the President of the United States [McKinley], representing a great party known as the war party in the civil war [again, Gen. Lee is in error: During the War the two major parties were reversed, only becoming the parties we know today in 1896—making Republican President McKinley, at the time of this writing, a Conservative; L.S.],[124] and speaking publicly in a Southern city could express the sentiment that the North should assist the South in caring for the graves of the

Confederate soldiers, and the expression of that sentiment, touching every Southern heart, drew forth patriotic response which showed the Southern love for a common country, surely we are again a reunited people, and Southern loyalty can no longer be questioned.[125]

It is also a source of great pride to the people of the South, that, although her volunteer soldiers did not have an opportunity to display their gallantry on the field of battle, yet among the heroes of the short war with Spain none are more conspicuous than Southern men who had an opportunity to manifest their soldierly qualities. The President of the United States, in making his appointments in the volunteer army organization for the war, gave some appointments to Southern men who had been ex-Confederate soldiers. This action on his part gave much satisfaction to the people of the South, and it is with pride that they can point to these soldiers and sailors as having well performed the duties devolving upon them wherever opportunity permitted.

Gen. Joseph Wheeler, who had been a lieutenant-general in the Confederate army, was appointed a major-general in the volunteer army of the United States. His enthusiasm, his patriotism, his good generalship, his good common sense in every emergency, stamped him as one of the noted heroes of the war, and his popularity at the North is not surpassed even in his own native South. His coolness at Santiago [Chile] at the moment when everything looked dark, possibly was the turning point to success on that field. He remembered that in the mighty struggle of 1861-65, when two American armies met in deadly conflict, generally both sides were paralyzed for a time; and after he carried the San Juan hills near Santiago, when for a time things looked blue, he recalled how it was in the great civil war, and said,

> "If we are so badly hurt, you may rest assured that the Spaniards are worse hurt, and we must hold our lines and not yield an inch."

His services in the field were not surpassed by his good sense and administrative talent in caring for the sick soldiers of the Union at Montauk Point [New York].

We are proud of Fitzhugh Lee [a cousin of both Gen Robert. E. Lee and the author of this essay Stephen D. Lee], another appointment as major-general of President McKinley. Amid all the fault finding (whether true or false), regarding the administrative direction in the care of our troops, he alone has not been criticised on account of the care and management of the soldiers under his charge. He was ever ready to obey the orders of the President, and go to Cuba or wherever, as a soldier, he could have been sent. He, too, has won the admiration of the people of the United States everywhere.

Maj. Gen. M. C. Butler was, like Lee and Wheeler, a distinguished Confederate soldier who performed his part well, not only in camp with the soldiers intrusted to his care, but as a statesman and a member of the evacuation commission at Havana. These three ex-Confederate generals have enjoyed the confidence of the President [McKinley] possibly as much as any other of the numerous appointments made in the volunteer army by him. Among the brigadier-generals of volunteers appointed from the South, were W. C. Oates of Alabama, H. T. Douglas of Maryland, T. L. Rosser of Virginia, and W. W. Gordon of Georgia, all noted Confederate officers who won distinction in the Confederate army.

Lieut. Richmond Pearson Hobson, of the navy (an Alabamian), is probably the hero of the war, by virtue of sinking the *Merrimack* in the channel leading to the harbor of Santiago de Cuba amid the shot and shell of Spanish heavy guns. Lieut. A. S. Rowan, of the United States army (a Virginian), is another Southern hero in the short war; while North Carolina has added to the above Worth Bagley and South Carolina Lieut. Victor Blue. There were many other heroes who deserve mention. The officers of the army and navy of the United States have never failed to do their whole duty wherever duty called them, but in this brief war with Spain, so far as individuals are concerned, the Southerners mentioned, have received enthusiastic appreciation from the whole people of the United States.

It should not be thought strange that the people of the South would burn with patriotic ardor against a foreign foe. While giving full credit to the South for her patriotism in the recent war with Spain, it is with pride that she can point to her past history in every instance where national honor and national statesmanship were needed to defend the flag of the Union, or be aggressive for its advancement. Leaving out her record of the great civil war, she points back to the spirit of the Southern colonial people, as broad and liberal, active in the general defense against the Indians and in the French wars. The first battle of the revolutionary war was fought on Southern soil, and the signal for resistance came from the South. The most critical and pressing struggle of the revolutionary war was carried on in the South and in the face of continual disaster. The devastations of that war were nearly all on her soil. A Southern colony furnished most of the soldiers in the army of the American revolution, and a Southern State finds a place in her soil for the bones of more revolutionary soldiers than any other State.

A Southern State was the first to organize an independent State government. The union of the thirteen revolting colonies, under the articles of confederation, was only made possible by the self-sacrifice of Virginia, who, to allay the fears of the smaller commonwealths, gave up her large northwestern territory to common ownership. The federal convention that gave us that greatest of all documents ever drawn by the hand of man, was presided over by a Southern member. And finally, when the ship of state was launched, with singular unanimity a Southern hand was called to the helm. With the exception of Alaska, no acquisition of territory had been made except through the effort of Southern statesmen, and generally in opposition to those of the North. It was [Thomas] Jefferson, who, by the purchase of Louisiana, extended the domain of the United States to the Rocky mountains, notwithstanding the violent threats of secession which came from the Northeast. Oregon, Florida, California and Texas—purchases and annexations—extended her domain to the Pacific, when Southern men occupied the presidential chair. In every war the national honor has been practically upheld by the South [my emphasis, L.S.]. In the cause of the national government in 1812, [in order to secede and form their own confederacy] New England responded with the Hartford convention, looking to the dismemberment of the Union. Impartial history will show that our "Southern ancestors were not drones in the hives and mere participants in the blessings which other sections have conferred," but on all occasions they did their duty like manly men and were leaders in all that "has largely made the United States, governed her, administered justice from her judicial tribunal, commanded her armies, created her greatness." It should not be forgotten that the States of Virginia, North Carolina, South Carolina and Georgia, at the close of the revolutionary war, had over two-thirds of the territory acquired by the United States from Great Britain by the treaty of Paris, and gave it up to the general government. The South, standing by its patriotic record, and tendering all its resources to the government, cordially bids our reunited country God-speed.[126] — CONFEDERATE GENERAL STEPHEN DILL LEE

CHAPTER 2
THE TRAGIC ERA

FROM A 1929 BOOK BY MIDWESTERN NEWSPAPER EDITOR & AUTHOR
Claude Gernade Bowers

IN THE DAYS FOLLOWING THE FALL OF RICHMOND
☛ ... FOR SOME TIME NOW A straggling procession of emaciated, crippled men in ragged gray had been sadly making their way through the wreckage to homes that in too many instances were found to be but piles of ashes. These men had fought to exhaustion. For weeks they would be found passing wearily over the country roads and into the towns, on foot and on horseback. It was observed that "they are so worn out that they fall down on the sidewalks and sleep." The countryside through which they passed presented the appearance of an utter waste, the fences gone, the fields neglected, the animals and herds driven away, and only lone chimneys marking spots where once had stood merry homes. A proud patrician lady [Mary Boykin Chesnut] riding between Chester and Camden in South Carolina scarcely saw a living thing, and "nothing but tall blackened chimneys to show that any man had ever trod this road before"; and she was moved to tears at the funereal aspect of the gardens where roses were already hiding the ruins. The long thin line of gray-garbed men, staggering from weakness into towns, found them often gutted with the flames of incendiaries or soldiers. Penniless, sick at heart and in body, and humiliated by defeat,

Right, Claude G. Bowers; Left, Rep. Edith Rogers.

they found their families in poverty and despair. "A degree of destitution that would draw pity from a stone," wrote a Northern correspondent. Entering the homes for a crust or cup of water, they found the furniture marred and broken, dishes cemented "in various styles" and with "corn cobs substituting for spindles in the looms." The houses of the most prosperous planters were found denuded of almost every article of furniture, and in some sections women and children accustomed to luxury begged from door to door.

In the larger towns the weary soldier found business prostrate, except with the sutlers, in full possession now that the merchants were ruined, and these were amassing fortunes through profiteering without shame. In Charleston [SC] the shops were closed, the shutters drawn. There was no shipping in the harbor, where the piers were rapidly decaying. Cows were feeding on the vacant lots and grass was growing between paving-stones in the principal streets. Warehouses were deserted, and the burnt district looked like a vast graveyard with broken walls and tall blackened chimneys. The once aristocratic clubs were closed, along with the restaurants, and it was noted that "no battle blood" mantled "the face of the haggard and listless Charlestonians one meets." One, who momentarily rejoiced in what he saw, found that "luxury, refinement, happiness have fled from Charleston and poverty is enthroned there." Columbia [SC] was one mass of ruins, and only the majestic columns of what had once been Wade Hampton's hall of hospitality remained. There, the prostration complete, intellectuals of the college faculty in rags were supplied with underclothing by a benevolent society of women. Thus it was in towns and cities generally. Everywhere destitution, desolation, utter hopelessness. In some of the cities brave attempts were being made to restore something of business prosperity, but this rested almost wholly on the speculators from the North. The natives were literally without money, their Confederate paper and bonds now worthless. The banks had closed their doors—ruined. The insurance companies had failed. The one hope for the restoration of the cities was the resumption of normal activities in the country, the cultivation of the plantations, as of old.

But in the country the situation was desperate, for the herds, cattle, sheep, and horses had been driven away. The master of one of the best plantations in Mississippi had returned to find only a few mules and one cow left. Houses, fences, and barns, destroyed, had to be rebuilt—and there was no money. Farming implements were needed and there was no credit. But the gravest problem of all was that of labor, for the slaves were free and were demanding payment in currency that their old masters no longer possessed. The one hope of staving off starvation the coming winter was to persuade the freedmen to work on the share, or wait until the crops were marketed for their pay. Many old broken planters called their former slaves about them and explained, and at first many agreed to wait for their compensation on the harvest. Many of them went on about their work, "very quiet and serious, and more obedient and kind than they had ever been known to be." It was observed that with the pleasure of knowing they had their freedom there was a touch of sadness. Some Northerners, who had taken Mrs. [Harriet Beecher] Stowe's [fictitious anti-South] novel too literally, were amazed at the numerous "instances of the most touching attachment to their old masters and mistresses." One of these was touched one Sunday morning when the negroes appeared in mass at the mansion house to pay their respects. "I must have shaken hands with four hundred," she wrote. Something of the beautiful loyalty in them which guarded the women and children with such zeal while husbands and fathers were fighting far away persisted in the early days of their freedom. Old slaves, with fruit and gobblers and game, would sneak into the house with an instinctive sense of delicacy and leave them in the depleted larder surreptitiously. Occasionally some of these loyal creatures, momentarily intoxicated with the breath of liberty, would roam down the road toward the towns, only to return with childlike faith to the old plantation. But for the suggestions of [U.S.] soldiers and [Left-wing] agitators, the former masters and slaves might easily have effected a social readjustment to their mutual benefit, *but this was not the game intended. The negroes must be turned against their former masters* [my emphasis, L.S.]; it was destiny perhaps that the carpet-bagger should be served. Quite soon an extravagant notion of proper compensation for services was to turn the freedmen adrift. Soon they were drunk with a sense of their power and importance.[127]

INDOCTRINATED FREEDMEN & "FREEDOM"
☛ One day a South Carolina woman [Chesnut] wrote in her diary that "negroes are seen in the fields plowing and hoeing corn," and a month later that "the negroes have flocked to the Yankee squad." The [Left-wing Republican] revolution had been wrought. The first evidence that outside influences had been at work upon the freedmen was furnished in their bizarre notions of labor, that under freedom all system ceased. At all hours of the day they could be seen laying down their implements and sauntering singing from the

fields. If freedom did not mean surcease from labor, where was the boon? And since they had changed their condition, why not their names? Former owners, meeting negroes born on their plantations and addressing them in the familiar way, were sharply rebuked with the assurance that they no longer responded to that name. "If you want anything, call for Sambo," said a patronizing old freedman. "I mean call me Mr. Samuel, dat my name now." Had the intoxication of the new freedom worked no more serious changes in the negro's character, all would have been well, but he was to meet with [radical socialist and communist] influences designed to separate him in spirit from those who understood him best.

Very soon they were eschewing labor and flocking to [U.S.] army camps to be fed, and here they were told, with cruel malice, that the land they had formerly cultivated as slaves was to be given them. Accepting it seriously, some had actually taken possession and planted corn and cotton. The assurance was given them solemnly that when Congress met, the division would be made. Quite soon they would have it on the authority of [radical New England socialist] Thaddeus Stevens. Convinced of the ultimate division, they could see no sense in settling down to toil for the meager wages the impoverished planters could afford to pay. There was pathos in their faith, in the blue coat, and their congestion about the army posts soon tested the patience of the commanders. Even the negro women were wont to array themselves in cheap, gaudy finery, and carry bouquets to soldiers in festive mood. When military orders drove them from the camps, they flocked to villages, towns, and cities, where, in the summer of 1865, they lived in idleness and squalor, huddled together in shacks, and collecting in gangs at street corners and crossroads. So sinister was the tendency that he who was to become their political leader in North Carolina on their enfranchisement warned them against "crowding into towns and villages, subsisting on Government rations, contracting diseases, and incurring fearful risks to their morals and habits of industry." But warnings and pleas were of no avail to turn them back to the fields. They were to become the owners of the land, their former masters dispossessed, and while waiting for the possession of their property they could depend on Government rations, and their wits. Hearken to the advice of their former masters and mistresses? Had not their new friends from the North been at pains to teach them these were enemies? Freedom—it meant idleness, and gathering in noisy groups in the streets. Soon they were living like rats in ruined houses, in miserable shacks under bridges, built with refuse lumber, in the shelter of ravines and in caves in the banks of rivers. Freedom meant throwing aside all marital obligations, deserting wives and taking new ones, and in an indulgence in sexual promiscuity that soon took its toll in the victims of consumption and venereal disease. Jubilant, and happy, the negro who had his dog and a gun for hunting, a few rags to cover his nakedness, and a dilapidated hovel in which to sleep, was in no mood to discuss work.

All over the South that summer the negroes held their jubilee. A weird wave of religious fervor swept them into a crazy frenzy, and day after day they gathered in groves where imported preachers worked on their emotions [indoctrination]. Shouting, praying, howling, they turned their backs on the old plantation preachers, who disapproved of the methods of the visiting evangelists, who in many instances turned out to be unscrupulous organizers [propagandizers] for the Northern Radicals [extreme Left-wing Republicans, then socialists and communists]. At night the vicinity of the revivals was pillaged of poultry and vegetables on the theory that the Lord should provide. Great black multitudes stood shouting on the banks of streams as preachers converted and immersed. "Freed from slavery" shouted an old woman emerging, dripping, "freed from sin. Bless God and General Grant."

And with it all went the feeling that the topsy-turvy world had just been righted, and that they, as God's chosen children, were to be the proprietors of the land and the favored of paradise. Thus groves rang with song:

> We'se nearer to de Lord
> Dan to de white folks an da knows it,
> See de glory gates unbarred.
> Walk in, darkies, past de guard.
> Bets yer dollah he won't close it.
>
> Walk in, darkies, troo de gate.
> Hark de cullid angels holler,
> Go way, white folks, you're too late.
> We'se de winnin' culler.

Soon celebrations of a more threatening sort were being held, demanding suffrage—a forerunner of much that was to come. For under the patronage of the new friends from the North, the negro had already become the equal of the white in blue [Yankees] and the potential master of the man in gray [Southerners]. Even their vocabulary had expanded in the light of freedom. "Where are you going?" asked a white man of a neighbor's former slave as he was striding militantly down the road. "Perusin' my way to Columbia," he replied, for "peruse" had a royal sound. Everywhere they were on the march. "My sister-in-law is in tears of rage and despair," wrote a lady [Chesnut] in her diary. "Her servants have all gone to a big meeting at Mulberry [SC] though she made every appeal against their going."

They were free waiting for the master's land, assured of heaven.[128]

THIEVERY, THUGGERY, RAPE, & MURDER

☛ If the negroes caused some uneasiness, many of the army of occupation [U.S. forces] were more disturbing. When the soldiers marched into a community, visions of rapine and rape terrorized the women. Unfounded as were these fears, *there were instances where soldiers, unworthily officered, maliciously frightened women and children by pushing into houses and jeering at the faithful negroes, who stood by to protect them. But the meanest offenses of soldiers were committed against the blacks who gathered about them in childish faith, to be worse maltreated than by former masters, who, in numerous instances, interfered to protect them from the cruelty of their "deliverers." Even more cruel was the persistent effort of [U.S.] soldiers to instill into the negro's mind a hatred of the men with whom he would have to live after the army should march away. The correspondent of* The Nation *ascribed the labor and race troubles to the bad influence of the negro's Northern friends, "particularly soldiers." Emissaries of radicalism [socialism and communism] were constantly inflaming the freedmen with a false sense of their importance, turning them against the native whites, encouraging their indolence with wild tales of the inevitable division of the plantation lands among them. Young colored women, gayly making their way to camps to "enjoy mah freedom" were frequently used for immoral purposes. "The negro girls for miles around are gathered to the camps and debauched," wrote an indignant citizen to [Union] General Sherman, in protest* [my emphasis, L.S.]. "It surely is not the aim of those persons who aim at the equality of colors to begin the experiment with a whole race of whores." Officers [U.S.], waiting to be mustered out, regaled themselves with women, cards, and whiskey, for there was an enormous sale of liquor in the vicinity of the camps. In Charleston, where only the taverns thrived, "flushed and spendthrift Yankee officers" were found by [Midwestern politician] Whitelaw Reid, "willing to pay seventy-five cents for a cobbler." Abandoned white women trailed the camps, and disreputable houses sprang up in the vicinity of the posts.

Other irritating features of the occupation there were in abundance such as the requisition of the finest private houses for the use of officers. And to this was added an unnecessary offensiveness toward the Southern whites taking the amnesty oath [my emphasis, L.S.]. An editor who wrote a harmlessly amusing editorial about it was pompously denounced by the commander of the post as "necessarily a bad man, incendiary in his character," and guilty of "a high crime," and he was arrested, his office seized, his paper suppressed. Thus the Southerner who was sober was meditating treason, and he who smiled was guilty of its commission. When, in taking the [U.S.] oath, one man laughingly asked if the dog that accompanied him should take it, too, he was arrested and thrown into jail.

Inevitably, under such conditions, conflicts between civil and military authorities were not rare. From every quarter protests poured into Washington against the high-handed tyranny of some of the military commanders. Ordinary thieves were wrested from the civil authorities, to be tried, or released, by military tribunals. Such incredible stupidity or tyranny as the release of a grafting treasury agent arrested for various crimes, on the ground that State courts had no authority over these petty officials, aroused the wrath of thousands [of Southerners].

It only remained for the Federal Government to drive the disarmed people to the verge of a new rebellion by stationing negro troops in the midst of their homes. Nothing short of stupendous ignorance, or brutal malignity, can explain the arming and uniforming of former slaves and setting them as guardians over the white men and their families [my emphasis, L.S.]. Even the patient [former Confederate General] Wade Hampton was moved to fury; and he wrote hotly to [U.S. President Andrew] Johnson denouncing "your brutal negro troops under their no less brutal and more degraded Yankee officers" by whom "the grossest outrages were committed . . . with impunity." This is not an exaggerated picture. Even Northerners, not prone to sympathize with the prostrate foe, were shocked and humiliated by the scenes they saw. In streets and highways they took no pride in the spectacle of thousands of blacks with muskets and shimmering bayonets swaggering in jeering fashion before their former masters and mistresses. These [communized] colored soldiers were not so culpable as the [radical Left-wing] whites who used them to torture a fallen enemy. These were children, acting as children would under the circumstances. Marching four abreast in the streets, they jostled the whites from the pavements. In rough and sullen tones the sentries challenged old crippled and emaciated men in tattered gray [elderly Confederate veterans]. So insolent did their conduct become in some communities that *women no longer dared venture from their doors, and citizens in the country no longer felt it safe to go to town* [my emphasis, L.S.]. Noisy—often, when intoxicated, dangerous they gave the freedmen refusing to work a sense of racial grandeur, and encouraged the dream of the distribution of the white man's land.

Worse than the men were the degraded white officers who commanded them. From every quarter appeals reached Washington for their removal, for the fears of the whites were not of the imagination. Thus, at Chester [SC] they clubbed and bayoneted an old man; at Abbeville white men were ordered from the sidewalks; in Charleston they forced their way into a house, ordered food, and, after partaking, felled the mistress of the household. In retaliation, for the blow of a white man entrusted with the guardianship of a young woman who had been insulted, negro soldiers dragged him to camp, murdered him in cold blood, and danced upon his grave. *These are not carefully selected cases to make the picture black—the evidence is overwhelming that they do not exaggerate the peril thus placed at the doorsteps of the whites* [my emphasis, L.S.]. Here and there were colored troops, under the discipline of decent white [U.S.] officers, who conducted themselves with propriety and without offense. There was such a regiment in Florida. But always, with these newly freed negroes armed and in easy reach of liquor, the shadow of an awful fear rested upon the women of the communities where they were stationed.[129]

PUBLIC HUMILIATION, SORROW, & POVERTY

☛ Nothing could have been finer than the spirit and courage with which the [Southern] women faced defeat and misfortune, and yet, despite their simulated smiles in that spring that came unusually early in, 1865, there was bitterness and sorrow in their hearts. Not only had they lost husbands, sons, brothers, and sweethearts, but they were impoverished and their cause had failed. Even so there was no bending of their pride. A correspondent traveling in South Carolina noted their "superior presence" and a "certain, air of vehemence or pertness." Disaster and poverty could not rob them of their charm. For the sake of the returning warriors, humiliated by defeat, they made merry over the makeshifts imposed upon them in matters of dress, wearing their homespun and their calico with a regal grace. And though it was observed that "hardly anyone at church is out of mourning" by one who thought "it piteous to see so many mere girls' faces shaded by deep crape veils and widow's caps," they turned bravely to the soothing of the wounded spirits of their men. Within two weeks of the surrender, a traveler [Chesnut] was amazed to see the young people at Winnsboro [SC] gayly celebrating May Day amid the still smoking ruins. In midsummer a young girl was writing in her diary that, "we are trying to help our soldiers forget, and are having picnics and parties all the time." Popular were the "starvation parties," where no refreshments were served, and picnics where young folks danced to the music of fiddles. Soon they were turning to tournaments where riders, armed with hickory lances, rode past posts collecting rings suspended to them on the end of the lance for the glory of their ladies. There was billing and cooing, even among the graves.

But toward the conquerors they were implacable. The rumor, false, no doubt, that [Union] General Sherman had boasted he would bring every Southern woman to the washtub, intensified their hatred of the army of occupation. Sometimes [U.S.] soldiers would amuse themselves by sitting on back fences to jeer the former mistress of slaves as she washed the family linen. Thus the attempts of the younger subordinate [U.S.] officers to enter the social circles of the [Southern] communities where they were stationed were rebuked. The Southern men treated the soldiers and Northerners, flocking into the South to profit on the necessities of a stricken people, with courtesy in business, but the women were the rulers of the homes. Many of the [U.S.] soldiers were undeserving of social courtesies. When women crossed the street to evade them, or swept their skirts aside in passing, they were met with insulting comments on their clothes and ankles. And woe to the woman who succumbed to a Northern officer in romance.

During both the War and Reconstruction, Union soldiers continually violated the rights of Southern people. One of the more common unconstitutional outrages was, as this old illustration shows, entering homes without warrant, ransacking and pillaging the contents, and terrorizing the occupants. According to eyewitnesses, families were often driven out into the streets, then forced to watch as their houses were robbed of valuables, then intentionally burned to the ground in front of them.

When the daughter of a former Governor of North Carolina married a dashing Yankee officer who had entered her village at the head of cavalry, the wedding invitations were generally ignored, and when the bride departed for her Northern home, it was said that a daughter of the South had gone away loaded with jewelry and finery that had been stolen from women in States farther south.

With the women moved by emotions, memories of the dead, pity for the living, the Southern men, facing realities, had accepted defeat as final, and asked nothing better than a speedy removal of the [U.S.] soldiers and the restoration of normal conditions. Here and there could be heard the defiant cry of an irreconcilable [restoration of the Southern states]; ever and anon the thoughtless gave utterance to a foolish thought; but among men of sobriety and judgment there was a general acquiescence in the verdict of the battle-field. [Prussian-born socialist, radical Left newspaper editor, South-hating Union General] Carl Schurz, eager to justify the policy of the Radicals [his fellow Republican socialists and communists], treasured up every idle gesture and foolish word of irresponsible and unimportant [Southern] men as proof that the mailed hand could not be withdrawn with safety. But Grant, with a better understanding of the people, was "satisfied that the mass of thinking men . . . accept the present situation in good faith"; and [Conservative Southerner and Kentucky Representative Henry] Watterson found "unmistakable evidence [across the South] of a determination to renew in good faith their former relations." More impressive and conclusive to the President and posterity was the report of Benjamin P. Truman, which was a sharp contradiction of the extravagant partisan findings of Schurz. In truth, nothing was more remote than politics from the minds of [Southern] men threatened with economic ruin. "Politics are never mentioned and they know less of what is going on in Washington than in London," wrote Mrs. Leigh.[130]

LIES, PILLAGING, & MORE LEFT-WING YANKEE MADNESS

☛ . . . Meanwhile the Southern people were fighting for the preservation of their civilization. The negroes would not work, the plantations could not produce. The freedmen clung to the illusion planted in their minds by [Left-wing] demagogues that the economic status of the race was to be reversed through the distribution of the land among them. This cruelly false hope was being fed by private [U.S.] soldiers, [U.S.] Bureau agents, and low [that is, criminal-minded Left-wing] Northern whites circulating among the negroes on terms of social equality *in the cultivation of their prospective votes* [as today, the Victorian Left, then the Republicans, used minorities to advance their own political careers, not out of true concern for civil rights]. "Nothing but want will bring them to their senses," wrote one Carolinian to another. *At the time, however, the negroes were warding off want by prowling the highways and byways in the night for purposes of pillage. In one week, in one town in Georgia, one hundred and fifty were arrested for theft* [my emphasis, L.S.].

More serious than this annoying petty stealing was the wholesale pillaging by [U.S.] Treasury agents, who swarmed over the land like the locusts of Egypt following the order confiscating all cotton that had been contracted to the fallen Confederacy. It mattered not whether the cotton had been contracted for or not; these petty officials rumbled over the roads day and night in [U.S.] Government wagons with [U.S.] soldiers, taking whatever they could find. One agent in Alabama stole eighty thousand dollars' worth of cotton in a month. The burden of proof was put upon the owner, and the [anti-South] agent in Arkansas enforced rules of evidence no [Southern] planter could circumvent. When, in Texas, [U.S. Treasury] agents caught red-handed were indicted, the [U.S.] army released them. When, as in Alabama, the stealing was so flagrant that prosecutions were forced, proceedings were suddenly stopped as the trail of crime led toward politicians of importance.

This, then, was the combination against the peace of a fallen people—the soldiers inciting the blacks against their former masters, the [Freedmen's] Bureau agents preaching political and social equality, the white scum of the North fraternizing with the blacks in their shacks, and the thieves of the Treasury stealing cotton under the protection of Federal bayonets. And in the North, demagogic politicians and fanatics were demanding immediate negro suffrage and clamoring for the blood of Southern leaders. Why was not Jeff Davis hanged; and why was not [Confederate General Robert E.] Lee shot? [my emphasis, L.S.].

The gallant figure of the latter had ridden quietly out of the public view. No word of bitterness escaped his lips, and he sought to promote harmony and good feeling. His own future was dark enough, the fine old mansion at Arlington gone [stolen by the U.S. government], and he had no home. Sometimes, astride old [warhorse] Traveller, he cantered along country roads looking for a small farm. "Some quiet little home in the woods," he wrote, declining the offer of an estate in England. June found him settled in a four-room house in a grove of oaks near Cartersville [VA], with his wife and daughters. Then came the offer of the presidency of Washington College [now Washington and Lee University,

Lexington, VA]. Should he accept? Was he competent? Would it injure the institution? He would like to set the young an example of submission to authority. One September day, his decision made, found him mounted on old Traveller riding toward Lexington. The ladies of the town helped furnish his little office, and admirers sent articles of furniture for his house and the family took possession. In old letters we have a vision of Lee, the sinister conspirator pictured in the Northern papers, proudly displaying to his wife and daughters the pickles, preserves, and brandied peaches the neighbors had sent in, and the bags of walnuts, potatoes, and game the mountaineers had given. But the patriots of the North were not to be deceived by appearances. "We protest" said *The Nation* "against the notion that he is fit to be put at the head of a college in a country situated as Virginia is." And [New England socialist] Wendell Phillips was exclaiming to a cheering crowd at Cooper Union [NY] that "if Lee is fit to be president of a college, then for Heaven's sake pardon [Confederate Captain Henry] Wirz [commander of the Confederate prison camp, Andersonville Prison, at Andersonville, Georgia] and make him professor of what the Scots call "the humanities."[131] — CLAUDE GERNADE BOWERS, 1929

Contrary to the Left's fake Civil War history, Southern "slaves" were allowed, and even encouraged, by their owners to produce foods, such as vegetables and meat, that they could sell at market. The profits they netted were either reinvested by them into food production or used to buy personal items, such as clothing, tools, fishing poles, or various fineries.

CHAPTER 3
THE RECONSTRUCTION ERA

FROM A 1901 BOOK BY CONFEDERATE GENERAL
Samuel Gibbs French

SUPREME MALIGNITY

☞ WHEN I COMMENCED WRITING THE narrative of my observations in early life and the incidents of service in the United States army and my diary of the civil war, I did it to preserve for my children the record of these events, but in volume it has increased more than at first intended; and as it may perhaps some day be made public, I feel it incumbent on me to give my experience under the workings of reconstruction as being of more value than a description by any historian of a later age who would have no enlightenment by living under its arbitrary rule.

An act creating the Freedmen's Bureau was passed March 3, 1865. The commissioner was authorized to set apart for the use of loyal refugees and freedmen abandoned lands, also confiscated lands, and assign forty acres for three years, etc., to families.

In 1866 a supplementary bill was passed over a veto to extend the act. Among other things the bill subjected any white person, who might be charged with depriving a freedman of civil rights or immunities to imprisonment or fine or both, without defining the meaning of "*civil rights or immunities.*" The jurisdiction of the agents extended to all contracts, and without a written contract and the agent's approval no freedman could be employed. No indictment by a grand jury nor a trial by a jury was necessary. The *ipse dixit* [a

Confederate General Samuel G. French.

statement made based on one's own authority, without supporting evidence] of an ignorant negro was cause for fine or imprisonment without appeal.

[Union] Gen. O. O. [Oliver Otis] Howard, noted for exuberant piety, was made Commissioner, and his career, his establishing of the Howard University in Washington for the higher culture of the negro, the cottages he built for them, the aid he gave the Church, the land he bought, and the Freedman's Bank he established, which blew up or burst [due to widespread, entrenched Yankee fraud and corruption], can be found in a report of a congressional committee. Under this bill the annual expenditure was $11,750,000.

An article published in the [Left-leaning Yankee periodical] *Atlantic Monthly* for August, 1865, sounded the keynote for the action of the United States government in legislation for the "rebels," wherein it is stated:

> "We are placed by events in that strange condition in which the safety of the republican form of government we desire to insure the Southern States has more safeguards in the INSTINCTS OF THE IGNORANT than in the INTELLIGENCE OF THE EDUCATED." And furthermore it is declared that "the highest requirements of abstract justice coincide with the LOWEST REQUIREMENTS of political prudence, and the LARGEST JUSTICE to the loyal blacks is the real condition of the WIDEST CLEMENCY to the rebel whites."

This declaration proclaims that the Southern States would be safer if their governments were established on the ignorance of the blacks than on the intelligence of the whites. Could malignity go any farther? On this degrading plane were the [Reconstruction] State governments established.

They had called for blood, and got none, save in the case of [Confederate Captain Henry] Wirz [commander of the Confederate prison camp, Andersonville Prison, at Andersonville, Georgia], who was given to the mob as a "sop."[132] As they could not indict a whole nation, they arrested [Confederate] President [Jefferson] Davis, and, discovering no grounds for conviction, *he was released, because a failure to convict would establish legally the right of secession, and thus prove the North to be the aggressor* [my emphasis, L.S.]. Failing on this line, the human passions and human prejudices of the people arrayed under the higher law of conscience *swayed them like a mob, and, failing to find any lawful means to spill blood, sought vengeance in the enacting of partisan laws for plunder of wealth, and the humiliation of the whites. To this end the Freedmen's Bureau was created,* and President [Andrew] Johnson's proclamation was issued disfranchising the whites on fourteen different counts: among them was one that made the possession of twenty thousand dollars worth of *property a crime* that disfranchised the owner. Then came the ironclad [U.S.] oath, which debarred all persons from taking it

> "who had ever borne arms against the United States since they have been citizens thereof, or who have voluntarily given aid, countenance, counsel, or encouragement to persons engaged in armed hostility thereto; that they have never sought, nor accepted, nor attempted to exercise the functions of any office whatsoever under any authority, or pretended authority, in hostility to the United States," etc.

All men above twenty-one years of age who could take this oath could vote, and no others. As there were very few white men who could take this oath, the elections fell, as intended, into the hands of the negroes, carpet-baggers, and the United States troops on duty South.

The enactment of the [anti-South] fourteenth amendment to the Constitution of the United States was regarded in the North as a magnanimous exhibition of philanthropy toward the untutored slaves, and it was so accepted by nations; but *in reality it was an insidious mode of punishing the Southern people* [my emphasis, L.S.].

The white people who owned the land and paid quite nine-tenths of all the taxes were now disfranchised, and the amendment was intended as a punishment by denying them a voice in legislation.

[Liberal Indiana] Senator [Oliver P.] Morton and [radical Left-wing Yankee] Thaddeus Stevens, like the Roman augurs, could not look in each other's face without laughing at the success of their machinations.[133]

NEGRO OFFICERS

☛ Two years later (in 1870) the [anti-South] fifteenth amendment to the Constitution was passed. *These last three articles placed the Anglo-Saxon people in the South under the rule of their former slaves! This was the Sin that started the race problem. The freedmen, left to themselves, would have settled the labor question, and their social position and the race issue; but for aggrandizement of power and acquisition of wealth he was dragged into the halls of legislation and flattered into the belief that also socially he was on an equality with the whites [not out of concern for black civil rights, but for the purpose of forwarding Left-wing political power]. From this sprung unmentionable crimes, and daily lynchings followed as a remedy* [my emphasis, L.S.].

What a change! As a slave he was the faithful protector of his mistress and her family; his children the terror now of unprotected women!

And here I will tell you how the voting was done. The negroes had, previously, been required to take the oath. At my home a table was placed on the gallery, and there the registrars were seated. The negroes were called up; as many as could touch the Bible were asked if they "had ever held office under the United States or given aid," etc. Some said "No," some said "Yes," and some were silent. At last they were told to say "No," and registration papers were given them, with the charge not to lose them. There I sat, no more a citizen than if I had been born in China, while my negroes were made eligible to almost any office in the country.

It is now generally acknowledged that all the negro received was by the force of environments; and now he has discovered that he has been grateful to the radical [Left-wing] party [part of the then Liberal Republican Party], and *payed them for a debt of love that had no foundation except in hypocrisy* [my emphasis, L.S.]. They were told that they were now American citizens, endowed with all their moral and civil rights.

> "The *natural rights* of a solitary individual have no connection whatever with the *moral and civil rights* of the man who has entered into association with others."[134] [Thomas Henry Huxley]

The dominant party [the then Left-wing Republican Party] entertained the belief that the slaves would politically always belong to the party that "confiscated"[135] them; and confounding natural rights with civil rights, they forced the Southern States to pass the fourteenth amendment to the Constitution, which made them citizens of the United States and the State wherein they reside.

As vultures sail in long lines from their roost (countless in numbers) to where the carcass is, so came the harpies and political adventurers to the carcass (the South) to embrace the colored citizens; and, hand in hand, cheek by jowl, they entered the political arena, and filled the capitols of the South. Every [Conservative Southern] officer in the State from governor to coroner was dismissed, and new [Left-wing] appointments made. The Legislatures became bacchanalian feasts to divide the spoils of office and increase the debts of the States by selling State bonds to the amount of countless millions. They subsidized everything they could; in short, they ate up or took possession of all that was left after the war ceased; and at last departed with stolen wealth, and the execrations of all the honest people [of the South].

[Uneducated, communized] negroes were appointed or elected to such offices as Senator, Governor, members of Congress,[136] and the judiciary of the States and county officers.

June 13, 1865, [liberal Southerner] William L. Sharkey was appointed provisional governor of the State of Mississippi, and he ordered an election of delegates to the convention, and here is the way the members were elected:

On the appointed day the new-made citizens went to the precincts to vote. When they came home I asked my servant Levi, who had been with me through the war, how many persons were at the polls, and he said "about two hundred, that only two white men were there, and they were inside the house." When asked who he voted for, he replied "he voted for that thing, you know, called *invention*," and the way they voted was this: "You remember the paper we had (registration); I handed it to two white men inside the room, through a window; they looked at it, handed it back to me, and said open your hand; I did so, and one of the men then put a little folded paper in my hand, then took it out and put it in a box and said, 'Move on'" This was a Republican [Liberal] free election, peaceful, quiet, and decisive, based on ignorance. The complexion of the convention was dark, of course. This ungenerous revenge taken against a conquered people will ever remain a dark shadow over the generosity and Christian spirit of the Northern people. It, however, must be attributed to uncultured minds and want of knowledge of history. The masses did not know that New England's ablest statesmen always claimed their right of secession, as the debates in Congress show.[137] Besides, they were unmindful that opinion at the North was about equally divided on this question.

When the revolutionary war was ended, and the cry for persecution, and confiscation of property of the *Tories* was raised, our Minister to France, Ben Franklin, put that as a trump card in his pocket to win against England; and Gens. Alexander Hamilton and Nathanael Greene and other liberal [that is, empathetic] gentlemen declared it would be "an outrage to punish them for holding the *same opinion* that we all held only a few years ago, before the war commenced." What a contrast between the age of honor and the age thirsting for gold!

Perhaps in all the wide world never again will be seen such malignant legislation, and maladministration of law, such trials in the courts, speeches in legislative halls, preaching by illiterate negroes, mode of getting religion, idleness of the laborers, immorality taught by men from the slums of Northern cities, thirst for money, howling for office, insolence in office, with upheaval of society, creating constant anxiety of mind as to what a day might bring forth [my emphasis, L. S.].[138]

THE FREEDMEN'S BUREAU

☞ Add to these the formation of loyal league societies of negroes, by politicians swearing them to obedience to orders, bands of brothers and sisters, composed of blacks under white villains, to burn our towns, and murder the whites; the Kuklux Klan of the whites for protection, and other kindred vexations and trials that made the South the home of the spirits of pandemonium; so one could truly exclaim with Ariel,

"Hell is empty and all the devils are here."[139]

As I have said, they came like vultures to the carcass to devour the substance of the helpless South, and they were unblushingly successful. Under the Freedmen's Bureau and the military governors, those who could not take the ironclad oath were helpless.

The agent of the Freedmen's Bureau in our county (Washington, Miss.) who came first was desirous to aid the planters and freedmen to make a crop; and as this required reliable labor, the planters in the neighborhood agreed to give him cotton to the value of $5,000 if he would visit the plantations, when necessary or convenient, to encourage the hands to work faithfully, under the contracts that he had approved, and I will most cheerfully say that without this aid and influence the negroes would have been unprofitable producers.

The agents were changed, and in 1867 an Irishman came, who could handle the shillalah, drink whisky without the smell of peat, sing the "Irish Dragoon" or the "Widow Malone," and run the Freedmen's Bureau. And here is a little of my own experience under it with him.

In renting out the land on shares, among the squads was one squad of thirteen hands, with two negroes named Miles and Derry as head men. They had about eighty acres put in cotton. The recorded contract required them to work under my direction, and I was to furnish means to raise the crop, and their share was half the cotton. Owing to the almost constant spring rains, their crop became hopelessly overgrown with weeds and grass. I vainly tried to induce them to abandon the lowest part of the land and save about sixty acres; they refused. I then wrote a note to the agent. He came out late in the evening with the deputy sheriff and sent for

Miles and Derry, heard what they had to say; then severely reprimanded them; took Miles by the ears and backed him against the side of the house and pounded his head against the wall vigorously; then taking Derry by the ears, he pounded his head as he did Miles's. By this time near a hundred negroes were on the lawn peeping up over the gallery, which was the arena of the acts.

Then he made a five minutes' talk to the people, giving them some good advice. He then took Miles and Derry through the same enlivening bout, ordering them to be at his office the next day at 10 A.M. Again he spoke to the crowd, telling them how he had "fought, bled, and died that they might be free," etc.

While this was going on, to stop such proceedings, I took the deputy sheriff, Wilson, into the dining room, put a decanter of whisky on the sideboard, and told him to get the agent in there, give him a glass to sober him, and, when he came out, take his arm and go direct for the horses. Much to my relief, he got him on his horse and they returned to Greenville. Miles and Derry went to Greenville next day, as ordered. The former came back much subdued and Derry went to an adjoining plantation to work. Ridiculous as the performance was, which lasted over an hour, it had a good effect on the deportment of all the hands on the place.[140]

ARRESTED BY A NEGRO

☛ The military governor had commissioned a man from the North named Webber as sheriff of the county. Bolton, an Irishman, Harris, an educated negro from Ohio, and Horton, a cotton field negro without education, were appointed justices of the peace in Greenville. I will very briefly give you an idea of the administration of justice in a few cases out of many brought before them.

Ed Chamberlain, who had been a negro soldier in the United States army, occupied a house at the southern gate of the plantation, and he was instructed to keep the gate shut on account of cattle. Twice *without cause* he had told H. N. Hood, a neighboring planter, in an insolent manner: "Shut the gate after you." On a third occasion he repeated the remarks, whereupon Hood and a friend with him gave him a trouncing. They then went to Justice Harris, told him what they had done, and settled the case by each giving him five dollars. On trial day Chamberlain went to court, and when the court adjourned he asked the justice why he did not try his case, and the answer was: "Go home; I tried your complaint long ago."

Another freedman on the place named Nelson one morning got into a triangular fight with his wife and a colored girl. They all started for Greenville to lay their respective grievances before Judge Harris. However, they met Harris on horseback on the road running through the plantation, and he accosted them: "Good morning, ladies and gentleman; where are you going?" They told him that they were going to see him in Greenville, and all made complaint to him there in the road; whereupon he fined each the sum of five dollars, and I had to advance the money or they would have left the plantation. That was summary justice, and an examination of the books by the grand jury showed that he had credited the county with the fifteen dollars.

A third case worthy of notice as illustrating the vigilance of the colored brethren as magistrates is the trial of what may be termed "State of Mississippi vs. S. G. French." John Dixon, a freedman, about Christmas stole two bales of cotton from the ginhouse in open daylight, and being pursued by my manager, threw the bales off his wagon, and they were recovered. I went to Greenville, and before Bolton, the justice of the peace, swore out a warrant for the arrest of Dixon. A number of days passed and he was not arrested. So I sent for Dixon, and settled money accounts with him, and told him to leave the plantation.

Some days after this a deputy negro constable was sent to arrest Dixon; but, meeting one of my hands on the road and making known to him the purport of his visit, he was told: "Go home, nigger; de ginneral done gone settled with John long ago, and John have left the place." So the deputy returned and reported accordingly.

Perhaps it was a week after this that a negro constable came to my house with a warrant to arrest me issued by the cotton field justice, Horton, charging me with having compounded a felony. Who prompted Horton to issue the warrant I never knew; but, as he employed a "jack-leg" lawyer to keep his docket and act as legal adviser, he may have induced Horton to act in the matter. I asked Frank Valliant, a distinguished lawyer, to take my case and defend me. He said that he had resolved not to argue any case where a negro presided, for he disliked to say, "May it please your honor," to an illiterate negro. However, out of friendship, he said that he would appear for me if I would pay any fine imposed upon him for contempt of court.

Some two weeks after this the trial day came. Valliant and I went to the room where Horton dispensed justice, and found him behind a railing seated at a small table with the Mississippi code in his hand. John Dixon and "Jack-leg" were there, but no lookers-on. After turning the code first one end up and then the other several times, he announced: "Dis court am assembled to hear the case of Gen. French for composing a felony with John Dixon."

Valliant seemed to be swallowing something that was swelling in his throat, but he rose and went near the table and said: "Will your honor let me have the papers in this case?"

"What papers you want? I am done hab none."

"Where is the affidavit made against Gen. French?"

"I just told you, Mr. Valliant, I done hab none."

"Well, how could you arrest a person without charge being made?"

"Sir, dis court has been informed dat Gen. French swore John Dixon stole two bales ob his cotton, which am an offense, and then done settled and composed it, which am a crime against the law, and an insult to the majesty ob de State of Mississippi."

Here the "jack-leg" injected a remark to the judge, when Valliant asked him: "Are you engaged as an attorney in this case?"

He replied: "I am."

"Then I wish to see your license."

At this Horton said: "De gentleman wants to see your license. Go and get it, sir."

While he was absent in quest of the paper Valliant read the law to the court, showing his honor that the license must be granted by the Circuit Court.[14]

COMPOSING A FELONY

☛ When the license was handed to Valliant he read it to the court, and, it being one granted by the Chancellor, was of no authority. At this information Horton rose from his seat, and in a loud voice said: "Sir, you will stand aside. You have imposed on dis court, and am no more a lawyer in any case in court here."

When this incident was over, and the indignant court had composed itself, Valliant tried again to satisfy the judge that there was no case before the court; but he insisted that I had *composed* a felony, and that his court was bound to "'vestigate what am a crime in de eye of de law." Under the argument and showing of my attorney, however, the judge began to weaken, especially when told that he would be held responsible for this unwarrantable arrest.

Valliant now whispered to me: "We will have to buy out of this."

"All right," was the reply.

Then my attorney went to the table, and quietly whispered to Horton: "Will ten dollars settle expenses?"

A ten-dollar bill was handed the judge, and that sum *composed* the felony, the feelings of the court, and the offended majesty of the State.

Valliant was the wit of the Greenville bar, and a true friend. Some years ago he was called from his field of usefulness and sorrowing friends to

Sleep the sleep that knows no breaking.

These are not a tithe of my personal experience with the Bureau and the courts. They were almost daily annoyances to all.[142]

EXPOSING VILLAINY

☞ One day I received a note from the agent of the Freedmen's Bureau to come to his office if convenient. I went as requested; found there one of my hands, who had no common sense, told he complained that I had not settled with him agreeably to the contract; and when the agent asked him what complaint he had to make he said that I had paid him only a *half*, whereas I had promised him a *fourth*, and insisted that four was more than two.

But I pass from the recital of these petty annoyances to larger ones. The circuit judge *appointed* was named S_____, and in political parlance he was a "scallywag" [that is, Southerner who sided with the North]. It would seem that, to make his loyalty apparent, he imposed harsh sentences or punishments on nearly every white person convicted, and he committed personally some criminal offenses.

It was, I believe, in the winter of 1876 or 1877 that I was a member of the grand jury of Washington County. All those who were summoned—twelve whites and six negroes—answered to their names. The judge excused one member, and accepted another person, who was sworn in. The matter of a murder was among other things brought to the notice of the grand jury. All voted against finding a true bill except two other members and myself. This same day (Saturday) we were about to find an indictment against the judge for falsely representing himself as surety on the bond of the notorious Bolton, who was appointed county treasurer, the facts in the case being that the judge did not sign his name to the bond, but told his clerk of the court to sign it for him. To this the clerk made oath, but excused himself by informing us that "it is common practice now."

On Sunday Bolton gave a champagne dinner to the judge, and it was there arranged that the judge should dismiss the grand jury on Monday morning to prevent indictments being found against *himself and Bolton.* The excuse offered was that putting a juror on in the place of one excused was irregular, and their findings would be void, and also we had failed to find a true bill against a certain man. And so we were all discharged without retaining *the three* who voted to find a true bill, and a new jury was empaneled. That night the negroes called a mass meeting to condemn these proceedings of the judge; but the meeting was captured through the influence of two negroes—Gray, the state senator, and Ross, a negro from Kentucky—and resolutions passed complimenting the judge. The fine hand of Bolton was seen in this. Some months after, the judge called on me,

Senator George E. Spencer. Senator Willard Warner.

C. W. Buckley. John B. Callis.

J. T. Rapier. Charles Hays.

A few examples of far Left Republican Congressmen (dishonestly called "Radicals" in mainstream history books) who helped oversee the so-called "Reconstruction" of the South.

and said he wished to say that he discharged that grand jury because they did not find an indictment against S_____ who had killed a man in an altercation. I replied: "Judge, no person in Greenville believes that to be true."

The judge was afterwards petitioned by the members of the bar to resign. The list was headed by the distinguished attorney, William A. Percy. *Six* months after this a person appeared in Greenville with a challenge [to a pistol dual] for Col. Percy. For amusement Percy said: "The judge has had six months to practice at a target, and I also want a little time to practice; then I will accommodate him." After worrying the bearer of the cartel some time he accepted the challenge, the fight to take place on an island in the Mississippi river. Nothing further was heard from the challenger, and he died soon after, it is reported, from mortification.

Before the judge had dismissed the grand jury it had found a number of indictments against persons who belonged to a secret association of freedmen, known as the [Left-wing] "Band of Brothers and Sisters," *bound by oaths to rob, burn the town, and murder the whites* [my emphasis, L.S.]. The day these disclosures were made the witnesses were shot at in the night, and claimed protection.

Bolton, who had been an officer in the United States volunteers during the war, was president of the band; Gray, negro state senator, vice president; and a scallywag named Brentlinger, from Kentucky, was treasurer. He was also postmaster, through Bolton's influence. Bolton spent most of his time in the post office, and induced Brentlinger to lend him public funds to the amount of about $3,000. An effort was made to destroy the post office books by setting fire to the office, but a man fortunately saved the books. Bolton, however, got them from the office as a package purporting to have come by mail, and destroyed them.

Then came a United States post office inspector, who discovered the loss of funds, books, etc., and removed or suspended the postmaster. Bolton went on Brentlinger's bond, and accompanied him to Jackson, Miss., where he was tried before Judge Hill. Bolton told Brentlinger that he had arranged it with the judge. If he would remain silent, and make no disclosures, he would be acquitted. He was found guilty, and sent to the penitentiary at Albany, N.Y.

In hope of convicting some of these scoundrels, I wrote to President Grant for permission to visit the penitentiary and obtain Brentlinger's testimony, and the attorney-general, Alphonso Taft, to whom the request was referred, gave permission.

In due time I made the visit to Albany, and with the keeper, Pillsbury, saw Brentlinger. He wrote out what he knew about the society, acknowledged that he was treasurer; but from timidity would give but little testimony of his own knowledge, and made it mostly hearsay evidence. It corroborated exactly what we learned in the jury room. No use was made of this testimony, because all who were implicated agreed to quit the State and never come back. I have this testimony and the attorney general's letter.

The military governor appointed one T. L. Webber sheriff of the county. Without the knowledge of any one, he falsely reported thousands of acres of plantation lands, and other sections of land, sold for taxes. This he did for two years. Not a name of any delinquent taxpayer was ever published, and no one attended any sale. Planters continued paying their taxes regularly. At last it was discovered that the reported list of taxable lands did not embrace half the lands on which taxes were paid. A list was obtained for the grand jury. I found that six hundred and forty acres out of the heart of my plantation had been reported sold; Bourge's plantation of two thousand acres, all sold, and so on; yet we were paying taxes all the same.

Next year I know of but two planters who paid any taxes in the county. Had Gov. A_____ remained, there would not have been any taxes paid in the State. He wrote to Bolton to know how he was to get any salary, or any courts could be held, or Legislatures meet, etc., and was told that the services of all such were not required, etc.

The *auditor* had been receiving from the sheriff only the money received from lands *on the tax list*, while he (the sheriff) pocketed all money paid on lands that he pretended were sold and not taxable—by "sold" meaning forfeited to the government. To escape perjury, Webber's *reports* of taxable lands were not signed by him, but by his brother, a worthless fellow.

When the people elected a negro sheriff over Webber, he bought the office of sheriff from him for $1,000 and the negro sheriff (O. Winslow) appointed him his deputy. Webber, when detected, turned into the bank $40,000 out of perhaps $150,000 stolen, and went to Florida. The ablest lawyers said he could not be convicted under the existing condition of affairs.

Those who would not pay taxes were permitted to redeem their lands by act of the Legislature, by paying back taxes, the title coming from the State. The $10,000 was distributed among the owners of the forfeited lands, and used in part payment of the taxes. O reconstruction, what a curse thou wast![143]

UNCERTAIN HELP
☛ Had Ames remained, there would have been presented a singular revolution—the people of the State peacefully pursuing their avocations without a government; every function of state government would have been suspended. When the governor applied to Grant for troops he was refused. Grant telegraphed that "the public was tired of the annual autumnal outbreaks in the South."

Another source of annoyance to the planters—nay, it was ruinous—was the want of reliable labor. Capital could not command labor in the rich Yazoo bottoms, and it had to be obtained from a distance.

I went to Wytheville, Franklin, and Danville, Va., for labor. In Danville I made a contract with a man named Wilson to bring me some thirty hands. About the middle of February he arrived with the negroes. I paid him $1,040 for transportation and services. One pleasant noon in May a servant came in and told me a certain negro was leaving the place; he was the last of the men that Wilson brought, except a Spanish negro, who was painting my house.

My neighbor Jackson went to Richmond, Va., and obtained some forty hands; paid their way to Greenville. Their contract made was that they were to raise a crop of cotton and corn, and out of their share of the crop they were to repay expenses of transportation, provisions, etc. Gradually they began to leave him, and went into the employment of negroes who had rented land. They were hired for two bales of cotton. By this proceeding they escaped paying transportation. One day in May the last of Jackson's hands (on Monday) went to the smokehouse and obtained their rations for the week, and then quit the plantation. They were arrested for breach of contract and obtaining supplies under false pretenses, and were tried before the notorious Judge Bolton. Whilst the trial was going on, Bolton asked my views of the matter. I told him if they were acquitted every contract recorded in court would be worthless, and it would damage the planting interest in the county perhaps two hundred thousand dollars. Nevertheless, he decided that there was no evidence to prove that the hands had any intention of leaving when they drew their rations, although they had a place engaged and left as soon as they got the provisions. For months I never retired to rest without apprehension that some of my hands would leave during the night, at the persuasions of visiting spies.

Another trouble was to check the thoughtless extravagance of the freedmen. If they were largely in debt, when fall came, they would not gather their cotton, believing it mortgaged to the merchants for all it would bring, but quit, and pick cotton on some other place, by the hundred, for cash. Of these things there was no end.

The counties of Bolivar, Washington, and Issaquena composed a levee district in Mississippi, and had for years protected the lands from overflow by constructing levees. Funds were obtained by tax on lands and by sales of bonds. When the war ended, I was elected president of the board. Gen. Alvan C. Gillem was military governor, and gave me all the aid he could to rebuild the levees. I negotiated the bonds in New York City at par, and repaired the levees and saved the plantations from overflow. When Ames became military governor, he one day sent a man to Greenville with an order dismissing us, and required the office to be turned over to the bearer, etc.; and this, too, when the river was at its highest stage. I went to Jackson to see him. I demanded the grounds for his action in the matter, and was refused. At this time the river was out of its banks everywhere, except in our district. I wrote to President Grant, and he answered: "You should have telegraphed at once." [Union] Gen. Sherman wrote, "Yours is not a public office, and Ames is wrong, etc., meddling with private corporations," or words to that effect.

Whilst in Jackson, the capital of Mississippi, I was offered the opportunity of seeing the legislators who made our laws, composed mainly of carpet-baggers and negroes. For this purpose I obtained a seat by the sidewalk on the main street leading to the capitol.

As the hour to meet had arrived, down this street could be seen the members approaching. Generally they came two together, arm in arm, a carpet-bagger and a negro in close confab. The whites were clothed in garments of various makes and colors; the negroes rejoiced in black clothing, with Prince Albert coats and silk hats and gold-headed canes. Down the avenue and far away could be seen the white of their eyes, teeth, shirts, and enormous collars.

The carpet-bagger was generally holding on to the arm of his colored brother, and engaged in conversation; and, judging from the gestures, they were advocating some benevolent measure for the benefit of the "wards of the nation," and their own prosperity. One other observation I made: there were no small feet, and not an arched instep; flap, flap, came down their flat feet. I had seen enough; I thought the negro had the more honest face.[144]

SCENES IN THE HOUSE

☛ Thence I went into the House [of Representatives in the State Capitol]. Ye gods, what a sight! The floor was dirty, the many spittoons were all filthy-filled with quids of tobacco, stumps of cigars, pieces of paper around them were cemented to the floor by dried tobacco juice; fumes of tobacco filled the house, so that the air was foul and unpleasant.

The members were seated, black and white side by side, all over the house, perhaps to guide them in voting; and they lolled on the desks and chairs. A negro would lay his head on the desk of his white neighbor, look him in the face, and laugh with great glee at what was told him; the conversation was so loud and the laughter so boisterous that the Speaker could not command silence: he pounded with the gavel, and shouted "Order! order!" till his voice was drowned by the cries of "Master Speakyar!" from the negroes, while the whites shouted and waved their arms frantically to catch the Speaker's eye for recognition. The whole scene was one of confusion not unlike the Gold Exchange, New York, in days of yore, or the Stock Exchange.

I then went to the Senate chamber. It was cleaner than the House, and better order was preserved; but what a travesty on intelligence and decorum, and shame on the government of the United States, [the Liberal] North, that made this not only possible but common, and laughed at it with joyous hearts; and wherefore? *It was an assembly of mostly dishonest white men influencing the uneducated negro members to enact laws whereby the State was, by bonded indebtedness, plundered of millions of dollars* [my emphasis, L.S.]. Their reign is ended.

> "I myself have seen the ungodly in great power and flourishing like a green bay tree: I went by again, and lo, he was gone."

Adieu! The royal Bengal tiger, when he once tastes human blood, will depopulate a village; so the loyal carpet-bagger, having tasted Southern plunder, went home and devised a scheme of trust companies now in operation.[145]

THE SHOTGUN POLICY

☞ Then came taxation. On this matter I will merely remark that on realty it was about ten per cent. Government tax on cotton, in the aggregate, was sixty-seven million dollars. On cotton it was (all told), including charges by the government, about twenty dollars per bale. There should now be on file in the Department of Agriculture a letter written by me to Mr. Isaac Newton, commissioner, telling him that, were it practical, I would deed to the United States the land planted in cotton, if it were exempted from taxation one year, which meant—the market value of the land was twenty dollars per acre; and as one acre would produce a bale of cotton, and the tax on the bale was twenty dollars, the tax was equal to the value of the land—that was confiscation. An acre in cotton, if it produced a bale, was, taxed, as I have related; but if planted in corn or sown in wheat, the produce was free. *All these legal pilferings, vexations, insults, arrogance, and trials to our families were in silence and poverty submitted to, that our children might have food and clothing. Our patience in adversity, amidst trials and sufferings, gives greater evidence of elevation and dignity of character than did matchless achievements in arms. In the tented field we found redress for wrongs; in reconstruction years we lived in expectancy, as the Christians lived in the years of Nero, not knowing what would befall us next* [my emphasis,

L.S.].

The negroes, when set free, became very pious, and gave more time to their devotions than to the crops. After the Freedmen's Bureau agents took their departure, nearly all of them "got religion" and wanted to preach. Their protracted ("distracted" they called them) meetings continued all night long, for five and six weeks continuously. Men and women would leave the church (I had one on the plantation) after sunrise, go to the field direct, and sleep leaning on their hoes. I found one sleeping on the creek bank, and on asking him what was the matter, he said: "O, I have got religion in me as big as a yearling calf." And thus piety impaired industry to an alarming extent, without improving morality.

Bishop Wilmer (Episcopal), during the war, had omitted the usual prayer "for the President of the United States and all others in authority," and this continued after the surrender. For this offense [Union] Maj. Gen. George H. Thomas was so distressed that he, by orders, caused the bishop and the clergy in the diocese to cease from preaching; and this gave rise to a discussion, which was terminated by the President denouncing the silly order and revoking it. I have no doubt of Gen. Thomas's sincerity, for he was prudent and cautious, and he must have been really convinced that President Johnson, and all others in authority with him, needed the prayers of the Episcopal clergy to bless them and replenish their grace.

The Bishop was not as desirous of praying for the President of the United States as was a young priest after the surrender. He had omitted praying for [Confederate] President [Jefferson] Davis since his capture, and had not decided what to do when the Sabbath came; but found relief, when asked by a United States army officer if he had any objection to using the old prayer for the President of the United States, by answering: "No, none whatever; for I know of no one who needs our prayers more than he."

The few incidents of my own experience that I have narrated are to illustrate the condition of the people of the South during the years of reconstruction (annexation), and for preservation for future ages; to show the ills, vexations, humiliations, and indignities so unjustly and designedly imposed upon them as a spiteful punishment for daring to assert their rights and defend their homes. The fifteenth amendment to the Constitution has brought forth bitter fruit to the progress of the freedmen and the peaceful progress of the whole country by offering the negro a dependent support on polities rather than labor. Their votes were generally in the market, and their sale at the presidential nominations for office in the Federal service in the South consolidated the white people against them when harmony would otherwise have existed [my emphasis, L.S.].

The State of Mississippi was saved from utter ruin by what the North called "the shotgun policy." Seeing nothing but poverty and wretchedness before us, it was determined to rescue the State from the hands of the carpet-baggers and negroes by a compromise with the freedmen. In our county we offered them the offices of congressmen, the sheriff of the county, clerk of the chancery court, clerk of the circuit court, and justice of the peace, but not a member of the Legislature. The educated whites were to redeem the State from perdition in the halls of legislation.[146]

IN THE UNION OR OUT OF IT

☛ In the hustings absolute protection by arms was pledged to all freedmen who voted the Democratic [then Liberal] ticket, and to those who voted the radical [the socialist-communist wing of the then Left-wing Republican Party] ticket, not a hair of their heads should be touched, if order was maintained by them; but under all circumstances *a free election should be held, and peace preserved*. Every one knew that a disturbance imperiled life. The consequence was that a more cheerful, peaceful election never was held. One party had yellow tickets and the other white, open in their hands, and the vote could be counted as well outside as inside at the polls; and furthermore the radical [socialist-communist] white carpet-baggers were in an unmistakable manner informed that they would be held responsible if peace at the polls was not maintained. Thus was the State redeemed from the hands of the corrupt carpet-baggers and corrupt *followers* of the United States army, and all cried: "Amen!" The joy that followed cannot be realized, and cheerful industry commenced. *The suffering, vexations, and agony of mind of the people South during reconstruction years, unless written by those who endured them, will no more be known in history than are the cries for mercy uttered in the chambers of torture in the prisons and baronial castles of Europe during the Middle Ages. And now for all these malicious tortures, for the state debts, for the enfranchising of the negro, and the race problem the harshest condemnation I have known to be expressed by the party which imposed them on us is: "It was a blunder!"* [my emphasis, L.S.].

In a statesman "*a blunder is a crime*," said Napoleon [III]. So by parity of reasoning, you can discover in what class you have placed yourselves. This election is the hegira of misrule and vampirism.

It is difficult to subscribe to the dogma of "an indissoluble union of indestructible States." It is at variance with the foundation of all government;

"for governments are founded on superior force that subjects everything to the will of the governor, or it is founded on a compact, express or tacit. . . . When founded on force, resistance is implied. . . . In a government founded on an express agreement, or compact, resistance is unlawful while the ruler maintains his part of the contract. When he violates those rules resistance is legal and justifiable. Hence in all governments resistance is naturally inherent." (Lord Woodhouselee)[147]

In the twelfth century, for instance, there "was in Aragon the Justiza, an officer elected by the people, who was the supreme interpreter of the law and protector of the people. . . . This great officer had likewise the privilege of receiving in the *name of the people* the king's oath of coronation, and during the ceremony he held a naked sword pointed at the heart of the sovereign, whom he thus addressed: 'We, your equals, constitute you our sovereign, and we voluntarily engage to obey your mandates on condition that you protect us in the enjoyment of our rights; if otherwise, not.'" *Here we find reserved rights of the people, as in our Constitution* [my emphasis, L.S.].

States appear to be destructible. From the Pillars of Hercules, all around the shores of the Mediterranean Sea—where dwelt the people to whom God gave laws amidst the thunders of Horeb and others, whence came language and most of our civilization and religion—are found the ashes of dead empires [my emphasis, L.S.].

The Confederate States must have been out of the *Union*, unless we admit that the English language is not expressive enough to clearly describe events. *To me the act of Congress passed February 17, 1870, to "admit the State of Mississippi," the proclamations to "come back,"*[148] *to "restore the State," etc., are but a few of the proofs that we were out of the Union; and the declaration of war, the blockade, belligerent rights show that the Confederate States were independent* [my emphasis, L.S.]. We were "rebels"(so called) designedly to enable the United States to escape paying Confederate bonds held by foreign powers, and to settle other international questions with them. We were in the Union or out of the Union, as the exigency of the occasion required.[149]

AN INALIENABLE RIGHT
☛ And this reminds me of an incident that occurred in the section room at the United States Military Academy in 1841. Capt. J. A. Thomas was assistant professor of ethics. The subject: "The Constitution of the United States." He there said: "Gentlemen, there are latent powers in this Constitution that will be found to

meet every emergency that may arise." And now, behold, since then! "The higher law," " the *extra* constitutional measures," the confiscation of property," "green backs a legal tender," etc., the wealth of the nation made exempt from taxation by the supreme court, and the trusts, etc. *Truly we were a conquered nation, because the United States had to resort to all the constitutional requirements of foreign warfare* [my emphasis, L.S.].

In the platform accepted by Mr. Lincoln is this resolution:

> "*Resolved*, That we maintain inviolate the rights of the States, and especially the right of each State to order and control its own domestic institutions, according to its own judgment exclusively." And in his inaugural he said: "I have no purpose, directly or indirectly, to interfere with slavery in any of the slaveholding States of the Union."

Then Congress passed, February 11, 1861, the following:

> "*Resolved*, That neither Congress, nor the people, nor the government of the nonslaveholding States have the right to legislate upon or interfere with slavery in any of the slaveholding States of the Union."

These resolutions and promises were brushed aside like reeds in the path of conquest. Their armies marched on without any check by the act of *habeas corpus*, as it was suspended by article 2 in the President's proclamation of September 22, 1862, which reads:

> "That the writ of *habeas corpus* is suspended in regard to all persons arrested, or who are now or hereafter during the rebellion shall be imprisoned in any fort, camp, arsenal, military prison, or other place of confinement by any military authority or by sentence of any court-martial or military commission."

I remember a story on the Committee of the French Academy appointed to prepare the "Academy Dictionary." Their definition of a *crab* was "a small, red fish which walks backward." "Gentlemen," said [French naturalist Georges] Cuvier, "your definition would be perfect, only for three exceptions: The crab is not a fish, it is not red, and it does not walk backward."

So, *if the Union was indissoluble, and the States were indestructible, how could they be reconstructed and readmitted?* [my emphasis, L.S.]. It is as erroneous as the definition of the crab.

It may be said, almost literally, that the administration for the expansion of war power deposited the Constitution in the State Department for the use of the supreme court after the war. They now ordained a despotic policy as being more expedient to run the government, because it could be changed, like a vane on a house top, according to the breath of public opinion or the exigency of the times. To confine their troops to the duty of destroying the regular Confederate forces, according to the usages of civilized war, had been tried in vain; but once freed from the restraints of the Constitution and modern rules of war, the work of desolation commenced to the extent that a ruthless [Union] general [Sherman] reported that a crow would have to carry its provisions if it crossed the valley he had laid waste. His example was excelled by others. *The truth is that if the North had not disregarded the Constitution, it would have ruined them. It was a government of opportunism* [my emphasis, L.S.].

German revolutionary Carl Schurz, one of many socialists who worked in the Lincoln administration. A member of the then Left-wing Republican Party, the staunch Radical served as both a Union General and as U.S. minister to Spain under Lincoln. Not only did Schurz diligently campaign for Lincoln's reelection in 1864, he was known to have heavily influenced every presidential election from 1860 to 1904.

As regards reconstruction (so called), I will only observe that a conquered people are obliged to accept such terms as the conqueror offers.

In our case the separate or sovereign States that withdrew from the Union were the parties conquered. The negotiators for peace on the one part were the Congressional Committee on Reconstruction, and on the other each one of the sovereign States for itself. The terms offered the States respectively were embodied in the last three amendments to the Constitution. As these were accepted they were admitted into the Union, each a sovereign State. So the thirteenth, fourteenth, and fifteenth articles of the Constitution, when accepted, became virtually a treaty of peace between the North and the South, made State by State. Virginia, Texas, and Mississippi were the last, and they did not accept the terms offered until 1870, when they were admitted into the Union

As Minerva sprung from the brain of Jupiter, full grown, robed in the panoply of war, and took her seat among the gods, so the Confederate States—born in a day, clothed in all the attributes of government, complete in every department—took her station among the nations of the earth [my emphasis, L.S.]. She exacted from the United States the observance of international law on war and official intercourse. After four years of the most sanguinary war of modern times she fell, white and pure, before the mercenary hosts of the nations arrayed against her. She died for the priceless heritage wrung from tyrants "*that all just power's of government are derived from the consent of the governed.*"

For this inalienable right—a right that has been exercised by almost every nation on earth, and for which millions and millions of lives have been sacrificed—the States seceded, and it will never die. It was implanted by Providence like religion in the hearts of mankind. It is an invisible power behind a veil that will break through as certainly as the soul at death lifts the dim veil that hides the life beyond the grave. It is an occult power pervading the air, and gentle until developed by oppression, whether by bad government or remorseless tyranny incident to aggregated wealth or other causes. It was not the victories of the Confederate armies; it was not because they gave the world a Lee, a Johnston, a Forrest, and a Stonewall Jackson that won the admiration of the nations; but because over all these the South was true to her convictions of right. Their achievements were great, but their cause was greater; their deeds are immortal, their cause eternal, and paid for in blood. It will exist till the leaves of the judgment book unfold [my emphasis, L.S.].[150]

A PROGRESSIVE AGE

☞ I must now take my farewell of the good Confederate soldiers with whom I have had the honor to serve. I know their valor and their worth. Like the sibylline books, as they diminish in numbers they will increase in value, and with the last veteran the order will end—then silence! Their valor will be the common heritage of mankind. Their memory will be revered by their posterity, and linger in the mind as sweetly as the fragrance of flowers. Their cause let none gainsay; it is the birth right of all the ages.

To you, my children, I have related some of my observations, and given a little of my experience in this wonderful nineteenth century.

In my youth dwellings were lit up with candles; then came gas and kerosene; now electricity illumes cities and streets, cars and ships. Steam power was known, but it had not been applied to railroads or steamships on the ocean, or to many mechanical purposes. How well do I remember the many journeys I made over the Allegheny Mountains by stage to Pittsburg, Brownsville, and Wheeling, and how steam power superseded horse power in ferryboats, treadmills, and sailing vessels on the ocean!

I have told you how I went with Prof. [Samuel] Morse to

receive what may be deemed the first message of the telegraph; now we send messages around the world.

In 1862 I saw a telephone established from one house to another, distant about fifty yards, by two young ladies in Wilmington, N.C., to communicate with each other. To-day we talk face to face a thousand miles.

The discovery of anæsthetics has alleviated the pain of the surgeon's knife, and with the X ray he looks through the human body, and makes visible the location and cause of pain, etc.

During this century the map of the world has had many changes by the Napoleonic wars, the upheaval of 1840 by [Italian socialist revolutionary Giuseppe M.] Garibaldi, [German Chancellor Otto von] Bismarck, Germany, and France; and all Africa is subjugated. In the Orient—that empire of occult science and mystery, of magic, fakirs, castes, and barbaric wealth; six times invaded from the West through the gates of India by Alexander, Mahmoud, Genghis Khan, Tamerlane, Monguls, and Persians—at last, in this century, with a population of over 300,000,000, has passed into the possession of England, and Queen Victoria is Empress of India! What destiny awaits China, with her 400,000,000 people?

We have witnessed Spain lose possession of all her colonies in South America, Mexico, and her West Indies possessions and the Philippine Islands; the slave trade, conceded to New England, ended only in 1808; imprisonment for debt was in existence when I was young in some of the States—in short, such has been the progress of liberty during this closing century that it has turned the world upside down, and to all oppressors from any cause the spirit of liberty cries:

"By all ye will or whisper, by all ye leave or do,
"The silent sullen people, shall weigh your God and you."[151] — SAMUEL GIBBS FRENCH, 1901

Baton Rouge, Louisiana.

Rutherford Birchard Hayes of Ohio, a former Union general and America's 19th president. Though a Yankee Liberal (that is, a member of the then Left-wing Republican Party), Hayes remains a hero in the South to this day, for it was he who officially ended Reconstruction when he pulled the remaining U.S. soldiers out of Dixie on April 24, 1877. Thus ended *Twelve Years of Hell* across the South.

CHAPTER 4
THE PRIVATION OF A CITIZEN

FROM A 1905 BOOK BY CONFEDERATE PRIVATE
Marcus Breckenridge Toney

AFTER THE WAR

☛ ... ON REACHING HOME [THE NASHVILLE, TN, area] we found change written upon everything. During our four years and three months' absence the city government was in control of aliens or carpet-baggers who ground out checks and bonds with a lavish hand. After paying out my last fifty cents for dinner at the Commercial Hotel, I borrowed five cents from a friend, and proceeded across the ferry, which was just above the L. and N. railroad bridge. I trudged along the White's Creek Pike and finally stopped and tried to locate myself. When I left home, the whole country around Edgefield was a vast forest of large poplars, sweet gum, hackberry, hickory, and walnut. There never was a country that produced such a fine and diversified timber as this. It was all gone, and the stumps dug up. I looked for the old homestead, and there was a piece of house that resembled it; but the weather boarding had been stripped off for some distance, and not apiece of fence was in sight. The trees my mother planted in 1845, the year before she died, were all gone. I walked near the old house, where some mulatto children were playing on the porch. I stopped to look at, but could not recognize, them. Presently a white woman came out on the porch, and I said: "Who are you?" She replied: "I am Jim's wife." I saw at once that she was a Northern woman. The "Jim" she had reference

Confederate Private Marcus Breckenridge Toney.

to was one of my former faithful slaves. As soon as I got one dollar and twenty-five cents I went before Mr. R. McPhail Smith and took the amnesty oath, and Jim and his wife had to vamoose the ranch. I trudged along for four miles farther to the home of Judge Whitworth, on the Brick Church turnpike, which I reached early in the evening. The family were all glad to see me; and after supper, feeling very tired, I went to the office room to bed, but could not sleep. Man is a creature of habit, and I had been so used to sleeping on a hard surface that I got up, took a quilt, and slept well in the front yard under the apple trees. James, George, and Leonard followed me, and it was nearly a month before I got used to a bed.

After helping on the farm for a month I came to the city and went to work for the Express Company. No one who had participated in the war on the Southern side could vote. *In order to vote, a man had to subscribe to an oath that he had not aided, abetted, or sympathized with secession. Of course that disfranchised nearly all of the whites, and no one could vote save carpet-baggers and the colored population* [my emphasis, L.S.]. Those that had real estate at that time, in addition to the city, county, and State tax, had a special tax to pay on the Edgefield and Kentucky and the Tennessee and Pacific Railway. So we had taxation without representation. The city was in the hands of a [U.S.] military post and metropolitan police; the railroads were United States military roads, and were managed by superintendents. *It took nearly the entire police force to look after the lawless [U.S.] soldiers, who would rob and in some instances murder inoffensive citizens. We had no law or order; everything was in a chaotic state* [my emphasis, L.S.]. In the meantime [what I call the Reconstruction KKK, that is, the original] . . . Kuklux Klan [which has no connection to today's KKK] and Palefaces were a law unto themselves. The object of the [this the original] Kuklux Klan [which began as a Conservative, pro-South, pro-Constitution organization] was a laudable one. It was to intimidate the evildoer and to protect the weak against the strong. No one knew who the Grand Cyclops was unless he recognized his voice in the giving of the oath, as it was administered in a deep guttural voice, and with hoodwink. The Palefaces were auxiliaries of the Kuklux, and were composed of young men who were too young to go in the war of 1861.[152] Any Kuklux could join the Palefaces. Their mode of initiation was quite tragic. A large tent was in the hall room, and a sentinel paced to and fro; near by was a gallows, and before the initiate was to be hanged there was a terrible scuffling and firing of pistols. This was done to try the mettle of the young candidate. The Kuklux ceremony was quite tame compared with that of the Palefaces. The Kuklux Klan were supposed to have been tried by the fires of battle, and no other kind of firing was required in their initiation. I recollect five meeting places: in the powder magazine of Fort Negley, Masonic Temple, under the old Olympic, a store on Market Street, and over the Evans, Fite, Porter & Company's store, and the Grand Cyclops were Player Martin, E. R. Richardson, Frank Anderson, [Confederate] Captain [John W.] Morton, and Judge Hales, of the Palefaces. There were about four thousand members of the Kuklux Klan and Palefaces in the city and county. Each Klan had a Grand Cyclops, and many of their names I have forgotten. I never heard of a large procession of Kuklux riding through our city intimidating the metropolitan police. There were some eighteen in the squad, and they were not trying to intimidate the police. On the other hand, I have always thought that *the Kuklux Klan were auxiliaries to the police in suppressing crime* [my emphasis, L.S.]. Columbia and Pulaski [Tenn.] would sometimes have a horseback procession of some one hundred and fifty or two hundred horsemen, the men all heavily gowned and the horses' hoofs muffled, and they presented quite a weird troop as they noiselessly marched through the towns, which would strike awe to the evil doers. It was not done especially to intimidate the blacks, but whites as well, if guilty of wrongdoing. *The blacks who behaved themselves [that is, obeyed the law] had the best of friends in the Kuklux Klan* [my emphasis, L.S.]. I never heard of but two deeds of violence in our midst. During the existence of the Klan one was that of a white man who was mistreating his wife. The Klan to which Capt. P. M. Griffin belonged took the man out, gave him a good whipping, and sent him home. The man afterwards always behaved himself, and I think he died a good citizen. The Klans were located in all parts of the city and country, and kept up with their neighbors' doings. When a man was doing wrong a note [pinned to his front door] saying "Beware," and signed "Kuklux Klan," was enough. The fellow's guilty conscience would say, "I am the man," and thus a reformation in his conduct would take place. So I have always maintained that *the Klans were great conservators of law and order* [my emphasis, L.S.]. The next deed of violence was the case of Mr. Barmore, of Indianapolis. It was said that [radical Left-wing, South-hating Tennessee] Governor [William G.] Brownlow had offered a large reward to any one who would ferret out the Klan, and Mr. Barmore came to Nashville. He soon called at the express office for a package, and I asked for identification, and he brought in Mr. Sparling, who was at that time agent for the Knickerbocker

Life Insurance Company. Mr. Barmore would attract attention anywhere. He was a man of fine physique, and dressed very conspicuously for a detective. He wore a fur cap, velvet jacket, and pants with high-top patent leather boots, with pants stuffed in bootlegs, and carried under his arm a large silver-mounted cane. After his first introduction he frequently called at the office for packages, and talked with me, but never mentioned the Kuklux Klan, although he knew that I had been in the Confederate army. One day he went to Columbia, and the Klan gave him a mock and asked him not to come to that section any more. A few weeks later he was in Pulaski [Tenn.], but did not get any information, and left on the train for Nashville. The Pulaski Klan wired Columbia: "Barmore is on the train." Four men in Columbia bought tickets to Godwin, and took seats near Barmore. I think Pitts Brown was the conductor. Just before Duck River bridge was reached one of the men pulled the bell cord and said to Barmore: "We want you." They carried him below the turnpike bridge, put a rope around his neck, and, notwithstanding his plea for mercy, they deposited his body in Duck River.

In 1870 our franchise was restored while D. W. C. [Dewitt Clinton] Senter was Governor, and the Kuklux Klan was disbanded forever.

Another great privation, and I shall have finished. On December 4, 1868, I was returning home from Cincinnati on the steamer *United States*. It was a cold, stormy night, and we had thirty barrels of coal oil on our bow. At 11:20 the steamer *America* collided with us, knocking a large hole in our bow, igniting the coal oil, and our vessel commenced to burn and sink at the same time. We had quite a passenger list, one hundred and thirty of whom were lost. As soon as I felt the shock of the collision I rushed up to the hurricane roof to see what had struck us. I saw the *America* standing out between us and the shore, and there was no sign of fire about her except the lights from the cabin. From the light of our fire I read her name distinctly. I rushed at once to the ladies' cabin and said to Rev. J. P. McFerrin and wife: "Get out on the guards quick; the *America* will save us." I then rushed back to my stateroom, which was near the office, to get my watch and money. When I came out of my room, the vessel was afire from stem to stern, and on account of the dense coal oil smoke I came near suffocating, and had to crawl some one hundred and fifty feet to the ladies' cabin, where all was in great confusion. Mothers were calling for husband and children, husbands shrieking for wife and children. In all my privations in life I have never witnessed such a heartrending scene, and I was powerless to aid any one. When I reached the outer guard, aft of the wheelhouse and near where I left Mr. McFerrin and wife, the bow of the *America* was passing by, and the fire was nearly to the top of her chimneys. I started to jump on the stage plank space, but all around were burning piles of baled hay. Soon as her bow passed I took a plunge, and went down, I suppose, some twelve feet; and when I struck the bottom, I shot up like a rocket, and struck out for the shore, which I soon reached. But I got very cold when a few feet up the bank, and could go no farther. I had on nothing but my underclothes, and but for a flatboatman who carried me on his back some two hundred yards to the burning *America* I believe I would have succumbed to the cold. On my berth that night was my Baltimore overcoat, which I had worn in General [Robert E.] Lee's army and had sent to relatives in Virginia before the Wilderness campaign. My relatives had forwarded it to me at Nashville in the fall of 1865, and it was lost in that terrible holocaust; but I was glad to get out.

I was sick for quite a while after the wreck, and the doctor said that one of my lungs was involved, but I said, "Doctor, I am too young a man to give up so early," and I have been leading an active life to this date (October 3, 1905).[153]

A UNITED CITIZENSHIP

☞ When the reconstruction of the Southern States had been accomplished by our Representatives taking their seats in the halls of legislature, then we felt that we were again a part of this great nation. The South then started on an era of prosperity; *it was not the new South, but the old South, with new life infused into it. We had been slaves to our slaves, and now we were freemen, as the yoke of slavery had been lifted from our necks* [my emphasis, L.S.]. Whatever of bitterness had been felt was fast disappearing; in fact, there was always less prejudice between the men who fought each other than by the noncombatants of both sides. Between the old soldiers it was as with the schoolboys—one a stalwart, the other a weakling engaging in a fight. The stalwart overpowers the puny one, and feels sorry, and they make up, and are now faster friends than before. Such was the case with many of *the boys in blue,* who said: *"We fought you with all the Americans we could muster, and then gave bounty to all foreigners we could get, and also armed many of your former slaves to fight. We overpowered you, boys, and are sorry for it." And you know sympathy begets love, and that is why the boys in blue, when we go North of the river and attend their camp fires, make us welcome guests. Some of them felt so sorry for us that they suggested that we ought to receive pensions [from the U.S.*

government], and when the matter was agitated in certain sections the bivouacs [Confederate camps] of the South were unanimous in repudiating it. We have condemned pensions, except in cases of disability, because it discounts patriotism, and a Southern soldier who deserted his flag and joined the enemy and now receives a pension is getting a premium on perjury [my emphasis, L.S.].

When the Spanish-American War came on [1898], the men of the blue and the men of the gray stood shoulder to shoulder, the sons of the men who wore the blue and the gray in 1861-65 marched step with step, and won the victory that made us feel proud that we were Americans. Thus was cemented this country as never before, and prejudices gave way to an era of good feeling throughout this Union.

I wish that every American citizen could have been with Comrade S. A. [Sumner Archibald] Cunningham [editor of *Confederate Veteran*] and me and witnessed the unveiling of the bronze statue erected to the memory of the private Confederate soldier over the graves of our two thousand two hundred and sixty dead at Camp Chase, near Columbus, Ohio, June 14, 1902. The history of the monument is as follows: [Union] Colonel W. H. Knauss was a member of a Pennsylvania regiment, and was badly wounded at Fredericksburg, Va., the wound being so severe that the surgeons said he could not recover, and he was unconscious for some weeks. He finally recovered, and after the war moved to Columbus, Ohio, and engaged in the real estate business. Soon after he reached Columbus he commenced to look after the graves of our two thousand two hundred and sixty dead at Camp Chase, four miles from Columbus. He found the graves in a common overgrown with bushes and weeds, which he soon had cut and the ground put in good shape, and asked Governor [Joseph B.] Foraker to recommend to the Legislature an appropriation of $4,000, which was made, and the cemetery was inclosed in a substantial fence. Colonel Knauss then got an oval stone which, I think, would weigh about two tons. On this stone he inscribed:

> "Two thousand two hundred and sixty Confederate soldiers buried here; died in Camp Chase Prison, 1861-65."

He then commenced to send appeals to the South each June, and he called public meetings of G.A.R. [Grand Army of the Republic, Union war veterans] men, the Daughters of the Confederacy, the Bivouacs and Daughters of the Grand Army Circle, and he put these combined influences to work, and for years has had each June a successful decoration. He then conceived the idea of erecting a monument to the private Confederate soldier, and he had all his plans made, and approached Mr. W. H. Harrison, a wealthy manufacturer of Columbus, and said:

> "Mr. Harrison, here are the plans for the monument. These men fought for what they thought was right, and were as much entitled to their opinions as I was to mine, and they died away from home and amongst strangers and foes."

Mr. Harrison was so struck with Colonel Knauss's enthusiasm that he said: "Build the monument according to your plans, and send me the bill."

Therefore, on that bright June day was assembled a vast multitude of citizens, Grand Army men, and ex-Confederates. A special train was run from Charleston, W. Va., bringing the boys in gray and their families to the unveiling. We met and clasped hands with Governor [George K.] Nash and Judge Pugh, both of whom had followed [Union] General Grant at Vicksburg [MS]. We were accorded a place on the programme, and followed Governor Nash and Judge Pugh, and spoke in the uniform of Company B, Confederate Veterans, and did our best to picture the deeds of the boys in gray. On the platform with us were the Daughters of the Confederacy and Grand Army Circle. We could not tell one from the other as far as enthusiasm went. We did recognize them, however, from their badges. Just before the service commenced Colonel Knauss came to each of the Confederates on the platform and whispered: "Boys, when the veil is removed from the statue, I want you to give us the old-fashioned Rebel yell." So we did our best, and the entire throng appeared to enjoy it. We heard the Ohio State band play "Dixie," we saw the Ohio State Guards fire a volley over the graves of our dead, we saw the [Confederate] statue standing out like a life figure. The monument had two bases, each starting out on a side of the oval rock, about nine feet high, joined together by an arch. On the arch was inscribed "Americans;" I guess Colonel Knauss did not wish to offend any oversensitive people by calling them Confederates. On the apex of the arch was the bronze figure of the boy in gray. It was typical of the Confederate private. The empty haversack, the full canteen, the old blanket twisted, tied at both ends, and thrown around the shoulders, pants stuffed in socks, and shoes well-nigh worn out, he was standing at order arms, and his body was facing his Southland. When I saw this statue I thought of William Stewart Hawkins, the author of *Behind Prison Bars*, a volume he wrote in Camp Chase. Many will recollect his "letter that came too late." He died in Nashville November 5, 1865, of the seeds of disease sown in Camp Chase. The last verse he wrote was a few days after the surrender of [Confederate] General Lee, and was written from behind prison bars as he looked out upon the graves of the two thousand two hundred and sixty dead, who preceded him only a short while. It was entitled "Defeated Valor":

> Sleep sweetly in your humble graves;
>   Sleep, martyrs of a fallen cause;
> Though yet no marble column craves
>   The pilgrim here to pause.
>
> In the seeds of laurel in the earth,
>   The blossom of your fame is blown;
> And somewhere, waiting for its birth,
>   The shaft is in the stone.[154] —MARCUS B. TONEY, 1905

As this old illustration shows, many Southern blacks, being first and second generation immigrants, knew little if anything about Western, European-American, or even Southern culture. This young 19th-Century black girl, for example, is pondering the meaning and uses of an ordinary baptismal font, something well familiar to Christians the world over. Under their racially discriminatory Reconstruction program, Yankee Liberals purposefully placed such "ignorant" blacks in positions of power, in particular political and legal power, where it was intended that they abuse, punish, and torture their former allies and best friends: Southern whites. The devilish plan worked—for a few years at least, after which, thanks to such unprejudiced Conservative organizations as the original Ku Klux Klan (not in any way connected to the modern KKK), the North's oppressive and sadistic Left-wing misgovernment, along with its outrageous racist black supremacy policies, came to an ignoble and sudden end.

CHAPTER 5
POSTWAR DIXIE

FROM A 1907 BOOK BY SOUTHERN PROFESSOR & HISTORIAN

John Lesslie Hall

A PROSTRATE NATION
☛ [AS IS WELL-KNOWN, CONFEDERATE General Robert E. Lee]. . . surrendered April 9, 1865. On April 26, followed the surrender of General Joseph E. Johnston in North Carolina; in May, that of General Richard Taylor in Mississippi, and that of General E. Kirby Smith west of the Mississippi river. By the last of June, there was not a Confederate soldier in arms against the United States government. Never did an army lay down its arms in better faith, or with more sincere acceptance of the terms offered by the conqueror. How these terms were kept by some of the conquerors, history will tell in flaming letters, calling to her aid essay, fiction and drama, and the eloquence of tongues yet unborn. [Union] General Grant acted honorably and kindly. Mr. Lincoln seems to have nursed no mean grudge against the fallen foe; but, *if General Lee could have foreseen the events of the years from 1865 to 1876, he would have hidden his ragged remnant in the Appalachian mountains, and two new generations of Southern youth would have kept up the contest to the present moment* [my emphasis, L.S.]. *But for the personal influence of General Grant, General Robert E. Lee would have been prosecuted for treason. [Confederate] President Davis, [Confederate] Vice President Stephens, Governor [Joseph E.] Brown, of Georgia, Governor [Charles] Clark, of Mississippi, General Howell Cobb, Senator [Benjamin H.] Hill, of Georgia, and other prominent men were

Dr. John Lesslie Hall.

arrested and put in prison. The greatest sufferer was President Davis. His treatment by some government officials at Fortress Monroe reads like a chapter from the Spanish Inquisition or from a history of the Indians [my emphasis, L.S.]. *Mrs.* [Varina] *Davis's account of that treatment and of the disrespect shown her by one or two prominent officials at Fort Monroe, challenges the credulity of mankind. Mr. Davis was never brought to trial. The United States Government knew that an impartial jury might well fail to find him guilty of treason against the government, and that eminent lawyers were ready to argue his case before the world. The failure to try Mr. Davis was a great constitutional victory for the South, and posterity will so regard it. The North could not have proved that he had committed treason against the government* [since secession was legal—and still is] [my emphasis, L.S.].

The cost of the war is almost beyond calculation. Besides slaves worth about two thousand million dollars, the South lost values of every kind, footing up at least two thousand million more. There was practically no money in circulation, her banks had gone to ruin, her credit was totally gone, all basis of credit was destroyed, her stocks and bonds were utterly worthless, provisions almost exhausted, bankruptcy was universal. The whole land lay in utter paralysis and ruin.[55]

THE WOLF AT THE DOOR

☛ The soldier, returning to his dismantled home, saw starvation standing at his door, shaking his gaunt finger at wife and little ones. Soon a worse sight met his gaze: an idle, shiftless mass of freedmen hung around the courthouse, the post office and other public places, wondering when they could crowd the soldier's family out of their home, and move into it. Some of the slaves were still faithful and respectful; many were sullen, suspicious, grum; some insolent. Many looked on with maudlin curiosity and with ill-suppressed delight as they saw the gentlemen of the South hoeing their gardens, ploughing the fields, driving their own ox carts, or hiring themselves to some neighbor that could manage to give them three meals a day and a few dollars a month to work as laborers. The freedmen crowded to the towns and cities. Freedom they thought meant eternal rest. Wonderful stories came to them of bounteous stores from the boundless treasury in Washington; and visions of forty acres and a mule; or, grander yet, of roving into the "big house" of their bankrupt masters, where they might smoke their pipes in the library of the "effete aristocrats," lie on old Marster's feather beds, and use the master's silver.

Agriculture was totally demoralized, factories generally

destroyed, railroads worn out and useless, farming implements gone, neither ox nor mule nor horse left to plough with; fences had been burnt by the armies; many houses were totally dismantled, the whole land lying under the curse of Nineveh.

Having made a heroic fight, the South determined to accept heroically the arbitrament of war. Slavery she willingly surrendered [since she had been trying to rid her region of it since the 1600s];[156] secession as a remedy for grievances, she embalmed among the mummies of Egypt; the right of a state to judge of infractions of the constitution, she marked "obsolete," and laid on the shelf with [William] Lilly's Latin grammar. She threw herself on the mercy of her conquerors.

The Southern people were willing and anxious to settle down and begin life over again. They were willing to accept any fair government that would protect their persons, and the little property the war had left them; believed that Mr. Lincoln would treat them humanely if not kindly; and were ready to bear anything to which self-respecting men could submit.

Mr. Lincoln had already shown that his plan of restoring the Union was not one of cruelty.[157] On December 8, 1863, he had offered "full pardon" to all persons (except the leaders of the "rebellion") that would lay down their arms, swear allegiance to the constitution, and promise to obey all acts of Congress that had been passed up to the date of his amnesty proclamation (December 8, 1863). He further said that, if one-tenth of the votes of 1860 in any seceded state should establish a government upon the basis outlined above, he would recognize it as "the true government of the state." Representation in Congress, he said, did not rest with him, but with Congress. No mention was made of negro suffrage. Indeed, *we have it on record that Mr. Lincoln did not believe that the negro should be a voter or a juror, or be put upon any political or social equality with the white man* [my emphasis, L.S.].

When the war closed, Mr. Lincoln said, "Let 'em up easy, let 'em up easy." When the question was raised whether to regard the Southern states as never out of the Union but as having temporarily cut themselves off as aliens, Mr. Lincoln brushed it aside as not a practical question, but as rather what is called "academic," that is, technical and not worthy of serious discussion at such a crisis. His idea was to bring the seceded states into practical touch with the other states and restore them as soon as possible to their place in the Union, on condition that they surrender slavery and the right of secession and accept the constitution of the United States as the fundamental law of the land. His method was one of conciliation and of restoration [this was what he presented to the public, but behind closed doors he had very different plans for the South]. When violent men wished to treat the states as conquered provinces that had forfeited all the rights of statehood, he said, "We shall sooner have the fowl by hatching the egg than by smashing it."[158]

THE HOUNDS OF PEACE

☛ This policy did not please Congress. A large number in both houses thought that Mr. Lincoln was too lenient, and that he was violating "the rights of humanity" and "the principles of republican government." Chaos reigned supreme. Many were so angry with the South that they could not hear the voice of mercy, which "droppeth as the gentle dew from heaven." Shylock was whetting his knife, not on his sole but on his soul, demanding his pound of flesh from Antonio, whose argosies had gone to the bottom of the ocean. Mr. Lincoln was firm and inflexible, and, on April 11, 1865, said publicly that he still clung to his plan of restoration.

To add fuel to the flame, came the assassination of President Lincoln. None deplored this wild act more than the South and her noble ex-president [Jefferson Davis]. It now seems incredible that Andrew Johnson, the successor of Mr. Lincoln, offered a reward of $100,000 for the capture of Mr. Davis as an accomplice of the assassin. Nor was the South in any sense responsible. John Wilkes Booth was not strictly a Southern man, did not represent the South, but killed the president on his own motion, and probably from personal motives.

While deploring the assassination and regretting that Mr. Lincoln did not live to carry out his policy, the South has never professed to love Mr. Lincoln. To do so would be arrant hypocrisy. She cannot put him along with Washington, and rank him with the demigods. She cannot forget his campaign cry of 1858; his leading a ticket avowedly hostile to her institutions; his saying that he had no authority to interfere with slavery, and yet issuing the [illegal] Emancipation Proclamation; and his straining and rending the constitution that he promised in his oath of office faithfully to maintain [my emphasis, L.S.]. She, however, admires his great ability, his shrewd common sense, his keen sagacity, and believes that he had more of "the milk of human kindness," less small bitterness, less desire to gloat over a fallen foe, than Andrew Johnson, or than the Radical [socialist-communist] majority in Congress.

The poet [John Milton] tells us of fearful creatures that, "never ceasing, barked with wide Cerberean mouths full loud, and rang a hideous peal." Not to push the comparison to the very farthest, we may say that such a chorus broke upon the ears of the prostrate South after Lincoln's assassination. Many believed that Booth was her appointed agent. Many accused Jefferson Davis of being an accomplice, and, as said already, President Johnson offered $100,000 reward for his arrest; and smaller amounts were offered for other Southern gentlemen equally above such atrocious crimes as assassination. Thank Heaven that such charges found little credence even in those fearful days! We regret that history has to notice them in this better era; but the historian more than the poet must deal with "the unrelenting past," enter its most ghastly precincts, and walk with shuddering horror among its grinning sepulchre.

We have all heard of "the dogs of war;" but the South suffered more from the hounds of peace.[139]

THE REIGN OF TERROR
☞ With the accession of Andrew Johnson to the presidency, the South had new visions of horror. Harsh measures were in the air. The imprisonment of Jefferson Davis and of others already mentioned, the summons issued against General Lee by the United States court at Norfolk, and the violent language used by the new president—all these things alarmed those that had figured prominently in the war; and a number of them left the United States, and went, some to Cuba, some to Egypt, some to Mexico, and some to Europe.

The Radical party in Congress [that is, the socialists and communists in the then Left-wing Republican Party] thought that providence had come to their assistance. Now should the conquered South lick the dust at the feet of her enemies. Soon their faces fell. The president's tone changed; he became less bitter; it was soon found out that he would not hang, draw and quarter all the Confederate leaders, but that "my policy" would be more human and humane than he first intended. This change is generally attributed to the influence of Mr. [William H.] Seward, secretary of state, who is said to have urged Mr. Johnson to pursue milder methods.

If Congress was dissatisfied with Mr. Lincoln's leniency, they raved at Mr. Johnson's mildness. Then began the deadlock between the legislative and the executive branches of the government which culminated in the unsuccessful impeachment and trial of the president. There was a roaring chaos of opinions. No two men in Congress agreed as to how the South should be got back into the

Union; whether she should be hung, drawn, and quartered first, and then brought back in a million coffins; or brought back first, then tied to a post, whipped till the blood flowed in streams, and then carried off to execution. All the Radical party [socialists and communists] agreed that the president had nothing to do with it; that he was not in the game even as referee or umpire, certainly not as captain. Meantime the South was lying in "misery and irons, hard by at death's door." Her brave sons had gone to work; but the negroes were totally demoralized, and little labor could be had to work the crops. Untold thousands of freedmen threw down all work, flocked to the towns, cities and camps, expecting to be supported if not made rich from the Federal [U.S.] treasury.[160]

THE FREEDMAN'S BUREAU

☛ This state of affairs, Mr. Lincoln had already foreseen and tried to provide against. Among the negroes that had followed the Federal armies, especially Sherman's army in its march through Georgia, there had been great suffering and destitution. To keep these runaways from starving, Congress, on March 3, 1865, established the Freedman's Bureau, but did not make any adequate appropriation; so that at first the act did little towards relieving want, but a great deal towards making the negroes feel and know that they were, in some sense, "the wards of the nation," and believe that the Southern people were their worst enemies. [This entitlement-victim mentality, found among many 21st Century blacks, is just one example of how remnants of Reconstruction have carried on into the modern era.]

This act, with amendments and "variations," was in force till 1872, and relieved a great deal of suffering among the blacks, and among whites that had "stuck" to the Union. It also established schools, colleges, and universities for the freedman, and spent a good many million dollars in caring for the negro. So far so good. *The abandoned and deserted lands which this Bureau took charge of to give the negroes, was the property of the wretched, impoverished people of the South, and much of it was recovered by the owners only after great delay and after grievous treatment at the hands of some of the [U.S.] officials* [my emphasis, L.S.].

Theoretically, this Bureau sounds very noble. As described by [Union] General O. O. [Oliver Otis] Howard, the commissioner appointed by President Johnson, it reads like an extract from the writings of John Howard, Elizabeth Fry, or some other great philanthropist. Practically, however, it did not work so well. To disburse all these millions and see that hundreds of thousands were fed daily required a very large corps of assistants; and many of these were very questionable characters. All this, however, might have gone on without adding to the woes of the South; and we must refer briefly to the reasons why *the name Freedman's Bureau is unsavory in the nostrils of the Southern people* [my emphasis, L.S.].

One of its clauses made its agents "guardians of freedmen, with power to settle their disputes with employers;" and thereby hangs a tale ghastlier than any that ghost or goblin damned ever hissed into the ear of Hamlet. Under this clause, our fathers suffered untold annoyance, indignity, and insult. Any shiftless negro girl could threaten her employer with arrest by the provost-marshal, and all through the South cases of this kind were of daily occurrence. Our people in these years drank the cup of humiliation to its very dregs, the "wine of astonishment" to its very bottom.[161]

THE SCHOOLMARM IN TRADITION

☛ At this time, and as part of the machinery of this Bureau, appeared "the Yankee schoolmarm," famous in Southern tradition. Under the ægis of the provost-marshal and his assistants, who protected her from the imaginary bullets of the imaginary assassin and from the real contempt of our [Southern] mothers and grandmothers,

> In her noisy mansion, skilled to rule,
> The village schoolmarm taught her little school.

Ladies of refinement there may have been among these [Yankee] teachers; but many of them came for what they could make by it. We shall describe "the schoolmarm" as the older people generally remember her. She came as a philanthropist, but had her eyes on the loaves and fishes. She told the little "darlings" what sacrifices she had made to come South to raise them to a level with the "proud aristocrats over yonder;" and, at the end of the session, took up a collection in which forks, spoons, and family heirlooms figured instead of silver dollars. She brought a stigma upon the sacred name of teacher, and left behind her the flavor of asafoetida.

The last interview of one of these "marms" with old Aunt Susan [a black Southern servant] is interesting:

"Good-bye, Mrs. Brown; remember now what I say: You are as good as any of these white people, and have a perfect right to eat with them and sit in the parlor with them. Do you understand?"

"Yes'm," replied Aunt Susan, alias Mrs. Brown.

"Now, Mrs. Brown," continued the retiring head of Cross Roads College, "I want you dear people to know what brought me down here. I used to make dresses and bonnets up in my own state, but came South to help elevate your precious children to equality with the proud aristocracy of the South. Understand?"

"Yes'm," said Aunt Susan; "lemme see. Does you say I is good as my ole mistis?"

"Oh, yes, certainly," answered the philanthropist.

"An' you sez yo' biz'ness at home wuz to make dresses and bonnits?"

"Yes," answered the schoolmarm.

"Well, my white folks never 'sochiates wid dressmakers and millners, an' I ain't gwine do it; good mornin', marm. " (Exit Mrs. Brown, usually known as Aunt Susan.)

This illustration is taken from an article published by a Southern lady in 1885, after the heat of passion had subsided. It represents exactly the [Yankee] schoolmarm in tradition.[162]

RECONSTRUCTION THROUGH DESTRUCTION

☛ President Johnson soon showed that he thought the president was "in the saddle." He proposed to carry on the policy of "restoration"—what is called in our history presidential reconstruction; but Congress violently opposed his policy. Most of the seceded states accepted the new president's suggestions, called conventions, adopted constitutions, repealed their ordinances of secession, accepted the thirteenth amendment abolishing slavery forever, and elected representatives and senators to seats in Congress. Here came the rub. When these representatives and senators got to Washington, they met with a cold reception from the Northern members, and found that their names were not on the roll of Congress. The clause of the constitution making each branch of Congress the judge of the eligibility of its members was used as a pretext to reject these Southern representatives and senators.

Then began the contest between Congress and the president. February 26, 1866, Congress appointed a committee of fifteen, twelve Republicans [then Liberals] and three Democrats [then Conservatives], to look into Southern affairs. On June 18, this committee reported against the president's policy, treated the South as still in a state of rebellion, and, under the leadership of violent South-haters, entered upon a new era of persecution.

Meantime, the prostrate South was fast in the grip of the [antiwhite, socialist-run] Freedman's Bureau, the shiftless freedman himself, and the schoolmarm, and could not be reinstated in the

Union. Her great offenses—what led Congress to denounce her as still in rebellion—were first, that she had passed laws against vagrancy; but this had been done to protect property from millions of idlers, mostly of the freedman class; and, second, that she was unwilling to receive the slaves as political equals, competent to vote and to hold public office. These bitter pills she could not swallow in a moment. After a while, however, she submitted to the inevitable, and, in order to get some kind of government and go to work to rebuild her shattered fortunes, accepted the fourteenth and fifteenth amendments to the constitution. These two amendments, with the thirteenth abolishing slavery, are the constitutional results of the War between the States, alias the "Rebellion."

The thirteenth amendment confirmed the [unconstitutional, and therefore illegal] Emancipation Proclamation. No one wishes to see it repealed.

The [anti-South] fourteenth amendment brought a new being into existence, that is, a citizen of the United States. Before its adoption, men were citizens of their respective states, and incidentally residents of the United States. Its object of course was to make citizens of the negroes emancipated by the war [and permanently disrupt and destroy the culture of the Old South].

The [anti-South] fifteenth amendment went farther, and gave votes to all negro males over 21 years of age. For thirty years or more, these votes were cast almost solidly in the interests of one political party, and the Southern people saw that there was no probability that the negro vote would ever be divided between the parties. This led to the restriction of the suffrage in several Southern states. The results are excellent. As said elsewhere, a good many whites are disfranchised by the new constitutions of the Southern states. The best class of colored men retain their votes, and the mass of idle and vicious ones are disfranchised. In these results, the North has practically acquiesced, and the Supreme Court of the United States has shown no inclination to upset the new constitutions. All this is a happy omen. It is one of the most significant signs that "the war is at last over."

March 2, 1867, is the "Black Friday" of the South. On that day, Congress passed, over the president's veto, a bill dividing the territory of secession, except Tennessee, into five military districts, to be commanded by generals of the United States army. These military governors were ordered to ignore the state governments and the state officers as illegal and as insufficient to protect the freedman in his rights under the constitution. Under this act, the mass of intelligent white men in the South were disfranchised, and all negro males over twenty-one were given the ballot. The results may be imagined.[163]

THE CARPET-BAGGER & THE SCALAWAG

☛ In the midst of this hurlyburly of wrack and ruin, and as a part of the diabolical [Left-wing Yankee] machinery, appears that monstrosity, that vulture of society, the "carpet-bagger." He is the product of putrefaction, the child of carrion and decay. In our day, he packs his bag and speeds to the sister isle of Cuba, and his odor is even now borne to us on the southern zephyr. When the Philippines are "pacified," he will take ship to "loot" the treasury of that territory.

The carpet-bagger of 1865 was the lowest of his ilk, the basest of his species. Often he was an apostate in religion, a preacher driven out of some community for political corruption, for immorality, or for robbing his church's treasury. He refugeed to the prostrate South to recoup his fortunes by plundering bankrupt commonwealths.

Grant and Lee discussing the terms of surrender.

To inflame the negroes against their former masters; to speak contemptuously of the "poor white rebel trash;" to point the negro to the home of "that broken-down aristocrat" and ask him how he would like to have it; to ogle him and embrace him, calling him "Mister" and "Brother," and count upon his vote at the next election,—such was the employment of this bird of prey, this cross between the cormorant and the buzzard.

Forth from this cesspool of corruption, sprang another creature forever infamous as the "scalawag." He is a renegade Southerner, who joined the carpet-bagger and the negro in dividing offices, plundering citizens, and robbing the public treasury. Before the war, he was a blatant "day before-yesterday secessionist." During the war, he probably held a bomb-proof position far from the post of danger. When Congress quarrelled with the president, he saw the opportunity of his life, sneaked slimily out of his hole, and with oily tongue ingratiated himself with the August representatives of the conqueror, while gleams of the gubernatorial mansion and of senatorial honors flashed before his snaky vision.

The carpet-bagger is no new character in history. He has lived in all periods and among all nations. He crossed the Mediterranean, and checked his carpet-bag for Utica and Magnesia. He was with the infamous [ancient Roman magistrate Gaius] Verres, whom [Marcus Tullius] Cicero denounced for plundering Sicily. He crossed the [English] Channel with William the Norman, and battened on the decaying carcass of Anglo-Saxon civilization. History repeats itself.

Scalawags, also, were produced in earlier ages; but ours seem fouler. Sicily, Africa, and Asia Minor had them in abundance; but those were pagan days, and men were sunk in superstition and brutality. England under the Conqueror had them in plenty; but that was before the days of nice honor and chivalric ideals. The scalawag of 1865, we repeat, was "the basest of his species."[164]

THE THIRD TRIUMVIRATE

☛ When [Julius] Caesar, [Marcus Licinius] Crassus, and Pompey [the Great] divided the Roman world among them, they were indulging "that vaulting ambition which o'erleaps itself," but were themselves the worst sufferers. When [Roman Emperor Gaius] Octavius [Caesar Augustus], [Mark] Antony, and [Marcus Aemilius] Lepidus drew up their deadly proscription, they were but following the precedents of a pagan age; but their deeds, though bloody and heinous, did not undermine the civilization of the Roman world. Not so with the third triumvirate, composed of the carpet-bagger, the scalawag, and the [communized] negro. They rode roughshod over private rights, piled up huge debts for posterity, plundered the public treasury, and made heinous plots against the hearth and home of the Southern family.

We must say, however, that *the poor ignorant freedman was but a pliant tool in the hands of unprincipled [Left-wing] men of the other two classes* [my emphasis, L.S.]. Rascality and robbery ran riot. Enormous debts were piled up against the states; the bonds were sold cheap to adventurers from every section; and colossal fortunes were made by depraved and corrupt men like [Simon] Legree, famous in *ante-bellum* fiction. The debt of Alabama increased from about six million to about thirty-eight million; that of Florida from two hundred and twenty-one thousand to nearly sixteen million; that of South Carolina from five million to thirty-nine million; and the debts of other states in about the same proportion. The debts of the eleven seceding states were increased from eighty-seven million to three hundred and eighty million.[165] A former congressman from Maine says that the military government of South Carolina in 1867 was "a carnival of crime and corruption," "a morass of rottenness," "a huge system of brigandage." Justice L. Q. C. Lamar says that *the reconstruction policy of Congress was intended to reverse every natural, social, and political relation on which the civilization not only of the South, but of the whole Union rested* [my emphasis, L.S.].

The black man was stirred up against the white man by incendiary [communist] speeches in public and by the basest suggestions in private. To get the "proud aristocrat's" house and home was held up as immediately possible; to get his daughter in marriage was to follow. Compared with the last suggestion, all others sank into insignificance. To stand by disfranchised and see great masses of ignorant and insolent men of an inferior race casting their votes against one's property, and laying up boundless debts and burdens for posterity—this was bad, yet for a time endurable; but the attack upon the home, upon the racial integrity of the Anglo-Saxon—this would make every Southern father draw the sword of Virginius, and smile with joy that he yet lived to thrust it into the vitals of his daughter.

Behind all this reign of atrocity, stood the Radical [that is, socialist-communist] majority in Congress. In this era of better feeling, it is almost incredible that men of Anglo-Saxon blood could have given countenance to plans of reconstruction that could lead to such results. In their fury, they [the far Left members] impeached President Johnson because his plan seemed too lenient; possibly they would have impeached even Abraham Lincoln, had he lived to urge his temperate and humane policy.

A quotation from the records of that period will interest the student. Let us see what Mr. D. [Daniel] H. Chamberlain, of Massachusetts, attorney-general of South Carolina from 1868 to 1872, writes of the situation. First, as to the "unwise and unfortunate" conduct of the white men of that noble old commonwealth, sprung from the best blood of the French Huguenot and of the Anglo-Saxon. Says Mr. Chamberlain:

> "One race (that is, the whites) stood aloft and haughtily refused to seek the confidence of the race which was just entering on its new powers."

Shades of Alfred [the Great] and of [George] Washington! Men of the great Anglo-Saxon race expected to "seek the confidence," to acknowledge the leadership, of a race known to history only as "hewers of wood and drawers of water" through all the ages!

So much for Mr. Chamberlain's knowledge of history. Now for his opinion of the carpet-bagger and the scalawag.

> "Three years have passed," says he, "and the result is—what? Incompetency, dishonesty, corruption in all its forms, have 'advanced their miscreated fronts,' have put to flight the small remnant that opposed them, and now rules the party that rules the State."

Mr. Chamberlain's candor and truthfulness compel our admiration, in spite of his monstrous twaddle about the Anglo-Saxons of Carolina.[166]

THE KU KLUX KLAN

☛ This state of affairs could not last; moderate wickedness might have lasted longer. Respectable Northern men living in the South revolted against it, and began to think about their Anglo-Saxon civilization. As a result, there sprang up the Ku Klux Klan,[167] a secret order instituted by the whites in self-preservation, but later on used [by imposters and infiltrators] for unworthy purposes. Great throngs of men clothed in white sheets rode single file on horseback through negro sections of the country; their horses drank water by the barrel, and the riders, by the bucketful; skulls and crossbones were drawn on the doors and walls, and on all the voting places: the appeal to superstition won the victory; the great reign of terror was over.[168]

It was anarchy; but self-preservation is the first law of nature. Let him that is without sin among us throw the first stone, we say reverently. The nation that holds the continent bought from the Indian with beads and bracelets, or taken from him at the point of the bayonet, the nation that gave Spain twenty million dollars for a principality, can ill afford—whether North or South—to blame the Anglo-Saxon for using ghosts and goblins to save his property and maintain his civilization.

This fearful period may be said to have lasted from 1865 to 1876. During these years, many of the young men went to new states to seek their fortunes; capital shrank from the South as men shrink from a leper; two-thirds of the wealth of the South had been swept away; money, if anyone would lend it, was held at the fabulous rate of 75 percent or 80 per cent; colossal ruin reigned supreme.

Even [former Union General] President [Ulysses S.] Grant, so kindly in some ways, had kept soldiers in the South to terrorize elections. [U.S. President Rutherford B.] Hayes relieved the South of this incubus.

From his accession to the presidency [in 1877], the new era of reconstruction set in—*reconstruction by the Southern people, the only kind that could be sound or permanent* [my emphasis, L.S.].

Of the "black-and-tan" conventions that drafted the new constitutions, we have already briefly spoken. Virginia's great (!) convention was probably more decent, or less barbarous, than some others; that worthy body drafted the constitution under which Virginia lived till July 10, 1902. A handful of Virginia gentlemen of brains and character were powerless against the enormous black-and-tan majority in the "famous" Underwood convention [named after the radical, then Left-wing, Republican John C. Underwood]. An anecdote of two of the statesmen will lighten up our ghastly narrative. The question of issuing certain stock and bonds was being discussed by the carpet-baggers and the scalawags, when one ebony statesman turned to another and said, "What is disyere storck de is talkin' about so much? Whar's de gwineter put all dat storck?" "Oh, shur! Jim, ain't you done listen to de 'schusion? De storck is gwine ter be kep in de barns." Both solons were ready to vote; carpet-bagger and scalawag were ready to divide the office and the plunder.[169]

RECONSTRUCTION BY THE SOUTHERN PEOPLE

☛ The real restoration of the South may be said to have begun about 1880. In that year, she had about 171 per cent of the assessed property of the whole country, against 44 per cent in 1860. By 1890, she had added $3,800,000,000 to her assessed values, a gain of more than 50 per cent in ten years. In farm products, she gained 16 per cent in the same period. In 1896, she made one-third of the corn crop of the country; she now makes more than half the total wheat crop. In the period 1880-1895, she increased her cotton crop from five million to almost ten million bales. In 1894, she manufactured 718,515 bales; in 1903, 2,000,729 bales. In 1903, her cotton crop was nearly eleven million bales; in 1904, more than ten million; in 1905, nearly fourteen million; and in 1906, it was more than eleven million bales.

In the *ante-bellum* period, the South grew rich on grains, sugar, rice, indigo, and tobacco. Now she has all these sources of wealth, and many others. Since 1863, the wheat shipments of New Orleans have increased from 2,744,581 bushels to 15,643,745 bushels a year, and the corn shipments from less than 1,000,000 bushels to 12,832,139 bushels. The shipments from Galveston have increased in the same proportion. In 1902, the shipments from these two ports together almost equalled those from New York. Cotton mills are springing up in all directions. New England mills, also, are moving south, so as to save freights, and thus be able to compete better with Southern mills. In 1902, for the first time, the number of bales and pounds used by Southern mills exceeded those of the North and East.

Before the war, the seed of the cotton was fed to the hogs. To-day, it is used for fertilizing after a valuable oil has been extracted. The income from this new source of wealth increased almost ten-fold in fifteen years.

The South is developing vast mines of coal and of iron. In fifteen years, the output of coal from her mines increased fivefold. She is "sending iron to Pennsylvania and coal to Newcastle," says a distinguished educator.[170] By putting iron ore, coke, coal, and limestone close together, nature enables the South to undersell the world in manufactured iron.

The railroads of the South are developing rapidly. Since 1894, the Southern Railway has increased in mileage from 4,159 to 7,550; the Louisville and Nashville, from 2,673 to 4,279; the Norfolk and Western, from 1,327 to 1,861. In the same period, the united earnings of these three systems have more than doubled.

Cotton will yet be "king." By building mills near the cotton fields, the South can soon dictate the price of cotton to the world. The proposed canal across Central America, by bringing the Southern states much closer to China, will greatly promote the cotton interests of the South, and in various ways add to the wealth of the whole nation.

In farm produce, in garden products, in foreign commerce, in banking, and in many other sources of wealth, the South is making substantial progress in building up her waste places and restoring her shattered fortunes. She is no longer dependent upon negro labor, though she prefers the negro for her rice, her sugar, and her cotton fields. Her farmers are rapidly learning to diversify their crops so as to be less injured by the decline in this or that market. The brains and the energy formerly devoted to politics will soon make the South wealthy, and make her educational institutions equal to those of any other section in training intelligent citizens.

In educational matters, also, the South has made most substantial progress. A Northern expert says that the South is spending as much on public education as Great Britain, though the population is little more than half. *The magnanimity of the Southern people in giving negro children the same advantages as their own, in spite of the fact that the whites pay over 90 per cent of the taxes, is one of the greatest proofs of the true nobility of our people. The South has forgiven the poor hoodwinked freedman, but despises the [radical Left-wing] white men that used him as a cat's-paw* [my emphasis, L.S.].

The colleges and the state universities of the South are doing a great work in training the youth of both sexes, proving that our people believe in an intelligent citizenship. It is said that no Southern college was extinguished by the war, but that the people, by private and by state funds, have revived all that were closed or seriously crippled by war and its results. In the twenty years from 1875 to 1895, school attendance increased 130 per cent, while population increased only 54 per cent; the value of school property more than trebled; the attendance upon the colleges and universities increased in fifteen years 150 per cent.

To the buoyancy and the hopefulness of our people; we have referred in foregoing pages. The power of recuperation, with peoples as with individuals, is one of the sweetest gifts of Heaven; and this gift in large measure has been bestowed upon our people. The French people, also, have wonderful recuperative power, but the South has eclipsed that nation. After the Franco-Prussian War (1870-1871), France lay apparently prostrate and helpless at the feet of the new German Confederation. It seemed as if all were lost including honor; and a superficial observer might have thought that France might never resume her place among the "great powers of Europe." Such gloomy fears were soon dissipated. In a short time, France paid a war indemnity of over a billion dollars, and, in spite of the loss of valuable territory ceded to the conqueror, soon resumed her place among the great nations of Europe. Even greater power of recuperation has been shown by our noble people. *Though one-third of her able-bodied men had died from the effects of war; though she had lost two-thirds of her assessed property by the forcible confiscation of her slaves, by plunder, and by the legitimate results of failure; though the era of reconstruction had paralyzed her energies and made life a mere existence—yet, since her people regained control of their local governments, the South has rallied beyond expression, and now her pulses throb with the fullness of the spring and with the buoyancy of a new vitality* [my emphasis, L.S.].

The war was worth all it cost. It has made labor more universal. Before the war, a good many young men lived on their fathers and helped languidly to manage the plantation. Now every young man is expected to adopt a trade, a business, or a profession, and the first question asked of a young man of twenty-five is, "What is your business or profession?" Gentlemen of easy leisure are little respected. Labor is more honored than ever before.

Being cut off from political honors and preferment, the brains of the South have been devoted to other matters. Politics used to be the bane of her civilization; to every statesman, she had a thousand small politicians. Now our people are as a rule too busy to go into politics, and it is very hard to induce good business men, or men of standing in the professions, to take public office. Consequently, we are producing great leaders of industry, great financiers, fine lawyers, noble educators, and excellent scholars. Statesmen we can hardly hope to produce while occupying our isolated position, politically, in the Union. A [Henry] Clay or a [John C.] Calhoun from the South could not muster a majority in the Senate.[171]

THE RACE PROBLEM
☛ The "negro question" is one of the great problems now awaiting solution. Not whether the negro shall sit at the white man's table, smoke in his library, and marry his daughter—that question is never discussed south of the Potomac [River]; but whether he shall take part in the government of the Southern people, and hold public office and other positions of honor and responsibility. This race question is one that vitally concerns the individual states, and must be left to them for solution. *If many negroes are disfranchised by the new constitutions of North Carolina, Virginia, Louisiana, Alabama, and other Southern states, it is because they cannot meet the requirements as to intelligence and as to amount of property laid down by those constitutions. That no man can be deprived of his vote on account of race, color, or previous condition of servitude is known to everyone who has ever heard of the war amendments to the constitution of the United States, or who ever reads a newspaper. A good many whites lose their votes under the new constitutions of the South, but vastly more negroes are disfranchised* [my emphasis, L.S.]. It is needless to say that the South believes that this is a white man's country; and it would seem that the North is rapidly coming to the same opinion.
    This race question has been a bone of contention ever since the formation of our government. In 1787, it came near defeating the plan for a "more perfect union;" and the so-called "Federal ratio," whereby five slaves were counted as three citizens in fixing the number of representatives in Congress, was resorted to as a compromise. Then came the long wrangle as to "free states" and "slave states;" the Missouri compromise of 1820; the angry debates in Congress; the rise of the Abolition party; the publication of [the fictitious, anti-South novel] *Uncle Tom's Cabin*; John Brown's raid, and, to cap the climax, the great war outlined in foregoing chapters. Worse than all that, came the era of reconstruction, when

a merciless Radical [socialist-communist Republican] majority in Congress attempted to put the freedman in control of millions of what an English historian has called the flower of the Anglo-Saxon race. This problem long refused to admit of solution. White men in the South used this negro vote to elevate themselves into public office, until the South was driven to the conclusion that the negro must get out of politics and let the white man govern both races unassisted. This is the true solution. Since retiring largely from the field of statesmanship, the negro is less objectionable to his Anglo-Saxon neighbor; and, if the United States government and its courts will let the South alone and not interfere in her suffrage questions, we shall have peace, happiness, and fraternal union.

What I have termed the Reconstruction Ku Klux Klan has no connection to today's modern KKK. The original group was a creation of the then Right-wing Democratic Party, and was a direct response to the then Left-wing Republican Party's inhumane and illegal Reconstruction program. A Conservative, pro-law, pro-Constitution, paramilitary organization, it was not racially motivated, but instead focused its attention on anti-South individuals and groups (mainly white Yankees and radical Leftists), which it strove to drive out of Dixie in order to regain control of its own region. Also a social welfare organization operating on behalf of Confederate vets, widows, and orphans—of all races—the Reconstruction KKK was so successful that by 1869 it was closed down.

As said before, the negro question has long been the apple of discord between the sections of our country. How preposterous it seems for brethren of the great Anglo-Saxon race to quarrel over a race so manifestly inferior, and so clearly intended by providence to occupy a position of inferiority! It simply proves the perversity and the stupidity of human nature.

As said in an earlier chapter, many of the ablest men of the *ante-bellum* period were in favor of colonizing the negroes in Africa [foremost among them was Abraham Lincoln].[772] Some of the thoughtful men of our day are in favor of deportation. At present, however, the cotton states are opposed to the separation of the races. They believe that the labor of the negro is indispensable on the rice and cotton plantations; but the time may come soon when this idea will vanish before statistics.

Rudimentary education the Southern people intend to give the negro if he stays cut of politics; but, if his so-called friends in other sections should upset the suffrage laws now prevailing in the South, the next step would probably be to let the colored children have no schools except those that could be maintained by the taxes of the colored people alone. This would give them one school where they now have ten. At present, comparatively few Southern whites favor a division of the school tax on the basis of color; if, however, the United States courts should interfere with suffrage laws in the South, there would be a tidal wave of indignation that would submerge the colored schools sustained by the whites, and produce other results too painful to predict.

Bad advice and pernicious leadership have injured the colored man beyond expression. Alienated from his white neighbors, first by scalawags and carpet-baggers, more recently by artful politicians, he has left the white man's church, protested against white teachers, and lost the training that contact with a higher civilization used to give him. The difference between the old colored people and the younger is very noticeable, and to this deterioration is due the present state of feeling between the races.

. . . At school and at church, also, he is often woefully misled, even totally ruined. Many of his [Left-wing] teachers set him against his white neighbors. Instead of reminding him that the schoolhouse was built with the white man's money and the teacher's salary paid out of the white man's treasury, the [Left-wing] teacher too often plants the seeds of race bitterness in the black child's bosom. At home, too, a great many parents are doing the same thing, thus sowing the wind to reap the whirlwind in the future. We are glad to say, however, that there are some wiser teachers and some wiser colored parents. A most respectable colored teacher in Virginia, on being asked quite recently why his pupils were so offensive to white citizens on the streets, replied, "I try to teach them right at school, but they are taught wrong at home."

At church, also, they get some pernicious instruction, though we rejoice to say that there are a number of faithful colored ministers trying to lift their people to a higher moral level. To illustrate our statement as to pernicious instruction, we cite an incident related to us by a Virginia gentleman of high Christian character. His family had but one servant, a colored woman, whom they trusted as a member of the family and for whom they all felt a deep affection. Handkerchiefs, pieces of jewelry, and other things disappeared mysteriously; but at first no one suspected the servant.

Finally, the losses became so heavy that they were compelled to suspect her, as she was the only person that had access to the trunks and bureaus. One day they searched her trunk, and in it found the missing articles. They called her up, told her how they had felt towards her and how they had trusted her, and asked her why she had betrayed their confidence. She replied: "Well, my preacher tells us that the Lord told the Jews, when they went out of Egypt to plunder the Egyptians, to get even with them for keeping them in bondage; and he says that we have a right to get all we can out of the white people for having kept us in slavery." [The weapon of black victimization continues to be used to this day by the Left to stir up racial animosity. L.S.]

Shakespeare makes one of his characters say that the devil can cite scripture for his purpose. So with this negro preacher. He might be pardoned for not understanding the command given by Moses to the Jews in verse 22 of the 3rd chapter of Exodus; but the application of it to the colored race is a clear perversion of scripture. How shall the blind lead the blind?

A strong feeling for employing white teachers for negro children is developing in parts of the South. There are many ladies in the Southern states who would take charge of schools for colored children, and thus guarantee them several hours a day of good moral teaching and moral influence.

What the negro needs is kind but firm restraint such as he had in slavery. He is the child-race of the world. Instead of letting him live in idleness, or work only one day in six, as numbers of them do, many are in favor of putting him under tutelage, and compelling him to earn honest wages. If his hands and his brain were employed, his evil propensities would be to a large degree curbed, and thus the most potent cause of bad feeling between the races would be removed, partially if not entirely.

He needs, also, good leaders of his own race. Most of his representative men, when they meet, pass resolutions against lynching, but rarely condemn the monstrous crimes that drive the white man to such frenzy.[173]

MORALS & RELIGION

☛ In morals and religion, the Southern people are still quite sound at bottom. Divorce, though more common than before the war, still puts one on the defensive, if not under asocial stigma.

Immorality is condemned; drunkards are despised; the temperance movement is sweeping large parts of the country, the elimination of the vicious vote giving the temperance cause a wonderful impetus, even in such conservative states as Virginia. The negro vote always went in the main on the side of liquor; and in temperance elections the colored preacher could not control his members.

To decline a drink used to cause duels. Now, duelling is put among the antiquities, and liquor is rarely offered in private houses.

In religious matters, the Southern people are still very conservative. New fads and isms find little favor among them. To go to church at least once on Sunday is expected of every good citizen, and a public violation of the Sabbath injures a man's standing in most communities. *The two races no longer worship together. The colored race demand their own churches, and preachers of their own color* [my emphasis, L.S.] Many of the preachers were used by the white politicians, and lost caste with their white neighbors; but some of them have been very useful in maintaining law and order.

The people of the so-called "New South" still honor religion, respect the Sabbath, and despise cant and hypocrisy.

Social swearing, if we may coin the phrase, is no longer "good form" in the South. An oath uttered audibly in the Westmoreland Club of Richmond would cause amazement; swearing is relegated to the barroom and other haunts of the sons of Belial. Gentlemen of standing rarely swear in public; but most youths have a touch of the habit just after measles and roseola.

Lynching is just now bringing censure upon some Southern communities; but it is an erroneous idea that it is confined to the South or that negroes are the only victims. It is true, however, that about three-fourths of the lynchings occur in the South, and that over half of the victims are negroes. It is equally true that the principal cause of lynching is the freedman's crime; and it may be added that, as long as this cause continues, lynching will be resorted to. Southern men will not allow certain facts to be dragged through the courts, while police-court lawyers delight police-court rabbles with their indecent questions. *We regret to say, moreover, that the colored people as a rule do not condemn the crimes leading to lynching half as vigorously as they do the lynching* [my emphasis, L.S.]. The colored man does not seem to have the least conception of the awful sanctity of the white man's home: the chasm at this point is as wide as eternity.

As some of the brutal element of the negro race move north and west, these sections are resorting to lynch law almost daily. The people there are beginning to sympathize with the South considerably. Foreigners, however, do not understand the awful situation. Says an Englishman living in Mississippi:

> "It is perfectly useless to try to explain to a foreigner the true inwardness of lynch law. I do not uphold them in wrong-doing, and yet I tell my English kinsmen and friends that, if they were surrounded by the same conditions, they would undoubtedly act just as the Southerners do. Human nature, especially Anglo-Saxon nature, is the same in all lands."

In the matter of honor, we still have much to be proud of. We cannot claim, however, that we are as strictly scrupulous as the generations before us. Civil wars always affect the honor and the morals of a people, and we cannot claim total exemption from this law of nature. While our election officers have, in many cases, used very questionable methods to maintain the political supremacy of the white race, our people as a mass regret that such methods were considered necessary, and are recasting their constitutions so as to eliminate the vicious and purchasable vote by fair and honorable means. Upon the youth of our day devolves the responsibility of carrying out hereafter the election laws created under these new state constitutions. The temptation to corrupt methods will exist no longer. Cheating in elections will train our people to cheat in other matters. The habit of dishonesty and prevarication grows into a second nature.

Though making the concessions in the last paragraph, we can still say that we have not been "sinners above all the Galileans."

The young men of the South are still sound in the essentials of honor. The college honor spoken of in our second chapter is still maintained to a degree that augurs well for the future. While cheating on examinations is more frequent than "before the war," it is generally condemned by the public sentiment of the students, and the student body will often secure the necessary evidence and present the culprit before the faculty for trial. Northern colleges and universities have been trying recently to introduce the honor system: prominent students sometimes write south to inquire as to its details, and its methods of operation.

Municipal corruption figures a good deal in our daily papers. Councilmen are bought up; some are convicted of bribery, and others go unpunished. In this matter, also, we are not "sinners above all the Galileans." Some of the pious and self-righteous cities of the other sections are worse than those of the old "slave-driver" and "lashing-planter." Two wrongs, however, do not make a right. We must make our town councils and our legislatures, like [Julius] Caesar's wife [Pompeia], above reproach. It devolves upon us to elect men of character to these positions. If such men say that they are too busy to accept office, our boys must determine, first to be men of character, and then to make some personal sacrifice in order to serve the city and the commonwealth. We still have much to be thankful for. In these cases of municipal corruption, the men under suspicion rarely represent the real civilization of our communities. They are generally men of little previous standing, itching for public office, and using it, when gained, for their own personal ends and objects.

Our educated men are generally men of honor. The teachers and the scholars of the South are as a rule highly respected as representing the best type of the citizen and of the gentleman. Few of them can be bought at any figure. A few Southern states have been accused of rottenness and corruption in the matter of "book adoptions;" but the men suspected of selling their votes are generally not educators and scholars, but men of the type described in the foregoing paragraph pushing their way into school boards and state boards of education. We must mark these men, and by our votes bury them in the obscurity from which they sprang.[174]

ZACCHEUS IS COMING DOWN
☛ Love for the Union is increasing in the South. Though she is practically ignored in the national government, and though many objectionable men represent the Federal government in Southern communities, the South is proud of the Union, would fight for it against any foreign nation, and welcomes overtures from friendly Northerners like Mr. Charles Francis Adams [Sr.] and others that are leading the way to full reconciliation. The young men love the Union more than the older; but state loyalty is still very strong among all classes. If compelled to choose between the State and the Union, the men of the South would undoubtedly "go with the state;" but the possibility of a rupture is never discussed with any seriousness. The right of secession, "though not by gunpowder determinable," is not regarded as a live question, but rather as what editors call "dead matter." It would take a number of wild-cat presidents and pestiferous politicians to resurrect the doctrine of secession as a burning question.

A Southern youth, if asked which he loves most, the state or the Union, would probably say, "I love not Cæsar less but Rome more," Cæsar being the Union, and Rome his native state. Possibly we should say he loves the Union well, and his state better.

[U.S.] President [Grover] Cleveland's official recognition of Southern men did no little to cement the sections. In his cabinet, sat several Southern men of high standing; and, during the great naval review in 1893, when the fleets of the world met our navy in Hampton Roads, a Confederate veteran, who was secretary of war, was welcomed to the harbor by the screaming of hundreds of whistles, American and foreign.

[U.S.] President [William] McKinley was respected, if not loved, by the Southern people. His tragic death was greatly deplored by our people, and public sentiment in the South demanded the execution of the assassin.

In the war with Spain in 1898, the South showed great loyalty to the Union. The greatest diplomat of that era was Fitzhugh Lee, consul-general to Havana. This noble son of Virginia was selected for this position when the relations between Spain and the United States were becoming "strained" on account of our sympathy with Cuba. General Lee was a brilliant success, and helped to distinguish Mr. McKinley's administration. The president, it is thought, permitted small politicians to "sidetrack" this eminent Southerner and Democrat in the slashes of Florida, instead of sending him as the liberator of Cuba.

In the war with Spain, Worth Bagley, of North Carolina, was the first man killed in battle. The heroic deed of [Richmond P.] Hobson, of Alabama, in attempting to block up the harbor of Santiago; the bravery of "Little Joe Wheeler" in the same campaign; the gallantry of [Winfield S.] Schley, the noble son of Maryland—all helped to unite the different sections of our country.

If we may judge by the signs of the times, the day of true union and full reconciliation is fast approaching. Mr. Charles Francis Adams's Charleston [SC] address, in which he said that both sides were right in 1861; Mr. Cleveland's Madison Square Garden speech, in which he praised the magnanimity of the South towards the negro, and urged the North to leave the solution of the negro problem to the Southern people; the endorsement of that speech by the Philadelphia *Press*, long the exponent of the warmest anti-Southern sentiment; the addresses made in Richmond, Va., in April, 1903, by Mr. St. Clair McKelway, editor of the Brooklyn *Eagle*, and by Dr. Lyman Abbott, in which they spoke tenderly of Southern heroes and sympathetically on Southern questions—these and other significant events have made the heart of the South beat faster, and prepared the way for a union not "pinned together by bayonets," but "resting upon the consent of the governed."

Mutual forgiveness and reparation! This, as already said, is the open sesame to fraternal union and to the full measure of our national greatness. If such Northern men as those named above could write our histories, compile our encyclopedias, and edit all our great journals, this book might not be needed, or certainly many of its paragraphs might be dispensed with. *Alas! however, ink-pots of Liliput and pygmy politicians have so shaped public sentiment, so filled our bookshelves with pestilential libels, that, unless Southern men write the truth, the South will be handed down to infamy. Books are still pouring from the press, encyclopedias still being printed, that demand refutation from Southern writers* [my emphasis, L.S.].

We are not waving the "bloody shirt" [that is, trying to inflame the passions surrounding the "Civil War"], but telling the truth, "naught extenuating and naught setting down in malice." Truth is the great healer. Truth crushed to earth will rise again. To tell the truth to the people of the South, and to all elsewhere that care to know it,—such is the object of this volume, and we invoke upon it the blessing of high Heaven, that it may increase the self-respect of our beloved South, disabuse some fair minds in other sections of false ideas as to her history, her customs, her institutions, and her motives, past and present, and hasten the day when "Ephraim shall not envy Judah and Judah shall not vex Ephraim."[175]

RECAPITULATION

☞ We have finished our talks. Before parting, let us take time for a few words of review, of recapitulation, and a few words by way of warning to the young reader of these pages.

We have tried to show the Southern youth how much he has to love and to be proud of, and how much there is to inspire him. In our earlier talks, we dwelt upon some of the poetic features of our country, and tried to appeal to the sentiment for the venerable, the lofty, in our history. . . .We passed rapidly in review the career of some of her greatest soldiers, spoke briefly of some of the critical battles of the [American] Revolution, and saw clearly that the South played a noble and heroic part in achieving American independence.

. . . Then came the era of constitutions. The South's part in drafting the Federal constitution of 1787, we found to be very great; and we saw later on that the violation of this great compact or agreement by many Northern and Western states led eleven Southern states to secede from the Union in 1861.

Between the formation of the Union (1789) and its dissolution (1861),[176] came, it will be remembered, the War of 1812 and the Mexican [American] War (1846). That our states did nobly in these wars, we showed very clearly. We then reviewed the cause of ill-feeling between the sections. We showed that the South bore patiently for many years the attacks made by fanatics upon her people and her institutions, bore slurs and abuse from many quarters, bore the nullification on the part of many Northern and Western states of clauses of the constitution and of acts of Congress in which she was deeply interested. We saw that, *when, in 1860, a great party [the newly created, then Left-wing, Republican Party] avowedly hostile to her and her interests got possession of the government, seven Southern states seceded, and that four others, because they did not believe in coercion, joined the secession movement* [my emphasis, L.S.].

That the doctrine of secession was not confined to the South but was also a New England doctrine, we proved conclusively; and that nullification, also, was a New England doctrine, we showed very clearly.

We then gave a rapid sketch of the great war for Southern independence. We discussed the rearing, the motives, the courage, and the self-sacrificing heroism of the soldiers and the sailors of the Confederacy; gave a rapid outline of the campaigns of Lee, Jackson, and Albert Sidney Johnston, and of the sufferings of the noble women of the South, the wives and the mothers of heroes.

We wrote as a Southern man for Southern youth. While glorifying the South, we did not heap maledictions and denunciations upon every one in the North, but upon those alone that came under the head of fanatics, vilifiers, marauders, plunderers, and heroes of "triumphal" marches over women, children, and graves. Any one that takes offense must either belong to one of these classes or condone the crimes referred to. "If any, speak, for him have I offended." Hatred towards any section, we have not encouraged. Love for the South, admiration for her heroes, belief in her sincerity, and in the eternal justice of her cause—all this we have taught to the best of our ability and with all the earnestness of conviction. "If this be treason, make the most of it."[177]

PATRIOTISM

☛ What we all, old and young, need, is real patriotism. We need a larger vision of our relation to our country. Local patriotism killed ancient Greece, and, if encouraged, may kill modern America.

In ancient Greece, men used to say, "I am an Athenian," "I am a Spartan," "I am a Theban;" and the system of city states indicated by these phrases led Greece to disintegration, decay, and ruin.

General Henry Lee in 1798 needed a larger vision when he cried in the Virginia legislature, "Virginia is my country." John

Randolph, of Roanoke [VA], needed it. We in the twentieth century need it also. Let us lift up our eyes unto the hills and catch the inspiration.

Patriotism means love of country, love of one's native land. Some men spell *country* without *r*; but even Westmoreland county [PA] is no man's country. If we love only Texas, Georgia, or Virginia, we cannot say that we are patriotic. We must love our country as a whole. We must love the flag that has braved a hundred years the battle and the breeze. If we have not this love, we are orphans in the universe, we are cut off from one of the deepest sources of joy. A man without patriotism is a man without a country, and a man without a country is more to be pitied than the man without a shadow—the famous but wretched being of German literature.

A great German author depicts in vivid language the sufferings of the man without a shadow; how he was pursued by the sidelong glances of every passer-by and by the curious stare of vulgar mobs, and so driven to desperation. Worse than this is the suffering of the man without a country. Better migrate to the bleak hills of Labrador [Canada] and, sitting on the shivering edges of a glacier, cry, "My country 'tis of thee I sing," than live in a land of perpetual sunshine and of golden harvests, with lips that cannot sing that thrilling anthem.

Already I hear your comments, "gentle" reader. The Northern sympathizer is saying, "Good; he's advising the youth of the South to forget the war and love the Union." The overzealous Southerner is saying, "Bah! he's gone over to the enemy, and is catering to the majority."

Both are wrong, especially the Southerner. His sneer is as false as Lucifer's when he told the Almighty that Job knew which side his bread was buttered on, and that he served God for the loaves and fishes. Wrong, too, was the Northerner, when he thought that this writer was urging the Southern youth to "forget the war." When I forget the war, let my tongue cleave to the roof of my mouth, and let my right hand forget its cunning.

What, then? Both are wrong, I repeat. I am just where I started: we need a larger vision of patriotism.

Virginia is not your country. Carolina is not your country. Alabama, Florida, Tennessee, though all call up sweet and solemn memories, are not your country. You need what the Romans call *patria* and the Germans fatherland—and would that we had the word, and the same lofty sentiment that thrills the bosom of the German as he sings, *What is the German's Fatherland?*

A man may say that the old Abolition party destroyed his love for this country. That party is out of date, but the fatherland still lives. Another may say that he does not love the [U.S.] flag because so many South-haters have sung of that flag in verse or have glorified it in their orations. Rise to a larger vision. Do you hate the Bible because many blatant and pernicious sects have quoted it as authority for their perverted teachings?

We can denounce the abolitionists, but love our country. We can denounce the slurs of pestiferous poets, pulpiteers, and orators, but still love the flag which our fathers helped to make respected and feared on land and ocean. It is our country, our flag. Shall we let these men and their modern imitators scratch our names out of the old family Bible and drive us out of the halls of our fathers, and leave us shivering in the cold without a home where we may meet around the old hearth and the old Yule log?

For forty years, this has been our blunder; let us up and rectify it. Let us go up and keep the feast. If some of the family give us cold looks and treat us as the prodigal son who has wasted his substance with riotous living, let us not be driven from the ancestral halls and the graves of our fathers; but, led by Virginia, the oldest of all the sisters, and "Carolina bright and fair," let us take our place at the old fireside and sing together the songs of "Auld Lang Syne."[178] — JOHN LESSLIE HALL, 1907

For the most part in antebellum times, unlike in the predominately monoracial North, the racially diverse South operated smoothly and efficiently. The American abolition movement, which got its start in the South, was on everyone's mind, with plans—as individuals such as Confederate Generals Robert E. Lee and Patrick R. Cleburne repeatedly emphasized—for complete emancipation as soon as was practicable. The War, and more especially Reconstruction, changed all that, leaving social devastation, homelessness, and poverty in its wake. Was this all intentionally planned by the then Left-wing Republican Party? The words of Victorian Southerners in this book provide the answer.

CHAPTER 6
RECONSTRUCTION

FROM A 1907 BOOK BY NORTHERN ATTORNEY

Leon Cushing Prince

FALL OF THE CONFEDERACY
☞ ... NO SOONER HAD THE CONFEDERACY fallen than the national Government was confronted with the perplexing question, What shall be done with the Southern States? The Republican Party [then Liberal or Left-wing] was completely dominant and its decision would be final. But on this point the party was not united.

President Lincoln, Secretary Seward, Grant, Sherman, and other generals favored admitting the Southern States at once to full representation in the Government, conditioned on their acquiescence in the results of the war. Actuated by the spirit of Lincoln's noble motto, "with charity for all, with malice toward none," they said in substance: The South was sincere in its devotion to the Confederacy. But the war is over and the South is defeated. Slavery is abolished, the Union is saved. We can afford to be generous, but we cannot afford to be unjust. The surest way to establish fraternal relations with our late foes is to let by-gones be by-gones and devote our united effort to building up our common country.

Yankee Liberal Charles Sumner, one of the main proponents of dictatorial post-Lincoln Reconstruction policies.

This was also the attitude of the soldiers and of the great majority of Northern people.

The strongest and ablest opponent of this liberal policy was Thaddeus Stevens of Pennsylvania, [radical socialist] Republican leader of the House of Representatives. Stevens declared that the South was nothing more than conquered territory to be disposed of in the way that would best suit the purposes of its conquerors and benefit the [then Left-wing] Republican Party. In this design and policy he had the effective coöperation of Charles Sumner, the distinguished abolitionist Senator from Massachusetts, and the support of a [U.S.] Congressional majority.[179]

THE ASSASSINATION OF LINCOLN

☞ Before the Government could determine upon any policy, an event occurred which plunged the country into blackest gloom and destroyed all possibility of a fraternal adjustment of this delicate matter.

On the evening of April 14th President Lincoln was shot through the brain while attending a play in Ford's Theatre in Washington [D.C.]. The assassin was John Wilkes Booth, an actor, and chief conspirator in an infamous plot to murder the President and his Cabinet. The blow fell with crushing force upon the North, which had learned to admire Abraham Lincoln for his integrity and common-sense and to love him for his magnanimous and sympathetic nature. Born under the humblest conditions he had risen by sheer force of surpassing character to be the foremost ruler of his time and one of the most impressive figures in the history of mankind.[180]

THADDEUS STEVENS SUPREME

☞ The assassination of Lincoln was the worst calamity that could have befallen the prostrate South. Outside of its own borders he was the best and wisest friend it had in a crisis when a powerful advocate was most needed. So strong was Lincoln in the confidence of the Northern people that Congress probably could not have offered effective opposition to his Southern policy had he remained at the helm of state.

The atrocious deed was ascribed by the Northern press to the instigation of Jefferson Davis and the Confederate leaders. The whole North called for summary and speedy punishment. It is now known that the crime originated in the wicked hearts and disordered brains of a few desperadoes. Instead of rejoicing, mass-meetings were held in Southern cities, where indignant sorrow voiced unfeigned regret.

But Northern passion, inflamed by rumor and suspicion, demanded vengeance. The death of [Liberal Republican] Lincoln removed the only check upon the purpose of the Stevens radicals [socialists and communists] who came into full control of the [then Left-wing] Republican Party and of the nation.[181]

OUR 17TH PRESIDENT
☞ Andrew Johnson, who now stepped into Lincoln's place, is the most striking example of rapid promotion from obscurity to exalted political rank which the history of our country affords. He was born in North Carolina, of the despised "poor white" stock, and migrated to Tennessee in his boyhood. He never attended school and could not even write his name until after he was married. A tailor by trade, he entered politics and served in many distinguished offices. He possessed great natural ability and courage, but he was deficient in tact, and being a Southern Democrat [then a Conservative] he never had the confidence of the [then Liberal Republican] party which elected him.[182]

THE PRESIDENT & CONGRESS
☞ When Andrew Johnson became President of the United States Congress was not in session. The new President started to carry into effect the generous policy of his predecessor. In a few weeks the Southern States were reorganized on lines embodying the ideals of Abraham Lincoln. Nothing was said about negro suffrage. Political power remained in the hands of white men.[183]

The President, however, reckoned without Congress and its powerful leader. When that body met in December, 1865, the Southern Senators and Representatives who had been elected under Johnson's plan were refused admission to Congress. The work of the President was ignored and Congress, under the merciless direction of Thaddeus Stevens, put into operation an altogether different and drastic plan of reconstruction.[184]

THE FOURTEENTH AMENDMENT
☞ In South Carolina, Mississippi, and Louisiana the black population exceeded the white. These States, foreseeing the peril sure to arise in Southern communities from the presence of a great mass of ignorant and lazy negroes without legal restraint and unable to realize the obligations which freedom imposed, passed laws requiring idle negroes to work. Some of the laws were very severe.

Congress interpreted the action of these States to signify a deliberate purpose to reduce the "freedmen," as the emancipated slaves were called, to a condition of dependence upon the whites which would approximate their former servitude, and thus practically nullify the Thirteenth Amendment, which had forbidden the reëstablishment of slavery. Congress then proposed another amendment to the Constitution, which would place the freedmen under the protection of the Federal Government.

The Fourteenth Amendment defined citizenship in such a way as to include the negroes, and then forbade any State to abridge the privileges of citizens or to deprive them of life, liberty, or property without due process of law. When the proposed amendment was submitted to the people the Northern and Border States ratified it, but the Southern States, with the exception of Tennessee, rejected it.[185]

THE RECONSTRUCTION ACTS

☞ In refusing to give their assent to a legislative proposition unanimously disapproved by the judgment of their section the Southern States acted strictly within their Constitutional right. But Thaddeus Stevens and the [then Left-wing] Republican leaders resented this independent attitude on the part of the conquered [Conservative] South.

Desiring above all things the permanent triumph of their [Left-wing] party these men proceeded to carry into effect a plan which was nothing less than conspiracy against the liberties of the [Conservative] Southern people and the rights of the Southern States, and a plain subversion of the Constitution itself. They resolved to take from the educated, intelligent white men of the South, trained for two hundred and fifty years in the science of government, all political rights and power and give the South over to the control of a vast and irresponsible horde of negroes, all of them ignorant and inexperienced and many of them vicious. The whites, who were Democrats [Conservatives] almost to a man, were to be disfranchised, and the [largely communized] freedmen given the ballot [my emphasis, L.S.].

By this measure the [then Left-wing] Republican Party expected to build up a negro organization which would transfer permanently the Southern States into the Republican column and destroy the [then Right-wing] Democratic Party beyond all possibility of resurrection. Thaddeus Stevens openly declared such to be his purpose.

To insure complete success and to prevent the opposition which the Southern white people would naturally attempt, the United States Army was to take military possession of the entire region and support by force the experiment of negro rule [my emphasis, L.S.].

In 1867 [the U.S.] Congress passed two acts by which the ten Southern States that had rejected the Fourteenth Amendment were divided into five military districts and each district placed under an army officer who was to act in the capacity of military governor.

This official was directed to hold an election for delegates to a State convention. A test oath was required which practically debarred the whites and permitted only negroes to take part in the election. Each State convention must then frame a constitution which would extend the franchise to freedmen. If the new constitutions were approved by the colored voters and accepted by Congress the States would thereupon be admitted to the Union after their legislatures had ratified the Fourteenth Amendment.

The President vetoed both reconstruction bills but Congress by an overwhelming vote passed them over his veto.[186]

THE FIFTEENTH AMENDMENT

☛ The [anti-South] Fourteenth Amendment became a part of the Constitution in 1868. But the [then Left-wing] Republican leaders were not satisfied. *Knowing that their party in the South depended wholly upon negro dominance, they feared that if the white [then Right-wing] Democrats should regain control of their States they would disfranchise the negroes and make the South again Democratic [more proof that the Victorian Left was simply using blacks as political pawns]* [my emphasis, L.S.].

Another amendment was accordingly drafted with the intent of forever insuring negro suffrage. It denied to Congress or to any State the power to disfranchise a man "on account of race, color, or previous condition of servitude." The negro governments of the South ratified the [anti-South] Fifteenth Amendment, which became a part of the law of the land in 1870.[187]

ANARCHY IN THE SOUTH

☛ *It is now agreed by nearly all historians and statesmen that the reconstructive measures of Congress were a series of tragic blunders. They engendered a bitterness of feeling against the North which would have been impossible under the humane and generous policy of Lincoln or Johnson. Nor did they accomplish their purpose-which was to make the South permanently Republican [that is, at the time, Liberal or Left-wing]. Not one of the negro governments endured after the Federal troops, upon which they depended, were withdrawn. They were corrupt and scandalous beyond all precedent or parallel. The whole ill-fated region was flooded with unscrupulous adventurers from the North, called "carpet-baggers," who took advantage of the helplessness of the whites and the unfitness of the negro to fill the offices and grow rich on public plunder. The freedman was taught to rely for the vindication of his newly acquired political rights not upon the fruits of character but upon force bills and Federal bayonets [tactics still in use by the Left today]* [my emphasis, L.S.].

The States of the "black belt" [that is, those with the highest black populations] fared worst. [The Left-wing "Robber"] Governor [Franklin J.] Moses [Jr.] of South Carolina was a professional crook, whose photograph may be seen to-day in the Rogues' Gallery of New York. *The South Carolina Legislature during a single session spent $350,000 for whiskey, cigars, and kindred luxuries for its colored members. Taxable values in this State dropped from $490,000,000 in 1860 to $184,000,000 in 1871, while in the same period taxes increased from less than $400,000 to $2,000,000. In South Carolina there were two hundred negro trial judges who could neither read nor write* [my emphasis, L.S.].

At the close of Reconstruction the average debt of each State subjected to its blasting regime was nearly five times as great as at the close of the Civil War—with nothing to show for it but demoralization and ruin [my emphasis, L.S.].[188]

THE FAILURE OF RECONSTRUCTION

☛ Several additional laws were passed by Congress designed to bolster up negro rule, but they were rendered ineffective or declared unconstitutional by the [U.S.] Supreme Court of the United States.

Gradually the whites recovered control of their State governments. This was accomplished largely by means of the Ku-Klux-Klan, a powerful [Conservative] secret [pro-Constitution, counter-Reconstruction] fraternity which sprang up all over the South. Its members wore disguises and operated by night in armed bands. The huts or houses of the negro rulers were visited and the occupants taken out and flogged or else frightened with a show of "magic." Sometimes they were killed.[189] The mysterious character of the fraternity appealed to the superstition of the negroes, who yielded at once. The Ku-Klux-Klan directed the same effective policy of intimidation against the "carpet-baggers." At first its membership was confined to *conservative* men who were driven to these measures in necessary self-protection. Later it passed into the control of a different element [villainous imposters who infiltrated the organization], and was finally broken up by Federal marshals—but not until it had achieved its purpose, which was to save the civilization of the South.[190]

The Fourteenth Amendment was greatly weakened by several Supreme Court decisions, which limited its scope and confirmed the Southern States in the possession of the powers of which Congress had tried to deprive them.

The Fifteenth Amendment has likewise become a dead letter. The later State constitutions, drafted by white men, have practically disfranchised the negro.

It is absolutely essential to the progress and welfare of the South that white men shall rule it. In no other way can its resources be developed and its general advancement keep pace with the rest of the nation. Even the North now recognizes this fact and is no longer disposed to interfere in those problems which public opinion has acknowledged the South alone is competent to solve.

The harsh and futile measures of the Republican radicals [socialists and communists] not only dimmed the glory which their party had won by its successful conduct of the Civil War, but it resulted in committing the Southern whites almost unanimously to the support of the [then Right-wing] Democratic Party; not primarily because Democratic policies were better suited to Southern interests than Republican policies, but because the [then Left-wing] Republican Party was associated with the vindictive and disastrous experiment of negro rule.

Since, however, the Republicans [the Liberals of that period] have given up serious thought of enforcing negro equality, it is likely that their party will eventually command a liberal [that is, generous] Southern support on the strength of its own merits. Already we can discover a definite movement in that direction, and the "solid South" shows signs of breaking up.

Vast sums of money have been expended upon negro education. Part has been contributed by Northern philanthropists, but by far the greater portion has been the voluntary gift of the [white] Southern people out of their poverty [my emphasis, L.S.].[191]

THE NEGRO OF TO-DAY

☛ With the exception of an exceedingly small class of intelligent and efficient colored people, the negro exhibits none of the results that forty years of freedom and industrial opportunity under the tutelage of education are popularly supposed to have produced.

The domestic and commercial requirements of slavery, necessitating as they did careful attention to hygiene and moral culture as well as a thorough training in the useful arts, produced a being in whom bodily strength was united to a considerable degree of moral virtue. But with the passing of slavery the beneficent and humanizing influence of white control disappeared, with the consequence that the original elements of negro character, hopelessly rooted in countless centuries of jungle life, at once asserted themselves, and have wrought sad havoc with the manhood and the prospects of the race.

The overwhelming tendency to herd in cities, aggravated by a constitutional inability to resist the peculiar temptations of urban life, is having a rapidly disastrous effect upon both physical and moral character. The extraordinary proclivity of the negro to find his keenest enjoyment in sensual gratification, together with the entire absence of self-control, renders him the inevitable and easy prey of drunkenness, tuberculosis, and those diseases most demoralizing to the soul and destructive to the body of man. His mortality has increased above one hundred per cent.

Crime is alarmingly on the increase, not only in the region known as the "black belt," but throughout the entire area of the former slave States. Although the whites in the South outnumber the blacks three to one, yet the latter furnish from eighty-five to ninety-three per cent of the convict class. Even in the city of Washington, the colored "Mecca," the negroes furnish eighty-six per cent of the criminals, while comprising less than one-third of the population. And the fact of most tragic import is that this amazing criminal activity is almost wholly the work of the generations born in freedom [that is, after 1865] and whose education has thus far cost $150,000,000.

The productive capacity of the negro is everywhere of the lowest. He owns but three per cent of the taxable property of the South, and most of that represents the accumulations of the older members of the race who were bred to the habits of industry which slavery promoted. He has had wide opportunities to prove his industrial fitness in the manufactures which are springing up all over the South, but he has failed in factory and in mill because he cannot be relied upon to keep his contract. The average negro has not the first notion of moral responsibility. He possesses neither strength of will nor power of conscience to resist the inclinations of his baser nature. He knows no motive to industry beyond the simple barbaric impulse to fill his stomach or to decorate his person. With these primitive wants temporarily satisfied, he will knock off work with as little compunction as he would steal a chicken or sell his vote.

The appalling disregard of moral obligations, plus his hand-to-mouth philosophy of existence, is the secret of the negro's indisputable failure in the serious pursuits of life. At his present rate of deterioration the American negro is destined to a certain and not distant extinction. The mere fact that the race numbers about nine millions in the United States, so far from indicating a future of promise, signifies rather the contrary, for if the rate of increase which prevailed before the Civil War had continued to the present time, the numerical strength of the negro would have far exceeded that figure.

Left to the "uncovenanted" mercy of a superior race, and exposed to the untempered severities of natural law without the safeguards of physical oversight or moral restraint, the ultimate disappearance of the negro from this continent is only a matter of time.[192] — PROFESSOR LEON CUSHING PRINCE, DICKINSON COLLEGE, PENN., 1907

Left: This article was printed in the *Independent Monitor* (Tuscaloosa, Alabama), on April 1, 1868, and is titled "The Ku Klux Phylarchy." The writer has included a "true copy" of several anonymous "Ku Klux Orders." Written on posters, "headed with large letters of blood," they were found one morning mysteriously pasted on various walls around town. Meant for Left-wingers, socialists, communists, carpet-baggers, Yankees, and South-haters in general, these "terrible scribbles" are typical of the Reconstruction KKK: much of it is plain gibberish, generously sprinkled with alarming, eerie, ominous, and intimidating language, the main intent being to frighten off, or preferably drive out, anti-South individuals—whatever their race or origins. The authors of such weird fantastical writings must have had a good laugh over the panicked reactions of their intended targets—many who were highly superstitious city-slickers from the Northeast. How well this ploy worked can be seen in the fact that the original KKK was closed after being in operation for only three years, late 1865 to early 1869.

Two photographs of Radical Socialist Thaddeus Stevens of New England. The South-hating Vermonter, a member of the then Left-wing Republican Party, was the chief proponent of extremist autocratic Reconstruction policies and led the (unsuccessful) attempt to impeach Conservative Southerner, U.S. President Andrew Johnson (a member of the then Right-wing Democratic Party). Yankee Stevens did more damage to Dixie, to North-South relations, and to the U.S. Constitution than any other single individual up to that time. Like many other polarizing Northern figures (e.g., Union war criminals William T. Sherman, Henry W. Halleck, John M. Palmer, Edward M. McCook, Philip H. Sheridan, Andrew J. Smith, John W. Geary, David Hunter, Benjamin F. Butler, John T. Croxton, Robert H. Milroy, John W. Phelps, Edward Hatch, James H. Wilson, William Sooy Smith, and John Pope), to this day "evil genius" Stevens continues to be reviled across the South.

CHAPTER 7
PERSONAL REMINISCENCES OF THE WAR, 1861-1865

From a 1911 Book by Confederate Soldier
William Henry Morgan

LINCOLN'S ASSASSINATION

☞ . . . WHEN THE NEWS OF THE assassination of Lincoln, which occurred on the night of the 14th of April, 1865, reached [us Confederate prisoners at] Fort Delaware [DE] the next morning, there was great excitement among the Yankee guards and prisoners also. The Yankee soldiers looked mad and vindictive, and the guards were doubled. Visions of retaliatory measures—banishment to Dry Tortugas, or worse—rose up before the Confederate officers. If retaliation was resorted to, no one knew how many Southern lives it would take to appease the wrath and vengeance of the North. If lots were cast for the victims, no one knew who would draw the black ballots. While all were discussing these questions in all seriousness, Peter Akers, the wit of the prison, broke the tension with the remark, "It was hard on old Abe to go through the war and then get bushwhacked in a theater."

The Yankees almost moved heaven and earth to implicate the Confederate authorities in the assassination of Lincoln, but failed most signally. No doubt, they would have given worlds, if at their command, if President Jeff Davis and other leaders could have been connected with the plot and crime. As is well known, [John Wilkes] Booth, the assassin, was shot dead in the attempt to capture him, and that a man named [David E.] Harold, who was with Booth when killed; [Lewis] Payne, who the same night attempted to assassinate Secretary of State, Wm. H. Seward, and Mrs. [Mary] Surratt—were hung, the latter in all probability innocent of any crime; there was no evidence to connect her with the assassination or the plot. Some of the assassins boarded at her house and her son fled.

The assassination of U.S. President Abraham Lincoln by Yankee madman John Wilkes Booth was considered a great tragedy, not only by most Liberal Yankees, but by many Conservative Southerners as well. Among the latter group was Confederate President Jefferson Davis. Confederate General Stephen Dill Lee strongly condemned the crime, believing that Lincoln's death would prove disastrous for the South.

The assassination of Lincoln was the act of a scatter-brained actor, John Wilkes Booth, and did the South no good, if, indeed, it was so intended. *Many people think that if Lincoln had lived the South would have fared much better after the war. I do not think so.* Lincoln might have been disposed to have dealt more justly with the South, but in my opinion he would have been overruled by the Sewards, the Stantons, the Mortons, the Garrisons, and the Thad Stevenses, and many more of that ilk, who lived and died inveterate haters and vilifiers of the Southern people. Meanness is bred in the bone of some people. *If Lincoln ever did a kindly or generous act in behalf of the South, I do not recall it.* [My emphasis. Note: The editor fully agrees with this paragraph. L.S.].

When Gen. Joseph E. Johnston surrendered on the 26th day of April, 1865, the last vestige of hope against hope vanished. We felt like saying, "Tis the last libation that Liberty draws from the heart that bleeds and breaks in her cause."[193]

OUT OF PRISON AND AT HOME

☛ I remained [a prisoner] at Fort Delaware until the 21st day of May, 1865, when I was released by a special order from Washington, which my brother had procured, and who brought the order to Fort Delaware and accompanied me to New York and to his home in Brooklyn. So that I was a prisoner of war one year to a day. I came out of prison in a much worse condition, physically, than when captured. Three years of active service in the field was as nothing to my experience in prison, although I did not suffer as much as thousands of poor fellows who received no aid from friends. I was sick several times while in prison, but had no serious illness, but was much debilitated at the end.

We left Fort Delaware on the steamer *Mentor*, going up Delaware River to Philadelphia, and thence by train and boat to New York.

After remaining in New York about two weeks recuperating, my brother and family and myself left for Virginia and home, going by steamer to Norfolk; thence up James River to Richmond, where we found a large part of the city in ashes. Gloomy and distressing was the scene. Here I met [Confederate] General [James L.] Kemper and other comrades. The next day we took the train for Lynchburg—on the old Richmond and Danville Railroad. At Burkeville [VA] we found the road to Farmville [VA] destroyed. My brother and family went by private conveyance to Farmville, while I remained at Burkeville, sitting up all night guarding the baggage, as the railroad system was so out of joint and deranged that no care could be taken of baggage by the officials. The next morning I went by wagon to Farmville with the baggage, when we again took the train to another break in the road at James River below Lynchburg. Here we got aboard an old-fashioned canal boat, drawn by an old mule or two, which landed us at Lynchburg. The next day we went to my father's, twenty-one miles, in Campbell County, and joined the loved ones there. The reunion was a happy one. But what a change! Scores of thousands of dollars' worth of property gone forever, and the future, with reconstruction and attempted negro domination, staring us in the face, the prospect was anything but encouraging. But all was not lost; honor and truth still lived, though might had triumphed over right.

Thus ended my four years of service to the Confederacy, which I served loyally and willingly, and my only regret is that we all could not have rendered our dear Southland more efficient service, even to the full fruition of our fondest hopes in the beginning.

I had three brothers in the army, all of us escaping without the loss of life or limb. The youngest, Taylor, was only in service a short time, being only thirteen years of age when the war began. He was in the cavalry service, as was my brother, Coon, towards the end.[194]

RECONSTRUCTION & SINCE

☛ As a fit climax to, and exhibitory of, Yankee hatred, malice, revenge, and cruelty practiced during the war, the North bound the prostrate South on the rock of negro domination, while the vultures, "carpet-baggers" and "scalawags," preyed upon its vitals. Unlike Prometheus, however, the South did not have its chains broken by a Hercules, but rose in its own might and severed the fetters that bound it, and drove away the birds of prey, and her people are now free and independent, controlling their own state affairs without let or hindrance; though many at the North are still growling and snarling, threatening reduction of representation in Congress, howling about negro disfranchisement, and the separation of the races in schools and public conveyances.

Let it never be forgotten that in Virginia in 1868, 80,000 carpet-baggers, scalawags, and negroes voted to disfranchise every Confederate soldier who fought for home and native land, and every man in the State, young or old, who would not swear that he had never given aid or comfort to the soldiers in the field, or sympathized with the Southern cause [my emphasis, L.S.]. Armed Yankee soldiers were posted at every courthouse in the land. Civil law gave place to arbitrary military rule. The names of states were obliterated, the states being designated as "Military Districts Nos. 1, 2, 3," etc. Detectives were abroad in the land. *Everything that [Left-wing] Yankee ingenuity and malignancy could conceive of was done to humiliate the Southern people* [my emphasis, L.S.]. This service was very distasteful to some of the Yankee officers and soldiers, but they were urged on by the venom of a [Left-wing] majority at the North. Peaceful citizens were hauled up before the military courts on complaints of worthless and vicious negroes, whose word was taken before that of the white man.

The carpet-baggers were unprincipled [Left-wing] Northern men who came South after the war—political adventurers and freebooters—to steal and plunder as office-holders. The scalawags were native [Southern] white men, many of them skulkers and deserters during the war, who, like the carpet-baggers, sought political office—"apostates for the price of their apostasy." They took sides against their kith and kin, fawning on the Northern South-haters and traducers, joining in with the despoilers of the South, "that thrift might follow fawning."

And all these atrocities practiced by the North in the name of "liberty and freedom," and, as it was often expressed, that, "treason might be made odious." "Oh, Liberty, what crimes are enacted in thy name!" Treason, indeed! Lee and Jackson "traitors"? Blistered be the tongue that utters it. The brave men of the South who for four years fought as never men fought before. "Traitors"? Palsied be the hand that writes it. The charge of treason against the South is as black as the hearts that conceived it, and as false as the tongues that uttered it.

Henrich Heine, in speaking of England's banishment of Napoleon [III] and his death on the lonely island of St. Helena, says,

> "Britannia! thou art queen of the ocean, but all great Neptune's ocean can not wash from thee the stain that the great Emperor bequeathed thee on his deathbed."

Well might it be said of the Washington Government, both during the war and afterwards, that not all the waters of all the oceans can wash away the stains of infamy practiced by it upon the South and her people. The cruel torture of [Confederate] President Davis at Fortress Monroe [VA] is a "damned spot that will not out," along with thousands of other acts, some of which I have enumerated.

A large majority of the Northern people were bitter enemies of the South, vilifying and slandering the Southern people, and sought to degrade and oppress them in many ways, but not all of them were so disposed, and many others are beginning to see the heinousness and folly of Reconstruction.

A late Northern paper, the Brooklyn *Eagle*, says:

> "Under Reconstruction the [then Left-wing] Republican party outlawed character, dispensed with fairness, degraded decency, elevated ignorance and invested in barbarism, under all the forms of politics which covered the fact of brigandage."

A true and just arraignment by a Northern man, it gives a true statement of facts in a few words.

No wonder, then, the great mass of the people of the South have stood together for their section, and are political opponents of their traducers and persecutors.

There are, however, many just and good men at the North who were opposed to the invasion of the South by the Northern armies and the waging of that cruel war, who have, since the war, battled for the rights of the South, and held in check, to some extent, that puritanical element which, like the Pharisee, ascribes to itself all the virtue and intelligence of the land.

The original Puritans came to this country, as they said, to escape persecution. I think the truth is, they left their native country for that country's good. I have often thought that if the *Mayflower* had landed at the bottom of the ocean instead of on Plymouth Rock, it would have been much better for this country.

The New England Yankees [that is, Northeast Victorian Liberals] are, in a large measure, responsible for the events that brought on the war, and for the atrocities committed in the South during and since the war. I don't believe the West and South would ever have gone to war had it not been for this puritanical spirit of New England. Envy is the ruling attribute of the Puritan; magnanimity is foreign to the Puritan nature. One thing formerly practiced by the New Englanders, they utterly failed to establish in this country. A good thing it was too for the old women, or else many more of them might have been burned, hanged or drowned as witches, as was done in New England when the Puritan spirit prevailed in its undiluted state.

The following is a copy of an old-time Massachusetts legal document, reproduced here that early history may be perpetuated:

"EXECUTION FOR WITCHCRAFT: To George Corwin Gent'n, High Sheriffe of the County of Essex Greeting: WHEREAS Bridgett Bishop al's Olliver, the wife of Edward Bishop of Salem in the County of Essex Lawyer at a special Court of Oyer and Terminer held at Salem the second Day of this instant month of June for the Countyes of Essex, Middlesex and Suffolk before William Stoughton Esque. and his associates of the said Court was Indicted and arraigned upon five several Indictments for using practising and exerciseing on the . . . last past and divers other dayes and times the felonies of Witchcraft in and upon the bodyes of Abigail Williams, Ann Puttnam, Mercy Lewis, Mary Walcott and Elizabeth Hubbard of Salem Village . . . single women; whereby their bodyes were hurt, offlicted, pined, consumed and tormented contrary to the forme of the statute in that case made and provided. To which Indictm'ts the said Bridgett Bishop pleaded not guilty and for Tryall thereof put herselfe upon God and her Country whereupon she was found guilty of the Felonyes and Witchcrafts whereof she stood indicted and sentence of Death accordingly passed ag't her as the Law directs. Execution whereof yet remaines to be done. These are therefore in the names of their maj'ties William and Mary now King and Queen over England &c. to will and command That upon Fryday next being the Tenth Day of this instant month of June between the hours of eight and twelve in the aforenoon of the same day you safely conduct the s'd Bridgett Bishop al's Olliver from their maj'ties Gaol in Salem afores'd to the place of execution and there cause her to be hanged by the neck untill she be dead and of your doings herein make returne to the clerk of the s'd Court and of this pr'cept. And hereof you are not to faile at your peril. And this shall be your sufficient warrant Given under my hand & seal at Boston the eighth of June in the fourth year of the reigne of our Sovereign Lords William and Mary now King and Queen over England &c.

Annoq'e Dom. June 10, 1692. Wm. Stoughton."

"According to the within written precept I have taken the body of the within named Brigett Bishop out of their majesties goal in Salem and safely conveighd her to the place provided for her execution and caused s'd Brigett to be hanged by the neck untill she was dead and buried in the place all which was according to the time within required and so I make returne by me. George Corwin, Sheriff."

As before said, the sentiment at the North is changing in favor of the South; many are beginning to learn the true history of the past and present state of affairs, though the South still has its traducers and slanderers there, for in this year of grace, 1907, a Sunday-school magazine up North printed in its columns the following:

"And when General Lee invaded Pennsylvania, at the time of the battle of Gettysburg, destruction and rapine followed in the wake of the invaders. There was evil and misfortune at every turn."

A bigger lie was never told. A fouler slander was never uttered.
The South, despite its enemies, is advancing rapidly in material interests, and is destined to be the most prosperous portion of the United States. "King Cotton" is coming to his throne again. *The South has always been the most chivalrous, conservative and American-like, holding more closely to the traditions, customs, and manners of the old days, where the high and unselfish principles of right, justice and honor, which go to make up the true gentleman and patriotic citizen, have always prevailed* [my emphasis, L.S.]. The pure Anglo-Saxon blood still predominates in the South, as well as the spirit of the cavalier. Blood will tell.

The average Yankee [that is, the Northern Liberal, socialist, or communist] has a very poor conception of what is right and honorable in his transactions and intercourse with his fellow-man, and very faint conceptions of those principles of right and justice which are the same among men of honor, world without end. To drive a sharp bargain, to get money no matter how, but to get money, and diffuse and enforce his own ideas and notions, seem to be the summa summorum *of all his ends—as witness the developments in the past few years of rascality and thieving being brought to light at the North, as it exists among the "great captains of finance," as they are wont to be called; I think "great thieves" would be a much more suitable appellation. The foundations of many of the great, overgrown fortunes at the North were laid during the war by swindling and stealing by Government contractors, and they are still at it. Graft, graft; fraud, fraud, everywhere and in everything they touch* [my emphasis, L.S.].

As before said, the South is coming to its own again. I firmly believe the days of retribution will come when the evil deeds the North perpetrated in the South during and since the war, will be avenged, not in kind perhaps, but in some way. "The gods wait long, but they are just at last;" their "mills grind slowly, but they grind exceeding fine." God is just; His will be done.

I have written much more than I anticipated in the beginning the subject and occurrences opened up the "cells where memory sleeps." The more I wrote, the more I recalled.

These reminiscences were commenced several years ago and virtually completed last February. Since then they have been gone over, revised, added to and some parts rewritten, and now on this, the 31st day of December, in the year of our Lord, 1907, the last day of the year, are completed.[195] — WILLIAM HENRY MORGAN, 1907

Yankee actor and assassin John Wilkes Booth of Maryland. A hero to some, a villain to others.

CHAPTER 8
AFTER THE WAR

FROM A 1912 BOOK BY CONFEDERATE SOLDIER
Augustus Pitt Adamson

☛ THE SURRENDER OF [CONFEDERATE] GEN. Lee's army, at Appomattox, April 9, 1865, and [Joseph E.] Johnston's on April 26, was soon followed by the surrender of all the small detachments in different places through the South. The prisoners were paroled, as well as those in Northern prisons, and at once began to return to their homes. Only a small remnant of the proud army who had four years before gone out with flying colors to resist the invasion of their native land, were present at the surrender. They had during these trying years battled for principles which they believed right; they had in hundreds of hard fought battles, contended against largely superior numbers, in most of which they had been victorious. They had left many of their comrades dead on these gory fields, many had died from disease and many were languishing in Federal prisons. They had patiently endured many hardships, often making long and weary marches, ragged and barefooted, with scanty food, over rugged roads, covered with mud and ice. No soldiers ever made greater sacrifices, or fought with more valor. The suffering of [George] Washington's army, at Valley Forge; or of Napoleon's on the retreat from Moscow, were no worse than [Confederate General John Bell] Hood's army endured in Tennessee. The charge of Napoleon's men at Lodi, and Austerlitz was not equal to [Confederate General George E.] Pickett's charge at Gettysburg; or that of [Confederate General John C.] Breckinridge, at

Augustus Pitt Adamson.

Murfreesboro. The heroism displayed by the Southern soldiers at Gettysburg, Sharpsburg, around Richmond, Chickamauga, Jonesboro and Franklin has never been surpassed by the soldiery of any land; but the sacrifice and bravery of this immortal band could not withstand the great disparity of numbers arrayed against them. It seemed that the South had the world to contend with, and 600,000 men could not overcome 2,500,000, so their cause went down in defeat.

The war over, they turned their faces homeward; with mingled joy and sadness they wended their way through the land made desolate by the marauders of [Union Generals] Sherman and Sheridan. The loving welcome they received from mothers, wives and sisters awakened springs of joy in their breasts; but this joy was marred by the sad reflections of missing comrades left behind, and the gloomy scenes which met their view on every hand; of devastated fields, ruined homes and blackened chimneys, standing as grim sentinels, in the midst of the ruins of burned cities. Gen. Sherman, upon leaving Atlanta, in November, 1864, ordered it destroyed, and that place was left a mass of smoldering ruins. In his march through Georgia, like a besom of destruction, he swept a path nearly thirty miles wide, in which little of value was left. Subsistence of all kinds, horses, cattle and hogs were taken; houses were pillaged, and in many instances trunks and wardrobes of ladies were broken open and robbed of valuable articles highly prized as family heirlooms, which had been handed down from past generations. Families that had been in affluent circumstances were in a day reduced to hunger and want; and in many places women and children had to gather up the waste corn, left by the horses, and use it for food. History furnishes no parallel to the acts of vandalism, and wanton destruction of private property, and homes of defenseless women and children, perpetrated by Sherman's army in his "march to the sea." The rules of civilized warfare were disregarded, and but little attempt made to prevent these atrocities. It was in striking contrast to the conduct of Gen. Lee's army in 1863, upon its invasion of Pennsylvania, when private property was protected.

Such was the condition, in most of the Southern States when her soldiers arrived at their homes. It was indeed a gloomy outlook for the future, with nothing to subsist upon,—all lost except honor, and their proud record. But they knew that it would not do to indulge in useless repinings; but with the same courage that had characterized them as soldiers, went at once to work to build up the waste places; remembering the parting words of their great chieftain, Robert E. Lee, who said,

> "You have done all you could; go home, and make as good citizens as you have been soldiers."

President Lincoln had been assassinated on April 15, 1865, and [Southern Democrat, then a Conservative] Vice-President Andrew Johnson had succeeded him. He announced that he would endeavor to carry out the policy of his predecessor, and at once took steps to establish orderly civil government in the Southern States, and during the year 1865, Conventions were held and Constitutions framed in accordance to the changed condition of affairs. But this policy of President Johnson was too conservative for the extreme Republicans in Congress and was rejected by them; the senators and representatives elected were denied admission. Intense excitement, madness and wild fanaticism prevailed and Congress seemed determined to reduce the Southern people to a state of vassalage and force upon them negro equality. In opposition to the wishes of the President, and over his veto, [the Republican, then Left-wing, controlled] Congress passed what was known as the Reconstruction Bill, which was in subversion to the Constitution and the rights of the people. By this odious measure many of the best people of the South were disfranchised and ignorant negroes given the right to vote. During the war the negroes had, as a race, conducted themselves well, and had given very little trouble; but as soon as the war closed, instigated by [radical Left-wing] emissaries from the [Liberal] North, they were made to believe they were entitled to both civil and social equality; and in many places became impudent and troublesome. Elections were held in pursuance of these laws, the polls being opened at the county sites only, and guarded by armed soldiers. Power unheard of before was given military commanders, they being authorized to declare the result. By this means the government of the Southern States, was for a time, completely dominated by military authority, negroes and carpet-baggers. Civil law was subordinated to military law and great excitement and indignation existed everywhere., In many places carpet-baggers and negroes were declared elected to offices which had been filled by great statesmen. In Georgia a mulatto negro named Jeff Long, was sent to Congress from a district once represented by David J. Bailey and Thomas Hardeman. The district once represented by [former Confederate Vice President] A. H. Stephens, was now misrepresented by a carpet-bagger, and a little later on a negro was sent to the United States Senate from

Mississippi, occupying a place once held by Jefferson Davis. *These days of reconstruction were awful dark, and more terrible than war* [my emphasis, L.S.]. The Southern people had not lost their instinct for local self-government, and it now became more intensified than ever before. Three million of their former slaves were turned loose upon them, and given the right to govern their former masters, many of whom were denied the right to vote. For a time misrule, rottenness and corruption reigned supreme. A new issue now faced the people of the South. They were a knightly race who knew how to govern and were determined, by the help of God, to govern. Like men who had been true in the war, they faced the issue, and with hope, courage and determination wrested their beloved Southland from the clutches of the rapacious and motley crowd of corruptionists. Of the part the Southern soldier took in this struggle for local self-government, Gen. Clement A. Evans says:

> "Was there ever a prouder display of civic government? The marvel of their battles was great. The marvel of their sufferings was greater; but greatest of all was their firm endeavor to avert dishonor, and prevent abhorrent social order and blend the broken sections into a government of brothers."

Thus the South was saved from corruption and negro domination, and at once began to grow in prosperity.

The land, which was made desolate by war, and left in ruins, has, by the efforts of her people, been converted into prosperous cities, fertile fields and flowery gardens. If space permitted, many pages could be written in relation to the dark days—of anxiety and suspense of the reconstruction period. It is due President Johnson, to say that he opposed these measures and did all he could to prevent their enactment, using the veto power invested in him as long as he could. The differences between [Conservative Democrat] President Johnson and [Liberal Republican] Congress increased, and finally articles of impeachment were adopted charging the President with high crimes and misdemeanors. Upon these charges he was tried by the Senate of the United States, sitting as a court of impeachment, and acquitted by a vote of 35 to 19, two-thirds being required to convict. His course has since been vindicated, and after the madness and excitement of that dark period had cleared away a returning sense of right compelled many who were opposed to him, to admit that his impeachment would have been a great mistake. It had taken several years to accomplish the final overthrow of the corrupt regime organized under the reconstruction measures; but as soon as the power passed into the hands of our people, peace and order was restored. The negroes began to find out who were their best friends and went [back] to work; and a better feeling existed between the races. During all these years it was a hard struggle to live, money was scarce and provisions were sold at exorbitant prices.

There were many things to discourage our people, but they were equal to the occasion; and notwithstanding, the venom of the extremist the injustice heaped upon them, and the many obstacles they encountered, with a united and determined purpose they brought order out of chaos and prosperity out of adversity, and won the respect of their former foes; proving to the world how great they were in the midst of severe trials.[796] — AUGUSTUS PITT ADAMSON, 1912

U.S. General William Tecumseh Sherman. The socialist-leaning South-loather, a member of the then Left-wing Republican Party, was responsible for untold profane outrages against the South, including the harming and even murder of noncombatants and the wanton, unnecessary, and widespread destruction of private property—both unconstitutional and both violations of the Geneva Conventions. Due to his racial views, by today's standards the Yankee war criminal would be considered a white racist, a white separatist, and a white supremacist. Despite his beliefs and actions, Sherman continues to be lauded as a hero-patriot in our mainstream history books.

"RADICAL [SOCIALIST] MEMBERS OF THE LEGISLATURE OF SOUTH CAROLINA"

Original caption: "These are the photographs of sixty-three members of the 'reconstructed' Legislature of South Carolina. Fifty of them were Negroes or Mulattos; thirteen were white men. Of the twenty-two among them who could read and write only eight used vernacular grammatically. Forty-one made their mark [signature] with the help of amanuensis [an assistant or secretary]. Nineteen were taxpayers to an aggregate of $146.10. The other forty-four paid no taxes, and yet this body was empowered to levy on the white people of the states taxes amounting to $4,000,000 [$100,000,000 in today's currency]."

CHAPTER 9
THE BLACK TERROR

FROM A 1919 BOOK BY ENGLISH JOURNALIST
Cecil Edward Chesterton

Cecil Edward Chesterton, British political commentator and brother of G. K. Chesterton.

☞ ... THE SURRENDER OF LEE AND his army was not actually the end of the war. The army of [Confederate] General [Joseph E.] Johnston and some smaller Confederate forces were still in being; but their suppression seemed clearly only a matter of time, and all men's eyes were already turned to the problem of reconstruction, and on no man did the urgency of that problem press more ominously than on the President [Abraham Lincoln].

Slavery was dead. This was already admitted in the South as well as in the North. Had the Confederacy, by some miracle, achieved its independence during the last year of the war, it is extremely unlikely that Slavery would have endured within its borders. This was the publicly expressed opinion of [Confederate President] Jefferson Davis even before the adoption of Lee's policy of recruiting slaves and liberating them on enlistment had completed the work which the Emancipation Proclamation of Lincoln had begun. Before the war was over, Missouri, where the Slavery problem was a comparatively small affair, and Maryland, which had always had a good record for humanity and justice in the treatment of its slave population, had declared themselves Free States. The new Governments organized under Lincoln's superintendence in the conquered parts of the

Confederacy had followed suit. It was a comparatively easy matter to carry the celebrated Thirteenth Amendment to the Constitution declaring Slavery illegal throughout the Union.

But, as no one knew better than the President, the abolition of Slavery was a very different thing from the solution of the Negro problem. Six years before his election he had used of the problem of Slavery in the South these remarkable words:

> "I surely will not blame them (the Southerners) for not doing what I should not know how to do myself. If all earthly power was given I should not know what to do as to the existing institution."

The words now came back upon him with an awful weight which he fully appreciated. All earthly power was given—direct personal power to a degree perhaps unparalleled in history—and he had to find out what to do.

His own belief appears always to have been that the only permanent solution of the problem was [Thomas] Jefferson's. He did not believe that black and white races would permanently live side by side on a footing of equality, and he loathed with all the loathing of a Kentuckian the thought of racial amalgamation. In his proposal to the Border States he had suggested repatriation in Africa, and he now began to develop a similar project on a larger scale. [Lincoln was, in fact, a lifelong member and a one-time official of the American Colonization Society, whose stated mission was to make the U.S. "white from coast to coast."][197]

But the urgent problem of the reconstruction of the Union could not wait for the completion of so immense a task. The seceding States must be got into their proper relation with the Federal Government as quickly as possible, and Lincoln had clear ideas as to how this should be done. The reconstructed Government of Louisiana which he organized was a working model of what he proposed to do throughout the South. All citizens of the State who were prepared to take the [U.S.] oath of allegiance to the Federal Government] were to be invited to elect a convention and frame a constitution. They were required to annul the ordinances of Secession, to ratify the Thirteenth Amendment, and to repudiate the Confederate Debt. The Executive would then recognize the State as already restored to its proper place within the Union, with the full rights of internal self-government which the Constitution guaranteed. The freedmen were of course not citizens, and could, as such, take no part in these proceedings; but Lincoln recommended, without attempting to dictate, that the franchise should be extended to "the very intelligent and those who have fought for us during the war."

Such was Lincoln's policy of reconstruction. He was anxious to get as much as possible of that policy in working order before Congress should meet. His foresight was justified, for as soon as Congress met the policy was challenged by the Radical [that is, the socialist and communist] wing of the [then Left-wing] Republican Party, whose spokesman was Senator [Charles] Sumner of Massachusetts.

Charles Sumner has already been mentioned in these pages. The time has come when something like a portrait of him must be attempted. He was of a type which exists in all countries, but for which America has found the exact and irreplaceable name. He was a "high-brow" [in today's parlance, a Liberal elitist]. The phrase hardly needs explanation; it corresponds somewhat to what the French mean by *intellectuel*, but with an additional touch of moral priggishness which exactly suits Sumner. It does not, of course, imply that a man can think. Sumner was conspicuous even among politicians for his ineptitude in this respect. But it implies à pose of superiority both as regards culture and as regards what a man of that kind calls "idealism" which makes such an one peculiarly offensive to his fellow-men. "The Senator so conducts himself," said [William P.] Fessenden, a Republican [then Left-wing], and to a great extent an ally, "that he has no friends." He had a peculiar command of the language of insult and vituperation that was all the more infuriating because obviously the product not of sudden temper, but of careful and scholarly preparation. In all matters requiring practical action he was handicapped by an incapacity for understanding men; in matters requiring mental lucidity by an incapacity for following a line of consecutive thought.

The thesis of which Sumner appeared as the champion was about as silly as ever a thesis could be. It was that the United States were bound by the doctrine set out in the Declaration of Independence to extend the Franchise indiscriminately to the Negroes.

Had Sumner had any sense it might have occurred to him that the author of the Declaration of Independence might be presumed to have some knowledge of its meaning and content. Did Thomas Jefferson think that his doctrines involved Negro Suffrage? So far from desiring that Negroes should vote with white men, he did not believe that they could even live in the same free community. Yet since Sumner's absurd fallacy has a certain historical importance through the influence it exerted on Northern opinion, it may be well to point out where it lay.

The Declaration of Independence lays down three general principles fundamental to Democracy. One is that all men are equal in respect of their natural rights. The second is that the safeguarding of mens natural rights is the object of government. The third that the basis of government is contractual—its "just powers" being derived from the consent of the governed to an implied contract. The application of the first of these principles to the Negro is plain enough. Whatever else he was, the Negro was a man, and, as such, had an equal title with other men to life, liberty, and the pursuit of happiness. But neither Jefferson nor any other sane thinker ever included the electoral suffrage among the natural rights of men. Voting is part of the machinery of government in particular States. It is, in such communities, an acquired right depending according to the philosophy of the Declaration of Independence on an implied contract.

Now if such a contract did really underlie American, as all human society, nothing can be more certain than that the Negro had neither part nor lot in it. When [Conservative Yankee Stephen A.] Douglas pretended that the black race was not included in the expression "all men" he was talking sophistry, but when he said that the American Republic had been made "by white men for white men" he was stating, as Lincoln readily acknowledged, an indisputable historical fact. The Negro was a man and had the natural rights of a man; but he could have no claim to the special privileges of an American citizen because he was not and never had been an American citizen. He had not come to America as a citizen; no one would ever have dreamed of bringing him or even admitting him if it had been supposed that he was to be a citizen. He was brought and admitted as a slave. The fact that the servile relationship was condemned by the democratic creed could not make the actual relationship of the two races something wholly other than what it plainly was. A parallel might be found in the case of a man who, having entered into an intrigue with a woman, wholly animal and mercenary in its character, comes under the influence of a philosophy which condemns such a connection as sinful. He is bound to put an end to the connection. He is bound to act justly and humanely towards the woman. But no sane moralist would maintain that he was bound to marry the woman—that is, to treat the illicit relationship as if it were a wholly different lawful relationship such as it was never intended to be and never could have been.

Such was the plain sense and logic of the situation. To drive such sense into Sumner's lofty but wooden head would have been an impossible enterprise, but the mass of Northerners could almost certainly have been persuaded to a rational policy if a sudden and tragic catastrophe had not altered at a critical moment the whole complexion of public affairs.

Lincoln made his last public speech on April 11, 1865, mainly in defence of his Reconstruction policy as exemplified in the test case of Louisiana. On the following Good Friday he summoned his last Cabinet, at which his ideas on the subject were still further developed. That Cabinet meeting has an additional interest as presenting us with one of the best authenticated of those curious happenings which we may attribute to coincidence or to something deeper, according to our predilections. It is authenticated by the amplest testimony that Lincoln told his Cabinet that he expected that that day would bring some important piece of public news—he thought it might be the surrender of [Confederate General Joseph E.] Johnston and the last of the Confederate armies—and that he gave as a reason the fact that he had had a certain dream, which had come to him on the night before Gettysburg and on the eve of almost every other decisive event in the history of the war. Certain it is that Johnston did not surrender that day, but before midnight an event of far graver and more fatal purport had changed the destiny of the nation. Abraham Lincoln was dead.

A conspiracy against his life and that of the Northern leaders had been formed by a group of exasperated and fanatical Southerners who met at the house of a Mrs. [Mary] Surratt in the neighbourhood of Washington [D.C.]. One of the conspirators was to kill [William H.] Seward, who was confined to his bed by illness, but on whom an unsuccessful attempt was made. Another, it is believed, was instructed to remove [Union General Ulysses S.] Grant, but the general unexpectedly left Washington, and no direct threat was offered to him. The task of making away with the President was assigned to John Wilkes Booth, a dissolute and crack-brained actor. Lincoln and his wife [Mary Todd Lincoln] were present that night at a gala performance of a popular English comedy called *Our American Cousin*. Booth obtained access to the Presidential box and shot his victim behind the ear, causing instant loss of consciousness, which was followed within a few hours by death. The assassin leapt from the box on to the stage shouting: "*Sic semper Tyrannis!*" and, though he broke his leg in the process, succeeded, presumably by the aid of a confederate among the theatre officials, in getting away. He was later hunted down, took refuge in a bar, which was set on fire, and was shot in attempting to escape.

The murder of Lincoln was the work of a handful of crazy fools. Already the South, in spite of its natural prejudices, was beginning to understand that he was its best friend. Yet on the South the retribution was to fall. It is curious to recall the words which Lincoln himself had used in repudiating on behalf of the [then Left-wing] Republican Party the folly of old [Yankee socialist and South-hater] John Brown, words which are curiously apposite to his own fate and its consequences.

> "That affair, in its philosophy," he [Lincoln] had said, "corresponds to the many attempts related in history at the assassination of kings and emperors. An enthusiast broods over the oppression of a people till he fancies himself commissioned by Heaven to liberate them. He ventures the attempt, which ends in little else than his own execution. [Italian revolutionary Felice] Orsini's attempt on Louis Napoleon [Napoleon III] and John Brown's attempt at Harper's Ferry were, in their philosophy, precisely the same. The eagerness to cast blame on Old England in the one case and on New England in the other does not disprove the sameness of the two things."

It may be added that the "philosophy" of Booth was also "precisely the same" as that of Orsini and Brown, and that the "eagerness to cast blame" on the conquered South was equally unjustifiable and equally inevitable.

The anger of the North was terrible, and was intensified by the recollection of the late President's pleas for lenity and a forgetfulness of the past. "This is their reply to magnanimity!" was the almost universal cry. The wild idea that the responsible heads of the Confederacy were privy to the deed found a wide credence which would have been impossible in cooler blood. The justifiable but unrestrained indignation which Booth's crime provoked must be counted as the first of the factors which made possible the tragic blunders of the Reconstruction.

Another factor was the personality of the new President. [Southern Democrat, then Conservative] Andrew Johnson occupied a position in some ways analogous to that of [John] Tyler a generation earlier. He had been chosen Vice-President as a concession to the War Democrats [then Conservatives] and to the Unionists of the Border States whose support had been thought necessary to defeat [George B.] McClellan. With the Northern [then Left-wing] Republicans who now composed the great majority of [the U.S.] Congress he had no political affinity whatever. Yet at the beginning of his term of office he was more popular with the Radicals [that is, the socialists and communists of the then Left-wing Republican Party] than Lincoln had ever been. He seemed to share to the full the violence of the popular mood. His declaration that as murder was a crime, so treason was a crime, and "must be made odious," was welcomed with enthusiasm by the very [Left-wing radical] men who afterwards impeached him. Nor, when we blame these men for trafficking with perjurers and digging up tainted and worthless evidence for the purpose of sustaining against him the preposterous charge of complicity in the murder of his predecessor, must we forget that he himself, without any evidence at all, had under his own hand and seal brought the same monstrous accusation against Jefferson Davis. Davis, when apprehended, met the affront with a cutting reply:

> "There is one man at least who knows this accusation to be false—the man who makes it. Whatever else Andrew Johnson knows, he knows that I preferred Mr. Lincoln to him."

It was true. Between Johnson and the chiefs of the Confederacy there was a bitterness greater than could be found in the heart of any Northerner. To him [Johnson] they [Southerners] were the seducers who had caught his beloved South in a net of disloyalty and disaster. To them [Southerners] he [Johnson] was a traitor who had sold himself to the Yankee oppressor. A social quarrel intensified the political one. Johnson, who had been a tailor by trade, was the one political representative of the "poor whites" of the South. He knew that the great slave-owning squires despised him, and he hated them in return. It was only when the issues cut deeper that it became apparent that, while he would gladly have hanged Jeff Davis and all his Cabinet on a sufficient number of sour apple trees (and perhaps he was the one man in the United States who really wanted to do so, he was none the less a Southerner to the backbone; it was only when the Negro question was raised that the Northern men began to realize, what any Southerner or man acquainted with the South could have told them, that the attitude of the "poor white" towards the Negro was a thousand times more hostile than that of the slave-owner.

Unfortunately, by the same token, the new President had not, as Lincoln would have had, the ear of the North.

Had Lincoln lived he would have approached the task of persuading the North to support his policy with many advantages which his successor necessarily lacked. He would have had the full prestige of the undoubted Elect of the People—so important to an American President, especially in a conflict with Congress. He would have had the added prestige of the ruler under whose administration the Rebellion had been crushed and the Union successfully restored. But he would also have had an instinctive understanding of the temper of the Northern masses and a thorough knowledge of the gradations of opinion and temper among the Northern politicians.

Johnson had none of these qualifications, while his faults of temper were a serious hindrance to the success of his policy. He was perhaps the purest lover of his country among all the survivors of Lincoln: the fact that told so heavily against his success, that he had no party, that he broke with one political connection in opposing Secession and with another in opposing Congressional Reconstruction, is itself a sign of the integrity and consistency of his patriotism. Also he was on the right side. History, seeing how cruelly he was maligned and how abominably he was treated, owes him these acknowledgments. But he was not a prudent or a tactful man. Too much importance need not be attached to the charge of intemperate drinking, which is probably true but not particularly serious. If Johnson had got drunk every night of his life he would only have done what some of the greatest and most successful statesmen in history had done before him. But there was an intemperance of character about the man which was more disastrous in its consequences than a few superfluous whiskies could have been. He was easily drawn into acrimonious personal disputes, and when under their influence would push a quarrel to all lengths with men with whom it was most important in the public interest that he should work harmoniously.

For the extremists, of whom Sumner was a type, were still a minority even among the [then Left-wing] Republican politicians; nor was Northern opinion, even after the murder of Lincoln, yet prepared to support their policy. There did, however, exist in the minds of quite fair-minded Northerners, in and out of Congress, certain not entirely unreasonable doubts, which it should have been the President's task—as it would certainly have been Lincoln's—to remove by reason and persuasion. He seems to have failed to see that he had to do this; and certainly he altogether failed to do it.

The fears of such men were twofold. They feared that the "rebel" States, if restored immediately to freedom of action and to the full enjoyment of their old privileges, would use these advantages for the purpose of preparing a new secession at some more favourable opportunity. And they feared that the emancipated Negro would not be safe under a Government which his old masters controlled.

It may safely be said that both fears were groundless, though they were both fears which a reasonable man quite intelligibly entertains. Naturally, the South was sore; no community likes having to admit defeat. Also, no doubt, the majority of Southerners would have refused to admit that they were in the wrong in the contest which was now closed; indeed, it was by pressing this peculiarly tactless question that Sumner and his friends procured most of their evidence of the persistence of "disloyalty" in the South. On the other hand, two facts already enforced in these pages have to be remembered. The first is that the Confederacy was not in the full sense a nation. Its defenders felt their defeat as men feel the downfall of a political cause to which they are attached, not quite as men feel the conquest of their country by foreigners. The second is that from the first there had been many who, while admitting the right of secession—and therefore, by implication, the justice of the Southern cause—had yet doubted its expediency. It is surely not unnatural to suppose that the disastrous issue of the experiment had brought a great many round to this point of view. No doubt there was still a residue—perhaps a large residue of quite impenitent "rebels" who were prepared to renew the battle if they saw a good chance, but the conditions under which the new Southern Governments had come into existence offered sufficient security against such men controlling them. Irreconcilables of that type would not have taken the [U.S.] oath of allegiance, would not have repealed the Ordinances of Secession of repudiated the Confederate Debt, and, if they had no great objection to abolishing Slavery, would probably have made it a point of honour not to do it at Northern dictation. What those who were now asking for re-admission to their ancient rights in the Union had already done or were prepared to do was sufficient evidence that moderation and an accessible temper were predominant in their counsels.

The other fear was even more groundless. There might in the South be a certain bitterness against the Northerner; there was none at all against the Negro. Why should there be? During the late troubles the Negro had deserved very well of the South. At a time when practically every active male of the white population was in the fighting line, when a slave insurrection might have brought ruin and disaster on every Southern home, not a slave had risen [against his or her white or black owners]. The great majority of the race had gone on working faithfully, though the ordinary means of coercion were almost necessarily in abeyance. Even when the Northern [U.S.] armies came among them, proclaiming their emancipation, many of them continued to perform their ordinary duties and to protect the property and secrets of their masters. *Years afterwards the late [black educator and orator] Dr. Booker [T.] Washington could boast that there was no known case of one of his race betraying a trust. All this was publicly acknowledged by leading Southerners and one-time supporters of Slavery like [former Confederate Vice President] Alexander [H.] Stephens, who pressed the claims of the Negro to fair and even generous treatment at the hands of the Southern whites* [my emphasis, L.S.]. It is certain that these in the main meant well of the black race. It is equally certain that, difficult as the problem was, they were more capable of dealing with it than were alien theorizers from the North, who had hardly seen a Negro save, perhaps, as a waiter at an hotel.

"The Black Terror" was not a reference to blacks in general. It was a Reconstruction term specifically used for those African-Americans who had been gaslighted, indoctrinated, and generally communized by Radical Liberals and Socialists to view Southern whites as racist enemies. In truth, nearly all of the racism in Dixie was being generated by extremist white members of the then Left-wing Republican Party, who promoted, not racial equality, but black supremacy—a detestable attempt to destabilize the South.

It is a notable fact that the soldiers who conquered the South were at this time practically unanimous in support of a policy of reconciliation and confidence. [Union General William T.] Sherman, to whom [Confederate General Joseph E.] Johnston surrendered a few days after Lincoln's death, wished to offer terms for the surrender of all the Southern forces which would have guaranteed to the seceding States the full restoration of internal self- government. Grant sent to the President a reassuring report as to the temper of the South which Sumner compared to the "whitewashing message of [U.S. President] Franklin Pierce" in regard to Kansas.

Yet it would be absurd to deny that the cleavage between North and South, inevitable after a prolonged Civil War, required time to heal. One event might indeed have ended it almost at once, and that event almost occurred. A foreign menace threatening something valued by both sections would have done more than a dozen Acts of Congress or Amendments to the Constitution. There were many to whom this had always appeared the most hopeful remedy for the sectionable trouble. Among them was [William H.] Seward, who, having been Lincoln's Secretary of State, now held the same post under [President Andrew] Johnson. While secession was still little more than a threat he had proposed to Lincoln the deliberate fomentation of a dispute with some foreign power—he did not appear to mind which. It is thought by some that, after the war, he took up and pressed the *Alabama* [a C.S.S. war ship] claims with the same notion. That quarrel, however, would hardly have met the case. The ex-Confederates could not be expected to throw themselves with enthusiasm into a war with England to punish her for providing them with a navy. It was otherwise with the trouble which had been brewing in Mexico.

Napoleon III had taken advantage of the Civil War to violate in a very specific fashion the essential principle of the Monroe Doctrine. He had interfered in one of the innumerable Mexican revolutions and taken advantage of it to place on the throne an emperor of his own choice, Maximilian [I, Austrian emperor of Mexico], a cadet of the Hapsburg family, and to support his nominee by French bayonets. Here was a challenge which the South was even more interested in taking up than the North, and, if it had been persisted in, it is quite thinkable that an army under the joint leadership of Grant and Lee and made up of those who had learnt to respect each other on a hundred fields from [the Battle of First] Bull Run [which we Southerners call the Battle of First Manassas] to [the Battle of] Spottsylvania [Courthouse] might have erased all bitter memories by a common campaign on behalf of the liberties of the continent. But Louis Napoleon was no fool; and in this matter he acted perhaps with more regard to prudence than to honour. He withdrew the French troops, leaving Maximilian to his fate, which he promptly met at the hands of his own subjects.

The sectional quarrel remained unappeased, and the quarrel between the President [Johnson] and [the U.S.] Congress began. Congress was not yet Radical [that is, socialist and communist], but it was already decidedly, though still respectfully, opposed to Johnson's policy. While only a few of its members had yet made up their minds as to what ought to be done about Reconstruction, the great majority had a strong professional bias which made them feel that the doing or not doing of it should be in their hands and not in those of the Executive. It was by taking advantage of this prevailing sentiment that the Radicals [the socialists and communists of the then Left-wing Republican Party], though still a minority, contrived to get the leadership more and more into their own hands.

Of the Radicals Sumner was the spokesman most conspicuous in the public eye. But not from him came either the driving force or the direction which ultimately gave them the control of national policy.

Left to himself, Sumner could never have imposed the iron oppression from which it took the South a life—and death wrestle of ten years to shake itself free. At the worst he would have been capable of imposing a few paper pedantries, such as his foolish Civil Rights Bill, which would have been torn up before their ink was dry. The will and intelligence which dictated the Reconstruction belonged to a very different man, a man entitled to a place not with puzzle-headed pedants or coat-turning professionals but with the great tyrants of history.

Thaddeus Stevens of Pennsylvania was in almost every respect the opposite of his ally, Charles Sumner of Massachusetts. Sumner, empty of most things, was especially empty of humour. Stevens had abundance of humour of a somewhat fierce but very real kind. Some of his caustic strokes are as good as anything recorded of Talleyrand [French diplomat Charles Maurice de Talleyrand-Périgord, 1st Prince of Benevento]: notably his reply to an apologist of Johnson who urged in the President's defence that he was "a selfmade man." "I am delighted to hear it," said Stevens grimly; "it relieves the Creator of a terrible responsibility." With this rather savage wit went courage which could face the most enormous of tests; like [François] Rabelais, like [Georges J.] Danton, he could jest with death when death was touching him on the shoulder. In public life he was not so much careless of what he considered conventions as defiantly happy in challenging them. It gave him keen delight to outrage at once the racial sentiments of the South and the Puritanism of the North by compelling the politicians whom he dominated and despised to pay public court to his mulatto mistress.

The inspiring motive of this man was hatred of the South [my emphasis, L.S.]. It seems probable that this sentiment had its origin in a genuine and honourable detestation of Slavery.

As a practising lawyer in Pennsylvania he had at an earlier

period taken a prominent part in defending fugitive slaves. But by the time that he stood forward as the chief opponent of the Presidential policy of conciliation, Slavery had ceased to exist; yet his passion against the former slave-owners seemed rather to increase than to diminish. I think it certain, though I cannot produce here all the evidence that appears to me to support such a conclusion, that it was the negative rather than the positive aspect of his policy that attracted him most. Sumner might dream of the wondrous future in store for the Negro race—of whose qualities and needs he knew literally nothing—under Bostonian tutelage. But I am sure that for Stevens the vision dearest to his heart was rather that of the proud Southern aristocracy compelled to plead for mercy on its knees at the tribunal of its hereditary bondsmen.

Stevens was a great party leader. Not such a leader as [Thomas] Jefferson or [Andrew] Jackson had been: a man who by bribery or intrigue induces his fellow-professionals to support him. He was one of those who rule by personal dominance. His courage has already been remarked; and he knew how much fearlessness can achieve in a profession where most men are peculiarly cowardly. It was he who forced the issue between the President and Congress and obtained at a stroke a sort of captaincy in the struggle by moving in the House of Representatives that the consideration of Reconstruction by Congress would precede any consideration of the President's message asking for the admission of the representatives of the reorganized States.

By a combination of forceful bullying and skilful strategy Stevens compelled the House of Representatives to accept his leadership in this matter, but the action of Congress on other questions during these early months of the contest shows how far it still was from accepting his policy. The plan of Reconstruction which the majority now favoured is to be found outlined in the Fourteenth Constitutional Amendment which, at about this time, it recommended for adoption by the States.

The provisions of this amendment were threefold. One, for which a precedent had been afforded by the President's own action, declared that the public debt incurred by the Federal Government should never be repudiated, and also that no State should pay or accept responsibility for any debt incurred for the purpose of waging war against the Federation. Another, probably unwise from the point of view of far-sighted statesmanship but more or less in line with the President's policy, provided for the exclusion from office of all who, having sworn allegiance to the Constitution of the United States, had given aid to a rebellion against its Government.

The third, which was really the crucial one, provided a settlement of the franchise question which cannot be regarded as extreme or unreasonable. It will be remembered that the original Constitutional Compromise had provided for the inclusion, in calculating the representation of a State, of all "free persons" and of three-fifths of the "other persons"—that is, of the slaves. By freeing the slaves the representation to which the South was entitled was automatically increased by the odd two-fifths of their number, and this seemed to Northerners unreasonable, unless the freedmen were at the same time enfranchised. Congress decided to recommend that the representation of the South should be greater or less according to the extent to which the Negro population were admitted to the franchise or excluded from it. This clause was re-cast more than once in order to satisfy a fantastic scruple of Sumner's concerning the indecency of mentioning the fact that some people were black and others white, a scruple which he continued to enforce with his customary appeals to the Declaration of Independence, until even his ally Stevens lost all patience with him. But in itself it was not, perhaps, a bad solution of the difficulty. *Had it been allowed to stand and work without further interference it is quite likely that many Southern States would have been induced by the prospect of larger representation to admit in course of time such Negroes as seemed capable of understanding the meaning of citizenship in the European sense. Such, at any rate, was the opinion of General Lee, as expressed in his evidence before the Reconstruction Committee* [my emphasis, L.S.].

The South was hostile to the proposed settlement mainly on account of the second provision. It resented the proposed exclusion of its leaders. The sentiment was an honourable and chivalrous one, and was well expressed by Georgia in her protest against the detention of Jefferson Davis: "If he is guilty so are we." But the rejection of the Amendment by the Southern States had a bad effect in the North. It may be convenient here to remark that Davis was never tried. He was brought up and admitted to bail (which the incalculable [Yankee socialist Horace] Greeley [and others] found for him), and the case against him was not further pressed. In comparison with almost every other Government that has crushed an insurrection, the Government of the United States deserves high credit for its magnanimity in dealing with the leaders of the Secession. Yet the course actually pursued, more in ignorance than in malice so far as the majority were concerned, probably caused more suffering and bitterness among the vanquished than a hundred executions.

For the Radicals were more and more gaining control of Congress, now openly at war with the Executive. The President [Johnson] had been using his veto freely, and, as many even of his own supporters thought, imprudently. The [then Left-wing] Republicans were eager to obtain the two-thirds majority in both Houses necessary to carry measures over his veto, and to get it even the meticulous Sumner was ready to stoop to some pretty discreditable manœuvres. The President had taken the field against Congress and made some rather violent stump speeches, which were generally thought unworthy of the dignity of the Chief Magistracy. Meanwhile alleged "Southern outrages" against Negroes vigorously exploited by the Radicals [the socialists and communists in the then Left-wing Republican Party], whose propaganda was helped by a racial riot in New Orleans, the responsibility for which it is not easy to determine, but the victims of which were mostly persons of colour. The net result was that the new Congress, elected in 1866, not only gave the necessary two-thirds majority, but was more Radical in its complexion and more strictly controlled by the [then Left-wing] Republican machine than the old had been.

The effect was soon apparent. A Reconstruction Bill was passed by the House and sent up to the Senate. It provided for the military government of the conquered States until they should be reorganized, but was silent in regard to the conditions of their re-admission. The [then Left-wing] Republican caucus met to consider amendments, and Sumner moved that in the new Constitutions there should be no exclusion from voting on account of colour. This was carried against the strong protest of John Sherman, the brother of the [Union] general [William T. Sherman] and a distinguished Republican Senator. But when the Senate met, even he submitted to the decision of the caucus, and the Amendment Bill was carried by the normal Republican majority. [President] Johnson vetoed it, and it was carried by both Houses over his veto. The Radicals [Republican socialists and communists] had now achieved their main object. Congress was committed to indiscriminate Negro Suffrage, and the President against it; the controversy was narrowed down to that issue. From that moment they had the game in their hands.

The impeachment of Johnson may be regarded as an interlude. The main mover in the matter was [Thaddeus] Stevens. The main instrument [South-hating Union General] Ben Butler—a man disgraced alike in war and peace, the vilest figure in the politics of that time. It was he who, when in command at New Orleans (after braver men had captured it), issued the infamous order which virtually threatened Southern women who showed disrespect for the Federal uniform with rape—an order which, to the honour of the Northern soldiers, was never carried out. He was recalled from his command, but his great political "influence" saved him from the public disgrace which should have been his portion. Perhaps no man, however high his character, can mix long in the business of politics and keep his hands quite clean. The leniency with which Butler was treated on this occasion must always remain an almost solitary stain upon the memory of Abraham Lincoln. On the memory of Benjamin Butler stains hardly show. At a later stage of the war Butler showed such abject cowardice that Grant begged that if his political importance required that he should have some military command he should be placed somewhere where there was no fighting. This time Butler saved himself by blackmailing his commanding officer. At the conclusion of peace the man went back to politics, a trade for which his temperament was better fitted; and it was he who was chosen as the chief impugner of the conduct and honour of Andrew Johnson!

The immediate cause of the Impeachment was the dismissal of [Edwin M.] Stanton, which Congress considered, wrongly as it would appear, a violation of an Act which, after the quarrel became an open one, they had framed for the express purpose of limiting his prerogative in this direction. In his quarrel with Stanton the President seems to have had a good case, but he was probably unwise to pursue it, and certainly unwise to allow it to involve him in a public quarrel with Grant, the one man whose prestige in the North might have saved the President's policy. The quarrel threw Grant, who was already ambitious of the Presidency, into the hands of the [then Left-wing] Republicans, and from that moment he ceased to count as a factor making for peace and conciliation.

[Southern Conservative Democrat] Johnson was acquitted, two or three honest Republican [then Left-wing] Senators declaring in his favour, and so depriving the prosecution of the two-thirds majority. Each Senator gave a separate opinion in writing. These documents are of great historical interest; Sumner's especially—which is of inordinate length and intensely characteristic—should be studied by anyone who thinks that in these pages I have given an unfair idea of his character.

In the meantime far more important work was being done in the establishment of Negro rule in the South. State after State was "reconstructed" under the terms of the Act which had been passed over the President's veto. In every case as many white men as possible were disfranchised on one pretext or another as "disloyal." In every case the whole Negro population was enfranchised. Throughout practically the whole area of what had been the Confederate States the position of the races was reversed.

So far, in discussing the Slavery Question and all the issues which arose out of it, I have left one factor out of account the attitude of the slaves themselves. I have done so deliberately because up to the point which we have now reached that attitude had no effect on history. The slaves had no share in the Abolition movement or in the formation of the [original] Republican Party [by Liberals and Socialists in 1854].[198] Even from John Brown's Raid they held aloof. The President's [Lincoln] proclamation which freed them, the Acts of Congress which now gave them supreme power throughout the South, were not of their making or inspiration. In politics the negro was still an unknown factor.

There can be little doubt that under Slavery the relations of the two races were for the most part kindly and free from rancour, that the master was generally humane and the slave faithful. Had it not been so, indeed, the effect of the transfer of power to the freedmen must have been much more horrible than it actually was. On the other hand, it is certain that when some Southern apologists said that the slaves did not want their freedom they were wrong. Dr. Booker [T.] Washington, himself a slave till his sixth or seventh year, has given us a picture of the vague but very real longing which was at the back of their minds which bears the stamp of truth. It is confirmed by their strange and picturesque hymnology, in which the passionate desire to be "free," though generally apparently invoked in connection with a future life, is none the less indicative of their temper, and in their preoccupation with those parts of the Old Testament—the history of the Exodus, for instance—which appeared applicable to their own condition. Yet it is clear that they had but the vaguest idea of what "freedom" implied. Of what "citizenship" implied they had, of course, no idea at all.

It is very far from my purpose to write contemptuously of the Negroes. There is something very beautiful about a love of freedom wholly independent of experience and deriving solely from the just instinct of the human soul as to what is its due. And if, as some Southerners said, the Negro understood by freedom mainly that he need not work, there was a truth behind his idea, for the right to be idle if and when you choose without reason given or permission sought is really what makes the essential difference between freedom and slavery. But it is quite another thing when we come to a complex national and historical product like American citizenship. Of all that great European past, without the memory of which the word "Republic" has no meaning, the Negro knew nothing: with it he had no link. A barbaric version of the more barbaric parts of the Bible supplied him with his only record of human society.

Yet Negro Suffrage, though a monstrous anomaly, might have done comparatively little practical mischief if the Negro and his white neighbour had been left alone to find their respective levels. The Negro might have found a certain picturesque novelty in the amusement of voting; the white American might have continued to control the practical operation of Government. But it was no part of the policy of those now in power at Washington to leave either black or white alone. "Loyal" [that is, Liberal leaning] Governments were to be formed in the South; and to this end [Left-wing] political adventurers from the North—"carpet-baggers," as they were called—went down into the conquered South to organize the Negro vote. A certain number of disreputable Southerners, known as "scallywags," eagerly took a hand in the game for the sake of the spoils. So of course did the smarter and more ambitious of the freedmen. And under the control of this ill-omened trinity of Carpet-Bagger, Scallywag, and Negro adventurer grew up a series of [Left-wing oriented] Governments the like of which the sun has hardly looked upon before or since.

The Negro is hardly to be blamed for his share in the ghastly business. The whole machinery of politics was new to him, new and delightful as a toy, new and even more delightful as a means of personal enrichment. That it had or was intended to have any other purpose probably hardly crossed his mind. His point of view—a very natural one, after all—was well expressed by the aged freedman who was found chuckling over a pile of dollar bills, the reward of some corrupt vote, and, when questioned, observed: "Wal, it's de fifth time I's been bo't and sold, but, 'fo de Lord, it's de fust I eber got de money!" *Under administrations conducted in this spirit the whole South was given up to plunder. The looting went on persistently and on a scale almost unthinkable. The public debts reached amazing figures, while Negro legislators voted each other wads of public money as a kind of parlour game, amid peals of hearty African laughter* [my emphasis, L.S.].

Meanwhile the Governments presided over by Negroes, or white courtiers of the Negro and defended by the bayonets of an armed black militia, gave no protection to the persons or property of the whites.

Daily insults were offered to what was now the subject race.

What I have termed the Reconstruction Ku Klux Klan was not even remotely similar to what is taught and believed by the mainstream today. This Conservative Southern organization consisted of members of all races (Nashville, for example, had its own all-black KKK den), whose main purpose was to force socialists and communists (whatever their race) out of Dixie and regain political, economic, educational, and social control of the South.

The streets of the proud city of Charleston [SC], where ten years before on that fatal November morning the Palmetto flag had been raised as the signal of Secession, were paraded by mobs of dusky freedmen singing: "De bottom rail's on top now, and we's g'wine to keep it dar!" It says much for the essential kindliness of the African race that in the lawless condition of affairs there were no massacres and deliberate cruelties were rare. On the other hand, the animal nature of the Negro was strong, and outrages on white women became appallingly frequent and were perpetrated with complete impunity. *Every white family had to live in something like a constant state of siege* [my emphasis, L.S.].

It was not to be expected that ordinary men of European origin would long bear such government. And those on whom it was imposed were no ordinary men. They were men whose manhood had been tried by four awful years of the supreme test, men such as had charged with [Confederate General George E.] Pickett up the bloody ridge at Gettysburg, and disputed with the soldiers of Grant every inch of tangled quagmire in the Wilderness. They found a remedy.

Suddenly, as at a word, there appeared in every part of the downtrodden country bands of mysterious horsemen. They rode by night, wearing long white garments with hoods that hid their faces, and to the terror-stricken Negroes who encountered them they declared themselves—not without symbolic truth—the ghosts of the great armies that had died in defence of the Confederacy. But superstitious terrors were not the only ones that they employed.

The mighty secret society called the Ku-Klux-Klan was justified by the only thing that can justify secret societies—*gross tyranny and the denial of plain human rights. The method they employed was the method so often employed by oppressed peoples and rarely without success—the method by which the Irish peasantry recovered their land. It was to put fear into the heart of the oppressor* [my emphasis, L.S.]. Prominent men, both black and white, who were identified with the [Reconstruction and carpetbaggism] evils which afflicted the State, were warned generally by a message signed "K.K.K." to make themselves scarce. If they neglected the warning they generally met a sudden and bloody end. At the same time the Klan unofficially tried and executed those criminals whom the official Government refused to suppress. These executions had under the circumstances a clear moral justification. Unfortunately it had the effect of familiarizing the people with the irregular execution of Negroes, and so paved the way for those "lynchings" for which, since the proper authorities are obviously able and willing to deal adequately with such crimes, no such defence can be set up.[199]

Both sides appealed to Grant, who had been elected President on the expiration of Johnson's term in 1868.

Had he been still the Grant of Appomattox and of the healing message to which reference has already been made, no man would have been better fitted to mediate between the sections and to cover with his protection those who had surrendered to his sword. But Grant was now a mere tool in the hands of the [then Left-wing] Republican politicians, and those politicians were determined that the atrocious [far Left] system should be maintained. They had not even the excuse of fanaticism. [South-hating Yankee socialist Thaddeus] Stevens was dead; he had lived just long enough to see his [radical Left] policy established, not long enough to see it imperilled. [Charles] Sumner still lived, but he had quarrelled with Grant and lost much of his influence. *The men who surrounded the President cared little enough for the Negro. Their resolution to support African rule in the South depended merely upon the calculation that so long as it endured the reign of the [then Left-wing] Republican party and consequently their own professional interests were safe* [my emphasis, L.S.].[200] A special Act of Congress was passed to put down the Ku-Klux-Klan, and the victorious army of the Union was again sent South to carry it into execution. But this time it found an enemy more invulnerable than Lee had been—invulnerable because invisible. The whole white population was in the conspiracy and kept its secrets. The army met with no overt resistance with which it could deal, but the silent terrorism went on. The trade of "Carpet-bagger" became too dangerous. The ambitious Negro was made to feel that the price to be paid for his privileges was a high one. Silently State after State was wrested from Negro rule.

Later the Ku-Klux-Klan—for such is ever the peril of Secret Societies and the great argument against them when not demanded by imperative necessity—began to abuse its power. Reputable people dropped out of it, and traitors [that is, imposters] were found in its ranks. About 1872 it disappeared [Nathan Bedford Forrest closed it down in 1869]. But its work was done.[201] In the great majority of the Southern States the voting power of the Negro was practically eliminated. Negroid Governments survived in three only—South Carolina, Florida, and Louisiana. For these the end came four years later.

The professional [Liberal] politicians of the North, whose motive for supporting the indefensible [Left-wing Republican] *régime* established by the Reconstruction Act has already been noted, used, of course, the "atrocities" of the Ku-Klux-Klan as electioneering material in the North. "Waving the bloody shirt," it was called. But the North was getting tired of it, and was beginning to see that *the condition of things in the conquered States was a national disgrace* [my emphasis, L.S.]. A [then Conservative] Democratic House of Representatives had been chosen, and it looked as if the [then Conservative] Democrats would carry the next Presidential election [with Conservative Democrat Samuel J. Tilden of New York as their candidate]. In fact they did carry it. But fraudulent returns were sent in by the three remaining Negro Governments, and these gave the [then Liberal] Republicans a majority of one in the Electoral College. A Commission of Enquiry was demanded and appointed, but it was packed by the Republicans and showed itself as little scrupulous as the scoundrels who administered the "reconstructed" States. Affecting a sudden zeal for State Rights, it declared itself incompetent to inquire into the circumstances under which the returns were made. It accepted them on the word of the State authorities and declared [Rutherford B.] Hayes, the Republican candidate, elected.

It was a gross scandal, but it put an end to a grosser one. Some believe that there was a bargain whereby the election of Hayes should be acquiesced in peaceably on condition that the Negro Governments were not further supported. It is equally possible that Hayes felt his moral position too weak to continue a policy of oppression in the South. At any rate, that policy was not continued. Federal support was withdrawn from the remaining Negro Governments, and they fell without a blow. *The second rebellion of the South had succeeded where the first had failed* [my emphasis, L.S.]. Eleven years after Lee had surrendered to Grant at Appomattox, Grant's successor in the Presidency [Hayes] surrendered to the ghost of Lee.

Negro rule was at an end. But the Negro remained, and the problem which his existence presented was, and is, to-day [1919], further from solution that when Lincoln signed the Emancipation Proclamation. The signs of the Black Terror are still visible everywhere in the South. They are visible in the political solidarity of those Southern States—and only of those States—which underwent the hideous ordeal, what American politicians call "the solid South." All white men, whatever their opinions, must vote together, lest by their division the Negro should again creep in and regain his supremacy. They are visible in those strict laws of segregation *which show how much wider is the gulf between the races than it was under Slavery—when the children of the white slave-owner, in Lincoln's words, "romped freely with the little negroes"* [my emphasis, L.S.]. They are visible above all in acts of unnatural cruelty committed from time to time against members of the dreaded race. These things are inexplicable to those who do not know the story of the ordeal which the South endured, and cannot guess at the secret panic with which white men contemplate the thought of its return.

Well might [Thomas] Jefferson tremble for his country. The bill which the first [American] slave-traders [all Northern in origin] ran up is not yet paid.[202] Their dreadful legacy remains and may remain for generations to come a baffling and tormenting problem to every American who has a better head than Sumner's and a better heart than Legree's....[203] — CECIL EDWARD CHESTERTON, 1919

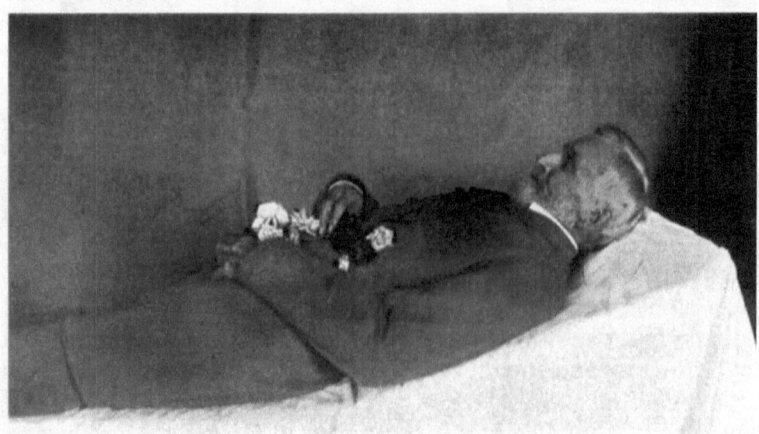

The body of Confederate president, Southern hero, and American patriot and statesman, Jefferson Davis, lying in state; from an unpublished photograph by E. F. Blake, December 1889.

CHAPTER 10
IN THE DAYS OF RECONSTRUCTION

FROM A 1920 ESSAY BY CONFEDERATE SOLDIER
Reverend James Hugh McNeilly

Confederate chaplain James Hugh McNeilly. A native of the Volunteer State, he served with the 49th Tennessee Regiment during Lincoln's War and was a strong Southern defender during and after Reconstruction.

☞ TO THOSE WHO PASSED THROUGH the experiences of Reconstruction in the South after the War between the States the memory of those evil days lies on heart and mind "with a weight heavy as frost and deep almost as life." They can never forget the cruel humiliations to which they were subjected, the stupendous iniquities perpetrated in the name of law, the pitiful and cowardly tyrannies inflicted on them by adventurers who followed in the wake of war and who were backed by all the powers of the [then Left-wing Republican] government. Well might they cry, "*Vae victis*" ("Woe to the vanquished"), *for the war for the Union turned out to be a war of conquest, which the conquerors used to despoil their victims not only of all political and civil rights, but of the remnants of their poverty which were left after the invading armies had plundered and burned their way through the whole land. It was called "Reconstruction." It was really destruction on a national scale* [my emphasis, L.S.].

It was the nightmare period of Southern history. A radical and fanatical [socialist and communist] majority in the United States Congress, moved and inspired by leaders who were themselves the embodiment of frenzied and malignant hatred of the South, trampled on and flouted the very foundation principles of liberty and exercised a despotism as brutal as the oppression of Turk or Russian. The coryphaeus [leader] of this Congressional chorus was Hon. Thaddeus Stevens, ably assisted by the Hon. John Sherman. It was the deliberate attempt of abolitionism to destroy every vestige of a noble civilization and to place the ignorance and stupidity of the negro over the culture and refinement of Southern whites. Such an effort was bound to fail in the long run, and it is to be said to the credit of the majority of the Southern people that as soon as they realized the real nature of Reconstruction they repudiated it. In 1876, by the aid of several Northern States, a President [Rutherford B. Hayes] was elected who was opposed to the Reconstruction measures. It is true that by the skill and craft of Hon. John Sherman the Presidency was stolen from [then Conservative Democrat] Mr. [Samuel J.] Tilden, but the President who was counted in was forced by public sentiment to nullify the very measures by which he got his office. *That rape of the Presidency was the end of Reconstruction, and that period of corruption, oppression, cruelty, and injustice is now generally recognized, North as well as South, as the darkest stain on the record of the United States* [my emphasis, L.S.].

It may be properly asked: "If it is all over and gone, why recall the story to a new generation which is free from its evils?" There are two answers: First, the truth of history demands and justice requires that the character and deeds of the Southern people of that day be vindicated against the falsehoods by which Northern speakers and writers try to justify or excuse the wrongs then forced on the South; and, second, the present generation is not free from the evils brought on by Reconstruction. Its fruit largely remains, and a knowledge of the source of present ills may help toward correcting them.

Reconstruction was the legitimate outcome of a war born of hatred, nursed in hypocrisy, waged with cruelty, and under the plea of Union ending in the subversion of the Constitution framed by the fathers of the Union. And so Reconstruction sowed the seeds of social and political ruin which to-day are springing up everywhere and threatening the very existence of government and of society [my emphasis, L.S.]. The spirit of those measures was a revolt against the divine order. It was putting ignorance and brutality in the seat of authority. It was making might the measure of right. It released the conquerors from all obligations of justice to the conquered. Under pretense of protection to the negro, it destroyed every safeguard of the white man. That spirit subtly infused itself into the new order of things and has made the United States more prolific and more tolerant of crime than any other civilized nation on earth. Disregard of law by railroads resulted in the death or wounding of over one hundred thousand persons in one year. The lawless liquor traffic brought misery to a million homes. Law-defying combinations of capital poison the food or increase the cost of living for the poor.

I believe that the South was fighting for the true principles of constitutional government—for liberty, righteousness, honor, truth, for racial integrity and Anglo-Saxon supremacy and a spiritual civilization, for the purest social order—and I believe it was better to have fought and lost than to have submitted to a false and wrong theory of government without a fight. Better to die for the right than to triumph in iniquity. *I therefore believe that Reconstruction was the application of the wrong principles, and the only hope for the country is to expose to the present generation the practical results in the past of those false principles in the hope that there may be a reaction in favor of the return to those principles that inspired the fathers of the republic in framing the original Constitution* [my emphasis, L.S.].

I write these "Recollections" as I wrote "Reminiscences of the War," in no spirit of hatred or vindictiveness against the Northern people, as individuals or as a section, but simply to show the difficulties we had to contend with in saving our civilization and to warn our people against those ideas and practices that were prevalent in Reconstruction days and which are now subtly permeating the spirit of the people North and South.

In these recollections I record not only what came under my own personal observation, but also things told me by trustworthy persons of their knowledge and experience. My object is not so much the criticism of those who oppressed us as to state the actual facts and set forth the conditions that really existed in those troublous times, for the facts themselves are sufficient to condemn.

I begin, therefore, in my own home. I was brought up in the little village of Charlotte, the county seat of Dickson County, Tenn.; but after the fall of Fort Donelson, in 1862, my father removed his family to his farm on Jones Creek, about six miles distant from the town.

I was paroled at Tuscaloosa, Ala., on the 20th of May, 1865, and it was near the middle of June when I reached home. I found that the Hon. W. G. Brownlow was Governor of the State. He had been for years before the war an influential [Leftist] figure in State politics. As editor of the Knoxville *Whig* he was one of the most fearless and able advocates of the Whig party [Liberal], particularly sharp and severe in his denunciations of the opposite party. My memory is that he had a public debate in Philadelphia with a noted abolitionist, and he did not come out second in the end of it. He was intensely devoted to the Union, and in the early days of the war he had suffered for his faith. The Reconstruction measures found in him a sympathetic supporter.

Among other things, I found that under the Brownlow administration all Confederates and their sympathizers were excluded from the ballot box. I don't know whether they could gain the right to vote by taking any kind of oath, for I made no experiment in that direction.

When I reached home nearly everything had been taken from the farm. The mules, horses, oxen, cows, hogs were all gone. A good small crop was growing, tended by my father and two younger brothers with a mule and a plow, loaned by my uncle, whose farm was off of the main road. The negroes were all gone except the cook, a faithful woman about forty years old. My father was a lawyer, but he could not practice his profession under the requirements of the Reconstruction acts. Everything was in confusion. No one knew just what to do. The amnesty proclamations of the President, Andrew Johnson, exempted most of the private citizens from prosecutions, but under the State administration there were some magistrates in the county, who were appointed by the Governor, as no election could be held, and they were anxious to show their patriotism by listening to and giving judgment on petty charges that were trumped up against Southern sympathizers. One of these magistrates was at the beginning of the war an ardent secessionist. The [radical Left] Freedman's Bureau agents were active in stirring up the negroes to bring charges against the white people. There was a general feeling of uneasiness, men not knowing when they might be arrested and brought before some government official to answer any sort of a charge that ignorance or malice might devise.

The negroes generally were eager to realize their freedom by leaving their old homes and setting up for themselves. A number of them gathered at White Bluff, a station on the railroad some ten miles from Charlotte, where there was a company of negro troops commanded by a white man; and to slap an impudent negro child or to dispute a negro's account brought a white man to answer at once before the Freedman's Bureau.

After the crop began to come in and father had succeeded in

getting his disabilities removed so as to practice his profession he soon got provisions for the family on hand to meet all their needs. Mother saw that our cook, Betty, was getting restless. The White Bluff negroes would meet her occasionally, and they had wonderful stories to tell of the sweets of liberty, of how they were making money by washing for the soldiers, and how all the men had government jobs. Visions of an easy life, with plenty of money easily earned, disturbed her mind. So mother said to her: "Betty, I see you want to set up for yourself, and you won't be satisfied until you have tried freedom. Go to White Bluff and pick you out a cabin, for the government has many empty ones at small rent, and I will furnish you provisions for six months until you see what you can do." Betty went off in high feather, and the mule drew a spring wagon in which she sat with a supply of bacon, meal, coffee and sugar, some jars of preserves, which she had helped to put up, and a little money for "extras." There was enough to have kept her comfortably for six months at least. She was welcomed tumultuously by her friends, who visited her often and always stayed to meals. She was hospitable, and they accepted her hospitality cheerfully, and at the end of six weeks "Sis" Betty's larder was exhausted. She told father a pitiful tale as he passed the station one day on his way to Nashville. As soon as he got back home the wagon was again sent to White Bluff, and Betty's wants were generously met, but in about a month she was again destitute. She was saying to the other darkies that she didn't have to work unless she wanted to. "As long as Marse Robert has anything my white folks ain't gwine to see me suffer." Again the wagon went to White Bluff, but this time to bring Betty home. It was too costly an experiment to care for her in freedom. She remained at home for some years, until an ancient colored swain, "a gander old and gray, took her for his mate," and she did his cooking and mending until his death. But until the day of her death she drew on my brothers and me when she was in need, and her drafts were always honored.

By the way, there was a little episode in Betty's life in our family which probably Northern people cannot understand, but which added a touch of peculiar tenderness to my mother's feeling for her.

During the winter of 1863-64, while father was a prisoner at Nashville, my mother and two little brothers were on the farm without any protector except Betty, the only one of the negroes who remained. At night before retiring mother usually went over the yard and outbuildings to see that everything was secure. One night as she was passing among the cabins, all of them except

Betty's being deserted, she heard very earnest conversation going on in a low tone in her cabin. Of course mother was alarmed, thinking there might be some plot brewing. She stepped lightly to the window, and, looking in, she saw by the light of a candle Betty on her knees praying most fervently, and the burden of the prayer was that the Lord would spare the lives of her three young [white] masters in the [Confederate] army and bring them home in safety. Mother slipped away and never told Betty that she had heard her prayer, but ever after that there was a tenderness in her dealing with the old servant and patience and charity in judging Betty's faults and infirmities, a tenderness all the greater, it may be, because one of the young masters never came back home, but sleeps in a soldier's grave on the battle field of Franklin.

While Betty was at White Bluff I went back and forth to Nashville frequently to supply one of the city Churches, and I never went without a commission from her, generally to get medicine—some advertised cure-all. She was very stout, weighing over two hundred pounds, and not very tall. She was sensitive as to her size and personal appearance. On one occasion as I stepped off of the train she met me, with her face greatly swollen from toothache. She certainly presented a funny aspect, with her cheek like a big, husky hemisphere, her eye nearly closed, her head tied up in a big red flannel cloth, the ends of the tie sticking nearly a foot above her head. I cried out in surprise: "Why, Betty, what in the world is the matter with your face?" There were several Yankee soldiers on the train, and they crowded to the car windows to see her. She answered me in a hoarse whisper with a lisp, "It thwaled" (it's swelled). One of the soldiers said, "Auntie, you look like you are swelled all over," and they all laughed. She regained her voice instantly, and the way she denounced all Yankees as "pore white trash who didn't have no feeling for colored folks" was a caution and showed that she was not duly thankful to the heroes who "died to make men free" as they went "marching through Georgia."

Indeed, one of the inconsistencies of negro character I noticed during those days of Reconstruction was that, while they stood politically with the Yankees and were ready to do their bidding, yet when they wanted a favor of a real kind they applied to the Southern man; and while they admired the Yankee people in mass as their deliverers, they yet had a contempt for the Yankee as an individual and down in their hearts they had a greater genuine respect, even love, for the old master than they had for the Northern leader of their party [Lincoln] [my emphasis, L.S.].

There was deep pathos in the patience and self-restraint of the majority of our people under the oppressions they endured. There was inspiration in the heroic courage with which they undertook to rebuild the wastes and repair the desolations of war. But in the midst of the tragedy of Reconstruction there were comic features that somewhat relieved the burdens of care. The makeshifts that took the place of comforts or conveniences of life were often so in contrast with the elegance or the handiness of the things of the old time that we had to laugh at our awkwardness in using them. Sometimes the effort to appear fine would put a shining silk hat over a coat shiny from long wear, or a handsome gown would be surmounted by headgear that was made over from some old bonnet that was resurrected from old finery of "before the war." This was in the country. Of course in the city it was easier to adapt one's dress to one's means and position. My Uncle Thomas McNeilly was a member of the State Senate in 1861. He was very determined to have our rights at any cost. He owned fifty or sixty negroes and two farms, besides his home in the village. He had all the conveniences of comfortable living, among other things fine saddle horses, a necessity in a country of rough roads. In his public speeches and in private talks he would not hear to compromise. If we would just stand firm, those Yankees would yield us all our rights. With him liberty with poverty was better than luxury and ease in subjection. I was enjoying my right of walking to town for lack of a horse, and sometimes I spent the night with him. One day he was going to his farm, two or three miles distant. He had been telling how much was still left to us. Even though we had lost so much, it was best to have made the fight for our rights. He called one of the negroes who remained with him to bring his horse to the door. Directly the darky came leading the most forlorn, lean, mangy-looking little mule that shambled along as if utterly discouraged. The saddle was a Mexican without skirts, and the seat was not padded. It nearly covered the little beast. As my uncle mounted, the linen duster he wore spread out to the tail of the mule, his feet came nearly to the ground, and a rather battered plug hat completed the ridiculous figure. I called to him as he rode off: "Uncle Tom, are you going after your rights on that little donkey?" It was a sore subject. He replied: "Jimmy, there is no sense in treating our misfortunes with levity." So I became duly solemn, but his daughters and I had a good laugh after he got out of hearing. It was well that we could get some fun out of our calamity.

But there were other things that came upon us far worse than having to ride on donkeys and wear patched clothes, and these other things were no laughing matter—*the humiliations and insults, the oppressions and injustices we had to endure at the hands of carpetbaggers and scalawags, who reveled in corruption and thievery while we were helpless* [my emphasis, L.S.]. These made the blood boil.

One of the demoralizing features of the times was the case with which men swore to loyalty [to the U.S.] in order to get pay for supplies taken or property destroyed by the Federal army. I remember seeing three commissioners going to and fro between the courthouse and the hotel. They were appointed to hear the claims of citizens and recommend or reject them. While I heard charges that *any claim would be allowed if the commissioners got a divide* [my emphasis, L.S.], yet the worst thing was that men who were notoriously disloyal to the United States would present claims that were false and then swear they were loyal.

In one case a claim agent came to my father proposing to collect his claim for forage taken and amounting to several hundred dollars. My father said: "But I can't swear that I was loyal." The fellow said: "You can swear that you were loyal to the true idea of the government." The reply was: "That would be a dodge. The [U.S.] oath means that I was loyal to the United States government at Washington, and you see every one of these receipts has on it 'This man has three sons in the Rebel army.' I was not loyal according to the terms of the oath." The man seemed astonished that anyone should stand on a quibble like that when money was at stake, and finally he proposed that if father would put the claims in his hands he himself would do all the necessary swearing, only he would sign father's name to the oath. When he made this proposition he was ordered out of the office instantly. But he seemed to think this was a foolish regard for a mere form. I am proud to say that there were but few in the old county who could be persuaded to violate conscience for the sake of money, although many of them had been forced to furnish supplies to the government. If I remember correctly, there was so little doing by the three commissioners that their daily tramp to and from the courthouse became a joke, and they were guyed about the hard work they had to do to earn their salaries. Still, there were several claimants who found out that they were Union men only after they found there was money in it.

One of the saddest things in the Reconstruction madness was that the Church tried to give the sanctions of religion to the efforts made to steal our property and to disfranchise us in favor of the carpetbagger, the scalawag, and the negro.

The General Assembly of the Presbyterian Church had been very bitter during the war denouncing the "rebellion," as they called it, and in advising and encouraging the [then Left-wing

Republican] government in all its measures, however cruel and oppressive. In May, 1865, the Assembly met in Pittsburgh, Pa., and passed a series of resolutions practically suspending all Presbyterian ministers from the ministry until they had repented of the sin of rebellion; and as those in the South almost to a man were strong supporters of the Confederacy, this action declared every pulpit vacant and meant that the North had the right to take over all our Churches, with their property. The Southern ministers in 1861 had protested against the Church taking sides in the political question dividing the country, and when the Assembly demanded that all ministers under its jurisdiction should support the cause of the Union those in the Confederate States withdrew and organized a separate Church. This action in Pittsburgh in 1865 was then a distinct refusal to acknowledge the Southern General Assembly as having any rights that the Northern body was bound to respect.

The First Presbyterian Church of Nashville was probably the first to resist the effort of the Northern Church to get possession. This Church had called the Rev. R. F. Bunting, the noted chaplain of the Texas Rangers, to be their pastor. He had gone to Ohio to meet his family and to bring them to Nashville, and it would be some weeks before he could enter on his work. In the meantime the Northern Board of Home Missions appointed a minister, a Mr. Brown. I think, to come to Nashville and take charge of the First Church. The elders of the Church had been notified of this appointment, and they were expecting him any day. But they determined that he should not have charge. So they employed me to hold the fort until Dr. Bunting came.

The church building had been used as a hospital by the Federal army. It required some time after getting possession for the main auditorium to be fitted for service, and the basement was used for worship. I had preached for four or five weeks when Dr. Bunting and Mr. Brown reached Nashville on the same day, and on Sunday morning both were present to take charge. I, of course, cheerfully stepped aside and was only an interested spectator, while the session settled the question between the two claimants of the pulpit. Dr. Bunting declined to argue the case, leaving it to the elders to say whether they would stand by their call. But the Northern claimant was rather persistent. There was a full meeting of the session. If my memory serves me, there were in the session then Dr. Paul F. Eve, Mr. Daniel F. Carter, Mr. John M. Hill, and two of the elders. Col. R. H. McEwen and Prof. Nathaniel Cross, had been very pronounced Union men, and to them was left the talking. No two men stood higher in the community for integrity and purity of character, and they had the confidence and the respect of the whole Church, a majority of which was warmly Southern. Besides, they thoroughly understood the principles of Presbyterian Church government.

They told Mr. Brown that the First Presbyterian Church had never given up its organization nor forfeited its rights, and it claimed the right, fundamental for Presbyterianism and dearest of all to Presbyterian people—the right to choose their own officers: that the congregation had freely chosen Dr. Bunting as pastor; that they could support him; therefore they declined any outside interference with their rights.

Now, while most of the ministers were away in the South during the war a small minority—five ministers—voted the Presbytery of Nashville into the Northern Assembly, and two of those ministers opposed the action, and only one of the five was a pastor. But Mr. Brown on this account insisted that the Northern Assembly had the right to declare all the Churches of the Presbytery vacant, take charge of them, and appoint supplies for them. The session was very courteous, but obdurate, and told him very positively that Dr. Bunting must have charge and would begin his work that morning.

After awhile, when Mr. Brown realized that his cause was hopeless, he seemed to lose patience and spoke with some heat to this effect: "Gentlemen, you seem to forget that the rebellion is crushed and that Nashville is in the hands of the Union army." I shall never forget the reply of Professor Cross. He was not a large man, slender, rather delicate in appearance, a gentleman of mild and refined manners, an elegant scholar, a modest, sincere, exemplary Christian. In all his talk he had been calm, courteous, quiet; but suddenly something happened to the surprise of Mr. Brown. Rising from his seat, drawing himself to his full stature, and looking straight into the eyes of the other, his own eyes blazing, with vibrant voice he said: "Do you mean to threaten us, sir? Is it your purpose to use military force to compel us to accept you as our pastor?" I have no idea that the minister intended a threat. He was only vexed at what seemed to him the Rebel spirit, and he did not think how his words sounded, and he hastened to disclaim any purpose to threaten. Colonel McEwen was as firm as Professor Cross, and the interview ended in Dr. Bunting's preaching that morning, and for several years he continued as pastor of the Church, until he was succeeded by the saintly Dr. Moore, of Richmond, Va.

The sequel of the rejection of Mr. Brown by the session was

told me by Mr. Andrew J. Smith, one of the deacons, with whom I was boarding. He spoke of it during the following weeks as of a thing he knew. He said that Mr. Brown went to [Union General] Gen. George H. Thomas, who was in command of the military department, and asked him to interfere in behalf of loyalty, telling the General that the spirit of rebellion was still strong in this Church, which had refused to receive him, although he was sent by the highest authority in the Church. The soldier was a just man and unwilling to act on an *ex parte* statement. He was anxious also to conciliate the Southern people. So he told the preacher that the military had no right to interfere with the ecclesiastical authority, that he had no knowledge of the questions at issue, and that he believed in leaving all such matters to the Church. It was reported that the minister was so persistent that he at last became offensive, intimating that the General's patriotism was at fault. And then the soldier grew indignant and told the preacher to go to that warm region from which he professed to save men and that it was not the business of the army to run the Churches.

Mr. Smith also told me that on the Sunday of the interview with the session Mr. Brown dined at Colonel McEwen's. Mrs. McEwen, known to her friends as "Aunt Hetty," was a devoted Unionist, as brave and true a woman as ever lived. She was also a woman of strong common sense and loved her Church as she loved her country. When the minister told his woes to her, she said: "If you want to preach the gospel, there is a great need here in Nashville, and you say your Board will support you. We do not need you in the First Church. Why not stay and gather a congregation from those who have no pastor?" But that was not what the brother was after. He came to get the large and influential First Church, and it was that or none. So he went back North a sadder if not a wiser man.[204] — REVEREND JAMES HUGH MCNEILLY, NASHVILLE, TENN., 1920

Bristol, Virginia.

THE STARS AND BARS.

First flag of the Confederate States, adopted by the Congress at Montgomery, Ala., and raised at the capitol, March 4, 1861, by the granddaughter of President John Tyler.

THE BATTLE FLAG.

Designed by General Beauregard, to avoid the resemblance of the Stars and Bars to the Stars and Stripes; adopted after the battle of First Manassas, and used thereafter in the army.

THE NATIONAL FLAG.

Adopted by the Congress of the Confederate States of America, May 1, 1863.

THE NATIONAL FLAG.

Adopted by the Congress March 4, 1865, the red stripe being added to the National Flag of 1863, because the latter, when furled, showed only white.

A Victorian era pictorial, with descriptions, of the First, Second and Third Confederate National Flags and the Confederate Battle Flag, used by the C.S. military.

CHAPTER 11
DESTRUCTION & RECONSTRUCTION

FROM AN 1879 BOOK BY CONFEDERATE GENERAL
Richard Taylor

INTRODUCTION
☛ DURING ALL THESE YEARS [1865-1877] THE conduct of the Southern people has been admirable. Submitting to the inevitable, they have shown fortitude and dignity, and rarely has one been found base enough to take wages of shame from the oppressor and maligner of his brethren. Accepting the harshest conditions and faithfully observing them, they have struggled in all honourable ways, and for what? For their slaves? Regret for their loss has neither been felt nor expressed. But they have striven for that which brought our forefathers to Runnymede [where the Magna Carta was signed in 1215], the privilege of exercising some influence in their own government.[205]

RECONSTRUCTION UNDER JOHNSON
☛ The following considerations induced me to make a pilgrimage to Washington [D.C.], where, by accident of fortune, I had a larger acquaintance with influential politicians than other Southern commanders. When the [Left-leaning] Whig party dissolved, most of its Northern members joined the [then Left-wing] Republicans, and now belonged to the reigning faction; and I had consorted with many of them while my father [Zachary Taylor] was President and afterward.

Mention has been made of the imprisonment of Governors [Charles] Clark and [Thomas Hill] Watts for adopting my advice, and it was but right for me to make an effort to have them released. Moreover, Jefferson Davis was a prisoner in irons, and it was known that his health was feeble. [Robert E.] Lee, [Joseph E.]

Confederate General Richard Taylor, son of U.S. President Zachary Taylor and brother of Sarah Knox Taylor—the first wife of Confederate President Jefferson Davis.

Johnston, and I, with our officers and men, were at large, protected by the terms of our surrenders—terms which [U.S.] General [Ulysses S.] Grant had honourably prevented the civil authorities from violating. If Mr Davis had sinned, we all were guilty, and I could not rest without making an attempt for his relief.

At the time it was understood that prisoners on parole should not change their residence without military permission, and leave to go to New York was asked and obtained of [Union] General [Edward R. S.] Canby. By steamer I reached that place in a week, and found that General [John A.] Dix had just been relieved by [Union] General [Joseph] Hooker, to whom I at once reported. He uttered a shout of welcome (we were old acquaintances), declared that he was more pleased to see me than to see a church (which was doubtless true), made hospitable suggestions of luncheon, champagne, etc., and gave me a permit to go to Washington, regretting that he could not keep me with him. A warmhearted fellow is "fighting Joe," who carried on war like a soldier.

In Washington, at Willard's—a huge inn, filled from garret to cellar with a motley crowd—an acquaintance whom I chanced to meet informed me that a recent disturbance had induced the belief of the existence of a new plot for assassination, and an order had been published forbidding rebels to approach the capital without the permission of the War Secretary. Having been at sea for a week, I knew nothing of this, and Hooker had not mentioned it when he gave me the permit to come to Washington. My informant apprehended my arrest, and kindly undertook to protect me. Through his intervention I received from the President, Andrew Johnson, permission to stay or go where I chose, with an invitation to visit him at a stated time.

Presenting myself at the "White House," I was ushered in to the President—a saturnine man, who made no return to my bow, but after looking at me, asked me to take a seat. Upon succeeding to power, Mr. Johnson breathed fire and hemp against the South, proclaimed that he would make treason odious by hanging traitors, and ordered the arrest of General Lee and others, when he was estopped by the action of General Grant. He had now somewhat abated his wolfish desire for vengeance, and asked many questions about the condition of the South, temper of the people, etc. I explained the conduct of Governors Clark and Watts, how they were imprisoned for following my advice, submitted to and approved by General Canby, who would hardly have abetted a new rebellion; and he made memoranda of their cases, as well as of those of many other prisoners, confined in different forts from Boston to Savannah, all of whom were released within a short period. Fearing to trespass on his time, I left with a request that he would permit me to call again, as I had a matter of much interest to lay before him, and was told the hours at which I would be received.

Thence to the Secretary of State, Mr. [William H.] Seward, who in former Whig times, as Senator from New York, had been a warm supporter of my father's administration. He greeted me cordially, and asked me to dine. A loin of veal was the *pièce de résistance* of his dinner, and he called attention to it as evidence that he had killed the fatted calf to welcome the returned prodigal. Though not entirely recovered from the injuries received in a fall from his carriage and the wounds inflicted by the knife of [Lewis] Payne, he was cheerful, and appeared to sympathise with the objects of my mission—at least, so far as I could gather his meaning under the cloud of words with which he was accustomed to cover the slightest thought. One or two other members of the Cabinet, to whom Mr. Seward presented me, were also favourably inclined. One, the War Secretary [Edwin M. Stanton], I did not meet. A spy under [U.S. President James] Buchanan, a tyrant under Lincoln, and a traitor to [U.S. President Andrew] Johnson, this man was as cruel and crafty as [Roman Emperor] Domitian. I never saw him. In the end, conscience, long dormant, came as Electro, and he was not; and the temple of Justice, on whose threshold he stood, escaped profanation.

In a second interview, President Johnson heard the wish I had so much at heart, permission to visit Jefferson Davis. He pondered for some time, then replied that I must wait and call again.

Meantime an opportunity to look upon the amazing spectacle presented by the dwellers at the capital was afforded. The things seen by the Pilgrims in a dream were at this Vanity Fair visible in the flesh:

"all such merchandise sold as houses, lands, trades, places, honours, preferments, states, lusts, pleasures; and delights of all sorts, as bawds, wives, husbands, children, masters, servants, lives, blood, bodies, souls, greenbacks, pearls, precious stones, and what not."[206]

The eye of the inspired tinker had pierced the darkness of two hundred years, and seen what was to come. The martial tread of hundreds of volunteer generals, just disbanded, resounded in the streets. Gorged with loot, they spent it as lavishly as Morgan's buccaneers after the sack of Panama. Their women sat at meat or walked the highways, resplendent in jewels, spoil of Southern matrons. The camp-followers of the army were here in high carnival, and in character and numbers rivalled the attendants of [King] Xerxes. Courtesans [prostitutes] swarmed everywhere, about the inns, around the Capitol, in the antechambers of the "White House," and were brokers for the transactions of all business. Of a tolerant disposition, and with a wide experience of earthly wickedness, I did not feel called upon to cry aloud against these enormities, remembering the fate of Faithful; but I had some doubts concerning divine justice; for why were the "cities of the plain" overthrown and this place suffered to exist?

The officers of the army on duty at Washington were very civil to me, especially General Grant, whom I had known prior to and during the Mexican [American] war as a modest, amiable, but by no means promising, lieutenant in a marching regiment. He came frequently to see me, was full of kindness, and anxious to promote my wishes. His action in preventing violation of the terms of surrender, and a subsequent report that he made of the condition of the South—a report not at all pleasing to the radicals [the socialists and communists in the then Left-wing Republican Party]—endeared him to all Southern men. Indeed, he was in a position to play a *rôle* second only to that of [George] Washington, who founded the Republic; for he had the power to restore it. His bearing and conduct at this time were admirable, modest, and generous; and I talked much with him of the noble and beneficent work before him. While his heart seemed to respond, he declared his ignorance of and distaste for politics and politicians, with which and whom he intended to have nothing to do, but confine himself to his duties of commander-in-chief of the army. Yet he expressed a desire for the speedy restoration of good feeling between the sections, and an intention to advance it in all proper ways. We shall see when and under what influences he adopted other views.

The President [Johnson] put me off from day to day, receiving me to talk about Southern affairs, but declining to give an answer to my requests. I found that he always postponed action, and was of an obstinate, suspicious temper. Like a badger, one had to dig him out of his hole; and he was ever in one except when on the hustings addressing the crowd. Of humble birth, a tailor by trade, nature gave him a strong intellect; and he had learned to read after his marriage. He had acquired much knowledge of the principles of government, and made himself a fluent speaker, but could not rise above the level of the class in which he was born and to which he always appealed. He well understood the few subjects laboriously studied, and affected to despise other knowledge, while suspicious that those possessing such would take advantage of him. Self-educated men, as they are called, deprived of the sidelight thrown on a particular subject by instruction in cognate matters, are narrow and dogmatic, and, with an uneasy consciousness of ignorance, soothe their own vanity by underrating the studies of others. To the vanity of this class he added that of the demagogue (I use the term in its better sense), and called the wise policy left him by his predecessor "my policy." Compelled to fight his way up from obscurity, he had contracted a dislike of those more favoured of fortune, whom he was in the habit of calling "the slave-aristocracy," and became incapable of giving his confidence to any one, even to those on whose assistance he relied in a contest, just now beginning, with the Congress.

President Johnson never made a dollar by public office, abstained from quartering a horde of connections on the Treasury, refused to uphold rogues in high places, and had too just a conception of the dignity of a chief magistrate to accept presents. It may be said that these are humble qualities for a citizen to boast the possession of by a President of the United States. As well claim respect for a woman of one's family on the ground that she has preserved her virtue. Yet all whose eyes were not blinded by partisanship, whose manhood was not emasculated by servility, would in these last years have welcomed the least of them as manna in the desert.

The President, between whom and the Congressional leaders the seeds of discord were already sown, dallied with me from day to day, and at length said that it would spare him embarrassment if I could induce [South-hating Yankee radicals] Thaddeus] Stevens, [Henry Winter] Davis, and others of the House, and [Charles] Sumner of the Senate, to recommend the permission to visit Jefferson Davis; and I immediately addressed myself to this unpleasant task.

Thaddeus Stevens received me with as much civility as he was capable of. Deformed in body and temper like [Shakespeare's monstrous character] Caliban, this was the Lord Hate-good [a John Bunyan character] of the fair; but he was frankness itself. *He wanted no restoration of the Union under the Constitution, which he called a worthless bit of old parchment. The white people of the South ought never again to be trusted with power; for they would inevitably unite with the Northern "Copperheads" and control the Government. The only sound policy was to confiscate the lands and divide them among the negroes, to whom, sooner or later, suffrage must be given. Touching the matter in hand, Johnson was a fool to have captured Davis, whom it would have been wiser to assist in escaping* [my emphasis, L.S.]. Nothing would be done with him, as the executive had only pluck enough to hang two poor devils such as [Confederate Captain Henry] Wirz and Mrs. [Mary] Surratt. Had the leading traitors been promptly strung up, well; but the time for that had passed. (Here, I thought, he looked lovingly at my neck, as Petit André was wont to do at those of his merry-go-rounds.) He concluded by saying that it was silly to refuse me permission to visit Jefferson Davis; but he would not say so publicly, as he had no desire to relieve Johnson of responsibility.

There was no excuse for longer sporting with this radical Amaryllis either in shade or in sunshine; so I sought Henry Winter Davis. Like the fallen angel, Davis preferred to rule in hell rather than serve in heaven or in earth. With the head of Medusa and the eye of the Basilisk, he might have represented Shiva in a Hindoo temple, and was even more inaccessible to sentiment than Thaddeus Stevens. Others, too numerous and too insignificant to particularise, were seen. These were the cuttlefish of the party, whose appointed duty it was to obscure popular vision by clouds of loyal declamation. As Sicilian banditti prepare for robberies and murders by pious offerings on shrines of favourite saints, these brought out the altar of the "nation," and devoted themselves afresh, whenever "Crédits Mobiliers" and kindred enormities were afoot, and *sharpened every question of administration, finance, law, taxation, on the grindstone of sectional hate* [my emphasis, L.S.]. So sputtering tugs tow from her moorings the stately ship, to send her forth to winds and waves of ocean, caring naught for the cargo with which she is freighted, but, grimy in zeal to earn fees, return to seek another.

Hopeless of obtaining assistance from such statesmen, I visited Mr. Charles Sumner, Senator from Massachusetts, who received me pleasantly. A rebel, a slave-driver, and, without the culture of Boston, ignorant, I was an admirable vessel into which he could pour the inexhaustible stream of his acquired eloquence. I was delighted to listen to beautiful passages from the classic as well as modern poets, dramatists, philosophers, and orators, and recalled the anecdote of the man sitting under a fluent divine, who could not refrain from muttering, "That is Jeremy Taylor; that, South; that, Barrow," etc. It was difficult to suppress the thought, while Mr. Sumner was talking, "That is Burke, or Howard, Wilberforce, Brougham, Macaulay, Harriet Beecher Stowe, Exeter Hall," etc.; but I failed to get down to the particular subject that interested me. The nearest approach to the practical was his disquisition on negro suffrage, which he thought should be accompanied by education. I ventured to suggest that negro education should precede suffrage, observing that some held the opinion that the capacity of the white race for government was limited, although accumulated and transmitted through many centuries. He replied that "the ignorance of the negro was due to the tyranny of the whites," which appeared in his view to dispose of the question of the former's incapacity. He seemed overeducated—had retained, not digested his learning; and beautiful flowers of literature were attached to him by filaments of memory, as lovely orchids to sapless sticks. Hence he failed to understand the force of language, and became the victim of his own metaphors, mistaking them for facts. He had the irritable vanity and weak nerves of a woman, and was bold to rashness in speculation, destitute as he was of the ordinary masculine sense of responsibility. Yet I hold him to have been the purest and most sincere man of his party. A lover, nay, a devotee of liberty, he thoroughly understood that it could only be preserved by upholding the supremacy of civil law, and would not sanction the garrison methods of President Grant. Without vindictiveness, he forgave his enemies as soon as they were overthrown; and one of the last efforts of his life was to remove from the flag of a common country all records of victories that perpetuated the memory of civil strife.

 Foiled in this direction, I worried [pestered] the President [Johnson], as old Mustard would a stot, until he wrote the permission so long solicited. By steamer from Baltimore I went down Chesapeake Bay, and arrived at Fortress Monroe [Hampton, VA] in the early morning. [Union] General [Henry S.] Burton, the commander, whose civility was marked, and who bore himself like a gentleman and soldier, received me on the dock and took me to his quarters to breakfast, and to await the time to see Mr. Davis.

 It was with some emotion that I reached the casemate in which Mr. Davis was confined. There were two rooms, in the outer of which, near the entrance, stood a sentinel, and in the inner was Jefferson Davis. We met in silence, with grasp of hands. After an interval he said, "This is kind, but no more than I expected of you." Pallid, worn, grey, bent, feeble, suffering from inflammation of the eyes, he was a painful sight to a friend. He uttered no plaint, and made no allusion to the irons (which had been removed); said the light kept all night in his room hurt his eyes a little, and, added to the noise made every two hours by relieving the sentry, prevented much sleep; but matters had changed for the better since the arrival of General Burton, who was all kindness, and strained his orders to the utmost in his behalf. I told him of my reception at Washington by the President, Mr. Seward, and others; of the attentions of [Union] Generals Grant and [Andrew A.] Humphreys, who promoted my wish to see him, and that with such aid I was confident of obtaining permission for his wife [Varina] to stay with him. I could solicit favours for him, having declined any for myself. Indeed, the very accident of position that enabled me to get access to the governing authorities, made indecent even the supposition of my acceptance of anything personal while a single man remained under the ban for serving the Southern cause; and therefore I had no fear of misconstruction. Hope of meeting his family cheered him much; and he asked questions about the condition and prospects of the South, which I answered as favourably as possible, passing over things that would have grieved him. In some way he had learned of attacks on his character and conduct, made by some Southern curs, thinking to ingratiate themselves with the ruling powers. I could not deny this, but remarked that the curse of unexpected defeat and suffering was to develop the basest passions of the human heart. Had he escaped out of the country, it was possible he might have been made a scapegoat by the Southern people, and great as were the sufferings that he had endured, they were as nothing to coward stabs from beloved hands. The attacks mentioned were few, and too contemptible for notice; for now his calamities had served to endear him to all. I think that he derived consolation from this view.

 The day passed with much talk of a less disturbing character, and in the evening I returned to Baltimore and Washington. After some delay Mr. Davis's family was permitted to join him, and he speedily recovered strength. Later I made a journey or two to Richmond, Virginia, on business connected with his trial, then supposed to be impending.

 The slight service, if simple discharge of duty can be so called, I was enabled to render Mr. Davis, was repaid ten thousand-fold. In the month of March [16,] 1875, my devoted wife [Louise Marie Myrthé Bringier] was released from suffering, long and patiently endured, originating in grief for the loss of her children and exposure during the war. Smitten by this calamity, to which all that had gone before seemed as blessings, I stood by her coffin, ere it was closed, to look for the last time upon features that death had respected and restored to their girlish beauty. Mr. Davis came to my side, and stooped reverently to touch the fair brow, when the tenderness of his heart overcame him and he burst into tears. His example completely unnerved me for the time, but was of service in the end. For many succeeding days he came to me, and was as gentle as a young mother with her suffering infant. Memory will ever recall Jefferson Davis as he stood with me by the coffin.

Duty to imprisoned friends and associates discharged, I returned to New Orleans, and remained for some weeks, when an untoward event occurred, productive of grave consequences. The saints and martyrs who have attained worldly success have rarely declined to employ the temporal means of sinners. While calling on Hercules, they put their own shoulders to the wheel, and, in the midst of prayer, keep their powder dry. To prepare for the re-election of President Lincoln in 1864, *pretended State governments had been set up by the Federal [U.S.] military in several Southern States, where fragments of territory were occupied. In the event of a close election in the North, the electoral votes in these manufactured States would be under the control of the executive authority, and serve to determine the result. For some years the Southern States were used as thimble-riggers use peas: now they were under the cup of the Union, and now they were out* [my emphasis, L.S.]. During his reign in New Orleans, the Federal General [Nathaniel P.] Banks had prepared a Louisiana pea for the above purpose.

At this time negro suffrage, as yet an unaccomplished purpose, was in the air, and the objective point of Radical [that is, socialist-communist] effort. To aid the movement, surviving accomplices of the Banks fraud were instigated to call a "State Convention" in Louisiana, though with no more authority so to do than they had to call the British Parliament. The people of New Orleans regarded the enterprise as those of London did the proposed meeting of tailors in Tooley Street; and just before this debating society was to assemble, the Federal commander, General [Philip H.] Sheridan, selected especially to restrain the alleged turbulent population of the city, started on an excursion to Texas, proving that he attached no importance to the matter, and anticipated no disturbance.

Living in close retirement, I had forgotten all about the "Convention." Happening to go to the centre of the town, from my residence in the upper suburb, the day on which it met, on descending from the carriage of the tramway I heard pistol-shots and saw a crowd of roughs, Arabs, and negroes running across Canal Street. I walked in the direction of the noise to inquire the cause of excitement, as there was nothing visible to justify it. The crowd seemed largely composed of boys of from twelve to fifteen, and negroes. I met no acquaintance, and could obtain no information, when a negro came flying past, pursued by a white boy, certainly not above fifteen years of age, with a pistol in hand. I stopped the boy without difficulty, and made him tell what he was up to. He said the niggers were having a meeting at Mechanics' Institute to take away his vote. When asked how long he had enjoyed that inestimable right of a freeman, the boy gave it up, pocketed his "Derringer," and walked off.

By this time the row appeared to be over, so I went on my way without seeing the building called Mechanics' Institute, as it was around the corner near which the boy was stopped. Speedily the town was filled with excitement; and [Union General Absalom] Baird, the Federal commander in the absence of Sheridan, occupied the streets with troops and arrested the movements of citizens. Many poor negroes had been killed most wantonly, indignation ran high among decent people, and the perpetrators of the bloody deeds deserved and would have received swift, stern punishment had civil law been permitted to act. But this did not suit the purposes of the [Republican] Radicals, who rejoiced as [Spanish Grand Inquisitor Tomás] Torquemada might have done when the discovery of a score of heretics furnished him an excuse to torment and destroy a province. *Applying the theory of the detective police, that among the beneficiaries of crime must be sought the perpetrators, one would conclude that the Radical leaders [that is, the socialists and communists in the then Left-wing Republican Party] prompted the assassination of Lincoln and the murder of negroes; for they alone derived profit from these acts* [my emphasis, L.S.].

[Editor's note: *General Taylor wrote the following paragraph as sarcasm.* L.S.] From this time forth the entire white race of the South devoted itself to the killing of negroes. It appeared to be an inherent tendency in a slavedriver to murder a negro. It was a law of his being, as of the monkey's to steal nuts, and could not be resisted. Thousands upon thousands were slain. Favourite generals kept lists in their pockets, proving time, place, and numbers, even to the smallest piccaninny [a black child]. Nay, such was the ferocity of the slave-drivers, that unborn infants were ripped from their mothers' wombs. Probably these sable Macduffs were invented to avenge the wrongs of their race on tyrants protected by satanic devices from injury at the hands of Africans of natural birth. Individual effort could not suffice the rage for slaughter, and the ancient order of "assassins" was revived, with an "Old Man" of the swamps at its head. Thus "Ku Klux Klan" originated, and covered the land with a network of crime. Earnest, credulous women in New England had their feelings lacerated by these stories, in which they as fondly believed as their foremothers in Salem witches.

Scenes showing black supremacy in the 1870s. Reconstruction failed in great part because its primary tenets and policies could not stand then anymore than they could if they were enacted across the South today. In essence, the basic foundation of the socialist and communist-inspired Reconstruction program was black supremacy, a racist ideology that violates reason, the Constitution, and Christian teaching (Galatians 3:28).

As crocodiles conceal their prey until it becomes savoury and tender and ripe for eating, so *the Radicals [Republican socialists and communists] kept these dark corpses [that is, fabricated stories] to serve up to the public when important elections approached, or some especial villainy was to be enacted by the Congress* [my emphasis, L.S.]. People who had never been south of the Potomac and Ohio rivers knew all about this Ku Klux Klan; but I failed, after many inquiries, to find a single man in the South who ever heard of it, saving in newspapers. Doubtless there were many acts of violence. When ignorant negroes, instigated by pestilent [Left-wing] emissaries, went beyond endurance, the whites killed them; and this was to be expected. The breed to which these whites belong has for eight centuries been the master of the earth wherever it has planted its foot. A handful conquered and holds in subjection the crowded millions of India. Another and smaller bridles the fierce Caffre tribes of South Africa. Place but a score of them on the middle course of the Congo, and they will rule unless exterminated; and all the armies and all the humanitarians cannot change this, until the appointed time arrives for Ham to dominate Japhet.

Two facts may here be stated. Just in proportion as the whites recovered control of their local governments, in that proportion negroes ceased to be killed; and when it was necessary to Radical success to multiply negro votes, though no census was taken, formal statistics were published to prove large immigration of negroes into the very districts of slaughter. Certainty of death could not restrain the coloured lambs [uneducated blacks], impelled by an uncontrollable ardour to vote the [Republicans'] Radical [socialist-communist] ticket, from travelling to the wolves. Such devotion deserved the tenderest consideration of Christian men and women, and all means of protection and loving care were due to this innocent, credulous race. A great bureau, the Freedmen's, was established; and in connection with it, at the seat of government, a bank. It was of importance to teach the freedmen, unused to responsibility, industry and economy; and the bank was to encourage these virtues by affording a safe place of deposit for their small savings. To make assurance doubly sure, the "Christian soldier of the United States army" was especially selected to keep the money, and he did—so securely, in point of fact, that it is to be apprehended the unfortunate depositors will never see it more. After so brilliant an experience in banking, prudence might have suggested to this officer the wisdom of retiring from public view. Fortune is sometimes jealous of great reputations and fresh laurels. The success of his first speech prevented "Single-speech Hamilton" from rising again in the House of Commons; Frederick [the Great] failed to repeat [the Battle of] Rossbach, and Napoleon [III], [the Battle of] Austerlitz; but the "Christian soldier" rushed on his fate, and met it at the hands of the Nez Percés. The profound strategy, the skilful tactics, the ready valour that had extinguished bank balances, all failed against this wily foe [that is, the socialists and communists of the then Left-wing Republican Party].

While the excitement growing out of the untoward event mentioned was at its height, President [Andrew] Johnson summoned me to Washington, where I explained all the circumstances, as far as I knew them, of the recent murders, and urged him to send [Union] General [Winfield S.] Hancock to command in New Orleans. He was sent, and immediately restored order and confidence. A gentleman, one of the most distinguished and dashing officers of the United States army, General Hancock recognises both the great duties of a soldier of the Republic—to defend its flag and obey its laws, discharging the last with a fidelity equal to his devotion to the first in front of battle.

The contest between the [U.S.] Congress and the President now waxed fierce, and Thaddeus Stevens, from his place in the House, denounced "the man at the other end of the avenue." The President [Johnson] had gone back to wise, lawful methods, and desired to restore the Union under the Constitution; and in this he was but following the policy declared in the last public utterance by President Lincoln. Mr. Johnson could establish this fact by members of his predecessor's Cabinet whom he had retained, and thus strengthen his position; but his vanity forbade him, so he called it "my policy," as if it were something new.

At his instance I had many interviews with him, and consulted influential men from different parts of the country. His Secretary of War [Edwin M. Stanton] was in close alliance with his enemies in the Congress, and constantly betraying him. This was susceptible of proof, and I so informed the President, and pointed out that, so far from assisting the people of the South, he was injuring them by inaction; for the Congress persecuted them to worry him. He was President and powerful; they were weak and helpless. In truth, President Johnson, slave to his own temper and appetites, was unfit to control others.

General Grant yet appeared to agree with me about "reconstruction," as it was called; and I was anxious to preserve good feeling on his part toward the President. In the light of subsequent events, it is curious to recall the fact that he complained of Stanton's retention in the Cabinet, because the latter's greed of power prevented the Commander-in-Chief of the army from controlling the most minute details without interference. I urged this on the President as an additional motive for dismissing his War Secretary, and replacing him by some one agreeable to General Grant; but all in vain. This official "old man of the sea" kept his seat on the Presidential neck, never closing crafty eye nor traitorous mouth, and holding on with the tenacity of an octopus.

Many moderate and whilom [that is, erstwhile] influential Republicans determined to assemble [in 1866] in convention at Philadelphia, and invited delegates from all parts, North and South, to meet them. The object was to promote good feeling and an early restoration of the Union, and give aid to the President in his struggle with extremists. Averse to appearing before the public, I was reluctant to go to this Convention; but the President, who felt a deep interest in its success, insisted, and I went. It was largely attended, and by men who had founded and long led the Free-soil party. Ex-members of Lincoln's first Cabinet, senators and members of the Congress, editors of Republican [Left-wing] newspapers (among whom was Henry J. Raymond, the ablest political editor of the day, and an eminent member of Congress as well), Southern men who had fought for the Confederacy, were there. Northern Republicans [then Liberals] and Democrats [then Conservatives], long estranged, buried the political hatchet and met for a common purpose, to restore the Union. Negro-worshippers from Massachusetts and slave-drivers from South Carolina entered the vast hall arm in arm. The great meeting rose to its feet, and walls and roof shook with applause. [Union] General John A. Dix of New York called the Convention to order, and, in an eloquent and felicitous speech, stated the objects of the assembly—to renew fraternal feeling between the sections, heal the wounds of war, obliterate bitter memories, and restore the Union of the fathers. Senator [James R.] Doolittle of Wisconsin was chosen permanent president, and patriotic resolutions were adopted by acclamation. All this was of as little avail as the waving of a lady's fan against a typhoon. Radical [socialist-communist] wrath uprose and swept these Northern men out of political existence, and they were again taught the lesson that is ever forgotten—namely, that it is an easy task to inflame the passions of the multitude, an impossible one to arrest [subdue] them. From selfish ambition, from thoughtless zeal, from reckless partisanship, from the low motives governing demagogues in a country of universal suffrage, men are ever sowing the wind, thinking they can control the whirlwind; and the story of the Gironde and the Mountain [the Girondins and La Montagne, two political groups that operated in France during the French Revolution] has been related in vain.

The President [Johnson] was charmed with the Convention. Believing the people—his god—to be with him, his crest rose, and he felt every inch a President. Again I urged him to dismiss his War Secretary [Stanton] and replace Mr. Seward, Secretary of State—now in disfavour with his own creation, the Radical [socialist-communist] party—by [Union] General Dix, who was rewarded for his services at Philadelphia by the appointment of Naval Officer at New York. He was an exception to the rule above mentioned. A more cautious pilot than Palinurus, this respectable person is the "Vicar of Bray" of American politics; and like that eminent divine, his creeds sit so lightly as to permit him to take office under all circumstances. Secretary of the Treasury in the closing weeks of President Buchanan, he aroused the North by sending his immortal despatch to the commander of a revenue cutter: "If any man attempts to haul down the American flag, shoot him on the spot." This bespoke the heart of the patriot, loving his country's banner, and the arm of the hero, ready to defend it; and, clad in this armour of proof, he has since been invulnerable. The President took kindly to the proposition concerning General Dix, and I flattered myself that it would come off, when suddenly the General was appointed Minister Plenipotentiary to France. I imagine that Mr. Seward had got wind of the project and hurried Dix out of the way. Thus, in a few days General Dix had the offer of the Netherlands, Naval Office, and France. "Glamis, and thane of Cawdor;" and his old age is yet so green, mayhap "the greatest is behind."

To air his eloquence and enlighten the minds of his dear people, the President made a tour through the North and West, in which his conduct and declarations were so extraordinary as to defeat any hopes of success for "my policy."

A circumstance connected with the [the then Left-wing Republicans' 1866] Philadelphia Convention made an impression on me at the time. [Liberal-leaning Yankee] Mr. [Henry Jarvis] Raymond was [a cofounder of the then Left-wing Republican Party and a cofounder and] editor of the [Left-leaning] New York *Times*, the most powerful [then Liberal] Republican journal in the North. Among many who had gained large wealth by speculations during the war was Mr. Leonard Jerome, a Republican [then a Liberal] in politics. This gentleman spent his fortune so lavishly that his acquaintances and the public shared its enjoyment. With other property, Mr. Jerome owned the controlling interest in the *Times*, then very valuable. Dining in New York with him and Mr. Raymond, the latter told me it was useless to support the President [Johnson], who was daily becoming more unpopular, and that the circulation and influence of his paper were rapidly diminishing in consequence of his adherence to "my policy." Whereupon Mr. Jerome replied:

> "I know but little about politics; but if you think it right to stand by the President, I will pay all losses that the *Times* may suffer to the other proprietors."

This was unselfish and patriotic; and I record it with the more pleasure, because Mr. Jerome has lost much of his wealth, and, I fear, like many another Timon [that is, respected individuals], some friends with it.

After this period I saw little of President Johnson, who fought his fight in his own way, had his hands completely tied, and barely escaped impeachment; the Congress meanwhile making a whipping-post of the South, and inflicting upon it every humiliation that malignity could devise.²⁰⁷

RECONSTRUCTION UNDER GRANT

☛ Before the conventions to nominate candidates for the Presidency met in 1868, I had much intercourse with [Union] General [Ulysses S.] Grant, and found him ever modest and determined to steer clear of politics, or at least not permit himself to be used by partisans; and I have no doubt that he was sincere. But the Radical [that is, the socialists and communists in the then Left-wing Republican Party] Satan took him up to the high places and promised him dominion over all in view. Perhaps none but a divine being can resist such temptation. He accepted the nomination from the Radicals [socialists and communists], and was elected; and though I received friendly messages from him, I did not see him until near the close of his first administration. As ignorant of civil government as of the characters on the Moabitish stone, President Grant began badly, and went from bad to worse. The appointments to office that he made, the associates whom he gathered around him, were astounding. All his own relatives, all his wife's relatives, all the relatives of these relatives, to the remotest cousinhood, were quartered on the public treasury. Never since King Jamie [Scottish King James IV] crossed the [River] Tweed with the hungry Scotch nation at his heels has the like been seen; and the soul of old Newcastle, greatest of English nepotists, must have turned green with envy. *The influence of this on the public was most disastrous. Already shortened by the war, the standard of morality, honesty, and right was buried out of sight* [my emphasis, L.S.].

For two or three years I was much in the North, and especially in New York, where I had dear friends. The war had afforded opportunity and stimulated appetite for reckless speculation. Vast fortunes had been acquired by new men, destitute of manners, taste, or principles. The vulgar insolence of wealth held complete possession of public places and carried by storm the citadels of society. Indeed society disappeared. As in the middle ages, to escape pollution, honourable men and refined women (and there are many such in the North) fled to sanctuary and desert, or, like early Christians in the catacombs, met secretly and in fear. The masses sank into a condition that would disgrace Australian natives, and lost all power of discrimination.

The Vice-President of the United States [Schuyler Colfax] accepted bribes, and perjured himself in vain to escape exposure. President Grant wrote him a letter to assure him of his continued esteem and confidence; and this Vice-President has since lectured before "Young Men's Christian Associations [YMCA]." Plunderings by members of the Congress excited no attention so long as they were confined to individuals or corporations. It was only when they voted themselves money out of taxes paid by the people, that these last growled and frightened some of the statesmen into returning it. A banker, the pet of the Government, holding the same especial relation to it that the Bank of England held to William of Orange, discovered that "a great national debt was a blessing," and was commended and rewarded therefor. With a palace on the shores of the Delaware, this banker owned a summer retreat on a lovely isle amid the waters of Lake Erie. A pious man, he filled this with many divines, who blessed all his enterprises. He contributed largely, too, to the support of an influential Christian journal to aid in disseminating truth to Jew, Gentile, and heathen. The divines and the Christian journal were employed to persuade widows and weak men to purchase his rotten securities, as things too righteous to occasion loss.

 The most eloquent preacher in the land, of a race devoted to adoration of negroes, as [Carthaginian General] Hannibal to hatred of Rome, compromised the wife of a member of his congregation. Discovered by the husband, he grovelled before him in humiliation as before "his God" (his own expression). Brought before the public, he swore that he was innocent, and denied the meaning of his own written words. The scandal endured for months, and gave an opportunity to the metropolitan journals to display their enterprise by furnishing daily and minute reports of all details to their readers. The influence of the preacher was increased by this. His congregation flocked to him as the Anabaptists to John of Leyden, and shopkeepers profitably advertised their wares by doubling their subscriptions to augment his salary. Far from concealing this wound inflicted on his domestic honour, the injured husband proclaimed it from the housetops, clothed himself in it as in a robe of price, and has successfully used it to become a popular lecturer.

 To represent the country at the capital of an ancient monarchy, a man was selected whom, it is no abuse of language to declare, [English priest] Titus Oates after his release from the pillory would have blushed to recognise. On the eve of his departure, as one may learn from the newspapers of the day, all that was richest and best in New York gathered around a banquet in his honour, congratulated the country to which he was accredited, and lamented the misfortune of their own that it would be deprived, even temporarily, of such virtue. Another was sent to an empire which is assured by our oft-succeeding envoys that it is the object of our particular affection. To the aristocracy of the realm this genial person taught the favourite game of the mighty West. A man of broad views, feeling that diplomatic attentions were due to commons as well as to crown and nobles, he occasionally withdrew himself from the social pleasures of the "West End" to inform the stags of Capel Court of the value of American mines. Benefactors are ever misjudged. Aristocracy and the many-antlered have since united to defame him; but Galileo in the dungeon, [Blaise] Pascal by his solitary lamp, More, Sidney, and Russell on the scaffold, will console him; and in the broad bosom of his native Ohio he has found the exception to the rule that prophets are not without honour but in their own country.

The years of Methuselah and the pen of Juvenal would not suffice to exhaust the list, or depict the benighted state into which we had fallen; but it can be asserted of the popular idols of the day that, unveiled, they resemble Mokanna, and can each exclaim—

"Here, judge if hell, with all its power to damn,
Can add one curse to the foul thing I am!"

The examples of thousands of pure and upright people in the North were as powerless to mitigate the general corruption as song of seraphim to purify the orgies of harlots and burglars; for they were not in harmony with the brutal passions of the masses.

In Boston, July 1872, as co-trustees of the fund left by the late Mr. [George] Peabody for the education of the poor in the Southern States, President Grant and I met for the first time since he had accepted the nomination from the Radical party [that is, the then extreme Left-wing of the then Liberal Republican Party]. He was a candidate for re-election, and much worshipped; and though cordial with me, his general [Left-wing] manner had something of "I am the State." Stopping at the same inn, he passed an evening in my room, to which he came alone; and there, avoiding public affairs, we smoked and chatted about the Nueces, Rio Grande, Palo Alto, etc.—Mexican-American War-related] things twenty-five years agone, when we were youngsters beginning life. He was re-elected in November by a large majority of electoral votes; but the people of Louisiana elected a Democratic Governor and Assembly. When, in January following, the time of meeting of the Assembly arrived, the country, habituated as it was to violent methods, was startled by the succeeding occurrences.

The night before the Assembly was to meet, the Federal Judge in the city of New Orleans, a drunken reprobate, obtained from the commander of the United States troops a portion of his force, and stationed it in the State House. In the morning the members-elect were refused admittance, and others not elected, many not even candidates during the election, were allowed to enter. One [Stephen B.] Packard, Marshal of the Federal Court, a bitter partisan and worthy adjunct of such a judge, had provided for an Assembly to suit himself by giving tickets to his friends, whom the soldiers passed in, excluding the elected members. The ring-streaked, spotted, and speckled among the cattle and goats, and the brown among the sheep, were turned into the supplanters' folds, which were filled with lowing herds and bleating flocks, while Laban had neither horn nor hoof. There was not a solitary return produced in favour of this Packard body, nor of the Governor subsequently installed; but the Radicals [Republican socialists and communists] asserted that their friends would have been elected had the people voted as they wished; for every negro and some whites in the State upheld their party. By this time the charming credulity of the negroes had abated, and they answered the statement that slave-drivers were murdering their race in adjacent regions by saying that slave-drivers, at least, did not tell them lies nor steal their money.

All the whites and many of the blacks in Louisiana felt themselves cruelly wronged by the action of the Federal authorities. Two Assemblies were in session, and two Governors claiming power in New Orleans. Excitement was intense, business arrested, and collision between the parties imminent. As the Packard faction was supported by Federal troops, the situation looked grave; and a number of worthy people urged me to go to Washington, where my personal relations with the President might secure me access to him. It was by no means a desirable mission; but duty seemed to require me to undertake it.

Accompanied by Thomas F. Bayard, Senator from Delaware, my first step in Washington was to call on the leader of the Radicals in the Senate, [Oliver P.] Morton of Indiana, when a long conversation ensued, from which I derived no encouragement. Senator Morton was the [French politician Georges A.] Couthon of his party; and this single interview prepared me for one of his dying utterances to warn the country against the insidious efforts of slave-driving rebels [that is, Southern Conservatives] to regain influence in the Government. The author of the natural history of Ireland would doubtless have welcomed one specimen, by

South-loathing, Radical Liberal, Indiana Senator Oliver P. Morton, a member of the then Left-wing Republican Party.

describing which he could have filled out a chapter on snakes; and there is temptation to dwell on the character of Senator Morton as one of the few Radical [socialist-communist] leaders who kept his hands clean of plunder. But it may be observed that one absorbing passion excludes all others from the human heart; and the small portion of his being in which disease had left vitality was set on vengeance. Death has recently clutched him, and would not be denied; and he is bewailed throughout the land as though he had possessed the knightly tenderness of Sir Philip Sidney and the lofty patriotism of [the First Earl of] Chatham [William Pitt].

The President [Grant] received me pleasantly, gave much time to the Louisiana difficulty, and in order to afford himself opportunity for full information, asked me frequently to dine with his immediate family, composed of kindly, worthy people. I also received attention and hospitality from some members of his Cabinet, who with him seemed desirous to find a remedy for the wrong. More especially was this true of the Secretary of State, Hamilton Fish, with whom and whose refined family I had an acquaintance. Of a distinguished Revolutionary race, possessor of a good estate, and with charming, cultivated surroundings, this gentleman seemed the Noah of the political world. Perhaps his retention in the Cabinet was due to a belief that, under the new and milder dispensation, the presence of one righteous man might avert the doom of Gomorrah. An exception existed in the person of the Attorney-General, a man, as eminent barristers declare, ignorant of law, and self-willed and vulgar. For some reason he had much influence with the President, who later appointed him Chief Justice of the United States; but the Senatorial gorge, indelicate as it had proved, rose at this, as the easy-shaving barber's did at the coal-heaver, and rejected him.

Weeks elapsed, during which I felt hopeful from the

earnestness manifested in my mission by the President [Grant] and several of his Cabinet. Parties were in hostile array in New Orleans, but my friends were restrained by daily reports of the situation at Washington. Only my opinion that there was some ground for hope could be forwarded. Conversations at dinner-tables, or in private interviews with the Executive and his advisers, could not, then or since, be repeated; and this of necessity gave room for misconstruction, as will appear. At length, on the day before the Congress was by law to adjourn, the President sent a message to the Senate, informing that body that, in the event the Congress failed to take action on the Louisiana matter, he should esteem it his duty to uphold the Government created by the Federal Judge. I left Washington at once, and did not revisit it for nearly four years.

I believe that President Grant was sincere with me, and went as far as he felt it safe. No doubt the Senatorial hyenas brought him to understand these unspoken words:

> "We have supported your acts, confirmed your appointments, protected and whitewashed your friends; but there are bones which we cannot give up without showing our teeth, and Louisiana is one of them."

The failure to obtain relief for the State of my birth, and whose soil covered the remains of all most dear, was sad enough, and the attempt had involved much unpleasant work but I had my reward. Downfall of hope, long sustained, was bitter to the people, especially to the leaders expectant of office; and I became an object of distrust. "Nothing succeeds like success," and nothing fails like failure, and the world is quite right to denounce it. The British Ministry shot an admiral for failing to relieve Minorca—to encourage others, as Voltaire remarked. [British Admiral John] Byng died silent, without plaint, which was best. The drunken Federal Judge, author of the outrages, was universally condemned, with one exception, of which more anon. Both branches of the Congress, controlled by Radicals [the socialists and communists in the then Left-wing Republican Party], pronounced his conduct to have been illegal and unjust, and he was driven from the bench with articles of impeachment hanging over him. *Nevertheless, the Government evolved from his unjudicial consciousness was upheld by President Grant with Federal bayonets* [my emphasis, L.S.].

Two years later the people of Louisiana elected an Assembly, a majority of whose members were opposed to the fraudulent governor, [William Pitt] Kellogg. The President sent United States soldiers into the halls of the Assembly to expel members at the point of the bayonet. [U.S.] Lieutenant-General [Philip H.] Sheridan, the military maid of all (such) work, came especially to superintend this business, and it was now that he expressed the desire to exterminate "banditti." The destruction of buildings and food in the Valley of Virginia, to the confusion of the crows, was his Salamanca; but this was his Waterloo, and great was the fame of the Lieutenant-General of the Radicals [the socialists and communists of the then Left-wing Republican Party].

This *Governor* Kellogg is the senator recently seated, of whom mention has been made, and, if a lesser quantity than zero be conceivable, with a worse title to the office than he had to that of Governor of Louisiana. So far as known, he is a commonplace rogue; but his party has always rallied to his support, as the "Tenth Legion" to its eagles. Indeed, it is difficult to understand the qualities or objects that enlist the devotion and compel the worship of humanity. Travellers in the Orient tell of majestic fanes, whose mighty walls and countless columns are rich with elaborate carvings. Hall succeeds hall, each more beautifully wrought than the other, until the innermost, the holy of holies, is reached, and there is found enshrined—a shrivelled ape.

The sole exception referred to in the case of the drunken Federal Judge was a lawyer of small repute, who had been Democratic in his political tendencies. Languishing in obscurity, he saw and seized his opportunity, and rushed into print in defence of the Judge, and in commendation of the President [Grant] for upholding such judicial action. It is of record that this lawyer, in the society of some men of letters, declared Dante to be the author of the Decameron; but one may be ignorant of the Italian poets and thoroughly read in French memoirs. During the war of the Spanish succession, [Louis Joseph] the Duke of Vendôme, filthiest of generals, not excepting Suvaroff [Alexander Suvorov], commanded the French army in Italy. To negotiate protection for their States, the Italian princes sent agents to Vendôme; but the agents sent by [Alexander Farnese] the Duke of Parma were so insulted by the bestialities of the French commander as to go back to their master without negotiating, and no decent man would consent to return. A starving little abbé volunteered for the service, and, possessing a special aptitude for baseness, succeeded in his mission. Thus [Guilio] Alberoni, afterward Cardinal and Prime Minister of Spain, got his foot on the first rung of the ladder of fame. The details of the story are too gross to repeat, and the Memoirs of [Louis de Rouvory] the Duke of St. Simon must be consulted for them; but our lawyer assuredly had read them. Many may imitate Homer, however feebly; one genius originated his epics.

Having entered on this lofty career, our Alberoni stuck to it with the tenacity of a ferret in pursuit of rabbits, and was rewarded, though not at the time nor to the extent he had reason to expect. The mission to England was promised him by the reigning powers, when, on the very eve of securing his prize, a stick was put in the wheels of his progress, and by a brother's hand. Another legal personage, practising at the same bar—that of New York—and a friend, did the deed. "Chloe was false, Chloe was common, but constant while possessed;" but here Chloe was without the last quality. In 1868, General Grant's election pending, Chloe was affiliated with the Democratic party, and had been chosen one of the captains of its citadel, a sachem of Tammany. Scenting success for Grant, with the keenness of the vulture for his prey, he attended a Radical meeting and announced his intention to give twenty thousand dollars to the Radical election fund. This sum appears to have been the market value of a seat in the Cabinet, to which ultimately he was called. When the English mission became vacant by the resignation of the incumbent, disgusted by British ingratitude, Chloe quitted the Cabinet to take it, and Alberoni, was left wearing weeds. Yet much allowance is due to family affection, the foundation of social organisation. Descended from a noble stock, though under a somewhat different name, Chloe from mystic sources learned that his English relatives pined for his society, and devotion to family ties tempted him to betray his friend. Subsequently Alberoni was appointed to a more northern country, where he may find congenial society; for, in a despotism tempered only by assassination, the knees of all become pliant before power.

It is pleasant to mark the early steps of nascent ambition. In the time of the great Napoleon every conscript carried the baton of a marshal in his knapsack; and in our happy land every rogue may be said to have an appointment to office in his pocket. This is also pleasant.

Since the spring of 1873, when he gave himself up to the worst [socialist and communist] elements of his party, I have not seen President Grant; but his career suggests some curious reflections to one who has known him for thirty-odd years. What the waiting-woman promised in jest, Dame Fortune has seriously bestowed on this Malvolio; and his political cross-garterings not only find favour with the Radical Olivia, but are admired by the Sir Tobys of the European world. Indeed, Fortune has conceits as quaint as those of [the Arabian ruler] Haroun al-Raschid. The beggar, from profound sleep, awoke in the Caliph's bed. Amazed and frightened by his surroundings, he slowly gained composure as courtier after courtier entered, bowing low, to proclaim him King of kings, Light of the World, Commander of the Faithful; and he speedily came to believe that the present had always existed, while the real past was an idle dream. Of a nature kindly and modest, *President Grant was assured by all about him that he was the delight of the Radicals* [my emphasis, L.S.], greatest captain of the age, and saviour of the nation's life. It was inevitable that he should begin by believing some of this, and end by believing it all. Though he had wasted but little time on books since leaving West Point, where in his day the curriculum was limited, he had found out to the last shilling the various sums voted by Parliament to the Duke of Wellington, and spoke of them in a manner indicating his opinion that he was another example of the ingratitude of republics. The gentle temper and sense of justice of Othello resisted the insidious wiles of Iago; but ignorance and inexperience yielded in the end to malignity and craft. President Grant was brought not only to smother the Desdemona of his early preferences and intentions, but to feel no remorse for the deed, and take to his bosom the harridan of Radicalism. As [European tyrant] Phalaris did those of Agrigentum opposed to his rule, *he finished by hating Southerners and Democrats* [that is, Conservatives; my emphasis, L.S.].

During the struggle for the Presidency in the autumn of 1876, he permitted a member of his Cabinet, the Secretary of the Interior, to become the manager of the Radicals [the socialists and communists of the then Left-wing Republican Party] and use all the power of his office, established for the public service, to promote the success of his party's candidate.

Monsieur [Oscar Bardi de] Fourtou, Minister of the Interior, removed prefects and mayors to strengthen the power of De Broglie; whereupon all the newspapers in our land published long essays to show and lament the ignorance of the French and their want of experience in republican methods. One might suppose these articles to have been written by the "seven sleepers," so forgetful were they of yesterday's occurrences at home; but beams near at hand are ever blinked in our search of distant motes. The election over, but the result in dispute, President Grant, in Philadelphia, alarmed thoughtful people by declaring that "no man could take the great office of President upon whose title thereto the faintest shadow of doubt rested," and then, with all the power of the Government, successfully led the search for this non-existing person. To insure fairness in the count, so that none could carp, he requested eminent statesmen to visit South Carolina, Florida, and Louisiana, the electoral votes of which were claimed by both parties; but the statesmen were, without exception, the bitterest and most unscrupulous partisans, personally interested in securing victory for their candidate, and have since received their hire. *Soldiers were quartered in the capitals of the three States to aid the equitable statesmen in reaching a correct result by applying the bayonet if the figures proved refractory* [my emphasis, L.S.]. With equity and force at work, the country might confidently expect justice; and justice was done that justice ever accorded by unscrupulous power to weakness.

But one House of the Congress was controlled by the Democrats [then the Conservative Party]; and these, Herod-like, were seeking to slay the child, the Nation. To guard against this, President Grant ordered other troops to Washington, and a ship of war to be anchored in the Potomac, and the child was preserved. Again, the 4th of March, appointed by law for the installation of Presidents, fell on Sunday. President Grant is of Scotch descent, and doubtless learned in the traditions of the land o' cakes. The example of Kirkpatrick at Dumfries [Scotland] taught him that it was wise to "mak sicker;" so the incoming man and the Chief Justice were smuggled into the White House on the Sabbath day, and the oath of office was administered. If the chair of George Washington was to be filched, it were best done under cover. The value of the loot inspired caution.

In Paris, at a banquet, Maître Gambetta recently toasted our ex-President "as the great commander who had sacredly obeyed and preserved his country's laws." Whether this was said in irony or ignorance, had General Grant taken with him to Paris his late Secretary of the Interior, the accomplished Zachariah Chandler, the pair might have furnished suggestions to Marshal [Patrice de] MacMahon and Fourtou that would have changed the dulcet strains of Maître Gambetta into dismal howls.[208]

CONCLUSION

☛ Dismissing hope of making my small voice heard in mitigation of the woes of my State, in May 1873 I went to Europe, and remained many months. Returned to New York, I found that the characters on the wall, so long invisible, had blazed forth, and the vast factitious wealth, like the gold of the dervish, withered and faded in a night. The scenes depicted of Paris and London, after the collapse of Mississippi schemes and South Sea bubbles, were here repeated on a greater scale and in more aggravated form. To most, the loss of wealth was loss of ancestry, repute, respectability, decency, recognition of their fellows—all. Small wonder that their withers were fearfully wrung, and their wails piteous. Enterprise and prosperity were frozen as in a sea of everlasting ice, and guardians of trusts, like [Italian naval officer] Ugolino [della Gherardesca], plunged their robber fangs into the scalps and entrails of the property confided to them.

A public journal has recently published a detailed list, showing that there has been plundered by fiduciaries since 1873 the amazing amount of thirty millions of money; and the work goes on. Scarce a newspaper is printed in whose columns may not be found some fresh instance of breach of trust. As poisoning in the time of [Marquise de] Brinvilliers [Marie-Madeleine d'Aubra], stealing is epidemic, and the watch-dogs of the flocks are transformed into wolves.

Since the tocsin sounded we have gone from bad to worse. During the past summer (1877), labourers, striking for increased wages or to resist diminution thereof, seized and held for many days the railway lines between East and West, stopping all traffic. Aided by mobs, they took possession of great towns and destroyed vast property. At Pittsburgh, in Pennsylvania, State troops attempting to restore order were attacked and driven off. Police and State authorities in most cases proved impotent, and the arm of Federal power was invoked to stay the evil.

Thousands of the people are without employment, which they seek in vain; and from our cities issue heartrending appeals in behalf of the suffering poor. From the Atlantic [Ocean] as far to the west as the young State of Nebraska, there has fallen upon the land a calamity like that afflicting Germany after the Thirty Years' War. Hordes of idle, vicious tramps penetrate rural districts in all directions, rendering property and even life unsafe; and no remedy for this new disease has been discovered. Let us remember that these things are occurring in a country of millions upon millions of acres of vacant lands, to be had almost for the asking, and where, even in the parts first colonised, density of population bears but a small relation to that of Western Europe. Yet we daily assure ourselves and the world that we have the best government under the canopy of heaven, and the happiest land, hope and refuge of humanity.

Purified by fire and sword, the South has escaped many of these evils; but her enemies have sown the seeds of a pestilence more deadly than that rising from Pontine marshes. Now that Federal bayonets have been turned from her bosom, this poison, the influence of three-fourths of a million of negro voters, will speedily ascend and sap her vigour and intelligence. Greed of office, curse of democracies, will impel demagogues to grovel deeper and deeper in the mire in pursuit of ignorant votes. Her old breed of statesmen has largely passed away during and since the civil war, and the few survivors are naturally distrusted, as responsible for past errors. Numbers of her gentry fell in battle, and the men now on the stage were youths at the outbreak of strife, which arrested their education. This last is also measurably true of the North. Throughout the land, the experience of the active portion of the present generation only comprises conditions of discord and violence. The story of the six centuries of sturdy effort by which our English forefathers wrought out their liberties is unknown, certainly unappreciated. Even the struggles of our grandfathers are forgotten, and the names of [George] Washington, [John] Adams, [Alexander] Hamilton, [John] Jay, [John] Marshall, [James] Madison, and Story awaken no fresher memories in our minds, no deeper emotions in our hearts, than do those of Solon, Leonidas, and Pericles. But respect for the memories and deeds of our ancestors is security for the present, seed-corn for the future; and, in the language of [Edmund] Burke,

> "Those will not look forward to their posterity who never look backward to their ancestors."

Traditions are mighty influences in restraining peoples. The light that reaches us from above takes countless ages to traverse the awful chasm separating us from its parent star; yet it comes straight and true to our eyes, because each tender wavelet is linked to the other, receiving and transmitting the luminous ray. Once break the continuity of the stream, and men will deny its heavenly origin, and seek its source in the feeble glimmer of earthly corruption.[209] — CONFEDERATE GENERAL RICHARD TAYLOR, 1879

Appomattox Court House, Virginia, site of Lee's surrender.

This illustration is from an early American novel by pro-South author Thomas Dixon Jr. It depicts a meeting between Radical Socialist Thaddeus Stevens (whom Dixon has given the fictional name "Austin Stoneman") and big government Liberal Abraham Lincoln, both members of the then Left-wing Republican Party. Though a creation of Dixon's imagination, it is likely that such a meeting between the nefarious pair actually took place. Dixon's original caption has Stevens (as "Stoneman") saying to Lincoln: "The South is conquered soil. I mean to blot it from the map." In 1862, Lincoln said nearly precisely the same thing to Interior Department official T. J. Barnett, during a private conversation. According to Barnett, after declaring that he was going to alter the purpose of the war to one of "subjugation," Lincoln blurted out: "The South is to be destroyed and replaced with new propositions and ideas."

SECTION 2

RECONSTRUCTION: PERSONAL VIEWS

CHAPTER 12

HOW THE WAR ENDED

☛ . . . On the 1st of March [1865], [Union] General [Ulysses S.] Grant's armies, under [Union Generals George G.] Meade, [Edward O. C.] Ord and [Philip H.] Sheridan, all of which were available in the attack on [Confederate General Robert E.] Lee, contained an effective total of over 162,000, according to the official reports. It has been stated that Grant moved upon Lee April 1st with an actual force of 120,000. His cavalry, commanded by Sheridan, was the best that had been put in the field on the Federal [U.S.] side, and doubled the force under [Confederate Generals Wade] Hampton and Fitzhugh Lee. His infantry, freshly uniformed and equipped, made a superb appearance in their compact and well-supported advance against the gallant foe which had so long and well defended the land they loved. It was not physically possible for the reduced army of Northern Virginia to resist on April 2nd the Federal heavy columns which assailed them along the entire front from the Appomattox river to the exposed flank which had been turned on the day before. The ratio of physical force on that day was fully four [U.S.] to one [C.S.].

Robert E. Lee: West Point graduate, Mexican-American War veteran, superintendent of the United States Military Academy, Confederate general, head of the Army of Northern Virginia, Commander-in-Chief of the Confederate military, and later President of Washington College (now Washington and Lee University). Not mentioned in most mainstream history books: Lee never personally owned slaves, freed his wife's family slaves four months before Lincoln issued his illegal Emancipation Proclamation, and campaigned to abolish slavery and enlist Southern blacks in the Confederate military long before the War ended.

Lee withdrew from all the defenses of the Confederate capital, and sought the way for junction with [Confederate General Joseph E.] Johnston, but while delayed at Amelia Court House by the necessity of securing rations for his small army, was overtaken and turned from his chosen course. The fighting in retreat resulted in the reduction of his army by the 9th of April to about 10,000 men, with which small force he essayed to cut through toward Lynchburg, and that last recourse becoming futile, this remnant of a great army was surrendered by the noble chieftain whom all nations admire and revere. The terms of the surrender were highly honorable to General Grant, the victorious Federal general, and greatly promoted the rapid cessation of the long, bloody, costly struggle. The armies parted in mutual respect, and notwithstanding there were other forces in the field, the conviction was settled in the public mind that the Confederate movement had been effectually checked. Over twenty small engagements occurred after the battle of Appomattox in various parts of the Confederacy, but none was important. General Johnston surrendered his forces, April 26th, to [Union] General [William T.] Sherman in North Carolina, and [Confederate] Gen. [Edmund] Kirby Smith surrendered the Trans-Mississippi department [C.S.] on the 26th of May. President Lincoln was murdered by an assassin on the 14th of April—an untimely death, deplored, not only South and North, but throughout the civilized world. [Confederate] President [Jefferson] Davis, well worthy of the high honors which are paid to his memory, in attempting to reach the West beyond the Mississippi [River], was captured and imprisoned, but afterward released. *Trial on the indictment against him could not result in conviction* [my emphasis, L.S.]. The presidency of the United States passed, under the provisions of the Constitution, to Andrew Johnson. The Confederate States government ceased to exist. *Serious errors were committed by Washington politicians, in reconstruction policies that fostered feeling which could have been easily allayed by wiser action* [my emphasis, L.S.], and notwithstanding Southern protestations and proof of fidelity to the faithful recognition of the real results of the war, it required the struggle with Spain [Spanish-American War], after the passing of a generation, to bring to the States of the Confederacy a just recognition of their true attitude toward the Union.[210] — CONFEDERATE GENERAL CLEMENT ANSELM EVANS

CORRECTING A FEW YANKEE FALLACIES

☞ After the overthrow of the Confederate Government and the surrender of the Confederate armies the work of the restoration of Federal authority in the Southern States was commenced while the excitement, the passions, and prejudices of the war were in full blaze, and were intensified by the assassination of President Lincoln, with which it was then unjustly assumed the Confederate authorities had some connection, but which was regarded by them as most unfortunate for all the people who had adhered to the fortunes of the Confederacy.

Under the state of feeling which then existed on both sides it was hardly to be expected that a wise and temperate policy of reconstruction would be adopted, *while many of the Churches of the Northern States were resolving and some of their ministers of the religion of Christ were preaching a crusade of hate, proscription, and revenge against the Southern people* [my emphasis, L.S.].

The plan adopted for the restoration of the Union and the pacification of the Southern people was to deprive them of all political rights, put them under military rule, and suspend the right of the writ of habeas corpus, so that there could be no relief or redress for any wrong done to a citizen, however unlawful or outrageous. Our citizens were subject to arrest by the military authority without an affidavit or formal charge or legal warrant, and to detention, without knowing what the charges against them were, and to a trial by a drumhead court-martial, without the intervention of a jury [my emphasis, L.S.].

A large part of the Southern States had been devastated by war; the people had exhausted their resources in the endeavor to maintain their cause, and tens of thousands of their bravest and best men had either fallen in battle or died in the service. Beaten in battle, denied political rights and the protection of law, governed by an unfriendly military authority, by the [communized] negroes, by carpet-baggers and scalawags—and I mention them in the order of their respectability—plundered and robbed by employees of the Treasury Department, and constantly menaced by loyal leagues [organized socialists and communists] composed of the elements above named, their condition seemed to be as hopeless as can well be imagined.

If, under the providence of God, the life of President Lincoln could have been spared, so that reconstruction and the restoration of the Union could have been brought about under his supervision and that of the officers and soldiers who fought the battles of the Union, I believe the country would have been saved from the introduction of abnormal military governments, which are so unfriendly to civil rights and political liberty and so contrary to the genius of our government, and that the people of the Southern States would have been saved from much of the enormous sacrifices and suffering which they were compelled to endure during the period of reconstruction; the demagogue in politics, the unchristian persecutions by religious bodies, and the thieving treasury officials would not have had so wide a field for their operations."[211]

It is unpleasant to me to make the foregoing recitals, and the more so because the purpose for which they are made may be misunderstood or misrepresented. The restoration of peace, good government, the rule of law and of good will between those who were once enemies is as gratifying to me as it can be to any other citizen. But the charge has been constantly made since the war that the Confederates were rebels and traitors, and the effort is all the time being made to educate the rising generation into the belief that their fathers and their mothers were rebels and traitors, and therefore lawless criminals. Without malice against any of our fellow-citizens, I feel it to be my duty to the memory of our heroic dead, to their surviving associates, and to those who are to come after us to make these statements in vindication of the truths of history and in justification of the patriotism, the manhood, and love of justice of those who defended the "Lost Cause" and offered their all in an effort to preserve their constitutional rights against the aggressions of a hostile majority.

And now that we are again citizens of the United States, living under the same government and constitution and flag, our late adversaries ought not to desire to degrade us in the eyes of posterity; and, if they would be wise and just, they should not wish to place our people in history in the position of being unworthy of the rights, liberty, and character of citizens of our great and common country.

And while I have accepted and do accept in good faith the legitimate results of the war, and while I am and will be as true to my allegiance and duty to our common government as any other citizen can be, *I shall insist on my right to tell the truths which show that in that great struggle we were guided and controlled by a sense of duty and by a spirit of patriotism which caused us to stake life, liberty, and property in a contest with a greatly superior power rather than basely surrender our rights without a struggle* [my emphasis, L.S.].

It is fitting and proper at this point that I should refer to a matter which fitly illustrates the character of the Southern people. There never was a time during all the perils and suffering of reconstruction that men of prominence who had been on the Confederate side could not have obtained positions of honor and emolument under the Federal Government if they would have consented to surrender their convictions and betray their people—a very few did so, and thereby earned an everlasting infamy—but nearly all of them stood by their convictions and preserved their honor, and thereby proved themselves worthy of citizenship in the greatest and proudest government on earth.

Having attempted to fulfill an unpleasant duty in what I have so far said, I now turn to the consideration of more pleasant subjects.

The War for the Constitution, 1861-1865, pitted Northern Liberals (then known as Republicans) against Southern Conservatives (then known as Democrats). This age-old sociopolitical divide carried into the Reconstruction era, and is, in fact, still very much evident to this day—despite the reversal of the two party platforms in 1896.

From the desolation, absence of civil government and political rights and of law throughout the Southern States less than thirty years ago we now in all these states have good civil government, good laws faithfully enforced, liberty protected, society reorganized, peace and industry reestablished, with many valuable enterprises put into successful operation, and with a steady and wonderful increase in population, wealth, and the comforts of civilized life. This constitutes the greatest and proudest vindication of the capacity of our people for local self-government, and is a grander and nobler achievement by them than was obtained even by war. It is the triumph of their capacity for self-government, and shows that our people are worthy of the possession of the political power and religious liberty which they now enjoy, and which shows them worthy of political equality with those who were once our enemies. This great Centennial Exposition of Tennessee we have before us is a magnificent exhibition of the results of Southern enterprise and prosperity to gladden the hearts of our people and to gratify the pride of the people of this great state. And to-day the people of the South are as earnest in their attachment to our common government as those of any other part of the Union, and would make as great sacrifices, if need be, in defense of our government as could be made by any other part of the American people. Enjoying peace and liberty to-day, we can refer with pride to the courage and heroism of our soldiers in the late war and to the gallantry and skill of our officers. And when impartial history comes to be written we do not doubt but that it will be seen that they were never excelled in the qualities of patient endurance and manly courage.

The names of Jefferson Davis, R. E. Lee, Stonewall Jackson, and many others of our heroic leaders will go into history illumined by a halo of courage and skill and purity of life and patriotism unsurpassed by any other names in history. As indicating the faith of President Davis in God and his devout earnestness, I recall attention to the closing sentence of his inaugural address after his election under the constitutional government of the Confederacy, made on the 22nd day of February, 1862. Raising his hands, at the close of his address, and looking toward the heavens, he said: "And now, O God, I commit my country and her cause into thy holy keeping." Thus showing the solemnity with which he assumed anew the duties of President of the Confederacy.[212] — CONFEDERATE POST MASTER GENERAL, TEXAS SENATOR JOHN H. REAGAN, 1897

HOW THE SOUTH WEATHERED RECONSTRUCTION

☞ The world's history can hardly show an instance in which such courage and constancy and devotion has been shown by both men and women, in the face of so powerful an enemy. And I predict that in the not distant future some Macaulay [British historian Thomas B. Macaulay] will be found who will do justice to their patriotism and skill and courage; and that, the citizens of all parts of the Union, North and South, will feel a just pride in the facts that such men and women and their descendants form a part of the population of this great republic; as we of the South shall feel a just pride in being citizens of a country which produced a Davis and a Lincoln, a Lee and a Grant, a Stonewall Jackson and a Sherman, and their respective compatriots. With all our pride on account of the qualities exhibited by our people during the war, perhaps the most striking illustration of their capacity for self-government is shown by their conduct since it ended. Their country desolated by the war; their wealth and resources exhausted; tens of thousands of their best men filling honorable graves on the fields of battle; their social and domestic institutions destroyed; their local governments annulled under the policy of reconstruction; denied the blessings of civil government; the military made paramount to the civil authorities; the right of the writ of *habeas corpus* suspended; arrests

without affidavits of guilt and without warrant; citizens liable to be tried by drum-head military courts; freedmen's bureaus established everywhere, under the control of the military and of a set of lawless camp followers of the army, stimulating the negroes to hostility to the whites; with an alien race made dominant who were unused to the exercise of the duties of citizenship, and unqualified for self-government; with no security for life, person or property; overwhelmed by all these calamities, that the people should have been able to reorganize society, and to reestablish civil government, revive the ordinary industries of the country, and in less than thirty years, reach the condition of general prosperity which now prevails throughout the Southern States, furnishes the strongest possible proof of the capacity of our people for the preservation of social order and for self-government; and cannot fail to secure for them the good opinion of the civilized world.[213]
— CONFEDERATE POST MASTER GENERAL, TEXAS SENATOR JOHN H. REAGAN, 1894

ABOUT RECONSTRUCTION TIMES
☞ Col. C. B. Howard has written of the time, in June, 1867, when the State of Georgia was under military rule and the citizens were being annoyed with all sorts of indignities. Judge W. W. Clayton, a prominent citizen, had just been turned out of house and home because his daughters refused to pass under the United States flag, and hid their faces from yankee officers with their parasols. It was a few days before [Confederate Vice President] Alexander H. Stephens wrote a letter to Col. R. A. Alston, saying he considered the country in *articula mortis* ["at the moment of death"], that if the South resisted reconstruction they would he forced, and if they accepted it they were disgraced, and that it was a choice between martyrdom and suicide, and for himself he preferred martyrdom.[214]
— SUMNER A. CUNNINGHAM, EDITOR *CONFEDERATE VETERAN*, 1893

IN THE DAYS BEFORE RECONSTRUCTION
☞ . . . In these sordid, selfish, degenerate times, patriotism, chivalry, reverence, and many characteristics of the old times that have gone, and that helped to make our nation the grandest and best on the earth, are rapidly dying out.

The speaker who stands before you remembers, and with keenest longings, the good "old days" when religion, morality, virtue, honor, and patriotism and chivalry occupied high ground, and maintained it. Now they are, the things most often scoffed at.

God forgive us that it should be so! Living, as the speaker has, during four periods of the South's history, in the days of the old South, the Confederate South, the days of reconstruction, and since, she has seen many changes, some for the better; but many have been so deplorable that we seem a totally different people. Having lived in the days of the glorious old South, with associations, special and hallowed, of a time that has gone forever and a people that will soon have passed away, it is not strange that she loves it best and holds its memories in deepest reverence.[215] — MRS. W. C. SIBLEY AT THE STATE GATHERING OF THE DAUGHTERS OF THE CONFEDERACY, 1896

THE MEANING OF RECONSTRUCTION

☞ Reconstruction is not a well understood term. If it means acceptance of the "situation" simply, then most men are reconstructed. It does not imply uncompromising belligerence to say that one is not reconstructed. The meaning generally is to detest the sentiment of concession for policy, which some have done who breathe the fragrance of air in Dixie.[216] — SUMNER A. CUNNINGHAM, EDITOR *CONFEDERATE VETERAN*,, 1893

THE IRRATIONAL HATRED OF THE SOUTH

☞ . . . I think a hatred of the South began at the North only with the close of the war. Else, why the hanging of the helpless man [Confederate Captain Henry] Wirz, for not feeding sufficiently the prisoners of war that were refused exchange by their own people [Yankees], when our own soldiers were starving? Why the hanging of poor, innocent Mrs. [Mary] Surratt? Why the order commanding every rebel soldier to cut off the [Confederate] buttons from his old gray jacket? Why the manacling and chaining of Jefferson Davis in a casemate of a fort from which there could be no possibility of escape? And yet they dared not submit the question of his treason to the courts!

What a commentary it would have been—after fighting four years to make treason odious, after destroying the South—to find there had been no treason!

Why such expressions from representative men of the North like this from Henry Ward Beecher, who said in a sermon: "Those who suffered in the South were not martyrs in a good cause, but convicts in a bad one," and "who shall comfort them that sit by dishonored graves?"

Why should our brothers at the North approve the attempt by the old fanatic, [radical Left-winger] John Brown to massacre the slave holders of Virginia with the help of their slaves? Why do they eulogize him as the noblest of heroes? Why should the conquered South have been subjected to the bitterness of reconstruction, her people refused the privilege of the ballot, and the heel of the ignorant [that is, uneducated] negro placed upon the neck of the proudest people of all America? Why should the Secretary of State [William H. Seward] have informed the Pan-American Congress that there was nothing worth visiting South of the Potomac River?

A plantation house (the "big house") in the Old South. Under Reconstruction, Victorian Socialists and Communists (most members of the then Left-wing Republican Party) had such mansions seized and handed over to poverty-stricken blacks who could neither read or write. Thoroughly indoctrinated by the ethnomasochistic Freedmen's Bureau to despise white Southerners, such blacks were taught that whites owed them compensation for their past lives under slavery. Thus began the Left's victimization marketing of black people and the false communist concepts of "reparations" and "white privilege."

It has been said that the injured one can always forgive, but that he who maliciously wounds another can never forgive his victim.

[During Reconstruction] the writer saw armed Federal soldiers guarding the graves of the few Confederate soldiers buried in a corner at Arlington, on the 30th of May, 1868, *to prevent the Southern ladies of Washington from placing flowers on their graves.*

Is there any one in the whole South who can understand the wild frenzy and rabid utterances of a Governor of a Western State at the prospect of a return of some old [Confederate] flags to certain organizations in the South—who wished them as souvenirs—twenty years after the war was over? Why is it that partisan school books and histories must be continually written, filled with such falsehoods, when the authors could easily discover the truth if they desired it?

Why should continual effort be made to impress the seeker after truth with a belief that the South attempted to destroy the government by making war upon it, when that South attempted peaceably to secede from a contract after the conditions were broken? . . .²¹⁷ — DANIEL BOND, NASHVILLE, TENN., 1895

NOBLY SURVIVING "AN ODIOUS RECONSTRUCTION"

☞ . . . the course pursued by the Southern soldiery on parole and the Southern people in defeat has gained the respect of their countrymen and saved themselves from abject disgrace. Turning from the front of war, they faced the issues of peace at once, and, by bravely breasting all their obstacles, are finally ending them. They made a brave, necessary, and successful resistance to the policy of an odious reconstruction, but agreed to all measures necessary to the perfect fellowship of both States and people in an imperishable union. They taxed themselves to educate the negroes, who had been suddenly elevated into citizenship without preparation. They resumed their own political duties to the nation, and renewed commercial relations with the reunited country. Meanwhile they have maintained their true conviction in a most royal state; they have honored the ashes of their slain comrades; they have cherished the spirit of comradeship; but in all these things they have borne no malice toward our government, nor failed in loyalty to its constitution and laws. Thus have they established themselves in the good esteem of true men everywhere by maintaining the essential quality of self-respecting citizenship, and demonstrated that there are no nations on earth more fairly entitled to the admiring regard of mankind than these people of the Southern States, who bravely fought for their views in actual war, as earnestly contended for their political rights in peace, and are as persistently resolved to advance the interests and defend the honor of their country. . . .[218] — CONFEDERATE GENERAL CLEMENT ANSELM EVANS, 1896

THE RECONSTRUCTION BAN ON CONFEDERATE BUTTONS

☞ . . . During the awful days of reconstruction and negro rule in the South one, Col. William Betts, well known to me from his boyhood, continued to wear the gray [uniform], [Confederate] buttons, etc., despite the peremptory order of the military despot that they must all be taken off and put out of sight. Every railroad car, steamboat, or stage had a Yankee guard, with bristling bayonet, and a captain, to see that this order was executed. Col. Betts, as brave and fearless a little man as ever drew a sword, was on the cars, going from his home at West Point, Ga., to Montgomery, Ala., clad in his Confederate gray.

"You must take off those buttons, sir," said the Yankee captain.

"You had better take them off yourself," said Col. Betts.

After a short parley the officer cut off a button. Instantly Col.

Betts thrust a bowie-knife into his heart, jumped out of the window, the train running at full speed, and made his escape across the Chattahoochee River into Florida. He changed his dress from that time, and engaged in business with a firm in Quincy, Fla. A large reward was offered for him, and after several months he was captured, after stabbing two men to death, and carried to a military prison at Lagrange, Ga., where he was kept in "durance vile" for nearly a year. He was tried first by court-martial and sentenced to be hanged, but obtained a new trial before a civil tribunal, and was finally cleared by [Georgia Senator] Ben Hill and [former Confederate] Vice president Alex Stephens.[219] — DR. C. S. REEVES, LONE GROVE, TEX., 1897

CONFEDERATE CAPT. J. T. COBBS AFTER THE WAR
☞ In the days of reconstruction in Mississippi a war of the races was imminent. One negro insurrection followed another, and women and children were terrorized, and often in danger. Capt. Cobbs was sent for more than a hundred miles around to quell turbulent outbreaks among the negroes. His name was a terror, and they stood in awe of him. Yet more heroic than all his exploits in battle was the calm self- restraint that triumphed over revenge. A negro man cook in his own house ran his wife out of the kitchen with a butcher-knife one day, so dangerous had they become in their insolence and fury. It is but just to state, however, that he never knew of it until after the negro had been killed in a fight.

Becoming worn out with such recurrences, he returned to Waco, Tex., to live. On account of his wife's health he then removed to Comanche, where he remained a number of years, when, for the same reason, he sought the milder climate of the gulf coast, and is now an honored and influential citizen of Alvin.[220] — MRS. W. J. HAMLETT, HISTORIAN LAMAR-FONTAINE CAMP, UNITED DAUGHTERS OF THE CONFEDERACY, 1897

HOW GRANT ALMOST REOPENED THE WAR
☞ In the *Atlanta Constitution* of December 8, 1897, Mrs. Elizabeth Belt gave an account of reconstruction and the readmission of Georgia into the Federal Union. She told how [Union] General [Ulysses S.] Grant was affected by an appeal made by a Southern woman, and how he received it as "information in regard to affairs in Georgia," and sent a copy of her letter to the Reconstruction Committee. It contained the usual flavoring of Gen. Grant's "magnanimity" toward Southern soldiers and Southern people. This idea is magnified beyond its proper measure. Let us not detract one

iota from Grant's generous acts. Let us remember that President Grant was the general-in-chief of a victorious army of largely superior numbers when he received the capitulation of Gen. Lee. It may be that there was sufficient leniency, but it may be also that Gen. Grant was not alone or superior in his generous terms of surrender. The event was not so sudden as to cause general belief that it was on "the impulse of the moment." There may have been influences behind him which he adroitly utilized to his own personal advantage. He had been in communication by truce with Gen. Lee at least two days and nights, contemplating the surrender. In that time he had evidently conferred with his subordinate generals concerning the coming event, and he was manifestly anxious to crush Lee and his army.

Grant was reticent as to his general methods, but his trend indicated his purpose to defeat his adversary by astounding him with unexpected hard blows. He did not fight on the idea of being generous, but to compel surrender. He obtained a reputation for great will force, with a generous, even magnanimous, disposition. His unceasing hatred of [Union Chief of Staff Henry W.] Halleck and other generals of the Union army simply shows the true personal character of the man. He was vindictive in spirit, and at times subject to violent outbursts of a cruel temper. This was manifested about a week after the surrender of Gen. Lee. Lincoln had the night before been assassinated. Of course we all know that Gen. Lee and his soldiers had nothing at all to do with that horrible assassination. Gen. Grant knew it as well; yet he flew into a rage, and still desired to "crush the rebellion" by a strong blow upon his vanquished foe after the combat had closed and Lee and our soldiers of the South had gone on parole. The telegraphic order of Gen. Grant and the answer of [Union] Gen. [Edward O. C.] Ord demonstrate all that is claimed herein. My attention was recently directed to this by Capt. "Tip" Harrison, a brave Confederate soldier under Gen. Lee. The telegrams tell the whole story:

> Washington City, April 15, 1 865, 4 P.M. Maj.-Gen. Ord, Richmond, Va. Arrest J. A. Campbell, Mayor [Joseph C.] Mayo, and the members of the old council of Richmond who have not yet taken the oath of allegiance, and put them in Libby Prison [during the War a Confederate prison in Richmond, VA.]. Hold them guarded beyond the possibility of escape until further orders. Also arrest all paroled [Confederate] officers and surgeons until they can be sent beyond our lines, unless they take the [U.S.] oath of allegiance. The oath need not be received from any one who you have not good reason to believe will observe it, and from none who are excluded by the President's proclamation, without authority to do so. Extreme rigor will have to

be observed while assassination remains the order of the day with the Rebels. U. S. Grant, Lieutenant-General.

Gen. Ord's reply:

> Richmond, Va., April 15, 1865. Gen. U.S. Grant: Cipher despatch directing certain parties to be arrested is received. The two citizens I have seen. They are old, nearly helpless, and I think incapable of harm. Lee and staff are in town among the paroled prisoners. Should I arrest them under the circumstances, I think the rebellion here would be reopened. I will risk my life that the present paroles will be kept, and, if you will allow me to do so, trust the people here, who, I believe, are ignorant of the assassination, done, I think, by some insane Brutus with but few accomplices. Mr. Campbell and [Senator Robert M. T.] Hunter pressed me earnestly yesterday to send them to Washington to see the President. Would they have done so if guilty? Please answer. E. O. C. Ord, Major-General.
>
> Headquarters Army of the United States, Washington, April 15, 1865, 8 P.M. Maj.-Gen. Ord, Richmond, Va.: On reflection, I will withdraw my despatch of this date directing the arrest of Campbell, Mayo, and others so far as it may be regarded as an order, and leave it in the light of a suggestion, to be executed only so far as you may judge the good of the service demands. U. S. Grant, Lieutenant-General.
>
> Richmond, Va., April 15. 1865, 9:30 P.M. Received, 10:20 p.m. Lieut.-Gen. U. S. Grant: Second telegram, leaving the subject of arrest in my hands is received. E. O. C. Ord, Major-General.

These papers are in the [U.S. government's] Official Records, Series I, Volume XLVI, part 3, pages 762, 763.

Is it not apparent that Gen. Grant was mad or affrighted, and temporarily lost the equipoise with which he has been credited? The order was given on his own assumption of authority, as though he were the supreme commander or dictator. Was he mad or frightened? Was it magnanimous or malignant? One was calm in the midst of paroled prisoners, while the other was excited and petulant in the midst of victors fresh from the field, in their own capital. Which deserves the credit for generous spirit—he who would then and there risk his life on the parole of these people, or he who would arrest old men and paroled prisoners, without civil or military authority, and hold them in Libby Prison with military authority, and hold them in Libby Prison with "extreme rigor," because "some insane Brutus" had become a mean assassin? Give honor to whom honor is due.[221] — JUDGE ROBERT L. RODGERS, HISTORIAN, ATLANTA, GA. CAMP, U.C.V.

WHITES, BLACKS, & RECONSTRUCTION

☛ . . . The horrors of the civil war were nothing, dreadful as they were, compared with those which came upon us during the process of reconstruction. The right of franchise was conferred upon the negroes of the Southern States, who had no preparation for its exercise, and they easily became the victims of wicked and designing men who came down upon us to consume the little substance which had escaped the ravages of war. No good purpose would be subserved by enumerating the crimes which were committed in the Southern States during that dread period, and that under the form of [military] government. Let me say, however, that they are not justly to be attributed to the negro race. They were the work of bad white men [primarily Yankee socialists and communists belonging to the then Left-wing Republican Party] who preyed upon the superstitions and ignorance of that race, and made it a scapegoat for their own wicked performance. It may be that under the pressure of our environments at that time some things were done by our people which had better been left undone, but when I reflect upon the enormity of our provocation, I realize that if it had not been for the patience and fortitude displayed by the veterans of the Confederate armies, which had come to them through their years of discipline, there might, and probably would, have been such anarchy and bloodshed throughout the South as would have shocked the civilized world. We have before us the gravest social problems with which any people were ever confronted. If the negro belongs to the weaker race, so much the greater is the duty upon us of the white race, by the lessons of example, to prepare him for the proper discharge of the solemn duties of citizenship.

We must not judge the negro too hastily or too harshly, nor expect him, without that preparation which can come only from the long exercise of those duties, to measure up to the standard which we set for ourselves. If they do not understand now, they will in time, that they can have no separate foundation for happiness and prosperity from that upon which we build our own; that we must live and struggle side by side, all doing their best to work out a just solution of the problems which confront us; and that this can never be accomplished in a way which would bring the best results, except by the steady and persistent cultivation of peaceable and kindly relations.

Let us esteem ourselves fortunate that we have survived long enough to witness the total banishment of those asperities which so long existed between the different sections of our country. The mellowing influence of time has softened and cleared the vision of us all. We now see things clearly where once we could not see at all. We now know that good people are the same everywhere; that no section has a monopoly of patriotism or virtue; that our people, no matter whence they come, are flesh of one flesh and are inspired by the same lofty courage and noble purpose. . . .²²² — THOMAS CLENDINEN CATCHINGS

THE TRUE CAUSE OF POSTWAR RACIAL FRICTION
☛ The people of Virginia never blamed the negroes for the war and its evil consequences. In fact the fidelity of the great majority of them to their masters' families during the whole period of the war has always been remembered with appreciation by the white people of the South. The old servants still depended on their former masters for advice and aid. The press and the official reports of the Federal [U.S.] officers stationed in Virginia indicate an increasing spirit of harmony between the races from 1865 to 1867. It was the injection of the negroes into politics before they were sufficiently intelligent [that is, educated] to assume the responsibilities of the franchise, and the radical [that is, the socialist and communist element of the then Left-wing Republican Party] influence of the Freedmen's Bureau officials, Union Leaguers, Northern political adventurers of all kinds and [Liberal] Northern school teachers that caused the friction that existed between whites and blacks after 1867.²²³ — RICHARD LEE MORTON, 1913

C.S. cruiser *Georgia*.

Deleted from mainstream histories: These Southern black servants ("slaves" to Yankees) are praying for the safety and welfare of their friends, patrons, and neighbors, white Southerners. In turn, white Southerners prayed continually for the well-being of their African-American servants as well. This was common practice across antebellum Dixie, a time when blacks viewed whites as their advocates and benefactors, and whites registered black "slaves" as legal members of their own families at the time of purchase. This delicately balanced relationship dynamic was obliterated after the fall of Richmond in April 1865, leading to a 12 year period marked by social chaos, increased racial friction, financial stress, brutal lawlessness, and uncertainty for both races. Yes, of course, slavery had to end. But not in the manner it did. While the South had long been formulating its own gentle, legal, systematic, gradual, peaceful path to full emancipation, the ultimate course of Southern abolition was pre-planned by the North to be purposefully harsh, illegal, disorderly, abrupt, and even violent (see, for example, Lincoln's January 1, 1863, Emancipation Proclamation, second paragraph); which is why many of the effects of the draconian Reconstruction measures put in place between 1865 and 1877, *Twelve Years in Hell*, are with us still. Moreover, they continue to be exploited by the originators of that scandalously unlawful and repressive era: the far Left. One only need read the daily headlines.

CHAPTER 13

HONORING THE CONFEDERATE DEAD

☛ . . . They gave up their lives in defense of home and loved ones, to drive back the hirelings who sought to despoil our altars and devour our substance. Amid the roar of battle and the clash of arms their souls took flight. They were spared the ignominy and degradation of the days of reconstruction. We are not called upon to prove they were right; we know they were. They fought for a principle [constitutionalism] that is as eternal as the stars. Sacred ties bind us to their memory. Side by side we toiled with them on the weary march, and stood shoulder to shoulder with them where battle raged and death reveled in the slaughter. We can vouch for their valor as they faced and fought the foe, and can testify to their good names. In obedience to a sentiment of honor and a call of duty, they made the last human sacrifice: they gave up their lives for a grand and glorious cause. It was such courage as this, my comrades, that has made the "boys who wore the gray" the immortal heroes of our Southland, and as long as life lasts we will honor them in their grand achievements.[224] — CONFEDERATE OFFICER R. H. LINDSAY

PLEA FOR UNITY OF ACTION IN THE SOUTH

☛ Let us be thankful for respite from political wrangle for a few years, during which time let us get the bearings in the South whereby unity of sentiment and action may be continued. One of the most grievous things that could happen in the South would be disruption of methods whereby the white people, after having wrested their State governments from carpet-bag rule, achieved the wonderful result of restoring public credit after the general bankruptcy brought about by devastating war and "reconstruction."

Good men differ about the purposes and character of the late candidates for President [Republican, now Conservative, William McKinley, versus Democrat, now Liberal, William Jennings Bryan], and now that the [1900] election is over, let us all take a rest. Sufficient unto the day is the evil that is to come. The purpose of this writing is to plead that our people stand together for the good of our common country. Race issues demand this, even should the people become lukewarm in the associations whereby we have been so constantly and universally sympathetic through more than three decades. The severity and bitterness of the long years of reconstruction may have had greater compensation than we realized through the devotion of the Southern people to each other. Those attachments should continue as long as there be memories to revere of sacrifice in a common cause. No issues having pecuniary consideration should ever cause a breach among our people. All lines of patriotic life were above that so long that the surrender would lower our political morality below what we can afford. The people of the Southern States should meet in convention, if necessary, to maintain the solidarity of the section. "Solid South" is a term used in intended discredit to the people of the South, but results have caused that sentiment to be a benefit to the section, and thereby a blessing to the nation. In this connection the most hopeful sign of the race problem is the action of prominent negroes in publicly advocating the wisdom and the justice of their race, looking to the white people of the South as their best friends.[225] — SUMNER A. CUNNINGHAM, EDITOR *CONFEDERATE VETERAN*, 1900

Turning angry, indoctrinated, white-hating blacks into Southern police officers was a recipe for social, racial, and judicial disaster. But that is the exact result that Yankee Socialists and Communists intended.

UNITY OF THE SOUTHERN PEOPLE

☛ Nearly forty years have intervened in the memory of all who were Confederate soldiers, taking them in turn through the thrill and the havoc of war—the four years being an age—the long, bitter period of reconstruction, and the subsequent years of peace. The four decades have bound men together in a sympathy that only makes the condition good faith precedent to unstinted sacrifice for each other. Wealth even to multimillions does not dwarf the possessor to narrowness in affectionate regard for his true comrade who has struggled on and on through adversity. It would exalt the minds of others to know with what unselfish regard the rich, in a quiet way, share with the unfortunate when their merit is unquestioned. That more of this is not done is rather from lack of opportunity than inclination. Approach the richest of these men so they will know of true merit, and the response is sure and liberal. The best way understood, more and more of this unselfish liberality will be continued until time is no more. The shame of reconstruction days, while dishonoring the "top rails," was such a blessing to those at the bottom that it is not well to overlook, and the steadfastness of Confederates to principle sealed their devotion to each other. Let us pray that these relations may continue, for they have maintained the exaltation of ancestral patriotism, and have been a pride to that class on the other side who fought only for the Union and with whom the war ended in 1865.[226] — SUMNER A. CUNNINGHAM, EDITOR *CONFEDERATE VETERAN*, 1900

CONFEDERATE SOLDIERS AFTER THE WAR

☛ . . . I honor the old Confederate soldier for the courage, with which he fought and suffered for four long years, for what he thought was right during the war, but I doubly honor him for the brave and manly fight he made for home rule and free government after the war. When bitterness and strife prevailed, when reconstruction hung like a pall over the fair but prostrate South, and when the Southern people were disfranchised and denied the right of citizenship in their own land, the old Confederate soldier, with a patience, a conservatism, and a moral courage that was sublime, fought for home rule and the right of the Southern people to vote and control their own affairs, and he won a victory no less splendid in peace than those which he had achieved in war. For this we young men owe him a lasting debt of gratitude.[227] — HONORABLE J. B. FRAZIER

A WOMAN'S VIEW OF RECONSTRUCTION

☛ . . . When the war was over and arms had been surrendered and the oath of allegiance taken, our soldiers returned to their homes, when homes were left, with heavy hearts. In many cases they found loved ones gone. Heaps of ashes were piled where once their homes had stood. Was it not natural that, out of heart, out of money, and with hope itself almost gone, they should have despaired?

A period of darkness followed—the reconstruction period—and one can well understand how much courage it needed in that hour of despair to contemplate living, much less thinking of rearing monuments to the dead. And yet this is just what was done. The conditions to be met were far more trying than the perils encountered on the field of battle; and yet these brave men endured want without a murmur and submitted to oppression with a patience rarely equaled and never surpassed in the history of the world. True it was they were in honor bound not to resist, on account of the obligations implied in their paroles; but there are ways and ways of bearing wrongs, and they were verily brave in the bearing of theirs. Those who never had known what it was to toil before toiled now with their own hands to keep the wolf of hunger from the door of their loved ones. They put discouragement's behind them, and they moved forward resolutely in the path of love and duty.

And while I would not detract one iota from the courage required of these brave men at this time, I must in justice pay a tribute where it rightfully belongs—to the wives and mothers who sustained and cheered them during these days of gloom and despondency. In times of danger, if danger threatens physical harm, women is a natural coward; but if the danger threatens the moral nature or inner life, she becomes heroic, and meets adversity with a braver heart than man. And so it was at this period of our history, for verily it was when hope had well-nigh vanished and these women saw loved ones cast down, with spirit gone, they said:

> "The cause is not lost. We will build monuments to our loved dead, to let the world see that we believe they died for what was just and right. We will keep in tender remembrance these dead heroes of ours."

Hope begets hope, and when the women became hopeful then the hearts of the men revived and became full of hope. Lofty shafts began to be erected all over our beloved Southland, to stand in mute and eloquent evidence of the loving devotion they bore the Confederate cause. From the very commencement of this memorial work every obstacle was thrown in the way by the Federal [U.S.] authorities. At New Orleans July 6, 1866, the following official order was issued:

> "Notification is hereby given for the information of all concerned that no monument intended to commemorate the late rebellion will be permitted to be erected within the limits of the military division of the Gulf."

The soldiers on parole said: "We cannot even give encouragement to this work, for our word of honor forbids." But the women said:

> "We are under no parole, we have taken no [U.S.] oath of allegiance; we will give entertainments, we will not ask your aid, we will sell our

own handiwork and get the means whereby our dead shall be honored."

And they did. These wives and mothers began to formulate plans and to raise funds to honor the fallen brave. They took upon themselves the duty of locating and removing the scattered Confederate dust. With the scantiest means at their disposal and under the most discouraging conditions, they entered upon this labor of love. So general became the custom of erecting monuments throughout the South that it is now regarded as a stigma of reproach to that town or city where no monument has been raised. . . . [228] — MILDRED LEWIS RUTHERFORD, STATE HISTORIAN GEORGIA DIVISION, U.D.C.

THE "EVIL INFLUENCES" OF RECONSTRUCTION
☞ It would indeed have been a happy fate for the country if the example of the Southern hero [Robert E. Lee], after Appomattox, which has secured for him for all time a recognition that makes him only second in war, second in peace, and second in the hearts of his countrymen, had been followed by the North and its commander. It is difficult to speak with calmness or moderation of the scenes enacted in the decade following 1865. No appeals could check the wild orgy into which the controlling [Left-wing] powers in the North had rushed. A South so plundered that all the ruins of the war appeared as nothing! A North reeking with corruption until the records of Credit Mobiler Frauds and Black Friday tumults made the people doubt the integrity of all! The terrible scourge of so-called reconstructions, as directed by the distorted brain of [radical socialist Yankee] Thaddeus Stevens, and the iniquities of the "Freedmen's Bureau" aroused not only the South, but the North itself. Even those apostles of the cause that produced the war, [Yankee socialist Horace] Greeley, [Salmon P.] Chase, [George] Julian, the war governors [John A.] Andrew of Massachusetts and [Andrew G.] Curtin of Pennsylvania, and many others rebelled against the actions of their old political associates. Few governments have survived such evil influences as culminated in the great crime of [the contentious presidential election of] 1876 [when Liberal Republican Rutherford B. Hayes defeated Conservative Democrat Samuel J. Tilden], when even the will of the people overwhelmingly asserted at the polls was ruthlessly disregarded. The sad story is now, I hope, nearing the end.

Slowly but surely the truth is being recognized and public sentiment is approving the assertion of their powers by the several

States over their domestic concerns. It has been a strange anomaly that at a time when the right of local self-government is the cry of every State, this very right has been denied to the States themselves. In the vast growth of this great power among nations it becomes more and more necessary that the Federal Government should exercise full powers in our external affairs and in those specific fields assigned to it by the Constitution; but *it is even more vitally necessary that in their internal affairs and in those fields retained by the States there should be no Federal interference* [my emphasis, L.S.].

More than ever before will it be impossible to secure peace and contentment throughout this vast territory, extending from ocean to ocean, with its infinite variety of climate, conditions and the occupations of its peoples, *unless these peoples are left to themselves to determine and control their private interests* [my emphasis, L.S.]. The language of Thomas Jefferson in his first inaugural, defining the essential principles of our government, it is well to repeat. He expressly declares as of the first importance the "support of the State governments in all their rights as the most competent administrations for our domestic concerns and the surest bulwarks against anti-republican [anti-Conservative] tendencies . . . the preservation of the general government in its whole constitutional vigor, as the sheet anchor of our peace at home and abroad."[229] — HONORABLE JOHN CADWALADER

HOW A GERMAN BECAME A PRO-SOUTHER

☞ There is now residing in Mexia, Tex., a German whom we will call Schmidt, because that isn't his name. He has been a prominent business man and a good citizen a number of years, and is intensely Southern in his sentiments. Having learned that he was born in Germany, I asked him how it was that his sympathies were so strongly in favor of the South. He replied substantially as follows:

> I was born in Germany, and left there when I was nine years old, and landed in Galveston, Tex., in 1868. I could speak only two English words, yes and no. One day, soon after my arrival, I was in company with five or six other boys about my age, and they proposed that we play "Yankee and Rebel." It was during reconstruction days, and owing to the fact that the Yankees were trying to force on the white people, through the aid of Federal soldiers, the social equality of the negro and negro domination, the feeling against the Yankees was very bitter. So the other boys asked me which side I would take. Not knowing what Yankee or Rebel meant, and somehow associating in my mind the word Rebel with a word in German meaning robber, I told them I would take the Yankee side. "All right," they said, and immediately the whole crowd pounced on me, and they gave me the worst licking I

ever had. When they got through with me I knew the difference, and have never tried to play on the Yankee side since. They got in their work in good shape, and it has stuck good and fast. Ever since then I have been a Rebel and my children are all of the same breed.[230] —
SUMNER A. CUNNINGHAM, EDITOR *CONFEDERATE VETERAN*, 1903

A SOUTHERN DOCTOR ADDRESSES RECONSTRUCTION

☛ . . . Recall the awful years of reconstruction, when the sole comrades you envied were those dead on the field of battle, when to live was a far more grievous fate than to have died for Dixie, when by outrageous taxation you were robbed of the scanty products of your toilsome poverty; when your rights as pardoned prisoners of war with restoration to citizenship were desecrated; when you, the descendants of a long line of freemen, you who had during four of the bloodiest years in history proved that the sons of your forefathers had not degenerated, you who had given such daring to the Army of the Confederacy that even its victors had trembled, you, even you, were made subservient to your own black slaves, led by those hyenas of the North called carpet-baggers and by those buzzards of the South called scalawags. Would to God we could forget that behind these villains and their ignorant, venal followers stood the victorious soldiers of the United States, and that over them all flaunted the [U.S.] flag that could never have existed but for the valor of our sires, the flag crimsoned with their blood shed for liberty, independence, and a fraternal union! In those woeful days it seemed to Confederate patriots that hell had disgorged all its fiends to devastate the South, and that Satan had at last vanquished God. Then the torturing iron of humiliation scared your souls, and then the "Solid South" was born that still survives.

But slowly, very slowly, you began to realize that all men of the North were not animated by hatred, malice, and revenge, that there were some [mainly fellow Democrats, then America's major Conservative Party] who loved justice, loved the South, and were incensed at the outrages inflicted by the victors on the vanquished. It is a source of just pride to recall that the first manifestation by any prominent class of men of the justice and mercy of God and of the charity of Christ issued from those whose lives are dedicated to the service of humanity, the men of the medical profession. In 1869 there assembled in New Orleans the American Medical Association, bringing with it from Northern homes proffers of sympathy, encouragement, influence, and aid; led by him who was the worthy leader of our profession. For he was the nation's greatest surgeon, and a man unsurpassed for nobility of character and for a patriotism broad enough to clasp in loving arms the patriots of the Confederacy. This great and good man was Samuel D. Gross, of Pennsylvania, whose memory should be cherished by every son of the South.

Another ray of hope came, in 1872, to New Orleans and the South, for it proved that the unconquerable spirit that sustained the Confederacy still lived, that surviving Confederates and their sons could still strike a deadly blow for their right as freemen to openly purchase and to wear arms for their own defense. On the bank of the Mississippi, at the foot of the street you are now seated by, stands Liberty Place, where a scanty number of patriots promptly drove the armed mercenaries of the carpet-baggers into the near-by customhouse, where, under the folds of the stars and stripes [U.S. flag], they cowered for protection. Sixteen patriots [Conservative Southerners] were killed in giving this needed lesson to the United States. The lesson thus taught was that the reconstruction governments, based on carpet-baggers, renegades, and ex-slaves, were flimsy houses of cards that the crook of the fingers of a few patriots would topple to the ground but for the support of the army. Therefore, that these governments were not the strong, civil governments hoped for by a revengeful [U.S.] Congress, but the very worst of all military governments, one executed by selfish scoundrels, sustained by millions of semi-barbarians who cared much for license, nothing for liberty, and who knew naught of the patriotism that passionately faces death to secure the rights of freemen.

And so, at last, justice, sound policy, and some fear that the Lion of the Confederacy, exhausted by starvation and bleeding wounds, was regaining strength and might, in desperation, renew his dreaded roar in battle, regained our ancestral rights as freemen. For in this State, in 1876, a Confederate veteran, grievously mutilated and permanently disabled in battle (Gen. Francis T. Nicholls, now Chief Justice), became the Governor of Louisiana. Then hope, confidence, and progress revived, after fifteen of the most trying years that any patriots ever endured. . . .[231] — DR. STANFORD E. CHAILLÉ, NEW ORLEANS, LOUISIANA, 1903

MORNINGS DURING RECONSTRUCTION DAYS

☛ . . . Every morning before the Preacher could finish his breakfast, callers were knocking at the door—the negro, the poor white, the widow, the orphan, the wounded, the hungry: an endless procession.

The spirit of the returned soldiers was all that he could ask. There was nowhere a slumbering spark of war. There was not the slightest effort to continue the lawless habits of four years of strife. Everywhere the spirit of patience, self-restraint and hope marked the life of the men who had made the most terrible [that is, ferocious] soldiery. They were glad to be done with war and have the opportunity to rebuild their broken fortunes. They were glad, too, that the everlasting question of a divided Union was settled and settled forever. There was now to be one country and one flag, and deep down in their souls they were content with it.

The spectacle of this terrible army of the Confederacy, the memory of whose battle-cry yet thrills the world, transformed in a month into patient and hopeful workmen, has never been paralleled in history.

Who destroyed this scene of peaceful rehabilitation? Hell has no pit dark enough, and no damnation deep enough, for these conspirators when once history has fixed their guilt.

The task before the people of the South was one to tax the genius of the Anglo-Saxon race as never in its history, even had every friendly aid possible been extended by the victorious North. Four million negroes had suddenly been freed, and the foundations of economic order destroyed. Five billions of dollars' worth of property were wiped out of existence, banks closed, every dollar of [Confederate] money worthless paper, the country plundered by victorious armies, its cities, mills and homes burned, and the flower of its manhood buried in nameless trenches, or worse still, flung upon the charity of poverty, maimed wrecks. The task of organising this wrecked society and marshaling into efficient citizenship this host of ignorant [that is, illiterate] negroes, and yet to preserve the civilisation of the Anglo-Saxon race, the priceless heritage of two thousand years of struggle, was one to appal the wisdom of ages. Honestly and earnestly the white people of the South set about this work, and accepted the Thirteenth Amendment to the Constitution abolishing slavery without a protesting vote.

The President [Andrew Johnson] issued his proclamation announcing the method of restoring the Union as it had been handed to him from the martyred Lincoln, and indorsed unanimously by Lincoln's Cabinet. This plan was simple, broad and statesmanlike, and its spirit breathed Fraternity and Union with malice toward none and charity toward all. It declared what Lincoln had always taught, that the Union was indestructible, that the rebellious states had now only to repudiate Secession, abolish slavery, and resume their positions in the Union, to preserve which so many lives had been sacrificed. . . .[232] — THOMAS DIXON JR., 1902

SOUTHERN WOMEN DURING RECONSTRUCTION

☛ . . . The women of the South gave all they had to their country. They saw their fathers, husbands, and brothers depart to the field of battle, and they saw them no more forever. They put away their imported and store-bought garments and dressed in clothes that were woven and made by their own hands. They tore the carpets from the floors of the mansion and cottage, and sent them to the camps to be used as blankets by the soldiers. Hands that never knew the task of an hour's labor were willingly turned to daily and nightly toil. They wove blankets, knit socks, made over and patched old garments and sent them to clothe a half-naked army. They took charge of the hospitals and nursed the sick and wounded back to life and health, or, with gentle and loving hands, they dressed the dead and laid them away in their last resting places. They followed the army on the field of battle and hung like ministering angels at the side of the wounded and dying. They bound up the wounds of friend and foe alike, and cheered them with words of sympathy and kindness. They heard the last wish of the dying boy, and sent it with a lock of hair and his words of undying love to the mother at the far-off home. When the Southern army gave way before the overwhelming hosts that surrounded it, the women of the South bore the great disaster and met their fate with as much courage as the men; and when the governments of the Southern States, in violation of the terms under which their armies in the field had surrendered, were overthrown by military violence, their territory held under martial law and reduced to the condition of conquered provinces, they passed through the dark days of the desolating reconstruction, and met with resolute fortitude the triumphant presence of the foe that had invaded their land, destroyed their institutions, usurped their governments, bonded their property, and held them beneath their slaves in social and political bondage. And when at last their political thralldom ended and local self-government was once more recognized in the land, they made haste to care for the maimed and needy heroes who had fought in their defense, and to preserve the memory of the dead who had died for them on the field of battle. They organized associations that extended over every Southern State and had members in every Southern home, and under the name of the Daughters of the Confederacy they went forth on their holy mission of mercy and of love. By lectures, festivals, and entertainments

Before Reconstruction, the vast majority of white Southern slave owners (less than 5 percent of the total population) and their indentured black servants lived in relative harmony with one another in the leisurely, slow-paced manner that was endemic to Old Southern society. In exchange for his or her comparatively short work week (often less than 40 hours), a black servant's every need was met and paid for by his white (and sometimes black and Indian) owners—from cradle to grave. This all changed under Reconstruction, however. In the New South, uneducated and untrained former black servants, unfamiliar with the many serious responsibilities of freedom, were released from one form of bondage only to be returned to another: poverty, disease, hunger, malnutrition, homelessness, mental illness, increased family dysfunctionality and divorce rates, crime, drug use, alcoholism, safety issues, prostitution, lack of sanitation, stress, depression, and an overall decrease in quality of life and life span.

they enlisted the patronage of the people and collected large sums of money and expended them in building retreats where the decrepit soldiers could find the care and comforts of a home. They gathered together the scattered remains of their dead heroes and gave them burial in places beautified by their own hands and made attractive by magnificent and costly monuments that will mark their last resting place and perpetuate their glorious fame.

All hail to the Daughters of the Confederacy! May the great God of mercy bless them! They have built well and wisely and better than they knew. They have laid the foundation of a work of gratitude, a labor of love that will be continued by their children and their children's children, until a monumental memorial shall crown every battlefield and every cemetery where their martial heroes lie, and their glorious work and self-sacrificing labors will be linked with the deathless fame of their fallen heroes and be made to live forever.

The annals of the human race will show that our sex have ever been true and loyal to those who in the time of trouble and peril and war have stood high in the councils of the nation, and have sacrificed much for its welfare and defense. Jefferson Davis, as the chosen leader of the Southern Confederacy, had their full confidence; and as time wore on and his great ability, patriotism, and courage were developed by the progress of the war, they learned to honor, admire, and love him; and when his armies were overwhelmed, and to symbolize the bondage of his people whom he had served so faithfully and so well, he was made a chained captive in the casemated cell of Fortress Monroe—then from that moment he became the object of their tenderest affection, and will for all time to come hold the first place in their memory as the beloved chief of their wrecked and ruined cause. And this kindly sympathy, this love, this admiration followed him through all the days of his illustrious and honored life; and when he died, high above the general sorrow of the people of the South could be heard the unfeigned grief of its women, as if the dark shadow of death had been cast athwart their own households.

Animated by a spirit of sectional hate, the political writers of the North, in order to degrade the cause of the South, have sought to cast reproach upon the name and fame of its chosen leader, Jefferson Davis, by seeking to hold him responsible for all the calamities that attended a bloody and destructive war; but *the great scholars of the globe have turned the search light of scientific investigation upon the constitutional history of this country, and, in vindication of the truth, have declared to the world that the parties to the constitutional compact were sovereign States, and had the right, as it was their duty, to withdraw from the Union whenever, in their judgment, it endangered their safety and happiness, and that Jefferson Davis was justified in all that he did to secure a political separation from a factional section of States that had for so many years violated and broken the fundamental agreement* [my emphasis, L.S.]. They exonerate him from all blame for the blood that was shed, and place its responsibility upon the heads of those who violated the Constitution of their country and inaugurated the war. They applaud him for the great part that he took in the greatest drama ever enacted in the history of the world, and now that he is dead they honor his memory for all that he sacrificed and suffered in the sacred cause of constitutional liberty. And thus it is that the whole world now knows that Jefferson Davis led only where the freemen of thirteen commonwealths were glad to follow, and that the six hundred thousand Confederate officers and soldiers who fought for home and friends and kindred and for separation from a broken and discarded Union would have followed the same flag and fought the same battles if their great leader in the contest and the greatest of his compeers had never been born. Time has shown that all those defeated Confederate veterans who still live take upon themselves all the responsibility for what they did as soldiers in the war between the States; and now that the mighty issue has been tried and the wager lost, they demand that they bear with their great leader their full portion of blame for its failure, and claim their share of the glory which was won on a thousand battlefields by those wondrous deeds of valor that astonished the nations of the earth and linked that gigantic struggle for constitutional independence with a fame that will be immortal.

And the women of the Southland, true to their love for the triumph of justice and right, will denounce the untruthful writings against the fair name of Jefferson Davis. They will defend all the great acts of his illustrious life, and keep ever bright and green their love for his memory. They will remember the purity of his private life, his fortitude under many trying difficulties, his indomitable courage throughout all the vicissitudes of his eventful career, and, above all, his suffering as a vicarious victim for the cause of the people; and should they forget all this, the cruel scene enacted within the casemated cell of Fortress Monroe would rise up as a vision and remind them of the duty they owe to the memory of the most illustrious of their dead. . . .[233] — MISS EDMONDA AUGUSTA NICKERSON, WARRENSBURG, MISSOURI, 1902

CONFEDERATE SOLDIERS AFTER THE WAR

☛ . . . Sour and sullen, did he turn to his desolated home to sit idly down and curse the fate that had wrought such wreck and ruin? Disfranchised, pursued, and harassed through all those dark reconstruction days by the cruel hate not of his soldier foes but of corrupt and scheming politicians, with few resources save his own brave heart and indomitable will and the recuperative powers of a land on which shone the Southern sun—see him take up and manfully bear the burdens of life until wasted lands again waved with bountiful harvests, cities rose from their ashes and, with new ones that sprang from his enterprise and energy, adorned the land as busy marts of trade, while field and forest echoed and reechoed with the roar of the multitudinous wheels of prosperous industry.[234]
— REVEREND G. W. FINLEY, VIRGINIA

THE OLD ORDER CHANGETH

☛ . . . The breaking up of camps throughout the South necessarily led to much moving of tents among all classes. The old home life was a thing of the past. The laborer was no longer worthy of his hire, and had he been worthy his former owner could not have afforded to "keep" him.

Many, indeed, had been the hearts anxious for the war to cease; but, weary as the waiting was at home, the earnest exhortation to loved ones in the army had been, "Stay on till all is over; we can endure." Nor was this spirit lacking when the remnants of the

Southern army returned, and had to begin the battle for bread without hoe or plow or horse; for though the last was a concession at the surrender, such were the obstructions on the part of speculators already hungry and ready to take advantage of the helpless, that not many reached home with a horse. Truly, the old order was passing, "giving way to new," the like of which had not been seen, and from the like of which "may the good Lord deliver us!" The visage of the times was rough indeed. There were wild rangers in every forest claiming that the land was forfeited to the [U.S.] government and forty acres and a mule would be given to each freedman. War at its worst estate was scarcely so bad as the troublous times known as, "reconstruction." Domestic affairs were in a deplorable condition.

This "mixed-race" jury, the first of its kind ever formed in the U.S., was impaneled to try Confederate President Jefferson Davis for "treason." At the top, from left to right, is: Chief Justice Salmon P. Chase, Davis, and the presiding judge, John C. Underwood. The U.S. government could not find a single attorney willing to prosecute Davis. Why? Because it was well-known, and accepted, that secession was legal (as it still is today). Thus, the case was dropped and Davis was quietly released from prison. It is obvious why these facts are never discussed in conventional, Left-wing authored history books.

In December (18), 1865, the thirteenth amendment, abolishing slavery, was adopted as part of the Constitution, and at once there was an exodus of many of the old-time faithful attachés of the fallen fortunes of their masters, and who would have remained faithful but for the evil counsels of bad white men [that is, the socialists and communists of the then Left-wing Republican Party] come hither from the ends of the earth to prey, to plunder, and for political purposes.

Fluentes Omnium ("ragged robins") and vultures, whose sharp beaks found no dead body too filthy for picking, if perchance some morsel could be found to appease for a time the insatiable appetite. The [radical Left-wing, anti-white] Freedmen's Bureau, Civil Rights, and Tenure of Office bills were all extremely oppressive measures upon the former [Southern] land owners and slaveholders. The Tenure of Office bill especially, because, while the second bill guaranteed to the negroes the rights of citizenship, the last virtually disfranchised their former owners, "as a requisite demanded by Congress for holding office was that every candidate should swear that he had not participated in the secession movement. This virtually excluded Southern men from holding office, and was the sowing of dragon's teeth that gave for successive years a wild crop of adventurers known as "carpet-baggers" or beggars.

Nor was the Church exempt from the evils that infested the State. Every available means was used to retain possession of our churches (many of which had been used as hospitals), even when soldiers had gone and we were no longer under military rule. "Absorption" was a much-mooted theme in certain clerical circles. I know an instance in which a missionary came "to take possession" of one of our wealthiest and most influential Methodist churches![235]
— SUE F. DROMGOOLE MOONEY

NASHVILLE ADDRESSES CONFEDERATE VETERANS

☛ . . . When the Confederates reached their desolate homes after the war, their war had really only begun; there is no use to tell lies about it. It had taken all that was in them to learn to love that old [U.S.] flag again, carpet-baggery and free niggery [abolition] had been almost too much for their patience and fortitude. Yet under such conditions they finally restored the South to its old place in the Union and supplanted negro slavery with white civilization.

Were I Demosthenes or Cicero to-day, I could not overpraise the Confederate veteran. His courage has no equal and his endurance knew no end.

Nashville has decked her homes with brilliant bunting, has entwined the flags of the Confederacy and of the Union together—the flag of our Union, which no Confederate will ever dishonor. But I speak the sentiment of every Southern soldier when

I say that while one is the flag of our country, that we honor and obey, the other little flag of the stars and bars is the flag of our hearts. (The wildest enthusiasm greeted this sentiment.)

I don't know where we will meet next year, but Nashville extends you an invitation to meet here until the last Confederate soldier is laid in his grave. You saved the country; you saved it from the horrors and barbarities of reconstruction, and it is yours; you are welcome here whenever you may come."[236] — ESQUIRE TULLY BROWN, NASHVILLE, TENN.

LEFT-WING MENACING & HUMILIATION

☞ . . . You will remember the ten long years of so-called reconstruction which made the four long years of war itself seem tolerable by comparison, the ten long years during every day and every night of which Southern womanhood was menaced and Southern manhood humiliated. . . . The brethren of our own race, in our own country—the country whose pen had been [Thomas] Jefferson, whose tongue had been Patrick Henry, and whose sword had been [George] Washington—were against not only us but the [white] race itself—its past, its future—were seemingly bent only on two things—our humiliation as a race in the present, our subordination as a race in the future. . . .[237] — MISSISSIPPI REPRESENTATIVE JOHN SHARP WILLIAMS

A YANKEE SOLDIER WHO REGRETTED RECONSTRUCTION

☞ . . . I was a member of [Union Admiral Samuel F.] Dupont's fleet that reduced and took possession of Port Royal, S.C., and St. Augustine and Fernandina, Fla., in 1861-62. I was in command of Camp Chimborazo after the fall of Richmond, in 1865. Into Camp Chimborazo we gathered the floating contrabands [the North's derogatory name for Southern blacks] and refugees, and utilized them in cleaning up and rebuilding the historic city. In July, 1865, I was relieved at Chimborazo, and as military commandant ordered to a sub-district with headquarters at Point of Rocks, on the Appomattox [River], where I met my Rebel half [Southern wife], who still insists that she knows of one "Yank" that was and is conquered. On being ordered to Washington in the fall of 1865, I visited Richmond, and there met relatives of my wife that I paroled from the Point of Rocks military prison, Maryland. In obedience to orders, I finally found myself in the city of New Orleans, La., where I resigned the service to engage in civil affairs under the sign of attorney and counselor, advocate. My, what a whirl there was in those days of so-called reconstruction—re-destruction!

New Orleans then was the Mecca of ex-Confederates, as well as many others. There I often met and was pleased to have on my list of friends two [Confederate] generals, John B. Gordon and [James] Longstreet; also Gens. [Pierre G. T.] Beauregard, [John Bell] Hood, [Braxton] Bragg, [Jubal A.] Early, and others. [Liberal] Govs. [Daniel H.] Chamberlain, of South Carolina, and [Adelbert] Ames, of Mississippi, and other Governors of reconstruction days could occasionally be seen at the clubs. [Confederate] Gen. [William] Mahone, of Virginia, and the late [Conservative] Justice [Lucius Q. C.] Lamar, of the United States Supreme Court, did not forget to visit the Crescent City during the Mardi Gras season.

Of them all, I saw most of Longstreet and knew him best. During the great riot of the 14th of September, 1874, I was holding court in the parish of St. Bernard, adjoining the city of New Orleans on the south. On the evening of the 12th of September I had a long talk with Gen. Longstreet, Chief of Police Badger, and two others, whose names I do not now remember, but who were officers of the State militia and metropolitan police. I think the police officer was Capt. [Michael K.] Lawler, an ex-officer of the Union army. At that meeting it seemed to be understood that if trouble came and the militia were called into action, Gen. Longstreet would take active command of the State military forces. He was looked upon by every one who hoped for peace as the man of the hour and to whose advice the opposing elements would listen. He certainly was the man to command the forces of the government; and when the order (which it was) was handed to him to take command, while it was seen that he did not relish the order, he, soldierlike, obeyed and did his duty as he understood it. In this he believed he was right, as on the same belief of right action, he, in the hour of need, stood by the Confederacy. Gen. Longstreet was not a party to the hatreds or political troubles then existing.

It was not the fault of the people, but rather of the policy of reconstruction, that sought to put the "bottom rail on top" under the promise of "forty acres and a mule," regardless of the lessons of history, the weakness, inexperience, and ignorance of an inferior race. Section two of the Fourteenth Amendment and the Fifteenth Amendment to the United States Constitution are to-day nullities. They cannot, will not, be enforced. Reconstruction [along with its Left-wing institutional racist policies] should have failed as it did.[238]
— FORMER UNION SOLDIER, JUDGE P. P. CARROLL, SEATTLE, WASH., 1905

EXAMPLES OF

ALABAMA RECONSTRUCTIONISTS

Examples of Reconstructionists, that is, Radical Left-wing Liberals, in postbellum Alabama. Top left: Alabama Republican (then Left-wing) Governor Lewis E. Parsons; top right: Alabama Republican (then Left-wing) Governor William H. Smith; top middle: Alabama Republican (then Left-wing) Governor David P. Lewis. Bottom image (original caption): "Negro members of the convention of 1875 are on the left. The white man in the back row [top right] is Samuel Smith."

CHAPTER 14

A YANKEE POLITICIAN WHO REGRETTED RECONSTRUCTION

☞ ... No people were ever brought face to face with more utter desolation than that which confronted the men of the South on their return from Appomattox. It was not alone that they had lost the fight; that their ranks had been sadly thinned by the war; that their lands had been laid waste, their properly confiscated or destroyed. Their whole social, industrial, and political fabric lay in ruins. Their task was not the hopeful one of restoring an old order, but the well-nigh hopeless one of bringing a new order out of chaos. But they set to work with the courage and patience that create hope and defy failure. And they have triumphed gloriously. To-day they are enjoying the fruits of a victory greater than was ever won in warfare. And we of the North rejoice with them in their prosperity; for are they not our people, bone of our bone and flesh of our flesh?

On friendly terms for several centuries, Southern whites and blacks were turned against one another by Left-wing Republicans for one reason and one reason only: political ambition.

The leaders of Southern thought in 1865 accepted the results of the war, and were willing to set to work to create a new order of things on the ruins of the old. They should have been allowed to retain their natural leadership over the ignorant whites and blacks. *The most unfortunate result of our miserable reconstruction policy was that it destroyed the influence of the old leaders, instilled into the minds of the blacks feelings of "hatred, malice, and all uncharitableness" toward their natural and wisest guides, and arrayed the whites of all classes in solid opposition to the negroes [fomenting racial divisiveness has long been a staple of the Left-wing—and it continues to this day]. The fear of ignorant negro domination has persisted long after the danger of such domination has passed, working often an injustice to the negro and always a greater injury to the whites* [my emphasis, L.S.].

The amelioration of the political situation in the South is a problem that must for years to come tax the wisdom and patience of our greatest statesmen and philanthropists. We of the North have in years past made the solution of this problem more difficult for our Southern brethren. We now owe them generous sympathy and patient forbearance. Their task is a long one, and beset with peculiar difficulties. We should concede that they have done and are doing what we would do under similar circumstances. The solution of this grave and complicated problem cannot be hastened by [further] coercion, threats, or abuse.

But whatever we of the North may do, whatever the government may accomplish, the real burden of this problem rests on our brethren of the South. In her work of solving this problem the South could have no better, no firmer friend than President [Theodore] Roosevelt; for all that the South needs, besides time, is a square deal, and no one knows better than the President that a square deal for the South means simply intelligent sympathy from Northern men, unprejudiced, evenhanded justice from the Federal [U.S.] government.[239] — ADDRESS BY CONSERVATIVE YANKEE ILLINOIS CONGRESSMAN, HONORABLE HENRY SHERMAN BOUTELL, CIRCA JANUARY 1905

THERE IS NO SHAME IN OBEYING ONE'S CONSCIENCE

☛ . . . Looking back then to-day my comrades, over the four and forty years which separate us from the acts of secession passed by the Southern States, we say to the men of this generation and to those who will come after us that the opprobrium heaped upon those who then asserted the right of secession is undeserved. That right had not then been authoritatively denied. On the contrary, it had been again and again asserted, North and South, by eminent statesmen for nearly sixty years after the formation of the Union. Those who held it had as good right to their opinion as those who denied it. The weight of argument was overwhelmingly in their favor. So clear was this that *the United States government wisely decided after the fall of the Confederacy that it was not prudent to put Jefferson Davis upon his trial for treason.* Let it be remembered that the formation of the United States, in 1788, was accomplished by nine of the States seceding from the [U.S.] Confederacy which had existed for eleven years, and which had bound the States entering into it to "a perpetual Union." *Thus the [United States] Union itself was the child of secession!* [my emphasis, L.S.].

There was a time during those dark years of reconstruction when public opinion in the North demanded that we who had fought under the Southern flag should prove the sincerity of our acceptance of the results of the war by acknowledging the unrighteousness of our cause and by confessing contrition for our deeds.

But could we acknowledge our cause to be unrighteous when we still believed it just? Could we repent of an act done in obedience to the dictates of conscience? The men of the North may claim that our judgment was at fault; that our action was not justified by reason; that the fears that goaded us to withdraw from the Union were not well grounded; but so long as it is admitted that we followed duty as we understood it they cannot ask us to repent. A man can repent, I repeat, only of what he is ashamed, and it will not be claimed that we should be ashamed of obeying the dictates of conscience in the face of hardship and danger and death.

Capt. Oliver Wendell Holmes, of Massachusetts, who now occupies a seat upon the Supreme Bench of the United States, uttered these generous words nearly a quarter of a century ago:

> "We believed that it was most desirable that the North should win; we believed in the principle that the Union is indissoluble; but we equally believed that those who stood against us held just as sacred convictions that were the opposite of ours, and we respected them as every man with a heart must respect those who give all for their belief."

All honor to the valiant soldier and accomplished scholar who uttered those words! All honor, too, to another noble son of New England, Charles Francis Adams [Sr.], who has more recently declared, recognizing the same principle, that both the North and the South were right in the great struggle of the War between the States, because each believed itself right. When Jefferson Davis and Robert E. Lee were cadets at West Point, the text-books in use on political science were by St. George Tucker, a Southern writer, and William Rawle, a Northern writer, and both taught the right of a State to secede. Can these illustrious men be attainted as traitors because they put in practice the principles taught them by the authority of the government of the United States? . . .[240] — REVEREND RANDOLPH HARRISON MCKIM, ADDRESS AT NASHVILLE CONFEDERATE VETERANS REUNION, CIRCA 1905

A UNION VETERAN VISITS THE SOUTH

☞ My trip of several weeks through the South proved one of the most interesting and pleasant episodes of my life. Knowing the proverbial geniality of Southern people, I had anticipated a fairly good time among them while looking over my old campaign and battlefields, unless perchance some one in certain localities should find out my former regimental relations and confront me with some musty old bills for chickens and other sundries that had been overlooked by us in our hurry to keep ahead of [Confederate] Gen. [Nathan Bedford] Forrest's cavalry. I was well pleased, however, that the old bills were forgotten and old scores buried. I met with most cordial greetings everywhere, and was the recipient of many courtesies at the hands of your people, especially the old Confederate veterans. I am free to admit that I am very much in love with the South.

It gave me no less pleasure to see general prosperity, good cheer, and progress in every direction. I observed with real satisfaction how your people have under way the solution of the serious and perplexing problems confronting them with so much level-headed practical wisdom and energy. No fairminded observer who has the least idea of the magnitude of the difficulties in the reconstruction and rehabilitation of your social fabric upon a new basis can fail to rejoice in the progress already made—your public schools open to all children, the ballot box open to all alike under similar conditions, and the rights of property and person guaranteed to all alike by the laws of your States.

I am profoundly convinced that the genuine efforts of the South to bring order out of the chaotic condition into which the vicissitudes of a disastrous war and the more disastrous blundering of politicians had plunged their States merits the best wishes and cooperation of every good and patriotic citizen of our beloved America. It would be a blessed event in our country's history if those of the North and the South who faced each other upon the field of battle would, with others of like mind, come closer together and learn each other's conditions, difficulties, and needs. This could not fail to promote the good will necessary to a rational solution of questions that seem to threaten interminable controversy.

In this connection it is well for us Yankees, when we become excited and raise our hands in holy horror at what we think is quite terrible in some of the social and economic institutions of the North, that we have a few bosses that are not angels and a few regrettable events taking place right here on our own enlightened Western reserve, notwithstanding we have no social conditions to contend with. The War between the States, its long duration and the intense struggle, instead of fostering malice, has created the liveliest interest in me for the South and its people. My growing conviction of late years that the Southern people were willing and most able, because best informed, to handle all questions of especial interest to them and their section was fully vindicated by what I saw on my recent visit among them.[241] — E. EBERHARD, AKRON, OH.

A SOUTHERN CONGRESSMAN PUBLICLY REBUKES HIS YANKEE COMPATRIOTS CONCERNING RECONSTRUCTION

☛ Mr. Speaker [Liberal Republican Thomas B. Reed]: Virginia has suffered indeed. Her fields have been laid waste; her bosom bears many a scar. Her sons and her daughters, too, have trod the thorny path of poverty; within her borders the owl hoots now where merry voices were once heard and her streams murmur the memories of once happy but now desolate homesteads; she has passed through the fiery furnace of reconstruction and she has drunk to the dregs the cup of Republican [then the Liberal party] misrule; but in all her history her spirit has never waned, the manhood of her sons has never weakened, and she stands to-day on this floor, through her Representatives, as proudly as when her voice was the most potential in this land, and in spite of the August gentleman from Illinois [Liberal Republican Joseph G. Cannon] she protests against the assumption of power of the Speaker and the tyranny of the Republican [Liberal] party in this House. (Great applause.) Nay, more, sir; the sons of Virginia feel they are in their father's house, under their father's roof, beneath their father's flag. In this house they intend to stay, under this roof they intend to live, beneath that flag above your head, Mr. Speaker, they intend to die; and as long as they have breath they will defend the Constitution of this land against any and all foes, foreign and domestic. (Applause.) And if the gentleman from Illinois expects less of them, he will soon be made a wiser man, if not a better friend of the rights of the people and of the Constitution.[242] — SENATOR BENJAMIN H. HILL OF GEORGIA, ON THE FLOOR OF THE U.S. HOUSE OF REPRESENTATIVES, FEBRUARY 11, 1890

A CONFEDERATE SOLDIER'S PLEA

☛ . . . Let me close [my address] with a Confederate sentiment: However expedient it may have been, the legal right of the Southern States to dissolve copartnership with those of the North was absolute. We recognize that it was God's will that our cause should go down in defeat, and we have long since forgiven our friends, the enemy—especially those who did the fighting—and we sincerely hope that those who controlled the conduct of the war and of the reconstruction following it have asked and received God's forgiveness for their manner of carrying out his will. But "right is still right, though its defenders fall."[243] — J. H. FOWLES, BIRMINGHAM, AL., ADDRESS TO CONFEDERATE VETERANS, CAMP HARDEE

PEACE MUST BE FOUNDED ON LIBERTY

☞ It was one of the wisest sayings of a very wise man, that "the price of liberty is eternal vigilance." This maxim of wisdom is peculiarly applicable to the present time. Ten States of this Union are to-night under revolutionary governments, originated and imposed upon them by an external power [the U.S. government], and supported only by the bayonet [U.S. military]. These revolutionary governments displace, repress, and, for the time, suppress the regular, republican, constitutional governments which have existed here [in the South] all the while with an unbroken succession. These revolutionary governments are in the hands of carpet-baggers and scalawags, who treat the laws of their own origination with disgraceful contempt; and, under the forms of official authority, heap upon our people injuries and insults which never before were borne by men born and bred and educated in the principles of Liberty. Shameless plunder, malignant slander, corrupt favoritism, impunity for crimes when committed by partisans of the [U.S.] Government, gigantic extension of the credit of the States to penniless adventurers who come among us under the false and fraudulent plea of "developing our resources," robbery of the very *negroes who are sought to be used [by the Left] as the chief instrument of upholding this gigantic system of revolutionary fraud* [my emphasis, L.S.] and force *these* are the fruits of these revolutionary governments. *These* are the products of reconstruction. *This* is the "Situation"! And yet there are those who say: "Let us *accept* the situation."

In the last Presidential campaign we heard the potent words: "Let us have Peace!" They had their effect. They carried the Presidential election. Yet wise men then knew, as *all* men now know, that they were a delusion and a snare.—"Let us have Peace!"—It *meant* that freemen, with their necks under the heel of despotism, should remain submissive and quiet. *Such* a peace Turkey has! *Such* a peace Poland has! *Such* a peace, thank God, Ireland *refuses* to have! No people trained in the principles of liberty will ever accept of any peace that is not founded on *liberty*. Tyrants and despots may reconstruct, and *re*-reconstruct, and *re-re*-reconstruct *ad infinitum*; but they will never have peace from

American-born freemen until they give them their rights![244] — HONORABLE LINTON STEPHENS (BROTHER OF CONFEDERATE VICE PRESIDENT ALEXANDER H. STEPHENS), SPEECH AT CITY HALL, AUGUSTA, GEORGIA, FEBRUARY 18, 1871

SOUTHERN RECONSTRUCTION
☛ Mr. President, my humble belief is, and I say it with no asperity of feeling, that no people in the history of the world have ever been so misunderstood, so misjudged, and so cruelly maligned as the people I represent on this floor. It is known to this country and to this body that since the war not a solitary arm has been raised throughout the extent of Southern territory against the power and authority of the Federal Government by a solitary white man of the South, and yet we are charged, because of riots at elections, with manifestations of hostility to the Government of the United States!

A State government is overthrown; a committee of the Senate report that the powers which hold it are usurpers; the people attempt to assert their rights with the broad declaration that they mean no war upon the United States Government, and will acquiesce in its demands; the Federal soldiery, who have no interest in the support of any political party, cheer the people as they move upon the usurpers; a conflict ensues; men are killed; —and the Southern people are branded as murderers!

A band of misguided, deluded, ignorant negroes march upon converging lines in the dark hours of the night, with arms to murder, with hearts for plunder, and wagons and sacks to bear away their spoils from a peaceful city; the whites arm for defence; a conflict ensues; men are killed; —-and the South is branded as a land of murderers and assassins!

An armed black militia rides in arrogance over a country in the midst of a disarmed people; rob, pillage, insult, drag innocent citizens from their beds at night, and perpetrate crimes not to be described on this floor; and when men resist, when they defend themselves, their wives, and their daughters, and conflict ensues, the South is branded as a land of murderers and assassins!

Men are sent among us—I do not care otherwise to characterize them—who have no permanent habitation, no interest, no property, no sympathy with us, and whose sole purpose is to hold the offices, to levy our taxes, to gather our taxes, to disburse our taxes, to make our laws, to govern our people, and then to malign our people. We protest; we strive by all the powers given us, under the laws of the land, to overthrow their power and recover our rights; riots ensue,—and we are charged with disloyalty to the Government of the United States, and outrage, and murder!

How long is this thing to last? How long are we thus to be the subjects of misrule and of misrepresentation—the football with which political adventurers play? How long is the American Senate to be the stage for such scenes as this? How long are the material interests of every section to suffer by bankrupting the South, and the very existence of our free institutions endangered by the military support of political usurpers?[245] — FORMER CONFEDERATE GENERAL, SENATOR JOHN BROWN GORDON, SPEECH BEFORE CONGRESS

AFTER LEE'S SURRENDER
☛ . . . I shall ever believe, from the hospitality and good feeling that was shown by both sides, that if the men and boys who carried the guns and bore the brunt of the strife could have had control of the national affairs, and have kept it out of the hands of crafty politicians, such a thing as reconstruction would never have been thought of in our beloved and great Southland.[246] — CONFEDERATE SOLDIER, P. M. VANCE, BIRMINGHAM, ALA.

THE CONFEDERATE PRESIDENT ON RECONSTRUCTION
☛ The faces I see before me are those of young men. Had you not been this I would not have appeared alone as the defender of my southland, but for love of her I break my silence and speak to you. Before you lies the future—a future full of golden promise, full of recompense for noble endeavor, full of national glory before which the world will stand amazed. Let me beseech you to lay aside all rancor, and all bitter sectional feeling, and take your place in the rank of those who will bring about a conciliation out of which will issue a reunited country.[247] — JEFFERSON DAVIS, FROM A SPEECH MADE TO THE YOUNG MEN OF THE SOUTH DURING HIS LAST YEARS

A WHITE SOUTHERN WOMAN'S VIEWS ON THE BLACK RACE BEFORE & AFTER RECONSTRUCTION
☛ As late as 1890, [anti-South] Senator [John J.] Ingalls said:

> "The use of the torch and dagger is advised. I deplore it, but as God is my judge, I say that no people on this earth have ever submitted to the wrongs and injustice which have been put upon the coloured men of the South without revolt and bloodshed."

Others spoke of the negro's use of torch and sword as his only way to right himself in the South. When prominent men in Congressional and legislative halls and small stump speakers everywhere fulminated such sentiments, the marvel would have been if race prejudice had not come to birth and growth. Good men, whose homes were safe, and who in heat of oratory or passion for place, forgot that other men's homes were not, had no realisation of the effect of their words upon Southern households, where inmates lay down at night trembling lest they wake in flames or with black men shooting or knifing them [my emphasis, L.S.].

But for a rooted and grounded sympathy and affection between the races that fierce and *newly awakened prejudice* [my emphasis, L.S.] could not kill, the Sepoy massacres of India would have been duplicated in the South in the sixties and seventies. Under slavery, the black race held the heart of the white South in its hands. Second only in authority to the white mother on a Southern plantation, was the black mammy; hoary-headed white men and women, young men and maidens and little children, rendered her reverence and love. Little negroes and little white children grew up together, playing together and forming ties of affection equal to almost any strain. The servant was dependent upon his master, the master upon his servant. Neither could afford to disregard the well-being of the other. *No class of labour on earth today is as well cared for as were the negroes of the Old South. Age was pensioned, infancy sheltered. There was a state of mutual trust and confidence between employer and employee that has been seen nowhere else and at no time since between capital and labour* [my emphasis, L.S.].

One of millions of black families living safely and comfortably in the Deep South before Reconstruction.

Had the negro remained a few centuries longer the white man's dependant, often an inmate of his home, and his close associate on terms not raising questions and conflicts, his development would have proceeded. Through the processes of slavery, the negro was peaceably evolving, as agriculturist, shepherd, blacksmith, mechanic, master and mistress of domestic science, towards citizenship—inevitable when he should be ready *for it; citizenship all the saner, because those who were training him were unconscious of what they were doing and contemplated making no political use of him. They were intent only on his industrial and moral education. His evolution was set back by emancipation* [my emphasis, L.S.].

Yet, if destruction of race identity is advancement, the negro will advance. The education which he began to receive with other Greek gifts of freedom has taught him to despise his skin, to loath his race identity, to sacrifice all native dignity and nobility in crazy antics to become a white man. "Social equality!" those words are to be his doom. It is a pity that the phrase was ever coined. It is not to say that one is better than the other when we say of larks and robins, doves and crows, eagles and sparrows, that they do not flock together. They are different rather than unequal. Difference does not, of itself, imply inequality. To ignore a difference inherent in nature is a crime against nature and is punished accordingly by nature.

The negro race in America is to be wiped out by the dual process of elimination and absorption. The negro will not be eliminated as was the Indian—though the way a whole settlement of blacks was made to move on a few years ago in Illinois, looks as if history might repeat itself in special instances. Between lynchings and race riots in the North and West and those in the South there has usually been this difference: in the former, popular fury included entire settlements, punishing the innocent with the guilty; in the latter, it limited itself to the actual criminal. Another difference between sectional race problems. I was in New York during Subway construction when a strike was threatened, and overheard two gentlemen on the elevated road discussing the situation: "The company talks of bringing the blacks up here." "If they do, the tunnel will run blood! These whites will never suffer the blacks to take their work." I thought, "And negroes have had a monopoly of the South's industries and have scorned it!" I thought of jealous white toilers in the slime of the tunnel; and of Dixie's greening and golden fields, of swinging hoes and shining scythes and the songs of her black peasantry. And I thought of her stalwart black peasants again when I walked through sweat-shops and saw bent, wizened, white slaves.

The elimination of the negro will be in ratio to the reduction of his potentiality as an industrial factor. Evolutionary processes reject whatever has served its use. History shows the white man as the exponent of evolution. There were once more Indians here than there are now negroes. Yet the Indian has almost disappeared from the land that belonged to him when a little handful of palefaces came and found him in their way. Had he been of use, convertible into a labourer, he would have been retained; he was not so convertible, and other disposition was made of him while we sent to Africa for what was required. The climate of the North did not agree with the negro; he was not a profitable labourer; he disappeared. He was a satisfactory labourer South; he throve and multiplied. He is not now a satisfactory labourer in any locality. What is the conclusion if we judge the white man's future by his past?

The white man does not need the negro as littérateur, statesman, ornament to society. Of these he has enough and to spare, and seeks to reduce surplus. What he needs is agricultural labour. The red man would not till the soil, and the red man went; if the black man will not, perhaps the yellow man will. Sporadic instances of exceptional negroid attainments may interest the white man—in circumscribed circle—for a time. But the deep claim, the strong claim, the commanding claim would be that the negro filled a want not otherwise supplied, that the negro could and would do for him that which he cannot well do for himself—for instance, work the rice and cotton lands where the negro thrives and the white man dies.

The American negro is passing. The mulatto, quadroon, octoroon, strike the first notes in the octave of his evolution—or his decadence, or extinction, or whatever you may call it. The black negro is rare North and South. Negroes go North, white Northerners come South. In States sanctioning intermarriage, irregular connections obtain as elsewhere between white men and black women; and, in addition, between black men and white women of most degraded type or foreigners who are without the saving American race prejudice. Recent exposure of the "White Slave Syndicate" in New York which kidnapped white girls for negro bagnios, is fresh in the public mind.

Under slavery many negroes learned to value and to practice virtue; many value and practice it now; but the freedwoman has been on the whole less chaste than the bond. With emancipation the race suffered relapse in this as in other respects. The South did not do her whole duty in teaching chastity to the savage, though making more patient, persistent and heroic struggle than accredited with. The charge that under slavery miscegenation was the result of compulsion on the part of the superior race finds answer in its continuance since. Because he was white, the crying sin was the white man's, but it is just to remember that the heaviest part of the white racial burden was the African woman, of strong sex instincts and devoid of a sexual conscience, at the white man's door, in the white man's dwelling.[248]

In 1900, negroes constituted 20.4 per cent of the population of Texas, the lowest rate for the Southern States; in Mississippi, 58.6, the highest. In Massachusetts, they were less than two per cent. Questions of social intermingling can not be of such practical and poignant concern to Massachusetts as to Mississippi, where amalgamation would result in a population of mulatto degenerates. Prohibitions are protective to both races. Fortunately, miscegenation proceeds most slowly in the sections of negro concentration, the sugar and cotton lands of the lower South. In these, it is also said, there is lower percentage of negro crime of all kinds than where negroes are of lighter hue.

Thinkers of both races have declared amalgamation an improbable, undesirable conclusion of the race question; that it would be a propagation of the vices of both races and the virtues of neither. In a letter (March 30, 1865) to the Louisville *Courier-Journal*, recently reproduced in *The Outlook*, [Left-wing Yankee preacher] Mr. [Henry Ward] Beecher said:

> "I do not think it wise that whites and blacks should mix blood . . . it is to be discouraged on grounds of humanity."

[Yankee] Senator [John J.] Ingalls said:

> "Fred Douglas [former Yankee slave Frederick Douglass] once said to me: ' The races will blend, coalesce, and become homogeneous.' I do not agree with him. There is no affinity between the races; this solution is impossible. There is no blood poison so fatal as the adulteration of race."

At the Southern Educational Conference in Columbia,1905, Mr. Abbott, in one of the clearest, frankest speeches yet heard from our Northern brotherhood, declared the thinking North and South now one upon these points: the sections were equally responsible for slavery; the South fought, not to perpetuate slavery, but on an issue "that had its beginning before the adoption of the Federal Constitution;" racial integrity should be preserved. In one of the broadest, sanest discussions of the negro problem to which the American public has been treated, Professor Eliot, of Harvard, has said recently:

> "Northern and Southern opinion are identical with regard to keeping the races pure—that is, without admixture of the one with the other . . . inasmuch as the negroes hold the same view, this supposed danger

of mutual racial impairment ought not to have much influence on practical measures. Admixture of the two races, so far as it proceeds, will be, as it has been, chiefly the result of sexual vice on the part of white men; it will not be a wide-spread evil, and it will not be advocated as a policy or method by anybody worthy of consideration."

"It will not be a wide-spread evil!" The truth star us in the face. Except in the lower South the black negro is now almost a curiosity. In any negro gathering the gamut of colour runs from ginger-cake to white rivaling the Anglo-Saxon's; and according as he is more white, the negro esteems himself more honourable than his blacker fellow; though these gradations in colour which link him with the white man, were he to judge himself by the white man's standard, would be, generally speaking, badges of bastardy and shame.

In Florida, a tourist remarked to an orange-woman: "They say Southerners do not believe in intermingling of the races. But look at all these half-white coons!" "Well, Marster," she answered, "don't you give Southern folks too much credit fuh dat. Rich Yankees in de winter-time; crap [crop] uh white nigger babies in de fall. Fus' war we all had down here, mighty big crapuh yaller babies come up. Arter de war 'bout Cuba, 'nother big crap come 'long. Nigger gal ain' nuvver gwi have a black chile ef she kin git a white one!" Blanch, my negro hand-maiden, is comely, well- formed, black; the descendant of a series of honest marriages, yet feels herself at a disadvantage with quadroons and octoroons not nearly her equals in point of good looks or principle. "I'd give five hundred dollars ef I had it, ef my ha'r was straight," she tells me with pathetic earnestness; and "I wish I had been born white!" is her almost heart-broken moan.[249] She would rather be a mulatto bastard than the black product of honest wedlock.

The integrity of the races depends largely upon the virtue of white men and black women; also, it rests on the negroid side upon the aspiration to become white, acknowledgment in itself of inferiority and self-loathing. The average negress will accept, invite, with every wile she may, the purely animal attention of a "no-count white man" in preference to marriage with a black. The average mulatto of either sex considers union with a black degradation. The rainbow of promise spanning this gloomy vista is the claim that the noble minority of black women who value virtue is on the increase as the race, in self-elevation, recognises more and more the demands of civilisation upon character, and that dignity of racehood which will not be ashamed of its own skin or covet the skin of another. The virtuous black woman is the Deborah and the

Miriam of her people. She is found least often in crowded cities, North and South; most often in Southern rural districts. Wherever found, she commands the white man's respect.

Hope should rest secure in the white man. If the faith of his fathers, the flag of his fathers, the Union of his fathers, are worthy of preservation, is not the blood of his fathers a sacred trust also? Besides, before womanhood, whatever its colour or condition, however ready to yield or appeal to his grosser senses, the white man should throw the ægis of his manhood and his brotherhood.

The recent framing of State Constitutions in the South to supersede the Black and Tan creations revived the charge of race prejudice because their suffrage restrictions would in great degree disfranchise the negro. As compared with discussion of any phase of the race issue some years ago, the spirit of comment was cool and fair. *The Outlook* led in justifying the South for protecting the franchise with moderate property and educational qualifications applying to both races, criticising, however, the provision for deciding upon educational fitness—a provision which Southerners admit needs amendment. One effect of these restrictions will be to stimulate the negro's efforts to acquire the necessary education or the necessary three hundred dollars' worth of property. Another effect will be decrease of the white farmer's scant supply of negro labour; this scarcity, in attracting white immigrants, provides antidote for Africanisation of the South.

As to whether negro ownership of lands improves country or not, I will give a Northern view. I met in 1903 at the Jefferson Hotel in Richmond, a wealthy Chicagoan and his wife (originally from Massachusetts), who were looking for a holiday residence in Tidewater Virginia. They made various excursions with land agents, and one day reported discovery of their ideal in all respects but one. "The people around are ruining property by selling lands to negroes. A gentleman at whose house we stopped, a Northerner, had just bought, as he told us, at much inconvenience, a plantation adjoining his own to make sure it would not be cut up and sold by degrees to negroes." I hear Southern farmers in black belts say: "I had much rather have a quiet, orderly negro for neighbour than a troublesome white." But the fact remains that negro ownership of property reduces value of adjoining lands. Besides the social reason, the average negro exhausts and does not improve lands.

Why don't the negroes live up North?" one is asked; "they go up there and make a little money and come back and buy lands."

"Land is cheap here. It is almost beyond their reach there. The climate here appeals. Then, this is home." Thus I answered in 1902, in Southside, Virginia. After further travel, I amend: Negroes do not wish to work for white land-owners; they wish to remain in the South or to return to the South as land-owners. They are acquiring considerable property. But, generally speaking, they are thinning out. One may journey miles along Southern railroads and see but few in fields where once were thousands. In Northern cities and pleasure resorts negroes increase. The race problem is broadening, changing territory.

The daughter of an Ohioan gave me a glimpse of this changing base.

> "Columbus negroes—those born there or who came there long ago, are very different from Southern negroes. They will have nothing to do with the negroes coming direct. The Southern negroes have nice, deferential manners; the Northern negroes hate them for it. Columbus negroes—why, they will push white ladies off the streets!"

In a New York store in 1904, I observed two negresses in a crowd near a window where articles of baggage were on check. They pushed their way to the front and demanded belongings without the courteous "please" which any Southerner, or which Northern gentlefolks, would have used; the young white girl in charge—it was a hot day and she looked faint—was doing her cheerful best to meet the noon rush, but was not quick enough for the coloured persons; they hurried and reproved her; as she turned about within, confused by their descriptions and commands, they exclaimed: "That's it! Right befo' you! Don't you see that case right there? What a fool!" She never thought of resenting; came up humbly, loaded with their property, glad to have found it. Their manners would have scandalised a black aristocrat of the Old South.

We cannot afford to wrong this race as we wronged the Indian. We must aid the negro's advancement in the right direction. But we should not discriminate against the white race. Educational doors are open to the negro throughout the land; the South is rich in noble institutions of learning for him; in black belts Southerners are paying more to educate black children than white. In black belts, in white belts, in the mountains, white children are put into fields and factories when they ought to be going to school. Educational odds are against the white children. In regard to schools of manual training, to limit the negro to these and these to the negro is to put a stigma on manual labor in the eyes of white youth and to continue the negro's monopoly of a field which he does not appreciate. We should do more educationally for the white child and not less for the negro. The negro pays small

The first Confederate Capitol, Montgomery, Alabama.

percentage of the Southern educational tax and enjoys full benefits. The negro needs to realize that if the white man owes him a debt, he owes the white man one; and that he cannot safely despise the school of service in house and field which white people from Europe and yellow people from the Orient are eager to enter.

I would close no door of opportunity to the negro. But I must say my affection is for the negro of the old order. I owe reverence to the memory of a black mammy and a debt to negroes generally for much kindness. The real negro I like, the poet of the veldt and jungle, the singer in field and forest, the tiller of the soil, the shepherd of the flocks, the herdsman of the cattle, the happy, soft-voiced, light-footed servitor. The negro who is a half-cut white man is not a negro, and it can be no offense to the race to say that he is unattractive when compared with the dear old darkey of Dixie who was worth a million of him! At Fort Mill, S. C., hard by a monument to a forgotten people, the Catawba Indians, stands a monument to the "Faithful Slaves of the Confederacy," type of a memorial many hearts yet hold. The new negro, in reaching out for higher and better things than the old attained, will be wise not to sacrifice those qualities which told in his ancestor in spite of all shortcomings.

The one true plane of equalisation is that of mutual service, each race doing for the other all it can. The old negro and the white man stood more surely on this plane than do their descendants, yet not more surely than all must wish their descendants to stand. My regard for the negro, my pride in what he has really accomplished under the hammering of civilisation, call, in his behalf, for a race pride and reserve in him which shall match the Anglo-Saxon's. There are negroes who have it and who deplore efforts placing them in the position of postulants for a social intermingling which they do not consider essential to their dignity or happiness. Between blacks and whites South we constantly see race pride maintained on one side as on the other while humanities are

observed in manifold exchanges of kindness and courtesy that make a bond of brotherhood. Whatever position the white Southerner takes theoretically on manufactured race issues, he will usually fight rather than see his inoffensive black neighbour or employee maltreated; his black neighbour or employee will often do as much for him. This attitude is sometimes an expression of the clan habit surviving the destruction of clan-life (old plantation-life in which the white man was Chief and his negroes his clansmen); also, it exists in the recognition of a common bond of humanity more than skin deep. Upon this rock the future may be builded.[250] As a useful, industrious, citizen, the negro is his own argument and advocate.[251]
— MYRTA LOCKETT AVARY, 1906

A black Confederate soldier regaling his fellow troops with humorous campfire stories. At least four times as many blacks fought for the Confederacy as fought for the Union, a bold fact purposefully excluded from our mainstream history books. Why? Because the idea of a non-racist South does not fit the current Left-wing/Socialist/Communist narrative.

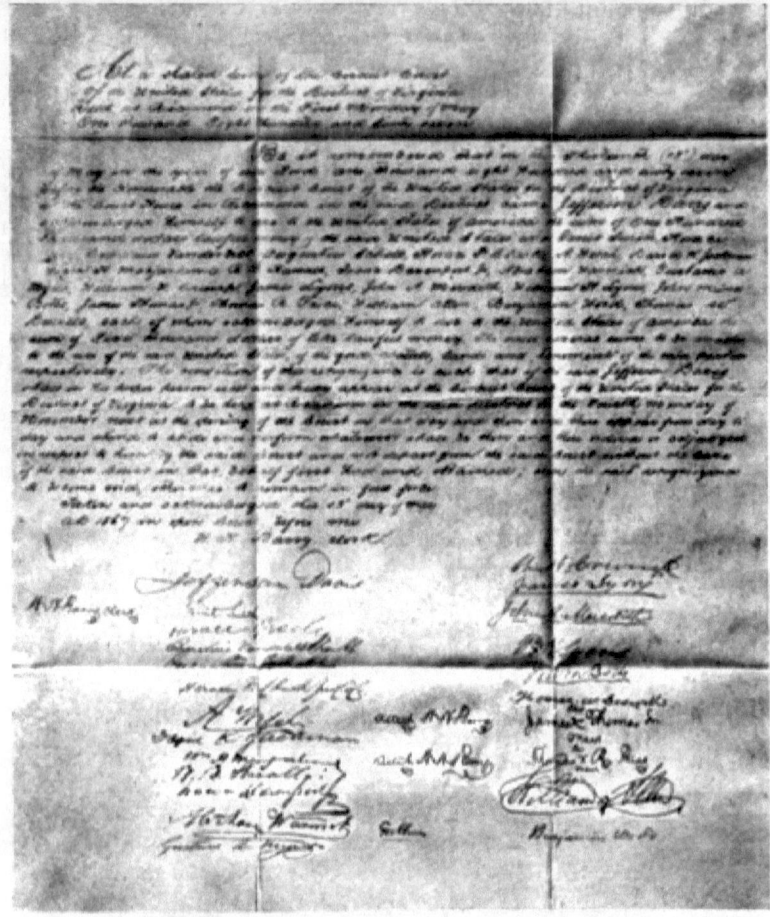

The bail bond of Jefferson Davis. The charge of treason that was brought against the noble former C.S. president was intentionally fabricated by amoral, corrupt, truth-hating, soulless Yankee reprobates. The indictment had absolutely no basis in either reality or law—which is why he was eventually released from prison without trial. The same manufactured charge was levied against the South as a whole, for the same reasons, and by the same dishonest malicious individuals who launched Reconstruction: Liberals, Socialists, and Communists, most of them members of the then Left-wing Republican Party—today, due to the platform switch in 1896, known as the Democratic Party. One curious footnote to this tragic chapter in American history is the inclusion on this document of the signature of Yankee Socialist and Left-wing newspaper editor Horace Greeley (the third signature below Davis'). A rare compassionate Northern Radical, Greeley saw through his comrades' villainous artifice, campaigned to have the innocent chief executive released from Fortress Monroe, and even donated to Davis' $100,000 bail bond.

CHAPTER 15

THE BEGINNING OF THE END
☛ A history of the stirring times of the city of Montgomery and of the State of Alabama has never been written. It is the purpose to write it now, while there are yet living witnesses to verify every statement. It is written too that it may he preserved for the education of our coming generations and for the vindication of Southern honor before the civilized world.

In tears and the agony of disappointment because of surrender and that the stars and bars [the Confederate States First National Flag] had gone down in defeat to rise no more the Confederate veteran made his way from North Carolina and Virginia afoot, riding when he could, inspired by the hope of being soon at home with his loved ones. He thought surrender was the end of the long years of his griefs and sorrows and a renewal of his allegiance to the stars and stripes [the United States National Flag]. He could not believe that free America would employ any policy or measure that did not promise sweet peace and the harmony and prosperity of a reunited country.

At the gate of his home, in smiles and gladness, he greeted wife and children with kisses and embraces. All along his way home were standing armies at every turn. Fortunately and pleasingly the United States regimental forces, both officers and privates, were polite, affable, and disposed to do anything comporting with the health, happiness, or prosperity of his fallen foe. Busy with his home interests, his energies were concentrated in his best efforts to make it what it was before grim-visaged war had defaced or destroyed its beauty and peace. He stopped the holes in his roof, filled up crevices through which the chilly winds of winter came, repaired his barns, remade his fences, and was in utter ignorance of the infernal fires being kindled at the National Capital [by the radical Left members, socialists and communists, of the then Liberal Republican Party].

When it was made known to him that Mr. [Jefferson] Davis was held a prisoner [at Fort Monroe, VA], bound with chains and fetters, his blood grew warm with the spirit of resentment.

Not content with the cowardly cruelty of incarcerating Mr. Davis and others, their venom rankled against even Gen. Robert E. Lee, who would have been their fellow-prisoner and fellow-sufferer had not [Union] General [Ulysses S.] Grant stood an impassable barrier, a wall of fire between them and him.[252]

Jealousy, envy, malice, and the direst poison of hate gathered in the halls of [the U.S.] Congress, growing into a mighty and consuming fire until our constitutional compact became only ashes, and the accursed spirit of reconstruction had so altered free America as to make it the foremost province of his Satanic Majesty. Then came swarms of locusts, clouds of vultures, and countless beasts of prey, each commissioned with authority to invade the sanctity of home, to look into all places, and to appropriate jewels, plate, gold or silver coin, cotton, or other things of value.

Radical Republican Socialist Thaddeus Stevens working hard to bring down both Conservative Democratic President Andrew Johnson and the Conservative South.

When that fire of Inferno had grown into its utmost proportions, all governments of Dixies, State, county, and municipal, were dissolved and an election ordered. Negroes in their ignorance, the contemptible scalawag who had turned his back on his country in her hour of need, and the carpet-bagger glorying in freedom and singing of the "bottom rail on top" migrated from county to county, town to town, and wherever there was a ballot box deposited a handful of illegal votes, unable to understand what their votes meant. "They obeyed the word that was saunt." Great haste was made in the inauguration of State, county, and municipal governments and the installment of officers. Stealage became their order of procedure, and so continued until there was no money to defray daily needs and darkness overspread their skies. In this emergency, on the suggestion of their white pilots, resort was had to the issuance of State, county, and city bonds, which were divided among those in power and by them bartered at any price in the markets of the North.

Alabama was bankrupt, being hopelessly involved in a bonded debt of nearly $35,000,000, and having neither money nor bonds in her treasury. Negroes became insolent and rapacious, with tendencies toward riot and disposition to appropriate the little left by the war upon which the [Southern] wives and children of the old [Confederate] soldiers were subsisting.

Such was the aspect of our political horizon when our people, without regard to gender or age, firmly resolved to resist the yoke of oppression at any cost. In conference it was proposed and agreed to outvote them in the ensuing city election, and so wrest from the dirty hordes the power they had usurped.

Organizations were perfected, fellow [Confederate] soldiers and their sons were called from our own and adjacent counties, and they came unbidden from other States; so that when the auspicious day came, in 1872, we were all at the polling places and in force, equipped with carefully correct lists of citizens who were legally entitled to suffrage.

That day the sun rose upon the heavens in beauty and splendor. Negroes were in swarms and militant, coming from other counties and towns to exercise their American freedom; nor were the hungry carpet-baggers or scalawags wanting.

Balloting was both rapid and continuous amidst imprecations and uncivil expressions of speech as some negro belonging anywhere outside of Montgomery City was challenged.

The writer found it necessary on that day to absent himself from the polls of Ward 2, going to Dexter Avenue. On his speedy return he was accosted by Col. H. C. Semple, who informed him that he was just from an investigating trip to the capitol; that *he had found recorded in the House Journal a bill which had become a law prohibiting the punishment of repeating or other illegal voting* [my emphasis, L.S.]. This information was manna falling to us from heaven. The efficient, good work of Colonel Semple was utilized at once, being conveyed to other polls, where our good people saw the dire necessity of driving the negro and his white [Left-wing] friends from all the voting places, of which they had taken possession, and permitting only Democratic [then Conservative] ballots to go into the box.

A negro came to the writer wanting to vote with the white people, the Democratic [then Conservative] ticket. He was pursued to the very polls by a pack of howling [Left-wing] devils, yelling: "Kill him! Kill him! This 'nigger' is here to vote the Democratic [Conservative] ticket." [Then, as today, the Left (now the Democrats) despised Conservative blacks. L.S.]

The fury and noise was so great as to be deafening, so that it was next to impossible to understand anything said to each other. Sticks, clubs, knives, and pistols were ready in hand for use, when Mr. "Billy" Ray, then an old [white] man, jerked off his coat, threw it on the ground, and exhorted the boys, saying: "Now is as good a time to die as any. Let the fight begin."[253]

Stonewall Jackson's invincibles never obeyed order to charge with more alacrity. The fight did begin in earnest. The Metcalfs in one place, the Caffeys in another, the Westcotts close by—all around old [Confederate] soldiers and boys who were too young for service when our country needed them were battling with great, burly [communized, Left-wing] negroes to drive them from the voting place. This determined effort was not without fruit. Messages were quickly sent to the other polls of what we had accomplished. Before the hour of 12 M. the enemy were routed, head, neck, and heels, and the polls were ours without dispute; but continuous and industrious work had to be kept up that we should have a majority of votes in the count at 8 P.M. Counting the ballot was enormous work, but its footings were honest and a righteous vindication of the good people of Montgomery.

Our good people rejoiced, and congratulations seemed to come from the civilized world. This signal triumph was quickly followed by a new [Conservative] city government and the speedy removal of the debased herd of [Left-wing] vultures from every place of trust or honor.

Holding the polls for ourselves only, voting thirty, fifty, one hundred times each, and cramming the boxes, was an invincible process; but it was inaugurated and made law by the Mongrel Legislature for its perpetuation, and without our knowledge Colonel Semple brought us the information necessary to our great triumph.

This election was an education to our county and State; so that when elections came later, Alabama's fetters were broken and she was herself again. Negro, scalawag, and carpet-bag politicians ceased to be a menace to our city or an offense to our people.

[Alabama] Governor [George S.] Houston was elected in 1874, and each county chose its own members of the General Assembly and its own county officers. But when attempt was made to oust the culprits from their usurpations, it looked again like bloody war. But the carpet-bagger, scalawag, and ignorant, impudent [communized] negro gave way to the inevitable, and sweet peace came to Alabama. The dust of battle was dissipated.

Our Governor was inaugurated, the Legislature met, and at once began looking into the unclean work of reconstruction. A true state of facts was presented to them in an empty treasury and evidence recorded in treasury books of $35,000,000 bonds sold or divided between such of them as had footing in or access to power.

Bankruptcy! repudiation! was heard in all our realm. Our stanch old Governor and his wise men applied themselves to the task of scaling or compromising for less than $8,000,000. They utterly refused to allow that Alabama was responsible for one dollar; but rather than have our State's good name dishonored by such association, this compromise was agreed to.

All of Dixie came into line with Alabama. Thus were broken the shackles riveted upon our homes by that unrighteous convention of Satanic spirits calling themselves "The Congress and Senate of Free America." So did Heaven thwart and bring to naught their wicked designs and cause the sun of liberty to roll in glory as it came to us from our Revolutionary fathers.

The writer assures the Christian world that every statement in this history is the truth and calls the living participants of that fearful, uncertain time as witness.[254] — JAMES W. POWELL, MONTGOMERY, ALA.

WHAT WAS ENDURED BY CONFEDERATE WOMEN

☞ [A personal letter addressed to] J. L. Thompson and other Missouri Confederates: My attention has just been called to your letter of inquiry published in the *Confederate Veteran*, of Nashville, Tenn. [seeking "survivors among the women who acted as nurses in the hospital at Somerville, Tenn." during the War], and as you request, I answer through the same channel.

Your pleasant surprise opens the avenues of many sad memories, yet my heart is thrilled with gratitude that we were enabled to do something to succor the brave [Confederate] men whom the disasters of war had rendered helpless and for whom Southern patriotism had provided an asylum at Somerville, Tenn.

Though separated widely from the friends of that war period, I have kept in close touch with many of the nurses and matrons of the old Hardwick—hotel hospital. Most of them have answered the call of the Master and gone home to glory. Miss Lucy Dillard, that intelligent, wide-awake Dixie lover, sleeps among Confederate comrades in the Somerville Cemetery. Mrs. Pulliam, Mrs. Williamson, and Mrs. Scott are sweetly resting in the same inclosure and waiting for the resurrection which is to reward useful and godly lives. Miss Bertie Miner, the tireless reader and letter writer for the sick soldiers, and who was so savagely treated by marauding Northern soldiers, has gone too to her Father's house. And Mrs. Virginia Lucas, the active benefactor and zealous friend of all Confederate soldiers, went to her reward from Russell's Valley, North Alabama, several years ago. I alone, as far as I know, am the only surviving member of that Woman Corps that presided at the West Tennessee refuge for soldiers forty-five years ago. Then you see how time is gathering us into the fold, and there I hope to meet the valorous [Southern] men who defended womanhood in the South against a cruel and barbarous invasion.

"Am I still a friend of the Confederate soldier?" Yes, and shall ever be. I regard patriotism among the loftiest possessions in the keeping of man, and the soul which does not know much of that fine fervor has missed one of the distinctions of pure manhood. Neither victory nor defeat can impair, nor can conditions change it.

"Am I still loyal to the flag of Dixie?" I love it with as much fervid zeal as in my young womanhood. And why should I not love it? I gave four years of tears and prayers for its success, four years of tireless toil to its vindication; while for full three years I was the victim of cruel and barbarous outrages at the hands of soldiers who invaded Southern homes under an alien flag [the U.S. flag].

When I recollect these wrongs perpetrated upon defenseless women and children, my very soul revolts at the reckless barbarity of Northern soldiers [my emphasis, L.S.]. While I suffered personal indignities from these "knights in blue," I am really glad that Northern women escaped the ravages of vandal hordes and knew so nearly nothing of the horrors of war. Such scenes as we in the South were forced to witness blunt the finer sensibilities of woman and put her out of her natural sphere.

Three days after the hospital at Somerville was closed and the remaining sick and wounded Confederates had been removed a raiding squad of eighty Federal [U.S.] soldiers dashed into the town and drove the old [Confederate] men into the courthouse. Then they began a system of robbery, pillage, and plunder that beggars description. Wardrobes were smashed to pieces, trunks broken open, feather beds ripped up and contents scattered—in fact, nothing of value escaped the vigilance of the [Yankee] barbarians. The principal sufferers were those who had been conspicuously active about this old Hardwick—hotel hospital. Somerville people will never forget the wanton destruction of their household goods and the total disregard of every sentiment of decency [my emphasis, L.S.].

Having a home just outside of Memphis and fearing similar outrages, I moved there under the false impression that places inside the Federal [U.S.] pickets would give some security to person and property. But it was a delusion, and I determined to move down the Mississippi River upon our plantation, where we had the promise of corn bread and bacon from the faithful negroes who still stayed on the farm. The [U.S.] cavalry at Helena [AR] soon found us out and daily raided us, taking just what they wanted, even down to woman's wearing apparel. To give us a taste of "Pelion on Ossa piled," the Federal [U.S.] gunboats on the river picked us out for target practice [my emphasis, L.S.]. Of all terror-inspiring things to an unskilled woman, nothing exceeds those fiery-tailed monsters as they crash through buildings and explode in open air so violently that earth and air tremble with the shock.

Our only safety was in a "dugout" beneath the ground, with negro women and their children and two white women all huddled in confusion, waiting for the cessation of bombardments [see the illustration on the cover of this book, L.S.]. With such memories you surely will not insist upon a specific answer to your question: "Are you reconstructed yet?"

While the war developed many phases of human depravity evidenced by the fiendish deeds of a barbarous [U.S.] soldiery, the reconstruction acts passed for our humiliation and the destruction of all our social, industrial, and commercial resources was the crowning ignominy of despotism, and furnishes a painful contrast between a monarchy and a republic [my emphasis, L.S.].

When England in vindication of her colonial unity made war upon the Boer republic and wasted it into submission then the purposes being accomplished, the war not only ended, but a system of wise and humane rehabilitation for the land of [white South African politician] Oom Paul [a nickname for Stephanus J. P. Kruger] was immediately started by the British Parliament. Instead of vindictive legislation imbued with bitter hatreds, as was administered to us [by the U.S. government], England wisely and in a spirit of Christian humanity saw the advantage of pacification, and did all that was possible to build up the wasted country and inspire the brave Boers with a capacity for a new uplift. Horses, mules, cows, hogs, agricultural implements, medicine, with spinning wheels, looms, carding machines, and other household necessities, were supplied in lavish profusion, and thereby in all that makes up national greatness the monarchy of Queen Victoria excelled the Lincoln republic too far for comparison.

Now, my old friends, while I have not said half I wanted to say, it would make my letter a bore perhaps to continue it and tell you about the work of the carpet-baggers, the Federal [U.S.] judges, and the bogus Governors sent down upon us as vampires; so I close.

May that Almighty Providence who shielded you so signally in defense of the constitutional rights of the South in the cruel war protect you and all the remnant of the brave Confederates and bring you at last to the beautiful city![255] — MRS. LIZZIE LUCAS DILLARD, MERIDIAN, TEX.

SHOULD THE SOUTH HONOR THE BIRTHDAY OF THE ARCHITECT OF RECONSTRUCTION?

☞ The question of honoring the birthday of Abraham Lincoln by the Southern people is a question indeed. At first blush it would seem meet and proper that the day should be honored inasmuch as it is generally agreed that "the war is over." That Lincoln was a fairly good man, certainly a rare genius in a way, is admitted by nearly every one in the South as well as in the North; this, too, despite the fact that he unquestionably violated the Constitution and willfully assumed powers not rightfully his as President and acting upon which he plunged this country in a bloody war the like of which was never before recorded in history. Half a million of the flower of the young manhood of this country were cut down, and their bones now lie bleaching upon every hill from Gettysburg to the Rio Grande. The beautiful Southland was ruthlessly overrun, plundered, and devastated, vividly recalling the atrocities of the barbarous Goths and Vandals in Italy a thousand years ago. Southern manhood was prostrated and crushed and Southern womanhood everywhere outraged and insulted, and for what? For a sentiment called Union.

Southern people, in my opinion, are ready for the olive branch at any time the people of the North may extend it in honesty and genuine sincerity, but not until then. Whenever the people of the North are ready to honor June 3, the birthday of Jefferson Davis—as gallant a knight as ever drew a sword and as pure a statesman as ever championed the rights and liberties of a free people—then, but not one hour sooner, should the people of the South honor February 12 as Lincoln's anniversary.

Magnanimity and charity are all right and proper within certain bounds; but I respectfully submit that it is ill becoming a high-minded people to "bow low and kiss the great toe" of the idol of the white people of the North and the negroes of the South, while their own matchless leader, champion, and hero continues to be denounced as a "Rebel and a bloody traitor." Let's maintain our self-respect at all hazards.[256] — ANONYMOUS SOUTHERNER, CIRCA 1909

SOUTHERN PATRIOTISM IS NOT TO BE QUESTIONED
☞ . . . The protest of the South in reconstruction times was against being treated as conquered provinces. The South considered that secession having failed by the arbitrament of arms, then the States in what the North called rebellion having laid down their arms were back in the Union with all the constitutional rights they had always enjoyed. It was the anomalous view of the reconstructionist [the socialists and communists in the then Left-wing Republican Party] opposing this view that created more sectional hard feeling than actual [wartime] hostilities had done. The South did not manifest its patriotism in the Spanish-American war for the purpose of showing good will to the North, but because that patriotism was as genuine here then as it was in every foreign war in which the nation had ever engaged.[257] — SECRETARY OF WAR, SOUTHERNER JACOB MCGAVOK DICKINSON (UNDER PRES. WILLIAM TAFT)

A YANKEE COMMENTS ON SOUTHERN EDUCATION & RECONSTRUCTION
☞ The war and then the reconstruction dealt Southern education a blow which put upon an impoverished people the cost of educating millions of a non-taxpaying population [Southern freedman] and which deprived two generations of people of a fair opportunity to obtain an education.

The struggle of the South under the calamities which have been put upon her has been heroic, and the other sections of the Union have never fully comprehended it all.[258] — NEW ENGLANDER DR. CHARLES W. ELIOT, PRESIDENT OF HARVARD UNIVERSITY FROM 1869 TO 1909

THE SOUTH IN HISTORY
☞ Half a century, less five years, has passed since the South emerged from a war which, viewed from any standpoint that war may be considered, left immeasurable havoc and awful desolation and a destruction of life and property which it is difficult in figures

to calculate. Within a brief period of four years that war had robbed the South of one-third of its men capable of bearing arms; more than 200,000 of her most chivalrous, patriotic, distinguished, cultured sons had gone down to death in battle or from wounds received in battle. Half of its property had been destroyed, its resources in a large part obliterated, its entire labor system disorganized, and helpless and well-nigh hopeless it lay prostrate at the feet of its conqueror. The best terms which could be gotten in this hour of darkness were protection from arrest and punishment and the preservation of the side arms of its officers and the right to take for their use the horses which its soldiers owned and had ridden to battle. Beyond this nothing was promised. Its legions had been reduced by starvation and death until its ranks were so thinned and decimated that there remained merely the skeleton of an army. *With the South nothing had been held back in this gigantic struggle for national life. Farms, cities, and homes had been desolated by war's exactions. In addition to this, the purposes of its people were misrepresented, and designing [Left-wing] politicians [then the Republicans] fanned sectional hate into flames, hoping to ride into political power* [my emphasis, L.S.].

Then came the horrors of reconstruction. A brave, generous, intelligent, and proud people were by the bayonet forced to submit to a government controlled by conscienceless carpet-baggers, aided by home scalawags and supported by newly liberated [and heavily indoctrinated] slaves. Their former servants became the political masters, and this mastery was embittered and controlled by the rapacity and greed of a class who had come down from the land of their enemies to feed and fatten on their misfortunes and to extract from them

McLean's House, Appomattox Court House, Virginia, where Generals Lee and Grant arranged the terms of surrender.

under the forms of government the little that could be found after the ravages of the war. The struggle for food was hard enough. There was but little provision for even the seed which would produce a crop, and the dreadful calamity had come at a period of the year when food supply was least and when months must necessarily intervene before the land could be cultivated and a living extracted from the soil. While the people of the Southland accepted the result heroically and philosophically, their defeat was enough to crush the stoutest heart and to eliminate hope in the bravest breast. Added to this came political sorrows, only a little short of the plagues which Divine Justice sent down on Egypt to force it to allow God's chosen people to depart from its borders. The land was full of mourning.

DAYS OF DARKNESS

☛ . . . In those days of darkness and almost impenetrable gloom there was no time to make defense of or to exercise care for the reputation and fame and honor of the people of the Confederate States. The cruelties and oppression, which were backed up by bayonets, and the struggle for existence and political rights consumed more than ten years of the lives of those who had engaged in that awful war.

After this long period, reason returned; a spirit of justice again pervaded the land. The carpet-bagger hied himself away from the borders of what was once the Confederacy, and the slave, made by force an enfranchised freeman, after the experience of a decade, realized that his own people [that is, Southerners] were his best friends and that peace with them and trust in them was the safest and wisest policy.

Then men came to think upon what the past was and what its history meant and what it was worth to them to vindicate the patriotism of their motives, the justice of their cause, and the sublime courage which animated them and their associates in the greatest war the world has ever seen. They had offered and sacrificed on their country's altar one thousand men a week for four years. They had yielded and surrendered and used in their defense hundreds of millions of dollars, or the equivalent of $700,000 each day during this long and ever-lengthening period. But now as tyranny and oppression had lifted off the face of the earth as a fog disappears before the rising sun, with the assurance of political liberty there came a fixed and immovable purpose to present for the consideration of mankind the motives which impelled them in their struggle and to tell the world what magnificent courage had been manifested in the battles that had been fought, what splendid endurance in the marches that had been made, and what patriotism in the sacrifices which had been suffered for four brief but terrible years.

When these brave people began to read the stories that had been prepared for the study of their children, they discovered the grossest misrepresentation of their principles and their purposes. They found perversion of truth on many pages; and in addition to all the horrors of defeat, they saw themselves as courageous men, as true women, as liberty-loving Anglo-Saxons, traduced, slandered, vilified, misrepresented. In a little while it was found that success lay only through the power and efficiency of a thorough organization. Substantial political freedom had been won. The carpet-bagger was a thing of the past. The scalawag had slunk into his hiding place of infamy, and the power of the government was again placed in the hands of white men, the owners of the wealth of the land and the possessors of nine-tenths of its intelligence. . . .[259] — GENERAL BENNETT H. YOUNG, LOUISVILLE, KY., CIRCA 1910

VALUABLE HERITAGE

☛ To the really brave there is something higher, better, and grander than money. Truth, honor, right, justice are more valuable than lands and houses, banks, factories, plantations, and farms; and in a brief while after the South was free her sons resolved that history should be true. They asked for nothing but truth. They demanded only that the world should judge them by what they did, what they dared, and what they endured. They neither sought nor desired exaggeration nor amplification, but staked their rightful place in history upon a true narrative of all that was done during those four years of darkness and gloom. Truth was to them nobler and more precious than all that imagination could bring to crown their lives, and they resolved at every cost and in the face of all difficulties to at least make the effort to be justified at the bar of mankind and to accept its final decision upon their history only when mankind fully understood for what they fought and how they fought and the purposes which induced them to fight. Under the power of organization and protest in a little while many false histories were banished from the schools of the South. Books which contained truth only were to be studied and read by Southern children. A nation that had Jefferson Davis for its President and Lee, Jackson, the Johnstons, Kirby Smith, the Hills, Breckinridge, Gordon, Hampton, Forrest, Taylor, Morgan, Stuart, and hundreds of others equally as brave for their generals and 600,000 heroes in the ranks of its armies need not fear to stand before the world and appeal to the judgment of their fellow-men upon the issues and conduct of a mighty war. . . .²⁶⁰ — GENERAL BENNETT H. YOUNG, LOUISVILLE, KY., CIRCA 1910

UNTIL RECONSTRUCTION . . .
☞ . . . This government was accepted as perfected until Reconstruction pitted the negroes, yeomen, and aristocrats against each other. . . .²⁶¹ — *CONFEDERATE VETERAN*, 1910

RACIAL DIVISION FOMENTED BY THE VICTORIAN LEFT
☞ . . . The negroes almost from the first were under the control of aliens and renegades, and the struggle for existence was on in earnest. Reconstruction, with its deliberate plan to subject the native white people to their former slaves, was an unspeakable horror, to be resisted to the death. . . .²⁶² — *CONFEDERATE VETERAN*, 1911

HOW LEFT-WING YANKEES SOUGHT THE SOUTH'S DESTRUCTION
☞ . . . Terrible as was the War between the States, hardly less so was the war of Reconstruction that followed. [Confederate] Captain [Daniel B.] Edwards, returning to his devastated home in '65, began hopefully—nay, cheerfully—to rebuild his shattered fortune. But the sky was soon overcast with clouds. Carpet-baggers, the scum of the human race, the refuse of the North, marshaled negro voters to the polls. The noblest men of the land charged with crimes they never committed, with manacles on their hand, were carried by negro guards before strange and infamous judges. The substance of the people was wasted in onerous taxes which were stolen by corrupt officials. The situation for eight years, twice as long as the war, was appalling, until finally it became intolerable. . . .²⁶³ — PROFESSOR D. M. CALLAWAY, CAMP JONES, SELMA, ALA., JUNE 3, 1911

HAD LINCOLN LIVED . . .
☞ . . . Soon after this [Lee's surrender] followed the infamous carpet-bag rule of plunder and murder throughout the Southern States. This was the greatest calamity, not excepting the war, from which we had just emerged, that ever befell the South. Her people lamented Mr. Lincoln's death almost as much as the North, not so much because they loved him, but because they detested and feared Andy Johnson. Mr. Lincoln visited Richmond only two days before his death, and was received more cordially than he anticipated. He had already promulgated his generous and humane policy of

reconstruction. The leading men of the South firmly believed that had he lived and been strong enough to have enforced his policies against bitter opposition there would never have been any carpet-bag or KuKlux Klan rule in the South, and she would have been twenty-five years farther advanced in every line of endeavor than she is to-day. . . .[264] — J. COLEMAN ALDERSON, CHARLESTON, WV.

PROCLAMATION BY THE 17TH PRESIDENT

☞ Whereas the President of the United States has heretofore set forth several proclamations offering amnesty and pardon to persons who had been or were concerned in the late rebellion against the lawful authority of the government of the United States; . . . and whereas . . . it is believed that . . . a universal amnesty and pardon for participation in said rebellion extended to all who have borne any part therein will tend to secure permanent peace, order, and prosperity throughout the land, and to renew and fully restore confidence and fraternal feeling among the whole people and their respect and attachment to the national government, designed by its patriotic founders for the general good; Now, therefore, be it known that I, Andrew Johnson, President of the United States, by virtue of the power and authority in me vested by the Constitution and in the name of the sovereign people of the United States, do hereby proclaim and declare unconditionally and without reservation to all and every person who, directly or indirectly, participated in the late insurrection or rebellion a full pardon and amnesty for the offense of treason against the United States or of adhering to their enemies during the late Civil War, with restoration of all rights, privileges, and immunities under the Constitution and the laws which have been made in pursuance

Confederate General Wade Hampton, a Southern hero who helped his people through the bitter times of Reconstruction.

thereof. By the President.[265] — U.S. PRESIDENT ANDREW JOHNSON, DECEMBER 25, 1868

WHAT THE SOUTH BORE

☞ . . . The bitterest aftermath of the Civil War was the period of "Reconstruction" falsely so called. The people of the Southern States were in many respects the richest and most influential politically of the nation. For the ideas peculiar to themselves they risked everything they had in life, and saw their wealth swept from them, their territory, fair as Eden, desolated, their children laid by thousands in the grave, and a scarcity of bread where opulence and plenty had prevailed. They sacrificed their political power, and by a cruel irony their slaves were exalted to become their masters. Yet this did not breed in them remorse; they neither mourned nor repined at their condition, but bore up bravely under the deprivation of everything that man holds dear. . . .[266] — REVEREND S. PARKES CADMAN (AN ENGLISHMAN)

STILL SUFFERING FROM RECONSTRUCTION

☞ . . . While I have suffered much and endured many hardships caused by that war, yet I have always felt sorry that any one was killed on my account. . . . I have never recovered from the losses of that period of war and reconstruction, but still feel that our people were in the right. We had justice on our side; and though defeated, we gained an imperishable heritage worth more than silver and gold. There is a high destiny awaiting our people. Let us teach our children that their fathers were not traitors but patriots.[267] — MRS. LOU MCCOY (WIFE OF MOSES MCCOY)

NO SUCH THING AS THE NEW SOUTH

☞ They call it the New South, those who would wipe us out and begin anew with their isms and schisms. It is not the new South; it is the same old South that needs must suffer for the sins of our fathers to render more perfect the Union aimed at in the very first line of our grand charter and by her crucifixion on the blood-red Southern cross as a vicarious offering on the altar of constitutional liberty and race purity to bring peace and reconciliation to us all. It is not a "lost cause," but one after laying in its grave has risen again with a glorified body, with healing in its wings, and is yet to stand as a balance wheel of power between the contending Northern factions who are kicking, having waxed fat on the spoils of the desolated South. The Old South is the stone cut out of the mountain without hands as a sign for all nations everywhere that home rule may live forever.[268] — AN ANONYMOUS VICTORIAN WRITER

WHAT IT WAS LIKE AT THE START OF RECONSTRUCTION
☛ Reconstruction, as it was called (ruin, desolation, and chaos were a better name for it), had just begun. The South was, as it were, in irons, waiting the executioner. The Constitution of the United States hung in the balance. The Federal Union faced a sectional despotism, the spirit of the time was martial law.[269] — COLONEL HENRY WATTERSON

LIVING UNDER A BRUTAL DESPOTISM
☛ ... We give those who defended the Union credit for sincere patriotism; but when they had gained the victory and the Union was triumphant, these patriots left us for [12] years the victims of the most brutal, conscienceless despotism that ever lorded it over a brave, honorable, upright people. This band of [Left-wing] plunderers under the name of Reconstruction completed the destruction wrought by the desolating march of the Federal armies through the South. . . .[270] — REVEREND JAMES HUGH MCNEILLY, NASHVILLE, TENN.

THE FAILED PLAN
☛ ... Then [came] so-called Reconstruction with its damnable and worse-than-war results. This was the "plan" of the so-called "wise" and "eminent" [Left-wing] statesmen then in power for ruin. But it ignominiously failed, and to-day the South is free again and prosperous. . . .[271] — JOHN COXE, GROVELAND, CAL.

Southern whites and blacks working in harmony together in the same field, another fact of history left out of our mainstream books.

CHAPTER 16

FOR RELIEF OF CONFEDERATE VETERANS & WIDOWS
☛ In the House of Representatives, in the first session of the Sixty-Fourth Congress, December 6, 1915, John M. Tillman, member of Congress from the Third Arkansas District, introduced the following bill, which was referred to the Committee on Invalid Pensions and ordered to be printed:

> *A bill to pay to Confederate soldiers and to widows of Confederate soldiers $500 and $30 per month during the remainder of their lives.*

Whereas a large amount of money, approximating $100,000,000, was secured and collected from the people of the South during the Civil War and the Reconstruction period that followed, from the following-named sources: First, from captured and abandoned property; second, from confiscated property; and, third, from the collection of cotton tax from eighteen hundred and sixty-three to eighteen hundred and sixty-eight; and

Whereas what is known as the "cotton tax" was illegally collected; and

Whereas the South prior to the Civil War and since that time abundantly proved her loyalty to the Union, gamely lost without murmuring four million slaves valued at $2,000,000,000, gave to the country much in military service, and added much territory through the genius and diplomacy of her statesmen;

Whereas fifty years after the unfortunate struggle between the States there exists only a scattered remnant of the gray chivalry that rarely lost a battle, many of whom are maimed and unable to work;

Whereas it is desirable to destroy the last vestige of sectional feeling and emphasize the fraternal spirit that should obtain in a happily reunited country and to permit a generous and a just government to recompense in part the South for her losses not justified by the stern demands of war;

Whereas it is practically impossible to restore the "cotton tax" illegally collected or other property confiscated to the people from whom it was taken during and after the war; and

Whereas the surviving soldiers of the Confederacy are conspicuous and deserving representatives of said section; therefore

Be it enacted by the Senate and House of Representatives of the United States of America in Congress assembled, That upon the passage of this act there shall be paid to each soldier who served in the Confederate army and to each widow of any Confederate soldier the sum of $500 and that in addition to this payment such soldiers and such widows shall be paid quarterly the sum of $30 per month each during the remainder of their lives.

Sec. 2. That this act shall be administered by the United States Pension Office.

Sec. 3. That to carry out the provisions of this act the sum of $100,000,000 be, and the same is hereby, appropriated.

Sec. 4. That this act shall be in force from and after its passage.[272]

— *CONFEDERATE VETERAN*, 1916

THE TRUTH ABOUT RECONSTRUCTION

☞ The "Reconstruction of the South" was, on the part of the [Liberal] people of the North at large, simply that which in national life is more than a crime, a blunder. On the part of the [Left-wing] leaders who planned it and carried it through, it was a cool, deliberate, calculated act violative of the terms on which the South had surrendered and disbanded her broken armies.[273] — THOMAS NELSON PAGE

Thomas Nelson Page.

WHY THE SOUTH FOUGHT

☞ For while those who were actors in the great drama are rapidly passing away, yet their children and their grandchildren, who inherit the noble heritage of principle bequeathed by them, heartily believe that *they contended for sacred rights guaranteed to them by the original Constitution of the United States and that they fought for the true principles of civil liberty* [my emphasis, L.S.]. And to every observant and thoughtful mind it must be still an open question whether the [Left-wing Yankee] triumph of a centralized government over the checks and balances of sovereign States has not introduced evils and dangers that threaten the very foundations of civil order. Our people accepted defeat with manly fortitude and patient resignation to the Divine will. They endured with dignified contempt the corrupt reign of the carpet-bagger, the scalawag, and the [communized] negro. They maintained their integrity for ten dreadful years of Reconstruction by Northern armies sent to force negro equality upon them. They answered not the falsehoods that were published as history, by which the conquerors sought to justify the brutalities of their war upon us. They set themselves with courage and industry to repair the waste and desolation of their country. They endeavored in good faith to adapt their lives to the new and strange conditions imposed on them.

But they never believed, and do not now believe, that material success and prosperity are tests of righteousness or that, because unlimited resources of men and munitions of war can triumph over a weaker government, therefore the weaker government was wrong and should have submitted without a conflict. Might does not make right, and our people felt that they fought for the right as it was guaranteed to them in the Constitution of their fathers; and, as Gen. Robert E. Lee expressed himself, they would have been false to duty if they had done otherwise.

Believing thus, that the South fought for the preservation of the original Constitution, I am bound to believe that the triumph of the Union was the overthrow of the Constitution, which was the bond of Union and was the forcing upon us of a government essentially different from the only one that could have been accepted by the States when they entered the Union. And I believe that this new government was in direct violation of the foundation principle of civil liberty, as announced in the Declaration of Independence, that governments "derive their just powers from the consent of the governed" [my emphasis, L.S.].

But the Southern people, having done their utmost to preserve their rights under the original Constitution and having been overpowered by brute force, could only surrender and yield to the arbitrament of war. In accepting the new order they now feel bound in honor to be loyal to the new government. It has become their government by the terms of capitulation, and they are duty bound to strive to make it a benefit and a blessing to all the people. Recognizing the difficulties and the dangers that threaten us under our new conditions. we should endeavor to ward off the evils and to make our government a real promoter of liberty and as far as possible to remedy the ruin brought by our defeat.[274] — REVEREND JAMES HUGH MCNEILLY, NASHVILLE, TENN., CIRCA 1916

THE CONFEDERATE SOLDIER

☛ . . . Poorly armed and equipped, without an organized commissary, quartermaster, or medical corps, without shops or arsenals, with her ports blockaded to the outer world, the Confederate government carried on a war for four long years against overwhelming numbers and unlimited resources and by the splendor of the valor and achievements of her soldiers compelled the respect and admiration of the civilized world. May not this laurel be laid upon his lowly mound?

The attempt to write into history the charge that the South went to war to perpetuate slavery is untrue; and since the passions of war have cooled, few, if any, believe it. When it is remembered that the people of the South accepted and carried out in good faith the great wrong done by the freedom and enfranchisement of the negro, although its effect was to bring to them financial and possibly social ruin, no further proof is needed in denial of the charge. The South went to war to defend her homes and institutions, and it was fought to the end with no other purpose.

The question of the right of the States to secede from the Union was submitted to the arbitrament of the sword. By the use of overwhelming numbers and resources and the slow process of attrition the South lost; and when valor and devotion could accomplish nothing more at the bidding of her commander [General Lee], whom she loved and whom her soldiers had followed with unswerving loyalty and devotion for four long years, the Confederate soldier laid down his arms and returned to the ways of peace, and on his flag might well be written: "for valor, for honor, for right." Then followed the Reconstruction days, the nightmare after the death of the Confederacy, when the great old mother of States and statesmen [Virginia] was known as Military District No. 1 and governed by a military satrap. The wolf and the hyena, who linger in the trail of an army, too cowardly to risk their carcasses in battle, were turned loose upon her people to destroy what little there was left.

On returning to his home after Appomattox the Virginia soldier found his house burned, his fences destroyed, and not a living thing to greet him save the faithful, loving eyes of his dear wife and little ones, who had worked and starved and hoped and prayed for four long years for the success of his cause. Without food, without shelter, with scant clothing, without seed, without stock or implements, and without means of purchase, without anything save that indomitable courage which had sustained him on the field of battle and which he exhibited, if possible, in a higher degree in caring for those loved ones when even God seemed to have deserted him, he began life anew. For years he and those loved ones suffered and endured without uttering a complaint. He had risked his all in the balance and lost; he accepted the result. God's mercy did not desert him. By slow degrees the bare walls of his home received a roof, the wild berries, nature's contribution to virtue and valor, gave them sustenance, seeds were planted and grew, and the sun of hope once again lit up that desolated home.

Half a century has passed since those colors carried to victory

on many a hard-fought field have been folded forever. Of that splendid army, of whom the historian and poet delight to write, a few gray-haired veterans remain, and soon there will be none left to recount their story. The descendants of those men and of those noble women have built anew their beloved South, until from its ashes it blooms again like its roses and has become once more a power in the government of this land. All honor to them! . . .[275] —
HENRY T. DOUGLAS, CIRCA 1916

ANTEBELLUM FRICTION & THE TERM CARPET-BAGGER
☞ The North and the South had been two households in one house, two nations under one name. The intellectual, moral, and social life of each had been utterly distinct and separate from that of the other. They no more understood or appreciated each other's feelings or development than John Chinaman comprehends the civilization of John Bull. It is true they spoke the same language, used the same governmental forms, and, most unfortunately, thought they comprehended each other's ideas. Each thought that he knew the thought and purpose of the other better than the thinker knew his own. The Northern man despised his Southern fellow citizen in bulk as a good-natured braggadocio, mindful of his own ease, fond of power and display, and with no animating principle which could in any manner interfere with his interest. The Southern man despised his Northern compeer as cold-blooded, selfish, hypocritical, cowardly, and envious.

. . . In order to express their abhorrence for such as dared to go from the North [after the War] to become residents of the South without an absolute surrender of principles, one who was of more intense virulence than the others invented a new term, or rather reapplied one which he had already helped to make infamous.

The name itself was a stroke of genius. In all history there is perhaps no instance of so perfect and complete an instrument. "Sans-culottes" is its nearest rival. "Abolitionist," its immediate predecessor, had the disadvantage of an etymological significance which sometimes interfered with its perfect application. "Carpet-bagger" had, however, all the essentials of a denunciatory epithet in a superlative degree. It had a quaint and ludicrous sound, was utterly without defined significance, and was altogether unique. It was susceptible of one significance in one locality and another in another, without being open to any etymological objection. This elasticity of signification is of prime importance in a disparaging epithet; there is almost always a necessity for it.

. . . So the South cursed carpet-baggers because they were of the North, and the North cursed them because the South set the example.

In nothing has the South shown its vast moral superiority over the North more than in this. "I pray thee curse me this people," it said to the North, first of the abolitionists [Yankee socialists and communists] and then of carpet-baggers; and the North cursed, not knowing whom it denounced and not pausing to inquire whether they were worthy of stripes or not. Perhaps there is no other instance in history in which the conquering power has discredited its own agents, denounced those of its own blood and faith, espoused the prejudices of its conquered foes, and poured the vials of its wrath and contempt upon the only class in the conquered territory who defended its acts, supported its policy, promoted its aim, or desired its preservation and continuance.[276] — ALBION W. TOURGEE, UNION SOLDIER & A SELF-PROFESSED CARPET-BAGGER (WHO EMPATHIZED WITH THE SOUTH)

THE HORRORS OF RECONSTRUCTION

☛ . . . No patriotic or well-thinking man justifies the horrors of Reconstruction. The outrages perpetrated by carpet-baggers, scalawags, and negro freemen upon the people of the South has long since been recognized by just and thinking men as a sad and baneful Story and the result of war's passion, prejudice, and bloodthirstiness. . . .[277] — GENERAL BENNETT H. YOUNG, COLUMBUS, OH., JUNE 10, 1916

THE END OF RECONSTRUCTION

☛ . . . The rule of the majority had been overthrown, the power of the [U.S.] government boldly defied, and its penalties for crime successfully evaded, that the enfranchisement of the colored man might be rendered a farce and the obnoxious amendments and Reconstruction legislation practically nullified. Read by the light of other days, the triumph of the ancient South was incredibly grand; in the then present there was little lacking to give it completeness; in the future—well, that could take care of itself.

Time went on, and twelve years from the day when Lee surrendered under the apple tree at Appomattox there was another surrender, and the last of the [U.S.] government organized under the policy of Reconstruction fell into the [Left-wing] hands of those who inaugurated and carried on war against the nation. . . .[278] — ALBION W. TOURGEE, UNION SOLDIER & A SELF-PROFESSED CARPET-BAGGER (WHO EMPATHIZED WITH THE SOUTH)

IF ABOLISHING SLAVERY HAD BEEN THEIR TRUE GOAL, YANKEES COULD HAVE DONE SO EVEN BEFORE SOUTHERN SECESSION BEGAN

☛ . . . We of the South fought for principle, and they of the North because of jealousy. Had Harriet Beecher Stowe, Mr. Lincoln, and the abolitionists [that is, socialists and communists] of the North been prompted by a true, pure motive of "all people being equal," they would have made it possible to abolish slavery without a Fort Sumter, an Appomattox, or a Reconstruction period.

If the United States government could pay $400,000,000 for the freedom of the slaves on February 3, 1865, at the Hampton Roads conference, after the heavy cost of millions of dollars and the appalling loss of life and injured, why could it not have paid before the secession of South Carolina! [my emphasis, L.S.]. Many of the abolitionists of the South, as well as those of the North [note that unlike in the North, most of the abolitionists in the South were not radical Left-wingers, socialists, or communists, but rather Conservatives, L.S.],[279] had freed their slaves and stood the criticism of those who did not believe as they did, and yet those same abolitionists took up their arms in defense of the right of secession. I know whereof I speak. My husband's father and mine both trod the road of battle, sons of Southern abolitionists who did not believe in slavery because their Christian consciences would not permit it. I say again that *the freedom of the slaves could have been bought, just as their slavery was bought, with money instead of with blood* [my emphasis, L.S.].

Could we cleanse our minds and hearts of all animosity and live the principle of true Christianity taught us by our leader, Robert E. Lee, the greatest leader that the world has ever known, how soon would truth shine out as the "Star of the East" did to the wise men.[280] — MRS. STEPHEN D. KNOX, LITTLE ROCK, ARK., 1916

RECONSTRUCTION DEFINED

☛ . . . the mad days of Reconstruction, when the South was under the despot's heel, who was endeavoring to Africanize her, disfranchising her bravest and best, and trying to republicanize her by giving political power to the negroes.[281] — CAPTAIN P. M. DE LEON, WASHINGTON, D.C.

THE COTTON TAX

☛ *The dreadful days of Reconstruction are passed, and reason has returned to the North, which as a whole is heartily ashamed of the history made at that period* [my emphasis, L.S.]. Should the [Southern] States be repaid the amount extorted from their citizens [via the North's onerous and unconstitutional cotton tax], they would, after paying proved claims, have perhaps $50,000,000 left to apply to the care of the aged men [Confederate veterans] and women [their widows] of the South who have made her immortal and illustrated *Americanism* [that is, conservative, all-American ideals], causing men of all sections now to admire and reverence her splendid record under our immortal leaders.²⁸² — CAPTAIN P. M. DE LEON, WASHINGTON, D.C.

Beauvoir ("beautiful view"), Biloxi, Mississippi, the final home of Jefferson Davis, where he wrote his opus magnum, *The Rise and Fall of the Confederate Government.*

A YANK'S IMPRESSIONS ON A FIRST VISIT TO THE WHITE HOUSE OF THE CONFEDERACY, RICHMOND, VIRGINIA
☛ [One of the many impressions I received during my visit] . . . was that slavery was but an incidental cause of the great fraternal strife. In this retrospect of half a century one cannot believe that two mighty sections of one blood and language could have hurled themselves in deadly combat at each other over an issue like that of African slavery. For slavery was doomed both for humane and economic reasons, and, as well, the cosmic law that transforms childhood and dependence into the estate of maturity and self-reliance was acting powerfully to free the bond-man. If slavery was an immediate irritant leading to the War between the States, it was so for the reason that one section attempted prematurely to hasten a process that human and economic and cosmic forces were fast consummating, and this prematureness that resulted in so much

loss of life and treasure led to the crime of an invasion that had no warrant in right and law and to repel which the South and her leaders drew the sword. [John] Randolph [of Roanoke] [note: actually, it was Thomas Jefferson] once declared: "We have a wolf (referring to slavery) by the ears; we fear to hold it, but dare not let it go." Certainly the deplorable experiences of Reconstruction gave ample justification to the fears and the judgment of the ante-bellum South.

No, the real cause of the war lay far deeper than slavery. As one hastened through this impressive repository of a cause which arises in perennial resurrection (two hours only were available for the visit where two weeks would be insufficient) one most profoundly realized that the differences created by the issues of Imperialism [defined as "a policy of extending a country's power and influence through diplomacy or military force"] and Republicanism [defined as "the doctrine that laws and the state properly exist only to serve the common good of a nation's people or citizens"], a controversy at least inherited from ancient Greece and Rome, were fundamentally the *casus belli* ["the case for, or cause of, war"] in 1861-65. So far as our nationality is concerned, these causes trace back to the Federalist [then Left-wing] and Democratic-Republican [then Conservative] parties and the two great statesmen, [Liberal Alexander] Hamilton and [Conservative Thomas] Jefferson, who, respectively, inspired and led them. Hamilton, the so-called Federalist, was in every fiber of his being an Imperialist. His great passion was for order; his chief mistrust, the people. While he fought to free the colonies from Great Britain, he cared nothing for popular liberty. Order was essential, and it could be had only (so taught Hamilton) under law administered by authority. Self-government and local autonomy he considered delusions, and centralization, civic and economic, was in his political and social philosophy the natural and inevitable tendency; order, centralization, and strong government were the foundations, according to Hamilton, of human well-being. He became [America's first] Secretary of the Treasury under the newly established national government [with George Washington as president]. On the other hand, Jefferson, Secretary of State [also under President Washington], was politically a Republican; socially, a Democrat. He knew the necessity for order, but he loved and advocated liberty; he trusted the people; he believed in self-direction and in local self-government; "the best government was that which governed the least;" decentralization, civic and economic, was his cherished policy; liberty and more liberty were the true goals of human ambition and human welfare, according to Jefferson. And, therefore, what more natural than that Washington's Secretaries of State and Treasury should be at swords' points with each other? In the light of these distinctions, what more inevitable than war, either of bullets or ballots, between the factions led by these two statesmen, the one imperialistic and centralizing [that is, essentially Left-wing], the other republican and decentralizing [that is, essentially Right-wing]?

Here, then, and not in slavery *per se*, were the roots of the struggle at arms in 1861-65. One could but reflect upon these things as one stood amongst the Confederate memorials in Richmond. And, too, the irony of the situation was brought to mind when one reflected that the Southern people held in bondage four millions of blacks, while at the same time they drew the sword in defense of constitutional Federalism, Republican self-government, and Jeffersonian ideals of human liberty. Yet the explanation is very easy. The whites were an old and mature race; the blacks a young and immature race. Of necessity, therefore, the one must dominate the other, as much so as that parents must control the children in the family life. And as children must perform household tasks unrequited save for care, so must an immature race do the same on a larger scale. If Southern plantations were carried on by slave labor, so Northern farms were largely carried on by the unpaid labor of sons and daughters and minor relatives until they reached legal majority. And the Confederate war, waged to maintain the right to regulate the affairs of the immature, was as justifiable as it would have been for a Northern farmer to resist by force of arms any invasion of his family intended prematurely to free his sons and daughters before they all attained legal majority. *The Southern people, guaranteed under the Constitution which they so willingly helped to form the right of regulation of their own local affairs, refused to tolerate invasion of either territory or legal rights. Hence the war then of bullets, now and for years to come of ballots* [my emphasis, L.S.].

And the remaining impression as one stood in that Museum and recalled Confederate memorials everywhere in the South, even the Confederate monument in the Arlington Cemetery, was to send mind and thought across the seas to that continent and the adjacent continents whereon is being waged an international war to determine which principle of human government shall prevail among men—Imperialism or Republicanism. And one may well imagine that the shades of Washington and Frederick the Great, of Jefferson and Hamilton, of Davis and Lincoln, and of Lee and Grant hover above those battle fields, solicitous as to the result. As one gazed at the gray and red and white symbolism in the former White House of the Confederacy one began to realize how close is the relation between the war of 1861-65 and the war of 1914. Furthermore, how much the rise of European Imperialism soon after the suppression of the Republican uprising of 1848 [fomented by European socialists and communists, many who then fled to America and, after 1854, joined the then Left-wing Republican Party, supporting Lincoln and the Union during the War] had to do with the failure of the Confederacy in 1865. [Note: as many of Europe's radical Left-wing "forty-eighters" ended up working in the Lincoln administration *and* serving in the Union army, they were indeed instrumental in the North's victory. See my Appendix.] Most significant reflection, is it not?

For, supposing the Confederacy had won, the power of the American people to resist foreign incursions would have been greatly weakened. Already Napoleon III had an army of occupation in Mexico; Germany had gotten ready to fight her short and successful war of 1866 and was soon (1870) to assault France successfully. In half a decade and a little more after Appomattox, William of Prussia was made Emperor William I in the great hall of Versailles, and German Imperialism was firmly established; the solid foundations for the assault of Imperialism (civic and economic) upon Republicanism were laid. Can one, then, fail to see that not only was fate against the South as to African slavery, but also against the political and economic ideals of Southern statesmen, from [Thomas] Jefferson and [John C.] Calhoun down? Preeminently so, it would seem. Just so long as imperialistic authority and centralization lurk in the bush, so long will it be impossible for Republican self-government to stalk in the open. The human sentiments of the world at large were against the South's maintenance of African slavery, and the imperialistic designs of Europe were against the South's aspirations and struggle for independence. In a word, the war of 1861-65 was fought too late to maintain slavery, too early to defend secession; this last the inalienable right of all peoples, if the preamble of the Declaration of Independence has any truth or significance whatever. In the large world sense the Confederate war was but one of the struggles to determine the status between Imperialism and Republicanism, while the present war [World War I, 1914-1918] is the latest of those struggles of liberty against authority. Therefore in 1861-65 the cosmic forces were arrayed against the South. The time was not yet ripe to substantiate the ideals of the Declaration of

Independence, the Federal Constitution, and the principles of local autonomy. Nevertheless, *the Southern cause is not lost, but sleepeth until the morning light of liberty shall awaken it* [my emphasis, L.S.]. Her battle was well fought in 1861-65; undoubtedly she prevented the complete overstepping of the line that divides Republican Federalism from imperial centralization. And her monuments and holy treasures will bear perennial testimony to this historic fact. Furthermore, the South's contention in the Confederate war will shortly become the great world question, seeing that time has arrived in human history when nations must either wage wars of extermination upon each other or form some sort of federation, just as Kant a century and a quarter ago stated. Shall it be world imperialism or world federation? Undoubtedly the South by her defense of her principles and her territory contributed immeasurably to the coming solution of that mighty issue in human affairs. May she ever remain true to herself and perpetuate to coming generations her ideals so splendidly commemorated in her memorials, her monuments, and her museums! They are not meaningless, for her cause was just and will rise some day into incomparable light and power. Such were some of the impressions received by a first visit to the Confederate Museum in Richmond. ...[283] — REVEREND A. W. LITTLEFIELD, NEEDHAM, MASS., AUGUST 1916

CONCERNING WORLD WAR II & CIVIL WAR RECONSTRUCTION

☛ [Rev. J. H. McNeilly:] In an article in *The Outlook* of December 20, 1916, on "Germany's Offer of Peace" the example of the North in its treatment of the South after the war of 1861-65 is commended to the belligerent nations of Europe when this great war [World War 1] shall end. The [uneducated] writer says: "The North made no attempt to punish the South or even the leaders of the Southern revolt." This statement called forth an indignant protest from a Virginian [J.N.W.] living in Tennessee, which was published in the Outlook of January 17, 1917, as follows:

> In your issue of December 20 [1916] you conclude your article on "Germany's Offer of Peace" with the following amazing statement:
>
>> "The example of the United States may be pointed out as one which worked well and is worth following. The North made no attempt to punish the South or even the leaders of the Southern revolt."

I would like to take up this paragraph *seriatim*. You say "it worked out well." Have you forgotten the ten ghastly years of reconstruction, the bitter feelings that were aroused in a moment and were allayed only after years, the shameless looting, the holding in bondage far worse than any Belgian deportation of a whole white race, the—but why continue? Surely you must remember something of all that, and if you weren't old enough at the time to remember it take some history and look it up or come down to the South and we will give you evidence. Belgian deportations make you indignant, and of the subjection of millions of your peers for a space of ten years you say the plan "worked out well." If reconstruction was the result of the North's "making no attempt to punish the South," we Southerners and you Northerners should be devoutly grateful that the North didn't really put its mind on the task.

Do you really think that the example is worth following? If the Central Powers know anything of our ten years after the Civil War, they will fight to the last man before delivering themselves into the bondage of Hottentots and Kaffirs and Zulus (to continue the parallel). Those ten years area burning memory to every Southerner and an eternal humiliation to every Northerner except, apparently, yourself.

And the leaders. Have you forgotten, or rather have you heard, that it was proposed to put General Lee and all other Confederate leaders on trial for their life on the charge of high treason? And that only General Grant's determined stand prevented it? And that President Jefferson Davis lay long months in chains and was tried for high treason and was acquitted; that [Yankee socialist] Horace Greeley went on his bond? Have you forgotten all these things? Because not all Southerners have.

And because you have many Southern readers you owe yourself, it seems to me, an explanation of this amazing misstatement of historical fact. You have completely destroyed the effect of this article, you have invalidated the editorial articles in this issue, and you have dropped suspicion in our minds as to your mental balance at the time you wrote these lines.

The writer is a Virginian and as such is not altogether foreign to these things, and he would certainly like to know how the editorial staff of the Outlook interprets post-bellum Southern history. — J.N.W.

[Rev. McNeilly:] To this in the same number the editor [of *The Outlook* piece] essays reply. While he agrees with his correspondent's view of reconstruction as "the ten ghastly years," he reaffirms that it was not the purpose of the reconstruction measures to inflict punishment on the South. He heads his defense of the policy "Not Malice, but False Philosophy," and he lays the blame of those "ghastly years" of ruin and oppression on a mistaken zeal for righteousness rather than on a malicious purpose to humiliate and punish the South. He says that only eight persons were punished, seven for "participation in the assassination of

Abraham Lincoln and one, [Confederate] Captain [Henry] Wirz, "for special brutal treatment of prisoners at Andersonville." But he ignores the fact that Mrs. [Mary] Surratt and Captain Wirz, two innocent persons convicted on suborned testimony, were sentenced to death by a military commission organized to convict. He also passes over the fact that Jefferson Davis was placed in irons by the order of the Assistant Secretary of War [radical Yankee socialist Charles Anderson Dana]. The editor especially declares that [radical Yankee socialist] Thaddeus Stevens was only actuated by a benevolent desire to "reform Southern society." Yet [Henry W.] Elson, partisan historian of the United States, bitter in his misrepresentations of the South, in his *Side Lights of [on] American History* says of Stevens:

> "He was extremely severe in denunciation, radical and intolerant. He belonged to that class in the North whose attitude toward the South was characterized by bitter personal feeling, who could not forgive a conquered and prostrate foe, but hastened to place the grinding heel upon his neck."[284]

In his history Elson says:

> "Congressional reconstruction was thorough, drastic, merciless. The governments (set up in the South) were the most corrupt in the annals of the United States."[285]

Surely if reconstruction was not designed in malice to humiliate and punish the South, it certainly had that effect.

In support of his position the editor of *The Outlook* quotes from [German revolutionary, socialist, Union general, and strong Lincoln supporter] Carl Schurz, that embodiment of sublimated German American philosophy, speaking of the course of the North with the South: "There is not a single example of such magnanimity in the history of the world." That is an opinion to be expected from one who fled his own country in 1848 to escape the wrath of an autocratic government against all liberals [and socialists and communists] and yet when he came to this country embraced the very principles of despotic power against which he had contended in his native land. He obtained large political reward for his devotion to coercion and despotism against the South.

We of the South may be excused if we adopt the sentiment of a Yankee soldier to a "Johnnie" in Richmond directly after the surrender. He said: "Come on, Johnnie, let's take a drink together. We are brothers now, you know." Johnnie replied: "If you are a brother of mine, you have had a mighty poor way of showing it for the past four years." Thaddeus [Stevens] and his followers may have been magnanimous with the South, but they had an awful poor way of showing it.

[*The Outlook*] editor's answer will scarcely soothe his correspondent's wrath or stir the gratitude of the Southern people for the blessings of Reconstruction.[286] — REVEREND JAMES HUGH MCNEILLY, NASHVILLE, TENN.

WHY THE SOUTH WENT TO WAR

☛ . . . Of course we know that there was a very large element in the North that was thoroughly opposed to the [radical Left-wing] theories, purposes, and methods of the party which forced the war upon the South; but they were held in subjection by the unscrupulous use of force and falsehood as to the purpose of the war. Our contention is that the South was justified in her heroic defense of the principles of constitutional liberty. And that we were right in interpreting the motives and aims of the [then Left-wing Republican] party of which [big government Liberal] Mr. Lincoln was the leader is clearly shown by the Reconstruction measures which followed the victory of the North. These measures, the shame of all good men in the North, were the logical outcome of the [radical Left-wing] policy of the abolitionized [then Liberal] Republican party in waging the war, for *the effort of the Reconstruction leaders was for a mighty centralized government at Washington, with absolute control of the Southern States as conquered provinces and ultimately of all the States, the central government to determine what rights might be given to the State, the right of unlimited taxation either directly or by tariff exactions, and the supremacy of the negro in politics and in social life* [my emphasis, L.S.]. Negro judges, negro legislatures, negro and white social intermingling were no accident; they were the logical result of abolition sentiment and legislation.

Against these things the South had to fight or be traitor to her traditions, to her blood, and to the true principles of civil and religious liberty. She fought "that government of the people, by the people, and for the people might not perish from the earth." And her defeat leaves it still in doubt whether the present regime of the trust or the labor union [socialism] is to prevail over liberty, equality, and fraternity. The South is proud of her record. Though defeated, she fought to the death for liberty, justice, and truth. . .
.[287] — REVEREND JAMES HUGH MCNEILLY, NASHVILLE, TENN.

New England Reconstruction missionary teacher Sarah Jane Foster. Like thousands of other meddling Yankee do-gooders, Foster traveled South after the War with the intent of educating the "backward" people of Dixie, and more specifically, their "ignorant former slaves." The problem was that her idea of education was Northern in perspective; that is, Liberal-minded. While Foster's personal aims may have been benevolent, the Conservative South did not appreciate such "charity," especially when it came from carpet-bagging educators whose primary goal was not to help the Southern people rebuild their shattered land, but purely to Northernize it through the Left-wing indoctrination of their children. Foster died of yellow fever in 1868. She was 28 years old.

CHAPTER 17

COMPARING LINCOLN'S ACTIONS DURING THE CIVIL WAR WITH THOSE OF WILSON DURING WORLD WAR I

☛ . . . To my mind, the present righteous war with Germany represents far more closely the Old South in 1861 than the Old North at that time. Indeed, no two men ever stood farther apart in principle than [U.S. President] Woodrow] Wilson and Lincoln. What does the war [World War I] stand for as currently stated in the United States?

U.S. President Woodrow Wilson. Though a Democrat, Wilson and Lincoln shared many of the same Liberal views, for the Democrats in Lincoln's day were known as Republicans, while the Republicans in the 1860s were known as Democrats. They would not switch platforms and become the parties we know today until the election of 1896.

1. The war stands for the rights of the "small nations" . . . By fighting a four years' war on equal terms with the powerful North it [the South] gave the best proof of its right to exist in the sun as an independent nation. After drawing in vain on his own population and that of Europe to suppress the South, Lincoln resorted to forcible enlistments from the South's own [black] population to achieve his victory, confessing that without the negro troops the North "would be compelled to abandon the war in three weeks."

2. The war stands for "government based on the consent of the governed. . . ." The sacred character of the principle is affirmed by Wilson in his inaugural address March 4, 1917, and in his letter to the new Russian government, but Lincoln and the North in 1861 denied its application to the South. . . .

3. The war stands for "humanity" as recognized by the international law. . . . Were Lincoln and his supporters humane? By an act of Congress approved July 17, 1862, and published *with an approving proclamation by Lincoln, death, imprisonment, and confiscation of property were pronounced on five million white people in the South and all their abettors and aiders in the North. To reduce the South to submission, Lincoln instituted on his own motion a blockade, a means of war so extreme that,*

despite its legality under the international law, it has evoked from the Germans the most savage retaliation when applied to them. He threatened with hanging as pirates Southern privateersmen and as guerrillas regularly commissioned partisans. He suspended the cartel of exchange; and when the Federal prisoners necessarily fared badly for lack of food on account of the blockade and the universal devastation, he retorted their sufferings upon the Confederate prisoners, thousands of whom perished of cold and starvation in the midst of plenty. Medicines [in the South] were made contraband, and to justify the seizure of neutral goods at sea great enlargement of the principle of the "ultimate destination" was introduced into the international law. The property of noncombatants was seized everywhere without compensation, and within the areas embraced by the Union lines the oath of allegiance was required of both sexes above sixteen years of age under penalty of being driven from their homes. Houses, barns, villages, and towns were destroyed, and the fiercest retaliation was employed by the Federal [U.S.] commanders to strike terror into Southerners. Even the act for which Lincoln has been most applauded in recent days, his [unconstitutional] Emancipation Proclamation, stood on no real humanitarian ground [my emphasis, L.S.].

Lincoln vacillated very much before deciding to put it [the Emancipation Proclamation] out. At a meeting of the cabinet on July 22, 1862, he announced tentatively his purpose of publishing such a paper; but on September 13, only ten days before his issuance of it, he absolutely ridiculed the thing, though not altogether committing himself against the step, pronouncing it as futile as "the pope's bull against the comet." He asked:

> "Would my word free the slaves when I cannot even enforce the Constitution in the Rebel States? Is there a single court or magistrate or individual that would be influenced by it there?"

The doubtful success of the battle of Antietam raised his spirits and decided him the other way; the Emancipation Proclamation was issued; but instead of taking the high ground of general liberty, he applied it to only that portion of the South over which he had confessed himself powerless, exempting from its application that part where he had real authority by means of Federal occupation.

Issued in this form, it could not have contemplated to any appreciable extent a moral effect in making friends for the government. What then? The Confederates denounced it as an effort to incite the negroes to rise and murder the women and children in the South, living lonely and unprotected while their men folks were at war.

In this light it was denounced severely in England and France. When the negroes did not rise, Lincoln denied that such was his purpose; but against this are his own words. After urging, as stated, the futility of the Emancipation Proclamation, he used this language:

> "Understand, I raise no objections against it on legal or constitutional grounds, for as chief of the army and navy in time of war I suppose I may take any measure which may best subdue the enemy. Nor do I urge objections of a moral nature in view of possible consequences of insurrection and massacre in the Southern States. I view this measure as a practical war measure, according to the advantages or disadvantages it may offer to the suppression of the rebellion."

Here there are a distinct recognition that insurrection and massacre were a possible consequence and a distinct affirmation that objections of every nature, legal, constitutional, or moral, had no weight as against the advantages or disadvantages of the measure as a practical *war measure* [my emphasis, L.S.]. This much, at least, may be said, that if there was any measure calculated to incite the negroes this was the one, and that if the dreadful consequences did not ensue it can never be credited to the humanity of Lincoln, who realized the peril. All the credit goes to the humanity with which the slaveowners treated their slaves.

As Lincoln said, he "wanted to beat the Rebels," and to win he resorted to the most extreme measures. When he thought that milder action might have a chance of prevailing, he tried that too, but seemingly without any particular preference. *He never understood the Southern people, and to him the whole question of secession seemed to be the money value of slaves instead of one of violated rights or self-government, as it undoubtedly was* [my emphasis, L.S.]. He is, therefore, much lauded for his humanity by those who take the same view of Southern men's motives as his own for suggesting on February 6, 1865, to his cabinet to pay the Southern people $400,000,000 if they would quit fighting, the money "to be for the extinguishment of slavery or for such purpose as the States were disposed." But his cabinet was opposed to the proposition, and Lincoln did not insist on it. It never got anywhere; but to show the light in which Lincoln regarded his offer it is interesting to notice that *he justified it to his cabinet, not on any generous or noble grounds, but on the mercenary one that the sum* "would pay the expenses of the war two hundred days." The proposition really contained a gross insult to the Southerners. Their men were not fighting for the money value of slaves, but for a national existence which they deemed menaced in the old Union.

There was no other meaning to their taking up arms, and there was no solution to the war except independence or absolute defeat. Their principles were not for sale. Suppose [George] Washington during the American Revolution had received from the British government a pecuniary offer to quit fighting, what would have been his reply? [my emphasis, L.S.].

Contrast with all this the record of [Confederate] President Davis and his generals on land and admirals at sea. The campaign of Lee in Pennsylvania and the victorious career of Raphael Semmes on the ocean were a contrast in every respect to the actions of the Federal commanders (George B. McClellan always excepted) and were about as far removed from the "frightfulness" of the [World War I] Germans as anything could be. And President Davis, although greatly blamed for his humanity from some quarters in the South, avoided in every way possible the practice of the doctrine of retaliation, which made the innocent responsible for the guilty. The only regrettable instance of severity by the Confederates was the burning of Chambersburg [Pennsylvania] by [Confederate] General [John] McCausland in retaliation for [Union] General [David] Hunter's campaign of fire and sword in the Valley of Virginia. It was not a part of any settled plan of destruction and occurred only after a demand for a moderate indemnity had been made of the inhabitants—an indemnity whose amount would make the [World War I] Germans smile—and had been refused by them.

4. Finally, the war [World War I] stands for democracy against autocracy. As already stated, the South was the champion of democratic principles when the North was wedded to those of an aristocratic character. The [Conservative] South had its [Right-wing political leaders Thomas] Jefferson and [James] Madison, and the [Liberal] North had its [Left-wing political leaders Alexander] Hamilton and John Adams. The difference between the rich and the poor was always greater in the North than in the South, so far as the whites were concerned. Lincoln adopted absolute autocratic principles during the war, making *necessity*[288] his plea, just as Germany has done. Despite the rulings of his own chief justice and the plain language of the Constitution, he assumed the power of suspending the writ of *habeas corpus* and under the pretense of the so-called war powers set aside any clause of the Constitution interfering with his will. He arrested thirty-eight thousand people in the North at different times and confined them in prison, subjected to great hardships, without any formal charge or trial, and in reply to a protest from a mass meeting at Albany, N.Y., used this extraordinary language:

> "The suspension of the *habeas corpus* was for the purpose that men may be arrested and held in prison who cannot be proved guilty of any defined crime."

After the war the South was held by the North under military government for twelve years, and the most ignorant elements of the population were intrusted with the power under the Reconstruction policy. If this does not signify autocratic rule similar to that which [World War I] Germany would impose upon the world, what does?

How utterly unlike Lincoln has been the conduct of [U.S.] President [Woodrow] Wilson, who has scrupulously consulted Congress one very important question concerning the war with Germany!

In conclusion, it is proper to state that it affords the writer no pleasure to indulge in recrimination; but as long as Northern writers will insist on misstating facts and rubbing the old sores the wrong way they need not expect absolute silence from the South. The North is to be congratulated upon its conversion to the principles for which the South contended both in the Revolution and the War between the States. The war with Germany [World War I] should be pushed to a successful conclusion, that the rights of small nations, the right of local self-government, the right of humanity, and the right of democracy be "rendered safe for mankind."[289] — LYON G. TYLER, PRESIDENT OF WILLIAM & MARY COLLEGE, WILLIAMSBURG, VA.

A PERIOD OF APPALLING MISGOVERNMENT

☛ . . . Then followed the period of Reconstruction, the horrors of which it has taken the people of the North forty years to begin to get some true conception of. . . . Dr. Lyman Abbott, in *The Outlook* of December 23, 1903, says of the Reconstruction period:

> "Then came what must be regarded in the light of to-day as one of the worst periods of misgovernment and maladministration in the history of any civilized community, a period of appalling misgovernment, a period which General Armstrong called a 'bridge of wood over a river of fire.'"

[German revolutionary, socialist, Union general, and strong Lincoln supporter] Carl Schurz says in *McClure's Magazine* for January, 1904:

> "It is difficult to exaggerate the extravagances, corrupt practices, and downright robberies perpetrated under the (Reconstruction)

governments. That the Southern people should be unwilling to tolerate such shameful and ruinous misrule is not surprising. But that statesmen of good character and high position in the national government should have been willing to sustain such misrule, the historians will find it difficult to explain. Expecting to keep the Southern States under Republican [then Left-wing] control and thus to fortify the Republican majority in Congress and in the electoral college, the party leaders insisted on supporting the carpetbag government to an extent now hardly credible."

The celebrated English historian [William E. H.] Lecky, in his *Democracy and Liberty*, gets the still clearer perspective of a foreigner on this period, which he characterizes as

"a grotesque parody of government, a hideous orgy of anarchy, violence, unrestrained corruption, undisguised, ostentatious, insulting robbery such as the world had scarcely ever seen."

We who lived through it know that it was a period of fearful compression, repression, suppression, depression, and oppression, when for the first time since time began a white race undertook to put the feet of a colored race on the necks of men and women of their own blood and breed. But the men of the South, of the purest Anglo-Saxon blood now left on the earth, inspired by the strongest instinct of this strongest of races, the intense instinct of local self-government, recovered what they had lost in the "imminent deadly breach"; and every Southern State has regained its autonomy, though at the cost of an entire change of the South's historical and traditional attitude toward politics. Before 1860 we had a leisure class with a genius for politics and with the highest positions open to us. Since 1860 we have had no leisure class, and the "door of hope" in national politics had been closed to Southern men by the sectionalism which has dominated the North since the outbreak of the war between the sections, and it will probably be many years before a man of Southern blood and antecedents can aspire to even the second place on the national ticket unless he had left the South and had gained name and fame for successful political leadership in some Northern State. A few of our foremost men have been so strongly demanded by their States that they served their States most ably, though with the certainty that they could aspire no higher. In order to regain our local autonomy, the thing of paramount importance, all our energies were concentrated on our local affairs, and national affairs were neglected. There were giants in the Old South in those days; there are giants in the South in these days. Against what seems overwhelming odds we overthrew negro and carpetbag domination. With no capital but the ground we stood on, in fifteen years we had doubled, and now we have more than tripled, the cotton crop, largely by white labor in some of the cotton States—a very significant fact. The wealth of the Old South from its very nature was unstable. Our wealth now is in the cotton mill, in the rice field, in the cotton field, in the cotton exchange, in the sugar mill, in the cattle ranch, in the smelting furnace, and is stable. . . .

. . . The people of the North [Liberal Yankees] settled their local white race problem by disfranchising all illiterate white men, their local black race problem by disfranchising all illiterate black men, their local red race problem by exterminating the red man, and their local yellow race problem by expelling the yellow man from the whole country at the dictation of a small minority of white men on the Pacific Coast. With this record of the disfranchisement of illiterates, white and black, at home, of extermination for the red man, and of expulsion for the yellow man, in 1867 they [Liberal Yankees] undertook to settle our local black race problem by enfranchising all black men among us. But we have reversed their proposed settlement of our black race problem, and all they propose to do about our following their example with their black illiterates is to cut down our representation in the Electoral College and in Congress. . . .[290] — COLONEL ROBERT BINGHAM, ASHEVILLE, N.C., 1904

A YANKEE ON SLAVERY, EMANCIPATION, & RECONSTRUCTION

☛ . . . In the North emancipation had been peacefully accomplished, mostly because it did not pay financially. In the South too it was destined to be achieved in the progress of events. As it was, at the time the Civil War broke out there were many thousands of colored men in the South who had already been freed by their Southern masters.

Now, as I said before, if emancipation had come about in that way [that is, *gradual emancipation*, as was done in the Northern states], as with wiser statesmanship and more mutual forbearance and faith it would have come about, [and] the negro in this country would be far ahead of where he is to-day. The Southern white man, having voluntarily ceased to be his master, would have continued to feel himself the guardian, and he would have continued to train this man from the point to which he had already brought him up to the point where he was capable of assuming the responsibility of citizenship. And the negro would have continued to look upon the

Southern white man as his best friend and counselor in politics, in industry, in religion, in every way.

The wholesale way in which [Southern] emancipation was finally brought about [that is, via *sudden emancipation*], with the consummate blunder on top of that of a wholesale enfranchisement and on top of that the crime of what by a woeful misuse of the term was called "Reconstruction," has not worked out eventually one-tenth of the harm to the white man that it has to the negro himself, who was supposed to be the beneficiary of all this. It separated him from his natural tutor and counselor; it put into his child's brain wrong notions which all the years since have not been sufficient to counteract and correct. And it took away from the Southerner by his impoverishment the ability to help and I think also something of that feeling of responsibility for this folk which he had always felt and which he would then still have continued to feel.

It was a dreadful burden which the North left the Southerner after the war to return to his ruined home, his devastated fortunes not only, but to an entirely changed industrial system, since the man who had been his slave was now free. But in the end the heaviest handicap fell upon the unprepared negro himself. He was turned loose an orphan now in a civilization that he had never yet been able to understand and which now in its utterly changed condition confused and deluded him altogether....[291] — PASTOR VANDER MEULEN, CHICAGO, ILL.

SOUTHERN WOMEN & RECONSTRUCTION
☛ ... No one knows what reconstruction means more than the loyal women of the South, when no hand was held out to us, and we had to make our beloved land to smile again unaided....[292] — MRS. HORACE L. SIMPSON, VICE PRESIDENT GENERAL OF FLORIDA, NATIONAL BOARD OF THE CONFEDERATED SOUTHERN MEMORIAL ASSOCIATION, 1919

ON WHETHER OR NOT TO PRESERVE THE FIRST WHITE HOUSE OF THE CONFEDERACY, MONTGOMERY, ALA.
☛ I have thought sometimes that the people of the South were sleeping on their rights. The salvation of the world to-day is due to the principles promulgated by the Southern Confederacy. The South should not hesitate to claim that the cause for which she fought was not and never will be lost. The first White House of the Confederacy, or rather the first home of true democracy, should be saved as a monument to the patriotic wisdom of the noble men of

the South, not only first promulgated the principles of world-wide democracy, but win fought, bled, and died for the same form of government and the same principles of life, which the world finally saw were just and right. The sons and grandsons of those who died and of those who lived and endured reconstruction rallied as a man.

The cause for which the Confederacy stood has finally prevailed. The patriotic, freedom-loving men of to-day should save this monument as an inspiration to all those individuals and to all those nations that are willing to sacrifice for the hope of humanity. This first While House was once the home of the greatest martyr the world has ever known [Jefferson Davis], excepting Jesus Christ. This is heresy to the ignorant and to those who still hate the South Mr. Davis was called unanimously against his will to take charge of a nation without one dollar, not a gun, no army, no ships, no quartermaster's department, no commissary, no hospitals, no Red Cross. He held the confidence and love of all the people. In all the annals of history no one ever accomplished so much with so little.

When overwhelmed by unnumbered hordes, called largely from foreign countries, principally from Germany, Mr. Davis, "like the Man of Sorrow," was crucified for his people.

If I forget thee, Southern Confederacy, let my right hand forget her cunning. If I do not remember thee, let my tongue cleave to the roof of my mouth.[293] — C. W. COOPER, COMMANDER, ALABAMA DIVISION, U.C.V.

THE SOUTH & REAL AMERICANISM

☛ . . . Since the beginning of the world war there has been marked tendency on the part of a certain class of prominent men up North to profit, as perhaps never before, by the abject use of sectionalism. How common it has been for those of the [socialistic Franklin D.] Roosevelt type to compare the Germany of to-day with the Southern Confederacy of sixty years ago, when a careful analysis by an unprejudiced mind will reveal absolutely nothing in common between the two!

. . . I contend that the War between the States viewed logically cannot be considered otherwise than the result of an old grudge toward the South, and that abolition was merely the instrumentality of its expression. In proof of this I can say that the North during the so-called Reconstruction period obtained a free and unhampered procedure in instigating and carrying to completion a policy which was not to the slight est extent actuated by lofty motives, but which for abject heinousness has never been excelled in the world's history. Not only was the ballot taken from the Southerner and

A Confederate chaplain blessing a Southern home and its inhabitants during Reconstruction. Only God could prevent its seizure or destruction by Left-wing controlled U.S. forces.

bestowed upon the [then uneducated] negro, but the two were literally forced into a relationship thought to be conducive to amalgamation and to the utter elimination of racial lines, this process being carried to the absurd extent of electing a negro Governor and two negro United States Senators. Was it her interest in the negro that prompted the North to this course of action? The love and friendship for the negro which she has so constantly proclaimed to the world from pulpit and platform when subjected to the test of sincerity is invariably found to be the rankest hypocrisy. She [the Liberal North] loves the negro as a race (which is in the South), but hates him individually. This accounts for the unsuppressed antipathy which exists in the North when the races are thrown together even commercially and which often assumes the proportions of outrage and murder. Hundreds [of blacks] were slain in East St. Louis two years ago for no other reason than that they were seeking employment. Many [blacks] were killed in Chicago a few weeks ago merely for an attempt to shift their dwelling places.

  As long as the South is attacked by [South-hating Left-wing] men . . . it behooves every old Reb to be ever on the defensive; for if there is any duty of an imperative character, it is the duty he owes his posterity to transmit his record unsullied and unstained.[294] — A. F. FRY, BENTONVILLE, ARK.

HOW YANKEE PURITANISM INFLUENCED SECTIONAL DIVISION, LINCOLN'S WAR, & RECONSTRUCTION

☛ . . . I believe I can say definitely that if sufficient diligence be exercised in the transmission to our children of undefiled records and substantiating data, fifty years from now, when all animosity shall have been allayed and racial questions shall have indeed assumed a national aspect, the story of the Confederacy, with its successes and failures, will adorn the brightest pages of American history. The New York *Herald* in an editorial on this subject recently said that the mystery as to how the South managed to obtain powder and lead with which to fight during the last two years of the war has not abated, but is assuming a more enigmatical aspect as time goes by. It is, indeed, a thing to be wondered at that seven hundred thousand men [Confederates], cut off from the world and living from hand to mouth, could have stood for four years against three million men (counting three hundred thousand marines) supported by inexhaustible resources drawn uninterruptedly from every port and clime. Some attribute it to the superior physique of the Southerner soldier, due to the fact that he was born and reared on the farm. Others attribute it to superior generalship, being supported in this contention by the leading military men of to-day. Of this I will cite proof: A correspondent of the *Saturday Evening Post* at the beginning of the world war [I] interviewed Generals [Charles D.] Roberts, [John] French, and [Joseph J. C.] Joffre individually as to whom they considered the greatest military genius of history. The reply in each case was forthcoming and emphatic, "Stonewall Jackson," all three putting forth the claim that Jackson's marvelous feat in Winchester Valley of crushing in rapid succession the three armies under [Union Generals John C.] Frémont, [Nathaniel P.] Banks, and [James] Shields, respectively, each being much larger than his own, is without parallel in the history of military maneuvers.

. . . The Puritanical spirit of hate, which for generations had contemplated with unsurpassed hilarity the Southerner's complete destruction, was astir as never before with the thrills of realization, and he [the Southern soldier] knew it. Viewing the world war from the standpoint of to-day, do the depredations committed by [Paul] Von Hindenburg and [Erich] Ludendorff assume greater proportions than those committed by [Union Generals William T.] Sherman and [Philip H.] Sheridan during the closing days of the War between the States? I contend again, knowing that the verdict of history will sustain me, that Sherman in his unopposed march to the sea—which is conspicuous not so much for its military strategy as for its devastations and atrocities, resulting as it did in thousands of innocent women and children, not to mention old men and cripples, being turned out of doors to endure hunger's pangs and winter's cold—was but the poignant instrumentality in the execution of infamous designs born generations before of Puritanical malignancy and which to-day reveal to the world the sordid depths of shame and depravity to which the human mind aflame with errant fanaticism can descend. What I have said of Sherman might apply to Sheridan also, for he openly boasted that his ravage of the Shenandoah Valley was so complete that a crow flying across would be compelled to carry its provisions with it. And thru, too (should I speak with hesitancy?), when we remember that Abraham Lincoln summoned [Edwin M.] Stanton, [Ulysses S.] Grant, and Sherman to the White House and there joined with them in planning these crimes, when we remember that he held a deaf ear to the piercing screams of frantic women and the heart-rending wails of little children, when a mere word from him would have sufficed for relief, we are prone to attune a contemplative attitude to this effect: if Lincoln personifies, as his worshipers claim for him, all that's good and just in human life, why did he with a stilled conscience hold aloof when purity and innocence were yearning for mercy?

During the last fifty years every effort has been made to strip Lincoln of his human characteristics and adorn him with the attributes of a god. Preachers and editors have vied with one another in the employment of lucid metaphors and nerve-tingling similes to give expression to their admiration and wonderment, which they at the same time, through the assumption of a sanctimonious demeanor or a holy, holy attitude, fain would impress upon all as being beyond the range of articulate utterance or symbolic transmission. From behind him thus deified men of exceptional ability (or opportunity), like the Rev. Newell Dwight Hillis and the editors of *Collier's Weekly* and the Chicago *Tribune*, have attained even international notoriety by casting slurs at the South and her traditions and picturing the Southern people as the very scum of humankind. The Northern youth is taught almost from his infancy to believe that Abraham Lincoln, "the man of sorrow and acquainted with grief," was foreordained of God to perform the greatest task known to history. To this end they claim it was part of the divine plan that he should have been born in a log cabin and should have endured through many long years the hardships and disappointments to which a soul enslaved to poverty and want is direct heir. He is taught to believe that Lincoln in espousing the cause of the poor slave loomed up "like some tall cliff that lifts its awful form," etc., the storm of opposition raging unabatingly around his head being characterized chiefly by vile denunciations, ridicule, and threats.

Such a policy is conspicuous for its misrepresentation. Lincoln was born in 1809, when pioneer days had not passed away. Do I exaggerate when I say that ninety-five per cent of the people of this country were then living in log cabins, of which the overwhelming majority neither exceeded the Lincoln cabin in size nor in magnificence of structure? And it may he said truthfully that long before Lincoln reached his majority Illinois had become a veritable rendezvous for abolitionists [that is, early socialists and communists]; therefore when he began his public career it was far more in accordance with political ethics for him to have espoused the cause represented by them than that of their adversaries, who were then rapidly dwindling in number. If Lincoln was the rail-splitter he is represented to have been, he must have done the splitting act while yet a mere boy, for it is a matter of record that he was elected to the legislature when only twenty-four years of age. As to the contention that Lincoln was altogether conservative in his views [in reality, as the Republican Party was then Left-wing, Lincoln was a Liberal] and never adhered to the doctrine of the ultra-abolitionists nor indorsed their plans, I might offer inexorable proof to the contrary, but the want of space forbids. A little incident, so often referred to, however, is significant within itself. It is said that once while attending a public reception he was introduced to Harriet Beecher Stowe, author of *Uncle Tom's Cabin*. Seizing her by the hand, he exclaimed with an outward show of exhilaration and esteem: "I am indeed glad to meet you, madam. I understand that you are responsible for this great war." Which remark was greeted with applause one very side.

    I do not mean to imply that Lincoln was altogether of the same cast as [South-hating Yankee socialist] William Lloyd Garrison, for on numerous occasions he gave evidence of real greatness which, in the estimation of the genuine Southerner, who is so little disposed to be swayed by prejudice, has ever had at least a tendency to lift him above the plane of pure demagoguery and selfish exploitation. Indeed, he may excuse certain acts of far-reaching consequence committed in direct violation of the principles of right and justice, believing that, perchance, Lincoln considered himself justified in adhering for a time to the old Jesuitical doctrine that the end justifies the means. Then, too, there are many things to indicate, inasmuch as he was born in Kentucky, of Southern lineage, that he really appreciated more than he dared make known the magnitude of the racial problem, with all of its intricate phases It may be true, as many have claimed, that he contemplated, after having freed the slaves, the inauguration of a recuperatory policy toward the South, cost what it might, which he calculated would do much to eliminate the contempt in which he was then held. In fact, a United States Senator from Ohio, who was closely associated with him for many years, said that had he even attempted to carry out his plans the North in turn would have rebelled, and in consequence he would have gone down in American history as the very personification of ignominy.

It is natural for the human mind to regard the instrumentality of a successful and long-yearned-for accomplishment with a reverence that may even transcend earthly limitations and assume the attributes of divineness. New England in her insatiable eagerness to see the execution of designs so long harbored, notwithstanding as years go by these designs assume a character of greater and greater malignancy and are sure to be interpreted by the future in terms of drastic contempt, entered into the war with a spirit of jocundity, which, however, was soon to yield to bewilderment and then to dismay. After the four years of fighting, which to her, considering the odds, must have been characterized by an inexplicable capriciousness, stirring as it did her very soul to its utmost depths, it is but natural, as suggested above, that she should have regarded Lincoln, the chief instrumentality of a successful though ofttime dubious accomplishment, with even a greater degree of reverence than had things moved in strict accordance with inviolate anticipation. To designate the extent of the departure from the paths of equitableness and veracity made by so many in seeking (principally for self-exaltation) to gratify a preternatural longing on the part of the public for eulogisms of Lincoln of an ever-extending scope and grandeur, a Northern writer a few years ago published to the world that after diligent study and close scrutinization of all the events given in connection with Lincoln's life, especially those told individually as being of unquestionable authority, he had come to the conclusion that Lincoln, provided his daily life conformed to the usual requirements of time and space, must have lived at least one hundred and fifty years.

Do Northern preachers, in holding Lincoln up as a model like unto Christ, give any consideration to the fact that there is no record of his ever having joined a Church? There is a tradition to the effect that his forefathers were Unitarians, some claiming that he in consequence more than once exhibited his preference for this denomination and creed. If this be true, does the fact of itself elevate him in the minds of Methodists, Baptists, and Presbyterians? And then the tales, so well verified, of his descending ofttimes in delivering speeches to male audiences and in telling private anecdotes to the level of obscenity and rank vulgarity are proof conclusive of his human characterization. The assassination of Lincoln was indeed a great misfortune to the South, inasmuch as voluminous measures of pent-up hate were poured out irrevocably upon her defenseless head. In looking back from the standpoint of to-day, however, we old Rebs can see fulfilled in many ways the Scriptural passage which says: "Those who kill by the sword shall die by the sword."

I should like to cite a few crimes of the awful period of Reconstruction which were committed in my own neighborhood to reveal, if possible, the full significance of its soul-staggering heinousness, but should I attempt such a thing the lack of an adequate power of expression would have a tendency, even at this late date, to force me into the use of vituperations. I contend, however, that the spirit of New England Puritanism is therein reflected and will be seen and marveled at by generations yet unborn. This aggressive hatred of the Southern blood, the offspring of envy, class inferiority, and fanaticism, had its beginning in England long before the Mayflower sailed and through succeeding years played an ever-increasing part, until finally it assumed a form of revengeful intriguery that was loath to establish any bounds to its operations. How strange it should have worn with complacency a sanctimonious demeanor, which in reality was naught but a surface gild under which was concealed, to the South's woeful detriment, a duplicity of character the import of which, particularly as respects the Confederacy, is as yet unappreciated by the outside world!

The Puritan, even while still posing as a heaven-bound pilgrim, in whom all earthly aspirations merged in a transcendental yearning for things celestial, became known to his business associates for a skillfully cultivated adroitness which when closely analyzed was found to contain none of the hand marks of sanctity. Indeed, a hundred years ago he was recognized for his penuriousness, avariciousness, and emphasized lack of hospitality, a fact of which more than one American writer of early date makes mention. A close study from the standpoint of morals or racial probity of the Puritanical and Cavalierish strains as developed in America will reveal as respects the two an intervening chasm of such colossal proportions as to seem inconsistent with the laws of social evolution. Nor was the Puritanical spirit of Reconstruction days a sudden outburst of righteous indignation, as the North once claimed, which gave absolution for adhering to a policy of justified retaliation, even though perchance the policy did for a time exceed the recognized bounds of discretion. It was rather, as its appearance even then indicated, the direct result of a close, obstinate adherency through generations to a wrong principle. Puritanism has, however, with the lapse of time opportunity for selfish aggrandizement becoming more and more rife, gradually, though unintentionally, bereft itself of its sanctimonious characterism and revealed itself to the world as being literally intoxicated with worldly ambition, in the gratification of which it uses without regard to honor's code every instrumentality that the human intellect can devise.

To the south of New England lay the Southern States, a region not only inhabited by a people whom she hated in compliance, as it were, with a sacred tradition, but one lying across her path as an inextirpable rival. Thus, I contend, the story of the war and Reconstruction may justly be considered the direct result of a historical antipathy interwoven as woof and warp in the social development of the South's most implacable foe. The word "reconstruction," as the whole world now knows, is merely another term for murder, rapine, and robbery—the commission of every crime known to the realms of jurisprudence.

When the Confederate soldier, having fought for principle to an extent almost incredible and in consequence bereft of everything of earthly value, staggered back home to his wife and children—provided they were still alive—it was with a steadfast resolution to make the most of fortune, to build the new on the ashes of the old, to exhibit the same courage in the humiliation of defeat as in the exhilaration of success, and to this end he set to work with as much vim and energy as his war-worn body could muster. But how vain were his resolutions! Simultaneous with the inauguration of this policy was the inauguration of another policy, the character of whose hellishness so far exceeds the capability of the human mind to describe as to make any effort along this line seem altogether futile. Nor can one cite a historic parallel in which the similitude of circumstance and deed is sufficiently marked as to prove of service. *The fact remains, however, that the Reconstruction period, whose horrors will in some way be transmitted to future generations, stands forth in itself, to the South's eternal vindication, a consummate symbolization of Puritanism unthwarted in the accomplishment of its agelong purpose* [my emphasis, L.S.].

The railings of [Yankee Liberals William Lloyd] Garrison, Phillips Brooks, [Henry Ward] Beecher, and innumerable others, so rampant as they seemed to be with piety and so expressive of an immeasurable love for the poor brothers in black, were the very essence of hypocrisy, for the fact is conclusive to-day as never before that the attitude of the North as a whole toward the negro, having been forced during the last decade into a conjunctional relationship with him on its own muchly vaunted plane of social and political equality, is not one of love and compassion, but one of execration and hate. The appeal of the Chicago Herald and other papers to the Southern governors, following the racial riots in Chicago and Washington, to offer inducements to the negroes in the North to return South is extremely pathetic and at the same time laughable. It is also virtually an acknowledgment that the Southerner is the negro's best friend [my emphasis, L.S.].

. . . Was New England Puritanism in its bloom, especially in its dealings with the South, actuated by good motives and influenced to the slightest extent by Scriptural precepts? *History will answer, Reconstruction* [my emphasis, L.S.].

Let me say again before leaving this subject that had the South remained undisturbed the slavery question would have been solved long before 1860, and that, too, in compliance with law, common sense, and equity. The Southern soldier did not fight for slavery as an institution; he fought for his home and his constitutional rights . . . . [my emphasis, L.S.].²⁹⁵ — A. F. FRY, BENTONVILLE, ARK.

This Right-wing Reconstruction broadside was published in 1866. It is entitled: "The Freedman's Bureau! An agency to keep the Negro in idleness at the expense of the white man. Twice vetoed by the President, and made a law by Congress. Support Congress & you support the Negro. Sustain the President & you protect the white man." The wood cut is promoting the gubernatorial election of Andrew Johnson supporter and Yankee Democrat (then Conservative) Hiester Clymer, who ran on a white supremacist platform.

This Thomas Nast wood engraving from 1866 is entitled "Andrew Johnson's Reconstruction and How It Works." Wholly anti-Johnson and anti-South in nature, this Left-wing political cartoon portrays Democrat (then a Conservative) President Johnson as Shakespeare's duplicitous character Iago, the betrayer of Othello, who is shown on the right as a black Union veteran. Other Left-wing propaganda can be seen, such as the horrors of the slave auction, European-Americans attacking African-Americans in Memphis and New Orleans, and Johnson playing a pungi as Copperhead and C.S.A. "snakes" entwine a helpless black man writhing on the ground. William H. Seward, Gideon Wells, and Edwin M. Stanton can be seen watching from the sidelines, all disgruntled Northern symbolism representing Johnson's alleged apathy toward the North and his sympathy toward the South.

CHAPTER 18

THE DIXIE COWORKERS

☛ For the benefit of the uninitiated let me say that the Dixie Coworkers are an unorganized band of Southern community builders who, loyal to truth and homeland, one in spirit and in purpose, work together while they work apart, each serving his own community. This is our creed:

"We believe in the reconstruction of the South by the South, because we know that development by self-activity is the law of life and growth.

"We believe that love is a constructive force of infinite possibilities, the power that makes and moves worlds, the power that can reconstruct a world that has been wrecked.

"We believe that the future of the South and the safety of the nation depend upon America's ability to create and maintain a contented, intelligent, self-respecting, God-worshiping, law-abiding, home-loving citizenship in our rural districts.

"We believe that each civil district should be a miniature republic, with machinery for local self-government.

"We believe that the South is the nation's greatest asset, and that the greatest asset of our Dixie Land is what is called the spirit of the Old South.

"We believe that the spirit of the Old South is a spirit of moral and civic righteousness, a spirit of love and loyalty to one's own, a spirit of freedom, the spirit of democracy.

"We believe that true democracy is Christianity, and that, no institution that is not founded upon the rock of eternal truth and righteousness can stand the test of time.

"We believe that it is the duty and the privilege of loyal sons and daughters of the Old South to take the initiative in reconstruction work, to interpret Southern ideals and point out

Varina Anne "Winnie" Davis, the youngest child of Jefferson Davis and Varina Howell Davis, was known as "The Daughter of the Confederacy," a title bestowed upon her by Confederate General John B. Gordon. Southern men viewed the women of their region as the bedrock of both Southern society and the Confederate States of America.

the sources of Southern weakness and Southern strength while we work with and for the youth of our land, the Southerners of the future.

"We believe that the Southern cause is and has always been the cause of Christian democracy and that Americanism [that is, conservative and traditional American ideals] in its essentials is a national expression of Southern ideals.

"We believe in our ability to build a greater nation through a greater South, and a greater South through loyalty to our standard and by the intelligent, sympathetic cooperation of district, county, State, and national forces.

"We believe that a new day has dawned for the South, for America, and for all the nations of the earth—the day of love and service—and we choose for our emblem of cooperative endeavor, in the spirit of faith, hope, and love, a single star in a field of blue, our Saviour's own sign.

"We believe that the need of the South of to-day is a getting together of home, school, and Church forces in every State, in every county, and in every district to work out community problems, and, in order that we may be unified in plans as well as in spirit and purpose, we believe we should establish and support a connectional organ.

"We believe that the South needs community songs expressing present-day purposes, songs that will fan into flame every spark of our smoldering patriotism, and until some member of our band puts into song our aims and ideals we will use what we have, believing that it is no desecration of a Confederate war song to adapt it to present needs. Are you with us?"[296] — ELIZABETH DENTY ABERNETHY, PULASKI, TENN.

THE ABRAHAM LINCOLN MYTHOS

☛ It involves an essential fallacy to assume that the myth creating faculty faded from the consciousness of our race as the world moved from the shadowy dream sphere of symbol, legend, and romance toward its modern secularized and empirical life in which types, visions, and fantasies wrought by the genius of romance serve no higher end than poetic illustration, social recreation, even to beguile weary hours in the nursery or by the fireside, as we recall snatches of witch lore, fragmentary, disjointed lines from chants drawn from fairyland, echoes and notes that bring back the day when superstition was a dominant and almost unchallenged power. Romulus and Remus may yet assume a renasence, and the peerless Idylls of [Alfred] Tennyson have invested Arthur, Lancelot,

Percival, and Galahad with a charm undreamed of in the mythic era until,

> "Substantialized in flesh and blood,
> They live from age to age upon the poet's page.
> And yet have never donned this mortal clay."

Within the last half century and in large measure under the eyes of a generation still in the vigor of manhood a transformation surpassing any of those I have indicated or any accomplished by the shaping spirit of dramatic imagination has become an assured, if not an abiding, invincible reality, in the apprehension or belief of the American people. Like Lord Tennyson's ideal statesman, Mr. Lincoln has "moved from high to higher" until, having attained the "crowning slope" of political ascendancy, at least in popular estimation, the hallucination, or delusion, acquires a most tenacious and apparently invincible character. The origin of the Lincoln cult, or, to describe it more accurately, the Lincoln mania, may be traced to the time of his tragic death, April 15, 1865, but its growth, or diffusion, as well as its unrestrained and often senseless manifestations or expressions, have received a marked impulse during a comparatively recent period. The war [World War I] with Germany, which, as contemplated from the viewpoint of the Northern press, was a phase of symbolical crusade against the ideals and the history of the South, tended in no small measure to stimulate the prevailing insanity and to invest it with renewed energy and vigor. From stage to stage it has advanced until every trace of reason, moderation, or discernment has ceased to exist in so far as it forms an element or an influence in determining the historic position of Abraham Lincoln or in attaining a just appreciation of his gifts as an orator, his character as a man, or his rank in the long array of administrative chiefs who "took occasion by the hand" in their endeavors "to make the bounds of freedom wider yet."

The fame of Lincoln concentrates its vital power upon his achievements in the sphere of oratory. Above all, does this criterion, or test, hold good of his much-vaunted Gettysburg address, delivered November 19, 1863. By one of those revealing ironies to which both literary and oratorical renown are ever subject the special phrase that has been most thoroughly ingrained and assimilated into the heart and speech of the world traces its suggestion, if not its specific origin, to [Yankee Daniel] Webster's memorable reply to [Southerner Robert Y.] Hayne during the historic debate of January, 1830. By reference to Webster's argument as edited by [British scholar Cornelius B.] Bradley, *Orations and Arguments*, the reader will discover at a glance the very essence of the language, "government of the people, by the people, and for the people," so intensely associated with the memory of Lincoln. Note the harmony existing between the words of Webster uttered in 1830 and those which fell from Lincoln at Gettysburg in November, 1863:

> "It is the people's government, made for the people, made by the people, and answerable to the people."

The resemblance existing between the passages cited is too minute and definite to admit of explanation as a mere coincidence of form or a simple analogy in the mode of exposition. Even if we waive the charge of willful plagiarism, the most exuberant charity cannot ignore or condone the palpable and wanton imitation of the thought and diction of Daniel Webster.

At the time of the delivery of the address at Gettysburg I was a prisoner in Federal [U.S.] hands, disabled from the effect of an almost fatal wound received on July 3 at Kulp's Hill, Gettysburg. A lad in my teens, I retain a vivid and graphic memory of that period of sorrow and gloom, remote from friends and home, devoid of all facilities for communication with them, and reckoned among the dead at my own fireside and my own family altar. I recall from out my valley of shadows that the Gettysburg oration when given to the world seemed to fall upon unheeding and irresponsive ears, "rousing no deed from sleep." Its celebrity was a development of later years and traces its origin, as well as its inspiration, to the tragedy linked with the fate of its author. "The deep damnation of his taking off" was a most auspicious creative agency and invested the name of Lincoln with a halo and sanctity that spring from martyrdom alone.

On March 4, 1861, while a student at the University of Virginia, in company with a party of my classmates, I attended the first inauguration of Mr. Lincoln and listened to his address upon assuming the functions of chief executive. It was a grim, bleak day, snow, rain, mist, all blending in the dissonance of elements marking the bodeful Monday morning which chronicled his advent to supreme official dignity. His manner of delivery was simple, earnest, unaffected, but lacking in every essential feature of rhetorical art or oratorical charm and grace. He displayed a tendency to "saw the air with his hand." I recall but a simple genuine gesture as he uttered the words: "No State has a right to leave the Union." No more consummate fiction has been devised since the age of [the ancient Greek storyteller] Aesop than that which attributes transcendent oratorical genius to Abraham Lincoln. The malignity constituting the vital essence of [Edwin M.] Stanton seems not to have determined his moral attitude, nor did he display his diabolic glee in the mere contemplation of human suffering. Still, it cannot be demonstrated by any form of proof or evidence that his voice or his influence, personal or official, was in one instance brought to bear in order to mitigate or restrain the barbarous excesses of his own commanders. The blood of the victims of [Union Generals Philip H.] Sheridan and [William T.] Sherman cries out from the earth against the memory of the "martyred President."

To my own apprehension, one of the most lamentable delusions prevailing in the South with reference to Lincoln relates to his fictitious or mythical oratory. Strange is it, even pathetic, that in the native source and fountain of American eloquence such fatal misconceptions should hold sway. The typical college or university president, the masters of assemblies, oracles of senates, lords of the forum, and beyond the Potomac the howling dervishes of the platform or the pulpit have exalted Lincoln's Gettysburg speech into a supreme criterion, a magical touchstone, by which ideal art in oratory is to be estimated and determined. Culture, literary discernment, reverence for our golden age have been renounced and abdicated in self-abasement before the shrine of Abraham Lincoln. The clarion tones, the remorseless logic, the invincible charm, the resistless grace which crowned the sovereign lights of a day that is dead have paled into shadow and eclipse. Alas for one trumpet note or even echo of [Robert Y.] Hayne, [Hugh S.] Legare, [William C.] Preston, Gaston, Badger, Davis, Dobbin!

> "They are all gone into the world of light,
> And we alone sit lingering here;
> Their very memory is clear and bright,
> And our sad heart doth cheer."

Most to be deplored of all the results or sequences associated with the deification of Mr. Lincoln is the tendency it has developed toward irreverence, if not in some instances a form of blasphemy, perhaps undesigned or unconscious, but none the less real in its nature, on the part of Northern authors, clerical lights, and popular lecturers. I am prepared to cite specific instances or illustrations in which he has been exalted to the same plane and assigned to the same supreme eminence with the incarnate God. In many circles, in the educational sphere, in life as affected by the influence of libraries, in the field of political activity, in the dominant mental attitude of the nation, to impeach or even question the sanctity and infallibility of Abraham Lincoln is construed as almost equivalent to a species of treason. Assuredly his apotheosis is fast attaining its final stage. In abject and sycophantic idolatry of a dead though sceptered sovereign the American of our own day has no rational or logical reason to hold in reproach the record of the Hohenzollern empire or to institute a contrast of self-adoration between Lincoln and William the Second. The admirable and unanswerable monograph of Dr. C. L. C. [Charles Landon Carter] Minor, *The Real Lincoln*,[297] is rigidly excluded from every Northern library. The fierce light that beats upon falsehood cannot be endured. "Touch not mine anointed; do my prophet no harm," such is the imperial strain. Even at this late stage a pleasing hallucination prevails in reference to the beneficent influence of Lincoln, had he survived the last act of the war drama, in tempering the wind to our prostrate and stricken Confederacy. A more baseless fantasy was never wrought by maudlin sentimentality or morbid sycophancy. The "red fool fury" and frenzy which swept an innocent woman [Mary Surratt] to the scaffold would have submerged like a tidal wave both President and the line of policy imputed to him by a gracious fiction that ascribes not evil to the dead. No earthly agency or power could have turned aside the carnival of infamy, the dance of death, revealed during the Saturnalian day of Reconstruction. As the ax of the headsman elevated Charles I almost to the saintly dignity in the roll of Anglican ecclesiastical worthies, so the dagger of [John Wilkes] Booth transformed Lincoln into a martyr and encircled his head with the halo and radiance of the amaranthine crown. His trivial utterances, his mere banality and jaded platitudes are conserved with fastidious devotedness and guarded from the assaults of time with pharisaic zeal and minuteness. To the Northern mind he has assumed the role of oracle and prophet, whose simplest deliverances carry with them a mysterious and inspired significance. In accord with one of those suggestive and logical ironies, so often marking the retributive character illustrated in the attitude of the human tragedy, Lincoln, untouched by any form of definite religious conviction or belief, met his fate in a theater on Good Friday, April 14, 1865, the most sacred and hallowed of the anniversaries commemorated by the homage and devotion of the Christian world.

"O eloquent, just, and mighty death!
What none hath dared thou hast done."[298] — DR. HENRY E. SHEPHERD, BALTIMORE, MD.

THE TRUTH ABOUT "OLD ABE"

☞ . . . [In 1864] we left our wounded at Frederick City [MD] to fall into the hands of the enemy, and the next day early we resumed our march [under Confederate General Jubal A. Early] to Washington [D.C.], which we reached unopposed. We were all anxious to capture the city, and especially to get "Old Abe" in our hands. We wanted him for the atrocities he allowed his armies to commit wherever they went in the South. He was aware of these, but never did he do or say a thing to abate these outrages against civilization—outrages equal to those of the Germans in France [World War I]. Much has been said of his kindness and sympathy, but as far as I could see from our standpoint his heart must have been as hard as flint. His assassination gave his friends cause to place his name among their deities, and many of his former enemies regretted his demise and thought it a calamity to the South; but Abe Lincoln had neither the will nor the ability to do anything for the people of the South. He always showed himself the willing tool of the extreme [Left-wing] element in his [then Liberal] political party [the Republican Party], and these he did not dare offend. He was taken off at the moment of his highest achievement, and his friends were then determined to have their own way with their fallen foes, and they would not allow any obstacle to curb their resentment in the passage and execution of their [radical Left-wing] Reconstruction measures. *These were the result of their hatred and were more grievous to the South than the war itself* [my emphasis, L.S.].[299] — CONFEDERATE SOLDIER, I. G. BRADWELL, BRANTLEY, ALA.

"EVERY DROP OF MY BLOOD BOILED"

☞ . . . It may be said—indeed, it is said—that these facts should be left to oblivion. I have tried in these sketches to give an accurate account of what I saw and heard. I have not grudged praise to Yankees for courage and deeds of kindness wherever it was due, and there were many noble, conscientious men among them, both officers and privates; but they were not the ones who made war on women and children, who burned homes and stole watches. When an ex-President of the United States, and probably the most popular man in the Union, at least in the North and West, glorifies an old cutthroat like John Brown as one of the great men of his day and whose only claim to that position was an attempt to arouse slaves to insurrection and to murder women and children, when large sections of the Grand Army of the Republic [Union veterans] strive to keep the grandest man in all history, Gen. Robert E. Lee, out of the National Hall of Fame, then I feel that our children and children's children ought to know the character of the war that was waged against us, and I have not hesitated to tell what I know. *The carnival of oppression, of robbery, of crime called Reconstruction was the expression of the real feelings of the majority of those who waged war on us. I have received letters of thanks for these sketches from all over the South, and especially from old comrades, who can confirm their truthfulness* [my emphasis, L.S.].

As to the period of Reconstruction, which I remember vividly, I think that for three or four years every drop of my blood boiled. It's over, and we all thank God that such a time can never come to us again.[300] — REVEREND JAMES HUGH MCNEILLY, NASHVILLE, TENN.

NOT BLACK EQUALITY, BUT BLACK SUPREMACY

☛ ... In 1861 it was said that the thermometer of the monetary and commercial power of the globe hung up in the London Exchange: the war for subjugation of the South had given the Northern States of the American Union power to hang the thermometer of money rule up in Wall Street, New York City. During this decade the grandest army [the Confederate military] that ever trod the soil of this same globe was surrendered to the might of militarism, and [our Southern] ... youths had seen every hope and ideal to which they were born trampled underfoot. After honorable defeat at arms the crushed South met the dishonorable warfare waged in the name of Reconstruction. The young South must fight with every force the Lord gives to right against wrong the destruction of the Reconstruction acts—acts to place the South, politically and socially, under the heel of the negro and to bring to hopeless ruin the most prosperous community in the world; not negro equality merely, but negro supremacy, and this at the sacrifice of humanity to both races, of citizenship under the Constitution, and of the civilization of society. . . .[301] — HOWARD MERIWETHER LOVETT, MACON, GA.

RELIGION & RECONSTRUCTION

☛ While most of the ministers of the Nashville Presbytery were in the Southern army, three out of five of those who remained in the city voted to carry the Presbytery into the Northern Church. When the Southern men returned they determined to undo the action of the rump Presbytery, but they had to be careful; for if a handful of members in any Church could be induced to claim that they were the true Church, the courts would he disposed to recognize them and give them the property, although the general government did not encourage such a course. The Presbytery had been represented in the General Assembly of 1865 at Pittsburgh. I was not present at the first meeting after the return of our men, but one of the members reported to me what occurred. The venerable Dr. R. A. Lapsley was Moderator. He had been a chaplain in hospitals. The clerk was one of those who voted to go into the Northern Church, and he had been a member of the 1865 Assembly. The Northern ministers and elders were present, but very largely in the minority. The motion to transfer the Presbytery back to the Southern Assembly was hotly discussed, the minority seeking to postpone action. Two of our ministers, Boude and Rosser, had been cavalry officers and were quite aggressive in the debate. It required all of Dr. Lapsley's tact and wisdom to keep order, so that the civil or military authorities should not be called in. Again and again as the temper of the brethren would threaten an explosion he would wave his hand gently and say in bland tones, "Order, brethren; keep order," or "Be quiet, brethren; remember we are in the Lord's house." But the two cavalrymen were springing up and propounding fierce questions so often that at last the old gentleman's patience gave way, and in tones of thunder, as if giving command on the field of battle, he cried out: "The cavalry will keep to the rear! I command this shebang!" This restored good humor for a while.

When the vote was taken transferring the body to the Southern Church, the Northern members withdrew, and the clerk took up the record book and started down the aisle to the door. That meant they would claim to be the legitimate Presbytery and that the others were seceders. For a moment no one moved to oppose, but about midway of the aisle Rev. H. B. Boude, a cavalry captain and an athlete, sprang in front of the clerk with the ringing command: "Hand me that book!" The clerk stopped and began to argue the case, while all were on their feet intently watching. Boude put an end to it by saying: "The time for argument is past. You have no right to that book. Give it to me at once." The clerk tried to push by, when the word came in no gentle tone: "Hand that book to me. There are not enough of your kind to take it out of this house." It was given up.

One of the effects of Reconstruction was to destroy the old-time religious ties that bound the white and black races together in the same Churches. The statement has been made and industriously circulated in professed histories that the Southern white people did practically nothing for the religious training of the negroes. The fact is that every denomination of Christians recognized the obligation to carry the gospel to the slaves, and some of the ablest Southern ministers gave their whole time to this work. As a result nearly half a million negroes were communicants in the Methodist and Baptist Churches, and the Episcopal and Presbyterian Churches gathered large numbers into their folds. One-seventh of the slaves were communicants in some Church. As soon as the war was over the Northern Churches sent missionaries to the freedmen as if they had never heard the gospel. They took the negroes out of those Churches in which they were gathered and formed them into separate organizations [my emphasis, L.S.]. In 1865 I saw the report of one of these missionaries. He told of his wonderful work in a certain district in South Carolina and how eagerly the poor creatures welcomed the gospel, so long withheld from them.

Christ Church, New Orleans, Louisiana.

It happened that I had preached in that district to the negroes, hundreds of whom were Church members, who were taught in a large Sunday school by white people. The missionary formed four Churches of them. A few years ago the work was a failure.

No doubt the Northern Churches were sincere in their belief of our neglect and in their desire to evangelize the negro, and many of the missionaries were honest and pious men. But there were also adventurers who used the religious need of the negroes as a cloak to cover up political schemes, and they organized leagues in secret, professedly for religious ends, but really to keep carpetbaggers in power and to loot the treasuries of the Southern States [my emphasis, L.S.].

Let me tell the story of how one of our ministers worked the religious traditions of the negroes to thwart these political schemes.

The Rev. Dr. R. K. Smoot was pastor of the Presbyterian Church in Bowling Green, Ky. He had preached frequently to the negroes. One night he called on an aged [black] brother to pray after the sermon, and the prayer was:

"O Lord, sen' your richest blessing on dis pure young brother what has dispensed wid de gospel to us dis night."

But he had great influence with them, and they came to him for advice. About the time the Baptist revision of the New Testament was published a very bright negro preacher came from Louisville ostensibly to introduce the new version, but really, as Dr. Smoot found out, he was organizing political clubs. Some of the old brethren had come to the Doctor for advice about the new Bible. He got them to appoint a meeting for the Louisville man to explain the value of the new version, and Dr. Smoot would be there to hear before he could advise. There was a big crowd. The preacher ridiculed the old Book, pointing out its errors and boosting the new. Then their white friend was called on. He praised the old Bible, which had shown them the way to heaven, by which their fathers and mothers had lived and died. When they were thoroughly aroused Dr. Smoot paused a moment and looked at the new preacher, then said: "But here comes a smart Aleck from Louisville to take your old Bible from you and put this newfangled thing in its place. What will you do with him?" They yelled: "Take him out! He ought to be killed!" The darky preacher went out of a back window and didn't stop till he got to Louisville.

During the months of July, August, and September, 1865, I spent a good deal of my time in Nashville. There were a great many Confederate soldiers in the city seeking positions or engaged in work of any honorable kind to make a living. My memory is that the metropolitan police was charged with keeping order and that this force was made up of appointees of the Governor and of course violent partisans of his administration. I heard frequent complaints of inefficiency, corruption, and tyranny exercised against our Southern sympathizers. Both in Nashville and Memphis I heard charges that this body were law breakers instead of law enforcers.[302]

At the time there were various entertainments gotten up by the ladies to raise money for the destitute or disabled Confederates. And I was told to be careful in my talk at or about these entertainments, for there were spies ready to report all disloyal utterances, and the police would interfere on any pretext.

Now, I don't know whether the dread was of [Left-wing] Governor [William G.] Brownlow or of the Federal authorities. I know that the [South-hating] Governor was considered very vindictive, and *it was said on the streets that if a man was convicted in the courts and sentenced to the penitentiary, if his crime was against a Confederate, he was met with a pardon at the door of the prison* [my emphasis, L.S.].[303] Let me say, on the other hand, that I heard much kind talk about a son of the Governor who had been a colonel in the

Union army. He was active and helpful in the entertainments for the relief of the Confederates.

For two or three weeks I was assisting the Rev. E. C. Trimble, pastor of the Edgefield Presbyterian Church, in a series of services. I was entertained in the homes of Col. William B. A. Ramsey and Mr. Robert S. Hollins, Sr., elders in that Church. I was indignant at things that I heard, petty tyrannies inflicted upon the people, and I was enthusiastic in my love for our cause, and in conversation among the friends gathered I was quick to express my sentiments. *While I always felt respect for every sincere Union man, I spoke freely my contempt for Yankees, whether Northern or home-bred, who stayed at home when war was going on and showed their patriotism by acting as spies and informers on Southern men and by stirring up the petty persecutions rife in the community* [my emphasis, L.S.].

I noticed that Mr. Hollins, himself a warm friend of the South, was quite uneasy when I indulged in this bitter talk and would change the subject or suggest that I ought to give up my harsh feelings, now that it would do no good. But as I did not heed his advice, he spoke to me very plainly on the subject. He said in substance:

> "Your talk is very imprudent and under our present conditions can bring no benefit, but only trouble. There are spies prowling about our homes at all hours ready to catch up and report every word that can be twisted into disloyalty. These spies lurk in all kinds of hiding places. It is possible that one is now under this gallery listening to you, and if you were reported you would be arrested and your friends would be subject to annoyance."

If was the twilight of a summer evening, and several of us were sitting on the gallery, raised two or three feet from the ground. Of course I was careful after that as to what and where I spoke of Yankees.

In a few days I had a chance to have practical demonstration of the system of espionage and persecution. Whether it was by the Federal authorities or by order of Governor Brownlow, as the family believed, I do not know. I give the facts as I knew them in part and as I got them from members of Colonel Ramsey's family. I was staying at Colonel Ramsey's, and his nephew, Maj. Crozier Ramsey, of Knoxville [TN], and I roomed together. He found that it would be dangerous for him to return to Knoxville after he was paroled, and he had secured some temporary position in Nashville. He went to work pretty early and returned for supper. One evening he failed to appear, and his uncle seemed very uneasy about him. He said that Crozier had hoped to live quietly in Nashville, unnoticed by those who were so bitter against him, until conditions in Knoxville became settled and it would be safe for him to return to his home. But his friends knew that spies were on his track to find something that would subject him to arrest. It was three or four days before it was found that he had been arrested at his place of business, and no chance was given him even to change his clothes. He was put on a flat car, and in his shirt sleeves at night he traveled to Chattanooga [TN] and Knoxville. It was not very long afterwards that the family heard of his death from pneumonia contracted in that night ride.

It will not be out of place for me to tell of other annoyances and persecutions which Nashville Confederates had to endure from the activities of these [Left-wing] busybodies. The system was inaugurated during the war, and the specimen here related was told me by a lady who was in the city at the time.

It seems that the girls, in a spirit of bravado probably, would combine the Confederate colors—red, white, and red in the trimmings of their dresses, and they were kept under close observation by detectives, so as to find excuse for banishing them beyond the Yankee lines. One of these girls wore rather flashy stockings of the obnoxious colors, and on one rainy day in crossing the muddy street she lifted her skirts above her shoes, and the awfully treasonable footgear was revealed. A spy who had made the dreadful discovery hastened to [Union] General [Lovell H.] Rousseau, who, I think, was then in command of the department, and reported the girl. The General was a Kentuckian, and he had no patience with such contemptible [and trivial] business. His reply was: "Well, if the United States government is in danger from a girl wearing red stockings, the infernal thing ought to fall—the quicker, the better." I understood that it was darkly hinted in loyal circles that General Rousseau was a traitor, in sympathy with the Rebels.

The whole incident, ridiculous as it may seem, was in thorough keeping with the boast of [Lincoln's] Secretary [of State William H. Seward] . . . about his little bell which by a ring of its little clapper could consign a man to prison without ever letting him know the charge against him, and the actual charges were often as trivial as this one. Surely no government claiming to be enlightened and Christian ever did such cruel things in such pitifully little ways. Picayune Butler in New Orleans was a correct type of the whole class.

During the summer I had occasion to go to Clarksville [TN] on some matter of business, now forgotten. A steamboat was going down the river, and, leaving Nashville late in the afternoon, I took passage. The boat was crowded, and I did not know a soul aboard. There was an air of constraint generally among the passengers. They seemed to be strangers to each other. Spies were suspected, who might report any disloyal utterance. There was a noticeable evidence of war talk. I was desirous of talking with some of them, for I was looking for a place where I could settle permanently as a minister, and I knew very little of the needs of the country. The question was to find out if the crowd was one that would sympathize with me. I found out by a simple expedient. There was a band of negro musicians on the boat. Their outfit was nothing extraordinary—a violin, guitar or banjo, a flute or clarionet, and a big cello. I am not strong in my knowledge of music nor of the names of instruments. But this band made up for any lack of art by immense enthusiasm as they played the old-fashioned tunes. So as the leader passed his hat for collections I asked if they could play "Dixie." He said they could, and I said: "I will give you half a dollar to play it good and strong." My finances were limited, but that investment paid. The band struck up in full blast. In a minute such a shout went up, and was repeated over and over, that there could be no further doubt as to their sympathies. The rest of my journey was enlivened with pleasant talk with men and women of my own kind.

There were compensations for even the evils of Reconstruction. In those first days after we got home, though defeated, ragged, penniless, and mulattos in complexion, yet we were all heroes in the eyes of our own people. And especially did the girls glorify us, and if one of us had a scar or went on crutches the admiration was so touched with pity that he was a kind of double hero.

The picture lingers in my memory of a scene very common in those early days. A young fellow sitting in the midst of a group of girls, one of whom, "nearer still and dearer yet than all others," was prompter for the story, and as they

> "Questioned him the story of his life
> From year to year—the battles, sieges, fortunes
> That he had passed—he ran it through
> To the very moment that they bade him tell it;
> Wherein he spake of most disastrous chances,
> Of moving accidents by flood and field,
> Of hairbreadth escapes i'th' imminent deadly breach."

And as "with greedy ear they devoured his discourse," it was enacting over again the [Shakespearian] story of Othello and Desdemona and no wonder that weddings were numerous, for the Moor of Venice did not press his suit more ardently than did these sun-burned veterans of the war. One of the most amusing things was to note how, if Othello hesitated from either modesty or conscience to make the most of his exploits, Desdemona with "sweet compulsion" brought it out. And it was a tacit understanding that no one of these youthful veterans should discount the story of another, and each could make it as vivid as he pleased without fear of contradiction, and each one of those girls was convinced that if all the soldiers had been as heroic as her own particular hero, then the Yankee army would have been whipped world without end and our independence won.

The women of the South not only took the returned soldiers to their hearts, but they did everything they could to secure places and employment for them. And they furnished them largely with decent outfits to take the place of the battered uniforms in which they came home.

I was peculiarly fortunate in this respect. In my war reminiscences I have told of the suit of clothes presented to me by a Church in Mobile [AL] at a cost of twenty-five hundred dollars in Confederate money. That suit, while it was of fine material, was woefully out of fashion. I also told of my handsome uniform of Confederate gray, presented to me by an Alabama regiment. But it was sure proof of disloyalty for me to wear that in public life before Yankees. My expensive suit was beginning to show the effects of constant wear when I became the recipient of so many good clothes that I was the best dressed of Rebel preachers in Nashville.

While I was preaching in the Edgefield [TN] Church an old lady who attended the services sent for me and in the most delicate way provided for me a more up-to-date outfit. Her son, a young man of about my age and size, had died a short time before, leaving a fine suit of clothes which he had worn but once before his fatal illness. His mother asked me as a favor to accept and wear the suit. She wished it to be of use to some one who had stood for the cause of the South. I accepted it with sincere thanks, both for the gift and the manner of the giving. That lady became one of the dearest friends I ever had, and for years I was her pastor. I violate no proprieties in mentioning her name, for she was known and loved by many of Nashville's best citizens of the older time. She was Mrs. Jackson, the grandmother of Miss Alicia Dyas, Miss Alicia Gibson, and Mrs. Jo B. Morgan, of this city. She was also a near relative of Mr. John Kirkman, and she was one of the noblest, brightest, most accomplished women I ever knew. Besides this, the ladies of the Edgefield Church found that I expected to be married as soon as I could secure a permanent charge, and they at once set out to provide for that interesting event. Their Presbyterian and Confederate sentiments combined on me, and they presented me with the finest suit of clothes that they could get in the city. Thus I was owner of four complete suits at one time—my handsome gray uniform, my twenty-five-hundred-dollar suit, my suit given by my old friend, and this bridal suit. Outwardly, at least, I was thoroughly reconstructed, and no one could have recognized the tramp of a few months before in ragged jacket and trousers, osnaberg shirt, brogan shoes, and brown jeans hat. But underneath all the finery there beat a heart as devoted to the Confederate cause as ever; and if that was rebellion, then I was still a Rebel, and the political reconstruction did not make me loyal to the government.

In mingling with those who had been devoted to the cause of the Confederacy, both citizens and soldiers, I was impressed with the spirit in which they accepted the results of the war. They felt that the cause was a righteous one and that they had done all that brave men could do to maintain it. Now, as that cause was overwhelmed, they accepted it as the will of Providence to be submitted to in good faith and while they still believed they had contended for their rights under the Constitution, and while they gloried in the fight they had made, yet they were ready with cheerful courage to repair the desolations of war and as good citizens of the United States to join in making this the greatest country and the best government on earth.

It was the terrible mistake of the Reconstruction policy that the Southern States were treated as conquered provinces, where people were ready to rise up in rebellion at the first opportunity. Their good faith was denied, and everything was done to goad them into resistance, and I can but believe that it was done to give excuse for taking possession of their property by greedy adventurers or to gratify the malice and hatred of the fanatical [Left-wing] leaders of abolitionism [my emphasis, L.S.].[304] — REVEREND JAMES HUGH MCNEILLY, NASHVILLE, TENN.

CHAPTER 19

DEIFICATION OF LINCOLN & RECONSTRUCTION

☛ . . . The [Left-wing] authors of the apotheosis [of the assassinated Abraham Lincoln] were those who hated Lincoln in life, but hated the South more. They used it to implicate the South and the South's great leader, Jefferson Davis, in Lincoln's assassination and gave what they viewed as justifiable causes for the horrors of the Reconstruction period which followed. It found large space in the literature and histories of the times and was extensively circulated. It was necessary to deify Lincoln in order to sacrifice the South. [But as Dr. A. W. Littlefield, of Needham, Mass., has said:] "Lee's shrine at Lexington, not Lincoln's tomb, will be the shrine of American patriotism when once history is told correctly."[305] — MRS. F. E. SELPH, U.D.C.

ROBERT E. LEE ON RECONSTRUCTION

☛ . . . After the war Lee used his great influence by precept and example to reconcile the South to her position. He never spoke bitterly of his late antagonists and invariably discouraged the use of such language by others. Nevertheless, the iron of the evil days of Reconstruction entered deeply into his soul, and his grief for the sufferings of his country was indubitably a contributory cause of his death [on October 12, 1870]. In 1869 he was passing through Richmond [VA] on his return to Lexington from a visit to the graves of his father and daughter and called upon [Confederate] Major [Thomas] Talcott, a former member of his staff. This gentleman remarked how ill and depressed he was looking.

General Lee in the heat of battle.

"Yes," the General replied, "I am not only somewhat apprehensive on account of my own health, but the sufferings of our people have deeply affected me. Major, if I could have foreseen the way in which those people [his usual way of speaking of the Yankees] would treat them, I would never have surrendered my army."

"Well, General," said Major Talcott, "you have only to blow the bugle." But the General said, "It is too late now," and shook his head sadly. It may not be generally known that, although Lee by way of example had taken the oath of allegiance to the United States government and had applied for pardon, no notice was taken of his application, and his actual status at the time of his death was that of a prisoner of war on parole.[306] — H. GERALD SMYTHE, HASTINGS, ENGLAND

RECONSTRUCTION WAS A COMMUNIST REVOLUTION
☞ . . . The present generation, even though natives of the South and descendants of those heroic sires who held for four trying years the Confederate battle lines, does not seem to have a full measure of realization of the beauties and glories of the land of their nativity as their progenitors knew it.

Radical [Left-wing] were the changes wrought by the terrible war, followed as they were by the red ordeal of "Bolshevik" [that is, communist] Reconstruction, which overturned all surviving conditions that could be obliterated, and by carpet-baggers and scalawags [my emphasis, L.S.]. I wonder that historical societies in this Southland do not awaken to the responsibility of taking up the urgent task of resurrecting, codifying, and editing the verities of Southern history and publish to the world to be transmitted to generations yet unborn the wonderful story of the Old South as it was when in its prime.

The scheme of Southern history should be undertaken and pushed with vigor while there are sources of truth yet to draw from, before fiction and fireside tales shall be canonized as truth. There are tangles of historic annals which ought to be straightened out, and facts which have been warped and twisted by sectional prejudices and by publicists and politicians to be corrected. . . .[307]
— CHARLES H. GOFFE, IN THE SAN ANTONIO *EXPRESS*

AT THE START OF RECONSTRUCTION
☞ . . . A battalion of infantry from Indiana, under Captain Mason, took the place of the Kentuckians, and during their stay our citizens began to realize the evils of reconstruction, the darkest page in all the history of our country. Our government was placed in the hands of carpet-baggers, negroes, and our own Southern traitors, many of whom had been prominent in the secession movement, but took no part in the fighting that resulted. They joined the Union League to get office and have a part in the robbery and plunder of their fellow citizens. Their management of the State government was so outrageous that we organized the [Conservative, pro-

Constitution] Ku-Klux Klan and redeemed the country. Since that time the South has remained solid.[308] — I. G. BRADWELL, BRANTLEY, ALA.

RECONSTRUCTION DAYS IN SOUTH CAROLINA

☛ There are hundreds—nay, thousands—of men and women who have grown up since the war closed in this beautiful Southland of ours who have but little idea of what their parents went through to bring about the prosperity they now enjoy. There are also thousands of true and noble men who wore the blue that have but little idea of the degradation heaped upon the Southern people by placing the ignorant negroes in power over their former masters.

I take it to be a duty I owe to the race of men who are rapidly passing away to record in my humble way from personal experiences some of the trials endured by them.

At the close of the war the Confederate soldiers with sorrowful hearts retraced their steps homeward. Great sacrifices they had made in behalf of their beloved country, but they had no regret for what they had given for the Southern cause, as, footsore and ragged, they plodded their weary way back to their native States and homes.

It is difficult to imagine a more deplorable state of affairs than existed at their homes. Thousands of them had not a single dollar, a bushel of corn, or a horse or mule; in most cases all that was left was the bare ground. Houses, furniture, fences, and everything that could be destroyed had been wantonly burned, all slaves freed, and they, exulting in their freedom, refused to work on any terms. All the Southern soldier had was the ground and the love of his wife and children.

With the same bold heart with which they had faced for four long years the columns in blue they now faced the wolf of poverty and fought to keep him from the door, and it was a hard, bitter fight. A still more bitter trial than defeat was before them, for as punishment for the South the [racist Left-wing] powers in Washington resolved to place the negro in power, giving him the right to vote without any qualifications whatever. It did not matter that he knew less than the beasts of the fields; all that was necessary was that he had once been a slave. *Armed troops were kept at every county seat to uphold negro rule and encourage him to vote the [then Left-wing] Republican ticket as often as he pleased, the Republicans by this means running up great majorities* [my emphasis, L.S.].

This state of affairs continued over all of the South from 1865 to 1876. Every office in South Carolina was filled by negroes, carpet-baggers, or renegade native whites known as scalawags.

> "The bottom rail was now on top, the negro proudly pranced,
> The authorities at Washington piped for him to dance."

From the close of the war until 1876 South Carolina was under negro rule upheld by Federal bayonets. Adventurers from the North, mostly from the lowest walks in life, flocked South with all their possessions packed in carpetbags, from which they derived the name of carpet-baggers. These [radical Left-wing] men encouraged the negro against his former master and instigated him to commit many heinous crimes.

The books written by Thomas Dixon [Jr.], such as *The Leopard's Spots*, etc., are not exaggerated conditions of this period.[309] *Crimes became so unbearable that the Confederate soldiers had to organize for the protection of their wives and daughters* [my emphasis, L.S.]. They joined together in the [counter-Reconstruction] Ku Klux Klans, which inspired terror in the negroes and checked somewhat the crimes that were being committed.

At every election for State and national offices the white (Democratic) party [then Conservative] put out a ticket, generally giving one-half of the offices to the best of the negroes, hoping in this way to get some of the whites into office; but they were continually defeated, as the negroes were taught that if the [then Conservative] Democrats ever got into power they would be put back into slavery.

As a rule the negroes did not pay taxes of any kind. All the expenses of government were paid by the whites, and three-fourths of it was openly stolen by the plunderers in office for this purpose alone. An account of the disgraceful scenes at the statehouse in Columbia would not be fit for publication [my emphasis, L.S.].

As all efforts of the whites to elect a mixed ticket had failed, in 1876 they determined to bring out a straight white man's ticket, and not to solicit a negro vote. That grand old [Conservative Confederate] cavalry officer, Wade Hampton, was nominated for Governor, and a full ticket for all other offices selected from men who had always been true to the South was placed in the field.

New life came into the hearts of the whites. A voice passed from the mountain to the sea, crying: "Arise, white men!" Like the dead arising from their graves, the Confederate soldier arose with his son, and all answered:

> "Yes, by the grace of God and with his help we shall redeem our land, fairly, if possible, but at any cost of blood or money."

In all counties cavalry companies were formed, arms secured, and a uniform, consisting of a red shirt and black hat, adopted. Weekly meetings were held at each county seat. It was resolved that the [racist, anti-white, and illegal] rule of the carpet-bagger and negro should end; that he should not longer be allowed to incite the negroes to violence at their political meetings; that if he would agree to have joint debates all would be quiet, and each speaker should have a respectful hearing, but if not there should be no speeches made by the [then Left-wing] Republicans.

These terms the [then Liberal] Republicans would not accept, so they were notified that their meetings should not be held, and in all cases where they attempted to speak the meetings were broken up by the "Red Shirts" making so much noise that the speakers could not be heard at all. One instance illustrating this will be cited.

Sumter, S.C., was a special stronghold of the [then Left-wing] Republicans, and they resolved to hold a mass meeting there, when Governor [Daniel H.] Chamberlain and other high officers of the State would address them. And they gave notice that if interfered with they would burn the town. The gage of battle being thus thrown down, the whites eagerly accepted it. The county chairman sent out messengers to all clubs and companies in Sumter, Kershaw, Lancaster, and adjoining counties, requesting full attendance and to come well armed and prepared for any emergency. Generals [Wade] Hampton, [Matthew C.] Butler, and many other distinguished ex-Confederate generals were to be present to make speeches and take command of the forces in case they were needed. The eventful day arrived that the carpet-baggers had set to intimidate or test the courage of the "Red Shirt" Brigade. The club I belonged to arrived in Sumter about 9 A.M. after a ride of twenty miles. We found awaiting us members of clubs from other parts of the county and others arriving every hour until we had a force of about one thousand men, all mounted and armed. Opposing us were at least fifteen thousand negroes. We seemed a mere handful compared to the black cohorts assembled, but there was no fear in the hearts that beat beneath the red shirts. The flower of South Carolina was in the field, and the old warhorse, Hampton, was at the head.

One or two hours were spent riding up and down the streets in close formation, the whites cheering for Hampton and the blacks for Chamberlain. About 11 A.M. the [then Left-wing] Republicans erected a platform in a grove of large trees near the depot, and Governor Chamberlain, surrounded by the thousands of negroes assembled, commenced his address. He was interrupted by a messenger from the [then Right-wing] Democratic assemblage requesting a joint debate, Chamberlain to be answered by Hampton, etc., but the request was refused. They declared that the [then Conservative] Democrats should never speak at any of their meetings. On this refusal the "Red Shirts" surrounded the crowd and made such a noise by shouting that it was impossible for the speakers to be heard, so the meeting was broken up. General Hampton was then called to the platform to address the whites, Chamberlain and all his blacks going back into the town. Hampton had hardly begun to speak before the fire bells rang a general alarm, which meant either a fight or a fire. Every "Red Shirt" wheeled his horse and dashed wildly toward the courthouse. Generals Hampton, [Johnson] Hagood, and other officers soon gained the head of the column and by entreaty and commands succeeded in checking the men and causing them to fall into order. We advanced on the courthouse, which was surrounded by a dense mass of negroes, while above their heads could be seen bright bayonets and troops formed into line. While we did not know whether these soldiers were friends or foes, we surrounded the negroes on all sides, and two or three old cannons were loaded down with nails, scrap iron, etc., and placed at the corners of the streets, the courthouse being in a square.

We found that the surrounded troops were a company of citizens of the town. A fight had started between a negro and a white man. The citizens had placed their guns in the courthouse, and when the disturbance began they rushed to the courthouse and had been surrounded by the negroes. Our coming up and surrounding the negroes on all sides, with the old cannons at each corner, made things look very squally. Through the coolness of our leaders the hotheads were kept quiet. The negroes, being caught between two forces of whites, were intimidated, and after a good deal of entreaty by the leaders of both parties the crowds were quieted.

I am sorry to say that all meetings in the State did not end so peaceably. There were several bloody riots in which a few white men lost their lives. These skirmishes and losses plainly showed the African that he was not a match for the white man; that the Anglo-Saxon was thoroughly aroused and determined to regain his land at any cost of blood or money. Their [Left-wing] leaders encouraged them on, but when trouble arose they took pretty good care to be elsewhere.

The elections came off in November, 1876. The negroes voted

the straight [then Liberal] Republican ticket, as usual; the white vote was solid for Hampton. By all kinds of devices the [then Conservative] Democrats poled a heavy vote. Both parties claimed to have carried the State by heavy majorities. Two sets of State officers and Governors were sworn into office. The whites refused to pay any taxes to the Chamberlain government, and great confusion existed.

This state of affairs existed in other Southern States. It was finally agreed that the electoral vote of these States should be allowed to be cast for [Rutherford B.] Hayes, and in return for this the national government would withdraw all Federal troops from these States, which was done and a fraudulent President [Hayes] was installed into office. But by this means war was averted, and the South was freed of negro rule.

Since 1876 the South has made rapid progress in wealth, which it would never have done under such a government as existed up to that time, and peace, happiness, and prosperity abound.

In 1878 the [then Left-wing] Republicans made their last attempt to regain control of the State and brought out the last Republican ticket for State and county offices that was ever put in the field in South Carolina. The whites again selected a straight [then Conservative] Democratic ticket. At this time the [then Liberal] Republican party was known only as the "negro party," and any white man voting that ticket was completely ostracized, both himself and his family. They were treated with the utmost contempt except those Northern men who had made their homes in the South and who voted only the national [then Left-wing] Republican ticket, voting always with the whites for all other offices. They were well treated and respected.

In 1878 we again brought out a white man's ticket. The result of this election was, of course, an overwhelming majority for the [then Conservative] Democrats. In the presidential election of 1890 we selected a new plan of carrying the election. Seven boxes in which the votes had to be deposited were put out, and on each box in large Roman letters the name of the office was printed, and each ticket had to go in the right box or it would not be counted. If the vote for Governor was placed in the box for a county officer, that vote was not counted at all. If a voter did not have education enough to read his ticket and the name on the box, the chances of it being counted was perhaps one in a hundred. This disheartened the negro from any further attempt to control elections.

The law in effect at present is that each voter shall register sixty days before election and shall produce his poll tax receipt; that he also must be able to read and write and to explain any paragraph in the Constitution to the satisfaction of the judges of the election. To keep from depriving any white men of their votes, the grandfather's clause was inserted, which is that if the grandfather or father fought in either the Revolutionary War or War between the States a man was entitled to vote on account of the services rendered to the State by that ancestor.

The first time I ever voted in South Carolina the negroes marched boldly to the polls with guns on their shoulders, stacked them in a hundred yards of the polls, placing a heavy guard over them, and kept the white men pushed away from the polls.

None of us will ever regret the part we took in these measures or would hesitate to do the same again or even worse should the same conditions arise.[310] — C. E. WORKMAN, GREENVILLE, S.C.

CONFEDERATE INDIAN GENERAL STAND WATIE HELPS HIS PEOPLE THROUGH RECONSTRUCTION

☛ Among the Confederate monuments that deserve notable mention is that recently erected [at Tahlequah, Georgia] by the Oklahoma Division U.D.C., to Gen. Stand Watie, the only full-blooded Indian brigadier general in the Confederate army.

> "... I must say ... as the chief reason for our monument that no man was ever more deserving a memorial from his people than General Stand Watie—a man whose character was above reproach and whose remarkable bravery and military prowess were known and felt far beyond the limits of his activities. The value of his services to the Indian Territory and the bordering counties of Arkansas and Missouri during the years of 1861-65 can never be estimated. During the baneful period at the close of the war and the beginning of reconstruction he was indeed a savior to his stricken people. For the Cherokee Nation, which had partially been occupied by both armies, had indeed suffered, and the Southern Cherokees were exiled and destitute. The great number he aided at this time will never be known. ..."[311] — MRS. MABEL W. ANDERSON, OF PRYOR, OKLA., 1921

RECONSTRUCTION & THE KU KLUX KLAN

☛ The darkest period of American history was that from 1866 to 1876, devoted by the Congress of the United States to restoring the conquered Confederate States to their place as members of the United States and removing the desolations of war.

It is not the purpose of this article to arouse again the bitterness and strife between the sections that prevailed immediately after the

War between the States. It is our privilege and our duty to accept results in the providence of God and to cultivate the spirit of peace and harmony.

Neither is it the purpose to condemn Mr. Lincoln for injustice and oppression in the conduct of the war; not to recall those violations of the laws of civilized warfare such as the making of medicines contraband of war, the refusal to exchange prisoners, when such exchange was dictated by every principle of humanity, and by the harsh and cruel treatment of noncombatants and the destruction of their property. We can give Mr. Lincoln credit for kindly personal feeling in his relations with his fellow men, his tender and sympathetic consideration of suffering everywhere, and for theoretical acceptance of the principles of morality and justice. But when we recall the outrages of [Union Generals Philip H.] Sheridan and [William T.] Sherman in Virginia, Georgia, and North and South Carolina, and that Mr. Lincoln approved of those outrages, it is hardly fair to expect the South to accept him as the highest type of Christian, as the national hero to be admired, and as the Christlike man to be imitated by all true patriots.[312]

It is true that the general sentiment of our country has come to condemn those outrages and the whole Congressional policy of reconstruction, yet within the last few years the tendency of the writers of the North has been to ignore or to condone the wrongs done or to justify them by false statements as to the attitude of the South after the war.

My object is to set forth the truths of history as to the conduct of the war, to vindicate the principles for which the Confederate States went to war, and our readiness at all times for peace and harmony with the Union.

It seems to me from a reading of history that when civilized governments are to be established two principles are in conflict, each laboring for supremacy, the great object being that each shall have its proper place in the life of the people. The first is the [Left-wing] principle of authority or autocracy, which asserts the supremacy of a central authority dependent upon physical force. The second great principle upon which the people are to depend for protection against oppression is the [Right-wing] principle of justice or righteousness, a spiritual principle, which, in the long run, will resist to the utmost all injustice and wrongdoing. These two principles and their antagonisms were manifest in the negotiations for the establishment of the Constitution of the United States. It was a question between a [Liberal-oriented] centralized government and the [Conservative-oriented] rights of sovereign

States, and the Constitution was a compromise or compact between these two great forces which must be dependent for success on the faithfullness of each party in observing it. But from the very beginning there was a tendency on the part of autocracy to emphasize its rights, and this tendency was especially cultivated in the [Liberal] Northern section, while the [Conservative] South emphasized State Rights. In 1854 the [then Left-wing] Republican party was organized [by Liberals and Socialists, who selected Radical (Socialist) John C. Frémont as their first presidential candidate], the declared purpose of which was to deprive the South of certain constitutional rights, setting aside the decisions of the Supreme Court. In 1860 Mr. Lincoln was elected as the avowed candidate of that policy. Under these circumstances there was only one thing for the South to do, which was to withdraw from the compact. This certain States attempted to do and to form a separate Confederacy. Their commissioners were sent to negotiate with the United States government for a settlement of all questions arising between the two governments. It all finally turned upon reenforcing Fort Sumter, in Charleston Harbor, and after various promises plainly made and unscrupulously broken, the United States government determined to reenforce the fort, and so the war was brought on.

In 1848 Mr. Lincoln was an able advocate in Congress of the doctrine of State Rights; by 1860 he declared that the attitude of a State to the general government was that of a county to a State, and upon this latter idea Congress acted, and its policy of reconstruction was but a carrying out of the wrongs and oppressions perpetrated during the war.

1. The Constitution was changed to give all the rights of citizenship to the negro.
2. White Southerners and their sympathizers were disfranchised and restrained from interfering with any of the negro's rights.
3. The country was divided into military sections, over each of which a [Union] general was placed in command, with [U.S.] troops at his disposal to enforce the decisions of the civil tribunals. *In a word, it was the legalizing of injustice and corruption before the courts of the country* [my emphasis, L.S.].

The result was that the South was overrun with an army of bummers [that is, drifters and grifters] and carpet-baggers from the North, coming ostensibly to see that the negro had his rights and to install him as ruler over the States. The result was a [racist, anti-white] rule of corruption, of graft, of loot, and of lust that to-day is recognized as the disgrace of all who took part in it.

In a single word, it was the malignant effort of the conquering section of the country, in obedience to a false and fanatical [Left-wing] ideal, to destroy an ancient [Western] civilization with its claims, its rights, its privileges, its ideals, and its principles. To change an order of nature and bring the highest elements—intellectual, social, religious, and political—into subjection to the very lowest elements that could be used for purposes of corruption and mere material profit. The negroes were organized into secret societies to put themselves in office and carry out the behests of their [Left-wing] carpetbag advisers [my emphasis, L.S.].

Confederate General Nathan Bedford Forrest did not found or lead what I have termed the Reconstruction Ku Klux Klan. However, he did shut the Conservative organization down in 1869 when it had accomplished its primary goal: driving meddling socialist and communist Republican do-gooders (called "Radicals" in mainstream history books) from the South.

Under these circumstances, every principle of self-respect, of honor, and of self-preservation demanded that the South should resist by all means in its power the destruction of its original ideals. It has been charged that the Ku Klux Klan made the reconstruction policy necessary.

The actual fact is that the Southern people were resorting to various plans to break up the influence of the carpet-baggers over the negroes, especially to break up the secret organizations. When suddenly it was found, by apparent accident, that an organization of young men, for their own amusement, could be used to appeal to the superstition of the negroes and to bring their dread of unseen world powers to protect the white people against their nightly machinations.

Against those unseen powers the carpet-bagger was held to be helpless. So the Ku Klux Klan was regularly organized with a head [the Grand Wizard], . . . its various officers and orders, it signs and watchwords to frighten the negroes into submission to the better elements of the community. It is probable that comparatively few suffered violence at its hands. There were two classes that were never spared—a negro assaulting a white woman or a white man stirring up negroes to outrages.

At the end of four years it was seen that the organization had accomplished its purpose, law and order were gradually restored, the better elements of the Northern people coming into the South became helpers in the work of restoration. The negroes gradually took their natural place, and so the organization, in 1870, was officially and formally dissolved by order of . . . [Confederate] General [Nathan Bedford] Forrest.

It is true that for several years afterwards there were organizations [comprised of imposters] calling themselves Ku Klux Klan and committing various outrages, but they were easily subdued.

In 1876 the Southern States that had entered the Confederacy were restored to their original position, and from that day, as a body, they have been thoroughly faithful to the new obligations assumed by them, and in two great wars have shown their loyalty to the Union. In the rape of Panama from Columbia, in the rescue of Cuba from Spain, and in the entrance of the United States in the great World War [I], the great principle for which the Confederate States contended is recognized as supreme. That is to say, the right of every people to determine their own form of government. So it is that God fulfills his purposes in various ways, and makes the "wrath of man to praise him, while the remainder of wrath he doth restrain."[313] — REVEREND JAMES HUGH MCNEILLY, NASHVILLE, TENN.

WAS LINCOLN A FRIEND OF THE SOUTH?

☛ During the war with Germany [World War I], this country fell into a panic over German propaganda. It was a serious matter then, and we all joined in fighting the German program of misrepresentation [that is, gaslighting]. But now that no danger to the country can result, we can see that this widespread apprehension had its comic side. As a matter of fact, the art of propaganda had its origin in America, and the Germans only employed our own weapons against us. In saying America, I mean the ruling North [that is, Liberal Yankees]. Propaganda is merely an organized form of advertisement, and this had its origin and highest development with the shrewd business men of the North. The chief characteristic of the propaganda was the sacrifice of everything to the humor of the public. And so the Germans, always ready enough to avail themselves of agencies which they did not possess, seized upon this American device and turned it to the purpose of their war. But it scared the country so that the joke was not appreciated.

Undeterred, however, by what may be considered a rebuke of

unscrupulous methods of popularizing one's wares, the [Liberal] North has kept up the old art [of gaslighting], and in these latter days many Northern writers and speakers are applying it to historical questions. The main purpose of the popular advertisement is to make people believe; and, in this historic application, truth becomes secondary to a sectional wish.

Of all the propaganda at work to-day, the glorification of Abraham Lincoln and the attempt to set him above [George] Washington are the most notable. In order to make this idealism of Lincoln general, this propaganda is trying its best to make it appear that Lincoln was a friend of the South. To accomplish this result, an entirely false construction is given to Lincoln's attitude and actions [my emphasis, L.S.].

For the sake of historic truth, let us look briefly into Lincoln's official conduct during the war for Southern independence, and see if there exists any real justification for this claim.

Well, one of the earliest of his official actions was to [unconstitutionally] denounce all Southern privateersmen as pirates, subject to the death penalty. Another was to approve an act of Congress denouncing death, imprisonment, or confiscation upon everybody in the South, including their sympathizers in the North [known as copperheads]. Another was to make medicine contraband of war, the first time it was ever done in the annals of warfare. Still another was to suffer [Union General] Benjamin F. Butler to go unrebuked after his infamous order at New Orleans, directed against the women of that city. The British Prime Minister, [3rd Viscount] Palmerston [Henry John Temple], characterized it in open Parliament as an order "too indecent to be put in the English language," and the British Minister at Washington protested to [William H.] Seward against it, but without effect. In the American Revolution some of the women of Boston spat at the British soldiers of [General John] Borgoyne's captured army, and went unrebuked; but Butler's order was directed against merely "any gesture or movement expressive of contempt of a Federal soldier."

At another time, when some ladies of England asked permission to distribute $85,000 among the Confederates in Northern prisons, the permission was refused by Seward, the Secretary of State, and Lincoln did not interfere. This was going far beyond the Germans, who permitted such gifts to be freely distributed among their prisoners during the World War.

Lincoln had plenty of opportunity to check Sheridan, Grant, and Sherman in their work of burning [Southern] houses and towns and destroying private property, but instead of blaming anyone of the three, he sent them congratulatory letters and telegrams. *It is difficult to find a greater act of cruelty perpetrated in any war than that of Sherman in driving away, in the midst of winter, the whole population of the city of Atlanta, numbering 15,000* [my emphasis, L.S.].

Property in the South was everywhere seized without compensation, and within the areas embraced by the Union lines, the people of both sexes above sixteen years of age had to take an oath of allegiance or quit their homes. Whatever may have been the origin of these orders, they were notoriously public, and Lincoln never interfered.

When we come to consider his emancipation policy, the facts are far from reflecting any honor upon him. He first declared the policy as "futile as the Pope's bull against the comet," but in ten days he reversed his decision and published his edict freeing the slaves. At the interview in which he expressed himself adverse to the policy, he observed that if he ever did issue such a proclamation it would be as a war measure, independent of its legal or constitutional character or "its moral nature in view of the possible consequences of insurrection or massacre in the South." Now, just here, I will ask the question, did this language show any friendliness to the South?

Had Lincoln taken the high ground of humanity in issuing his proclamation, I can understand how an incidental massacre might be excused as a very regrettable necessity; but his proclamation did not extend to slavery within such areas as were within the Federal lines, and where his authority might control the radical effects of his action. It professed to extend to areas entirely outside of his authority—areas where, in the interview referred to, he expressly admitted that his policy as an orderly measure could not be expected to go into effect.

What then? It became a favorite afterthought with modern writers that Lincoln issued his proclamation for the moral effect it might produce in Europe, but of this he said nothing in the interview mentioned, and his own words show that he had "the possible consequences of insurrection and massacre" directly in mind.

And what else could he have expected in view of Nat Turner's rebellion in Virginia in 1831 and the experience in Haiti and San Domingo in 1802, when sixty thousand white people were destroyed and scenes enacted too terrible for any human pen to describe?

Lincoln's proclamation was denounced both in England and France, and in the South its war character was construed to mean a scheme to break up the Confederate armies in the field by the menace of a frightful danger at home. *That the negroes did not rise in the South is not due to the humanity of Lincoln, who realized the peril and made it a menace; but the credit goes to the slave owners for the humane manner in which they had treated their slaves, and affords the most conclusive refutation of the misrepresentations of the abolitionists of cruelty on their part* [my emphasis, L.S.].

But this [gaslighting] propaganda tried to draw to its embrace Mr. [Jefferson] Davis and others who expressed regret at the assassination of Lincoln. Thus, Dr. N. W. Stephenson, born in Ohio, and now holding the chair of history in South Carolina College, declares in his "Abraham Lincoln and the Union," forming volume XXIX of the *Chronicles of America*:

> "It is recorded of Davis that in after days he paid beautiful tribute to Lincoln and said that next to the destruction of the Confederacy, the death of Abraham Lincoln was the darkest day the South had known."

Did Mr. Davis mean any compliment to Lincoln in these words? Only a victim of propaganda can imagine such a thing. If Mr. Davis is correctly quoted, as I presume he is, he referred merely to the opportunity which Lincoln's assassination gave to the South haters in the North to carry through their plans of reconstruction. Had Lincoln lived, though there is little assurance that he would have successfully opposed any plan of the radicals, the necessary stimulus to excessive cruelty afforded by the action of [John Wilkes] Booth would have been lacking. That is all Mr. Davis meant.

How little reliance was to be placed upon any policy of Lincoln, and how incapable he was of standing up against the "malignants" [that is, radical Left-wingers] around him is shown by perhaps his very last official acts. On the evacuation of Richmond by the Confederates, he visited the city, and, while there, was persuaded to give an order for the assembling of the Virginia Legislature. But he had hardly returned to Washington when, yielding to the vehement protest of [Edwin M.] Stanton, his Secretary of War, as Stanton himself says, he recalled his permission, excusing his action on grounds that are plainly afterthoughts.

In the light of the doctrine of self-determination, now so generally admitted, it appears one of the most astonishing things in history that eight millions of [Southern] people (now twenty millions), occupying a territory half the size of Europe, with a thoroughly organized government and capable of fighting one of the greatest wars on record, were not permitted to set up for

themselves. Having begun the war, Lincoln saw that there was no way out of it except to win the war. So unstable as he was in every other particular, a political dancer [that is, a demagogue] that veered about every other question in circles, he kept this one thing steadily in view. There is little doubt that had he to choose between the failure of his war and entire extermination of the Southern people, he would have chosen the latter alternative. *We have his own words to this effect, when, on August 3, 1862, he declared to his cabinet that he was "pretty well cured of any objections to any measure except want of adaptedness to putting down the rebellion"* [my emphasis, L.S.].[314] —
DR. LYON G. TYLER, HOLDCROFT, VA.

This pro-South, pro-Conservative, pro-Constitution wood engraving by Joseph F. Keppler is dated 1875 and is titled: "Grant's Last Outrage in Louisiana." It depicts Uncle Sam calling out Ulysses S. Grant with the words: "Hold there! Hold there, General! I have tolerated your abuses of your office long enough." In reply Grant says: "March those legislators out. I am going to have my way in this matter." The newspaper on the ground reads: "We are in the midst of a revolution tending fast to the concentration of all power in the hands of one man." The "revolution" and the "concentration of all power" spoken of here are references to communism.

CHAPTER 20

HAD HE LIVED LINCOLN WOULD NOT HAVE BEEN KIND TO THE SOUTH

☛ In the name of the Confederate soldiers who followed General [Robert E.] Lee in the War between the States and knew that they were right in fighting for their rights under the Constitution of the United States, let me thank you for your just and noble defense of the main object of the Committee's report at [the Confederate veterans] Richmond Reunion: to open the eyes of all men regarding the open and secret endeavors of [Left-wing] Northern fanatics to instill in the minds of our children, by textbooks and teachers, the false and pernicious doctrine that their fathers and kinsmen who followed Lee were traitors. As to the part of the report stigmatizing Lincoln as being "personally responsible for forcing the war upon the South," there is room for difference of opinion. I agree with you that "to put the blame on Lincoln alone for having conceived and inaugurated the War between the States, will need strong proof to sustain." With you, I would respectfully ask, why the protest of Generals Carr and Howry against that part of the report which they repudiated in the public press was not made in the meeting that adopted the report. Had I been present at the meeting, I would have sustained the purpose of the report, and have thanked the Committee for their labor of love in exposing the efforts of those people in the North to teach our children that our sacred cause was the cause of traitors; but would have suggested a change in the phraseology of a part of the report,

Lincoln was *not* who most people today think he was. He was not even what most Victorian Southerners thought he was: a charitable, empathetic Christian who was willing to let the South quickly rejoin the Union without punishment or recrimination. In fact, he was a tyrannical atheist who privately told his political colleagues that the South needed to be crushed and destroyed, then replaced with Left-wing Yankee "propositions and ideas"—that is, Liberalized and Northernized.

something like this: That *the War between the States was indorsed and commended by Mr. Lincoln because he made no effort to prevent it when the opportunity was offered him by the Peace Conference; and that he was responsible for the secession of Virginia by calling out 75,000 armed men to coerce the Southern States. More than that, he had it in his power at the Hampton Roads Conference in February, 1865, to end the cruel war, and thus prevent further suffering to our soldiers in the field, in the prisons, and to their loved ones at home* [my emphasis, L.S.]. The handing to [Confederate Vice President] Mr. [Alexander H.] Stephens a blank sheet of paper by Mr. Lincoln and saying to him, "Mr. Stephens, let me write 'Union' at the top of that sheet, and you may write anything you please under it," is sheer fiction, widely disseminated by the late Henry Watterson. On its face it is absurd to suppose that Mr. Lincoln would have committed himself to the retention in the Southern States of slavery, which he professed to abominate. Mr. Stephens says that the President's first and only proposition was "unconditional surrender of the States and their people." And he adds:

> "The conference reached the line where it seems the Southern Commissioners would have taken a step committing their government to dissolution without another battle, provided only they had been fully and frankly assured by authority to be trusted that the Union, even without slavery, would be at once reestablished, the States with all their rightful relations restored, the people of the South protected, the Constitution respected, and sectionalism ended forever."

Had these concessions of the Committee been accepted by Mr. Lincoln, ratified by President Jefferson Davis and the Confederate Congress, the awful and unequal conflict, with its terrible suffering of all concerned—North as well as South—would have been brought to an end; the horrors of the never-to-be-forgotten period of reconstruction would never have disgraced the [then Left-wing] Republican Party nor have humiliated the people of the South; and the glorious Union, founded by our Fathers "for, with, and by the consent of the people," would have been cemented by the cords of perpetual love. Then, we could, with commendable pride, have taught our children to reverence the name of Abraham Lincoln and acclaim him "a great and good man." But no; judging him by his actions—advising the [then Liberal] Republicans in Congress to vote against the Crittenden resolutions, the part he played at the Peace Conference, approving [William H.] Seward's deception in conferring with the committee from the Virginia convention, driving Virginia out of the Union by his proclamation for 75,000 men to coerce the Southern States, and not accepting the concessions made by the Committee at the Hampton Roads Conference—are we to be considered uncharitable in thinking that *Mr. Lincoln had but one idea from the beginning to the end of the unhappy struggle, and that idea was the subjugation of the Southern people?* [my emphasis, L.S.] And are Confederate veterans to be censured for resenting the false charge of being traitors, because we fought—under the leadership of our great and good President Jefferson Davis and the peerless Robert E. Lee—to defend our homes, and our Constitutional rights?[315] — REVEREND GILES B. COOKE, MATHEWS, VA.

PRESIDENT HARDING ON RECONSTRUCTION
☛ In my judgment, the reconstruction of the South by the people of the South, in the face of tremendous discouragements following the war, set the finest example that could be urged upon a war-wasted people to-day.[316] — U.S. PRESIDENT WARREN G. HARDING, CIRCA 1922

A CONFEDERATE CHILD'S VIEW OF RECONSTRUCTION
☛ Interesting and valuable articles are found in all departments of the *Confederate Veteran*, and I am going to suggest another department for the "Near Veterans"—that is, those of us who were here during the War between the States, too young to bear arms, yet who saw something of those times and what followed, Reconstruction, perhaps more horrible than the war.

I was born in Virginia, not in the United States; but in Virginia, *Confederate States of America*, having first seen the light of day during the war period. And I claim to be a "Near Veteran," as I was on the firing line toward the close of the war. To be exact, for history must be exact, I was an infant in the battle of Five Forks, Dinwiddie County, Va., C. S. A., which was fought on April 1, 1865. Bullets passed into the house, piercing furniture, etc., yet, I am told, I stood as stanch as Stonewall Jackson, and, moreover, I uttered the "Rebel Yell." All this is personal, but is necessary to establish my "near vet" identification.

Not long after the close of the war, while living at Dinwiddie Courthouse, I witnessed a scene that made a lasting impression on me, notwithstanding my youth.

While at play with some companions in the village, we heard loud singing from many voices, and saw a large company of negroes marching along the Plank Road bearing a [U.S.] flag and singing "We'll rally 'round the flag, boys." Some of the marchers wore gaudy sashes. We thought war had broken out again; in this frame of mind we ran home and told our parents that a large company of negro soldiers was coming up the road to the Courthouse; we were told that there was no war, that the negroes were only being marched up to the polls to vote. I had not up to that time ever heard of "polls" and "voting," and after this had been explained, I obtained permission to go to the polls to see the performance; and this is what I saw: A white man seated in a chair near the voting precinct. He was wearing a tall hat, as well as a long linen duster, and in his hands he had the [preassigned] ballots. The negroes would file by, receive a ticket [for the then Liberal Republican Party], which they deposited in the ballot box, then they formed in groups, all smiles, thinking perhaps of the "forty acres and a mule," which was a by-word among them then and after. I saw no native white men voting, for they were disfranchised because they had fought for State Rights, yet they were the educated people, taxpayers and property holders, but had no voice in any governmental affairs; the carpet-baggers and negroes [that is, Left-wingers] had everything their way. These negroes had assembled at Olive Branch Church, a few miles east of the Courthouse, and came from there along the old Petersburg-Boydton Plank Road, now a part of the tourist highway from the North through Washington, Richmond, Petersburg, and Dinwiddie County en route to Florida.

It was this very spectacular thing that made such an impression on me. As I grew older, the true significance dawned upon me. A black picture of the times fittingly set to the blacker background that brought it into being. Such was my first impression of Reconstruction. Is there any wonder that some forty years after, Ernest Crosby wrote in the *North American Review*[317] as follows:

> "We stabbed the South to the quick, and during all these years of reconstruction turned the dagger round in the festering wound. The spirit of war and imperialism has never yet settled any question, except the question as to which side is stronger; and now, after forty years, we are beginning to learn that the negro has yet to be emancipated. If the South had been permitted to secede, slavery would have died a natural death."[318] — A "NEAR VETERAN"

RECONSTRUCTION DAYS—1865-1876

☛ Lest my Northern friends may think that I have taken advantage of this opportunity to give vent to my feelings from the Southern point of view and what I may say will seem to be from prejudice, I shall quote only from fair-minded men of the North, nor will I even tell the worst things these men of the North have said.

Walter Henry Cook, a professor in the Western Reserve University, Cleveland, Ohio, a Northern man by birth and education, one who is trying to read history with his heart as well as his eyes, says:

> "The Northern soldier returned to his home to find every comfort and convenience. The North was more prosperous than when the war began. Manufactures had increased; railroads had opened up in the West; immigrants were supplying labor for factory and farm, and while the most destructive war in the history of the world had taken place, yet an increase in wealth, population, and power had been the result.
>
> "What a contrast to the South! The Southern soldier returned defeated, sorrowful, ill-clad, ill-fed, sick in mind and body, to find the South desolate and prostrate. The whole economic system had been destroyed or confiscated. Factories in ashes, railroads in ruin, bonds useless, currency valueless, a pitiable condition!
>
> "A new economic system could have been built up by the men and women of the South with freed slaves had they been let alone. The racist, anti-white] policy of Thad Stevens and Charles Sumner after Lincoln's death stirred up ex-slaves to hate the white men of the South . . ."

The next quotation is from Dan [W.] Voorhees, representative for many years, and later a United States senator from Indiana. In his speech, "Plunder of Eleven States," made in the House of Representatives, March 23, 1872, he pictures well the animus of reconstruction. He said:

> "From turret to foundation you tore down the government of eleven States. You left not one stone upon another. You not only destroyed their local laws, but you trampled upon their ruins. You called conventions to frame new constitutions for these old States. You not only said who should be elected to rule over these States, but you said who should elect them. You fixed the quality and the color of the voters [black supremacy]. You purged the ballot box of intelligence and virtue, and in their stead you placed the most ignorant and unqualified race in the world to rule over these people."

Then, taking State by State, he showed what Thad Stevens's policy had done.

> "Let the great State of Georgia speak first. You permitted her to stand up and start in her new career, but, seeing some flaw in your handiwork, you again destroyed and again reconstructed her State government. You clung to her throat; you battered her features out of shape and recognition, determined that your party [the then Left-wing Republican Party] should have undisputed possession and enjoyment

of her offices, her honors, and her substance. Then, bound hand and foot, you handed her over to the rapacity of robbers. Her prolific and unbounded resources inflamed their desires.

"In 1861 Georgia was free from debt. Taxes were light as air. The burdens of government were easy upon her citizens. Her credit stood high, and when the war closed she was still free from indebtedness. After six years of [then Left-wing] Republican rule you present her, to the horror of the world, loaded with a debt of $50,000,000, and the crime against Georgia is the crime this same party has committed against the other Southern States. Your work of destruction was more fatal than a scourge of pestilence, war, or famine.

"Rufus B. Bullock, governor of Georgia, dictated the legislation of Congress, and the great commonwealth of Georgia was cursed by his presence. With such a governor and such a legislature in perfect harmony, morally and politically, their career will go down to posterity without a rival for infamous administrations of the world. That governor served three years and then absconded with all of the gains. The legislature of two years spent $100,000 more than had been spent during any eight previous years. They even put the children's money, laid aside for education of white and black, into their own pockets."

When Senator Voorhees came to South Carolina, the proud land of [American Revolution Generals Francis] Marion and [Thomas] Sumter, his indignation seems to have reached its pinnacle:

"There is no form of ruin to which she has not fallen a prey, no curse with which she has not been baptized, no cup of humiliation and suffering her people have not drained to the dregs. There she stands, the result of your handiwork, bankrupt in money, ruined in credit, her bonds hawked about the streets at ten cents on the dollar, her prosperity blighted at home and abroad, without peace, happiness, or hope. There she stands, with her skeleton frame admonishing all the world of the loathsome consequences of a [Left-wing] government fashioned in hate and fanaticism, and founded upon the ignorant and vicious classes of manhood. Her sins may have been many and deep, and the color of scarlet, yet they will become as white as snow in comparison with those you have committed against her in the hour of her helplessness and distress."

Then he took in like manner State after State, and wound up with this:

"I challenge the darkest annals of the human race for a parallel to the robberies which have been perpetrated on these eleven American States. Had you sown seeds of kindness and good will, they would long ere this have blossomed into prosperity and peace. Had you sown seeds of honor, you would have reaped a golden harvest of contentment and obedience. Had you extended your charities and your justice to a distressed people, you would have awakened a grateful affection in return. But as *you planted in hate and nurtured in corruption* [my emphasis, L.S.], so have been the fruits which you have gathered."

I return now to quote from Walter [H.] Cook in regard to reconstruction graft.

"Governor [Henry C.] Warmouth, of Louisiana, accumulated one and a half million dollars in four years on a salary of $8,000 a year. Governor [Franklin J.] Moses [Jr.], of South Carolina, acknowledged that he had accepted $65,000 in bribes. *Governor [Powell F.] Clayton, of Arkansas, said he intended to people the State with negroes* [my emphasis, L.S.]. The carpet-bag government of Florida stole meat and flour given for helpless women and children. In North Carolina and Alabama, negro convicts were made justices of the peace, men who were unable to read or write. In the South Carolina legislature, ninety-four black men were members. The Speaker of the House, the Clerk of the House, the doorkeeper, the chairman of the Ways and Means Committee, and the chaplain, were all black men, and some of them could neither read nor write."

The next is an extract from the Chicago *Chronicle*, written by a Northern man:

"The Fifteenth Amendment to the Constitution grew out of a spirit of revenge, for the purpose of punishing the Southern people. It became a part of the Constitution by fraud and force to secure the results of war. The war was not fought to secure negro suffrage.
"The history of the world may be searched in vain for a parallel to the spirit of savagery which it inflicted upon a defeated and impoverished people, the unspeakable, barbarous rule of a servile race just liberated from bondage. Negro suffrage was a crime against the white people of the South. It was a crime against the blacks of the South. It was a crime against the whole citizenship of the republic. Political power was never conferred upon a race so poorly equipped to receive it."

Now a last quotation from Charles Francis Adams [Jr.], the grandson of John Quincy Adams:

"I have ever been one of those who have thought extremely severe measures were dealt the Southern people after the civil war, measures of unprecedented severity. The Southern community was not only desolated during the war, but $3,000,000,000 of property confiscated after the war. I am not aware that history records a similar act superadded to the destruction and desolation of war.
". . . Their manumitted slaves, belonging to an inferior and alien

race, were enfranchised and put in control of the whole administration. Is there a similar case recorded in history? If so, I have never heard of it. It was simply a case of insane procedure, and naturally resulted in disaster. We stabbed the South to the quick, and during all the years of reconstruction turned the dagger round and round in the festering wound. If the South had been permitted to secede, slavery would have died a natural death."

The United States government is the only government that ever freed her slaves without giving just compensation for them. Dr. [John Allan] Wyeth, an Alabamian, in his book, *With Saber and Scalpel*, says:

> "None but those who went through this period have any conception of it. Defeat on battle field brought no dishonor, but all manner of oppressions, with poverty and enforced domination of a race lately in slavery, brought humiliation and required a courage little less than superhuman."[319]

The trouble arose from interference on the part of the scalawags and carpet-baggers in our midst, and they were the ones to be dealt with first to keep the negroes in their rightful place.

After the surrender the soldiers returned to their homes, where homes remained. They literally had nothing left but the ground upon which they stood. Families scattered, negroes freed, banks closed, no currency available, the slave-holder knowing less than his overseer and slaves about the practical part of farming. The lawyer had no clients, the teacher had no pupils, the merchant had no credit, the doctor had no drugs. O! It was pitiful. Georgia and South Carolina suffered most on account of desolation caused by Sherman's march to the sea.

This was the time when those women of the Confederacy showed of what stuff they were made. They put their loving arms about those husbands, brothers, and sons, and they said:

> "We are not conquered, we are just overpowered, and we think it was better that you fought, even if you did not win, than never to have fought at all. The South is going to come out all right; you wait and see."

What prophets they were, for is not the South to-day the nation's greatest asset?

It was very hard for our Southern men, unused to manual labor of any kind, to try to adjust themselves to the new order of things in the South. It really was easier for the women than for the men, and some men never did get adjusted, and some women have never been reconstructed.

  The kitchens in the old civilization were never in the house, but some distance from it. There was no need that they should be in the house then, for there were plenty of young negroes to run back and forth with the hot waffles, the hot egg-bread, the biscuits, and the battercakes; but when the women of the South had to go into the kitchen after the negroes left, or had become too impertinent to be allowed around the house, the inconveniences were greatly felt. You must remember there was rarely such a thing as a cooking stove before the War between the States. All cooking had to be done in an open fireplace, with oven and pots. There were no waterworks, and all water had to be drawn from the well or brought from the spring. There were no electric lights, no gas lights, no kerosene lamps even, and lard lamps were really a rarity used only by the rich. The dependence for light were wax, tallow, and sperm [whale] candles. The wood had to be cut and the chips had to be picked up, and all this consumed time and required great patience. This was the beginning of the breaking up of home life in the South, and it proved the death blow to the old time Southern hospitality.

  So many men, the heads of the house, had been killed in battle or died in prison. How could the mother, in the kitchen away from the house, continue to gather the children for family prayers?

  How could hospitality, for which the Old South was so noted, continue under such changed conditions—with no servants to do the work and often no money to hire any or to buy necessary provisions?

  The education of the children was taken from the home and private schools to the public schools. There had been no public schools under the old regime in the South. A Southern gentleman resented having the State educate his child; but the changed condition forced this upon him, and it humiliated him. Free schools in the South had been only for those too poor to pay tuition or to employ a tutor.

  How could the husband, rushing off to his business office, and children rushing off to school, keep up the family altar or encourage that conversation around the family board so conducive to culture?

  Adjustment to new conditions came gradually. The kitchen became a part of the house; the introduction of waterworks relieved the labor of drawing the water; gas and electric stoves and the fireless cooker make now the preparation of meals a less perplexing question; gas and electricity have revolutionized the

South-hating Yankee Edwin M. Stanton, Lincoln's secretary of war, did much damage to the South and the Southern people during Reconstruction—all in the name of vengeance.

light situation; so the women of the South to-day are as independent as their Northern sisters and far ahead of them in dealing with negro help, for, say what you will, the women of the South, knowing these people, can better sympathize with them, and they do treat them with far more consideration than the people of other sections. There is no doubt that the negro finds his truest friends in the South, and that, too, with no social equality ideas to upset him.

The reconstruction period was not only a time of real oppression, but also a time of repression, suppression, and fearful humiliation. The South lost more than $2,000,000,000 by loss of slaves, together with confiscated and destroyed property. The South was also left with a bonded war debt of $300,000,000.

It is really refreshing to realize, even at this late day, that some of the leading negro leaders are conscious of the mistakes that have been made and are willing to acknowledge it. One of them, named Wilkins, at Little Rock, Ark., in 1915, said on Emancipation Day:

> "We are foolish for celebrating an event which has meant nothing to us but humiliation, persecution, alienation, degradation, obloquy, scorn, and contempt. We are celebrating a day that never took place, and you know it as well as I do."

By the freedom of the slaves and the estrangements that followed between them and their former owners, the civilization of the Old South gradually passed away.

Mark Twain said:

> "The eight years in America, 1860-1868, uprooted an institution centuries old, and wrought so profoundly upon the national character of the people that the influence will be felt for two or three generations."[320] — FROM THE "SCRAPBOOK" OF MILDRED LEWIS RUTHERFORD, STATE HISTORIAN GEORGIA DIVISION, U.D.C.

A LETTER TO *CONFEDERATE VETERAN* MAGAZINE

☞ I am eighty-one years old, and I lived through those four dreadful years of war with my husband with [Confederate General James] Longstreet in Virginia. I also remember the reconstruction era and our sufferings and humiliations. The *Veteran* brings to mind our struggles, and I want my grandchildren to know the truth while they are being taught untruth in the public schools. May God bless you and help you to broadcast the truth and honor of a fallen nation for a just cause.[321] — MRS. SARAH J. MCELVEY, QUINCY, FLA.

SOUTHERN BLACKS BEFORE & AFTER THE WAR

☞ . . . For months at a time there were numerous [white] families of women and children wholly dependent on the negroes for support and protection. Those women and children were cut off from their male relatives and friends, and yet, from the beginning to the end of the war, no such thing as an insurrectionary movement was known or heard of, nor the use of any incendiary language whatever charged, reported, or hinted against the negroes. As a matter of fact, the commands of the smallest child in the master's family were obeyed without a murmur.

True, a number of them left or were carried or enticed away, and many who went enlisted in the Federal army; but, on the other hand, a large majority of them remained at home and actually hid themselves and the stock of their masters whenever they heard the cry: "Yankees coming!" This is positively true; I could cite numerous instances and names were it necessary.

Not only did a large majority of the negroes remain at their homes, but they took care of the property and families of their masters, raised crops, and did all other customary and necessary work just as they had before the war, when owners and overseers watched over them. I personally know instances where the negro men alternately slept on the gallery or before the door of their master's home in order to protect the family against all harm.

These are facts that flatly contradict and give the lie direct to the oft-repeated assertions of the Abolitionists [that is, mainly socialists and communists] (slanders on the negroes) that the negroes hated the whites of the South and only worked for and obeyed them because they were compelled to do so. These are facts, and no matter what may be the outcome of the developments of the future, as a race the negroes, by their conduct and their fidelity in times and under circumstances that might well have, and did, put their allegiance and fidelity to the severest test, earned and entitled themselves to the kind consideration, the friendship, and love of our people.

True, after the war had ended and they became free, their ignorance was imposed upon and many of them allowed themselves to be duped and misled into a feeling of distrust and a course of antagonism to their former owners and the people of the South generally, which came very near causing a rupture that might have resulted in the destruction of all confidence, the severance of all ties, and creating a permanent animosity between them.

I do not envy the [Left-wing] men, or fiends, who could take advantage of the ignorant negroes and turn them against the white people and expose them to the possible dangers and evils of a bloody race conflict. The infamies practiced by the carpet-baggers engendered the feeling of hatred in the negro's breast, and I firmly believe that but for this we would not have felt the horrors of the so-called "Reconstruction," and that we would have no negro question now. *I do not believe that the effect those teachings had on the negro then will ever be eradicated from the present or future generations* [my emphasis, L.S.]. but whatever the future may develop, we must remember the loyalty of our good slaves....[322] — CAPTAIN JAMES DINKINS, NEW ORLEANS, LA

LINCOLN WAS NOT THE MAN OUR MAINSTREAM HISTORY BOOKS SAY HE WAS

☛ Lincoln's second election [in 1864] was largely committed to the War and Navy Departments of the Federal government, he having been nominated by the same radical [then Left-wing] Republican Party, practically, that nominated him at Chicago in 1860; and George B. McClellan was the nominee of the [then Right-wing] Democratic Party.

Lincoln made criticism of his administration treason triable by court-martial, and United States soldiers ruled at the polls. [Union] Gen. B. F. Butler's book gives full particulars of the large force with which he controlled completely the voters of New York City; and [Alexander K.] McClure's book, *Our Presidents*,[323] tells "how necessary the army vote was, and was secured"; and Ida Tarbell says: "It was declared that Lincoln had been guilty of all the abuses of a military dictatorship." R. M. Stribling's *From Gettysburg to Appomattox* gives undeniable proof of Lincoln's conspiracy with his generals to secure his reelection; and [Josiah G.] Holland's *Lincoln*[324] says that

> "when Lincoln killed, by pocketing it, a bill for the reconstruction of

the Union which Congress had just passed, Ben [F.] Wade, Winter Davis, and [Horace] Greeley published in Greeley's *Tribune* (August 6) a bitter manifesto, 'charging the President, by preventing this bill from becoming a law, with purposely holding the electoral votes of the rebel States at the discretion of his personal ambition.'"

And Usher tells how "pretended representatives from Virginia, West Virginia, and Louisiana were seated in Congress;" and (August, 1864) Schouler says:

> "An address to the people by the opposition in Congress accused Lincoln of the creation of bogus States."

[Union] General [John C.] Frémont, the preceding nominee of Lincoln's [Left-wing] party for the presidency, charged Lincoln with "incapacity, selfishness, disregard of personal rights, and liberty of the press;" also "with feebleness, want of principle, and managing the war for personal ends."

[James F.] Rhodes's *History of the Civil War* says:

> "Senator Wilson (Massachusetts) opposed Lincoln for reelection; and the official vote showed McClellan fell short of Lincoln's vote by only 20%, notwithstanding the unconstitutional and treasonable methods pursued by the administration."

The New York *World* (June 19, 1864) called Lincoln "an ignorant, boorish, third-rate, backwoods lawyer," and reported that the spokesman of a delegation of a great religious organization, sent to carry resolutions to the President "publicly denounced him as disgracefully unfit for the high office."

Rhodes's *History* states:

> "R. Fuller, a prominent Baptist preacher, wrote [Salmon P.] Chase: 'I marked the President closely. . . . He is wholly inaccessible to Christian appeals, and his egotism will ever prevent his comprehending what patriotism means."

And [Ward Hill] Lamon, his law partner, says:

> "Whenever he went to church at all, he went to mock and came away to mimic."

Gamaliel Bradford, in last September *Harper's*, states:

> "Thousands of pages have been written about Lincoln's religion; he still smiles, and remains impenetrable. Yet it is curious that, after all, the practical,

everyday, unmystical wife [Mary Todd Lincoln] should have given us, perhaps, what is the very best summary on this point: 'Mr. Lincoln had no faith and no hope, in the usual acceptation of those words. He never joined a Church; but still, as I believe, he was a religious man by nature. . . . But it was a kind of poetry in his nature; and he never was a technical Christian.'"

[George] Lunt, of Boston, in *The Origin of the Late War*,[325] says:

> "The new President was a person of scarcely more than ordinary natural powers, with mind neither cultivated by education nor enlarged by experience in public affairs. He was thus incapable of any wide range of thought, or, in fact, of obtaining any broad grasp of general ideas. His thoughts ran in narrow channels. He was of inferior purpose," etc.

In his Gettysburg speech, Lincoln quoted from [Daniel] Webster, of whose speeches he was a close student, when he said: "Government of the people, for the people, by the people."

[Union] General Donn Piatt ("Reminiscences of Lincoln")[326] denies the claim that Lincoln was of a kind or forgiving nature or of any gentle impulses; and that his insensibility to the ills of his fellow citizens and soldiers was extraordinary when the miseries of the war were at their worst; and, again, he is called the "Great Emancipator" in face of the letter he wrote Greeley saying: *"If I could save the Union without freeing any slaves, I would do it"* [my emphasis, L.S.].

Holland's "Lincoln" says, as to the indecency of Lincoln's jokes and stories:

> "It is useless for Lincoln's biographers to ignore this habit; the whole West (he is writing in 1866), if not the whole country, is full of the stories; and there is no doubt at all that he indulged in them with the same freedom that he did those of a less objectionable character."

And again:

> "Men who knew him throughout his professional and political life have said he was the foulest in his jokes and stories of any man in the country."

Lincoln's success was not won by the North, for a large part of its people were against Lincoln's policy of coercion. So, seeing voluntary enlistments ceasing, and the draft unpopular, by offering large bounties and other inducements, Lincoln secured recruits, as follows: 176,800 Germans, 144,200 Irish, 99,000 English and British-Americans, 74,000 other foreigners, 186,017 negroes, and from the border States 344,190, making a grand total of 1,151,660 men.

It is readily seen that without this great addition to Lincoln's Northern army he would have been "in bad," for, as it was, the North was almost on the point of "quitting" several times. If, for instance, [Confederate] General Lee had won an overwhelming victory at Gettysburg, as was certain had his orders to subordinates been promptly obeyed, peace soon would have followed, and the Confederacy established. Therefore, had Lincoln depended on Northern volunteers to extricate himself from the desperate toils in which he was involved by *his own willful and criminal war policy* [my emphasis, L.S.], he would surely have lost out; for, in 1864, there was great reaction against him.

In view of the foregoing arraignment of Lincoln, based on irrefragable proof, why do not present-day eulogists read reliable history, even the histories of those who knew him and were capable of judging of his real character? By so doing they would know the man and readily perceive the great difference between the real Lincoln and the myth they have created.

It must be remembered, however, that the [then Left-wing] Black Republican Party [that is, then Left-wing Republicans who advocated for black legislation] did not want the "real" Lincoln, the "ignorant, boorish, backwoods, third-rate lawyer;" and they conspired to have a myth before which they could bow the supple knee and worship; and so, with pen and ink in the hands of many subtle, scheming, and unscrupulous politicians, and others, the present [mythological] Lincoln was brought forth and placed in a Grecian shrine on the banks of the Potomac.

Can any sensible, sane man be found who would venture the assertion that a man of high ideals would approve of John Brown's career in "bleeding Kansas" and at Harper's Ferry? Lincoln did, and denounced, too, [then Conservative Democrat] Senator [Stephen A.] Douglas's resolution for the proper punishment of such interstate murderers as Brown and his gang.

Again: Would a man of high and Christian ideals allow the vile [anti-South, Hinton Rowan] Helper book (100,000 copies) [*Compendium of the Impending Crisis of the South*][327] to be used as free campaign literature to secure his election; and Lincoln was never known to repudiate it.

Again: Would a man of high ideals, in Lincoln's position, have secretly waged war of his own volition (as now proved by War and Navy Departments in the D.C., when the Constitution, which he had only a few days before sworn to support, required of him as his official duty to consult Congress and get authority as to what to do in the premises?

But Lincoln did not want Congress to know his secret moves for war. He was afraid it would not sanction them; his intention being, first, to commit the government to his war policy, hoping and expecting it would then not oppose it; and we know [William H.] Seward said that *"Lincoln had a political cunning that was genius"* [my emphasis, L.S.].

In an article in the *Confederate Veteran*, October, 1924 Dr. Scrugham, said:

> "These being the facts in the case, it can readily be seen how incorrect it is to jump to the conclusion that Lincoln saved the Union, what Lincoln saved was the [then] Republican Party. Very clearly the road to power is the road Lincoln took in calling for troops. To this day the Republicans are in power, still in Federal office as a result of Lincoln's course," etc. [Important note: The Republicans in Lincoln's day were the Liberals; the Republicans in 1924 were Conservatives. L.S.]328

Dr. Scrugham says further:

> "The United Daughters of the Confederacy have rendered a signal service to the perpetuation of government based on the consent of the governed by keeping alive the memory of the bravery of those who died that such a government might not perish from the Southern States. Their work will not be completed till they have convinced the world, after the manner of the Athenian Greeks, that the Greek memorial to Lincoln in Washington, D. C., is dedicated to the wrong man."

Amen.

Finally, let it not be forgotten, that this principle of government by consent of the people was the rock on which our fathers of 1776 built the "new and more perfect" Union of States; and, later, was the fundamental principle of the Union of the Southern Confederacy; and, still later, was reasserted in the World War [I] as the principle of "Self-Determination" with universal application and approval North, South, East and West; being the complete antithesis of Lincoln's unconstitutional war-cry: "Save the Union!"329 — CORNELIUS B. HITE, WASHINGTON, D.C.

CHAPTER 21

THE 1865 KKK & THE 1915 KKK ARE TWO DIFFERENT ENTITIES

☛ . . . To the Editor of the *Baltimore Sun*—Sir: Your dispatch from New York quotes Dr. Edwin Mims, professor of English at Vanderbilt University, as saying before the Southern Society:

> "There is a South that boasts of its original contribution to the nation in the organization of the Ku Klux Klan, and there is a South that believes that the Klan is un-American and un-Christian."

So dissimilar was the Reconstruction Ku Klux Klan (founded in 1865) with the modern KKK (founded in 1915) that these 1867 KKK members from Alabama would not recognize the latter version.

Now one may scarcely conceive of an assertion which is more historically unsound and presently misleading. Dr. Mims talks of two wholly different things belonging to different periods as if they were one and the same thing! [my emphasis, L.S.].

The [original 1865] Ku Klux Klan, [a Conservative, pro-Constitution organization] which rescued the South from the destructive forces of "reconstruction" misrule, is not to be thought of as in any way connected with the recently organized [1915] society which has assumed the nomenclature [as well as the clothing, signs, and symbols] of the erstwhile protector of political institutions. The old [original 1865 KKK] organization preserved for the good of the Federal republic what political scavengers were about to seize and destroy. The new [1915 KKK] organization appears to appeal chiefly to religious prejudices; and, in reaching for political power, it has expanded more successfully in the North than in the South.

Is it possible that Dr. Mims does not know these facts? Or was he careless in his phraseology in an effort to turn a striking antithesis or some other figure of speech? . . .[330] — HISTORIAN MATTHEW PAGE ANDREWS, 1927

OUR CONFEDERATE VETERANS

☞ ... These—'tis only a remnant now—are the gray-clad soldiers who came back foot sore, penniless, and weary to devastated homes, wasted fields, and facing an ignoble reconstruction. Through the years they have brought system and order out of chaos; their wisdom and guiding hand reestablished the South, and we rejoice that so many have lived to see the result of their efforts in a grander, greater, and more glorious Southland.

Theirs was a fight against the greatest odds ever faced by any people. Theirs the greatest determination that ever went forth to battle. Theirs the bravest hearts that ever fought for country, homes, and principles of right; and, when overcome by greater numbers and exhausted resources, they accepted the irony of fate and came home to begin a new life under entirely new conditions. And the South of to-day is their everlasting monument.[331] — MRS. VALLIE H. PERRY, HISTORIAN TAMPA FLORIDA CHAPTER, U.D.C., 1927

JEFFERSON DAVIS DURING RECONSTRUCTION

☞ ... After two years in prison, Mr. Davis was released [from prison] on bail. Amid the rejoicings of his people, white and black, he walked forth a free man. Of the first hour of this freedom his pastor [Rev. Charles Minnegerode, head of Saint Paul's Episcopal Church, Richmond, VA] tells us:

> "But Mr. Davis turned to me: 'Mr. Minnegerode, you who have been with me in my sufferings, and comforted and strengthened me with your prayers, is it not right that we should now once more kneel down together and return thanks?' There was not a dry eye in the room. [His wife] Mrs. [Varina Howell] Davis led the way into the adjoining room, more private; and there, in deep-felt prayer and thanksgiving, closed Jefferson Davis's prison life."

Mr. Davis had hoped, he once said, that the concentration of hate upon him would relieve the South somewhat. But with the progress of radical [that is, socialist and communist] reconstruction he began to fear the worst. From Montreal, [Canada], where he was living after his release from prison, he wrote to a friend in Richmond:

> "My trust in earthly powers is lost; but my sorrow is not without hope, for God is just and omnipotent. His ways are inscrutable, and history is full of examples of the greatest good being conferred upon a people by events which seemed to be unmitigated evil. Nations are not immortal, and their wickedness will surely be punished in this

world."³³² — DR. W. L. FLEMING, HEAD OF THE DEPARTMENT OF HISTORY, LOUISIANA STATE UNIVERSITY

WHY THE SOUTH RISKED ALL

☛ I have been living out here in Long Beach, a city of about one hundred and fifty thousand population, on the extreme western border of Southern California, for about ten years. I was born in Liberty, Clay County, Mo., in 1843, and am now eighty-four years of age, up and a-going, well and hearty; but I realize that I am old and will soon pass away.

I was a bit of a lad when the War between the States broke out, but I soon enlisted in the Confederate service, in Gen. Sterling Price's army, Shelby's Brigade, Shanks's Regiment, Company B, and served until the close of the war, surrendering at Shreveport, La., in June, 1865.

I am writing this communication to the *Confederate Veteran* because it may be the last opportunity that I shall ever have to express my love and admiration to the few remaining gallant and brave soldiers who wore the Confederate gray and fought during that bloody war. I wish also to be remembered by all the people of the South. I am proud of you and love you with all my heart.

I hardly know yet whether I have ever been fully reconstructed or not. I do not believe I have, when I come to think of how hard we tried to keep out of war with the North, to be let alone and to attend to our own affairs; but it was forced upon us. We had to defend our homes, our property, our rights, and the women and children of the South. The Yankee armies, with their millions of blue coats, overran the South, killed, burned, and destroyed everything of value they could find. We had to fight, and I have no apologies to make. I believed we were right in what we did, and I would do the same thing again under the same circumstances. The Confederate soldier is as loyal to this nation as any Northern soldier. That has been proved by the late wars. We worked and made our own living, and we never drew a cent of pension from the government either. A great wrong was done the South during Reconstruction days, and she feels it yet.

For seven years after the war, before I was allowed to cast a vote for anything, although I was qualified by age and citizenship, the registrar held that I was disloyal, and I was denied the right in all those many years just because I was a Confederate soldier....³³³

— W. J. COURTNEY, LONG BEACH, CALIF., 1927

PERVERSION OF THE SOUTH'S GOVERNMENT
☞ . . . The greatest blow the South suffered from the results of the war, from an economic standpoint, was not the destruction of her vast wealth, but the destruction of her strong men and the demoralization of business due to the perversion of her government as a factor in production, under the "Reconstruction" period.[334] — G. W. DYER, PH.D., NASHVILLE, TENN.

HOW WOMEN HELPED SAVE THE PROSTRATE SOUTH
☞ . . . When surrender was forced upon the South, it accepted in all good faith "the terms of surrender" agreed upon only to find their sought-for paths of peace were to lead through a Gethsemane of Reconstruction which was the cause and means that created the "Solid South." Might had enthroned a conquering political party at Washington [the then Left-wing Republican Party], which, to legalize its former acts of usurpation, ordered the Thirteenth and Fourteenth Amendments to be added to the Constitution of 1787, to which all conquered States were compelled to subscribe in order to exercise their statehood, so that the citizens of a State, by the vote of its citizens, should be governed by the citizens of that State, and the military control and carpet-bagger government of them be forever done away with.

. . . In 1865, when the South's disfranchised soldier citizens returned to their devastated homes in a sorely stricken land, they began to build upon the ashes of the old a South which has grown to be, as our government industrialists of to-day declare, the greatest of all American assets.

In the rebuilding of the South, its women took an active and glorious part and realized through it their broader service for Dixie. Into their rebuilt households these daughters of the South carried their Holy of Holies to again set up their family altars, whereon they placed with the open Bible, the Constitution of the country, with the thrilling story of the South's prestige and glory and their family traditions. . . .[335] — MRS. TOWNES RANDOLPH LEIGH, GAINESVILLE, FLA.

WADE HAMPTON & RECONSTRUCTION TIMES
☞ . . . [After the fall of Richmond] the Carolinians, who had fought so bravely for their country, returned now to their homes to find many of them burned and themselves in utter poverty. Mrs. [Mary] Chesnut, of South Carolina, tells in her "Diary" of their return to their plantation near Columbia, and, finding that among all the white people of the party, none had enough money to pay a

ferryman his fare, her negro maid put her hand in her pocket and brought out a sufficient amount to get them home.

After the third and last Confederate governor had been led from his office to a Federal prison, the country which had for so long borne the honorable name of the Commonwealth of South Carolina was called Military District No. 2 (which you know was also done in Virginia). Negroes were put into Federal [U.S.] uniforms and given entire charge of the affairs of the unfortunate State. It cannot be denied that there existed a feeling of deep enmity against the State [by the then Liberal Republicans] in Washington [D.C.] and that nothing was left undone there which would try to the utmost the patience and endurance of the people.

Every negro was given the right to vote, but this was denied to all white men who had in any way aided the Confederacy, which, of course, meant all the decent men of the State. This time, from 1868 to 1874, came to be known as the "Time of the Robbers." All power was in the hands of the Negroes and a few white men who had flocked to the State to enjoy the loot, which was to be found in abundance on all sides. The Federal [U.S.] judges were the most venal creatures possible, and no justice was to be had from any of them if the complainant was a native South Carolinian. If a negro stole from a white man, the latter invariably found, to his astonishment, that if the case came before the court, it was he who always received the punishment.

The political campaign of 1875-76 was probably the most exciting one that this or any other country ever went through; and it was a red-hot one in South Carolina, where the native born population was determined, cost what it would, to overthrow the carpetbag and negro government and to rid themselves of a tyranny that was no longer bearable. None but a desperate people would ever have thought it could be done, because the negroes greatly outnumbered the whites, and also because it was necessary to avoid any conflict with the United States government, which was *behind the negroes*. Gen. Wade Hampton, Gen. M. C. Butler, and Capt. Frank Dawson (editor of the *Charleston News and Courier*) were the leaders of that forlorn hope.

Rifle clubs were formed all over the State. The members of these were called by the carpet-baggers "Red Shirts," because, for economical reasons, they wore red shirts in place of more expensive uniforms. The carpet-baggers tried to give the national government the idea that these clubs were composed of bandits, when the truth was they were made up of veterans of the war and of young men who had grown up in the interval, and who came from the best families of the State. Where ever there was a political meeting, there "Red Shirts" would appear and insist on a division of time with the [then Left-wing] Republican orators.

I seem to have neglected to say that his was when [then Conservative Democrat] General Hampton was running for governor against a [then Liberal] Republican candidate. His friends had asked him to become the [then Conservative] Democratic candidate, and he consented. He went through the State and spoke to great crowds of people in every county. Companies of "Red Shirts" rode with him wherever he went. The negroes, who were much afraid of their former masters, as soon as these appeared, would slip away, but they voted the [then Left-wing] Republican ticket just the same, all except our Daddy Ned. You will pardon me, I am sure, if I tell you about him for just one minute. Daddy Ned was a "colored gentleman" of the best type. He grew up on my grandmother's plantation with my uncles; and when this crisis came, he said the ticket which suited his white people was good enough for him, and, *in spite of threats against his life* [by Left-wing Republicans] he went to the polls and voted the [then Conservative] Democratic ticket every time, and nobody dared molest him. He was very handy with a gun, Daddy Ned was, and a fine shot, and they were afraid of him. I am glad to pay this little tribute to a faithful friend and servant even at this late day.

[Confederate] Col. James Morgan, in his *Recollections of a Rebel Reefer*,[336] gives a fuller account of the condition of affairs in South Carolina than anyone else I know; and he says this:

"The story of the Reconstruction period in South Carolina has never been told in print, except in the files of the *News and Courier*, and now that nearly all of those who passed through that nightmare are dead, I fear that the present generation will never realize its horrors. But, believe me, South Carolina was the nearest approach to hell on earth, during the orgy of the carpet-baggers and negroes, that ever a refined people was subjected to.

"An imported negro sat on the Supreme Bench, his colleagues being carpet-baggers. A native-born South Carolinian who associated himself with these people was called a scalawag—Governor [Franklin J.] Moses [Jr.] was one of them. He fought bravely through the war for the South, married a woman of a respectable family, and then joined these creatures in robbing his native State. When he was governor the helpless whites were compelled to submit to outrages by the presence of United States troops, who were there to see that we did not run amuck among the carpet-baggers and scalawags. While these thieves lived in luxury, their lives must have been mentally very uncomfortable, for they well knew that if the [U.S.] troops should be removed for a moment their lives would pay the penalty of their outrages. But the swag was so rich that not even fear for their lives could induce them to let go, even after they had accumulated riches beyond their most extravagant dreams. Their only safeguard was the [U.S.] soldiers, the regular officers having such contempt for them that they would hold no social intercourse with them, and *the [U.S.] privates hated the negroes with a bitter hatred, and took no pains to disguise their feelings* [my emphasis, L.S.].

"White carpetbaggers seemed to have so much money that they did not know what to do with it. I have seen one of them walk into a drinking saloon by himself, and ostentatiously order a quart bottle of champagne, take one glass of it, and carelessly throw a ten-dollar bill on the counter and tell the barkeeper to keep the change; and this in a community where people, bred in affluence, were suffering for the very necessities.

"The salary of the comptroller was eighteen hundred dollars a year. Dr. Nagle, who held the office, had arrived in Columbia literally in rags. In the first year of his incumbency—out of his salary, of course—he bought a fine house and a carriage and horses, with gold-mounted harness among other things, and, incidentally, built a bridge across the Congaree River that must have cost thousands of dollars."

The [Left-wing] authorities in Washington were asked, of course, to lend their aid against Hampton and his [then Conservative Democratic] party, but they quickly realized that the people of the State were absolutely determined not to submit any longer to the rule of the carpet-baggers and negroes. As one of the South Carolinians expressed it, the people were grimly certain that the persecutors should go: in carriages if they would, or in hearses if they must. The Federal [U.S.] authorities, therefore, began to see that to enforce their rule would only mean the death of many an innocent negro, so Hampton was allowed to be inaugurated governor without interference.

From that time on the white people of the State have managed the affairs of the commonwealth to suit themselves, and thus, quite literally, Hampton, being the right man in the right place, became the leader of his people.[337] — MRS. JULIA PORCHER WICKHAM, GOOCHLAND VA. CHAPTER, U.D.C.

DEBUNKING THE MYTHS IN *UNCLE TOM'S CABIN*

☞ . . . My ancestors came to this country through Virginia and North Carolina before the [American] Revolution, and all were slave owners. My childhood and early youth was on a large Southern plantation, and I have most clear and accurate recollection of such plantations, not only of my own parents' and grandparents', but of a large planting community in which not less than a thousand negroes were owned on ten plantations varying in size from one thousand to three thousand acres. *If there ever was such a character as the Simon Legree, of Mrs. [Harriet Beecher] Stowe's [highly fictitious anti-South novel] Uncle Tom's Cabin, I never heard of one* [my emphasis, L.S.]. Then the overseers of Southern plantations, like the farmer of a New England home, was employed for his knowledge of cultivation and was under control of the owner. That there were no cruel owners I am not prepared to assert, but I never learned of one in my acquaintance with portions of four States—Tennessee, Mississippi, Alabama, and Georgia. At my former home, nearly half a century ago, I heard an intelligent negro man denounce as absurd the statements of abolitionists about cruel treatment of negroes, saying that common sense would make any owner know that his own interests required that the negro be kept in good condition for work. *Very many of the large slave owners were in favor of freeing their slaves when it could be done with justice to them through gradual emancipation* [my emphasis L.S.]. A planter who owned two hundred or more could not count on more than one hundred workers in the field, but all must be supplied with housing, clothing, food, [health and medical care,] and fuel, so that the total expense was more than would be required as wages for those engaged in productive labor.

The negro, being a more deliberate worker than a white man, none did so heavy a day's work as a white laborer of the North and West, and on most of the large plantations all work stopped from Saturday noon till Monday morning, except feeding the stock and milking the cows. During the afternoon of Saturday, the women washed the clothes of their families, the younger men went fishing or hunting (their master's boys often going with them), and many of the older men occupied themselves in working their own "patches" of land allowed to such of them as would cultivate cotton for themselves, and the annual Christmas shipment of cotton contained many bales of it owned by those industrious negroes [my emphasis, L.S.].

I can testify that all of the old slaves known to me were care-free, good-natured, and happy people. I never knew one that could not sing, and in their work about the house, in the quarters, or in the fields their songs were always heard. Their day's work over, and everything provided for them, they were free from cares about the future. The owners of plantations in our community gave first, second, and third liberal cash prizes for the best cotton pickers at Christmas, and alternated in having a big barbecue and dance on one of the plantations at the time of "laying by the crop," that being after the last working and while waiting for the cotton bolls to open. *I have been present when not less than a thousand were so gathered for a day and night of jollity and frolic* [my emphasis, L.S.].

Pride of family prevailed among those negroes as if they were of blood kin, and their owners cared for them as for children in sickness. There could be no better proof of the loyalty and friendliness of the slaves of the South for their owners than their actions during the war. When all of the white men (including overseers) from middle age to boys of fifteen years were in the army, the women and young children were left on the plantations dependent on their negroes to work the fields and care for them. Their faithful devotion was never forgotten by those of us who lived through those years. A Southern writer has said of them:

> "Faithful and trustworthy slaves, God and history know how well you, and all your color, kept the faith reposed in you during all those years of carnage and death. Whether masters returned or whether they died in distant prisons or were killed in battle, there is not recorded against you any wrong or evil toward your white mistress or her children and property left, in thousands of instances, solely in your care and under your protection."

Could there be better proof of the natural good qualities of the negroes of the South, uninfluenced by [Left-wing] white men of the baser sort in later years? That faithfulness continued after the close of the war until the carpet-baggers and [Left-wing] emissaries of abolitionists [mainly socialists and communists], in the years of the "reconstruction period," began their false teachings and falser promises, *using the uninformed, newly-freed negroes as instruments for their own gain* [my emphasis, L.S.]. This brought about conditions that caused the [Conservative, pro-Constitution, pro-law] organization of the Ku-Klux Klan for self-protection. That organization exerted its

Left-wing illustrator Thomas Nast titled this wood engraved Reconstruction cartoon from 1872: "The man with the (carpet) bags." It shows Prussian-born Union general and radical Socialist newspaper editor Carl Schurz (a member of the then Left-wing Republican Party) carrying a carpet bag marked with the words "C. Schurz, carpet-bagger South, from Wisconsin to Missouri."

influence on the freedmen through its mysterious and apparently supernatural character, causing them to stay in their homes at night and keeping the disaffected [that is, communized] ones from being used as instruments in further promotion of trouble by their infamous carpet-bag masters. The members of the K.K.K. knew the risk they ran if made known, with Congress then controlled as it was [by South-hating socialists and communists], but the situation in the South was desperate beyond endurance. *They avoided doing harm to the negroes* [my emphasis, L.S.], but soon convinced the white robber horde that had invaded the South for plunder that they had better get away. The relief of the South was due, in large measure, to the Ku-Klux Klan, and the former robber gang who had been forced to leave *devoted themselves largely to vicious misrepresentations about conditions in the South, which seem yet to influence the feelings toward us of uninformed people who are biased provincials* [my emphasis, L.S.].

Great changes in the negro population of the South have been made by their education in our schools, and they now are able to think and act on their own judgment or on the advice of those they know they can trust. We have been glad to get rid of some of those who have gone North, and many of a better sort who tried the experiment of such change have returned to remain among people they know.

With opportunity to make a living according to his ability, and equal rights under the law, no sensible negro wants social equality or any blood mixture of races, as may be learned by inquiry of any intelligent one of pure blood of the race.

We can assure our Northern friends that Southerners are not only friendly to the Southern negro, but that we appreciate the fact that fear of competition with negro labor has caused a vast number of undesirable immigrants from Southern Europe to prefer other sections of our country and avoid the South, and we are thankful for having the better class of negroes with us.[338] — CAPTAIN W. W. CARNES, BRADENTON, FLA., 1929

THE DAWN OF THE RECONSTRUCTION ERA

☛ . . . Numbers of our proudest, bravest, and best of men had been shot down and buried in unmarked graves. Sadness, mourning, and despair covered the land, for all over the Southern country was heard a cry like Rachel weeping for her children. Our property was gone; our liberties were gone; and the fair fabric of our institutions, which were heroically maintained, had fallen and were gone. Under the reconstruction era you all know how we were robbed, plundered, and oppressed, when men who had not known our soil came and planted their feet in our midst and set up their unrighteous claim to govern us. Our dear old mother State lay prostrate, weeping, bleeding—almost dying. But, thank God, since that time vast changes have taken place, and the minions of reconstruction days have been obliged . . . to fold their tents and steal away in the darkness of the night.[339] — CONFEDERATE VETERAN W. JASPER TALBERT, SOUTH CAROLINA, 1930

FROM A LETTER TO MASSACHUSETTS SENATOR & SOUTH-HATER CHARLES SUMNER

☛ My dear Sir: . . . Gradually was formed that party [the then Left-Wing Republican Party] of which [Yankee socialist] Wendell Phillips said: *"It is the first sectional party ever organized in this country. It is a party of the North [that is, Liberals] pledged against the South [that is, Conservatives]"* [my emphasis, L.S.]. These men adopted the "Higher Law,"[340] . . . ignoring their own laws and God's laws, for they were "a law unto themselves," and claimed the right of compelling everyone else to adopt their theory.

Did not [William H.] Seward tell the South, "Free your negroes at our dictation, or you shall have bullets instead of ballots, cannons and bayonets instead of words?" Are you, Sir, free from guilt in this matter? When you with others had thoroughly alarmed the South for the safety of their rights in the Union, when you had exasperated their passions to the highest degree—they saw no resource but to withdraw. Did they wish to go?

You heard, but ignored, the earnest and patriotic appeals from Southern men in Congress. You would give them no assurance that their rights under the bond would be respected by the incoming powers [the Lincoln administration]. You scorned and frustrated every effort made to prevent disruption! A Southern divine said in a sermon,

> "If I have to leave the Union, I shall go with a bleeding heart. I love the Union as our Fathers made it. I want no better government than that of the Constitution, but if we can not have that, let us exercise our right to withdraw and form such a government as we need."

The Southern people asked only for their rights—these were denied them. Were they "kicked out of the Union," as a member of Congress asserted when discussing reconstruction measures? Were the people of the seceding States "Rebels"? They broke no law. They only did what Massachusetts and other Northern States have always claimed as a right for themselves, a right which

Abraham Lincoln said in Congress in 1845 "could not be taken from the States"![341]

Did any of the original States delegate power to the Federal government to coerce itself? [Left-wing statesman] Alexander Hamilton said in the Convention that

> "an attempt to coerce a State for any supposed delinquency would be the maddest project ever devised. No State would allow itself to be so used, nor would any State allow its territory to be crossed for such a purpose."

If the Federal government really possessed the right to coerce a withdrawing State or States, why resort to a trick to induce a collision? Did not Seward admit to Mr. [Charles Francis] Adams [Sr.], *"We have contrived to throw the onus of beginning the war upon the South!"* [my emphasis, L.S.]. Can you find a parallel to this act in all history? Look at it — men calling themselves statesmen, men who had taken a solemn oath to support the Constitution, now resorting to trickery and deceit to bring on a civil war, a war which according to your own words in 1856 would be "a parricidal, a fratricidal war, with a wickedness beyond the wickedness of any war in human annals." Can words excuse the turpitude of such crimes? So-called statesmen, deliberately destroying that which the Fathers reared, would be philanthropists thirsting for blood! "Good! good! If blood comes (of this war of words), let it come; it can not come too soon," says a member of Congress from New Hampshire. And blood you had, the blood of your slaughtered brethren! Can you count the number? Do you know how many perished, through terror, exposure and want?

People ignorant of facts cannot conceive of the outrages and wrongs inflicted on the Southern people by Federal soldiers during the war, and by Federal officials since [my emphasis, L.S.].

A gentleman living in northwestern Georgia writes in the fall of 1865:

> "We are the carcass, they, the Federal [U.S.] officials, are the vultures, picking our denuded bones. The little that was left us after the war, they seized, and only release it after paying a heavy bonus into private pockets. I have even known them to steal by night from the pittance of damaged corn sent down by the [U.S.] government for distribution among our starving poor. They get richer and richer, and another horde of vampires takes their place. Not content with despoiling us, they annual our contracts, and take the laborers off under pretense of higher wages and under the patronage of a bureau [the radical Left-wing Freedmen's Bureau] whose promises are as rotten as the

promises of Pharaoh. While mourning the loss of thousands of the noblest of our race, while suffering the poverty and desolation with which our conquerors have visited us, while memory stings with the rape, the arson, which barbarians under arms enforced and heartless officers permitted, it is not inhuman nature not to feel resentment against those who would still play the tyrant and grind us in the dust."

At a picnic given in Ohio to the soldiers after the war, [Union] General [William T.] Sherman is reported as saying to them that he did not wish them to feel badly on account of anything they had done to the Southern people for they [Southerners], by their act of secession, had forfeited all right to anything, even their lives.

"All they have belongs to the Federal government, and I, as the government agent, gave you permission to take whatever the quartermaster did not need."

Facts, many of them in their nature so barbarous as to be incredible, confirm the sentiment uttered by Sherman, and lead all, who know those facts, to infer that the object and determination of the Federal soldiers, backed, of course, by the Federal [U.S.] government, was, while in the South,

"to destroy, to kill, to cause to perish all, both old and young, little children and women, and to take the spoil of them for prey."

Witness the wanton destruction of private property by the cavalry, their approach being heralded for miles by the light of burning buildings! Witness the fiend-like operations of [Union General Philip H.] Sheridan causing a desolation so complete that a crow, he boasted, in flying over the region invaded, would need to carry its own rations. Think of the wanton and persistent destruction of salt!

Listen to the spirited reply of a lady seventy years old to Sherman's men, who, after filling twenty-six army wagons with plunder, ordered her, with her weeping daughter and children out of the house that they might burn it: "If you burn this house, you burn me in it." This lady with all her family were Unionists, Unionists on the basis of the laws which made the Union.

These are but a few of thousands of similar outrages inflicted in the name of Union and Liberty. We slaughter our fellow men. We inflict inexpressible miseries upon the living, we break God's laws, we break almost every law which made the Union, to save it! Wonderful reasoning—worthy your Higher Law theory!

Can you save the life of anything by destroying that which

constitutes its life? The life of the Union was the Constitution, our decalogue. These laws you and your associates have broken both in letter and spirit. The government as our Fathers have made it, you have sought to change. Are you not therefore Rebels and Traitors? Will not those two terrible words adhere to you, and justly too, through all coming time? . . .[342] — MISS ELEANOR CLARK NOYES, CIRCA MID 1860S

THE SOUTHERN SOLDIER

☞ . . . I desire to pay tribute to . . . that group of boys who survived the battles and hardships of the war only to encounter the horrors of reconstruction.

You may recall the cadets of New Market—they were mere boys in the Virginia Military Academy who tossed aside their books to battle for the Confederacy. Their stand at New Market was a noble one—many died on the field—but others lived to build anew the stricken but undefeated South. These young men who survived the war led a life which should be a lesson to us to-day.

The young men and women who lived in the South after 1865 were tragic figures. They were the lost generation of the South, who led hard, bare, and bitter lives, when young people of the South before and since were at play and in school.

That Tragic Era from 1865 to 1880 was a period when the Southern people were put to torture so much so that our historians have shrunk from the unhappy task of telling us the truth. That was a black and bloody period—when brutality and despotism prevailed—a period to which no American can point with pride.

To the generation of Southerners who struggled in the years after the war in the sixties we owe the redemption of the South and the preservation of its society.

We shuddered at the destruction of France in the last war [World War I]; we shrank back when we contemplated the economic collapse of Europe. But recall what faced the young Southern women and the young Confederate soldier after the War between the States—theirs was the task to rebuild a new civilization upon a country laid waste by war, a country whose social order had been destroyed and whose economic structure had been swept away.

The Southern soldier was unable to comprehend his military reverses; we of to-day are unable to comprehend how the South lasted as long as it did. But equally marvelous was the quick rebuilding of the South.

I do not recall the horrors of reconstruction in order to revive bitter memories or to stir up sectional prejudices. To recall the past for such purposes would be harmful. The task before us is the future of the South. Therefore, one is justified in recalling the past so as to prepare for the future and to learn lessons from our own national history.

The War and Reconstruction obviously changed the course of our national history and made marked changes in our national state of mind.

Those two events cost the South heavily—but they also cost the nation. The South paid for theirs in an economic collapse and carpet-bag domination extending over a period of nearly thirty years. *But the nation also paid its price—it lost the powerful influence of the conservative Southern tradition. In ante-bellum times the South had steadied the nation's western expansion by its conservatism* [my emphasis, L.S.], *but when the South was broken and destroyed, we saw a period of western expansion, of European immigration, of speculation, of graft, and of greed—unknown before in the annals of our history. . . .*

Contrary to the Left's fake history, thanks to their beneficent, Christian, white Southern owners, before Reconstruction nearly all Southern black servants lived lives relatively free from care. Their sudden emancipation during Reconstruction threw them into a life of serious responsibilities, one they were completely unprepared for. Naturally, the outcome was disastrous for all concerned, with long-lasting effects that ripple into the present day.

But what are the lessons of reconstruction and of the War between the States?

. . . The eternal national values are then those intangible contributions to national life such as the old South gave—not wealth, not progress, but those great qualities of tradition and conservatism and individuality which neither depression nor hard times can destroy. . . .[343] — DR. JULIAN S. WATERMAN, DEAN OF LAW SCHOOL, UNIVERSITY OF ARKANSAS, CIRCA 1931

Thomas Nast entitled this 1868 wood engraving: "This is a white man's government." A typical far Left piece of misleading political propaganda, it shows Confederate General Nathan Bedford Forrest (center) holding a knife with the words "The Lost Cause" on it; an Irishman (left) holding a club with the words "A vote" on it; and a capitalist (right) holding a wallet with the words "capital for votes" on it. All have one foot on the back of a black U.S. soldier pinned to the ground. In the background African-American schools have been set ablaze and black children have been lynched. Full of disinformation and ridiculous fabrications, the major lie of this absurd gaslighting portrayal is obvious: White supremacy in the South was primarily a reaction to the black supremacy policies of Reconstruction, which was created by Radical racist, Liberal, Socialist and Communist politicians—most who were card-carrying members of the then Left-wing Republican Party. As for Forrest, during the War he enlisted 45 black men in his cavalry, seven who he chose to be his personal armed guards. After the War Forrest said of his African-American soldiers: "These boys stayed with me, drove my teams, and better Confederates did not live." In 1875, during a speech before an all-black civil rights group, Forrest declared to his audience: "I am your friend … I assure you that everyman who was in the Confederate army is your friend. We were born in the same soil, breathe the same air, live in the same land, and why should we not be brothers and sisters." So much for Left-wing "Civil War" mythology. (For more on the real Forrest see my book, A Rebel Born.)

CHAPTER 22

SETTING THE RECORD STRAIGHT
☛ ... [By 1860 slavery] became a very unpopular institution for sentimental reasons. The material interests of the North and East became antagonistic. Abolitionists [a Victorian, and modern, euphemism for socialists and communists] aroused much feeling against it. Self-seeking [Left-wing] politicians seized upon it to serve their ends. Jealous of the [Conservative] South's power, they sought to so direct affairs as to overcome the South and control the government, and particularly the offices. This finally led to a revolution against the Constitution by those [Northern Left-wing] agitators, selfish and party interests. This forced the South into a revolution to sustain and uphold the Constitution and laws of the country. We may call that secession.

An unbiased writer recently, looking over events, declares:

> "The Southern States had every legal right to retain slavery and to demand the return of fugitive slaves, and the Constitutional right to secede was incontestable."

I agree with Jay Hamilton. This is the absolute truth. It is unfair and unjust to blame the South for slavery [especially since both the American slave trade *and* American slavery got their start in the North].[344] When independence was declared, slavery was in existence in every State. When the Constitution was adopted in 1789, the institution still existed in every State except Massachusetts. Every State united in its recognition in the Federal compact. Three-fifths of the slaves were counted in the basis of representation in Congress; property in slaves was protected by rigid provisions regarding the rendition of slaves escaping from one State to another.

> "Thus embodied in the Constitution, thus interwoven in the very integrants of our political system, thus sustained by the oath to support the Constitution, executed by every public servant, and by the decisions of the Supreme tribunals, slavery was ratified by the unanimous voice of the nation and was recognized as an American institution and as a vested right by the most solemn pledge and sanction that man can give."

It would be tedious to consider factors in the development and the changes in the institution, *unsupported by any change in the*

Constitution or laws, and this probably states the case in the end:

> "But it was not hatred of the Union or love of slavery that inspired the South, nor love of the negro that inspired the North. Profounder thoughts and interests lay beneath these. The rivalry of cheap negro labor, *aversion to the negro* and to slavery alike, *were the spurs of North action*; that of the South was race integrity. Free white dominion! The question of slavery was one for the States" [my emphasis, L.S.].

It will be remembered that in the original draft of the Declaration of Independence, [Thomas] Jefferson included an indictment of King George [III] for his determination "to keep open a market where men could be bought and sold," and it was "stricken out, because New England was then profitably operating slave ships and practically all the colonies owned slaves.

After the war was over, *after* the South had been subjugated, the Constitution was amended in a way to support the contention of the North *before* it was changed.

Small government Southern Conservative and Founding Father Thomas Jefferson, a vocal proponent of secession, would have heartily approved of the formation of the Southern Confederacy in 1861, but would have been vehemently against the Left's postwar Reconstruction program.

The Thirteenth Amendment, abolishing slavery, was adopted December 18, 1865.

The Fourteenth Amendment, containing Sections 3 and 4, prohibiting, in effect, secession, was adopted July 18, 1868.

The Fifteenth Amendment was adopted March 30, 1870, *after* all the plans and activities in connection with reconstruction had been by force put into effect.

The terms of surrender had been ignored; the South was treated by those in power as conquered provinces; and although they had waged war on the claim that the States could not leave the Union, they proceeded to deny the Southern States the status of States, and to impose on them the rule of Federal bayonets, supporting gross ignorance, incompetency, rascality, carpetbag corruption, and the rankest possible oppression; in fact, all the horrors, atrocities, crimes, and suffering of which human nature is capable [my emphasis, L.S.].

Let the present-day historian speak:

"This, then, was the combination against the peace of a fallen people—the soldiers inciting the blacks against their former masters, the [Freedmen's] Bureau agents preaching political and social equality, the white scum of the North fraternizing with the blacks in their shacks, and the thieves of the Treasury stealing cotton under the protection of Federal [U.S.] bayonets. And in the North, demagogic politicians and fanatics were demanding immediate negro suffrage and clamoring for the blood of Southern leaders. Why was not Jeff Davis hanged, and why was not Lee shot? they said!"

I am tempted to call some names of these South haters, usurpers, and oppressors. A few of them have statues about Washington. They ought not to be there. It is the only way posterity will know of them. Very few of them are in Statuary Hall, if any—the Parthenon of the Great of the United States. But there will be found today Jefferson Davis, James Z. George, Robert E. Lee, E. Kirby Smith, and others of their type.[345]

You will not find [South-hating Yankee socialist] Thad Stevens there—that club-footed Caliban from Pennsylvania, who led in the Radical Republican movement which brought about the conditions mentioned. Three days before the deplorable death of Lincoln, Stevens had denounced the terms of [Union General Ulysses S.] Grant with Lee, said they were too easy, and that he would "dispossess those participating in the rebellion of every foot of ground they pretended to own." Supporting him were such delectable [Left-wing] characters as Ben Wade, Ben Butler, Seward, Charles Sumner, [Edwin M.] Stanton, Grant (note particularly his use of Federal troops in Louisiana, South Carolina, and Florida), [Salmon P.] Chase (who favored negro suffrage) [though not out of love for black people], [socialist Carl] Schurz, Oliver P. Morton, Roscoe Conkling, and Zack Chandler (the last three being Grant's "three musketeers"), Simon Cameron, W. E. Chandler, and Stanley Matthews (who did such dirty work in Florida), supported also by [famed Yankee atheist] Robert G. Ingersoll, James G. Blaine, and [Philip H.] Sheridan.

It is worth while to observe that Jay Cooke and Henry Clews were close to the Grant Administration, and urged that if he and the [then Left-wing] Republican Party prevailed in the national election, it meant the country would continue prosperous and a bright future of increasing prosperity would follow.

This was in 1873.

In 1874 both of these failed, and Grant himself, who had

acquired a desire for wealth, was financially involved in the crash.

Associated with these men were their agents and representatives in the Southern States, like [James W.] Hunnicutt in Virginia, [William W.] Holden in North Carolina, Scott, [Franklin J.] Moses [Jr.], and [John J.] Patterson in South Carolina, [Rufus B.] Bullock in Georgia, [Marcellus L.] Stearns and [Milton S.] Littlefield in Florida, [Adelbert] Ames in Mississippi, Powell Clayton in Arkansas, [Henry C.] Warmouth in Louisiana, Brownlow in Tennessee, [Elisha M.] Pease in Texas, [George] Harrington and [George E.] Spencer in Alabama—all spokesmen and practically all carpet-baggers.

It may be mentioned that *Harper's Weekly*, the Chicago *Tribune*, and the *Union League of Philadelphia* did their best for the Radical [then Left-wing] Republican cause. They were joined by the Grand Army of the Republic [Union army and navy veterans]—even then, in 1868, a political machine.

This disgraceful, outrageous work disgusted the decent people of the North, as well as all portions of the country. Public opinion revolted. This cruel, wicked, atrocious treatment of the South was about to come to an end.

It did when [Zebulon B.] Vance became Governor of North Carolina, [Wade] Hampton of South Carolina, [George F.] Drew of Florida, [Francis T.] Nicholls of Louisiana, followed by other changes in the same direction—in 1876.

The States were free again, and each State began to rule itself—in 1876—after eleven years of humiliating, torturing, harrowing experience.

No country ever suffered as did the South except Poland—just one hundred years ago—and she did not survive.

She has at last risen again! . . .[346] — UNITED STATES SENATOR DUNCAN U. FLETCHER BEFORE THE UNITED DAUGHTERS OF THE CONFEDERACY IN CONVENTION AT JACKSONVILLE, FLA., NOVEMBER 19, 1931

IF WE HAD KNOWN WE WOULD HAVE NEVER SURRENDERED

☛ . . . the greatest work done by [Confederate General Wade] Hampton was during the Reconstruction days in the South. It remained for the brutal Congress of the United States to drive the disarmed Southern people to the verge of a new war by stationing negro troops in the midst of their homes. Hampton was moved to fury, and wrote to President [Andrew] Johnson denouncing

"Your brutal negro troops under their no less brutal and more degraded Yankee officers [by whom] the grossest outrages are committed with impunity."

Hampton said, in effect, to [then U.S. President Ulysses S.] Grant: "If we had known that you were going to back with bayonets the carpet-bagger, the scalawag, and the negro in their infamous acts, we would never have given up our arms!"

At Chester, S.C., negro troops clubbed and bayoneted an old man; at Abbeville, white men were ordered from the sidewalks; in Charleston they forced their way into a house, ordered food, and after eating, felled the mistress of the home. In retaliation for the blow of a white man, entrusted with the guardianship of a young woman, who had been insulted, negro soldiers dragged him to camp, murdered him in cold blood, and danced upon his grave.

Is it any wonder then, that the [then Conservative, non-racial, Pro-Constitution] Ku-Klux Klan began to ride—and no doubt Hampton was riding with them. For eleven years, the carpetbag and negro government plundered and insulted the defenseless South Carolinians, largely because Grant, who was President and commander-in-chief of the United States army, did not have foresight enough to remove the negro troops. . . .[347] — MAJOR HENRY T. LOUTHAN, PROFESSOR OF HISTORY, STAUNTON MILITARY ACADEMY, CIRCA 1932

WHAT TRIGGERED VIRGINIA'S SECESSION

☛ [Confederate General] Jubal A. Early, an out-and-out-against-secession delegate, signed the Ordinance of Secession and asked permission to record his reasons. This was after Lincoln had called on Virginia for troops to put down the seceding States. Here is what Early wrote:

> "Abraham Lincoln, President of the United States, having set aside the Constitution and laws and subverted the government of the United States, and established in lieu thereof a usurped government, founded upon the worst principles of tyranny, the undersigned has, therefore, determined to sign the Ordinance of Secession adopted by the Convention on the 17th of April last, with the intention of sustaining the liberties, independence and entity of the State of Virginia against the said Abraham Lincoln, his [Left-wing] aiders and abettors, with the hope or desire of a reconstruction of the old Union in any manner that shall unite the people of Virginia with the people of the non-slave States of the North."

Thus, Mr. Lincoln's call on Virginia for troops changed the

complexion of the convention from a Union sentiment to one of secession.[348] — *RICHMOND TIMES-DISPATCH*, PRE-1930S, DATE UNKNOWN

IN RECONSTRUCTION DAYS
☛ . . . Now among the carpet-baggers were a number of [radical Left-Wing] white women from the North, who entered at once upon the task of teaching [indoctrinating] the many negro children. Their attitude was not such as to win the admiration or co-operation of the [Southern] citizens, and they resented the fact that they were ignored by the best people of the section. . . .[349] — ADA RAMP WALDEN

MEMORIES OF RECONSTRUCTION
☛ . . . Just about that time the news came of Lee's surrender, and in short order the men who had so gallantly worn the gray four trying years were homeward bound—to meet four or five more trying years of Reconstruction, harassed by carpet-baggers, scalawags, and negroes, voting themselves into office under protection of Federal [U.S.] soldiers, while they, the disfranchised Confederates, could only stand and look on—but for a while. Superior Southern intellect, aided by the [Conservative, non-racial, pro-Constitution] K.K.K. organization, at last redeemed the Southland from the second assault more terrible than the first. . . .[350] — C. E. GILBERT, HOUSTON, TEX.

A SOUTHERN WOMAN'S VIEW OF THE SOUTH'S EDUCATION SYSTEM DURING RECONSTRUCTION
☛ After the surrender at Appomattox, the Southern soldiers returned to their homes defeated, sorrowful, ill-clad, to find the South desolate and prostrate. Factories in ashes, railroads in ruin, bonds useless, currency valueless—with literally nothing left but the ground upon which they stood. This was the time when those splendid women of the Confederacy stood side by side with their men and, with renewed courage, helped to bring order out of chaos. The heroic past is our priceless heritage, and from the shadow of war and the reconstruction we swept into a new day. Our armies were destroyed, our land smitten, our homes ravaged, and we were then plundered by the hordes of reconstruction.

The history of the world may be searched in vain for a parallel to the spirit of savagery which inflicted on a defeated people the rule of a barbarous race just liberated from bondage. Truly the South's contribution to American life is not only its wonderful recovery from the ruins of war, but its spirit of silent strength in the hour of adversity—that spirit shown during this "Tragic Era."

The story of the recovery of the South from the war and subsequent reconstruction era is one of grinding, continuous work, of the severest economy, of determination to advance, of self-sacrifice, and of unparalleled courage, with education as the means to this recovery.

The war had swept away the endowments and exhausted the sources of annual income, wasted our school funds, and destroyed the beginnings of public education. Everywhere was chaos.

The South was left prostrated financially and industrially after the unequaled struggle. Property values had decreased by 1870 as a result of the war and reconstruction to the extent of $2,000,000. The cost of the war alone to the South was one-tenth of her male population and three billions of property. Reconstruction left upon the South in its impoverished condition a crushing bonded debt of over $300,000,000.

Let us remember that besides four years of demoralization during the war, there were ten years of unfortunate management following this, called "Reconstruction."

Reconstruction meant not only political, but also economical and social destruction; the work of a generation was wrecked, and the South was compelled to begin the process of rebuilding from the bottom. Political conditions made economic recovery difficult. Industry gone, banks ruined, farmers bankrupt, it took this State of ours until 1890 to regain the level of per capita wealth which she had reached in 1860.

The invested $250,000 educational fund of North Carolina had been rendered worthless by the conquest and overthrow of the State. This interruption of the schools had a deplorable effect on North Carolina, as it did on the other Southern States. With the loss of the State's school fund, white children found no school doors open to them. The Freedmen's Bureau and private gifts from the North furnished schools for the negroes. So for want of money, the entire system of schools of North Carolina was necessarily abandoned . . .

. . . The rebuilding and reorganization of the public school system was one of the many disheartening tasks which confronted the people of the South, the problem being complicated and discouraging. But the so-called Reconstruction period under military rule proved more destructive than the war to the resources of public education. Many of the richest portions of the South were wasted, industry was checked, fraud was encouraged, our people ruled by corrupt officials, and all tendencies to good government stifled. But for the [radical Left-wing] plan of the United States in governing the South, the [Conservative] leaders of the South would have restored the schools sooner. The poverty of the South resulting from the war, and the fact that the [U.S.] government was in the hands of the carpet-bagger and the [indoctrinated or communized] freedmen, are a sufficient explanation of the fact that rebuilding was necessarily slow, it appears to us of today. But the people of the South slowly and painfully were reaching again the place they had held in education in 1860....[351] — MRS. JOHN H. ANDERSON, HISTORIAN GENERAL, U.D.C.

A YANKEE'S VIEW OF LINCOLN & RECONSTRUCTION

☞ ... Hardly had the Compromise Bill [of 1850] become effective when the pious Massachusetts Abolitionists [that is, Yankee socialists and communists] suddenly discovered that the Constitution was

> "... a covenant with death and an agreement with hell—involving both parties in atrocious criminalities, and should be immediately annulled."

This was soon followed by a resolution of 250 to 24 that

> "it is the duty of every Abolitionist to agitate for the immediate dissolution of the Union"

Secession finally became a reality. For years New England had attempted to coerce the South to this final drastic step. Lincoln's war finally started, and again throughout this period we find the perpetual Northern inconsistency whenever the "pocket-book" was touched. That this inconsistency was not the prerogative of the lower classes, but extended so far as the White House, has been often referred to. A few quotations from Lincoln's speeches and letters will enlighten us as to his actual feelings, if such the thoughts of a mere politician may be called. Here are some of Lincoln's "sublime" thoughts:

> "This country, with its institutions, belongs to the people who inhabit it. Whenever they shall grow weary of the existing government, they can exercise their own constitutional right of amending it, or the revolutionary right to dismember or overthrow it."

> "The cause of civil liberty must not be surrendered. A majority held in restraint by constitutional check and limitations, and always

changing easily with the deliberate changes of the popular opinions and sentiments, is the only true sovereign of a free people. If by mere force of numbers a majority should deprive a minority of any clearly written constitutional right, it might, in a moral point of view, justify revolution—certainly would, if such right were a vital one."

". . . To give the victory to the right, not bloody bullets but peaceful ballots only are necessary. Thanks to our good old Constitution and organization under it, these alone are necessary. It only needs that every right-thinking man shall go to the polls and without fear or prejudice vote as he thinks."

As we gaze at these three quotations from the war President, we realize the tremendous inconsistency which pervades his whole expression. He openly espouses and acknowledges the right to protest, but refuses any such rights to a whole section of the country, because "the pocket-book" is affected! We can then easily realize what the Reconstruction period would have been under Lincoln.[352]

And thus, while the South was suffering and bleeding and starving, the Jeffersonian "common man" was gradually losing his rightful place, and Hamiltonianism soon superseded what was once called a "Government of the People, for the People, and by the People." The power of the Northern oligarchy assumed ever increasing proportions. Fortunes were made not merely by army contractors, but investors in stocks, bonds, and securities. Fortunes were made in oil, discovered in Pennsylvania in 1859, and they increased to almost unbelievable proportions during the war. The famous "Comstock Lode" of Nevada poured her riches into Northern pockets, strengthening her credit tremendously. Immigration rapidly increased the population of the North, while war, waged pitilessly and inhumanly, decimated the South. Labor in the North, blinded by false propaganda, added its force in aiding the Northern unscrupulous capitalist to increase his wealth on the blood and suffering of all.

Among the most vindictive men, we find one Thaddeus Stevens, of whom James Truslow Adams (a Northern historian) expresses himself in these words:

". . . Unfortunately, on [Confederate General Robert E.] Lee's dash into Pennsylvania, the ironworks of a man whose one idea had been to get rich as quickly as possible were destroyed. They belonged to Thaddeus Stevens, perhaps the most despicable, malevolent, and morally deformed character who has ever risen to high power in America."

This vindictiveness was shown throughout the whole Reconstruction period, and well characterizes the whole manner of warfare, of destruction, and elevation of the Northern capital. Jefferson's "common man," North and South, Middle West and West, was sacrificed on the altar of rapacious greed and money-lust of the capitalist.[353] — WOLFE A. LEDERER, PHILADELPHIA, PA

CONCERNING LUCIUS QUINTUS CINCINNATUS LAMAR

☛ . . . After the close of the war, Lamar practiced law and again became a teacher in the University at Oxford, Miss.

In 1870, he resigned his professorship and became active in the practice of law and the affairs of the state. During this year he wrote, in a private letter to a friend:

> "The country is in a deplorable state, and the people with all their sacred convictions scattered to the winds are absorbed in the prosaic details of making a living. Our public men have become bewildered in the wreck of all that they considered permanent and true, and know not what to do or advise. There is a perfect anarchy of opinion and purpose among us. We feel that the fate of our section is not in our hands; that nothing we can do or say would affect the results."

April 9, 1865, Appomattox Court House, Virginia: Confederate General Robert E. Lee bidding a sad farewell to his soldiers. It is the last time they would meet. Lee's surrender meant the fall of Richmond, the Confederate Capitol, which led to the collapse of the Confederate government. This, in turn, triggered the onset of the Reconstruction era, along with all of the ills, scandals, illegalities, horrors, and evils that accompanied it. The South has yet to receive an apology from the North for its inhumane, violent, and unconstitutional treatment and actions.

This political cartoon from 1868 satirizes the Left's failed impeachment of President Andrew Johnson (far right). Frustrated Socialist Thaddeus Stevens can be seen standing at center. By angering the Left, this loss only increased the barbarities and illegalities of Reconstruction.

In the study of the life of Mr. Lamar one is compelled to give considerable thought and attention to the reconstruction regime of the Federal government, particularly during the term of President Andrew Johnson and the eight years of President [Ulysses S.] Grant. At the time of the surrender at Appomattox nobody could have ever dreamed that Grant would have united with [radical South-hating, Yankee socialist Thaddeus] Stevens and his crowd to harass, plunder, and oppress the Southern people as was done during the days of the reconstruction—or so-called reconstruction. It seems certain that during those days (I refer to the days of the carpet-bagger and negro domination) there was no reconstruction, but on the other hand, plunder, theft, misrule, and continual retrogression until conditions became so bad that even the better class of Republicans in the South, whites and negroes, were compelled to abandon the Republican party and join with the Democrats to bring about better conditions. It was such a combination that first enabled the people of Mississippi to elect Mr. Lamar to the House of Representatives in 1872. It is heartbreaking to read the official records portraying the conditions in the Carolinas, in Louisiana, and Mississippi. . . .[354] — HON. LEVIN SMITH, BEFORE THE UNITED DAUGHTERS OF THE CONFEDERACY, PARKERSBURG, W.VA.

The End

This macabre pro-South wood engraving, published at the height of Reconstruction in 1871, is entitled: "Murder of Louisiana Sacrificed on the Altar of Radicalism." (Radicalism here refers to the socialist and communist movements within the then Left-wing Republican Party.) A Right-wing political cartoon, the artist portrays Liberal U.S. President Ulysses S. Grant (a member of the then Left-wing Republican Party) and U.S. Congress supporting Louisiana gubernatorial candidate, carpet-bagger William P. Kellogg. Kellogg can be seen above in a tuxedo holding the heart he has just cut from the living body of a female, a symbol of the state of Louisiana. She is being held down on the sacrificial altar by two recently freed black men. Behind this group, sitting on his throne brandishing a sword, is Grant. Directing his arm behind him is his attorney general, George H. Williams, depicted here as a winged demon. On the left we see three Republican (that is, Left-wing) officials watching the ghastly performance with obvious delight. On the right we see 13 women, symbols of the former 13 Confederate states (symbolized as 13 stars on the Confederacy's Third National Flag), in a state of shock and horror, while the kneeling woman at right, symbolizing South Carolina (the first state to secede), is wrapped in chains—symbols of Left-wing Yankee authoritarianism, intolerance, fanaticism, and oppression.

Appendix
COMMIES IN THE WHITE HOUSE
A HIGHLY ABBREVIATED LIST OF WELL-KNOWN 19ᵀᴴ-CENTURY SOCIALISTS & COMMUNISTS WHO WERE MEMBERS OF THE THEN LEFT-WING REPUBLICAN PARTY

RESEARCHED AND COMPILED BY LOCHLAINN SEABROOK

"The Republican Party was once Red." — Eugene V. Debs

WORKED IN THE LINCOLN ADMINISTRATION
- Charles A. Dana: Socialist. Assistant Secretary of War.
- Carl Schurz: Socialist. U.S. Secretary of the Interior; campaigned for Abraham Lincoln (see below).
- Reinhold Solger: Socialist. U.S. Treasury Dept.

SERVED IN THE UNION (U.S.) ARMY
- Anselm Albert: Communist. Adjutant.
- Alexander Sandor Asboth: Socialist. General.
- Fritz Anneke: Communist. Colonel.
- Isidor Bush: Socialist. Captain.
- Francis Channing Barlow: Socialist. General.
- Louis (Ludwig) Blenker: Socialist. General.
- Johan Fiala: Socialist. Topographical engineer.
- John Charles Frémont: Socialist (possibly communist). In 1856 Frémont became the first presidential candidate for the newly formed, then Left-wing, Republican Party. General.
- Friedrich Franz Karl Hecker: Socialist. In 1854 Hecker helped co-found the then Left-wing Republican Party. General.
- Richard Hinton: Socialist. Colonel.
- Fritz Jacobi: Communist. Lieutenant.
- Wladimir Krzyzanowki: Socialist. General.
- Thomas Francis Meagher: Meagher was a member of the Waterford Independent Labor Party (Ireland). General.
- Peter Joseph Osterhaus: Socialist. General.
- Allan Pinkerton: Socialist (possibly communist). Union military spy/intelligence agent.
- Henry Ramming: Socialist. Colonel.
- Robert Rosa: Communist. Major.
- Friedrich Salomon: Socialist. General.
- Herman Salomon: Socialist. Sergeant.

- Alexander Charles Schimmilfennig: Socialist. General.
- Albin Francisco Schoapfe: Socialist. General.
- William Tecumseh Sherman: Socialist (possibly communist). General.
- Carl Schurz: Socialist. General.
- Franz Sigel (or Siegel): Socialist. General.
- Julius Stahel: Socialist. General.
- Adolph von Steinwehr: Socialist. General.
- Gustav Struve: Socialist. Captain.
- Max Weber: Socialist. General.
- George Duncan Wells: Socialist. Colonel.
- Joseph Arnold Weydemyer: Socialist and Communist. General (some sources say Colonel).
- August von Willich: Communist. General.
- Charles Zagonyi: Socialist. Colonel.

EXTRAS
- Caspar Butz: Socialist. Butz campaigned for both Socialist John C. Frémont and Liberal Abraham Lincoln.
- Giuseppe Maria Garibaldi: Socialist. In July 1861, Lincoln asked European revolutionary Garibaldi to head the Union army—a position that eventually went to Ulysses S. Grant.
- Friedrich Kapp: Socialist. Kapp campaigned for Lincoln and served as one of Lincoln's presidential electors.*

A WORD ON LINCOLN
- Big government Liberal Lincoln himself, though not a socialist or a communist, seems to have strongly identified with the former ideology, for he was known to speak before socialist organizations, and once even accepted an honorary membership that was offered by one of them. It should also be noted that among others, Lincoln was admired by Vladimir Lenin, Adolf Hitler, and Marx, the latter who wrote him a personal letter congratulating him on his 1864 reelection.

*Notes: 1) We can safely assume that there were many hundreds of thousands of Socialists and Communists, not only in America, but worldwide, who supported Lincoln, and later Grant. 2) If we take my incomplete list of 19 Radical Union generals alone, nearly 3.5 percent of the total number of Union generals, out of approximately 560, were either Socialists or Communists. 3) Based on the number of Socialist and Communist Union generals who served, we can also be sure that there were thousands of Socialist and Communist privates in the Union army, men whose names have gone unrecorded. 4) Many of the men chronicled in my short list above were followers, or even personal friends, of ultra Left-wing Communist, white racist, and entrenched South-hater Karl Marx *and* his Radical Communist cohort Friedrich Engels—both who advocated the violent overthrow of capitalism. 5) A number of those listed here were "48ers": foreign-born Socialist and Communist Radicals who participated in the European Revolutions of 1848-1849; then as criminals they fled to, or were exiled to, America, where they were inevitably drawn to the "Red Party" of Abraham Lincoln, the then Left-wing Republican Party. 6) For more details on these topics, see my books *Abraham Lincoln Was a Liberal*, *Jefferson Davis Was a Conservative* and *Lincoln's War*.

NOTES

ALL FOOTNOTES, ENDNOTES, & NOTES ARE MINE, UNLESS OTHERWISE INDICATED. L.S.

1. Seabrook, *Abraham Lincoln Was a Liberal, Jefferson Davis Was a Conservative: The Missing Key to Understanding the American Civil War*, p. 55.
2. Schlüter, p. 23.
3. Woods, p. 47.
4. On Lincoln's socialistic, Marxist, and communist thoughts, ideas, and tendencies, see my books: 1) *Lincoln's War: The Real Cause, The Real Winner, the Real Loser*; 2) *Abraham Lincoln Was a Liberal, Jefferson Davis Was a Conservative: The Missing Key to Understanding the American Civil War*; 3) *Abraham Lincoln: The Southern View*. Also see McCarty, passim; Browder, passim; Benson and Kennedy, passim.
5. See J. W. Jones, TDMV, pp. 144, 200-201, 273.
6. Schlüter, p. 23. The then Left-wing Republican Party's first presidential nominee was Radical (that is, Socialist), and later Union general, John C. Frémont. As socialist Eugene V. Debs correctly asserted: "The Republican Party was once Red." *The Independent*, Vol. 102, No. 3724, June 5, 1920, p. 309. See my Appendix.
7. See Seabrook, *The Alexander H. Stephens Reader*, passim. See also, Pollard, LC, p. 178; J. H. Franklin, pp. 101, 111, 130, 149; Nicolay and Hay, ALCW, Vol. 1, p. 627.
8. *Confederate Veteran*, Vol. 12, 1904, p. 442.
9. Seabrook (ed.), *A Short History of the Confederate States of America* (J. Davis), p. 59.
10. Seabrook (ed.), *A Short History of the Confederate States of America* (J. Davis), pp. 55-56.
11. For more on this specific topic, see my book *Everything You Were Taught About the Civil War is Wrong, Ask a Southerner!*, pp. 34-39.
12. BISG (the "Book Industry Study Group"), for example—a Left-wing organization which describes itself as "the leading book trade association for standardized best practices, research and information, and events"—gives its BISAC ("Book Industry Standards and Communications") listing for works on the War for Southern Independence under the heading "Civil War Period, 1850-1877." Nearly all books published in the U.S.A. today are under the categorizational control of this progressive group located in New York City.
13. See e.g., Seabrook, *The Quotable Jefferson Davis*, pp. 30, 38, 76.
14. See e.g., Seabrook (ed.) *The Rise and Fall of the Confederate Government* (J. Davis), Vol. 1, pp. 55, 422; Vol. 2, pp. 4, 161, 454, 610. Besides using the term "Civil War" himself, President Davis cites numerous other individuals who use it as well.
15. See e.g., *Confederate Veteran*, Vol. 20, 1912, p. 122.
16. Minutes of the Eighth Annual Meeting, July 1898, p. 87.
17. For more on the nihilistic, atheistic, anti-life, anti-tradition, anti-American, anti-Constitution, anti-capitalism, anti-South agenda of the Victorian Republican Party (then the Liberal Party) and the modern Democrat Party (now the Liberal Party), otherwise known as "The Communist/Socialist Rules for Revolution," see Hasselberg, pp. 2350-2351; Lenin, passim; Marx and Engels, passim; B. Dodd, passim. Also see my book *What the Confederate Flag Means to Me: Americans Speak Out in Defense of Southern Honor, Heritage, and History*.
18. *Confederate Veteran*, Vol. 9, 1901, p. 318.
19. Minutes U.C.V., Vol. 2. *Proceedings of the Tenth Annual Meeting and Reunion of the United Confederate Veterans*, held at Louisville, Kentucky, May 30-June 3; 1900, New Orleans, LA: United Confederate Veterans, p. 25.
20. Gaslighting, one of the primary weapons of the Left, is defined as "deceiving a person or group of people through repetition of a constructed false narrative." Medically speaking it is defined as "a form of emotional abuse or psychological manipulation involving distorting the truth in order to confuse or create doubt in another person to the point where they begin to question their sanity or reality."
21. Seabrook, *Abraham Lincoln Was a Liberal, Jefferson Davis Was a Conservative: The Missing Key to Understanding the American Civil War*, pp. 77-78.
22. See Appendix.
23. See my book of the same name.
24. CNN, "Town Hall," interview with President Trump, May 10, 2023.

25. Seabrook, *Abraham Lincoln: The Southern View* (2021 ed.), p. 531.
26. Seabrook, *Rise Up and Call Them Blessed: Victorian Tributes to the Confederate Soldier, 1861-1901*, p. 503.
27. Ecclesiastes 10:2.
28. *Confederate Veteran*, Vol. 29, 1921, p. 420.
29. *Confederate Veteran*, Vol. 32, 1924, p. 136.
30. *Confederate Veteran*, Vol. 29, 1921, p. 16.
31. *Confederate Veteran*, Vol. 30, 1922, p. 58.
32. *Confederate Veteran*, Vol. 30, 1922, p. 96.
33. I am not the first to use this phrase. See *Confederate Veteran*, Vol. 24, 1916, p. 141; *Confederate Veteran*, Vol. 29, 1921, p. 178; *Confederate Veteran*, Vol. 30, 1922, p. 460. L.S.
34. Confederate Major Peter Pelham, as just one example, was noted for his sentiment that Lincoln's War was "unnecessary," and that "the South would have freed the negro in due time, and, in fact, was doing so when the war occurred." *Confederate Veteran*, Vol. 32, 1924, p. 236.
35. For more on these topics, see my book *Everything You Were Taught About American Slavery is Wrong, Ask a Southerner!*
36. *Confederate Veteran*, Vol. 4, 1896, p. 243.
37. Seabrook, *Rise Up and Call Them Blessed: Victorian Tributes to the Confederate Soldier, 1861-1901*, p. 351.
38. Seabrook, *Rise Up and Call Them Blessed: Victorian Tributes to the Confederate Soldier, 1861-1901*, p. 269.
39. Seabrook, *Abraham Lincoln: The Southern View* (2021 ed.), p. 532.
40. Seabrook, *Everything You Were Taught About African-Americans and the Civil War is Wrong, Ask a Southerner!*, p. 371.
41. Seabrook, *Abraham Lincoln: The Southern View* (2021 ed.), p. 532.
42. Seabrook, *Abraham Lincoln: The Southern View* (2021 ed.), pp. 532-533.
43. Seabrook, *Rise Up and Call Them Blessed: Victorian Tributes to the Confederate Soldier, 1861-1901*, p. 381. Note: This is my paraphrasal of the original quote. L.S.
44. McNeily, p. 375.
45. McNeily, p. 376.
46. Stevens, p. 1.
47. McNeily, p. 376.
48. Johnston, pp. 187-188.
49. Seabrook, *The Bittersweet Bond: Race Relations in the Old South as Described by White and Black Southerners*, p. 21.
50. Seabrook, *Abraham Lincoln: The Southern View* (2021 ed.), p. 533.
51. Yankee John Sherman is infamous for his Reconstruction era statement: "The negroes are not intelligent enough to vote." Bowers, p. 14.
52. *Confederate Veteran*, Vol. 4, 1896, p. 371.
53. Seabrook, *Rise Up and Call Them Blessed: Victorian Tributes to the Confederate Soldier, 1861-1901*, pp. 148-149.
54. *Confederate Veteran*, Vol. 32, 1924, p. 243.
55. *Confederate Veteran*, Vol. 13, 1905, p. 227.
56. Seabrook, *Abraham Lincoln: The Southern View* (2021 ed.), p. 532.
57. Seabrook, *Abraham Lincoln: The Southern View* (2021 ed.), p. 533.
58. See e.g., infra, p. 428.
59. I have heard Liberals and Socialists (today members of the now Left-wing Democratic Party) speak these exact sentiments before Congress. L.S.
60. Seabrook, *Abraham Lincoln: The Southern View* (2021 ed.), p. 533.
61. Seabrook, *Abraham Lincoln: The Southern View* (2021 ed.), p. 555.
62. Seabrook, *Abraham Lincoln: The Southern View* (2021 ed.), p. 533.
63. Seabrook, *Abraham Lincoln: The Southern View* (2021 ed.), p. 534.
64. Seabrook, *Abraham Lincoln: The Southern View* (2021 ed.), p. 534.
65. Seabrook, *Abraham Lincoln: The Southern View* (2021 ed.), p. 534.
66. As a writer of Southern history, I have experienced all of these practices myself, and continue to do so. L.S.
67. *Confederate Veteran*, Vol. 1, 1893, p. 149.
68. *Confederate Veteran*, Vol. 8, 1900, p. 530.

69. *Confederate Veteran*, Vol. 9, 1901, p. 469.
70. See my book *I, Confederate: Why Dixie Seceded and Fought in the Words of Southern Soldiers*. L.S.
71. Evans, Vol. 12, pp. 269-274. (Note: The title of this entry is mine. L.S.)
72. Evans, Vol. 12, pp. 274-278.
73. It is not true, as many continue to believe, that the Union was dissolved when the Southern states seceded. The original U.S. Union was, and still is, a voluntary and constitutionally formed compact between a group of states—a political system known as a confederacy, or more specifically, a "Confederate Republic," as the Founding Fathers referred to the U.S. in the late 1700s and early 1800s. Thus, the U.S. was originally known by the popular nickname "The Confederate States of America." This compact continued despite Southern secession, after which the Southern states created their own voluntary and constitutionally formed Union, and named it after the original name for the U.S.: The Confederate States of America. For more on these topics see my books: *Confederacy 101*; *America's Three Constitutions*; *The Articles of Confederation Explained*; and *The Constitution of the Confederate States of America Explained*. L.S.
74. Evans, Vol. 12, pp. 278-279.
75. Evans, Vol. 12, pp. 279-280.
76. For more on this sordid chapter in American history, see *Prison Life of Jefferson Davis*, by John J. Craven, edited by myself, published by Sea Raven Press. L.S.
77. Evans, Vol. 12, pp. 280-282.
78. Some of Lee's views concerning Lincoln have since been shown to be in error. As demonstrated in my Introduction, not only has new information arisen since the late 1800s (obviously Lee did not have access to late 20th- and 21st-Century research), but Lincoln's own words themselves have proven that he had no intention of ultimately forgiving the South or following the law. For an in-depth modern look at the actual man and his background, beliefs, statements, thoughts, and actions, see my book *Abraham Lincoln: The Southern View*. L.S.
79. Evans, Vol. 12, pp. 282-286.
80. To this day West Virginia remains an illegitimate state as her "statehood" was not constitutional. For more on this judicial travesty, see my book *Abraham Lincoln: The Southern View*. L.S.
81. This is false, as Confederate soldier Edmund Ruffin proves. L.S.
82. Evans, Vol. 12, pp. 286-291.
83. Evans, Vol. 12, pp. 291-294.
84. Evans, Vol. 12, pp. 294-296.
85. This was not based on Victorian white racism toward blacks, as mainstream historians continue to falsely teach. A majority of emancipated blacks remained uneducated until long after Reconstruction, and so were then not fully aware of the important power they wielded as individual voters in political elections. This left them open to the evil influences of the ethnomasochistic South-hating Freedmen's Bureau, which, as Gen. Lee points out, only stirred up hatred, division, and mistrust between Southern whites and blacks—one of the main weapons used by the Left to gain and maintain power, then as now. L.S.
86. Gen. Lee is being too lenient in his use of the word "forgetting." Northern Liberals were all too aware that the majority of blacks then lived in the South. L.S.
87. Evans, Vol. 12, pp. 296-297.
88. Gen. Lee once again underestimates the selfishness and cruelty of the Left—then politically represented by the Republican Party. L.S.
89. Evans, Vol. 12, pp. 297-300.
90. Evans, Vol. 12, pp. 300-305.
91. Gen. Lee's source for this quote is *Noted Men of the Solid South*, by Hillary A. Herbert (ed.).
92. Gen. Lee's source for this quote is *Noted Men of the Solid South*, by Hillary A. Herbert (ed.).
93. Evans, Vol. 12, pp. 305-309.
94. Evans, Vol. 12, p. 309.
95. For a detailed discussion of the original KKK (as opposed to the modern KKK, with which it has no connection), see my book *Nathan Bedford Forrest and the Ku Klux Klan: Yankee Myth, Confederate Fact*. L.S.
96. Gen. Lee's source for this quote is Isaac W. Avery's *The History of the State of Georgia From 1850 to 1881*.
97. Evans, Vol. 12, pp. 309-311.
98. Gen. Lee's source for this Thomas Norwood quote: Avery, p. 366.
99. Gen. Lee's source for this quote is *Noted Men of the Solid South*, by Hillary A. Herbert (ed.).
100. Evans, Vol. 12, pp. 311-314.

101. From a Conservative point of view, blacks are clearly still being used in the same way, for the same purpose, by the now Left-wing Democrats.

102. Gen. Lee's source for this quote is *Noted Men of the Solid South*, by Hillary A. Herbert (ed.).

103. Gen. Lee's source for this quote is *Noted Men of the Solid South*, by Hillary A. Herbert (ed.).

104. Gen. Lee's source for this quote is an author surnamed Judson.

105. Concerning this paragraph, I again ask the reader not to engage in presentism by mistaking the so-called "white supremacy" of the Old South with the white supremacy of modern times. This is not a black and white issue, as the Left would have the world believe. The two are very different, and for a host of complex reasons. For more on this topic see my books: *Everything You Were Taught About African-Americans and the Civil War is Wrong, Ask a Southerner!*; *Everything You Were Taught About American Slavery is Wrong, Ask a Southerner!*; *Slavery 101: Amazing Facts You Never Knew About America's "Peculiar Institution"*; *The Bittersweet Bond: Race Relations in the Old South As Described by White and Black Southerners*; *Nathan Bedford Forrest and African-Americans: Yankee Myth, Confederate Fact*; and *Nathan Bedford Forrest and the Ku Klux Klan: Yankee Myth, Confederate Fact*. L.S.

106. Evans, Vol. 12, pp. 314-323.

107. Gen. Lee is in error here. Many black servants ("slaves") owned property, and property of all kinds. For more on this topic, see my book *Everything You Were Taught About American Slavery is Wrong, Ask a Southerner!* L.S.

108. Although it is true that neither the antebellum U.S. government or the C.S. government provided black servants ("slaves") with a formal education, it is not true that they all were uneducated. Of their own accord, many slave owners (both white and black slave owners) taught their servants how to read and write, as well as a host of various professional trades. For more on this topic, see my book *Everything You Were Taught About American Slavery is Wrong, Ask a Southerner!* L.S.

109. Gen. Lee's source for this quote is R. H. Edmunds, 1896.

110. Evans, Vol. 12, pp. 323-327.

111. Evans, Vol. 12, pp. 327-340.

112. For more background on this and other Southern memorials, see my book *Confederate Monuments: Why Every American Should Honor Confederate Soldiers and Their Memorials*.

113. Evans, Vol. 12, pp. 340-343.

114. Evans, Vol. 12, pp. 343-346.

115. Gen. Lee is correct here. Lincoln referred to his illegal Emancipation Proclamation as both a "war measure" and a "military necessity," thoroughly debunking the widespread belief that he wanted to abolish slavery because "he loved black people." For more on this subject, see my book *Abraham Lincoln: The Southern View*. L.S.

116. *Daily Picayune*, New Orleans, April 9, 1897.

117. Evans, Vol. 12, pp. 346-351.

118. Evans, Vol. 12, p. 351.

119. Evans, Vol. 12, pp. 351-352.

120. Memphis *Commercial-Appeal*, January 5, 1897.

121. Evans, Vol. 12, pp. 352-360.

122. Were Gen. Lee alive today he would not and could not make such a statement. To this day, the descendants of the Victorian Left (now operating under the auspices of the Democratic Party), the same party that created and launched the horrors of Reconstruction (then under the auspices of the Republican Party), continues to fan the flames of hatred and sectional and racial divisiveness.

123. See my book, *Abraham Lincoln Was a Liberal, Jefferson Davis Was a Conservative: The Missing Key to Understanding the American Civil War*. L.S.

124. See my book, *Abraham Lincoln Was a Liberal, Jefferson Davis Was a Conservative: The Missing Key to Understanding the American Civil War*. L.S.

125. For more on this remarkable event, see my book *Confederate Monuments: Why Every American Should Honor Confederate Soldiers and Their Memorials*. L.S.

126. Evans, Vol. 12, pp. 360-368.

127. Bowers, pp. 45-48. (Note: The title of this entry is mine. L.S.)

128. Bowers, pp. 48-50. (Note: The title of this entry is mine. L.S.)

129. Bowers, pp. 50-53. (Note: The title of this entry is mine. L.S.)

130. Bowers, pp. 53-55. (Note: The title of this entry is mine. L.S.)

131. Bowers, pp. 60-62. (Note: The title of this entry is mine. L.S.)

132. Without any real evidence, but plenty of vengeance, the U.S. government hanged Captain Wirz for "war crimes" on November 10, 1865. The South has never forgiven the North for this outrage against truth, justice, and human decency. It can be truly said that his execution was motivated by nothing but pure malice.
133. French, pp. 328-330.
134. See Huxley, p. 101.
135. The confiscation of the slaves by act of Congress is an acknowledgment of the just decision made by Chief Justice [Roger B.] Taney in the Dred Scott case, that a slave was chattel, or personal property. [Gen. French's note.]
136. I know a man North who paid $6,000 to a Congressman for his son's appointment. This was excluding the South from positions in the army and navy. [Gen. French's note.]
137. For more on the New England secession movement, see my book *Confederacy 101*. L.S.
138. French, pp. 330-333.
139. Shakespeare, *The Tempest*, Act I.
140. French, pp. 333-334.
141. French, pp. 334-336.
142. French, p. 337.
143. French, pp. 337-340.
144. French, pp. 341-343.
145. French, pp. 343-344.
146. French, pp. 344-346.
147. Lord Woodhouselee: Alexander Fraser Tytler, Scottish historian and legal scholar.
148. Lincoln's December proclamation says: "Such States shall be received again into the Union." [Gen. French's note.]
149. French, pp. 346-347.
150. French, pp. 347-350.
151. French, pp. 350-351.
152. For a detailed look at the authentic history of what I have termed the Reconstruction KKK, see my book, *Nathan Bedford Forrest and the Ku Klux Klan: Yankee Myth, Confederate Fact*.
153. Toney, pp. 122-128.
154. Toney, pp. 129-133.
155. Hall, pp. 266-267.
156. See my book, *Everything You Were Taught About American Slavery is Wrong, Ask a Southerner!* L.S.
157. This is false. See my book, *Abraham Lincoln: The Southern View*. L.S.
158. Hall, pp. 268-270.
159. Hall, pp. 270-272.
160. Hall, pp. 272-274.
161. Hall, pp. 274-275.
162. Hall, pp. 275-277.
163. Hall, pp. 277-280.
164. Hall, pp. 280-281.
165. Dr. J. L. M. Curry's figures. [Hall's note.]
166. Hall, pp. 282-284.
167. In Thomas Dixon's play, *The Clansman*, Gen. N. B. Forrest is represented as the grand commander of the Ku Klux Klan. [Hall's note.] (Editor's note: Dixon casting Forrest as the Grand Wizard of the KKK is an example of extreme poetic license by a novelist who, understandably, wanted to add drama and flair to his work. The truth, however, is far different. For an in-depth discussion on this topic see my book, *Nathan Bedford Forrest and the Ku Klux Klan: Yankee Myth, Confederate Fact*. L.S.)
168. Halls' view of the original KKK, or what I call the Reconstruction KKK, does not agree with the facts as articulated by the then Conservative Democrats (former Confederate soldiers) who founded and operated it between 1865 and 1869. According to their own words, it was created as a Conservative, patriotic, pro-Constitution, pro-law enforcement, counter-Reconstruction, paramilitary unit and social aid society, one meant to benefit *all* loyal Southerners, whatever their race. As evidence, there was an all-black KKK chapter in Nashville. For an in-depth discussion on this topic see my book, *Nathan Bedford Forrest and the Ku Klux Klan: Yankee Myth, Confederate Fact*. L.S.
169. Hall, pp. 285-286.

170. Chancellor J. H. Kirkland, of Vanderbilt University. [Hall's note.]
171. Hall, pp. 287-291.
172. For more on Lincoln's lifelong support of the deportation of American blacks, see my book *Abraham Lincoln: The Southern View*.
173. Hall, pp. 291-296.
174. Hall, pp. 297-301.
175. Hall, pp. 301-304.
176. Hall is in error. The Union did not "dissolve" with the secession of the Southern states. For more on this topic see my books, *All We Ask is to Be Let Alone: The Southern Secession Fact Book*; *Lincoln's War: The Real Cause, the Real Winner, the Real Loser*; *Confederacy 101: Amazing Facts You Never Knew About America's Oldest Political Tradition*; and *Abraham Lincoln: The Southern View*. L.S.
177. Hall, pp. 305-307.
178. Hall, pp. 307-310.
179. Prince, pp. 259-260. (Note: The title of this entry is mine. L.S.)
180. Prince, pp. 260-261.
181. Prince, pp. 261-262.
182. Prince, p. 262. (Note: The title of this entry is mine. L.S.)
183. Andrew Johnson, unlike Lincoln, was exceedingly bitter against the prominent Confederate leaders and refused to include them in the general pardon extended to the rank and file of Southern people. This was probably owing to the traditional and ingrained jealousy of the "poor white" for the aristocratic class. Subsequently Mr. Johnson changed his attitude toward the Southern leaders and became more lenient. [Prince's note.]
184. Prince, pp. 262-263.
185. Prince, pp. 263-264.
186. Prince, pp. 264-267.
187. Prince, p. 267.
188. Prince, pp. 267-269.
189. Only known criminals were executed. See my book, *Nathan Bedford Forrest and the Ku Klux Klan: Yankee Myth, Confederate Fact*. L.S.
190. In reality, what I call the "Reconstruction Ku Klux Klan," a purely counter-Reconstruction group, was dissolved by Confederate General Nathan Bedford Forrest (in 1869). For more on this and related topics, see my book, *Nathan Bedford Forrest and the Ku Klux Klan: Yankee Myth, Confederate Fact*. L.S.
191. Prince, pp. 269-271.
192. Prince, pp. 271-274.
193. Morgan, pp. 267-269.
194. Morgan, pp. 269-271.
195. Morgan, pp. 272-280.
196. Adamson, pp. 136-140.
197. For more on Lincoln's real views concerning blacks, slavery, and abolition (as opposed to the fake views invented by Left-wing historians), see my book *Abraham Lincoln: The Southern View*. L.S.
198. See Appendix.
199. Some of Chesterton's remarks concerning the Victorian KKK are not historic. For an in-depth discussion on what I have named the Reconstruction KKK, see my book *Nathan Bedford Forrest and the Ku Klux Klan: Yankee Myth, Confederate Fact*.
200. Lincoln's chief justice, Yankee Liberal Salmon P. Chase, articulated the typical sentiment of Northern Leftists toward blacks. After stating that he would rather never see another black person "set his foot upon Ohio soil," he was asked why, to which he replied: "Because their moral influence is degrading. . . . I do not wish the slave emancipated because I love him, but because I hate his [white Southern] master." See Seabrook, *The Bittersweet Bond: Race Relations in the Old South as Described by White and Black Southerners*, p. 21.
201. Again, Chesterton is in error concerning some of his statements. See my book, *Nathan Bedford Forrest and the Ku Klux Klan: Yankee Myth, Confederate Fact*.
202. See my book, *Everything You Were Taught About American Slavery is Wrong, Ask a Southerner!* L.S.
203. Chesterton, pp. 203-226.
204. *Confederate Veteran*, Vol. 28, 1920, pp. 253-256. (Note: The title of this entry is mine. L.S.)
205. Taylor, pp. 319-320. (Note: The title of this entry is mine. L.S.)

206. From John Bunyan's 1678 novel, *The Pilgrim's Progress From This World, to That Which is to Come.*
207. Taylor, pp. 321-343.
208. Taylor, pp. 344-359.
209. Taylor, pp. 360-363.
210. Evans, Vol. 12, pp. 262-263. (Note: The title of this entry is mine. L.S.)
211. Reagan's assertion, that Reconstruction would have been much milder had Lincoln lived, is highly debatable, particularly in light of both the many anti-South comments Lincoln made and the numerous pro-North actions he took before and during the War. See my book, *Abraham Lincoln: The Southern View.* L.S.
212. *Confederate Veteran*, Vol. 5, 1897, pp. 346-347. (Note: The title of this entry is mine. L.S.)
213. *Confederate Veteran*, Vol. 2, 1894, pp. 148-149. (Note: The title of this entry is mine. L.S.)
214. *Confederate Veteran*, Vol. 1, 1893, pp. 214-215.
215. *Confederate Veteran*, Vol. 4, 1896, p. 214. (Note: The title of this entry is mine. L.S.)
216. *Confederate Veteran*, Vol. 1, 1893, p. 144.
217. *Confederate Veteran*, Vol. 3, 1895, p. 52. (Note: The title of this entry is mine. L.S.)
218. *Confederate Veteran*, Vol. 4, 1896, p. 224. (Note: The title of this entry is mine. L.S.)
219. *Confederate Veteran*, Vol. 5, 1897, p. 247. (Note: The title of this entry is mine. L.S.)
220. *Confederate Veteran*, Vol. 5, 1897, p. 575. (Note: The title of this entry is mine. L.S.)
221. *Confederate Veteran*, Vol. 6, 1898, pp. 51-52. (Note: The title of this entry is mine. L.S.)
222. *Confederate Veteran*, Vol. 8, 1900, p. 318. (Note: The title of this entry is mine. L.S.)
223. Morton, p. 22. (Note: The title of this entry is mine. L.S.)
224. *Confederate Veteran*, Vol. 8, 1900, p. 405. Lindsay's speech was addressed specifically to Company C, 16th Louisiana Regiment. (Note: The title of this entry is mine. L.S.)
225. *Confederate Veteran*, Vol. 8, 1900, p. 480.
226. *Confederate Veteran*, Vol. 8, 1900, p. 519.
227. *Confederate Veteran*, Vol. 9, 1901, p. 444. (Note: The title of this entry is mine. L.S.)
228. *Confederate Veteran*, Vol. 11, 1903, p. 17. (Note: The title of this entry is mine. L.S.)
229. *Confederate Veteran*, Vol. 11, 1903, p. 154. (Note: The title of this entry is mine. L.S.)
230. *Confederate Veteran*, Vol. 11, 1903, p. 202. (Note: The title of this entry is mine. L.S.)
231. *Confederate Veteran*, Vol. 11, 1903, p. 305. (Note: The title of this entry is mine. L.S.)
232. Dixon, *The Leopard's Spots*, pp. 34-35. Though this particular entry is from a novel by Dixon, he based the work on historical facts, figures, quotes, and events. (Note: The title of this entry is mine. L.S.)
233. *Confederate Veteran*, Vol. 11, 1903, pp. 499-500. (Note: The title of this entry is mine. L.S.)
234. *Confederate Veteran*, Vol. 11, 1903, p. 510. (Note: The title of this entry is mine. L.S.)
235. Mooney, pp. 196-197.
236. *Confederate Veteran*, Vol. 12, 1904, p. 325. (Note: The title of this entry is mine. L.S.)
237. *Confederate Veteran*, Vol. 12, 1904, p. 518. (Note: The title of this entry is mine. L.S.)
238. *Confederate Veteran*, Vol. 13, 1905, pp. 79-80. (Note: The title of this entry is mine. L.S.)
239. *Confederate Veteran*, Vol. 13, 1905, pp. 103-104. (Note: The title of this entry is mine. L.S.)
240. *Confederate Veteran*, Vol. 13, 1905, pp. 116-117. (Note: The title of this entry is mine. L.S.)
241. *Confederate Veteran*, Vol. 13, 1905, p. 125. (Note: The title of this entry is mine. L.S.)
242. *Congressional Record*, February 1890, p. 1223. (Note: The title of this entry is mine. L.S.)
243. *Confederate Veteran*, Vol. 14, 1906, p. 127. (Note: The title of this entry is mine. L.S.)
244. James, pp. 207-208. (Note: The title of this entry is mine. L.S.)
245. James, pp. 49-50.
246. *Confederate Veteran*, Vol. 14, 1906, p. 500. (Note: The title of this entry is mine. L.S.)
247. Avary, no page number. (Note: The title of this entry is mine. L.S.)
248. "The Negro in Africa and America," J. A. Tillinghast. On miscegenation see "The Color Line," W. B. Smith; also A. R. Colquhoun, N. Amer. Rev., May, 1903. [Avary's note.]
249. Fakirs, taking advantage of the general racial weakness, are selling "black skin removers," "hair straighteners," etc. [Avary's note.]
250. See Council, Penn, and Spencer, "Voice of Missions" (H. B. Parks, ed.), Sept., Nov., Dec., 1905. See Booker T. Washington's "Up from Slavery," "Character Building," "Future of the American Negro." [Avary's note.]
251. Avary, pp. 391-402. (Note: The title of this entry is mine. L.S.)

252. Despite his kindness in saving Lee (a Conservative Democrat) from prison, for most of his presidency former Union General Grant (a Liberal Republican) sided with the radicals in his party (that is, Republican socialists and communists), not only allowing their far Left Reconstruction program free reign, but enforcing it with brutal military might. L.S.

253. That many Southern whites, like those pictured here in Powell's article, risked their lives to ensure that black Conservatives were allowed to vote, is *never* mentioned in our mainstream history books. L.S.

254. *Confederate Veteran*, Vol. 16, 1908, pp. 185-186.

255. *Confederate Veteran*, Vol. 16, 1908, p. 649.

256. *Confederate Veteran*, Vol. 17, 1909, p. 154. (Note: The title of this entry is mine. L.S.)

257. *Confederate Veteran*, Vol. 17, 1909, p. 202. (Note: The title of this entry is mine. L.S.)

258. *Confederate Veteran*, Vol. 17, 1909, p. 204. (Note: The title of this entry is mine. L.S.)

259. *Confederate Veteran*, Vol. 18, 1910, p. 267.

260. *Confederate Veteran*, Vol. 18, 1910, p. 267.

261. *Confederate Veteran*, Vol. 18, 1910, p. 396. (Note: The title of this entry is mine. L.S.)

262. *Confederate Veteran*, Vol. 19, 1911, p. 177. (Note: The title of this entry is mine. L.S.)

263. *Confederate Veteran*, Vol. 19, 1911, p. 390. (Note: The title of this entry is mine. L.S.)

264. *Confederate Veteran*, Vol. 19, 1911, p. 466. (Note: The title of this entry is mine. L.S.)

265. *Confederate Veteran*, Vol. 19, 1911, p. 516. (Note: The title of this entry is mine. L.S.)

266. *Confederate Veteran*, Vol. 20, 1912, p. 217. (Note: The title of this entry is mine. L.S.)

267. *Confederate Veteran*, Vol. 20, 1912, p. 427. (Note: The title of this entry is mine. L.S.)

268. *Confederate Veteran*, Vol. 20, 1912, p. 566. (Note: The title of this entry is mine. L.S.)

269. *Confederate Veteran*, Vol. 21, 1913, p. 185. (Note: The title of this entry is mine. L.S.)

270. *Confederate Veteran*, Vol. 21, 1913, p. 556. (Note: The title of this entry is mine. L.S.)

271. *Confederate Veteran*, Vol. 22, 1914, p. 359. (Note: The title of this entry is mine. L.S.)

272. *Confederate Veteran*, Vol. 24, 1916, p. 8.

273. *Confederate Veteran*, Vol. 24, 1916, p. 28. (Note: The title of this entry is mine. L.S.)

274. *Confederate Veteran*, Vol. 24, 1916, p. 66. (Note: The title of this entry is mine. L.S.)

275. *Confederate Veteran*, Vol. 24, 1916, pp. 297-298.

276. *Confederate Veteran*, Vol. 24, 1916, pp. 308-309. (Note: The title of this entry is mine. L.S.)

277. *Confederate Veteran*, Vol. 24, 1916, p. 351. (Note: The title of this entry is mine. L.S.)

278. *Confederate Veteran*, Vol. 24, 1916, p. 360. (Note: The title of this entry is mine. L.S.)

279. For more on the differences between Southern servitude and Northern slavery, see my book *Everything You Were Taught About American Slavery is Wrong, Ask a Southerner!* L.S.

280. *Confederate Veteran*, Vol. 24, 1916, p. 388. (Note: The title of this entry is mine. L.S.)

281. *Confederate Veteran*, Vol. 24, 1916, p. 391. (Note: The title of this entry is mine. L.S.)

282. *Confederate Veteran*, Vol. 24, 1916, p. 391. (Note: The title of this entry is mine. L.S.)

283. *Confederate Veteran*, Vol. 24, 1916, pp. 438-439. (Note: The title of this entry is mine. L.S.)

284. Elson, *Side Lights*, Volume II, page 71. [McNeilly's note.]

285. Elson, *Side Lights*, Volume II, page 799. [McNeilly's note.]

286. *Confederate Veteran*, Vol. 25, 1917, p. 348. See *The Outlook*, Vol. 115, January-April 1917, pp. 98-99. (Note: The title of this entry is mine. L.S.)

287. *Confederate Veteran*, Vol. 25, 1917, p. 399. (Note: The title of this entry is mine. L.S.)

288. In his message to the extra session of Congress, July 4, 1861, Lincoln, after rather tamely attempting to defend his unconstitutional action, falls back upon "necessity" for justification, as follows: "These measures, whether strictly legal or not, were ventured upon under what appeared to be a popular demand and a public necessity, trusting then as now that Congress would readily ratify them." [Tyler's note.]

289. *Confederate Veteran*, Vol. 25, 1917, pp. 509-511. (Note: The title of this entry is mine. L.S.)

290. *Confederate Veteran*, Vol. 25, 1917, pp. 551-552. (Note: The title of this entry is mine. L.S.)

291. *Confederate Veteran*, Vol. 26, 1918, pp. 342-343. (Note: The title of this entry is mine. L.S.)

292. *Confederate Veteran*, Vol. 27, 1919, p. 157. (Note: The title of this entry is mine. L.S.)

293. *Confederate Veteran*, Vol. 27, 1919, p. 283. (Note: The title of this entry is mine. L.S.)

294. *Confederate Veteran*, Vol. 27, 1919, p. 328.

295. *Confederate Veteran*, Vol. 27, 1919, pp. 423-425. (Note: The title of this entry is mine. L.S.)

296. *Confederate Veteran*, Vol. 27, 1919, p. 474.

297. See my bibliography. L.S.
298. *Confederate Veteran*, Vol. 28, 1920, pp. 6-7. (Note: The title of this entry is mine. L.S.)
299. *Confederate Veteran*, Vol. 28, 1920, p. 177. (Note: The title of this entry is mine. L.S.)
300. *Confederate Veteran*, Vol. 28, 1920, p. 212. (Note: The title of this entry is mine. L.S.)
301. *Confederate Veteran*, Vol. 28, 1920, p. 257. (Note: The title of this entry is mine. L.S.)
302. The Left-wing practice of recruiting law enforcement for its own ends is not new or modern, as this paragraph clearly shows. L.S.
303. Another early example of the Left using its political power unjustly, immorally, unethically, and illegally. L.S.
304. *Confederate Veteran*, Vol. 28, 1920, pp. 296-298.
305. *Confederate Veteran*, Vol. 28, 1920, p. 465. (Note: The title of this entry is mine. L.S.)
306. *Confederate Veteran*, Vol. 29, 1921, p. 7. (Note: The title of this entry is mine. L.S.)
307. *Confederate Veteran*, Vol. 29, 1921, p. 16. (Note: The title of this entry is mine. L.S.)
308. *Confederate Veteran*, Vol. 29, 1921, p. 103. (Note: The title of this entry is mine. L.S.)
309. See my bibliography. L.S.
310. *Confederate Veteran*, Vol. 29, 1921, pp. 256-258.
311. *Confederate Veteran*, Vol. 29, 1921, p. 327. (Note: The title of this entry is mine. L.S.)
312. Lincoln was, in fact, a self-professed anti-Christian "infidel." See my book, *Abraham Lincoln: The Southern View*. L.S.
313. *Confederate Veteran*, Vol. 30, 1922, pp. 96-97. For a detailed discussion on what I call the Reconstruction KKK (separate and distinct from the modern KKK), see my book *Nathan Bedford Forrest and the Ku Klux Klan: Yankee Myth, Confederate Fact*.
314. *Confederate Veteran*, Vol. 30, 1922, pp. 365-366.
315. *Confederate Veteran*, Vol. 30, 1922, p. 437. (Note: The title of this entry is mine. L.S.)
316. *Confederate Veteran*, Vol. 31, 1923, p. 156. (Note: The title of this entry is mine. L.S.)
317. Vol. 177, p. 871. ["Near Veteran's" note.]
318. *Confederate Veteran*, Vol. 32, 1924, pp. 36-37. (Note: The title of this entry is mine. L.S.)
319. See my bibliography. L.S.
320. *Confederate Veteran*, Vol. 32, 1924, pp. 305-307.
321. *Confederate Veteran*, Vol. 33, 1925, p. 404. (Note: The title of this entry is mine. L.S.)
322. *Confederate Veteran*, Vol. 34, 1926, p. 20. (Note: The title of this entry is mine. L.S.)
323. See my bibliography. L.S.
324. See my bibliography. L.S.
325. See my bibliography. L.S.
326. See Piatt in my bibliography. L.S.
327. See my bibliography. L.S.
328. See my book, *Abraham Lincoln Was a Liberal, Jefferson Davis Was a Conservative: The Missing Key to Understanding the American Civil War*. L.S.
329. *Confederate Veteran*, Vol. 34, 1926, pp. 248-249. (Note: The title of this entry is mine. L.S.)
330. *Confederate Veteran*, Vol. 35, 1927, p. 4. (Note: The title of this entry is mine. L.S.)
331. *Confederate Veteran*, Vol. 35, 1927, p. 210. (Note: The title of this entry is mine. L.S.)
332. *Confederate Veteran*, Vol. 35, 1927, p. 422. (Note: The title of this entry is mine. L.S.)
333. *Confederate Veteran*, Vol. 35, 1927, p. 317. (Note: The title of this entry is mine. L.S.)
334. *Confederate Veteran*, Vol. 36, 1928, p. 220. (Note: The title of this entry is mine. L.S.)
335. *Confederate Veteran*, Vol. 36, 1928, pp. 342-343. (Note: The title of this entry is mine. L.S.)
336. See my bibliography. L.S.
337. *Confederate Veteran*, Vol. 36, 1928, p. 449-450. (Note: The title of this entry is mine. L.S.)
338. *Confederate Veteran*, Vol. 37, 1929, pp. 87-88. For more on the truth about both world slavery and American slavery, see my book *Everything You Were Taught About American Slavery is Wrong, Ask a Southerner!* (Note: The title of this entry is mine. L.S.)
339. *Confederate Veteran*, Vol. 38, 1930, p. 260. (Note: The title of this entry is mine. L.S.)
340. The "Higher Law" doctrine was an illegal and intentionally contrived sociopolitical invention of early American Liberals, Socialists, and Communists, mainly from the North. It stipulated that there was a law higher than the Constitution, *a law of conscience* regarding the need to abolish slavery in the South as quickly as possible, and by whatever means necessary. This view, adopted by millions of Victorian Left-wingers,

granted this radical group permission to ignore, violate, and trample over the U.S. Constitution in order to achieve their goal. Countless crimes and outrages were committed against the South and her people under its auspices. The Higher Law doctrine was one of the many minor elements that led to the secession of the Southern states and, ultimately, to war. L.S.

341. For more on the early New England secession movement, see my books *Confederacy 101: Amazing Facts You Never Knew About America's Oldest Political Tradition*; and *All We Ask is to be Let Alone: The Southern Secession Fact Book*. L.S.

342. *Confederate Veteran*, Vol. 38, 1930, pp. 385-386. (Note: The title of this entry is mine. L.S.)

343. *Confederate Veteran*, Vol. 39, 1931, pp. 275, 277. (Note: The title of this entry is mine. L.S.)

344. For a detailed examination of this topic, see my book *Everything You Were Taught About American Slavery is Wrong, Ask a Southerner!* L.S.

345. Sadly, as far as I have been able to tell, *all* statues of Confederate officials have since been removed from Statuary Hall in Washington, D.C. L.S.

346. *Confederate Veteran*, Vol. 40, 1932, pp. 10-11. (Note: The title of this entry is mine. L.S.)

347. *Confederate Veteran*, Vol. 40, 1932, p. 67. (Note: The title of this entry is mine. L.S.)

348. *Confederate Veteran*, Vol. 40, 1932, p. 128. (Note: The title of this entry is mine. L.S.)

349. *Confederate Veteran*, Vol. 40, 1932, p. 130.

350. *Confederate Veteran*, Vol. 40, 1932, p. 166. (Note: The title of this entry is mine. L.S.)

351. *Confederate Veteran*, Vol. 40, 1932, pp. 221-222, 223. (Note: The title of this entry is mine. L.S.)

352. In his April 19, 1861, "Proclamation" issuing an illegal blockade of Southern ports, Lincoln clearly states that his main concern with the secession of the Southern states is that "the collection of revenue cannot be effectually executed" by the United States. Seabrook, *Abraham Lincoln: The Southern View* (2021 ed), pp. 60-61.

353. *Confederate Veteran*, Vol. 40, 1932, pp. 261-262. (Note: The title of this entry is mine. L.S.)

354. *Confederate Veteran*, Vol. 40, 1932, p. 298. (Note: The title of this entry is mine. L.S.)

Both the War for the Constitution and the War of Reconstruction were unnecessary. But the Left needed both to remain in power. And so the wars came. The North then rewrote history and called them "irrepressible conflicts."

BIBLIOGRAPHY

And Suggested Reading

Adams, Charles Francis, Sr. *The Constitutional Ethics of Secession and War is Hell: Two Speeches of Charles Francis Adams*. Boston, MA: Houghton, Mifflin and Co., 1903.
Adamson, Augustus Pitt. *Brief History of the Thirtieth Georgia Regiment*. Griffin, GA: Mills Printing Co., 1912.
Alexander, Edward Porter. *Military Memoirs of a Confederate*. New York: Charles Scribner's Sons, 1907.
Anderson, John H. *Notes on the Life of Stonewall Jackson and on His Campaigning in Virginia, 1861-1863*. London, UK: Hugh Rees, 1904.
Anderson, Mabel Washbourne. *Life of General Stand Watie: The Only Indian Brigadier General of the Confederate Army and the Last General to Surrender*. Pryor, OK: self-published, 1915.
Andrews, Matthew Page. *The Dixie Book of Days*. Philadelphia, PA: J. B. Lippincott Co., 1912.
Armstrong, J. M. *The Biographical Encyclopedia of Kentucky of the Dead and Living Men of the Nineteenth Century*. Cincinnati, OH: J. M. Armstrong and Co., 1878.
Ashe, Samuel A'Court. *History of North Carolina*. 2 vols. Greensboro, NC: Charles L. Van Noppen, 1908.
Avary, Myrta Lockett. *Dixie After the War: An Exposition of Social Conditions Existing in the South, During the Twelve Years Succeeding the Fall of Richmond*. New York: Doubleday, Page and Co., 1906.
Avery, Isaac Wheeler. *The History of the State of Georgia From 1850 to 1881, Embracing Three Important Epochs: The Decade Before the War of 1861-65; The War; The Period of Reconstruction*. New York: Brown and Derby, 1881.
Benson, Al, Jr., and Walter Donald Kennedy. *Lincoln's Marxists*. Gretna, LA: Pelican, 2011.
Blaine, James G. *Twenty Years of Congress*. 2 vols. Norwich, CT: Henry Bill, 1886.
Bond, P. S. (ed.). *Military Science and Tactics: A Text and Reference for the Reserve Officers' Training Corps*. Washington, D.C.: P. S. Bond Publishing Co., 1938.
Bowers, Claude Gernade. *The Tragic Era: The Revolution After Lincoln*. Cambridge, MA: Riverside Press, 1929.
Boyd, James P. *Parties, Problems, and Leaders of 1896: An Impartial Presentation of Living National Questions*. Chicago, IL: Publishers' Union, 1896.
Bradley, Cornelius Beach (ed.). *Orations and Arguments by English and American Statesmen*. Boston, MA: Allyn and Bacon, 1895.
Brock, Robert Alonzo (ed.). *Southern Historical Society Papers*. 52 vols. Richmond, VA: Southern Historical Society, 1876-1943.
Browder, Earl. *Lincoln and the Communists*. New York, NY: Workers Library Publishers, Inc., 1936.
Bryan, William Jennings. *The First Battle: A Story of the Campaign of 1896*. Chicago, IL: W. B. Conkey Co., 1896.
Burgess, John William. *Reconstruction and the Constitution, 1866-1876*. New York: Charles Scribner's Sons, 1902.
Burns, James MacGregor. *The Vineyard of Liberty*. New York, NY: Alfred A.

Knopf, 1982.
Callahan, James Morton. *The Diplomatic History of the Southern Confederacy*. Baltimore, MD: Johns Hopkins Press, 1901.
Cantrell, Edward Adams. *Socialism and the World's Intellectuals: What Some Great Thinkers Have Said About Socialism and the Social Problem*. Los Angeles, CA: The Citizen Press, 1911.
Carpenter, Stephen D. *Logic of History - Five Hundred Political Texts: Being Concentrated Extracts of Abolitionism; Also Results of Slavery Agitation and Emancipation; Together With Sundry Chapters on Despotism, Usurpations and Frauds*. Madison, WI: self-published, 1864.
Chesterton, Cecil Edward. *A History of the United States*. London, UK: Chatto and Windus, 1919.
Christian, George Llewellyn. *Abraham Lincoln: An Address Delivered Before R. E. Lee Camp, No. 1 Confederate Veterans at Richmond, VA, October 29, 1909*. Richmond, VA: L. H. Jenkins, 1909.
———. *A Capitol Disaster: A Chapter of Reconstruction in Virginia*. Richmond, VA: self-published, 1915.
———. *Confederate Memories and Experiences*. Richmond, VA: self-published, 1915.
Commons, John R., David J. Saposs, Helen L. Sumner, E. B. Mittelman, H. E. Hoagland, John B. Andrews, Selig Perlman. *History of Labour in the United States*. New York: Macmillan Co., 1918.
Confederate Veteran (Sumner Archibald Cunningham, ed., 1893-1913; Edith Drake Pope, ed., 1914-1932). 40 vols (original forty year run). Nashville, TN: Confederate Veteran, 1893-1932.
Congressional Record: Containing the Proceedings and Debates of the Fifty-First Congress. Vol. 21, February 1890. Washington, D.C.: U.S. Government Printing Office, 1890.
Curry, Jabez Lamar Monroe. *The Southern States of the American Union Considered in Their Relations to the Constitution of the United States and to the Resulting Union*. New York: G. P. Putnam's Sons, 1894.
Davis, William Watson. *The Civil War and Reconstruction in Florida*. New York: Columbia University, 1913.
Dean, Henry Clay. *Crimes of the Civil War, and Curse of the Funding System*. Baltimore, MD: self-published, 1869.
Derry, Joseph T. *Story of the Confederate States; or, History of the War for Southern Independence*. Richmond, VA: B. F. Johnson, 1895.
Dixon, Thomas, Jr. *The Leopard's Spots: A Romance of the White Man's Burden—1865-1900*. New York: Grosset and Dunlap, 1902.
———. *The Clansman: An Historical Romance of the Ku Klux Klan*. New York: A. Wessels Co., 1907.
———. *The Southerner: A Romance of the Real Lincoln*. New York: D. Appleton and Co., 1913.
———. *The Black Hood*. New York: D. Appleton and Co., 1924.
Dodd, Bella. *School of Darkness*. New York, NY: P. J. Kennedy and Sons, 1954.
Early, Jubal Anderson. *A Memoir of the Last Year of the War for Independence, in the Confederate States of America*. Lynchburg, VA: Charles W. Button, 1867.
Eckenrode, Hamilton James. *The Political History of Virginia During the Reconstruction*. (Johns Hopkins University Studies in Historical and Political Science series). Baltimore, MD: Johns Hopkins Press, 1904.
Edmonds, George. *Facts and Falsehoods Concerning the War on the South, 1861-1865*. Memphis, TN: self-published, 1904.
Elson, Henry William. *Side Lights on American History*. 2 vols. New York:

Macmillan and Co., 1899.
———. *History of the United States of America*. 5 vols. New York: Macmillan and Co., 1904.
Evans, Clement Anselm (ed.). *Confederate Military History*. 12 vols. Atlanta, GA: Confederate Publishing Co., 1899.
Ewing, E. W. R. *Northern Rebellion, Southern Secession*. Philadelphia, PA: The John C. Winston Co., 1904.
Fiske, John. *American Political Ideas Viewed From the Standpoint of Universal History*. New York: Harper and Brothers, 1885.
Fitzhugh, George. *Cannibals All! Or, Slaves Without Masters*. Richmond, VA: A. Morris, 1857.
Fleming, Walter Lynwood. *Civil War and Reconstruction in Alabama*. New York: Columbia University Press, 1905.
———. *The Reconstruction of the Seceded States, 1865-1876*. Albany, NY: State Library and Home Education, 1905.
Flower, Frank Abial. *Edwin McMasters Stanton: The Autocrat of the Rebellion, Emancipation and Reconstruction*. Akron, OH: Saalfield Publishing Co., 1905.
Franklin, John Hope. *Reconstruction After the Civil War*. Chicago, IL: University of Chicago Press, 1961.
French, Samuel Gibbs. *Two Wars: An Autobiography of Gen. Samuel G. French*. Nashville, TN: Confederate Veteran, 1901.
Gardiner, C. *Acts of the Republican Party as Seen by History*. Washington, D.C.: self-published, 1906.
Garner, James Wilford. *Reconstruction in Mississippi*. New York: Macmillan Co., 1901.
Gordon, John Brown. *Reminiscences of the Civil War*. New York: Charles Scribner's Sons, 1903.
Greg, Percy. *History of the United States From the Foundation of Virginia to the Reconstruction of the Union*. 2 vols. London, UK: W. H. Allen and Co., 1887.
Hall, John Lesslie. *Half-hours in Southern History*. Richmond, VA: B. F. Johnson, 1907.
Hamilton, Joseph G. de Roulhac. *Reconstruction in North Carolina*. Raleigh, NC: Edwards and Broughton, 1906.
Hamilton, Peter Joseph. *The Reconstruction Period* (from *The History of North America*, Vol. 16). Philadelphia, PA: George Barrie and Sons, 1905.
Hancock, Richard R. *Hancock's Diary: or, A History of the Second Tennessee Confederate Cavalry*. Nashville, TN: self-published, 1887.
Hasselberg, P. D. (ed.). *Parliamentary Debates: First Session, Fortieth Parliament, 1982, House of Representatives* (Vol. 445). Wellington, New Zealand: Government Printer, 1982.
Helper, Hinton Rowan. *Compendium of the Impending Crisis of the South*. New York: A. B. Burdick, 1859.
Hill, Benjamin H., Jr. *Senator Benjamin H. Hill of Georgia: His Life, Speeches and Writings*. Atlanta, GA: T. H. P. Bloodworth, 1893.
Holland, Josiah Gilbert. *The Life of Abraham Lincoln*. Springfield, MA: Gurdon Bill, 1866.
Hollis, John Porter. *The Early Period of Reconstruction in South Carolina*. Baltimore, MD: Johns Hopkins Press, 1905.
Huxley, Thomas Henry. *Essays Ethical and Political*. London, UK: Macmillan and Co., 1903.
James, John Garland. *The Southern Student's Hand-Book of Selections for Reading and Oratory*. New York: A. S. Barnes and Co., 1879.

Johnson, Robert Underwood, and Clarence Clough Buel (eds.). *Battles and Leaders of the Civil War.* 4 vols. New York, NY: The Century Co., 1884-1888.

Johnston, Alexander (ed.). *American Orators: Studies in American Political History.* New York: G. P. Putnam's Sons, 1898.

Johnston, Joseph Eggleston. *Narrative of Military Operations, Directed, During the Late War Between the States.* New York: D. Appleton and Co., 1874.

Johnstone, Huger William. *Truth of War Conspiracy, 1861.* Idylwild, GA: H. W. Johnstone, 1921.

Jones, John William. *The Davis Memorial Volume; Or Our Dead President, Jefferson Davis and the World's Tribute to His Memory.* Richmond, VA: B. F. Johnson, 1889.

Kamman, William F. *Socialism in German American Literature.* Philadelphia, PA: Americana Germanica Press, 1917.

Keller, Martha Caroline. *Love and Rebellion: A Story of the Civil War and Reconstruction.* New York: J. S. Ogilvie, 1891.

King, Edward. *The Great South: A Record of Journeys.* Hartford, CT: American Publishing Co., 1875.

Lamon, Ward Hill. *Recollections of Abraham Lincoln, 1847-1865.* Chicago, IL: A. C. McClurg and Co., 1895.

Lee, Fitzhugh. *General Lee.* New York: The University Society, 1905.

Lenin, Vladimir. *"Left Wing" Communism: An Infantile Disorder.* Detroit, MI: The Marxian Educational Society, 1921.

Lindsley, John Berrien. *The Military Annals of Tennessee. Confederate. First Series: Embracing A Review of Military Operations.* Nashville, TN: J. M. Lindsley and Co., 1886.

Livermore, Thomas L. *Numbers and Losses in the Civil War in America, 1861-65.* 1900. Carlisle, PA: John Kallmann, 1996 ed.

Long, A. D., and Marcus J. Wright (eds.). *Memoirs of Robert E. Lee: His Military and Personal History Embracing a Large Amount of Information Hitherto Unpublished.* New York: J. M. Stoddart and Co. 1887.

Longstreet, James. *From Manassas to Appomattox: Memoirs of the Civil War in America.* Philadelphia, PA: J. B. Lippicott Co., 1896.

Lunt, George. *The Origin of the Late War: Traced From the Beginning of the Constitution to the Revolt of the Southern States.* New York: D. Appleton and Co., 1866.

Magliocca, Gerard N. *The Tragedy of William Jennings Bryan: Constitutional Law and the Politics of Backlash.* New Haven, CT: Yale University Press, 2011.

Marx, Karl. *Revolution and Counter-Revolution or Germany in 1848.* Chicago, IL: Charles H. Kerr and Co., 1907.

Marx, Karl, and Frederick Engels. *Manifesto of the Communist Party.* Chicago, IL: Charles H. Kerr and Co., 1906.

McCarty, Burke (ed.). *Little Sermons in Socialism by Abraham Lincoln.* Chicago, IL: The Chicago Daily Socialist, 1910.

McClure, Alexander Kelly. *The South: Its Industrial, Financial, and Political Condition.* Philadelphia, PA: J. B. Lippincott Co., 1886.

———. *Our Presidents and How We Make Them.* New York: Harper and Brothers, 1900.

McNeily, John Seymore. *From Organization to Overthrow of Mississippi's Provisional Government, 1865-1868.* Jackson, MS: Mississippi Historical Society, 1916.

McPherson, Edward. *The Political History of the United States of America During the Period of Reconstruction.* Washington, D.C.: James J. Chapman, 1880.

McPherson, James M. *Abraham Lincoln and the Second American Revolution.* New

York, NY: Oxford University Press, 1991.
Meriwether, Elizabeth Avery (pseudonym, "George Edmonds"). *Facts and Falsehoods Concerning the War on the South, 1861-1865*. Memphis, TN: A. R. Taylor and Co., 1904.
Miller, Francis Trevelyan, and Robert S. Lanier (eds.). *The Photographic History of the Civil War*. 10 vols. New York, NY: The Review of Reviews Co., 1911.
Milton, George Fort. *The Age of Hate: Andrew Johnson and the Radicals*. New York: Coward-McCann, 1930.
Minor, Charles Landon Carter. *The Real Lincoln, From the Testimony of His Contemporaries*. Richmond, VA: Everett Waddey Co., 1904.
Minutes of the Eighth Annual Meeting and Reunion of the United Confederate Veterans, Atlanta, GA, July 20-23, 1898. New Orleans, LA: United Confederate Veterans, 1907.
Minutes of the Ninth Annual Meeting and Reunion of the United Confederate Veterans, Charleston, SC, May 10-13, 1899. New Orleans, LA: United Confederate Veterans, 1907.
Minutes of the Twelfth Annual Meeting and Reunion of the United Confederate Veterans, Dallas, TX, April 22-25, 1902. New Orleans, LA: United Confederate Veterans, 1907.
Mooney, Sue F. Dromgoole. *My Moving Tent*. Nashville, TN: Methodist Publishing House, 1903.
Morgan, James Morris. *Recollections of a Rebel Reefer*. Boston, MA: Houghton Mifflin Co., 1917.
Morgan, William Henry. *Personal Reminiscences of the War of 1861-5*. Lynchburg, VA: J. P. Bell Co., 1911.
Morton, Richard Lee. *The Negro in Virginia Politics, 1865-1902*. Charlottesville, VA: self-published, 1913.
Muzzey, David Saville. *The United States of America: Vol. 1, To the Civil War*. Boston, MA: Ginn and Co., 1922.
——. *The American Adventure: Vol. 2, From the Civil War*. 1924. New York, NY: Harper and Brothers, 1927 ed.
Nicolay, John G., and John Hay (eds.). *Abraham Lincoln: A History*. 10 vols. New York, NY: The Century Co., 1890.
——. *Complete Works of Abraham Lincoln*. 12 vols. 1894. New York, NY: Francis D. Tandy Co., 1905 ed.
——. *Abraham Lincoln: Complete Works*. 12 vols. 1894. New York, NY: The Century Co., 1907 ed.
ORA (full title: *The War of the Rebellion: A Compilation of the Official Records of the Union and Confederate Armies*). 128 vols. Washington, DC: Government Printing Office, 1880.
ORN (full title: *Official Records of the Union and Confederate Navies in the War of the Rebellion*). 30 vols. Washington, DC: Government Printing Office, 1894.
Page, Thomas Nelson. *The Old South: Essays Social and Political*. New York: Charles Scribner's Sons, 1892.
——. *Red Rock: A Chronicle of Reconstruction*. New York: Charles Scribner's Sons, 1898.
Palmer, Beverly Wilson, and Holly Byers Ochoa (eds.). *The Selected Papers of Thaddeus Stevens*. 4 vols. Pittsburgh, PA: University of Pittsburgh Press, 1997.
Pease, Verne Seth. *In the Wake of War: A Tale of the South Under Carpet-Bagger Administration*. Chicago: George M. Hill Co., 1900.
Peek, Comer Leonard. *Lorna Carswell: A Story of the South*. New York: Broadway

Publishing Co., 1903.
Piatt, Donn. *Memories of the Men Who Saved the Union*. New York: Belford, Clarke and Co., 1887.
Pollard, Edward Alfred. *The Lost Cause*. New York, NY: E. B. Treat and Co., 1867.
Prince, Leon Cushing. *A Bird's-Eye View of American History*. New York: Charles Scribner's Sons, 1907.
Ramsdell, Charles William. *Reconstruction in Texas*. New York: Columbia University Press, 1910.
Randall, James Garfield. *Constitutional Problems Under Lincoln*. New York: D. Appleton and Co., 1926.
Rawle, William. *A View of the Constitution of the United States of America*. Philadelphia, PA: self-published, 1825.
Reynolds, John Schreiner. *Reconstruction in South Carolina, 1865-1877*. Columbia, SC: The State Co., Publishers, 1905.
Rhodes, James Ford. *History of the United States From Hayes to McKinley, 1877-1896*. New York: Macmillan Co., 1919.
Richardson, John Anderson. *Richardson's Defense of the South*. Atlanta, GA: A. B. Caldwell, 1914.
Rogers, William P. *The Three Secession Movements in the United States: Samuel J. Tilden, the Democratic Candidate for Presidency; the Advisor, Aider and Abettor of the Great Secession Movement of 1860; and One of the Authors of the Infamous Resolution of 1864; His Claims as a Statesman and Reformer Considered*. Boston, MA: John Wilson and Son, 1876.
Rove, Karl. *The Triumph of William McKinley: Why the Election of 1896 Still Matters*. New York, NY: Simon and Schuster, 2015.
Rutherford, Mildred Lewis. *Truths of History: A Fair, Unbiased, Impartial, Unprejudiced and Conscientious Study of History*. Athens, GA: n.p., 1920.
——. *Miss Rutherford's Scrap Book: Valuable Information About the South*. Athens, GA: self-published, 1924.
Schlüter, Herman. *Lincoln, Labor and Slavery: A Chapter From the Social History of America*. New York: Socialist Literature Co., 1913.
Schouler, James. *History of the Reconstruction Period, 1865-1877*. New York: Dodd, Mead and Co., 1913.
Schwab, John Christopher. *The Confederate States of America, 1861-1865*. New York: Charles Scribner's Sons, 1901.
Seabrook, Lochlainn. *Carnton Plantation Ghost Stories: True Tales of the Unexplained from Tennessee's Most Haunted Civil War House!* 2005. Franklin, TN, 2016 ed.
——. *Nathan Bedford Forrest: Southern Hero, American Patriot*. 2007. Franklin, TN, 2010 ed.
——. *Abraham Lincoln: The Southern View*. 2007. Franklin, TN: Sea Raven Press, 2013 ed.
——. *The McGavocks of Carnton Plantation: A Southern History - Celebrating One of Dixie's Most Noble Confederate Families and Their Tennessee Home*. 2008. Franklin, TN, 2011 ed.
——. *A Rebel Born: A Defense of Nathan Bedford Forrest*. 2010. Franklin, TN: Sea Raven Press, 2011 ed.
——. *Everything You Were Taught About the Civil War is Wrong, Ask a Southerner!* 2010. Franklin, TN: Sea Raven Press, revised 2019 ed.
——. *The Quotable Jefferson Davis: Selections From the Writings and Speeches of the Confederacy's First President*. Franklin, TN: Sea Raven Press, 2011.
——. *The Quotable Robert E. Lee: Selections From the Writings and Speeches of the South's

Most Beloved Civil War General. Franklin, TN: Sea Raven Press, 2011 Sesquicentennial Civil War Edition.

——. *Lincolnology: The Real Abraham Lincoln Revealed In His Own Words*. Franklin, TN: Sea Raven Press, 2011.

——. *The Unquotable Abraham Lincoln: The President's Quotes They Don't Want You To Know!* Franklin, TN: Sea Raven Press, 2011.

——. *Honest Jeff and Dishonest Abe: A Southern Children's Guide to the Civil War*. Franklin, TN: Sea Raven Press, 2012.

——. *Encyclopedia of the Battle of Franklin - A Comprehensive Guide to the Conflict that Changed the Civil War*. Franklin, TN: Sea Raven Press, 2012.

——. *The Quotable Nathan Bedford Forrest: Selections From the Writings and Speeches of the Confederacy's Most Brilliant Cavalryman*. Spring Hill, TN: Sea Raven Press, 2012.

——. *Forrest! 99 Reasons to Love Nathan Bedford Forrest*. Spring Hill, TN: Sea Raven Press, 2012.

——. *Give 'Em Hell Boys! The Complete Military Correspondence of Nathan Bedford Forrest*. Spring Hill, TN: Sea Raven Press, 2012.

——. *The Constitution of the Confederate States of America Explained: A Clause-by-Clause Study of the South's Magna Carta*. Spring Hill, TN: Sea Raven Press, 2012 Sesquicentennial Civil War Edition.

——. *The Great Impersonator: 99 Reasons to Dislike Abraham Lincoln*. Spring Hill, TN: Sea Raven Press, 2012.

——. *The Old Rebel: Robert E. Lee As He Was Seen By His Contemporaries*. Spring Hill, TN: Sea Raven Press, 2012 Sesquicentennial Civil War Edition.

——. *The Quotable Stonewall Jackson: Selections From the Writings and Speeches of the South's Most Famous General*. Spring Hill, TN: Sea Raven Press, 2012 Sesquicentennial Civil War Edition.

——. *Saddle, Sword, and Gun: A Biography of Nathan Bedford Forrest for Teens*. Spring Hill, TN: Sea Raven Press, 2013.

——. *The Alexander H. Stephens Reader: Excerpts From the Works of a Confederate Founding Father*. Spring Hill, TN: Sea Raven Press, 2013.

——. *The Quotable Alexander H. Stephens: Selections From the Writings and Speeches of the Confederacy's First Vice President*. Spring Hill, TN: Sea Raven Press, 2013 Sesquicentennial Civil War Edition.

——. *Give This Book to a Yankee! A Southern Guide to the Civil War for Northerners*. Spring Hill, TN: Sea Raven Press, 2014.

——. *The Articles of Confederation Explained: A Clause-by-Clause Study of America's First Constitution*. Spring Hill, TN: Sea Raven Press, 2014.

——. *Confederate Blood and Treasure: An Interview With Lochlainn Seabrook*. Spring Hill, TN: Sea Raven Press, 2015.

——. *Nathan Bedford Forrest and the Battle of Fort Pillow: Yankee Myth, Confederate Fact*. Spring Hill, TN: Sea Raven Press, 2015.

——. *Everything You Were Taught About American Slavery War is Wrong, Ask a Southerner!* Spring Hill, TN: Sea Raven Press, 2015.

——. *Confederacy 101: Amazing Facts You Never Knew About America's Oldest Political Tradition*. Spring Hill, TN: Sea Raven Press, 2015.

——. *The Great Yankee Coverup: What the North Doesn't Want You to Know About Lincoln's War!* Spring Hill, TN: Sea Raven Press, 2015.

——. *Slavery 101: Amazing Facts You Never Knew About America's "Peculiar Institution."* Spring Hill, TN: Sea Raven Press, 2015.

——. *Confederate Flag Facts: What Every American Should Know About Dixie's Southern Cross*. Spring Hill, TN: Sea Raven Press, 2016.

———. *Nathan Bedford Forrest and the Ku Klux Klan: Yankee Myth, Confederate Fact.* Spring Hill, TN: Sea Raven Press, 2016.

———. *Seabrook's Bible Dictionary of Traditional and Mystical Christian Doctrines.* Spring Hill, TN: Sea Raven Press, 2016.

———. *Everything You Were Taught About African-Americans and the Civil War is Wrong, Ask a Southerner!* Spring Hill, TN: Sea Raven Press, 2016.

———. *Nathan Bedford Forrest and African-Americans: Yankee Myth, Confederate Fact.* Spring Hill, TN: Sea Raven Press, 2016.

———. *Women in Gray: A Tribute to the Ladies Who Supported the Southern Confederacy.* Spring Hill, TN: Sea Raven Press, 2016.

———. *Lincoln's War: The Real Cause, the Real Winner, the Real Loser.* Spring Hill, TN: Sea Raven Press, 2016.

———. *The Unholy Crusade: Lincoln's Legacy of Destruction in the American South.* Spring Hill, TN: Sea Raven Press, 2017.

———. *Abraham Lincoln Was a Liberal, Jefferson Davis Was a Conservative: The Missing Key to Understanding the American Civil War.* Spring Hill, TN: Sea Raven Press, 2017.

———. *All We Ask is to be Let Alone: The Southern Secession Fact Book.* Spring Hill, TN: Sea Raven Press, 2017.

———. *The Ultimate Civil War Quiz Book: How Much Do You Really Know About America's Most Misunderstood Conflict?* Spring Hill, TN: Sea Raven Press, 2017.

———. *Rise Up and Call Them Blessed: Victorian Tributes to the Confederate Soldier, 1861-1901.* Spring Hill, TN: Sea Raven Press, 2017.

———. *Victorian Confederate Poetry: The Southern Cause in Verse, 1861-1901.* Spring Hill, TN: Sea Raven Press, 2018.

———. *Confederate Monuments: Why Every American Should Honor Confederate Soldiers and Their Memorials.* Spring Hill, TN: Sea Raven Press, 2018.

———. *The God of War: Nathan Bedford Forrest as He Was Seen by His Contemporaries.* Spring Hill, TN: Sea Raven Press, 2018.

———. *The Battle of Spring Hill: Recollections of Confederate and Union Soldiers.* Spring Hill, TN: Sea Raven Press, 2018.

———. *I Rode With Forrest! Confederate Soldiers Who Served With the World's Greatest Cavalry Leader.* Spring Hill, TN: Sea Raven Press, 2018.

———. *The Battle of Nashville: Recollections of Confederate and Union Soldiers.* Spring Hill, TN: Sea Raven Press, 2018.

———. *The Battle of Franklin: Recollections of Confederate and Union Soldiers.* Spring Hill, TN: Sea Raven Press, 2018.

———. *A Rebel Born: The Screenplay* (for the film). Written 2011. Franklin, TN: Sea Raven Press, 2020.

———. (ed.) *A Short History of the Confederate States of America* (Jefferson Davis, Belford Company, NY, 1890). A Sea Raven Press Reprint. Spring Hill, TN: Sea Raven Press, 2020.

———. (ed.) *Prison Life of Jefferson Davis: Embracing Details and Incidents in his Captivity, With Conversations on Topics of Public Interest* (John J. Craven, Sampson, Low, Son, and Marston, London, UK, 1866). A Sea Raven Press Reprint. Spring Hill, TN: Sea Raven Press, 2020.

———. *What the Confederate Flag Means to Me: Americans Speak Out in Defense of Southern Honor, Heritage, and History.* Spring Hill, TN: Sea Raven Press, 2021.

———. *Heroes of the Southern Confederacy: The Illustrated Book of Confederate Officials, Soldiers, and Civilians.* Spring Hill, TN: Sea Raven Press, 2021.

———. *Support Your Local Confederate: Wit and Humor in the Southern Confederacy.* Spring Hill, TN: Sea Raven Press, 2021.

———. *America's Three Constitutions: Complete Texts of the Articles of Confederation, Constitution of the United States of America, and Constitution of the Confederate States of America*. Spring Hill, TN: Sea Raven Press, 2021.
———. *Vintage Southern Cookbook: 2,000 Delicious Dishes From Dixie*. Spring Hill, TN: Sea Raven Press, 2021.
———. *The Bittersweet Bond: Race Relations in the Old South as Described by White and Black Southerners*. Spring Hill, TN: Sea Raven Press, 2022.
———. (ed.) *The Rise and Fall of the Confederate Government* (Jefferson Davis, D. Appleton, New York, 1881). 2 vols. A Sea Raven Press Facsimile Reprint. Spring Hill, TN: Sea Raven Press, 2022.
———. *I, Confederate: Why Dixie Seceded and Fought in the Words of Southern Soldiers*. Spring Hill, TN: Sea Raven Press, 2023.
Shaler, Nathaniel Southgate (ed.). 3 vols. *The United States of America: A Study of the American Commonwealth*. New York: D. Appleton and Co., 1894.
Sinclair, Arthur. *Two Years on the Alabama*. Boston, MA: Lee and Shepard, 1896.
Steel, Samuel Augustus. *The South Was Right*. Columbia, SC: R. L. Bryan Co., 1914.
Stephens, Alexander Hamilton. *Speech of Mr. Stephens, of Georgia, on the War and Taxation*. Washington, D.C.: J & G. Gideon, 1848.
———. *A Constitutional View of the Late War Between the States; Its Causes, Character, Conduct and Results*. 2 vols. Philadelphia, PA: National Publishing, Co., 1870.
———. *The Reviewers Reviewed*. New York: D. Appleton and Co., 1872.
———. *A Compendium of the History of the United States From the Earliest Settlements to 1883*. Columbia, SC: W. J. Duffie, 1875.
———. *Recollections of Alexander H. Stephens: His Diary Kept When a Prisoner at Fort Warren, Boston Harbour, 1865*. New York, NY: Doubleday, Page, and Co., 1910.
Stevens, Thaddeus. *Reconstruction: Speech by Hon. Thaddeus Stevens, of Pennsylvania* (delivered in the House of Representatives December 18, 1865). Washington, D.C.: self-published, 1865.
Stiles, Robert. *Four Years under Marse Robert*. New York: Neale Publishing Co., 1903.
Studies in Southern History and Politics (by pupils of Prof. William A. Dunning, Columbia University). New York: Columbia University Press, 1914.
Taylor, Richard. *Destruction and Reconstruction: Personal Experiences of the Late War*. New York: D. Appleton and Co., 1879.
The South: Some Addresses. Charlotte, NC: The Observer Printing House, 1910.
Thompson, Clara Mildred. *Reconstruction in Georgia: Economic, Social, Political, 1865-1872*. New York: Columbia University Press, 1915.
Thompson, Holland. *The New South: A Chronicle of Social and Industrial Evolution*. New Haven, CT: Yale University Press, 1920.
Toney, Marcus Breckenridge. *The Privations of a Private*. Nashville, TN: self-published, 1905.
Wallace, John. *Carpetbag Rule in Florida: The Inside Workings of the Reconstruction of Civil Government in Florida After the Close of the Civil War*. Jacksonville, FL: Da Costa, 1888.
Warner, Ezra J. *Generals in Gray: Lives of the Confederate Commanders*. 1959. Baton Rouge, LA: Louisiana State University Press, 1989 ed.
———. *Generals in Blue: Lives of the Union Commanders*. 1964. Baton Rouge, LA: Louisiana State University Press, 2006 ed.
Weik, Jesse W. *The Real Lincoln: A Portrait*. Boston, MA: Houghton Mifflin Co., 1922.

Wharton, Henry M. *White Blood: A Story of the South.* New York: Neale Publishing Co., 1906.

Wilson, Woodrow. *A History of the American People.* 5 vols. New York: Harper and Brothers, 1901.

Woods, Thomas E., Jr. *The Politically Incorrect Guide to American History.* Washington, D.C.: Regnery, 2004.

Woolsey, Theodore D., et al. *The First Century of the Republic: A Review of American Progress.* New York: Harper and Brothers, 1876.

Wright, Mrs. D. Giraud (Louise Wigfall Wright). *A Southern Girl in '61: The War-Time Memories of A Confederate Senator's Daughter.* New York: Doubleday, Page and Co., 1905.

Wyeth, John Allan. *With Saber and Scalpel: The Autobiography of a Surgeon and Soldier.* New York: Harper and Brothers, 1914.

The Left's execution of the innocent Mary Surratt, along with the other so-called "Lincoln assassin conspirators," on July 7, 1865, was inspired by nothing more than pure vengeance. A portent of the horrific Reconstruction era that was soon to come, it was a sadistic act that will go down in the annals of American history as one of the greatest follies, worst abuses of political power, and most unjust and cowardly crimes of all time.

INDEX

INCLUDES TOPICS, PEOPLE, KEYWORDS, SPELLING VARIATIONS, & KEY PHRASES

A Rebel Born (Seabrook), 444
Abbeville, SC, 126, 449
Abbott, Lyman, 186, 367
Abernathy, Elizabeth D., 382
abolition, 27, 179, 190, 216, 231, 294, 361, 371
abolition movement, 27, 190, 231
abolition of slavery, 216
Abolition party, 179, 190
abolitionism, 238, 396, 470
abolitionist, 19, 192, 240, 452
abolitionists, 19, 190, 352, 353, 375, 411, 423, 436, 437, 445, 452
Abraham Lincoln Was a Liberal (Seabrook), 17, 20, 458
account, 43, 70, 101, 116, 137, 158, 164, 179, 186, 195, 228, 229, 231, 240, 246, 284, 289, 298, 345, 364, 387, 397, 400, 404, 420, 434, 441
Adams, Charles F., Jr., 186, 419
Adams, Charles F., Sr., 185, 315, 440
Adams, James T., 453
Adams, John, 275, 366
Adams, John Q., 419
Adamson, Augustus P., 209, 213, 215, 237, 249
Aesop, 385
Africa, 31, 153, 173, 180, 216, 259, 323, 324
African Methodist Church, 103
African slavery, 354, 357
Africanisation, 326
Africanization, of the South, 353
African-American servants, 294
agitators, 71, 121, 445
agricultural exhibitions, 96
agricultural implements, 86, 90, 337
agricultural products, 86, 93

agriculture, 43, 84, 89, 102, 146, 164
agriculturists, 101
Akers, Peter, 201
al-Raschid, Haroun, 271
Alabama, 34, 35, 56-58, 64, 69-71, 75, 91, 107, 117, 129, 173, 179, 186, 189, 199, 225, 312, 328, 331, 333, 335, 336, 371, 395, 419, 429, 436, 471, 477
Alaska, 118
Albany, NY, 142
Alberoni, Guilio, 270
Albert, Anselm, 457
alcoholism, among freed black servants, 304
aldermen, 70
Alderson, J. C., 344
alethophobia, 28
Alexander the Great, 153
Alfred the Great, 174
all-black KKK chapter, 232
Allegheny Mountains, 152
Alston, R. A., 285
amalgamation, 216, 324, 372
Amelia Court House, 279
America, 2, 3, 6, 16, 18, 20, 27, 34, 42, 48, 84, 153, 158, 159, 177, 188, 217, 218, 287, 316, 322, 324, 331, 332, 335, 347, 357, 377, 381, 382, 408, 411, 415, 422, 453, 458, 470-477
America (steamer), 158
American abolition movement, 27, 190
American Colonization Society, 216
American Medical Association, 301
American Revolution, 187, 435
American Revolutionary War, 17

American slavery, 2, 27, 83, 86, 87, 236, 353, 438, 445, 475, 519
Americans, 2, 10, 19, 20, 22, 28, 38, 83, 101, 159, 160, 224, 380, 426, 476
Ames, Adelbert, 311, 448
Anabaptists, 265
anarchy, 175, 195, 292, 368, 454
anæsthetics, 153
ancestral patriotism, 297
Anderson, Frank, 157
Anderson, Mrs. John H., 452
Anderson, Mrs. Mabel W., 404
Andersonville Prison, 130, 132, 360
Andersonville, GA, 130, 132
André, Petit, 254
Andrew, John A., 299
Andrews, Matthew P., 429
Anglo-Saxon, 77, 105, 133, 175, 184
Anglo-Saxon civilization, 105
Anglo-Saxon race, 77
Anglo-Saxons, 342
Anneke, Fritz, 457
Anniston, AL, 95
Antietam, MD, 364
Antilles, 85
Antony, Mark, 173
Applegate, Andrew J., 71
apples, 89
Appomattox Court House, 275, 339, 454
Appomattox Court House, VA, 275
Appomattox River, 279, 310
Appomattox, VA, 24, 234, 313, 352, 357, 455
Arabs, 258
architects, 191
Arkansas, 34, 47, 55, 58, 69, 71, 87, 106, 129, 347, 404, 419, 443, 448
Arlington Cemetery, 356
Arlington House, 129
armies, 41-43, 45, 48, 49, 61, 85, 95, 96, 116, 118, 150, 152, 165, 168, 205, 223, 233, 237, 259, 279, 280, 292, 303-305, 331, 342, 346, 348, 373, 387, 404, 411, 431, 450, 473
army, 10, 19, 27, 32, 41, 42, 44, 45, 51, 66, 70, 73, 78, 99, 101, 112, 113, 116, 117, 122, 124, 127, 129, 131, 135, 137, 147, 148, 158-161, 163, 168, 171, 194, 203, 209, 210, 215, 225, 234, 242, 244-247, 252, 260, 261, 270, 279, 280, 285, 290, 291, 301-304, 307, 308, 311, 340, 347, 350, 351, 357, 365, 371, 388, 392, 395, 397, 404, 406, 409, 423, 424, 427, 431, 437, 441, 444, 448, 449, 453, 457, 458, 469
army contractors, 453
Army of Northern Virginia, 279
army of occupation, 124, 127, 357
army officer, 147, 194
Arthur, King, 382
Articles of Confederation, 2, 48, 118, 475, 477
asafoetida, 169
Asboth, Alexander S., 457
Asheville, NC, 369
Asia, 173
Asia Minor, 173
atheism, Northern, 37
Athens, Greece, 188
Atlanta exposition, 99
Atlanta, GA, 96, 99
Atlantic Ocean, 274
Atlantic ports, 100
Augusta, GA, 92, 319
Augustus, Caesar, 173
Austerlitz, Czech Republic, 209
Australia, 264
Australian aboriginals, 264
Austria, 71, 225
authoritarianism, 456
Avary, Myrta L., 329
Baba, Ali, 75
bacon, 241, 337, 469
Bagley, Worth, 117, 186
Bailey, David J., 211
Baird, Absalom, 258
bales of cotton, 92, 138, 144
Baltimore, MD, 100, 255, 256,

387
Band of Brothers and Sisters, 142
bank clearings, 93
Bank of England, 265
bankers' associations, 96
banking, 86, 93, 177, 260
banking capital, 86
Banks, Nathaniel P., 257, 373
Baptist Church, 390
barbarism, 29, 205
Barlow, Francis C., 457
Barmore, Mr., 157
Barnett, T. J., 33, 276
barroom, 183
Basilisk, 254
Battle of Antietam, 364
Battle of Austerlitz, 260
Battle of Chickamauga, 210
Battle of First Bull Run, 225
Battle of First Manassas, 225
Battle of Five Forks, 415
Battle of Fort Donelson, 239
Battle of Fort Pillow, 2, 475
Battle of Fort Sumter, 24
Battle of Franklin, 210, 242
Battle of Gettysburg, 210, 219, 233, 427
Battle of Jonesboro, 210
Battle of Murfreesboro, 210
Battle of Nashville, 2, 476
Battle of New Market, 442
Battle of Rossbach, 260
Battle of Sharpsburg, 210
Battle of Spottsylvania Courthouse, 225
Battle of Spring Hill, 2, 476
Battle of the Wilderness, 233
Battle of Thoroughfare Gap, 25
Bayard, Thomas F., 267
Beauregard, Pierre G. T., 311
Beecher, Henry W., 29, 286, 324, 378
beeswax, 86
Belt, Elizabeth, 289
Bentonville, AR, 372, 379
Betts, William, 288
Bhagavad Gita, 26
Bible, 3, 134, 190, 232, 391, 432, 476, 517
big government, 17, 24, 33, 276, 458

Biloxi, MS, 354
Bingham, Robert, 369
Birmingham, AL, 90, 95
Bishop, Bridgett, 206
Bishop, Edward, 206
Bismarck, Otto Von, 153
bivouacs, 160
black children, Left-wing indoctrination of, 450
black civil rights, 30, 133, 444
black Confederate, 329
black crime, 129, 198
black crime gang, 142
black crime statistics, 103, 104
black crimes, 111
black crimes against whites, 126
black equality, 388
black females, used as prostitutes by U.S. soldiers, 124
Black Friday, of the South, 171
black lifespan, 103
black lynchings, committed by Yankee Liberals, 258
black mammy, 321, 328
black man's party, 109
black population, 193
black racism, 181, 182
black racism among blacks, 325
black racism, stirred up by white Yankees, 174
black rape, of other blacks, 110
black rule, 194
black slave owners, 87, 304
black suffrage, 105
black supremacy, 38, 69, 71, 73, 80, 108, 109, 126, 129, 135, 137, 138, 171, 172, 194, 195, 197, 204, 211, 231-233, 236, 238, 239, 258, 388, 400, 401, 407, 433
Black Terror, 11, 215, 236
black victimization, 182
black welfare mentality, start of, 168
Black, J. C. C., 36
Black, Jeremiah S., 68
black-and-tan, 176
black-and-tan majority, 176
black-and-tan rule, 176
blacks, 29, 30, 35, 62, 63, 66, 69, 71, 74, 75, 77, 80, 94, 106,

109, 111, 112, 124, 125, 129, 132, 136, 157, 162, 168, 180, 195, 198, 216, 224, 234, 267, 279, 287, 292-295, 313, 322, 324, 328, 329, 334, 346, 356, 401, 402, 419, 423, 447
blacks, as political pawns of the Left, 77
blacks, U.S. government lies to, 122
blacks, used by U.S. to torment whites, 125
blacksmith, 321
Blaine, James G., 447
Blake, E. F., 236
bleeding Kansas, 427
Blenker, Louis, 457
blockade, 149, 363, 364, 453
Blue, Victor, 117
Boer republic, 337
Boers, 337
Bolivar County, MS, 144
Bolshevik Period, Reconstruction as the, 26
Bolshevik Reconstruction, 26
Bolshevik revolution, Reconstruction as a, 26, 398
Bond, Daniel, 287
bondage, 182, 304, 306, 356, 359, 419, 450
Booth, John W., 24, 166, 167, 192, 201, 202, 208, 219, 220, 386, 411
border states, 42, 73, 103, 194, 216, 220, 427
Borgoyne, John, 409
Boston, MA, 100, 206, 251, 254, 266, 409, 426
bottom rail on top, 311, 332
Boude, H. B., 389
Boutell, Henry S., 314
Bovay, Alvan E., 24
Bowers, Claude G., 10, 28, 130
Bowling Green, KY, 390
Bradenton, FL, 438
Bradford, Gamaliel, 425
Bradley, Cornelius B., 384
Bradwell, I. G., 387, 399
Bragg, Braxton, 32, 311
brains of the South, 179

Brantley, AL, 387, 399
Breckinridge, John C., 51, 209, 342
Brent, Robert J., 68
bribery, 71, 184, 227
bridges, 31, 122
Bringier, Louise M. M., 256
Brinvilliers, Marquise de, 274
Bristol, VA, 247
Britain, 17, 92, 118, 177, 355
British Empire, 17
British islands, 94
British Ministry, 269
British Parliament, 94, 257, 337
brogan shoes, 396
Brooklyn Eagle, 186, 205
Brooks, Phillips, 378
Brown, John, 220, 231, 286, 387, 427
Brown, Joseph E., 42, 163
Brown, Pitts, 158
Brownlow, William G., 157, 239, 391, 392, 448
Brunswick, GA, 100
Bryan, William J., 295
Buchanan, James, 24, 251
Buckalew, Charles R., 77
Buckley, C. W., 141
building material, 89
Bullock, Rufus B., 76, 418, 448
bummers, 406
Bunting, R. F., 245
Bunyan, John, 254
burglars, 266
Burke, Edmund, 275
Burkeville, VA, 203
Burton, Henry S., 255
Bush, Isidor, 457
business principles, 104
Butler, Benjamin F., 200, 229, 230, 409, 424, 447
Butler, Matthew C., 117, 401, 433
Butler, Picayune, 393
Butz, Caspar, 458
Byng, John, 269
C.S.A., 17, 380
cadets, 315, 442
Cadman S. P., 345
Cadwalader, John, 300
Caesar, Julius, 173, 184

Caffre tribes, 259
Cain (Bible), 75
Calhoun, John C., 179, 357
Caliban (Shakespeare), 254
calico, 126
California, 118, 431
Callaway, D. M., 343
Callis, John B., 141
Camden, SC, 119
Cameron, Simon, 447
Camp Chase, OH, 160, 161
Camp Chimborazo, 310
Camp Hardee, 318
Campbell County, VA, 203
Campbell, J. A., 290, 291
Canada, 107
Canby, Edward R. S., 250, 251
candles, 152, 421
Cannon, Joseph G., 317
Capel Court, 266
capital, 68, 75, 80, 82, 85-88, 93, 96, 100, 101, 143, 145, 175, 239, 250, 251, 265, 279, 291, 321, 331, 369, 454
capitalism, 20, 458
capitalists, 96, 100
Capitol, U.S., corruption in, 252
car wheels, 90
car works, 90
carding machines, 337
cards, 124, 302
Carnes, W. W., 438
Carnton, 3, 474
Carnton Plantation, 3, 474
carpet-bag governments, 97
carpet-baggers, 76, 79, 80, 82, 107, 204, 211, 232, 281, 309, 318, 340, 435
carpetbag government, 368
carpetbag rule, 477
carpetbaggers, 244, 390, 435
carpetbags, 400
carpet-bag politicians, 334
carpet-bag rule, 295, 343
Carroll, P. P., 311
cars, 106, 152, 288
Carter, Daniel F., 245
Cartersville, VA, 129
castes, 153
Catawba Indians, 328
Catchings, Thomas C., 26, 293

cattle, 89, 120, 137, 210, 267, 328, 369
cattle feed, 89
cat's-paw, 178
cavalry, 2, 128, 203, 279, 316, 337, 389, 400, 401, 441, 444, 471, 476
cavalrymen, 389
census, 44, 65, 82, 85-87, 103, 105, 260
Census Bureau, 103
Centennial Exposition of Tennessee, 283
Central America, 177
central government, 15, 16, 361
centralists, 15
centralization, 20, 355, 357, 358
centralized government, 348, 361, 405
Cervera, Pasqual, 112
Chaillé, Stanford E., 302
Chamberlain, Daniel H., 72, 79, 81, 174, 311, 401
Chamberlain, Ed, 137
Chambersburg, PA, 366
Chandler, William E., 447
Chandler, Zachariah, 273, 447
Charles I, King, 386
Charleston Harbor, SC, 406
Charleston, SC, 26, 120, 124, 126, 233, 449
Charleston, WV, 161, 344
Charlotte, TN, 239, 240
charm, 126, 383-385
Chase, Salmon P., 31, 234, 299, 308, 425, 447
Chatham, First Earl of, 268
Chattanooga, TN, 393
cheap iron, 90
Cherokee, 404
Cherokee Nation, 404
Chesapeake Bay, 255
Chesnut, Mary B., 119, 121, 124, 126, 432
Chester, SC, 119, 126, 449
Chesterton, Cecil E., 215, 236, 237, 249
Chesterton, G. K., 215
Chicago Tribune, 374, 448
Chicago, IL, 99, 100, 114, 372, 379

Chickamauga battlefield, 99
Chickamauga park, 114
Chickamauga, GA, 99
chickens, 316
Chicora (C.S. ironclad), 26
children, 2, 33, 94, 95, 106, 108, 109, 120, 121, 123-125, 131, 134, 146, 152, 155, 158, 170, 177, 181, 182, 188, 210, 236, 252, 257, 289, 301, 305, 316, 321, 327, 331, 333, 336, 337, 342, 345, 348, 356, 362, 364, 372-374, 387, 388, 399, 413, 414, 419, 421, 423, 431, 437, 438, 441, 444, 450, 451
Chile, 325
China, 134, 153, 177
Christ, 3, 281, 301, 371, 376, 390
Christian, 3, 20, 26, 27, 29, 32, 34, 74, 135, 181, 246, 259, 260, 265, 335, 337, 353, 382, 386, 393, 405, 413, 425-427, 429, 443, 470, 476
Christian humanity, 337
Christian ideals, 427
Christian world, 335, 386
Christianity, 3, 111, 353, 381, 515
Christmas, 3, 138, 436
church, 103, 111, 126, 132, 147, 156, 181, 183, 244-247, 250, 309, 376, 382, 388-390, 392, 395, 396, 416, 425, 426, 430
churches, 33, 35, 87, 106, 183, 242, 245-247, 281, 309, 390
Cicero, Marcus T., 173, 309
Cincinnati, OH, 158
citizens, 17, 29, 36, 42, 47, 48, 51, 53, 56, 57, 61, 62, 64, 66, 68, 70, 72, 74, 77-80, 82, 84, 99, 104, 111, 112, 114, 125, 133-135, 156, 161, 171, 172, 177, 179, 181, 194, 204, 211, 216, 240, 244, 258, 281, 282, 284, 285, 291, 319, 333, 354, 395, 396, 398, 402, 418, 426, 432, 450
citizenship, 60, 85, 98, 99, 104, 105, 107, 113, 159, 178, 194, 228, 232, 282, 285, 288, 292, 297, 301, 303, 309, 322, 369, 381, 388, 406, 419, 431
city bonds, 333
City Point, VA, 53
civic centralization, 355
civic decentralization, 355
civil rights, 30, 49, 131, 133, 134, 226, 237, 281, 309, 444
Civil War, 2, 3, 15, 17-20, 24, 28, 83, 115-117, 130, 131, 197, 198, 225, 275, 292, 344, 345, 347, 358, 359, 363, 369, 419, 425, 428, 440, 470-477, 517, 519
Civil War history, the Left's fake, 130
civilization, 22, 29, 78, 80, 83, 97, 105, 109, 128, 149, 173-175, 179, 181, 185, 196, 238, 239, 309, 351, 370, 388, 407, 421, 422, 442, 515
Clanton, James H., 515
Clark, Charles, 42, 163, 249, 251
Clarksville, TN, 393
clay, 77, 89, 179, 383, 431, 470
Clay, Henry, 179
Clayton, Powell F., 419, 448
Clayton, W. W., 285
cleaning, 310
Cleburne, Patrick R., 190
Cleveland, Grover, 95, 96, 98, 114, 185, 186
Cleveland, OH, 417
Clews, Henry, 447
climate, 84, 92, 93, 100, 289, 300, 323, 326
clothing, 130, 145, 146, 350, 429, 436
Clymer, Hiester, 379
coal, 84, 88, 90, 91, 158, 177, 268
coal fields, 91
coal oil, 158
Cobb, Howell, 42, 163
Cobbs, J. T., 289
coke, 90, 177
Colfax, Schuyler, 264
colleges, 95, 168, 178, 184
Collier's Weekly, 374

colonization, 216
Colorado, 111
colored race, 105, 182, 183, 368
Columbia, 33, 44, 64, 120, 123, 157, 158, 324, 400, 408, 432, 435, 470, 471, 474, 477
Columbia, SC, 120, 432
Columbus, MS, 100
Columbus, OH, 160, 161, 327
command centers, 35
commerce, 89, 93, 96, 101, 177
communism, 19, 412, 472
communist, 15, 19, 20, 26, 28, 33, 35, 36, 57, 69, 77, 148, 180, 259, 287, 293, 329, 398, 407, 444, 456-458, 472
communist uprising, Reconstruction as a, 398
communists, 17, 25, 26, 31, 38, 167, 199, 220, 226, 229, 232, 252, 258, 260, 264, 269, 270, 272, 287, 292, 295, 309, 330-332, 339, 353, 357, 439, 457, 458, 469
Compendium of the Impending Crisis of the South (Helper), 427
Compromise Bill, of 1850, 452
Comstock Lode, NV, 453
Confederacy, 2, 3, 29, 33, 34, 42, 46, 48, 60, 99, 115, 129, 135, 160, 161, 187, 188, 191, 203, 215, 216, 220, 221, 223, 233, 245, 262, 280, 281, 284, 286, 289, 301-305, 309, 311, 314, 328, 329, 341, 347, 350, 354, 357, 370, 371, 373, 377, 381, 386, 396, 406, 408, 411, 420, 427, 428, 433, 440, 442, 446, 448, 450, 455, 470, 475, 476
Confederate, 2, 3, 11, 13-16, 18-22, 24-29, 32-37, 41, 42, 45, 46, 48, 50, 51, 53, 56, 58, 73, 74, 79, 81, 83, 97, 99, 113-118, 120, 125, 130-132, 149, 151, 152, 155, 156, 158, 160, 161, 163, 167, 175, 180, 186, 190, 192, 193, 196, 201, 202, 204, 209, 211, 215, 216, 219, 223, 224, 231, 234-237, 245, 247-250, 275, 279, 280, 282, 284-293, 295-302, 306-311, 314-320, 328, 329, 331, 335, 336, 338, 339, 341-354, 356-359, 361, 364, 367, 369-372, 378, 379, 381, 382, 387, 388, 391, 393, 395-401, 404, 405, 407, 408, 411-416, 422-424, 428-433, 435, 438, 439, 442-444, 447-450, 452, 454-456, 469-478, 515, 517, 519
Confederate army, 116, 117, 158, 347, 404, 444, 469
Confederate bonds, 120, 149
Confederate buttons, 288
Confederate capitol, 328, 454
Confederate Capitol, first, 328
Confederate Cause, 298, 396
Confederate Congress, 42, 414
Confederate debt, 216, 223
Confederate flag, 2, 20, 475, 476, 519
Confederate flags, banned, 34
Confederate generals, 18, 99, 117, 190, 401
Confederate government, 3, 18, 42, 46, 51, 53, 56, 58, 81, 280, 349, 354, 454, 477
Confederate military, 36, 279, 471
Confederate money, 303
Confederate monument, 35, 114, 356
Confederate Movement, 280
Confederate museum, 358
Confederate prison camp, 130, 132
Confederate soldiers, 99
Confederate States, 2, 3, 16, 24, 42, 48, 79, 113, 114, 149, 231, 245, 280, 331, 341, 381, 404, 405, 408, 415, 456, 470, 474-477
Confederate States of America, 2, 3, 16, 42, 48, 381, 415, 470, 474-477
Confederate statue, 160
Confederate troops, 41

Confederate uniforms, banned, 34
Confederate Veteran magazine, 335
Confederate veterans, 18, 19, 21, 24, 161, 306, 309, 315, 316, 318, 347, 415, 430, 470, 473, 517
Confederate war, 356-358, 382
Confederates, 18, 49, 69, 114, 161, 225, 240, 282, 297, 302, 309, 311, 335, 336, 338, 364, 366, 391-393, 409, 411, 444, 450
confederation, 2, 48, 118, 178, 475, 477
confiscation, 30, 31, 134, 135, 146, 150, 178, 363, 409
Congaree River, 435
Congo, Africa, 259
Congress, 6, 28-30, 34, 42, 46, 49, 52-55, 57-62, 64-67, 69-74, 79-82, 97, 99, 113, 114, 122, 134, 135, 149, 150, 165-168, 170-172, 174, 179, 180, 188, 192-196, 204, 211, 212, 217, 220-222, 225, 227-231, 234, 238, 253, 259, 261-263, 265, 269, 273, 287, 302, 309, 320, 332, 335, 347, 363, 366-369, 379, 404, 406, 409, 414, 418, 425, 428, 438-440, 445, 448, 456, 469, 470
congressional committee, 132, 151
Congressional Committee on Reconstruction, 151
congressional reconstruction, 58, 62, 64-67, 113, 222
Conkling, Roscoe, 447
Connecticut, 107
consent of the governed, 152, 186, 218, 363, 428
conservatism, 297, 443
Conservatives, 15, 16, 37, 55, 70, 272, 283, 334, 353, 428, 515
consolidation, 16, 97
Constitution, 2, 9, 10, 18, 20, 21, 24, 26-28, 32, 37, 44-49, 52-56, 58, 60, 61, 67, 69-71, 73, 78, 79, 83, 98, 102, 115, 133, 134, 147, 149-151, 156, 165, 166, 170, 171, 175, 176, 179, 180, 187, 188, 194-196, 200, 211, 216, 225, 227, 238, 239, 254, 259, 261, 280, 282, 283, 288, 289, 300, 303, 306, 308, 311, 317, 324, 338, 344, 346, 348, 349, 356, 358, 364, 366, 388, 396, 404-406, 412-414, 419, 427, 429, 432, 437, 439, 440, 442, 445, 446, 449, 452, 453, 468-470, 472, 474, 475, 477
Constitution of the Confederate States, 2, 48, 475, 477
Constitutional Convention, 102
constitutional law, 472
constitutional liberty, 306, 345, 361
constitutional rights, 282, 338, 339, 379, 406, 415
contraband, 31, 364, 405, 409
contrabands, 310
Cook, Walter H., 417, 419
Cooke, Giles B., 415
Cooke, Jay, 447
cooking, 241, 421
Cooper Union, NY, 130
Cooper, C. W., 371
copper, 89
copperhead, 380
copperheads, 30, 64
corn, 86, 88, 89, 93, 121, 122, 144, 146, 176, 210, 275, 337, 399, 440
corn bread, 337
corruption, 38, 71, 75, 76, 78, 80, 81, 113, 172, 174, 175, 184, 185, 212, 238, 244, 266, 275, 299, 368, 391, 406, 407, 419, 446
corruptionists, 212
Corwin, George, 207
cotton, 31, 32, 86, 88-94, 100, 101, 122, 129, 136-139, 144, 146, 176, 177, 180, 323, 324, 332, 347, 353, 354, 369, 436, 447
cotton crop, 88, 89, 91, 94, 176, 369

cotton fields, 92, 177
cotton goods, 90, 92
cotton interests, Southern, 177
cotton manufacturing enterprises, 101
cotton plantations, 180
cotton products, 101
cotton tax, 347, 353
cotton-growing section, 92
cottonseed-oil mills, 88
councilmen, 184
counter-Reconstruction, 175, 196
county bonds, 333
county officers, 57, 58, 70, 135, 335
court judges, 70
Courtney, W. J., 431
cousinhood, 264
Couthon, Georges A., 267
Cowan, Edgar, 68
cows, 120, 240, 337, 436
Coxe, John, 346
Crassus, Marcus L., 173
Craven, John J., 50
Credit Mobiler Frauds, 299
Crédits Mobiliers, 254
Creek, 147, 155, 239
crime, 53, 69, 74, 104, 106-111, 125, 129, 133, 139, 148, 157, 174, 183, 192, 198, 201, 202, 220, 221, 239, 258, 259, 299, 304, 322, 324, 348, 352, 355, 367, 370, 378, 388, 391, 418, 419
crime, among freed black servants, 304
criminal statistics, 103
criminals, 103, 111, 196, 198, 200, 234, 282, 458
Crittenden Resolutions, 414
crop diversification, 177
Crosby, Ernest, 416
Cross, Nathaniel, 245
Crowe, James R., 515
Croxton, John T., 200
Cuba, 51, 112, 117, 167, 172, 186, 325, 408
Cunningham, Sumner A., 160, 285, 286, 296, 297, 301
Curry, J. L. M., 85
curse of Nineveh, 165

Curtin, Andrew G., 299
Cuvier, Georges, 150
Daily Picayune, 104
Dallas, TX, 95
Dana, Charles A., 360, 457
dancing, 127
Dante, 270
Danton, Georges J., 226
Danville, VA, 143
DAR, 233
Daughter of the Confederacy, 381
Daughters of the Grand Army Circle, 160
Davis, Henry W., 253, 254
Davis, Jefferson, 15, 16, 18, 42, 48, 50, 129, 132, 147, 163, 166, 167, 192, 201, 202, 205, 212, 215, 221, 228, 236, 249-251, 253-257, 280, 284, 286, 305-308, 314, 315, 320, 330, 331, 338, 342, 354, 356, 359, 360, 366, 371, 381, 397, 411, 414, 415, 430, 447, 458
Davis, Varina A. "Winnie", 381
Davis, Varina H., 164, 256, 381, 430
Davis, Winter, 425
Dawson, Frank, 433
De Leon, P. M., 353, 354
death, 3, 10, 31, 33, 42, 50, 53-55, 114, 152, 186, 192, 202, 205, 206, 219, 224, 226, 239, 241, 257, 260, 268, 280, 289, 295, 302, 306, 315, 340, 343, 350, 360, 361, 363, 383, 386, 387, 393, 397, 398, 409, 411, 416, 417, 420, 421, 435, 437, 447, 452, 515
Deborah (Bible), 325
Debs, Eugene V., 15, 457
debt, 45, 49, 75-77, 82, 95, 134, 144, 153, 173, 196, 216, 223, 227, 265, 297, 328, 333, 418, 422, 451
debts, 43, 57, 60, 69, 75, 80, 82, 97, 104, 134, 148, 173, 174, 232
decentralization, 355
Declaration of Independence, 17,

217, 218, 228, 349, 357, 358, 446
Decoration Day, 99
Deep South, 321
Delaware, 201-203, 265, 267
Delaware River, 203
demagoguery, 412
Democratic Party, 15, 16, 34, 78, 79, 113, 115, 180, 194, 197, 200, 271, 330, 424
Demosthenes, 309
Department of Agriculture, 146
deportation, 180, 359
Depression, 101, 304, 368, 443
depression, among freed black servants, 304
Derry (freedman), 136
Desdemona (Shakespeare), 395
despotism, 75, 238, 271, 318, 337, 346, 360, 442, 470
destruction, of the postwar South, 119
Devil, 182
devils, 136, 254, 334
Dewey, George, 112, 115
Dickinson College, Carlisle, PA, 199
Dickinson, Jacob M., 339
Dickson County, TN, 239
Dillard, Miss Lucy, 336
Dillard, Mrs. Lizzie L., 338
Dinkins, James, 424
Dinwiddie County, VA, 415
disability, 160
disaster, 85, 89, 117, 126, 221, 223, 295, 304, 420, 470
discrimination, 103, 264
disease, 96, 123, 162, 209, 268, 274, 304
disease, among freed black servants, 304
disinformationists, Left-wing, 25
disloyalty, 48, 221, 320, 392, 395
disorder, 35, 74, 106, 472
distrust, manufactured, 62
diversification, agricultural, 89
divorce rates, among freed black servants, 304
Dix, John A., 250, 262, 263
Dixie, 3, 6, 11, 21, 27, 29, 33, 34, 36, 37, 63, 154, 163, 180, 200, 224, 232, 286, 294, 301, 328, 335, 336, 362, 381, 432, 469, 477
Dixie Coworkers, 381
Dixiecrat, 25
Dixon, John (freedman), 138
Dixon, Thomas, Jr., 276, 304, 400
docks, 100
doctrine of secession, 185, 188
Domitian, Emperor, 251
Doolittle, James R., 262
Douglas, Henry T., 117, 351
Douglas, Stephen A., 218, 427
Douglass, Frederick, 324
Dred Scott case, 134
Drew, George F., 448
drug use, among freed black servants, 304
Dry Tortugas, FL, 201
duck, 158
Duck River, 158
due process, 194
duelling, 183
Dumfries, Scotland, 273
Dupont, Samuel F., 310
Dyas, Miss Alicia, 395
Dyer, G. W., 432
d'Aubra, Marie-Madeleine, 274
Earl of Oxford, 517
Early, Jubal A., 51, 311, 387, 449
Early, Mr., 71
East Tennessee, 91
Eastern markets, 90
Eberhard, E., 317
economic centralization, 355
economic decentralization, 355
economics, 27
Edgefield and Kentucky Railway, 156
Edgefield, TN, 395
educated class, 109
education, 20, 21, 27, 87, 94, 95, 98, 102-104, 111, 137, 177, 181, 185, 197, 198, 255, 266, 275, 322, 326, 331, 334, 339, 362, 403, 417, 418, 421, 426, 438, 450-452, 471
educational income, 87
educational institutions, 34, 177

educators, 179, 185, 362, 517
Edwards, Daniel B., 343
Egypt, 51, 129, 165, 167, 182, 341
election of 1876, 299
election of 1896, 16, 115
electioneering material, 235
elections, 34, 57, 62, 106, 133, 175, 183, 184, 211, 259, 319, 334, 402, 403
Electoral College, 235, 368, 369
electricity, 152, 421
elevators, 100, 101
Eliot, Charles W., 339
Elson, Henry W., 360
Emancipation Proclamation, 102, 166, 171, 215, 236, 279, 294, 364, 365, 410
empire, 17, 153, 266, 386
employment, 83, 89, 90, 102, 103, 144, 172, 274, 372, 374, 395
Encyclopedia Britannica, 29, 84
enfranchisement, 63, 107, 122, 350, 352, 370
Engels, Friedrich, 458
England, 29, 86, 88, 90, 92, 95, 118, 122, 129, 130, 135, 153, 173, 177, 188, 200, 206, 220, 225, 259, 265, 271, 315, 337, 362, 365, 376-379, 398, 409, 410, 436, 440, 446, 452
English, 15, 17, 19, 30, 72, 149, 180, 184, 215, 219, 264, 271, 275, 300, 368, 409, 426, 429, 469
English Channel, 173
Englishman, 93, 184, 345
enlisted men, 113
Enterprise, MS, 110
entitlement mentality, among blacks, 168
entitlement-victim mentality, 168
envy, 28, 187, 206, 264, 332, 377, 424
Ephraim (Bible), 187
Epic of Gilgamesh, 26
Episcopal Church, 390
equal rights, 438
ethnomasochism, 28, 58, 287

Europe, 51, 88, 100, 101, 148, 167, 178, 273, 274, 328, 357, 358, 363, 410, 411, 438, 442
European Imperialism, 357
European Revolution of 1848, 357
European Revolutions, 458
European socialists and communists, 357
European-Americans, 380
Evans, Clement A., 212, 280, 288
Evans, Fite, Porter & Company, 157
Eve, Paul F., 245
ex-Confederate soldiers, 113, 116
ex-Confederate States, 113, 114
Exodus, Book of, 182
faithful negroes, 124, 337
fake Civil War history, the Left's, 130
fakirs, 153, 325
Fall River, MA, 92, 101
family dysfunctionality, among freed black servants, 304
family heirlooms, 169, 210
family supplies, 89
fanaticism, 211, 234, 374, 377, 418, 456
farm assets, 88
farm produce, 177
farm products, 88, 176
farmer, 89, 356, 436
farmers, 27, 177, 326, 451
farmers' conventions, 96
farming, 88, 101, 104, 120, 165, 420
farming implements, 120, 165
farming land, 101
farmland, 30
farms, 32, 33, 42, 86, 105, 243, 340, 342, 356
Farmville, VA, 203
Farnese, Alexander, 270
fatherland, 189, 190
favoritism, 318
Federal authority, 280
federal government, 113, 125, 185, 194, 216, 227, 282, 300, 319, 424, 440, 441, 455
Federal ratio, 179
Federalism, 356, 358

Federals, 45
Fernandina, FL, 310
ferryboats, 152
fertilizer, 89
Fessenden, William P., 217
Fiala, Johan, 457
fiddles, 127
Fifteenth Amendment, 80, 83, 133, 147, 171, 195, 196, 311, 419, 446
fineries, 130
finery, 122, 128, 243, 396
finished products, 90
Finley, G. W., 307
First Presbyterian Church, 245, 246
Fish, Hamilton, 268
Fleming, W. L., 431
Fletcher, Duncan U., 448
Florida, 34, 47, 56, 58, 69, 76, 81, 118, 126, 143, 173, 186, 189, 235, 273, 289, 325, 370, 416, 419, 430, 447, 448, 470, 477
flour, 86, 419
Foraker, Joseph B., 160
Ford's Theatre, Washington, D.C., 192
foreign capital, 100
foreign commerce, 93, 177
foreigners, 36, 101, 159, 183, 223, 323, 426
Forrest, Nathan B., 18, 152, 175, 235, 316, 342, 407, 408, 444
Forrest's Cavalry, 316
Fort Delaware, DE, 201, 203
Fort Donelson, 239
Fort Mill, SC, 328
Fort Monroe, 164, 331
Fort Negley, Nashville, TN, 157
Fort Pillow, 2, 475
Fort Pulaski, 70
Fort Sumter, 17, 24, 353, 406
Fort Sumter, SC, 24
Fort Warren, 477
Fortress Monroe, 164, 205, 255, 307, 330
fortresses, 70
forty acres and a mule, 164, 308, 311, 416
forty-eighters, 357, 458

Foster, Sarah J., 362
Founders, 344
Founding Fathers, 15, 37, 48, 249, 428
foundries, 90
Fourierism, 29
Fourteenth Amendment, 60, 67-69, 80, 83, 133, 134, 171, 193-196, 311, 446
Fourtou, Oscar B. de, 272, 273
Fowles, J. H., 318
France, 135, 153, 178, 225, 262, 263, 357, 365, 387, 410, 442
franchise, 158, 195, 216, 217, 228, 292, 293, 326
Franco-Prussian War, 178
Franklin, Benjamin, 135
Franklin, TN, 210, 242
Franklin, VA, 143
fraternal union, 180, 186, 301
fraud, 132, 207, 257, 318, 419, 451
Frazier, J. B., 297
Frederick City, MD, 387
Frederick the Great, 260, 356
Fredericksburg, VA, 160
free America, 331, 332, 335
free labor, 29
free niggery, 309
free schools, 421
free states, 58, 179, 215
Freedman's Bank, 132
freedman's crime, 183
freedmen, 61-63, 121, 124, 126, 128, 131, 133, 136, 142, 144, 147, 148, 164, 168, 169, 194, 195, 216, 228, 231-233, 260, 390, 438, 452
freedmen, inflamed by Yankee Radicals, 124
Freedmen's Bureau, 43, 49, 57, 59-63, 71, 132, 136, 140, 147, 260, 287, 293, 309, 451
Freedmen's Bureau law, 43
freedom, 22, 26, 43, 49, 51, 63, 79, 80, 82, 98, 102, 108, 109, 121-123, 164, 193, 197, 198, 204, 222, 231, 240, 241, 304, 322, 332, 333, 342, 350, 353, 371, 381, 383, 399, 422, 426, 430

freight rates, 90
Frémont, John C., 15, 24, 373, 406, 425, 457
French Academy, 150
French and Indian War, 117
French army, 270
French Huguenots, 174
French people, 178
French, John, 373
French, Samuel G., 131, 153
fruits, 89, 195, 313, 318, 419
Fry, A. F., 13, 372, 379
Fry, Elizabeth, 168
fugitive slave laws, 46
fugitive slaves, 227, 445
Fuller, R., 425
furnaces, 90, 91
furniture, 89, 120, 130, 399, 415
G.A.R., 160
Gaines, W. J., 111
Gainesville, FL, 432
Galahad (knight), 383
Galileo, 266
Galveston, TX, 176
Gambetta, Maître, 273
garden products, 177
Garibaldi, Giuseppe M., 153, 458
Garnett, Henry, 103
Garrison, William L., 202, 375, 378
garrisons, 202
gas, 152, 421
gaslighting, 22, 25, 444
gaslighting, defined, 22
Geary, John W., 200
general assembly, 244, 245, 335, 389
Geneva Conventions, 213
Gentile, 265
George III, King, 17, 446
George, James Z., 447
Georgia, 34, 42, 44, 47, 51, 56-58, 68-70, 74, 76, 91, 94, 99, 101, 117, 118, 129, 163, 168, 189, 210, 211, 228, 242, 285, 289, 293, 299, 317, 319, 405, 417, 418, 420, 422, 436, 440, 448, 469, 471, 477
German Confederation, 178
German imperialism, 357

Germany, 153, 274, 300, 357, 363, 366, 367, 371, 383, 408, 472
Gettysburg Address, 383, 385
Gettysburg, PA, 209, 338, 384
Gherardesca, Ugolino della, 274
Gibson, Miss Alicia, 395
Gilbert, C. E., 450
Gillem, Alvan C., 144
Gironde, the, 262
Girondins, the, 262
goats, 267
God, 2, 3, 56, 118, 123, 149, 153, 189, 206, 208, 212, 281, 284, 286, 301, 305, 318, 320, 350, 371, 374, 381, 386, 388, 400, 405, 408, 423, 430, 437, 439, 476
Goffe, Charles H., 398
gold, 2, 5, 31, 135, 145, 146, 273, 332, 345, 435, 517
Gomorrah (Bible), 268
Good Friday, 219, 386
Gordon, John B., 18, 21, 311, 320, 342, 381
Gordon, W. W., 117
Goths, 338
government, 3, 15-18, 20, 24, 26, 32, 33, 36, 42-53, 55-58, 60-64, 67, 68, 72, 74, 76-79, 81, 82, 87, 97-99, 104, 107-109, 112-114, 118, 122, 125, 129, 132, 143, 146, 148-152, 155, 163-167, 171, 174, 179, 180, 185, 188, 191, 192, 194, 205, 207, 211, 212, 216, 218, 222, 224, 227-229, 232-234, 237-241, 244-246, 249, 253-255, 260, 264, 265, 267, 269, 272, 274, 276, 280-285, 287, 288, 292, 297, 300, 304, 308, 311, 314, 315, 318-320, 334, 340, 342-344, 347-349, 351-357, 360, 361, 363-368, 371, 381, 384, 389, 393, 396, 398, 400, 403, 405, 406, 408, 411, 414, 417-420, 424, 428, 431-433, 439-442, 444-446, 449, 452, 454, 455, 458, 470-473, 477,

515
governmental control, 29
grain, 89, 93, 100, 101
Grand Army Circle, 160, 161
Grand Army of the Republic, 99, 388, 448
Grand Cyclops, 156, 157
grand jury, 131, 138, 140-143
granite, 89
Grant administration, nepotism and cronyism in, 264
Grant, Ulysses S., 24, 31, 34, 48, 51, 61-63, 65, 66, 96, 114, 123, 128, 142, 143, 145, 161, 163, 172, 175, 191, 219, 224, 225, 230, 233-235, 250-252, 255, 256, 261, 264, 266, 268-273, 280, 284, 289-291, 332, 339, 356, 359, 374, 409, 412, 447, 449, 455, 456, 458
grass, 100, 120, 136
graves, 51, 115, 127, 160-162, 188, 190, 284, 286, 287, 397, 400, 438, 517
Great Britain, 17, 92, 118, 177, 355
Great Republic (river boat), 30
Greeley, Horace, 24, 228, 299, 330, 359, 425, 426
Greene, Nathanael, 135
Greenville, SC, 404
Griffin, P. M., 157
Gross, Samuel D., 302
Grow, Galusha A., 24
guerrillas, 41, 364
guilds, 103
Gulf ports, 100
gunboats, 337
habeas corpus, 48, 150, 281, 284, 366, 367
Hagood, Johnson, 402
Haiti, 29, 410
Hales, Judge, 157
Hall, John L., 163, 190, 191, 201, 209, 215, 237, 249
Halleck, Henry W., 200, 290
Ham (Bible), 260
Hamilton, Alexander, 135, 275, 355, 356, 366, 440
Hamilton, Jay, 445

Hamiltonianism, 355, 453
Hamlet (Shakespeare), 169
Hamlett, Mrs. W. J., 289
Hampton Roads, 186, 353, 414, 415
Hampton Roads Conference, 353, 414
Hampton, VA, 255
Hampton, Wade, 99, 120, 125, 279, 342, 344, 400-403, 433, 435, 448, 449
Hancock, Winfield S., 260
Hannibal, 265
happiness, 3, 120, 180, 218, 292, 306, 328, 331, 403, 418
Hapsburg family, 225
Hardeman, Thomas, 211
Harding, Warren G., 415
harlots, 266
Harold, David E., 201
Harper's Ferry, VA, 220, 427
Harper's Weekly, 59, 448
Harrington, George, 448
Harris, Isham G., 51
Harrison, Tip, 290
Harrison, W. H., 161
Hartford Convention, 118
Harvard University, Cambridge, MA, 339
Hastings, UK, 398
Hatch, Edward, 200
hate, 31, 33, 35, 190, 234, 254, 281, 306, 307, 327, 332, 340, 371, 373, 377, 379, 417-419, 430, 473
hatred, 22, 26, 38, 54, 62, 66, 113, 124, 127, 188, 204, 226, 238, 239, 265, 286, 290, 301, 377, 387, 396, 424, 435, 446, 515
Havana, Cuba, 112, 117, 186
Hawkins, William S., 161
hay, 15, 100, 159, 473
Hayes, Rutherford B., 24, 81, 97, 154, 175, 235, 238, 299, 403
Hayne, Robert Y., 383, 385
Hays, Charles, 141
heating, 92
Hecker, Friedrich F. K., 457
Heine, Henrich, 205
heirlooms, 169, 210

Helena, AR, 337
Helper, Hinton R., 427
Henry, Patrick, 310
Hercules, 204, 257
Herod, King, 273
heroism, 113, 188, 210, 284
higher law, 132, 150, 439, 441
Hill, Ambrose P., 342
Hill, Benjamin H., 42, 70, 163, 289, 317
Hill, Daniel H., 342
Hill, John M., 245
Hillis, Newell D., 374
Hindman, Thomas C., 51
Hinduism, 254
Hinton, Richard, 457
Hite, Cornelius B., 428
Hitler, Adolf, 458
Hobson, Richmond P., 117, 186
hogs, 86, 177, 210, 240, 337
Hohenzollern empire, 386
Holdcroft, VA, 412
Holden, W. H., 56
Holden, William W., 448
Holland, Josiah G., 424, 426
Hollins, Robert S., 392
Holmes, Oliver W., 315
home consumption, 101
home rule, 297, 346
homelessness, 32, 190, 304
homelessness, among freed black servants, 304
Homer, 271
homespun, 126
honey, 86
honor system, 184
Hood, H. N., 137
Hood, John B., 209, 311
Hooker, Joseph, 250
horse power, 152
horseback riding, 127
horses, 120, 137, 175, 210, 240, 243, 337, 340, 435
Horton (freedman), 137
Hottentots, 359
House of Representatives, 28, 30, 65, 192, 227, 235, 317, 347, 417, 455, 471, 477
household necessities, 338
houses, seizure of by U.S. troops, 124

Houston, George S., 335, 515
Houston, TX, 450
Howard University, 132
Howard, C. B., 285
Howard, John, 168
Howard, Oliver O., 132, 168
Hubbard, Elizabeth, 206
human nature, 180, 184, 446
Humphreys, Andrew A., 256
hunger, among freed black servants, 304
Hunnicutt, James W., 448
Hunter, David, 200
Hunter, Robert M. T., 291
Huxley, Thomas H., 134
Iago (Shakespeare), 272, 380
ignorance, 22, 23, 104, 113, 125, 132, 135, 205, 228, 238, 240, 252, 253, 255, 272, 273, 292, 311, 331, 332, 424, 446, 515
illegal votes, 332
Illinois, 99, 100, 111, 314, 317, 322, 375
Illinois Central Railroad, 100
Illinois National Guard, 99
immigrants, 82, 88, 103, 105, 162, 326, 417, 438
immigration, 75, 80, 82, 101, 260, 443, 453
immorality, 38, 135, 172, 182
Imperialism, 355, 357, 358, 416
income, 87, 101, 177, 451
Independent Monitor, 199
India, 153, 259, 321
Indian slave owners, 304
Indian Territory, 111, 404
Indiana, 111, 267, 268, 398, 417
Indians, 117, 164, 322, 328
indigo, 176
industrial development, 88, 96, 100
industrial upheaval, 96
industrialization, 36
industries, 35, 43, 87, 89, 100, 102, 285, 322
industry, 17, 62, 63, 75, 84, 86, 88-92, 100, 122, 147, 148, 179, 198, 260, 283, 307, 348, 370, 451
Ingalls, John J., 320, 324

Ingersoll, Robert G., 447
institutional black supremacy, 38
institutional racism, 29, 400
insurance companies, 120
insurrection, 35, 58, 60, 65, 107, 223, 228, 289, 344, 365, 388, 410
intelligence, 132, 146, 179, 205, 226, 275, 342, 417, 457
internal revenue, 71, 75
International Law, 152, 363, 364
intolerance, 36, 38, 456
investment, 86, 91, 96, 100, 107, 394
investors, 453
Ireland, 3, 267, 318, 457
Irish, 234, 426
iron, 72, 84, 86, 88, 90-93, 101, 177, 226, 301, 397, 402
iron fields, 91
iron goods, 90
iron industry, 86, 92
iron manufacturing enterprises, 101
iron ore, 177
iron pipe, 90
iron products, 101
Issaquena County, MS, 144
Italian poets, 270
Italy, 270, 338
Jackson, Andrew, 227
Jackson, Mrs., 395
Jackson, MS, 36, 142, 145
Jackson, Stonewall, 22, 24, 152, 188, 204, 284, 334, 342, 373, 415
Jacksonville, FL, 100
Jacobi, Fritz, 457
jail, 111, 125
James IV, King, 264
James River, 34, 203
James, John, 471
Japhet (Bible), 260
Jay, John, 275
jealousy, 26, 28, 193, 332, 353
Jefferson Davis Historical Gold Medal, 2, 5, 517
Jefferson, Thomas, 22, 118, 216, 217, 227, 236, 300, 310, 355-357, 366, 446
Jeffersonianism, 356

Jenkins, Charles J., 68, 70
Jerome, Leonard, 263
Jesus, 3, 371, 382
Jew, 265
jewelry, 128, 181
jewels, 252, 332
Jews, 182
Job (Bible), 189
Joffre, Joseph J. C., 373
John Brown's raid, 179, 231
John of Leyden, 265
Johnson, Andrew, 24, 34, 50, 51, 55-61, 64, 66, 69, 81, 113, 125, 132, 147, 166-168, 170, 171, 174, 193, 195, 200, 211, 212, 220-222, 225, 229, 230, 234, 240, 250-254, 260-263, 280, 303, 332, 343-345, 379, 380, 448, 455
Johnson, Bradley T., 28
Johnson, H. V., 70
Johnston, Albert S., 152, 188, 342
Johnston, Joseph E., 18, 41, 48, 163, 202, 209, 215, 219, 224, 250, 279, 342
Jones, John, 472
Joseph, Louis, 270
journals, 187, 265
Judah (Bible), 187
judges, 56, 70, 196, 338, 343, 361, 404, 433
judiciaries, 70
Julian, George, 299
Jupiter (god), 151
just powers, 349
Juvenal, 266
K.K.K., 438, 450
Kaffirs, 359
Kansas, 100, 225
Kansas City, MO, 100
Kapp, Friedrich, 458
Keifer, Mr., 71
Kellogg, William P., 269, 456
Kemper, James L., 203
Kentucky, 21, 32, 48, 73, 91, 128, 142, 156, 375, 469, 517
Keppler, Joseph F., 412
kerosene, 152, 421
Kershaw County, SC, 401
Khan, Genghis, 153
Kirkman, John, 395

KKK, 24, 74, 156, 162, 175, 180, 199, 232, 234, 408, 429
Knauss, W. H., 160, 161
Knickerbocker Life Insurance Company, 158
Knox, Mrs. Stephen D., 353
Knoxville Whig, 240
Knoxville, TN, 95, 392
Kruger, Stephanus, J. P., 337
Krzyzanowki, Wladimir, 457
Ku Klux Klan, 2, 24, 27, 74, 83, 156, 162, 175, 180, 196, 232, 234, 235, 259, 404, 407, 408, 429, 470, 476
Ku Klux Klan, all-black den, 232
Ku Klux Klan, differences between old and new, 429
Ku Klux Klans, 400
Ku Klux Orders, 199
Ku Klux Phylarchy, 199
Ku-Klux Klan, 399
Ku-Klux-Klan, 196, 233-235
Kuklux Klan, 136, 156-158, 344
La Montagne, 262
Laban (Bible), 267
labor, 29, 43, 63, 92, 103-105, 108, 121, 122, 124, 133, 136, 143, 147, 168, 177, 178, 180, 299, 304, 305, 327, 340, 356, 361, 369, 413, 417, 420, 421, 436, 438, 446, 453, 457, 474
Labor unions, 103
laborers, 90, 135, 164, 440
Lake Erie, 265
Lamar, Lucius Q. C., 44, 174, 311, 454
Lamon, Ward H., 425
Lancaster County, SC, 401
Lancelot (knight), 382
land transportation, 100
Lapsley, R. A., 389
lard, 421
law, 3, 6, 24, 27, 30, 34, 43, 48, 49, 54, 56, 58-60, 66-74, 78, 80, 97, 99, 109-112, 124, 132, 135, 139, 149, 150, 152, 156, 157, 165, 175, 180, 183, 184, 194, 195, 199, 204, 206, 211, 237, 239, 254, 255, 258, 268, 269, 273, 281-283, 304, 333, 334, 346, 354, 355, 363, 364, 379, 381, 391, 403, 408, 425, 438, 439, 441, 443, 454, 472
Lawler, Michael K., 311
lawmaking, 81, 107
lawyers, 143, 164, 179, 183
leaders of industry, 179
Lecky, William E. H., 368
Lederer, Wolfe A., 454
Lee, Fitzhugh, 116, 186, 279
Lee, Henry, 188
Lee, Robert E., 22, 24, 41, 48, 51, 113, 114, 116, 129, 130, 152, 159, 162, 163, 167, 172, 188, 190, 204, 207, 209, 210, 215, 225, 228, 234, 235, 249, 251, 275, 279, 284, 290, 291, 299, 315, 331, 339, 342, 343, 349, 350, 352, 353, 356, 359, 366, 388, 397, 413, 415, 427, 447, 450, 453
Lee, Stephen D., 74, 114, 116, 118, 202
Left's plan, to take control, 29
Left-wing, 15-17, 19, 20, 24-26, 28-31, 33-36, 38, 53, 59, 62, 77, 78, 109, 123, 128, 133, 134, 148, 150, 154, 157, 162, 167, 176, 180, 188, 190, 196, 200, 211, 213, 216, 221, 224, 226, 229, 237, 244, 252, 258, 260, 263, 264, 266, 268-270, 272, 276, 287, 292, 293, 308-313, 329, 330, 339, 343, 357, 361, 362, 371, 375, 380, 391, 413, 417, 427, 432, 434, 437, 439, 440, 444, 456-458
Legare, Hugh S., 385
legislation, 29, 54, 58, 60, 63, 64, 66, 67, 69-71, 73, 74, 78-82, 97-99, 111, 113, 132, 133, 135, 148, 337, 352, 361, 418
Legree, Simon (Stowe), 173, 236, 436
Lehigh Valley, PA, 90
Leigh, Mrs. Townes R., 432

Lenin, Vladimir, 458
Leonidas, King, 275
Lepidus, Marcus A., 173
Lewis, David P., 75, 312
Lewis, Mercy, 206
Lexington, VA, 130, 397
Libby Prison, 290, 291
liberalization, 20, 36
Liberalization, of the South, 413
liberals, 15-17, 25, 26, 34, 38, 63, 104, 162, 197, 224, 231, 283, 312, 330, 360, 378, 406, 428, 439
libertarian, 15
liberty, 47, 57, 121, 153, 194, 202, 204, 218, 238, 239, 241, 243, 255, 281-284, 301, 302, 306, 318, 335, 341, 342, 345, 348, 349, 355-358, 361, 364, 368, 425, 431, 441, 452, 469, 515
Liberty, MO, 431
life span, decrease of among freed black servants, 304
Lilly, William, 165
limestone, 90, 177
Lincoln cult, the, 383
Lincoln mania, 383
Lincoln, Abraham, 10, 15, 17, 19-22, 24, 25, 28, 29, 31-33, 37, 49, 50, 52-55, 58, 72, 81, 104, 113, 150, 163, 165-168, 174, 180, 191-193, 195, 201, 202, 211, 215, 217, 219-222, 224, 225, 230, 231, 236, 242, 251, 257, 258, 261, 276, 279-281, 284, 294, 303, 338, 343, 353, 356, 360, 361, 363-367, 372, 374, 376, 383-385, 387, 393, 397, 405, 406, 409-411, 413, 414, 417, 424-428, 439, 447, 449, 452, 457, 458, 478
Lincoln, Abraham, assassination of, 192
Lincoln, Mary T., 219, 426
Lincoln's War, 2, 3, 15, 17, 20, 21, 27, 187, 237, 372, 452, 458, 475, 476, 519
Lincoln's War (Seabrook), 20, 458
Lindsay, Robert. B., 515

Lion of the Confederacy, 302
liquor, 106, 124, 126, 183, 239
liquor business, 106
Little Rock, AR, 353, 422
Littlefield, A. W., 358, 397
Littlefield, Milton S., 448
livestock, 30
local autonomy, 355, 358, 368
locomotives, 90
Lodi, Italy, 209
log cabins, 375
London, UK, 128, 257
Long, Jeff, 211
Longstreet, James, 18, 311, 423
looms, 120, 337
Lord Hate-good (Bunyan), 254
Loring, William W., 51
Lost Cause, 14, 282, 345, 474
Lost Cause, term banned, 14
Louisiana, 34, 47, 55, 57, 58, 69, 70, 75, 76, 78, 81, 118, 153, 179, 193, 216, 219, 235, 257, 266-270, 273, 295, 302, 390, 412, 419, 425, 431, 447, 448, 455, 456, 477
Louisiana State University, 431, 477
Louisville and Nashville Railroad, 177
Louisville, KY, 95
Louthan, Henry T., 449
Lovett, Howard M., 388
loyal leagues, 281
Lucas, Mrs. Virginia, 336
Lucifer (Bible), 189
Ludendorff, Erich, 373
lumber, 86, 93, 94, 122
lumber manufacturing, 93
lumber resources, 94
Lunt, George, 426
lynch law, 183, 184
Lynchburg, VA, 34, 280
lynching, 106, 109-111, 182, 183
lynchings, 104, 106, 110, 111, 133, 183, 322
Macaulay, Thomas B., 255, 284
machine shops, 90
machinery, 86, 92, 169, 172, 218, 232, 381
machines, 90, 337
MacMahon, Patrice de, 273

Macon, GA, 388
Madison Square Garden, 186
Madison, James, 275, 366
magic, 95, 101, 153
Magna Carta, 2, 249, 475
Magnesia, 173
Magruder, John B., 51
Mahone, William, 311
Maine, 71, 107, 112, 174
Maine (warship), 112
Makepeace, C. R., 92
maladministration of law, 135
malice, 22, 122, 132, 187, 191, 204, 228, 240, 282, 288, 301, 303, 313, 316, 332, 359, 360, 396, 515
malnutrition, among freed black servants, 304
Malvolio (Shakespeare), 271
Manaway, L. W. W., 103
manhood, 85, 96, 113, 197, 233, 253, 282, 303, 310, 317, 326, 336, 338, 383, 418
Manila, Philippines, 112
manufactured iron, 177
manufacturing, 37, 83, 86-90, 92, 93, 101
manufacturing centers, 101
manufacturing industries, 87, 89
manufacturing interests, 90, 101
marble, 89, 162
March to the Sea, Sherman's, 210
Mardi Gras, 311
Marion, Francis, 418
Marshall, Arthur, 22, 32
Marshall, John, 275
martial law, 34, 48, 72, 304, 346
Martin, Player, 157
Marx, Karl, 19, 458
Maryland, 41, 45, 47, 48, 73, 117, 208, 215, 310
Mason, Captain, 398
Mason-Dixon Line, 85
Masonic Temple, 157
Massachusetts, 27, 85, 94, 107, 174, 192, 206, 217, 226, 254, 262, 299, 315, 324, 326, 425, 439, 445, 452
Massachusetts, and secession, 439
Mathews, VA, 415
Matthews, Stanley, 447

Maximilian I, 225
May Day, 127
Mayflower (ship), 206
Mayo, A. D., 94
Mayo, Joseph C., 290, 291
mayors, 70, 272
McCardle case, 68
McCausland, John, 366
McClellan, George B., 220, 366, 424
McClure, Alexander K., 424
McClure's Magazine, 367
McCook, Edward M., 200
McCoy, Moses, 345
McCoy, Mrs. Lou, 345
McElvey, Mrs. Sarah J., 423
McEwen, R. H., 245, 246
McFerrin, J. P., 158
McGavocks, 3, 474
McKelway, St. Clair, 186
McKim, Randolph H., 315
McKinley, William, 113, 115, 116, 186, 295
McLean's House, 339
McNeilly, James H., 13, 247, 346, 349, 359, 361, 388, 396, 408
McNeilly, Thomas, 243
Meade, George G., 70, 279
Meagher, Thomas F., 457
measles, 183
meat, 89, 130, 252, 419
mechanical exhibitions, 96
mechanical trades, 103
mechanics, 90, 103
Mechanics' Institute, 258
medical profession, 301
medicine, 337, 409
Medusa (deity), 254
Memphis, TN, 31, 337, 380
men, 10, 31, 33, 35, 36, 42, 43, 51-54, 56, 57, 59, 61, 62, 64, 68, 69, 71, 72, 74, 76-83, 85, 95, 96, 99, 102, 104, 106-108, 110, 111, 113, 116, 118, 119, 124-128, 133, 135, 136, 144, 146, 147, 156-161, 163, 165-167, 171, 173-175, 178-180, 182-190, 193, 194, 196, 197, 204, 205, 207, 209, 210, 212, 214, 217, 218, 221-223, 227, 230, 233,

234, 236, 240-242, 244, 245, 247, 250, 252, 253, 260-262, 264, 265, 270, 275, 280-282, 284, 286, 288, 289, 291, 292, 295-298, 301, 303, 304, 309, 313-315, 318-321, 323, 325, 335, 336, 340-344, 349, 351-354, 361, 363-365, 367-374, 381, 387, 389, 390, 392, 394, 396, 399-405, 407, 408, 413-417, 419-421, 423, 424, 427, 432, 433, 436-442, 444, 446, 448-450, 453, 454, 456, 458, 469, 474
mental illness, among freed black servants, 304
merchants, 31, 120, 144
Merrimack (steam frigate), 117
metropolitan police, 156, 157, 311, 391
Meulen, Vander, 370
Mexican-American War, 187, 252, 266
Mexico, 41, 51, 85, 153, 167, 225, 357
Middle Ages, 148, 264
Middle states, 86, 88, 93
Miles (freedman), 136
military authorities, 125, 389
military authority, 150, 211, 281, 291
military commissioners, 35
Military District No. 2, 433
military districts, 24, 34, 66, 67, 171, 194, 204
military events, 112
military governments, 281, 302
military governor, 137, 142, 144, 194
military roads, 156
military rule, 34, 35, 51, 56, 69, 204, 281, 285, 309, 451
military violence, 304
Miller, Mr., 71
mills, 88-90, 92, 101, 176, 177, 303, 469
Milroy, Robert H., 200
Milton, John, 166
Mims, Edwin, 429
Miner, Miss Bertie, 336
minerals, 89

Minerva (goddess), 151
mines, coal, 177
Minnegerode, Charles, 430
Minnesota, 111
Minor, Charles L. C., 386
minorities, 38, 129
Miriam (Bible), 326
miscegenation, 323, 324
misgovernment, 162, 367
Mississippi, 30, 34, 36, 41, 42, 47, 56-58, 68, 69, 74, 76, 103, 106, 120, 135, 138, 139, 141, 144, 145, 148, 149, 151, 163, 184, 193, 212, 273, 280, 289, 302, 310, 311, 324, 337, 354, 436, 448, 455, 471, 472
Mississippi River, 30, 41, 141, 163, 280, 302, 337
Missouri, 32, 47, 73, 179, 215, 307, 335, 404, 437
Missouri Compromise, 179
Missouri Compromise of 1820, 179
Mobile & Ohio Railroad, 100
Mobile, AL, 101, 395
Mokanna, 266
molasses, 86
monarchy, 17, 265, 337, 338
money, 32, 42, 69, 75, 80, 82, 89-92, 94, 99, 101, 102, 120, 135, 138, 143, 158, 164, 175, 181, 197, 207, 213, 232, 241, 244, 260, 265, 267, 274, 297, 303, 305, 326, 333, 342, 347, 353, 365, 388, 391, 395, 400, 402, 418, 421, 432, 435, 451, 454
Monguls, 153
Monroe Doctrine, 225
Montagne, La, 262
Montauk Point, NY, 116
Montgomery, AL, 35, 100, 328
Montreal, Canada, 430
monument, Confederate, 99
Mooney, Sue F. D., 309
morals, 38, 87, 110, 111, 122, 182, 184, 377
Morgan, Coon, 203
Morgan, James, 434

Morgan, John H., 342
Morgan, Mrs. Jo B., 395
Morgan, Taylor, 203
Morgan, William H., 201, 208, 209, 215, 237, 249
Morse, Samuel, 152
mortgages, 104
Morton, John W., 157
Morton, Oliver P., 133, 202, 267, 268, 447
Morton, Richard L., 293
Moscow, Russia, 209
Moses (Bible), 182
Moses, Franklin J., Jr., 72, 196, 419, 434, 448
mountaineers, 130
mulattos, 214, 394
Mulberry, SC, 124
mules, 120, 240, 337
municipal corruption, 184, 185
murderers, 319, 427
Murfreesboro, TN, 210
music, 127, 394, 517
musicians, 394
Nagle, Dr., 435
Napoleon III, 148, 205, 209, 220, 225, 260, 271, 357
Napoleonic wars, 153
Nash, George K., 161
Nashville, TN, 95, 159, 241, 245-247, 346, 349, 361, 388, 391, 392, 394-396, 408, 432
Nast, Thomas, 380, 437, 444
national banks, 87
national debt, 265
national government, 20, 97, 118, 185, 191, 344, 355, 368, 403, 433
national honor, 85, 95, 117, 118
national military park, 99
national patriotism, 95, 97, 112, 114
national statesmanship, 117
nationalism, 16
natural law, 199
natural resources, 27, 33, 96
natural rights, 134, 218
naval events, 112
naval review, of 1893, 186
navies, 473
navy, 45, 117, 135, 186, 225, 365, 424, 427, 448
Nebraska, 274
Needham, MA, 358, 397
negro, 27, 29, 30, 44, 49, 51, 57, 60, 63, 69, 71, 72, 74, 77, 79-83, 93, 94, 97, 98, 101-110, 113, 114, 122-126, 129, 132-134, 137, 138, 141-148, 165, 168, 169, 171-173, 175, 177, 179-183, 186, 193-199, 203, 204, 211, 212, 216-218, 221-224, 227-236, 238-240, 242, 244, 255, 257, 258, 260, 262, 267, 275, 287-289, 292, 300, 302, 309, 313, 321-329, 333-335, 337, 343, 348, 350, 352, 361, 363, 369, 370, 372, 378, 379, 388, 390, 391, 394, 399-403, 406, 407, 416, 419, 422-424, 433-436, 438, 446-450, 455, 473
negro crime, 324
negro domination, 63, 203, 204, 212, 300, 313, 455
negro government, 114, 433, 449
negro mechanics, 103
negro party, 403
negro politicians, 334
negro population, 228, 231, 438
negro rule, 194, 196, 197, 230, 234, 236, 288, 399, 400, 403
negro suffrage, 30, 81-83, 129, 165, 193, 195, 217, 229, 232, 255, 257, 419, 447
negro supremacy, 388
negro worship, 262, 265
negro-worshippers, 262
negroes, 30, 31, 43, 49, 55, 60, 62, 63, 68, 69, 71-75, 77, 79-83, 87, 94, 102-104, 106, 108-112, 121-124, 126, 128, 129, 133-137, 141, 144, 145, 147, 148, 168, 171, 172, 179, 180, 183, 193-196, 198, 204, 211, 213, 214, 217, 228, 229, 231-234, 240, 241, 243, 254, 258-260, 265, 267, 281, 285, 288, 289, 292, 293, 296, 303, 309, 313, 318, 319, 321-324, 326-329,

332-334, 337, 339, 343, 353, 364, 365, 379, 390, 398-402, 404, 407, 408, 411, 415, 416, 419-421, 423, 424, 426, 433-439, 450, 451, 455
negroes, adoration of, 265
negroid governments, 235
negroism, 98, 105
Nelson (freedman), 137
Neptune (deity), 205
Nero (Emperor), 146
Netherlands, 263
Nevada, 453
New England, 86, 88, 90, 92, 95, 118, 122, 135, 153, 177, 188, 200, 206, 220, 259, 315, 362, 376-379, 436, 440, 452
New England mills, 92, 177
New England secession movement, 118, 135, 440
New Englanders, 206
New Hampshire, 440
New Jersey, 91, 107
New Market, battle of, 442
New Orleans, LA, 96, 100, 176, 229, 257, 260, 267, 269, 298, 301, 310, 380, 390, 409, 424
New South, 14, 93, 94, 159, 183, 304, 345, 477
New South, term banned, 14
New Testament, 3, 26, 391
New York, 17, 29, 71, 91, 93, 100, 107, 111, 144, 146, 176, 196, 202, 203, 235, 250, 251, 262-265, 273, 322, 323, 327, 373, 388, 424, 425, 429, 469-474, 477, 478
New York City, NY, 100, 388
New York Herald, 29, 373
New York World, 425
Newcastle, UK, 177
Nez Percés, 260
Nicholls, Francis T., 302, 448
Nickerson, Miss Edmonda A., 307
Noah (Bible), 268
Norfolk and Western Railroad, 177
Norman invasion, 173
North, 2, 3, 21, 22, 27-30, 32, 34-38, 41, 43-45, 47, 48, 50, 53-55, 57, 58, 63-69, 72, 74, 76, 79, 80, 82-93, 95-104, 106, 110, 112, 115-118, 120, 122, 123, 128-130, 132, 133, 135, 137, 146, 148, 151, 159, 163, 164, 171, 175, 177, 179, 183, 186, 188, 190, 192, 193, 195, 197, 200, 201, 204, 205, 207, 208, 211, 215, 220, 221, 224-226, 228, 230, 235, 238, 239, 245, 247, 257, 261-264, 266, 275, 280, 281, 284, 286, 294, 299, 301, 303, 306, 313-317, 322-324, 326, 331, 333, 336, 338, 339, 343, 348, 351-353, 358-361, 363, 366-372, 376-380, 387, 400, 405, 406, 408, 409, 411, 413, 416, 417, 419, 426-429, 431, 435, 436, 438, 439, 445-451, 453, 454, 468, 469, 471, 475, 517
North American Review, 416
North Carolina, 34, 41, 44, 47, 53, 55, 57, 58, 72, 76, 91, 117, 118, 122, 128, 163, 179, 186, 193, 280, 331, 419, 435, 448, 451, 469, 471, 517
Northen, William J., 101
Northern abolitionists, 19
Northern capital, 82, 96, 454
Northern colleges, 184
Northern historians, 515
Northern merchants, 31
Northern mills, 92
Northern oligarchy, 453
Northern press, 192, 383
Northern racism, 106
Northern slavery, 353
Northern states, 63, 238, 281, 388, 439
Northern states, secession movement of the, 439
Northern universities, 184
Northern whites, 128
Northerners, 2, 14, 121, 125, 127, 185, 219, 222, 228, 323, 359, 475

Northernization, 20, 33-36
Northernization, of the South, 413
Northwest, 80, 82, 101
Norwood, Thomas, 75
Noxubee County, MS, 74
Noyes, Miss Eleanor C., 442
nullification, 188
nurses, 335
Oates, Titus, 265
Oates, W. C., 117
Oath of Allegiance, 115, 216, 223, 290, 297, 298, 364, 398, 410
oats, 89, 93
occult science, 153
occupation, 124, 127, 357, 364
Octavius, Gaius, 173
officers, U.S., using black women as prostitutes, 124
Official Records, 291, 455, 473
Ohio, 30-32, 71, 100, 107, 137, 154, 160, 161, 234, 245, 259, 266, 376, 411, 417, 441
Ohio River, 32, 259
Ohio State band, 161
Ohio State Guards, 161
oil, 88, 89, 158, 177, 453
Oklahoma, 111, 404
Oklahoma Territory, 111
Old North, 363
Old South, 2, 3, 20, 31, 83, 159, 234, 286, 287, 321, 327, 345, 363, 368, 369, 381, 398, 421, 422, 443, 473, 477
oppression, 36, 61, 152, 220, 226, 235, 238, 298, 333, 341, 359, 368, 388, 405, 422, 446, 456
option laws, 106
oranges, 89
Ord, Edward O. C., 34, 279, 290, 291
Ordinances of Secession, 48, 51, 58, 65, 170, 216, 223
Oregon, 118
ores, 91, 100
Orient, 270, 328
Orsini, Felice, 220
osnaberg shirt, 396
Osterhaus, Peter J., 457
Othello (Shakespeare), 272, 380, 395

overseer, 420
O'Connor, Charles, 68
Pacific coast, 93, 369
Pacific Ocean, 118
Packard, Stephen B., 267
paganism, 173
Page, Thomas N., 13, 32, 348
Palefaces, 156, 157, 322
Palinurus, 262
Palmer, John M., 200
Palmerston, Viscount, 409
Palmetto flag, 233
Panama, 252, 408
Panic of 1892, 101
Panic of 1893, 101
Paris, France, 118
Parkersburg, WV, 455
Parma, Duke of, 270
parole, 250, 288, 290, 291, 298, 398
Parsons, Lewis E., 312
party, 15, 16, 19, 20, 24, 25, 28, 30, 31, 34, 36, 38, 46, 49, 53-55, 57-59, 62, 64-66, 72, 73, 75, 77-82, 113, 115, 134, 148, 150, 154, 167, 168, 171, 175, 179, 180, 188, 190-195, 197, 200, 205, 213, 217, 220, 222, 224, 227, 231, 234, 240, 242, 249, 254, 255, 261, 263, 266-268, 270, 271, 276, 283, 287, 311, 317, 319, 330, 332, 357, 361, 368, 375, 384, 387, 400, 403, 406, 414, 417, 418, 424, 425, 427, 428, 432, 435, 437, 439, 444, 445, 447, 455-458, 471, 472, 515
party supremacy, 49, 65, 78
party supremacy, Left-wing, 78
Pascal, Blaise, 266
patria, 189
patriotism, 26, 45, 53, 79, 84, 95, 97, 112, 114-117, 160, 188, 189, 222, 240, 247, 268, 282, 284, 285, 293, 297, 302, 305, 335, 336, 339, 341, 346, 382, 392, 397, 425
patriots, 22, 36, 37, 49, 130, 301, 302, 345, 346, 405

patronage, 123, 305, 440
Patterson, John J., 448
Patton, Robert M., 515
Paul, Oom, 337
paupers, 103
Payne, Lewis, 201, 251
Peabody, George, 266
peace, 67, 72, 73, 75, 96, 109, 111, 129, 137, 138, 148, 151, 166, 167, 180, 213, 229, 230, 282-284, 288, 296, 297, 299, 300, 311, 318, 331, 335, 341, 344, 345, 350, 403, 405, 414, 418, 419, 427, 432, 447
peace officers, 111
peaches, 130
Pease, Elisha M., 448
Pease, Verne S., 13
peat, 136
Pelham, Peter, 27
Pennsylvania, 63, 90, 91, 107, 160, 177, 191, 207, 210, 226, 274, 299, 302, 366, 447, 453, 477
Pennsylvania regiment, 160
Pensacola, FL, 100
pensions, 159, 160, 347
Percival (knight), 383
Percy, William A., 141
Pericles, 275
perjury, 143, 160
Perry, Mrs. Vallie H., 430
Persians, 153
personal items, 130
personal property, 87, 134
perversion, 36
Phalaris, 272
Phelps, John W., 200
Philadelphia Convention, Republican, 1866, 261, 263
Philadelphia Press, 186
Philadelphia, PA, 100, 203, 240, 261, 262, 272, 454
philanthropist, 168-170
Phillips, Wendell, 130, 439
Piatt, Donn, 426
Pickett, George E., 209, 233
pickles, 130
picnics, 127
Pierce, Franklin, 224

Pierce, H. B., 94
Pierpont, Francis H., 55
pig iron, 88, 90, 91
Pilgrims, 251
Pinkerton, Allan, 457
pipe works, 90
Pitt, William, 268
Pittsburgh, PA, 245, 274, 389
plantation, 3, 75, 109, 121, 123, 124, 137, 138, 142-144, 147, 178, 287, 321, 326, 329, 337, 432, 434, 435, 474
plantations, 32, 120, 122, 128, 136, 144, 180, 342, 356, 435-437
planters, 120-122, 136, 142, 143
plunder, 69, 74, 132, 146, 176, 178, 182, 195, 204, 232, 268, 309, 318, 319, 336, 343, 398, 438, 441, 455
plunderers, 188, 346, 400
Plymouth Rock, MA, 206
Point of Rocks Military Prison, 310
Poland, 318
police, 26, 35, 156, 157, 183, 258, 274, 295, 311, 391
police powers, 35
police state, 26
police, weaponization of, 391
police-court lawyers, 183
political freedom, 342
political parties, 15, 16, 45, 99
political party, 19, 171, 319, 387, 432
political power, abuse of, 478
politically incorrect, 478
Pompeia, wife of Julius Caesar, 184
Pompey, the Great, 173
Pontine marshes, 274
poor white rebel trash, 172
Pope, John, 34, 70, 200
population, 42, 45, 65, 67, 73, 82, 85-87, 94, 95, 101, 103, 113, 153, 156, 177, 178, 193, 198, 215, 223, 228, 231, 234, 257, 274, 283, 284, 304, 324, 339, 363, 367, 410, 417, 431, 433, 438, 451, 453

Port Royal, SC, 310
potatoes, 86, 89, 93, 130
Potomac River, 28, 179, 259, 273, 287, 385, 427
poverty, 32, 65, 104, 120, 126, 146, 148, 190, 197, 237, 243, 287, 301, 303, 304, 317, 374, 399, 420, 432, 441, 452
poverty, among freed black servants, 304
poverty, of Reconstruction blacks, 122
Powell, James W., 335
Presbyterian Church, 244-246, 390, 392
presentism, 20, 83
presidential reconstruction, 52, 62, 63, 113, 170
Preston, J. R., 95
Preston, William C., 385
Price, Sterling, 51, 431
pride, 10, 112, 115-117, 125, 126, 283, 284, 297, 301, 328, 414, 437, 442
Prince, Leon C., 199
products, 38, 86-93, 100, 101, 176, 177, 301, 318
profiteering, 120
Prohibition, 106
Prometheus, 204
propagandizers, Northern, 123
proscription, 173, 281
prosperity, 43, 45, 56, 82-85, 94, 95, 99, 100, 113, 120, 145, 159, 212, 213, 274, 283, 285, 292, 313, 316, 331, 344, 349, 399, 403, 418, 447
prostitution, 3, 304
prostitution, among black women, 124
prostitution, among freed black servants, 304
protection of life and property, 109
provisions, 43, 60, 91, 144, 151, 164, 213, 227, 241, 280, 348, 374, 421, 445
provost marshals, 35
Prussia, 357
Pryor, OK, 404

public meetings, 96, 160
Pugh, Judge, 161
Pulaski, TN, 382
Pulliam, Mrs., 336
Puritans, 205, 206
Puttnam, Ann, 206
quality of life, decrease of among freed black servants, 304
Quincy, FL, 423
Rabelais, François, 226
race antagonization, 60
race bitterness, 181
race division, 181
race issue, 133, 326
race prejudice, 321, 323, 326
race pride, 328
race problem, 38, 112, 133, 148, 179, 296, 327, 369
race question, 179
race troubles, 124
race war, 62, 64, 313
race warfare, 78, 320, 321
race-baiting, 62, 124, 285, 321
race-hustling, 62, 64, 285, 321
racehood, 325
Rachel (Bible), 438
racial animosity, 182
racial conflict, manufactured, 74
racial discord, 30
racial division, 62
racial division, artificial, 240
racial division, manufactured, 71
racial divisiveness, 113, 313
racial friction, manufactured, 62, 121
racial grandeur, 126
racial hatred and division, manufactured, 74
racism, 29, 36, 38, 62, 224
racism, Left-wing, 29
racism, Liberal, 29
racism, reverse, 433
Radical party, 167, 168, 266
Radical Republican movement, 447
Radical Satan, 264
Radicalism, 124, 272, 456
Radicals, 123, 128, 192, 197, 220, 226, 229, 252, 258, 259, 264, 267, 269, 270, 272, 332, 407, 411, 458, 473

Radicals, responsible for Lincoln's death, 258
railroad builders, 71, 101
railroad cars, 106
railroad enterprises, 100
railroading, 86
railroads, 43, 71, 82, 86, 152, 156, 165, 177, 239, 327, 417, 450
rainfall, 84, 101
Ramming, Henry, 457
Ramsey, Crozier, 392
Ramsey, William B. A., 392
Randolph, John, of Roanoke, 189, 355
rape, 32, 74, 106-109, 111, 112, 124, 238, 408, 441
Rapier, J. T., 141
rapine, 13, 38, 124, 207, 378
rascality, 173, 207, 446
raw cotton, 92
Rawle, William, 315
Raymond, Henry J., 262, 263
Raymond, R. W., 90
Reagan, John H., 284, 285
Rebel Yell, 161, 415
rebellion, 56, 60, 107, 125, 150, 170, 222, 227, 235, 245-247, 251, 291, 298, 339, 344, 365, 396, 410, 447, 471-473
rebels, 30, 32, 36, 132, 250, 267, 282, 291, 365, 393, 442
Reconstruction, 2, 5, 6, 9, 11-13, 21, 24, 26-28, 30-39, 50, 52, 54-56, 58, 60-70, 72, 74-78, 80-83, 94, 96, 97, 102, 106, 113-115, 127, 131, 143, 146-148, 151, 154, 156, 159, 162, 168, 170, 174-176, 178-180, 190, 191, 193-196, 199, 200, 203-205, 211, 212, 215-217, 219, 220, 222, 224, 226-229, 232, 234, 235, 237-240, 242-244, 249, 259, 261, 264, 277, 280-289, 292, 294-297, 299-302, 304, 307, 310, 311, 313, 314, 316-321, 330, 332, 335, 337-340, 343-348, 350, 352, 353, 355, 358-362, 367, 369-372, 377-381, 386-389, 394, 396-399, 404-408, 411, 414-417, 419, 420, 422-424, 429-432, 434, 437-439, 442-444, 446, 448-456, 468-474, 477, 478, 515
Reconstruction Act of 1867, 24
Reconstruction Acts, 30, 69, 194, 240, 337
Reconstruction and communism, 398
Reconstruction Bill, 30, 211, 229
Reconstruction Bill of 1867, 30
Reconstruction KKK, 156, 175, 180, 199, 234, 408
Reconstruction Ku Klux Klan, 180, 232, 407, 429
Reconstruction, as a "red ordeal", 26, 398
Reconstruction, as a Bolshevik revolution, 26, 398
Red Party, the Republican Party, 458
Red Shirt Brigade, 401
Red Shirts, 401, 402, 433, 434
Reed, Thomas B., 317
Reeves, C. S., 289
refreshments, 127
refugees, 33, 63, 131, 310
Reid, Whitelaw, 124
religion, 135, 147, 152, 172, 182, 183, 244, 281, 285, 370, 388, 425, 517
religiosity, 27
religious denominations, 106
religious matters, 87, 183
Remus (myth), 382
reparations, 287
Republican leaders, 194, 195
Republican Party, 15, 16, 20, 24, 25, 28, 31, 36, 38, 62, 64-66, 72, 73, 75, 78, 79, 81, 113, 115, 150, 154, 190-194, 197, 200, 205, 213, 217, 220, 224, 231, 234, 263, 268, 276, 287, 357, 361, 375, 403, 406, 414, 424, 427, 428, 437, 444, 447, 455-458, 471
Republicanism, 355-357
reunion, 18, 21, 96, 203, 315, 413, 473

revenge, 30, 135, 204, 281, 289, 301, 419
reverse racism, 433
Revolutionary fathers, 335
revolutionary forefathers, 114
Revolutionary War, 16, 17, 117, 118, 135, 404, 517
Reynolds, Mr., 71
Rhodes, James F., 425
rice, 86, 89, 176, 177, 180, 323, 369
rice plantations, 180
Richardson, E. R., 157
Richardson, John, 474
Richmond and Danville Railroad, 203
Richmond Times-Dispatch, 450
Richmond, VA, 24, 53, 144, 183, 186, 203, 210, 256, 310, 326, 343, 354, 358, 360, 397, 411, 430
Rio Grande, 45, 266, 338
riots, 319, 320, 322, 379, 402
Ripon, WI, 24
Roanoke, VA, 95, 189
robbery, 13, 38, 173, 318, 336, 368, 388, 398
Roberts, Charles D., 373
Rocky Mountains, 118, 517
Rodgers, Robert L., 291
Rogers, Edith, 119
rolling mills, 90
Roman augurs, 133
Roman world, 173
Rome, 185, 265, 355
Romulus (myth), 382
Roosevelt, Franklin D., 371
Roosevelt, Theodore, 314
Rosa, Robert, 457
roseola, 183
Rosser, Mr., 389
Rosser, T. L., 117
Rousseau, Lovell H., 393
Rouvory, Louis de, 270
Rowan, A. S., 117
ruins, 32, 119, 120, 127, 210, 212, 299, 313, 417, 451
Runnymede, UK, 249
rural life, 103
Russell's Valley, AL, 336
Rutherford, Mildred L., 299, 422

Sabbath, 147, 183, 273
safety issues, among freed black servants, 304
sailing vessels, 152
Saint Paul's Episcopal Church, Richmond, VA, 430
Salamanca, 270
Salem, MA, 206
Salomon, Friedrich, 457
Salomon, Herman, 457
Sampson, William T., 112
San Antonio Express, 398
San Antonio, TX, 29
San Domingo, 410
sanitation, lack of among freed black servants, 304
Santiago, Chile, 116, 186
Satan (Bible), 33, 258, 301, 332, 335
Satan, metaphor for Left-wing Radicals, 264
Saturday Evening Post, 373
Savannah, GA, 251
scalawag, 172
scalawag politicians, 334
scalawags, 173, 176, 181, 204, 244, 301, 318, 333, 340, 352, 398, 400, 420, 434, 450
scallywag, 140
scallywags, 232
Schimmilfennig, Alexander C., 458
Schley, Winfield S., 112, 186
Schoapfe, Albin F., 458
Schofield, John M., 34
scholars, 110, 179, 185, 306
school, 73, 76, 94, 95, 103, 109, 169, 178, 181, 185, 193, 207, 287, 293, 327, 328, 382, 390, 421, 442, 443, 451, 470
school boards, 185
schoolmarm, 169, 170
Schurz, Carl, 128, 150, 360, 367, 437, 447, 457, 458
Schuylkill Valley, PA, 90
Scotland, 107, 264
Scots, 130
Scott, Mrs., 336
Scrugham, Dr., 428
SCV, 5

Sea Raven Press, 3, 5, 6, 18, 23, 50, 474-477, 519
Seabrook, Lochlainn, 37, 457, 517, 519
seasons, 101
Seattle, WA, 311
seceded states, 41, 42, 46-54, 58-61, 64, 66, 81, 165, 170, 471
secession, 2, 17, 35, 47-49, 51, 52, 57, 58, 63, 65, 118, 132, 135, 156, 164, 165, 170, 171, 185, 187, 188, 216, 222, 223, 225, 228, 233, 303, 308, 309, 314, 339, 353, 357, 365, 398, 414, 439-441, 445, 446, 449, 450, 452, 453, 469, 471, 474, 476, 519
secessionist, 172, 240
secret societies, 235, 407
sectional hate, 254, 306, 340
sectionalism, 368, 371, 414
securities, 76, 265, 453
seed, 89, 177, 275, 340, 350
segregation, 106, 236
self-government, 97, 212
Selma, AL, 343
Selph, Mrs. F. E., 397
Semmes, Raphael, 366
Semple, H. C., 333, 334
Senter, Dewitt C., 158
servant, 135, 144, 181, 242, 321, 434, 445
servants, 30, 78, 86, 87, 124, 252, 293, 294, 304, 340, 421, 443
servitude, 179, 193, 195, 353
Seward, William H., 28, 57, 67, 167, 191, 201, 219, 225, 251, 256, 262, 263, 287, 380, 393, 409, 414, 428, 439, 440, 447
sexual promiscuity, 123
sexual promiscuity, among emancipated blacks, 123
Shafter, William, 112
Shakespeare, William, 182, 254, 380, 395
Shanks's Regiment, 431
Sharkey, William L., 68, 135
sheep, 86, 120, 267

Shelby's Brigade, 431
Shenandoah Valley, 374
Shepherd, Henry E., 387
Sheridan, Philip H., 34, 44, 200, 210, 257, 258, 270, 279, 373, 374, 385, 409, 441, 447
Sherman bill, the, 70
Sherman, John, 31, 229, 238
Sherman, William T., 31, 32, 44, 48, 124, 127, 145, 151, 168, 191, 200, 210, 224, 229, 280, 284, 373, 374, 385, 409, 420, 441, 458
Sherman's March to the Sea, 44, 420
Shields, James, 373
shillalah, 136
shipping, 90, 101, 120
ships, 152, 371, 446
Shiva (god), 254
Shoeback, Mr., 71
shops, 90, 120, 322, 349
Shreveport, LA, 431
Sibley, Mrs. W. C., 286
Sicily, 173, 254
Sickles, Daniel E., 34
Sidney, Philip, 268
Sigel, Franz, 458
Simpson, Mrs. Horace L., 370
skilled labor, 92
skilled mechanic, 93
slander, 207, 318
slave, 22, 27, 31, 34, 46, 58, 82, 87, 102, 114, 123, 133, 134, 153, 198, 215, 218, 221, 223, 227, 231, 234, 236, 253, 254, 258, 261, 262, 267, 304, 323, 324, 341, 356, 370, 374, 380, 399, 411, 420, 435, 436, 445, 446, 449
slave insurrection, 223
slave labor, 356
slave states, 179, 198, 449
slave trade, 153, 445
slave-traders, 236
slavery, 2, 19, 25, 27, 35, 43, 46, 47, 49, 58, 66, 83, 86, 87, 102, 107, 108, 110, 150, 159, 165, 166, 170, 171, 182, 191, 194, 197, 198,

215, 216, 223, 224, 226, 227, 231, 236, 279, 287, 294, 303, 308, 309, 321, 323, 324, 329, 350, 353-357, 365, 369, 379, 400, 410, 414, 416, 420, 438, 439, 445, 446, 470, 474, 475, 519
slavery myths, debunked, 435
slaves, 32, 35, 43, 46, 56, 62, 77, 85, 86, 102, 108, 121, 122, 125, 127, 133, 134, 156, 159, 164, 171, 178, 179, 193, 212, 215, 227, 228, 231, 249, 279, 287, 301, 302, 304, 322, 328, 340, 343, 345, 347, 353, 362, 364, 365, 375, 388, 390, 399, 410, 411, 417, 419, 420, 422, 424, 426, 436, 437, 445, 446, 471
slaves, Southern, 130
slave-drivers, 258
Smith, Andrew J., 200, 247
Smith, Edmund K., 41, 163, 280, 342, 447
Smith, John, 200
Smith, Levin, 455
Smith, R. M., 156
Smith, Samuel, 312
Smith, William H., 71, 312
Smith, William S., 200
Smoot, R. K., 390
Smythe, H. Gerald, 398
social engineering, Left-wing, 31
socialism, 16, 19, 31, 470, 472
socialist, 15, 19, 20, 24, 28, 30, 35, 36, 57, 122, 128, 148, 153, 170, 174, 200, 207, 213, 217, 220, 225, 228, 234, 257, 259, 276, 293, 299, 329, 330, 332, 360, 367, 406, 407, 430, 437, 444, 455-458, 472, 474
socialists, 17, 25, 26, 31, 34, 38, 54, 123, 128, 150, 167, 199, 220, 224, 226, 229, 231, 232, 252, 258-260, 264, 267, 269, 270, 272, 281, 287, 292, 295, 309, 330-332, 339, 352, 353, 357, 360, 375, 406, 423, 437-439, 445, 452, 457, 458
soldiers, 2, 3, 27, 31-33, 37, 41, 43, 45, 50-52, 70, 97, 99, 109, 113, 116, 117, 119, 121, 122, 124-129, 152, 154, 156, 159, 160, 175, 187, 188, 191, 201, 204, 209-211, 224, 230, 233, 241, 242, 267, 270, 273, 281, 284, 286, 287, 289, 290, 296-298, 300, 301, 303-307, 309, 333, 334, 336, 340, 347, 349, 350, 391, 395, 396, 399, 400, 402, 409, 413, 414, 416, 420, 424, 426, 430, 431, 435, 440, 441, 444, 447, 449, 450, 454, 476, 477, 517
soldiers, Confederate, 99
soldiers, Union, 99
Solger, Reihold, 457
Solid South, 71, 72, 76, 79, 81, 236, 296
Solon, 275
Somerville, TN, 335
sons of Belial, 183
Sons of Confederate Veterans, 19
sorghum, 89
South, 2, 3, 5, 11, 13, 17, 18, 20, 22, 24-34, 36, 38, 41-45, 47-50, 52-54, 56-66, 68, 71-107, 111-119, 121, 123, 126-128, 132-136, 141, 143, 147, 148, 151-154, 156, 157, 159, 160, 164-200, 202, 204-216, 220, 221, 223-226, 228, 230-232, 234-239, 245, 246, 250, 251, 254-256, 258, 259, 261, 262, 264, 268, 273, 274, 276, 280, 281, 283-288, 290, 292-297, 299-304, 306, 307, 309, 311, 313-316, 319-330, 332, 336-340, 342-364, 366-375, 377-383, 385, 387, 388, 390, 392, 395, 397-401, 403-424, 427-456, 458, 469-474, 476-478, 515, 517
South Africa, 259
South America, 100, 153
South American ports, 100

South Carolina, 24, 26, 34, 44, 47, 56-58, 72, 75, 76, 79, 81, 111, 117-119, 121, 126, 173, 174, 193, 196, 214, 262, 273, 311, 353, 390, 399-401, 403-405, 411, 418-420, 432-434, 439, 447, 448, 456, 471, 474
Southern abolitionists, 353
Southern blacks, 162, 279, 423
Southern capital, 80
Southern Cause, 3, 204, 256, 358, 382, 399, 476
Southern centers, 90
Southern cities, 35, 192
Southern Confederacy, 2, 3, 29, 305, 370, 371, 428, 446, 470, 476
Southern cotton mills, 177
Southern education, 339
Southern Educational Conference, 324
Southern farmer, 89
Southern furnaces, 90
Southern homes, 336
Southern iron, 90
Southern patriotism, 335, 339
Southern plantations, 356, 436
Southern planter, 89
Southern point of view, 416
Southern ports, 453
Southern property-holders, 109
Southern railroads, 177
Southern Railway, 177
Southern slave owners, 304
Southern society, 29, 304, 360, 381, 429
Southern states, 24, 27, 28, 30, 31, 35, 45, 48, 52, 54, 61, 72, 80-82, 92, 94, 111, 113, 132, 134, 159, 165, 171, 177, 179, 182, 185, 187, 188, 191, 193, 194, 196, 210, 211, 228, 235, 257, 266, 280, 281, 283, 285, 288, 292, 296, 304, 314, 317, 324, 343, 345, 361, 365, 368, 378, 390, 396, 403, 408, 414, 415, 418, 428, 439, 445, 446, 448, 451, 453, 470, 472

Southern whites, 62, 64, 68, 74, 79, 105, 107, 125, 162, 181, 197, 224, 238, 313, 334, 346
Southern women, strength of, 126
Southerners, 2, 3, 5, 6, 17, 18, 20, 24, 26, 27, 29, 31, 33-38, 83, 97, 114, 117, 175, 184, 190, 202, 216, 219, 223-225, 231, 232, 234, 272, 287, 294, 325-327, 359, 364, 365, 382, 406, 413, 438, 442, 477
Southland, 161, 203, 212, 295, 298, 307, 320, 338, 341, 398, 399, 430, 450
Spain, 112-114, 116, 117, 150, 153, 175, 186, 270, 280, 408
Spaniards, 116
Spanish Inquisition, 164, 258
Spanish rule, 112
Spanish succession, war of, 270
Spanish-American War, 112, 114, 116, 117, 160, 186
Sparling, Mr., 157
Sparta, Greece, 188
speculators, 120, 308
Spencer, George E., 141, 448
sperm whale, 421
spies, 144, 391-394
spinning wheels, 337
St. Augustine, FL, 310
St. Bernard Parish, LA, 311
St. Helena, island of, 205
St. Louis, MO, 372
St. Simon, Duke of, 270
Stahel, Julius, 458
Stanton, Edwin M., 54, 55, 202, 230, 251, 261, 262, 374, 380, 385, 411, 447
staple crops, 89
Star of the East (Bible), 353
Stars and Bars, 310, 331
Stars and Stripes, 114, 115, 302, 331
starvation, 121, 164, 302, 340, 364
starvation parties, 127
state authorities, 51, 235, 274
state bonds, 333
State Department, 150
state sovereignty, 46
state universities, 178

statesmen, 50, 51, 77, 80, 83, 97, 99, 102, 112, 118, 135, 176, 179, 195, 211, 222, 254, 265, 273, 275, 314, 346, 347, 350, 355-357, 368, 440, 469
states' rights, 15, 16, 28, 98
states' rights movements, 28
Statuary Hall, 447
statue, Confederate, 161
Staunton Military Academy, 449
stealage, 333
steam power, 152
steamboat, 288, 393
steamships, 152
Stearns, Marcellus L., 448
Steinwehr, Adolph von, 458
Stephens, Alexander H., 15, 18, 42, 44, 48, 163, 211, 224, 285, 289, 319, 414
Stephens, Linton, 319
Stephenson, N. W., 411
Stevens, Thaddeus, 28, 30, 31, 63, 122, 133, 191-194, 200, 202, 226-228, 234, 238, 254, 261, 276, 299, 332, 360, 361, 417, 447, 453, 455
Stoneman, Austin (Dixon), 276
Stoughton, William, 206, 207
stoves, 90, 421
Stowe, Harriet B., 121, 255, 353, 375, 436
stress, among freed black servants, 304
Stribling, R. M., 424
strong government, 355
Struve, Gustav, 458
Stuart, James E. B., 342
Stubbs, William, 15
students, 184
subdistricts, 35
suffrage, 30, 55, 60, 62, 63, 67, 77, 81-83, 107, 129, 165, 171, 180, 181, 193, 195, 217, 218, 229, 232, 254, 255, 257, 262, 326, 333, 419, 447
suffrage laws, 181
sugar, 86, 89, 176, 177, 241, 324, 369
Sumner, Charles, 191, 192, 217, 219, 222-224, 226-229, 234, 236, 253-255, 417, 447
Sumter County, SC, 401
Sumter, SC, 401
Sumter, Thomas, 418
superior court judges, 70
superstition, 173, 175, 196, 382, 407
Supreme Court, 10, 46, 48, 52, 64, 68, 70, 79, 150, 171, 196, 311, 406
surplus crops, 89
Surratt, Mary, 201, 219, 254, 286, 360, 386, 478
suspicion, manufactured, 62
sutlers, 120
Suvorov, Alexander, 270
Swayne, Wager, 70, 73
swearing, 136, 183, 244
sweet potatoes, 86
Taft, Alphonso, 142
Taft, William, 339
Tahlequah, GA, 404
Talbert, W. Jasper, 439
Talcott, Thomas, 397
Talleyrand-Périgord, Charles M. de, 226
Tamerlane, 153
Tampa, FL, 100
Taney, Roger B., 134
Tarbell, Ida, 424
taxes, 76, 94, 133, 142, 143, 177, 181, 196, 214, 265, 319, 343, 400, 403, 418
Taylor, Frederick, 93
Taylor, Jeremy, 255
Taylor, Louise M. M., 256
Taylor, Richard, 18, 41, 163, 250, 275, 342
Taylor, Sarah K., 250
Taylor, Zachary, 249-251
teacher, 169, 181, 362, 420, 454
teachers, Left-wing, 181
Tecumseh, 31, 213, 458
telegraph, 153
temperance movement, 182
Temple, Henry J., 409
Tennessee, 3, 24, 31, 32, 34, 44, 47, 55, 57-60, 91, 156, 171, 189, 193, 194, 209, 237, 283, 336, 358, 448, 471,

472, 474, 517
Tennessee and Pacific Railway, 156
Tennyson, Alfred, 382
Tenure of Office bill, 309
terra cotta, 89
Texas, 29, 34, 47, 56, 58, 69, 70, 129, 151, 189, 245, 257, 284, 285, 324, 448, 474
Texas Rangers, 245
The Bittersweet Bond (Seabrook), 20
The Confederated Southern Memorial Association, 370
the East, 92
The Farmer, 436
The Federalist, 355
The Great Yankee Coverup (Seabrook), 25
the Left, 20, 22, 25, 26, 34, 35, 38, 53, 62, 83, 182, 195, 312, 313, 334, 362, 391, 455, 456, 468
The Leopard's Spots (Dixon), 400
The Liberator, 186
The New York World, 425
the North, 2, 22, 27-30, 35, 38, 43-45, 47, 48, 50, 53, 54, 63-69, 72, 74, 79, 80, 82-93, 95-98, 100-104, 106, 110, 115, 116, 118, 120, 122, 123, 129, 130, 132, 133, 135, 137, 148, 151, 164, 171, 177, 179, 186, 188, 192, 195, 197, 201, 204, 205, 207, 208, 215, 220, 221, 224-226, 228, 230, 235, 245, 257, 262-264, 266, 275, 286, 294, 299, 301, 306, 313-317, 322, 323, 333, 338, 339, 343, 348, 351-353, 358-361, 363, 366-372, 376-380, 387, 400, 405, 406, 408, 409, 411, 413, 416, 417, 426, 427, 429, 431, 436, 439, 445-451, 453, 454, 468, 475
The Rise and Fall of the Confederate Government (Davis), 18, 354
The South, 11, 13, 17, 18, 22, 24, 26-34, 36, 38, 41-45, 47-50, 52-54, 56-66, 68, 73, 74, 77-98, 100-107, 111-118, 123, 127, 128, 132-136, 141, 143, 147, 151, 152, 154, 159, 160, 164-171, 174-192, 194-198, 200, 202, 204-213, 215, 216, 220, 221, 223-226, 228, 230-232, 234-239, 245, 246, 250, 251, 254, 256, 258, 259, 261, 264, 274, 283-288, 290, 292-296, 299-304, 306, 307, 309, 311, 313-316, 319-324, 326, 327, 330, 336, 338-340, 342-361, 363, 364, 366-375, 377-383, 385, 387, 388, 392, 395, 397-400, 403, 405-411, 413-417, 419-424, 429-432, 434, 435, 437-446, 448, 450-455, 469-474, 477, 478, 515
the West, 55, 82, 85, 93, 100, 153, 206, 274, 280, 336, 417
Thebes, Greece, 188
thievery, 124, 244
thieves, 72, 75, 125, 129, 434, 447
Thirteenth Amendment, 58, 65, 67, 83, 170, 171, 193, 216, 303, 308, 446
Thirty Years' War, 274
Thomas, George H., 147, 247
Thomas, J. A., 149
Thompson, J. L., 335
thrift, 84, 87, 105, 204
Throckmorton, James W., 70
Tilden, Samuel J., 235, 238, 299
Tillman, John M., 347
timber, 84, 91, 100, 101, 155
timber products, 101
Time of the Robbers, 433
Timrod, Henry, 33
tobacco, 86, 89, 145, 176
Tompkins, D. A., 93
Toney, Marcus B., 155, 162, 163, 191, 201, 209, 215, 237, 249
tools, 36, 89, 130
Toombs, Robert A., 51
top rails, 297
Tories, 135

Torquemada, Tomás, 258
torture, 10, 125, 148, 162, 205, 442
Tourgee, Albion W., 352
tournaments, 127
traditionalism, 16
traitors, 22, 30, 235, 251, 254, 282, 315, 345, 398, 413, 415, 442
Traveller (Lee's warhorse), 129, 130
treadmills, 152
treason, 49, 125, 163, 164, 188, 204, 205, 221, 251, 286, 314, 330, 344, 359, 386, 424
Treasury Department, 281
Treaty of Paris, 118
Trimble, E. C., 392
Truman, Benjamin P., 128
Trump, Donald J., 25
Tucker, St. George, 315
Turkey, 318
Turner, Bishop, 111
Turner, Colonel, 99
Turner, Nat, 410
Tuscaloosa, AL, 199, 239
Twain, Mark, 422
Tweed River, 264
Tyler, John, 220
Tyler, Lyon G., 367, 412
tyranny, 125, 152, 233, 255, 317, 341, 391, 433, 449, 515
tyranny, Left-wing, 433
U.D.C., 299, 397, 404, 422, 430, 435, 452
U.S. Congress, 456
U.S. Constitution, 200, 439
U.S. forces, 371
U.S. government, 78, 87, 132, 308, 470
U.S. House of Representatives, 28, 317
U.S. Treasury, 457
U.S.A., 17, 84
Uncle Sam, 412
Uncle Tom's Cabin (Stowe), 179, 375, 435, 436
Underwood, John C., 176, 308
Union, 2, 6, 15, 16, 19, 24, 25, 27, 28, 30-33, 35, 41-53, 55-59, 61, 64-67, 73, 81, 85, 91, 94-97, 99, 101, 104, 111, 113-118, 127, 128, 130, 148-151, 154, 160, 165, 168, 171, 174, 175, 179, 180, 185-187, 189, 191, 195, 200, 216, 222, 223, 229, 234, 237, 238, 240, 244-246, 254, 257, 261, 262, 280, 281, 283, 284, 288-290, 293, 297, 301, 303, 306, 309, 311, 314, 315, 318, 325, 326, 329, 332, 338, 339, 345-347, 349, 350, 352, 357, 360, 361, 364, 365, 367, 380, 385, 387, 388, 392, 398, 405, 408, 410, 411, 413, 414, 425, 426, 428, 437, 439, 441, 442, 446, 448-450, 452, 457, 458, 469-471, 473, 474, 476, 477
Union army, 44, 101, 246, 290, 311, 357, 392, 458
Union generals, 99, 458
Union League, 73, 398, 448
Union League of Philadelphia, 448
Union Leagues, 73
Union Party, 30
Union soldiers, 99
Union war veterans, 448
Unionists, 220, 441
United Confederate Veterans, 19, 21, 473
United Daughters of the Confederacy, 289, 428, 448, 455
United States, 2, 6, 13, 16, 29, 34, 42-49, 51-53, 56, 58-60, 67, 73, 78, 79, 81, 87, 90, 91, 96, 107, 111-118, 131-134, 137, 142, 146-150, 152, 156, 158, 163-165, 167, 171, 179-181, 186, 193, 194, 196, 198, 207, 211, 212, 217, 221, 227, 228, 238, 239, 244, 253, 260, 264, 267-269, 279, 280, 282, 285, 291, 301, 302, 311, 314, 315, 319, 320, 331, 344, 346-348, 353, 358, 360, 363, 372, 376, 387, 393, 396, 398, 404-406, 408, 413, 415,

417, 420, 424, 433, 434, 447-449, 452, 453, 470-474, 477
United States (steamer), 158
United States government, 42-49, 132, 163, 164, 180, 244, 314, 319, 353, 393, 398, 406, 420, 433
United States Military Academy, 149, 279
United States of America, 2, 6, 347, 471-474, 477
urban life, 103, 198
Utica, 173
Valley Forge, PA, 209
Valliant, Frank, 138
Vance, P. M., 320
Vance, Zebulon B., 448
Vandals, 338
Vanderbilt University, 177, 429
vegetables, 89, 123, 130
Vendôme, Duke of, 270
Vermont, 107
Verres, Gaius, 173
Versailles, palace of, 357
Vicar of Bray, 262
Vicksburg, MS, 161
victim mentality, among blacks, 168
victimization marketing, of blacks, 287
victimization, black, 182
Victoria, Queen, 153, 338
Victorian Era, 248
Victorian white racism, 62
violence, 32, 38, 74, 157, 221, 259, 275, 304, 368, 401, 407
Virginia, 9, 24, 25, 27, 34, 41, 44, 47, 53-55, 58, 69, 73, 91, 113, 117, 118, 130, 151, 159, 176, 179, 181, 183, 186, 188-190, 203, 204, 247, 256, 270, 275, 279, 287, 293, 307, 311, 317, 326, 327, 331, 336, 339, 350, 354, 366, 384, 405, 410, 411, 414, 415, 423, 425, 433, 435, 442, 448, 449, 454, 469-471, 473, 517
Virginia Convention, 414
Virginia Military Academy, 442

Voltaire, 269
volunteer army, 116, 117
volunteer army organization, 116
volunteer organizations, 113
Von Hindenburg, Paul, 373
Voorhees, Daniel W., 417, 418
votes, 47, 55, 58, 67, 70, 71, 94, 106, 108, 129, 147, 165, 171, 174, 179, 185, 257, 260, 266, 273, 275, 332, 334, 403, 404, 425
voting polls, 404
Wade, Benjamin F., 425, 447
wages, 101, 122, 182, 249, 274, 436, 440
Walcott, Mary, 206
Walden, Ada R., 450
Walker, Mr., 68
Wall Street, NY, 388
walnuts, 130
war, 2, 3, 9, 11, 13, 15-21, 24, 26-28, 30-33, 35, 41-54, 56-62, 64-68, 70, 73, 75, 77-79, 81-85, 87, 89, 94, 95, 97, 99, 102, 104, 111-118, 127, 130, 131, 134, 135, 142, 144, 147, 149-152, 155, 156, 160, 164, 165, 167, 171, 172, 177-179, 182, 184, 186-191, 197, 198, 200-213, 215, 217, 219, 220, 225, 227, 229, 230, 237-240, 243, 244, 246, 250-252, 257, 261-264, 266, 270, 273-276, 279-284, 286-290, 292, 293, 295, 297, 299, 301, 303, 305-310, 313, 315-317, 319, 325, 331, 333, 335-341, 343-350, 352, 354-373, 375, 376, 378, 382, 383, 386-388, 390, 392-400, 403-406, 408-419, 421-428, 431-434, 437, 439-444, 446, 448, 450-454, 457, 458, 468-478, 515, 517, 519
War Against Northern Aggression, 18
war debt, 45, 49, 422
War for Southern Independence, 16-18, 188, 409, 470, 515
War for the Constitution, 9, 18,

24, 283, 468
war measure, 104, 365, 410
War of 1812, 187
War of Reconstruction, 9, 24, 27, 343, 468
warehouses, 120
Warmouth, Henry C., 419, 448
Warner, Albert, 71
Warner, Willard, 141
Washington and Lee University, Lexington, VA, 129
Washington College, 129, 279
Washington College, Lexington, VA, 129
Washington County, MS, 136, 144
Washington, Booker T., 224, 231
Washington, D.C., 6, 15, 53, 125, 128, 170, 202, 205, 219, 249, 250, 252, 256, 260, 267, 269, 273, 310, 353, 354, 361, 379, 387, 399, 428, 433, 447, 469-472, 477, 478
Washington, George, 16, 22, 174, 209, 252, 273, 275, 310, 355, 356, 366, 409
water transportation, 100
Waterford Independent Labor Party, 457
Waterloo, 270
Waterman, Julian S., 443
Watie, Stand, 404
Watterson, Henry, 128, 346, 414
Watts, Thomas H., 249, 251
wealth, 3, 27, 44, 45, 76, 81, 82, 85, 86, 91, 94-96, 100, 102, 105, 132-134, 150, 152, 153, 175-177, 263, 264, 273, 274, 283, 284, 296, 342, 345, 369, 403, 417, 432, 443, 448, 451, 453
Webber, T. L., 142
Weber, Maz, 458
Webster, Daniel, 383, 384, 426
weddings, 395
Weitzel, Godfrey, 53
welfare mentality among blacks, start of, 63
Wellington, Duke of, 272
Wells, George D., 458

Wells, Gideon, 380
West Indies, 153
West Point, 56, 272, 279, 288, 315
West Tennessee, 336
West Virginia, 55, 73, 91, 425, 517
Western Reserve University, 417
Western states, 187, 188
Westmoreland Club, 183
Westmoreland County, PA, 189
Weydemyer, Joseph A., 458
wharves, 100
wheat, 88, 89, 93, 146, 176
wheel works, 90
Wheeler, Joseph, 116, 186
Whig party, 16, 240, 249
whipping, 157, 264
whiskey, 124, 196
white belts, 104, 105, 327
White Bluff, TN, 240-242
White House, 12, 75, 273, 354, 357, 370, 374, 452, 457
White House of the Confederacy, 354
White House, U.S., 250, 252
white immigrants, 103, 105, 326
white labor, 369
white man's ticket, 400, 403
white mechanics, 103
white population, 85, 87, 223, 234
white privilege, 287
white race, 103, 184, 255, 258, 292, 327, 359, 368, 369
white slaves, 322
white supremacy, 38, 83, 444
whites, 29, 30, 34, 60, 62-64, 66, 68, 69, 71, 73-75, 77, 79, 80, 94, 103-111, 124-126, 128, 132, 133, 136, 140, 142, 145, 148, 156, 157, 162, 168, 171, 174, 175, 177, 179, 181, 193-198, 221, 224, 232, 238, 255, 259, 260, 267, 285, 287, 292-294, 313, 319, 322, 324, 328, 334, 346, 356, 366, 400-403, 423, 433, 434, 455
whites, racism against, 195
White's Creek Pike, Nashville,

TN, 155
Whitworth, Judge, 156
Wickham, Mrs. Julia P., 435
wild-cat presidents, 185
Wilderness campaign, 159
William I, Emperor, 357
William II, King, 386
William of Orange, 265
William of Prussia, 357
William the Conqueror, 173
Williams, Abigail, 206
Williams, George H., 456
Williams, John S., 310
Williamsburg, VA, 367
Williamson, Mrs., 336
Willich, August von, 19, 458
Wilmer, Bishop, 147
Wilmington, NC, 153
Wilson, James H., 51, 200
Wilson, Woodrow, 32, 65, 69, 363, 367
Winnsboro, SC, 127
Winslow, O., 143
Wirz, Henry, 130, 132, 254, 286, 360
Wisconsin, 24, 262, 437
Wise Men (Bible), 353
Witchcraft, 206
With Saber and Scalpel (Wyeth), 420
Woman Corps, 336
womanhood, 310, 326, 336, 338
women, 2, 3, 33, 36, 57, 107, 109, 120-122, 124-128, 134, 147, 188, 206, 210, 230, 233, 252, 259, 260, 264, 284, 289, 298, 304, 306, 307, 321, 323, 325, 335-337, 342, 351, 354, 364, 368, 370, 373, 374, 381, 387, 388, 394-396, 399, 409, 417, 419-423, 431, 432, 436, 437, 441, 442, 450, 456, 476
women, Southern, strength of, 126
wood products, 100
Woodhouselee, Lord, 149
woolen mills, 89
Workman, C. E., 404
World War I, 357, 363, 408, 442
World War II, 358

wounding, 239
wounds, 95, 251, 262, 287, 302, 304, 340
Wyeth, John A., 420
Wyoming, 5, 6, 37
Wytheville, VA, 143
X ray, 153
Xerxes, King, 252
Yankee myth, 2, 74, 83, 156, 175, 196, 234, 235, 408, 475, 476
Yankee officers, 204, 285, 449
Yankee schoolteachers, in the South, 169, 170
Yankeefication, 36
Yankees, 25, 28-30, 59, 180, 199, 201, 202, 206, 242, 243, 294, 300, 316, 325, 343, 353, 387, 392, 395
yarns, 92
yellow fever, 362
Young Men's Christian Associations, 265
Young, Bennett H., 20, 25, 342, 343, 352
Zaccheus (Bible), 185
Zagonyi, Charles, 458
Zulus, 359

TO ENEMIES OF THE TRUTH

"Let it be understood that it is no purpose of the Veteran to stir up hatred or perpetuate strife; but its chief mission is to secure true history, and history deals with the past. The South in the war fought for definite principles which she believed were essential to a free government, and she conducted the war on the highest plane of humanity and civilization with such resources as she had. Yet her motives and her conduct have been constantly, through ignorance or malice, misrepresented by Northern historians. So there is serious danger that the coming generations of the South will look upon their ancestors as a set of barbarians who made their terrible fight against history, civilization, and Christianity, actuated only by passion, greed, and brutality.

"Now, the object of the Confederate Veteran is to show by incontestable evidence the nature of the war for Southern independence, the provocation which led the South into war, the manner in which the war was conducted by each side, and the story of Reconstruction, which shows the spirit in which the war was waged upon the South. As to the future, the Veteran believes that a clear vindication of the principles for which the South fought is the best way to promote the highest interests of the nation. For if these principles are ignored or violated, the result will be the death of true liberty, the tyranny of the plutocrat or the proletariat." — Confederate Veteran, 1917

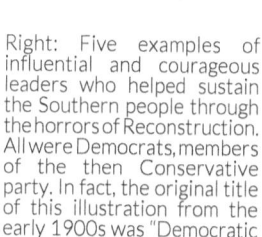

Right: Five examples of influential and courageous leaders who helped sustain the Southern people through the horrors of Reconstruction. All were Democrats, members of the then Conservative party. In fact, the original title of this illustration from the early 1900s was "Democratic and Conservatives Leaders."

GOVERNOR R. M. PATTON.

GENERAL JAMES H. CLANTON. Organizer of the present Democratic Party in Alabama.

GOVERNOR GEORGE S. HOUSTON.

GOVERNOR R. B. LINDSAY.

MAJOR J. R. CROWE, now of Sheffield, Ala., one of the founders of the Ku Klux Klan at Pulaski, Tenn.

MEET THE AUTHOR-EDITOR

NEO-VICTORIAN SCHOLAR LOCHLAINN SEABROOK, a descendant of the families of Alexander Hamilton Stephens, John Singleton Mosby, Edmund Winchester Rucker, and William Giles Harding, is a 7th generation Kentuckian and one of the most prolific and widely read writers in the world today. Known by literary critics as the "new Shelby Foote" and the "American Robert Graves," and by his fans as the "Voice of the Traditional South," he is a recipient of the United Daughters of the Confederacy's prestigious Jefferson Davis Historical Gold Medal. A lifelong writer, the Sons of Confederate Veterans member has authored and edited books ranging in topics from history, politics, science, religion, astronomy, military, and biography, to nature, music, humor, gastronomy, alternative health, genealogy, and the paranormal; books that his readers describe as "game changers," "transformative," and "life altering."

One of the world's most popular living historians, he is a 17th generation Southerner of Appalachian heritage who descends from dozens of patriotic Revolutionary War soldiers and Confederate soldiers from Kentucky, Tennessee, North Carolina, and Virginia. Also a history, wildlife, and nature preservationist, the well-respected polymath began life as a child prodigy, later transforming into an archetypal Renaissance Man. Besides being an accomplished and esteemed author-historian and Bible authority, he is also a Kentucky Colonel, eagle scout, screenwriter, nature, wildlife, and landscape photographer, videographer, artist, graphic designer, songwriter (3,000 songs), film composer, multi-instrument musician, vocalist, session player, music producer, genealogist, former history museum docent, and a former ranch hand, zookeeper, and wrangler.

Currently Seabrook is the author and editor of nearly 100 adult and children's books (totaling some 28,000 pages and 14,000,000 words) that have earned him accolades from around the globe. His works, which have sold on every continent except Antarctica, have introduced hundreds of thousands to vital facts that have been left out of our mainstream books. He has been endorsed internationally by leading experts, museum curators, award-winning historians, bestselling authors, celebrities, filmmakers, noted scientists, well regarded educators, TV show hosts and producers, renowned military artists, venerable heritage organizations, and distinguished academicians of all races, creeds, and colors.

Of northern, western, and central European ancestry, he is the 6th great-grandson of the Earl of Oxford and a descendant of European royalty through his Kentucky father and West Virginia mother. His modern day cousins include: Johnny Cash, Elvis Presley, Lisa Marie Presley, Billy Ray and Miley Cyrus, Patty Loveless, Tim McGraw, Lee Ann Womack, Dolly Parton, Pat Boone, Naomi, Wynonna, and Ashley Judd, Ricky Skaggs, the Sunshine Sisters, Martha Carson, Chet Atkins, Patrick J. Buchanan, Cindy Crawford, Bertram Thomas Combs (Kentucky's 50th governor), Edith Bolling (second wife of President Woodrow Wilson), Andy Griffith, Riley Keough, George C. Scott, Robert Duvall, Reese Witherspoon, Lee Marvin, Rebecca Gayheart, and Tom Cruise.

A constitutionalist, avid outdoorsman, and gun rights advocate, Seabrook is the author of the international blockbuster, *Everything You Were Taught About the Civil War is Wrong, Ask a Southerner!* He lives with his wife and family in the magnificent Rocky Mountains, heart of the American West, where you will find him hiking, photographing, and writing.

For more information on author Mr. Seabrook visit
LOCHLAINNSEABROOK.COM

LOCHLAINN SEABROOK ∽ 519

If you enjoyed this book you will be interested in Colonel Seabrook's popular related titles:

☛ Abraham Lincoln Was a Liberal, Jefferson Davis Was a Conservative
☛ Everything You Were Taught About the Civil War is Wrong, Ask a Southerner!
☛ All We Ask is to be Let Alone: The Southern Secession Fact Book
☛ Everything You Were Taught About American Slavery is Wrong, Ask a Southerner!
☛ Confederate Flag Facts: What Every American Should Know About Dixie's Southern Cross
☛ Lincoln's War: The Real Cause, the Real Winner, the Real Loser

Available from Sea Raven Press and wherever fine books are sold

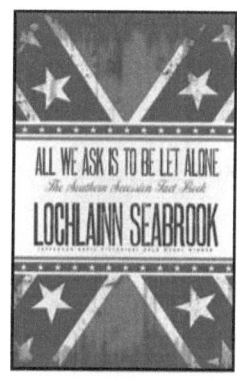

ALL OF OUR BOOK COVERS ARE AVAILABLE AS 11" X 17" COLOR POSTERS, SUITABLE FOR FRAMING

SeaRavenPress.com

www.ingramcontent.com/pod-product-compliance
Lightning Source LLC
Chambersburg PA
CBHW032008220426
43664CB00006B/175